HISTORY OF THE WEST TO 1500

Robert L. Cleve, Ph.D.

California State University

KENDALL/HUNT PUBLISHING COMPANY
4050 Westmark Drive   Dubuque, Iowa 52002

ISBN 13: 978-0-7575-3209-2
ISBN 10: 0-7575-3209-8

Printed in the United States of America
10   9   8   7   6   5   4   3

For Miwako
Friend, wife, life-long companion.

CONTENTS

PREFACE

During this first decade of the 21st century, dozens of textbooks designed for college history courses in Western Civilization are in print—this even as the Western Civilization course itself is rapidly being replaced by the more "politically correct" World History course. The opening paragraph of the preface of many, perhaps most, of these textbooks, offers an apology for the study of history in general[1] and for the study of Western Civilization in particular, a term which has now become a "dirty word" in the minds of many American intellectuals, especially the Social Studies establishment. This author wishes to make two things very clear at the beginning: (1) this book does not attempt political correctness; (2) it makes no apology for the study of Western Civilization, and indeed, if anything, it celebrates the history of the West.

Contemporary historical scholarship has become increasingly paralyzed by a crisis of self-confidence. Historians seem no longer to believe the human mind is capable of analyzing the past in valid or useful ways. History seems to have become altogether too complicated to decipher. Better to become absorbed in the complexities of the data than attempt to construct a coherent concept of past experience; better to lament the paucity of the evidence, to catalog all the missing items, to point out with great care and accuracy all that we *cannot* know, and thereby avoid the true work of the historian, which is analysis, explanation, and understanding. For example, a historian recently asserted that it is not valid to say that Christianity triumphed in the 3rd century because of "...any one of ten elements or factors. Such statements are unacceptable because, by their excessive clarification, they filter out too much fact."[2] Thus, any statement that does not include all the facts is invalid and because, on the face of it, we can never know all the facts, analysis and understanding of the past becomes impossible. Taken to its logical conclusion, this attitude means that the study of history is fruitless and unproductive and that, in effect, we can know *nothing* about the past because we cannot know *everything* about it. The very attempt at clarification becomes "unacceptable," and the historian had best not attempt to say anything of substance about past events lest he be rebuked and humiliated by his colleagues for saying too much, for being politically incorrect, for employing "defective" methods. The reader of this book should be aware that the author does not share this attitude.

One of the many serious problems inherent in the new politically correct World History courses is that they are not really part of a curriculum intended to acquaint the student with the past experiences of non-Western cultures, but rather indoctrination programs intended to produce unthinking, robot-like human beings capable of functioning in a politically and ethnically homogenized world that exists not in reality but only in the minds of the Social Studies advocates who promote these agendas. For them, everything revolves around equality and relativism, which they perceive as the only answer to the multiple claims to truth advanced by the various non-Western

---

1. The apology often begins with the quote (or the paraphrase of it) from Jane Austin's classic novel, *Northanger Abby*, which has become a cliché: "History tells me nothing that does not either vex or weary me. The quarrels of popes and kings, with wars or pestilences in every page; the men all so good for nothing, and hardly any women at all, it is very tiresome." The implication is, of course, that the political and intellectual heritage of the West is not only irrelevant to the modern world, but it is boring and uninteresting—it is not "entertaining," which is the greatest insult of all.

2. MacMullen, Ramsay, *Christianizing the Roman Empire*, New Haven, 1984, p. 102.

cultures. Their fantasy world is an ideal democracy of cultures in which all societies are of equal worth. The values and ideals of Western society are no more valid in this view than those of any other society—and indeed Western values are viewed as a hindrance, an impediment or obstruction to the realization of their ideal utopia, because the West's values appeal to the "good," or to "what is right." For the Social Studies advocates, the object of studying history is no longer to understand past experience, to correct mistakes, or even to discover what is morally right, but rather it is to not think that you are right at all.

The Social Studies approach presents the student with a stream of carefully selected, unrelated, and isolated facts, but the student is not allowed to analyze or integrate these facts into his own experience as a member of Western society. Rather, he is directed to process all this new information within the context of the Social Studies fantasy world of equality and relativism. His own system of values and morals are no longer a valid standard for assessing what is right. He learns that women in Muslim countries like Saudi Arabia are little more than sex slaves and what is called a "family" in the West is simply a man's private whore house in that society; he learns that the inhabitants of certain villages in New Guinea periodically hunt down and kill the inhabitants of neighboring villages, reduce their heads to the size of tennis balls and hang them on their walls as trophies. Never mind. One society's customs are as valid as those of all other societies, and the West's values are only relative. The Social Studies advocates of this "new world order" deeply believe this. If they are confronted with a simple question, such as, "If you were a British administrator in India in the 19th Century, would you have allowed the Indians under your governance to burn the widow at the funeral of a man who had died?," they deflect the question by insisting that the British should not have been in India to begin with, followed by an angry stream of accusations that racism, chauvinism, and bigotry are the motives for posing such a question. But they do not address the larger moral dilemma of what is right. Such questions are not permitted in their brave new world.

The author of this textbook rejects both the ideology and goals of the Social Studies establishment and in their place reasserts the ideals and aspirations of the classical liberal arts approach to the role of history in education. Up until the late 20th Century, education in the West was based on the "liberal arts" curriculum developed during the Italian Renaissance, which was in turn derived from the ancient Greek concept of *paideia*.[3] The purpose of a liberal education is not to produce a robotic-like individual who will serve as a subservient component of a new society still under construction, but rather to instill in the student those qualities that represent the best values of his own culture and to develop the social and ethical skills within the individual that permit him to operate freely, efficiently, and productively within his society—in other words, the purpose of liberal education is to liberate the individual into his society.

Paideia was not specifically "education" in the sense of the three "Rs," although education was an important element of the process. *Paideia* was the system of forming the young individual into an adult. The Greeks used an analogy to explain how the process worked. The young person, they said, is like an unworked lump of clay. The potential of a formless lump of clay can be realized only by the skill of the potter, who forms the clay—as nearly as his skill will permit—into a vessel that is the realization of the image of a pot he holds in his mind. In a similar process, *paideia* forms the young person into an adult that resembles—as nearly as the process can achieve—the image of the

---

3. See Jaeger, Werner W., Highet, Gilbert, Translator, *Paideia: The Ideals of Greek Culture: Archaic Greece and the Mind of Athens* (1939), Oxford U. Press; Robb, Kevin, *Literacy and Paideia in Ancient Greece* (1994), Oxford University Press.

ideal adult held in the collective mind of the community. The process was not in itself intended to reshape society into something new. It was rather intended to support and sustain the values and ideals of society, which the Greeks called *arête*. *Arête* is often translated as simply "virtue," but it means much more than that. It includes the attributes of beauty, honor, integrity, achievement—in short, *arête* includes all those qualities that separate human beings from the lower animals, all those characteristics that make us human.

The study of history occupies an important place in this process, especially the study of the history of one's own society. No one is qualified to understand the history of other societies until he knows his own. Before the Social Studies revolution of the late 20th Century in public education, the young student was immersed in the history of our nation, and this was presented against the background of the history of the Western Civilization. The intention was to give the student a firm footing in traditions of his own society, to give him a point of reference for the study of the wider world beyond his own origins. But the Social Studies curriculum gives the student no such preparation. Instead, the student is presented with an almost endless series of short, disconnected "sound-bites" of information selected from the histories of many different societies. These bits of information are juxtaposed in such a way that they form the most negative image possible of Western Civilization and at the same time exhibit non-Western societies in the most favorable way possible. The student emerges from this program with no firm knowledge of anything, but with a vague shame and dislike for his own origins. This, apparently, is exactly the result intended by the Social Studies establishment.

While this curriculum obviates any true education for the entire generation emerging from the public schools, it irritates and exaggerates another serious problem facing our nation. Our society is today under siege by a steady influx—a flood, really—of individuals from non-Western societies, many of whom do not understand and do not share our political and cultural traditions.[4] Until fairly recently, most immigrants entered our country with the intention of becoming a part of our society. No longer. Many, if not most, of the new immigrants are intent on transforming our society into a model of the society they left behind, or at a minimum on establishing independent beachheads of their societies within our midst—little states within our state. It is difficult to understand how this process will contribute to the health of our society, but even to observe that this problem exists is to invite accusations of racism and bigotry from the Social Studies establishment.

The purpose of this textbook is to provide the student who has emerged from the Social Studies curriculum of our public educational system with at least an introductory knowledge of the history of his own origins and at the same time provide the student who is new to our society with the beginnings of an understanding of Western origins and traditions—presumably the cultural environment in which he will live his life in the future. This is a tall order, and the author does not represent his effort as anything more than a small beginning. However, it is hoped that this course will inspire the student to pursue the study of Western Civilization more thoroughly on his own initiative and to enroll in more advanced college courses in history, literature, the humanities, the arts, or the classics. Beyond all this, however, the broad sweep of the history of Western Civilization is a saga that is interesting, uplifting, and inspiring in itself, and it is hoped that the

---

4. For example, the author recently experienced a strange conversation with a student form an Asian country. He said, "You Americans are insincere hypocrites. You do not really believe anything that you say, you have no values at all." When I asked him to be more specific, he replied "Your politicians are completely cynical. During a campaign they claim to hold certain opinions and beliefs, but even after winning an election they continue to permit opposing opinions to be advocated by their opponents. If they were sincere in their beliefs they would not permit this."

student will enjoy this exciting journey through time. Indeed, history is often far more fascinating than fiction and modern computer games like "Grand Theft Auto," which so sadly captivate our modern youth.

ACKNOWLEDGMENTS

I wish to thank the following individuals for their encouragement, support, and assistance in this project.

Prof. John Broesamle
Prof. Ronald Davis
Sir Rodney Hartwell
Prof. Charles Macune
Mr. Barry Rightman
Mr. Pantelis G. Spanos

Of course the opinions, errors, omissions, mistakes, and inaccuracies contained in this book are my own and are not to be ascribed to any of the above individuals.

1

Introduction

The Study of History

Before embarking on a journey, it is wise to decide exactly where one intends to go and give some thought as to the best method of travel and the most convenient and efficient route to take. Before embarking on a course of study, it is also wise to define exactly what one is going to study and devote some thought to how one will engage in the learning activity. The subject of this course of study is *The History of the West to 1500*. This title implies at least two simple questions: "What is history?" and "What is the West?"

Consider first the term, history. Regrettably, history textbooks do not provide the reader with a clear and lucid definition of their subject. This is due to the potentially controversial nature of the term.[1] The problem has become more difficult in recent decades because the profession of history has split into many diverse and often conflicting fields of study. Thus, there are now almost as many approaches and attitudes to history as there are historians: social history, political history, ethnic history, gender history, military history, and so on. Nevertheless, the student is entitled to a clear and unambiguous definition of the subject under study. Here is an attempt:

> History is the systematic and truthful record, analysis, and explanation of the past actions and events of humankind, based on the surviving evidence.

Although this appears to be a straightforward and simple definition, we immediately enter into controversy. The words "systematic," "truthful," "explanation," and "evidence" must be clarified. The phrase "systematic and truthful record" refers to what are often called historical facts, but what exactly is a historical fact, i.e. what is *historical truth*? Historians are rarely able to agree on an answer to this question.

Different individuals perceive the past quite differently, particularly when they hold dissimilar ideological or political views. For example, a Marxist ideologist perceives a very different history of the world than the Christian theologian, and the American politician, busily soliciting votes out in the U.S. heartland, visualizes a very different history of the past two millennia than does the Muslim

---

1. Publishers of general textbooks, i.e. textbooks for introductory courses like this one, attempt to avoid the treatment of controversial or politically incorrect material in their books because they do not wish to offend potential customers, the professors who adopt the books for their courses. After all, textbooks are published to make money for the publisher.

terrorist preparing to participate in a suicide mission. Yet, both individuals appeal to their own perception of the past to clothe their ideology, arguments, and actions in legitimacy. Accordingly, in order for our definition of history to be useful, we must bore deeper into the meaning of "historical truth." In other words, we need to come to at least a temporary agreement concerning the meaning of historical truth in order to proceed with our study of Western Civilization.

The renowned philosopher of history, Michael Oakshott, in his book *Experience and Its Modes*, suggested that historical truth, or fact, is "not 'what really happened'; it is 'what the evidence obliges us to believe.'"[2] A historical fact, then, is *what the evidence obliges us to believe*. This seems reasonable enough until we attempt to apply it to the real world. We then rapidly discover that this will not do. If we apply this standard of historical truth to the ancient world we can know almost nothing about the distant past except trivia. We could compile a catalog of place names and construct king lists; we could confirm a few isolated dates by the use of astronomical tables; and we might be able to arrange a small number of known events in approximate chronological order, but that would be the extent of our knowledge of the past. Almost all of the rest of what we think we know about antiquity would have to be abandoned.

Indeed, even the most elemental historical "facts" concerning the past are subject to doubt when subjected to Oakshott's standard. Public events which have occurred only recently are surrounded by disagreement and uncertainty. For example, eyewitnesses to the assassination of President John Kennedy in 1963—an event that occurred on a public street—could not agree on exactly what happened. Investigating this event has become an industry in itself. Hundreds of research papers, investigative reports, learned books, and Hollywood movies have been published seeking to expose the "truth," and almost all of them have reached different conclusions. No one can seem to agree on what really happened. The problem is not a shortage of evidence, there is even a photographic record of the event, provided by an amateur photographer who recorded the event with a movie camera. Yet if we apply the Oakshott standard, we can know almost nothing about the details of this momentous affair. Well, if historians cannot accurately reconstruct an event that occurred before hundreds of eyewitnesses only a few years ago, then how can the historians of the ancient world reconstruct the details of a meeting of the Roman senate, which took place over 2,000 year ago, in which important foreign policy decisions were taken, but which was so secret that details of the conclave were never released to the public? As you read further in this book you will discover that historians accomplish—or appear to accomplish—such feets all the time.

Historians in general, and historians of the ancient world in particular, obviously do not operate under Oakshott's strict standard. Thorkild Jacobsen, a well-known historian of ancient Mesopotamian civilization, pointed out that in practice historians have adopted a somewhat more flexible definition for historical truth. Jacobsen proposed that a historical fact, or truth, is simply "what the evidence makes it possible to believe."[3] A slight modification perhaps, but it opens the door for a degree of speculation that would not be tolerated by many other disciplines, especially the "hard" sciences. Historians, in fact, do not claim the status of science for their discipline. While historians do employ many scientific techniques to probe their evidence for accuracy and correctness, history is not an experimental science on the same level as physics, chemistry, biology, etc., because it is not, and cannot be, based on the same standards of evidence. History is classified as a "social science."[4]

---

2. Oakshott, Michael, *Experience and Its Modes* (1933), Cambridge University Press, Cambridge, England, pp. 112.

3. In a memorable lecture in 1972, attended by the author when he was a graduate student at UCLA.

4. The social sciences deal with the institutions and functioning of human society and with the interpersonal relationships of individuals as members of society. The branches or disciplines of social science include sociology, psychology, anthropology, economics, political science, and history.

However, history is subject to the same kind of constant review and revision that the hard sciences endure. The popular cliché, "each generation writes its own history," is at least partially correct. History, much like the hard sciences, is in a constant state of change. This is due in some degree to the discovery of new information, but continuous reinterpretation of the available information is an even more important factor. Each generation of historians views the past with a new perspective, based on its own experience, and then reinterprets history to meet the needs of its own age. Thus, history textbooks, like science textbooks, must frequently be revised and brought up to date.

"History is the systematic and truthful record, analysis, and explanation of the past actions and events of humankind, based on the surviving *evidence*." But exactly what is the evidence historians use to reconstruct the picture of the past? The evidence for ancient history is divided into five major categories, usually called sources. Each of the sources is the subject of a special field of study:

Source	**Field**
1. Artifacts:	Archaeology
2. Art:	Art History
3. Documents	
a. Inscriptions:	Epigraphy
b. Papyri:	Papyrology
4. Coinage:	Numismatics
5. Literature:	Philology

History is a picture of a vast landscape stretching from the present back over the horizon into pre-history. Historians labor to illuminate that landscape. Each of these sources contributes to the picture in a different way, each casts rays of light into different areas of the image. Together they help to illuminate the entire picture. Yet areas of darkness and obscurity remain throughout the landscape, and it is the job of the specialists in these various fields of study to illuminate those areas still obscured in darkness. It is a never-ending undertaking, a task that will never be complete, but it continues generation after generation.[5]

Archaeology

Archaeologists seek to discover knowledge about antiquity and pre-history through the study of the material remains, especially the artifacts and monuments, of past human life and activity. For example, artifact distribution can reveal the migration routes of peoples, ancient trade patterns, and even details of everyday life, such as hunting techniques, food preparation, etc. One example: during the 5th Century BCE, a distinctive type of earthenware known as Attic black figured pottery was manufactured in Athens (Fig. 1.1). Archaeologists have found this type of pottery, at least fragments of it, all around the shores of the Mediterranean and Black Seas. This is evidence of a wide-ranging Athenian trade during the 5th Century BCE, even though this activity is rarely discussed in the ancient literary sources.

Artifacts can reveal things about a people that can be learned from no other source. Pompeii, a city on the southwest coast of Italy, south of the modern city of Naples, was buried in a volcanic eruption of Mount Vesuvius in the year 79 BCE. In the mid 20th Century, archaeologists discovered a large number of sophisticated medical instruments during the excavations of a building they

---

5. For an overview of the sources for the history of the ancient world, see Crawford, Michael, editor, *Sources for Ancient History* (1983), Cambridge University Press, Cambridge.

Figure 1.1: The François Vase, black figured Attic pottery. Archaeological Museum, Florence.

named "The House of the Surgeon." These objects included scalpels, tweezers, forceps, and other instruments. Close study of them tells us much more about the state of medical science in the 1st Century of our era than we can learn from any other source. These are but two examples of the varied and important information archaeologists gather about the past. Thus, while archaeological information enhances and enriches the historical record, it cannot provide the detailed information about the specific events of a social and political history.

Art

The term art includes not only painting and sculpture, but architecture, monuments, and all forms of plastic art. Although some of the same limitations that apply to artifacts also apply to art objects, art historians can glean information about specific historical events from works of art. This is certainly important, but art does much more. Artists are often the most accurate observers of their contemporary social and political environment, and the medium of art can communicate information to us which is not available from any other source. Portraits of important historical figures often reveal not only their physical likeness, but psychological overtones of their personality not always evident from literature. For example, the portrait of the Roman general Pompey (Fig. 1.2), who styled himself "Pompey the Great," tempts us to speculate that his name is the root of our word pompous.[6]

---

6. Not quite the case. The modern word pompous and ancient Roman general's name, *Pompeius* (Pompey is the Anglicized form) are both related to the Latin word *pompa*, which means "solumn or religious procession; retinue; pomp; ostentation."

Figure 1.2: Pompey the Great.

After seeing his image we are certainly not surprised to learn that he was especially susceptible to flattery and ostentatious praise. And of course art provides us glimpses into the ordinary daily life of the people of the past. The scenes from Greek vase paintings, the frescos from the buildings of Pompeii, the bass-relief plaques and decorations from monuments give us important information about the ancient world not obtainable from any other source. The authors of ancient literature did not perceive these things worthy of description, and without art our perception of the ancient world would be dry and unappealing.

Art can also supply us with detailed facts and descriptions of specific historical events not available from any other source. One example: in modern Rome, adjacent to the Roman Forum, stands a commemorative column dedicated to the Emperor Trajan in the year 113 CE (Fig. 1.3) as a triumphal monument and a memorial to the Dacian Wars. The column soars over 100 feet high, and its surface consists of a 3 foot wide bass-relief ribbon, which is 670 feet long and twists around the column 23 times. The ribbon contains more than 2,500 figures, arranged in successive scenes which depict in minute detail the two Dacian Wars waged by Trajan. These wars were fought between 101 and 105 and resulted in the Roman annexation of the area of Europe known today as Romania. All the literary descriptions of this undeniably important event in the history of the ancient world and Europe are lost. The only remaining description of the war is contained in this visual document. Specialists in the military history of this period have been able to reconstruct an exhaustive narrative of the wars from this column. If we did not have this work of art, we would know next to nothing about these wars. Art, then, is a tremendously important source of evidence for the history of the ancient world.

Figure 1.3: Trajan's Column.

Written Documents

Historians of the ancient world group almost all types of surviving written material—except literary works—into this category. The term thus includes all of the written material that has come down to us from antiquity in its original form, such as official records, legal documents, laws, contracts, royal decrees, tombstone inscriptions, and even graffiti. The two most important ways this material survives is in the form of inscriptions on durable material, such as stone or bronze, and on papyrus, a paper-like material made from the fiber of the papyrus plant. Since the texts recorded on these two different materials present such dissimilar problems, the study of this category of evidence is divided into two sub-specialties: epigraphy, the study of inscriptions; and papyrology, the study of documents written on papyrus.

Epigraphy

Epigraphists study all types of texts inscribed on durable objects, most commonly on stone or bronze. Since these scholars are concerned with the form of the inscriptions as well as the content, their interests often impinge on other fields, such as art history and philology. Epigraphy excludes, but yet cannot ignore, texts on coins, gems, and pottery. The inscribed objects are frequently heavily damaged, and the first task of the epigraphists is to decipher all that can be read, which necessitates proposed restorations of what is illegible or lost. Recently, new technologies, such as digital image enhancement, computerized indices, and even x-ray techniques, have been employed to interpret epigraphical documents.

The Consular and Triumphal Fasti (Fig. 1.4) is an example of an important historical inscription. This inscription originally decorated the Arch of Augustus, dedicated in 19 BCE in the Roman Forum, but is now in the Capitoline Museum in Rome. It contains a list of Roman consuls[7] from

Figure 1.4: The Consular and Triumphal Fasti, now mounted on the wall of the Capitoline Museum in Rome.

---

7. The supreme magistrates of the Roman Republic. They were two in number, exercised equal power, and held office for one year.

483 to 19 BCE and a list of triumphators[8] from 753 to 19 BCE. The information in this priceless historical document has been used for centuries by scholars as an aid to the interpretation of Rome's political history.

Papyrology

Papyrologists study texts written on Papyrus in Egyptian, Hebrew, Aramaic, Greek, Latin, Pahlavi, and Arabic, but the vast majority of surviving papyri are written in ancient Egyptian or Greek. Every imaginable type of document, private, public, and official, have been discovered. Papyrus was manufactured in Egypt as early as 3000 BCE from a marsh plant *(Cyperus papyrus)* and was the most widely-used writing material in the ancient world, especially in the countries bordering the Mediterranean. The pith of the plant was cut into small strips and laid crossways in two layers and then pressed into sheets. The surface of these sheets were then polished and formed into the shape of roles by pasting the sheets together. It is these scrolls that are usually referred to as ancient "books." Due to the climatic conditions of the Mediterranean basin, papyrus was well preserved only in Egypt, where it is found in various places: ruins of buildings, trash heaps, coffin coverings, and other places. The mummies of animals were often stuffed with discarded papyri and frequently wrapped in the material. The condition in which the texts are found varies widely; long, undamaged rolls are rare.

By the end of the 5th century BCE, books were in general circulation in Greece, at least among the elite. There were book collectors but no institutional libraries in classical Greece. The most famous collector was the philosopher Aristotle (384–322 BCE), who founded the famous school of philosophy at Athens, known as the Lyceum. These collections remained private property, however.[9] Institutional libraries began under the Hellenistic monarchies. The most famous was the Library of Alexandria in Egypt, patronized by the Ptolemaic dynasty, which may have contained as many as 400,000 scrolls at its height. The fate of the Alexandrian Library is lost in legend, but it almost certainly did not survive into the common era.[10]

The value of papyrological material should be immediately evident. There is still much to be discovered. Not only are new papyri constantly uncovered, but there is a vast backlog of papyri in museum basements all over the world awaiting decipherment. What secrets these documents hold only the future can reveal.

---

8. A triumph involved the solemn procession of a victorious general, the triumphator, with his army and spoils into Rome. He entered the city in a chariot drawn by four white horses, dressed in purple with a golden wreath on his head. He proceeded through the city, receiving the adulations of the citizens, to the Sacred Way and thence through the Forum to the Temple of Jupiter on the Capitoline Hill.

9. The ancient Greek writer Strabo (*Geographia*, 13.1.54), writing in the 1st century BCE, describes the fate of Aristotle's library: Aristotle bequeathed his library (and school) to his pupil Theophrastus, who bequeathed it to Neleus, who took it to Scepsis (a small Greek city in Asia Minor), and it eventually fell into the hands of his heirs. They were "ordinary people" who stored the books carelessly "underground in a kind of trench," and they were damaged by moisture and moths. Their descendants sold them to Apellicon (died c. 84 BCE), who was "a collector rather than a philosopher." Apellicon moved the collection back to Athens and had the damaged parts restored, "filling in the gaps incorrectly." When the Roman general Sulla captured Athens (86 BCE), he carried Apellicon's library off to Rome as the spoils of war. There they passed through a succession of booksellers into the hands of Tyrannion, a grammarian.

10. Three stories are told over and over by both ancient and modern writers: (1) It was burned down by accident by Julius Caesar in 47 BCE during a battle in the city; (2) it was destroyed by Theophilus, the Patriarch of Alexandria, in 391 CE, "the vast structure was razed to its foundations and the scrolls from the library were burnt in huge pyres in the streets of Alexandria"; (3) in 640 CE, the Caliph Omar ordered the books and scrolls to be taken out of the library and distributed as fuel to the many bathhouses of the city, "six months were required for all of them to be burnt to ashes heating the saunas of the conquerors." None of these stories can be substantiated by the evidence.

Figure 1.5: Silver denarius of the Roman emperor Alexander Severus (BMC 6.268).

Numismatics

Numismatics is the study of coins. A coin is a piece of metal, usually silver, gold, or bronze, of a standard weight issued by a competent authority. Coinage was invented in Western Asia Minor around 600 BCE. The ancients had long been accustomed to using precious metal as a symbol of worth. Coinage made it possible to count, rather than weigh, a specific value, an obvious advantage in trade and exchange. The use of coinage spread rapidly throughout the Greek world and appeared at Rome about 300 BCE. As Rome became the master of the Mediterranean basin, the use of its coinage spread to the entire area. By the beginning of the common era Roman coinage was universal in the region, accept Egypt, where the coinage system of the Ptolemies continued. In the normal course of economic activity large collections of coins were transported, secreted, and sometimes lost. In fact, the chance discovery of large quantities (hoards) of coins, which were buried in antiquity but due to some mishap or disaster were never recovered by their owners, is the principle source of ancient coinage today.

Numismatic evidence is obviously a source of important information about the ancient world, but how does the historian interpret this data? Like the other categories of sources, numismatics is not an autonomous field of study. Numismatists are not isolated specialists who study only coins, but rather historians and archaeologists who use numismatics to contribute to the solutions of wider problems and issues.

Clearly coinage can tell us a lot about the ancient economy, the monetary system, the science of metallurgy, etc. Yet perhaps the most interesting information is contained in the coin's inscription, the message, so to speak, imprinted on the coin. We must bear in mind that in a world without any means of mass communication coinage was the only way the government could speak directly to the people. Ancient governments minted new coins very frequently—monthly, even weekly at times—in order to communicate their message to the public. Thus, the "message" on a coin is valuable historical data, but it must be evaluated carefully, because it is anything but objective.

For example, the silver denarius issued about 225 by the young emperor Severus Alexander (Fig. 1.5) seeks to reassure the people that the emperor has everything under control and they should feel secure in the power and protection of the government. On the obverse of the coin appears a handsome portrait of the emperor in profile, draped and wearing a laureate, the symbol of authority and power. The inscription around the portrait reads: IMP C M AVR SEV ALEXAND AUG, "Imperator (Emperor) Caesar Marcus Aurelius Severus Alexander Augustus," the full formal name of the emperor.[11] On the reverse we see a Winged Victory holding a wreath in her right hand and a palm branch in her left, the symbols of peace. The inscription here reads simply: VICTORIA AVG, "Victorious Augustus." While this coin does not memorialize any specific victory, it symbolizes the

---

11. The Romans were very fond of abbreviations.

strength and invincibility of the emperor and was undoubtedly intended to impart a feeling of well being and security to the public. This message does not necessarily reflect the reality of the state of the empire, but it does tell us the image the government sought to project at this particular moment. It informs us what the government was "thinking about," so to speak. Thus, it is significant historical information.

Literature

The study of ancient literature in its original languages is philology. Ancient literature is perhaps the most important, and at the same time the most abused, source of information about the ancient world. Every literary text reveals the personality, ideas, opinions, interests, and biases of its author, as well as the ideology, political outlook, and historical context of the author's culture and time. Every writer who ever wrote a single line was driven to do so by a motive, either conscious or unconscious, and that motive colored and injected bias into the resultant text. Thus, it is vitally important to understand the intentions behind the text. Also, there is a further complication. Ancient texts have not come down to us in their original form. All the ancient texts which survive today are the result of forces completely unrelated to the original intentions of the authors. The surviving texts have been copied numerous times throughout antiquity and the Middle Ages. Mistakes, intentional and unintentional, have crept into all texts. Indeed, preservation of an ancient text in anything close to its original form is rare.

A basic problem of interpreting with ancient literature is the question of objectivity. Inexperienced readers tend to instinctively trust ancient writings. Time imparts a sacrosanctity upon ancient writing. A statement written 2,000 years ago has "stood the test of time," as it were. But *age* does not equal *truth*; a lie is not magically transformed into truth by the passing of time. The reader must be vigilant. Ancient literature is loaded with lies and deceptions. And not infrequently the reader is confronted by what can only be called the "big lie." An illustrative example can be cited from a text written by the first Roman emperor Caesar Augustus. Augustus ruled the Roman Empire as an absolute monarch from the time he defeated Mark Antony in 31 BCE until his death in 14 CE. Near the end of his life he wrote the *Res Gestae*, his last will and testament, in which he listed his achievements. Here is a statement from that work:

> In my sixth and seventh consulships [28–27 BCE], after I had extinguished civil wars, and at a time when with universal consent I was in complete control of affairs, I transferred the republic from my power to the dominion of the senate and people of Rome. For this service of mine I was named Augustus by decree of the senate, and the door-posts of my house were publicly wreathed with bay leaves and a civic crown was fixed over my door and a golden shield was set in the Curia Julia, which, as attested by the inscription thereon, was given me by the senate and people of Rome on account of my courage, clemency, justice and piety. After this time I excelled all in influence, although I possessed no more official power than others who were my colleagues in the several magistracies.[12]

After this time. . . I possessed no more official power than others who were my colleagues in the several magistracies. How are we to interpret this statement? We know from all credible evidence Augustus exercised absolute power over the state and when he asserts that he had no more power than other

---

12. Brant, P.A. and Moor, J.M., Res Gestae Divi Augusti, *The Achievements of the Divine Augustus,* Oxford University Press, Glasgow, 1967, p. 35.

magistrates he is simply lying. Yet even this lie tells us something important about Augustus and his régime. It tells how he himself wished to be remembered, not as an autocrat, not as a tyrant, but as a very successful *republican* politician. This is the image that Augustus wished to project and although it is not the true image it is nevertheless an important facet of the historical truth about Augustus. He did not wish to be perceived as an despot ruling the state illegally and he believed, perhaps sincerely, that he was a constitutional head of state. This is a significant piece of historical information, but it warns us how carefully we must interpret the information we receive from the literature of the past.

Western Civilization

The term "Western Civilization"[13] refers much more to an idea than to a geographical location. For example, we instinctively include the people who live in places like Australia and New Zealand within this term and yet they are by no stretch of the imagination located in the "West." Indeed, no one can draw a line on a map, which accurately defines the location of Western Civilization. An astronaut, viewing the earth from space, can easily make out the continent of Europe, but he cannot see the Western Civilization, because it is not confined to Europe. In fact, Western Civilization has its earliest roots not in Europe itself but in the ancient Tigris-Euphrates river basin (modern Iraq), were the first cities appeared between five and six thousand years ago. Therefore, our history begins outside the area we normally think of as the "West," in that region referred to as

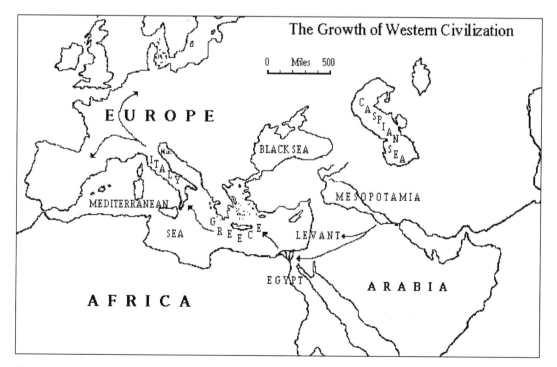

Figure 1.6: The geographical setting for the societies covered in this book.

---

13. The English word civilization derives from the Latin *civilis*, which means "civil," or "civic" and from *civilitas*, which means the art of government and politics.

Mesopotamia, the "land between the rivers." A few centuries later urban civilization also appeared in the Nile river valley and the region along the eastern Mediterranean coast called the Levant. Thus, it is here in the Middle East and North Africa, not in Europe, that the "cradle of civilization" is to be found, and it is here that we will begin our study of Western Civilization.

After the urban tradition developed for more than two thousand years in the environment of its Middle Eastern and North African origin, it began to move westward and northward, through the islands of the Aegean Sea, into the peninsula of Greece, where it flowered as never before—and possibly never since. In many ways the Greeks have never been surpassed in the quality of their culture and the intensity of their commitment to life. During a brilliant period of history known as the Hellenic Age, the Greeks founded and developed the essential elements of what we today know as modern Western Civilization, the elements that—for good or ill—have come to dominate the entire modern world: technology for harnessing nature; both the capitalist and socialist forms of economic and political organization; Western styles of music, theater, and art; the secular intellectual attitude. All of this seems completely natural to us today, but it represented a bold and original step, an unprecedented break with the past, for the ancient Greeks.

During the ensuing Hellenistic Age, this Greek culture was carried by Alexander the Great eastward into the Middle East as far as western India and then westward into north Africa, and western Europe by the Romans, who were perhaps the greatest empire builders of all time. As the Roman Empire grew to embrace the entire Mediterranean basin, it brought peace and order to that region for the only time during its long history. In the process, the Roman Empire became a crucible for the interaction of diverse cultures, languages, and religions. The result of all this interaction was a "Western" tradition, which survived the demise of Roman civilization and spread from the western Mediterranean into northern and western Europe. Here that Western Tradition was slowly transformed by the influx of several successive waves of semi-nomadic peoples, whom the Romans called "barbarians."

After more than a thousand years of incubation in western Europe, during the period known as the "Middle Ages," Western Civilization experienced a sudden flowering of creativity and genius that may, in some ways, be compared to the late Hellenic, or Classical Age of Greece. We call this period the Renaissance, the "age of rebirth." Then, with a renewed youth and vigor, Western Civilization exploded into the modern era, which spread Western influence across the entire earth, but this of course falls beyond the purview of the present volume.

Today, Western Civilization touches every human being in the world, whether they choose to be influenced by it or not. The remnants of European colonialism constantly push the developing, i.e. "Westernizing," nations toward an integrated world economy and the landscape of even the most ancient nations, like India, China, and Japan, have been transformed with highways, railroads, skyscrapers, airports, and other Western influences. Western technology has vastly increased the standard of living of the peoples of the entire world, carried human beings to the moon, and given us an image of our earth from outer space. However, that same Western technology has also poisoned our planet's air, water, and soil, while Western medicine has produced an unprecedented drop in the world-wide death rate, resulting in a sudden increase in life expectancy, which now plagues our earth with an uncontrolled population explosion. After all the triumphs of Western Civilization, this last, dark result of technology may prove to be the most terrible catastrophe ever to befall humanity.

No one can predict the future, and perhaps the historian, whose energy and expertise is directed toward the past, should not even try. Nevertheless, the human race has now entered the Twenty-first Century, and it is appropriate at this juncture to ask the question, "how did we get here?" The historian is especially well equipped to deal with this question and that is, in fact, what this book is all about, but just as important is the question "where do we go from here?" A knowledge of history—indeed of Western Civilization—is indispensable to the answer. If we wish to make intelligent choices concerning our future, concerning what road we should take into the future, we must first know where we have been, what roads we have traveled in the past and why. That is the purpose of this book—to go back and look at our past; to attempt to understand what choices we made in that past, why we made them, and what the consequences of those choices are for our present and our future. Only then can we hope to make intelligent decisions regarding our future. As the poet said long ago:

> I shall be telling this with a sigh
> Somewhere ages and ages hence:
> Two roads diverged in a wood, and I—
> I took the one less traveled by,
> And that has made all the difference.[14]

The Origins

The modern human being, species *homo sapiens sapiens,* is a member of the genus *homo,* which evolved in sub-Sahara Africa. Development of the genus spans a period of over 2 million years (Fig. 1.7). Although the fossil record is far from complete, paleoanthropologists constantly discover new evidence which is gradually making the picture more comprehensive. *Homo sapiens sapiens* is the most recent species of the genus *homo* to emerge. The earliest known example was found at Omo

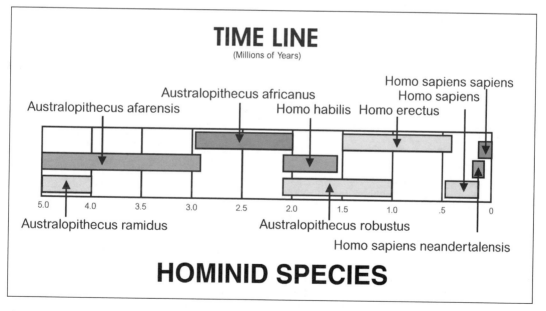

Figure 1.7

---

14. "The Road Not Taken," by Robert Frost.

in East Africa and is about 130,000 old. As historians, we need not unduly concern ourselves with those millions of years preceding the emergence of modern man—we may safely leave that to the paleoanthropologists.[15]

For most of what occurred in the beginning of human existence there is no evidence. The events that transpired in that obscure pre-historic age, a period far longer than the duration of recorded history,[16] are now lost forever. We can only guess and speculate. The first human beings obviously had to cope with their environment. Two of the major features which distinguished these early humans from other animals were language and tool making. The events surrounding the invention and development of language left behind no material remains.[17] The invention and development of tool making left behind a material residue which can be discovered, studied, and interpreted. It is much easier to study the origin of tool making than the origin of language, and for this reason it is in this context

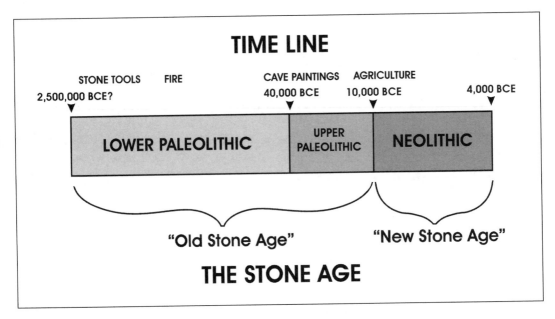

Figure 1.8

---

15. For an overview of the fascinating story of the origins of the human species, see Kennedy, G.E., *Paleoanthropology* (1980), McGraw Hill, New York.

16. Recorded history represents less than 1% of the time the human species has existed.

17. The span of time during which human language has existed is a subject of debate. The popular view is that it appeared rather suddenly about 200,000 years ago. In this view the archaeological evidence for a jump, or "revolution," in primitive technology and representational art, is also evidence for the appearence of human language. Another view, however, proposed by Terrence W. Deacon, *The Symbolic Species: The Co-evolution of Language and the Brain,* Penguin, 1997, holds that language evolved slowly over a period of 2,000,000 years or more and was triggered by the change humans made from a largely vegetarian diet to one that included meat. That change in behavior was accompanied by evolutionary changes in physiology, including the adoption of a bipedal gait and a change in the hand structure that allowed efficient gripping. All of this was accompanied by important changes in the size and structure of the brain. In other words, in Deacon's view, language developed as an integrated part of the development of all the other traits that distinguish the human species and was not simply an "invention."

that pre-history is most intently studied. The first tools were made of wood, bone, and stone, but since stone is the most durable, stone tools are the basis of the study of early humans. Thus, the pre-historic period of human development has been named the "Stone Age," which is dated from the beginning of hominid existence, (2,500,000 BCE?) to 4,000 BCE (Fig. 1.8). The Stone Age is traditionally broken up into two periods: The Paleolithic (Old Stone Age) and the Neolithic (New Stone Age).

Paleolithic Age

Human beings lived for hundreds of thousands of years by hunting and gathering. They stalked and killed animals large and small, including goats, pigs, horses, and buffalo. They took fish from the streams, rivers, and seashores. They gathered nuts, berries, fruits, grains, and green plants from the forests and meadows. But during the long Paleolithic Age, humans did not know how to raise animals or grow crops. They were totally dependant on hunting and gathering.

The chief activity of Paleolithic people was finding food, and success depended on adapting to their environment. This required the development of group behavior patterns and a social structure. Evidence provided by the size of campsites, etc. indicate that small nomadic bands of twenty to thirty people developed regular patterns of movement by following migrating animals and vegetable cycles. Very early tools were developed that made hunting and gathering more efficient. The invention of the spear and the bow and arrow made hunting more skilled, while harpoons and fish hooks increased the fish catch. All observation of contemporary human groups reveal a division of labor between the sexes. In the earliest societies, men must have done most of the hunting, while women, who bore and raised children, remained close to camp but were also responsible for gathering nuts, berries, and grains. In the past, archaeologists and anthropologists speculated that the men, because of their strength and aggressive nature, were dominant in Paleolithic society, but recently these scientists have argued that, because men and women both played important roles in providing for the community's survival, a rough equality existed between the sexes. Of course this is all pure conjecture, and it reveals more about the social environment and ideology of the scholars making these statements than it does about life in the Paleolithic Age. The fact is that we do not know and cannot know such details of the life of these peoples. Bone fragments and stone spear points do not speak to these questions, and speculation is useless.

Throughout the Paleolithic period humans continued to spread out in all directions from their point of origin in Africa and made slow but steady progress toward adapting to the various environments which they encountered. The creation of protective shelter and the effective use of fire were important aspects of the later stage of Old Stone Age, called the Upper Paleolithic (see Time Line II). Modern humans moved into Europe around 35,000 years ago at the latest, and that early group is known as Cro-Magnon man. The first skeletal remains and associated artifacts of these newcomers were found in 1868 in Les Eyzies, Dordogne, France. Later discoveries were made in a number of caverns in the Dordogne valley, Solutré, and in Spain, Germany, and central Europe. Cro-Magnon man is anatomically identical to modern humans, but differs significantly from Neanderthal man (*Homo sapiens neandertalensis*), who disappeared in the fossil record about 10,000 years after the appearance of Cro-Magnon man. The abrupt disappearance of Neanderthal populations, the sudden appearance of modern *Homo sapiens sapiens*, and the absence of transitional anatomical or technological forms have led most researchers to conclude that Neanderthal man was driven to extinction through competition with Cro-Magnon populations, but this cannot at present be conclusively proven by the available evidence. Greater linguistic competence and cultural sophistication are often suggested as characteristics tilting the competitive balance in favor of Cro-Magnon man.

As humans moved into the colder climate of Europe they found shelter in caves. Over time, however, they created new types of shelters, which amounted to artificial caves. Most common was a simple structure constructed of wood poles, or sometimes the bones of mammoths, covered with animal skins. Archaeologists believe the systematic use of fire dates back as early as 500,000 BCE. Fire provided a source of light and heat for the caves and man-made structures. Also, the use of fire made it possible for early humans to cook their food, which not only made it taste better and easier to digest but opened up new supplies of food, including some plants and animal parts which could not be consumed uncooked.

Paleolithic people did more than merely survive, they produced the first human culture. Beginning about 15,000 BCE, the cave inhabitants of southern France and northern Spain painted truly extraordinary pictures of animals, humans, and symbols (Fig. 1.9). For example, the walls of the cave at Lascaux, France, contain almost 600 depictions of animals identifiable by species. They include horses (about a quarter of the total), bison, ibex, aurochs, stags, mammoths, and, more rarely, birds and fish. A few carnivores, bears and felines, were painted in the remotest part of the cave.

Figure 1.9:
Cave painting from the Great Hall of the Bulls, Lascaux, France.

Human representations are rare in cave art, in fact there is only one anthropomorphic representation at Lascaux, in a part of the cave called the Shaft of the Dead Man. The symbols appear to be associated with animals and, although there is a vague resemblance between those found in other caves, the meaning and purpose of these symbols is controversial. Neither the landscape outside the cave nor any representation of vegetation is found in the cave paintings.

What was the purpose of this activity? Again, any answer to this question is the product of pure speculation. Paleolithic humans were still nomadic and visited these caves seasonally. Some caves show evidence of repeated painting over a period of thousands of years. These paintings were not likely produced as decorative art to enhance the decor of the cave dweller's home. They must have served some ritualistic function, perhaps to ensure the abundances of game animals, or even to give humans power over their prey in the hunt. But any attempt at understanding produces only conjecture, as none of the speculation is based on firm reality—which, of course, only increases the mystery.

The Neolithic Revolution

The climate of Europe was very cold during most of the Paleolithic. The term "Ice Age," known technically as the Pleistocene, refers to a period of marked climatic cooling that began some time before 1.5 million years ago. During this period, there were many fluctuations between warmer and cooler conditions. The cooling trend was more intense during the last 500,000 years, when massive ice sheets descended from the polar region at intervals, only to retreat during subsequent warmer periods. The last major glacial advance, known in Europe as the Würm glaciation, began about 75,000 years ago and ended about 10,000 years ago. The end of the last ice age ushered in the development of significantly new patterns of human existence. The most important change was an innovative method of food production, agriculture, which facilitated the beginnings of permanent settlements, the birth of trade, and, for the first time, the accumulation of wealth by communities and individuals, which in turn necessitated an increase in the complexity of social structure. This transformation is usually referred to as the "Neolithic Revolution."

Four different types of agriculture appear to have developed independently in four different areas of the world between 8000 and 7000 BCE:

1. The Near East (c. 8000 BCE), based on wheat, barley and lentils.
2. The Indus Valley (c. 5000 BCE), based on millet and yams.
3. Asia (c. 4000 BCE), based on rice and millet.
4. Middle America (c. 5000 BCE), based on bean, potatoes, and maize (corn).

As the last glaciers receded northward across Europe and Asia, the animals which had adapted to the cold climate, such as deer, elk, bison, and goats, moved north also. Some of the Paleolithic people moved north with the herds and continued to pursue the old way of life, but others remained behind and switched from the hunting and gathering mode of food production to agriculture. This was a momentous revolution in lifestyle.

2

The Ancient Near East

The Cradle of Western Civilization

The great arch of agriculturally-rich land stretching from the eastern Mediterranean coast through the Tigris-Euphrates river basin to the Persian Gulf is called the Fertile Crescent. It is here that the world's first civilization appeared around 3500 BCE, and it is here that our story begins. This was no accident. Civilization arose here because the conditions were right. Climatically, the highlands along the northern and eastern periphery of the Fertile Crescent received abundant rainfall throughout the year, and the prevailing temperature was conducive to farming. Just as important, however, the native flora and fauna included many species susceptible to domestication. Approximately 80% of the world's human diet consists of the products of only about a dozen plants, mostly cereals, domesticated from the hundreds of thousands of plant species found across the face of our planet. The Near East is the home of the largest number of these grains—wheat, barley, lentils and others. The picture is much the same for the domestication of animals. The Near East is the home of the ancestors of the most common domesticated animals, including dogs, pigs, sheep, goats, cows, donkeys, and horses. For these reasons, the Fertile Crescent used to be known as "the cradle of civilization," but this term is not used much anymore, probably because it appears somewhat politically incorrect nowadays. The Fertile Crescent is made up of two distinct geographical areas: The Levant, consisting of the area along the coast of the eastern Mediterranean Sea—the Palestine-Lebanon-Syria region—and Mesopotamia,[1] the region around the Tigris-Euphrates river system.

The "Invention" of Agriculture

The invention of agriculture, based on the cultivation of wheat, and the transition from a nomadic to a sedentary lifestyle occurred first in a narrow strip of land just inland from the coast of the eastern Mediterranean Sea, known as the "Levantine Corridor," (Fig. 2.1) rather than in the arid, desert-like region of the Mesopotamian plain itself. In addition to the domestication of plants and animals, another development was crucial to this transition: the ability to store food. Grain and other agricultural products are abundant at harvest time, but humans must, of course, have food supplies throughout the year, not just during the harvest season. A people known as the Natufians, who

---

1. From two Greek words, *mesos* "middle" and *potamos* "river," thus "land between the rivers."

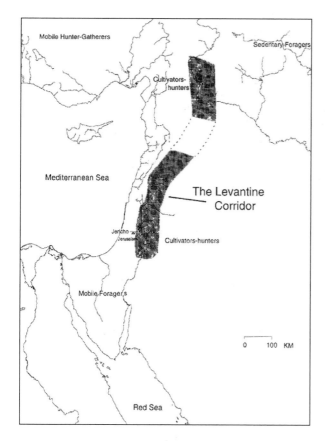

Figure 2.1: The Levantine Corridor.

inhabited the Levantine Corridor around 8500 BCE, seem to have first solved this problem by learning how to preserve grain by stockpiling it in underground storage pits. They were also the first cultivators of modern wheat.

All the evidence indicates that this is the place and time that agriculture began, but *how* did it happen? This is the mystery. Modern wheat is a mutation of wild wheat and it cannot survive on its own, it must be nurtured by humans or it will die out. The seeds of wild grains were small compared to modern wheat and they were dispersed by the wind. It was the wild grains that the Natufians gathered. Modern wheat is a mutation, a much richer and fatter grain and the seeds are bound firmly to the stalk and do not travel on the wind. Modern wheat cannot propagate itself, it must depend on humans for survival (Fig. 2.2). How did humans learn to cultivate the mutated wheat strains? Did a pre-historic genius figure out how to cultivate the wheat mutant and thereby establish the mutual dependence between humans and wheat? Once this link was established humans were bound forever to this new food supply by the technology of agriculture.

It was, indeed, once thought that a single individual, or at most a small group of individuals, were responsible for the discovery of agriculture in the Near East. It was even proposed that the women of the early Neolithic community discovered the technique of planting and harvesting plants, because of their familiarity with the grains, nuts, and fruits they were responsible for gathering while the men were off hunting, but archaeologists now believe that it was much more complicated than

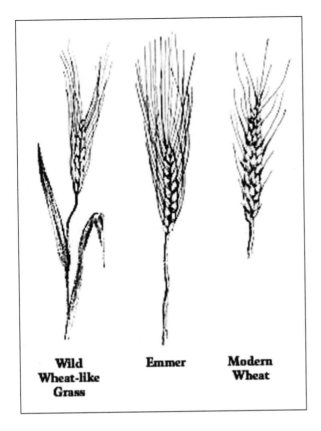

**Wild
Wheat-like
Grass**   **Emmer**   **Modern
Wheat**

Figure 2.2: The mutation of wheat.

that. Several hypotheses have been offered.[2] V.G. Childe proposed the "oasis theory." He believed the post-glacial warming resulted in humans and animals concentrating into river valleys, which forced on humans a new strategy of food production based on plant cultivation and animal domestication. Robert Braidwood proposed that agriculture originated not in the river valleys but the highland zones where wild grains flourish, and he proposed that evolving technology led humans to settle in villages and domesticate plants and animals.

Now Ofer Bar-Yosef and others offer the "historical narrative explanation," which takes into account the unique geographic conditions of the Levant and archaeological history of the region. According to this theory, toward the end of the last ice age the landscape of the Levant was quite different than it is today. It was the home of lush growths of numerous edible annual seed plants, including cereals, legumes, fruits, and game animals. This means that hunter-gather groups need not range over large territories. By about 12,500 BCE, humans occupied every environmental niche in the Levant. Hunter-gather groups inhabited the inland desert oases, but they were highly mobile and thinly distributed. Along the coast forager groups pursued a well-established semi-sedentary lifestyle. But about 11,000 BCE, there was a change in the climate. A short, cold period was immediately fol-

2. For an overview of theories explaining the origins of agriculture see: Childe, V.G., *New Light on the Most Ancient Near East* (1953), Praeger, New York; Braidwood, R.J., *The Near East and the Foundations for Civilization* (1952), Eugene, Condon Lectures, Oregon State System of Higher Education; Bar-Yosef, O., "The Natufian Culture in the Levant, Threshold to the Origins of Agriculture," *Evolutionary Anthropology*, 6.6 (1998) 159-177.

lowed by in increase in precipitation, which caused the forests to expand, and this had a major impact. The most practical response to this new environment was a sedentary settlement pattern within a definite homeland territory. This produced the people known as the Natufians who introduced a whole inventory of technological innovations, including sickles, picks, and food processing tools such as mortars and pestles. Competition for limited food resources resulted between the sedentary groups, and others who remained mobile, especially when a new climatic crisis, known as the "Younger Dryas,"[3] reduced the yields of the natural stands of cereals and fruits. This forced the sedentary groups to change their lifestyle, resulting in experimental planting, shifts in the location of their settlements, and clearing of patches of land for cultivation. The result was the appearance of the first Neolithic farming villages. The rapid return of wetter conditions around 8000 BCE produced an expansion of lakes and ponds which facilitated the cultivation of various annual plants along their shores, especially in the Levantine Corridor. The beginning of agriculture, according to the "historical narrative explanation," was a natural solution for a population who had become dependant on cereals for their food requirements. The domestication of wheat and other grains was an unintentional and even unconscious result of the process of survival. From this point onward, Neolithic villages, with populations of 300 to 500, began to appear throughout the Near East.

Still the mystery remains: Did the increase in human population at the end of the last ice age force humans to adopt the new technology of agriculture, force them to find a more efficient method of food production ("necessity is the mother of invention") in order to feed the increasing number of people, or did the invention of agriculture increase food supplies to the extent that a sudden increase in the population was the result? In other words, was this sudden population increase a cause or an effect? It is the old question of which came first, the chicken or the egg?

The Neolithic Village: Çatal Hüyük

The landscape along the Levantine Corridor and arch which forms the northern and northeastern periphery of Mesopotamia must have been dotted with countless Neolithic villages, but only a few of these sites have been excavated and studied extensively by archaeologists. Among the most

---

3. The Younger Dryas Period was a general warming trend about 9000 BCE, and it had a significant effect on the climate of the earth. Greenland ice core records of CO_2 levels indicate that mean temperatures dropped significantly, and all climates, including tropical and subtropical climates, became colder and dryer. Pollen records indicate that areas that were typically forests died off and made way for herbaceous plants, the type of low lying bushes that are very common on tundras and in tundra-like climates. Then after an estimated period of about 700 years, records indicate that the herbaceous plants disappeared and the common forests of before reappeared. This marked the end of the Younger Dryas, and when the warming resumed, temperatures rose 15 degrees C in about 40 to 50 years.

It is believed that the cause of the Younger Dryas period and the key to a global "cold spell" can be traced to the oceans and the circulation of ocean water. The warming trend caused larger amounts of ice to melt in the North Atlantic. So much fresh water was being poured by these ice sheets into the seas round Labrador and Greenland that it prevented the downturn of cold, salty ocean water to the ocean bottom. As a result, the global ocean conveyor halted and the circulation of warm water that typically was brought up to the North Atlantic was halted. The lack of ability to mix the ocean water and have an equilibrium sent the temperatures dropping.

All of this illustrates the fact that the earth experiences, often and quite naturally, large changes in temperature and climate. Is the current "global warming" trend a natural or a man-made event? Perhaps it is a bit arrogant of humans to think that they have control over such events.

important are Çatal Hüyük (6500 BCE), Jarmo (6000 BCE), Ain Ghazal (7200 BCE), and Jericho (8000 BCE). A brief description of Çatal Hüyük will provide an indication at least of what life was like in that New Stone Age long ago.[4]

Çatal Hüyük is situated on a double mound in the south Anatolian Plateau, in a region known as the Konya Plain. Almost all the excavation done so far has centered on the so-called west mound, and the term "Çatal Hüyük" generally refers to this area of the site. The Konya Plain has an elevation of 3,200 feet and is completely surrounded by mountains with no natural drainage. The 9.7 inches of annual precipitation flows mostly through the Çarsamba River into Lake Beysehir. Today the plain is an important producer of barley, wheat, rye, oats, beans, and lentils, and it must have been heavily cultivated during the Neolithic period also.

The buildings of Çatal Hüyük are arranged in a number of congested major blocks, with sizable open spaces between them. The houses are rectangular in plan—no evidence at all of circular construction—and have common walls, but true right angles are rare, since the shape of the individual houses are determined by the adjoining structures. Most houses have adjacent storerooms, which may be entered directly from the houses through entrances so low that a person would have to crawl. But such doorways never provide access to the outside. Abandoned areas are used as courtyards, refuse dumps, and probably toilets. Strangely, there is no evidence whatever of windows. The method of entry into the houses is not clearly established by the excavations so far, but must surely be from the roof. Although this compact method of construction obviously suggests a strong concern for community defense, no outer defensive wall has been located. Thus, there is the implication that warfare was not a major occupation of this society.

A ladder providing access to the roof is always positioned against the south wall. The hearths and ovens are also placed along this same wall, probably to take advantage of the opening in the roof. Permanent benches and low platforms are located along the walls of all houses. Wooden beams were used throughout the site and, at the high point in the town's history, the building structure was essentially a timber frame with mud brick filling between the tempers—no stone was used in the construction of Çatal Hüyük. The bricks were formed in molds and included a high percentage of straw. The walls and floors were coated with white mud plaster, which made a suitable background for painting. Amazingly, up to 120 layers of plaster have been found in some buildings and all the wooden elements of the buildings are always covered with plaster. The roofs consisted of a number of timber cross beams resting on the wall tops with matting supported by lighter beams and a thick mud coating on top. All roofs were flat and used for communication between the various buildings. They had to be strong enough to support relatively heavy loads. One wonders how often a stranger came crashing through a roof into the home of a family! There is no evidence of upper stories in any part of the town and no streets connect the various parts of the community.

The wall paintings at Çatal Hüyük are among the earliest yet found anywhere, and they are unique. Paintings are not found on the walls of all buildings, and many walls contain paintings that were covered over with layers of plaster. Indeed, several painted surfaces may be found on the same wall and are usually separated by multiple unpainted layers of plaster. Some archaeologists speculate that the walls were re-plastered annually, but why some layers were painted while others were not

---

4. For further reading concerning this interesting and important site, see: Mellaart, James, *Çatal Hüyük, a Neolithic Town in Anatolia* (1967), McGraw-Hill Book Company, New York; Todd, Ian A., *Çatal Hüyük in Perspective* (1976), Cummings Publishing Company, London; Hodder, Ian, editor, *On the Surface: Çatalhöyük 1993–95* (1996), British Institute of Archaeology at Ankara.

and why paintings still in good condition were plastered over is still a mystery. Subjects include geometric patterns, symbols, and animal and human figures. The paintings are polychrome, but the colors are clearly not meant to be naturalistic. As archaeologist James Mellaart puts it:

> Prima facie acceptance of the colours as naturalistic would create a naïve picture of a polychrome society of red or white women, red men with red or black hands pursuing blue cows and red and black bulls, which is anything but convincing.[5]

The reason for the use of a specific color, however, is unknown. Although the subject matter of many of the paintings appears to be religious in nature, only subjective interpretations can be made concerning the colors, symbols, and geometric patterns they employ. Some of the patterns are apparently purely decorative and even resemble the patters found on modern kilims (colorful modern Turkish mats) and are thus interpreted by some archaeologists as copies of woven textile patterns. It has even been suggested that some of the blank walls were originally covered with woven textile hangings and thus were left unpainted for this purpose. This is highly controversial, however, and none of the textile fragments found at Çatal Hüyük show any evidence of colored patterns.

Human figures in these scenes are almost always associated with birds and animals. Most of the paintings present the impression of cheerful humor: some figures seem to be dancing while others tease the animals by pulling their tails or tongues. Most commonly depicted animal species are the bull, wild donkey, bore, deer, bear, lion, dog, and wolf. Humans are painted in red, black, and pink—some figures are half pink and half black with multi-colored hands. Most are clearly male. A few scenes appear to depict the actual hunt itself. One impressive scene shows a man pursuing a stag and a fawn, armed with bow and arrow, accompanied by a dog.

Relief decorations also occur in association with many of the paintings. Subjects include human figures, animals, animal heads, and rows of what seem to be human female breasts. The horned bull is the most commonly represented animal head. They are made of clay, covered with plaster, and often painted decorations (handprints, net patterns, linear motifs) which differ from layer to layer. Reliefs of complete animals are rare. Horned pillars and benches appear along the east wall near the south end of some houses. The most complex benches have as many as seven pairs of horns mounted along their length. Horned pillars, called "bull-pillars," occur frequently. The structures in which these appear are assumed to be shrines by some archaeologists.

Large numbers of clay and stone statuettes were found at Çatal Hüyük, which the archaeologists believe depict "deities in anthropomorphic or near-anthropomorphic form," though they are able to produce little hard evidence to support this interpretation. Many of these objects are very primitive: "Often a little carving suffices to turn a pebble into a schematic seated goddess." But other figures are more sophisticated. The majority of them depict an obese human female, usually seated, with exaggerated breasts, buttocks, and thighs. This type is classified as the "Mother Goddess." Other figures depict males and a few seem to represent younger females and males. Mellaart groups these types into a "divine family" consisting of "four aspects. . . in order of importance: mother, daughter, son and father."[6] He, and other archaeologists, then proceed to draw conclusions such as:

> There can be little doubt that the people of Çatal Hüyük conceived their deities in human form endowed with supernatural power over their attributes and symbols taken from the animal world.[7]

---

5. Mellaart, James, *Çatal Hüyük, a Neolithic Town in Anatolia* (1967), McGraw-Hill Company, New York, p. 115.

6. Why the father ranks at the very bottom of the family hierarchy, even below his children, is not explained.

7. Mellaart, James, *Çatal Hüyük, a Neolithic Town in Anatolia* (1967), McGraw-Hill Company, New York, p. 181.

And:

> If the goddess presided over all the various activities of the life and death of the Neolithic population of Çatal Hüyük, so in a way did her son. Even if his role is strictly subordinate to hers, the male's role in life appears to have been fully realized.[8]

The Neolithic people of Çatal Hüyük buried their dead beneath the floors of their houses. The burials were multiple—as many as forty-two bodies were entombed beneath one house. This seems astonishing, even repulsive, to modern sensibilities. A great deal of obscurity and ambiguity surrounds what we know (or think we know) about these burial customs. That the people entombed their dead under the platforms of their houses and shrines, almost never under any other part of the floor and never under storerooms is clear, but ritual surrounding the burials, the method of preparing the body for entombment and religious beliefs which were a part of these customs can only be the subject of speculation. We can do little more than describe the evidence.

The condition of the remains makes it obvious that these burials were secondary, that is, the bodies of the deceased were, to varying degrees, stripped of soft tissue before burial inside the dwellings. This was probably not for hygienic purposes but the result of a highly developed rite of passage:[9]

> Upon death the corpse of the deceased was probably moved to a mortuary outside the settlement where vultures cleaned the corpses down to the bones and dry ligaments. Presumably the dead were exposed on platforms, accessible to the birds and insects, but not to dogs and other scavengers which carry off bones. Evidently care was taken to preserve the skeleton intact in anatomical position and a check was kept on their identity. Whether this was the duty of the relatives or that of a special class of undertakers is of course not known, but the former seems more likely. . . In a fair number of skeletons the brain was still in the skulls, but in one instance it was removed and a ball of fine cloth substituted.
> It seems extremely likely that the burial of the dead coincided with the annual spring or early summer redecoration of houses and shrines, when the population must have found other quarters for the duration of the burial rites, the white-washing and the time required for the plaster to dry out thoroughly. This implies that the dead were kept in the mortuary until the annual ceremony and it is therefore not surprising to find differences in the state of incarnation of the corpses.[10]

Of course this hypothesis is based on a great deal of speculation. For one thing, it postulates the existence of a mortuary enclosure somewhere outside Çatal Hüyük, and it is very unlikely that archaeological proof of such a facility will ever be discovered. However, Mellaart drew attention to a mysterious wall painting which appears to depict a lightly built gabled structure with human skulls laid out below it. The majority of the burials at Çatal Hüyük did not include grave goods, but some contained items such as weapons, tools, belt hooks and eyes for male bodies and jewelry, beads, pendants, obsidian mirrors, and cosmetic items for female bodies.

What does all of this say about the Neolithic person's religious beliefs? Again, all we can do is speculate. Mellaart states that "out of 139 rooms excavated at Çatal Hüyük. . .not less than forty and

---

8. Mellaart, James, *Çatal Hüyük, a Neolithic Town in Anatolia* (1967), McGraw-Hill Company, New York, p. 184.

9. Rite of passage: A ritual or ceremony signifying or facilitating an event in a person's life indicative of a transition from one stage to another, as from adolescence to adulthood.

10. Mellaart, James, *Çatal Hüyük, a Neolithic Town in Anatolia* (1967), McGraw-Hill Company, New York, p. 204-205.

probably more, appear to have served Neolithic religion." But this is based more on conjecture than evidence because he goes on to state:

> Such cult rooms or shrines are more elaborately decorated than houses and they are frequently, but not always, the largest buildings in the quarter. In plan and construction they are no different from ordinary dwellings and they include all the familiar built-in furniture, such as platforms, benches, hearths and ovens which we have already recognized as an integral part of the Çatal Hüyük building tradition.[11]

Elsewhere he states that the rooms contain "no provision for sacrifice," no alters, no "direct evidence for burnt offerings." So why are these rooms designated as shrines? And burials took place under these rooms just as did under the other dwellings, but never under storerooms. From the evidence presented by Mellaart himself then, it seems more likely these rooms he calls "shrines" were simply the dwellings of the elite upper class members of the community.

Although very little can be learned about the actual technology of Neolithic agriculture from Çatal Hüyük, we do learn from excavated residue that they cultivated at least twelve crops, including fruits, nuts, and three types of wheat. There is also evidence of domesticated animals, including cattle, sheep, goats, and dogs. Food surpluses made it possible for some members of the community to do something other than farming. This increased the social complexity of the community. There must have been at least a rudimentary class structure. In a community of this size there had to be leaders and followers, and this implies a political activity. There must also have been at least the beginnings of a division of labor. Obviously some people were artists, some crafted weapons, tools, and jewelry, while others worked in the fields. This social and political structure of the Neolithic period will be the basis for the development of civilization in later centuries.

Yet, the archaeological evidence does not present us with a detailed picture of the social events and the religious life of the people of Çatal Hüyük. Archaeology does not provide us with a social and political history, but only an out of focus snapshot of certain physical remains of the society. An analysis of the burial data appears to indicate that the inhabitants of Çatal Hüyük believed in some kind of afterlife—but what they imagined that afterlife to be like cannot be known. Some of them, at least, must have believed that they would have a need for the ordinary articles they had used in this life, thus the necessity to take these items into the grave. But again, this is little more than conjecture. They almost certainly practiced religious rituals and ceremonies, but whether they worshiped deities at indoor or open air shrines outside the building, we cannot know. There is no evidence of such activity in the courtyards, and the evidence that certain rooms served as shrines is ambiguous. The slim evidence uncovered from the ground seems quite adequate for archaeologists to make sweeping interpretations, but this is far too much speculation for the historian. There is simply no hard and specific evidence to support most of this assumption and conjecture.[12] The real importance of Çatal Hüyük is that the physical remains of this town built 8,500 years ago give us a hint, dim thought it may be, of how those first farmers lived, and it demonstrates that early Neolithic agriculture, primitive though it may have been, could support fairly large groups of people living in a quasi-urban environment. We cannot know what those people *thought* or what they *believed* in any detail, but we can certainly see and admire what they achieved—in the material aspects of their society, at least.

---

11. Mellaart, James, *Çatal Hüyük, a Neolithic Town in Anatolia* (1967), McGraw-Hill Company, New York, p.77.

12. If one did not fear to be labeled a cynic, one could just as easily conclude from the evidence that these figurines of the "Mother Goddess" were from the collections of pornographic objects stored up by the "dirty old men" of the community. But the author, who does not wish to known as a cynic, would never make such an assertion.

The Neolithic Experience

The invention of agriculture had far reaching consequences for the history of humanity, and the development is quite justly referred to as a "revolution." The social effects are easy to discern. The members of hunter-gather societies must carry everything with them, even their young, as they wander over the landscape in search of game or forage for plant food. Under these conditions, very little in the way of "possessions" can be accumulated, and members of the group are not differentiated from one another on the basis of wealth. Of course, the hunter-gather groups surely had leaders and a social structure, but the leaders could not have held their positions on the basis of how much property they managed to accumulate.

In contrast, settled, agricultural communities, by necessity, accumulated surpluses and stored commodities. There is an abundance of food at harvest time, but most of it must be stored in order to survive until the next harvest. Every house at Çatal Hüyük, for example, had an adjoining store-room. Quite naturally differences arose in the amount of surplus items an individual member of the community could acquire and store up for himself. Thus, the concepts of "property" and "wealth" were born, and they have been with us ever since. In time, the amount of wealth an individual (or a family) possesses can become quite divorced from the value of the contributions of the individual to the welfare and success of the community. So significant social and economic differences between individuals arose within human society for the first time. Agriculture also produced a more cohesive society. Once humans became accustomed to a sedentary way of life they became bound more tightly to the community, and it was much more difficult for an individual to split away. Each individual must sacrifice a certain amount of independence and freedom to function as part of a group.

Furthermore, this sedentary way of life sparked a new inventiveness. The first evidence of pottery occurred around 8000 BCE, and this allowed for more efficient storage of food. Eventually potters learned to fashion earthenware on a rotating wheel, which allowed them to create a pot in minutes that had previously required hours. Weaving appears to have been invented in Anatolia around 7000 BCE. The first cloth was linen, made from the fiber of the flax plant, which is native to the Near East. Flax seed may have originally been used for food. The plant grows to a height of from 12 to 40 inches, and the fiber used for cloth is contained in the stems. Twisting the flax fiber into the form of rope and twine was probably the first step and occurred as early as the Upper Paleolithic. The use of twine led naturally to the development of basket weaving. Perhaps necessity was the mother of invention. Pre-agricultural humans, living as hunter-gathers, clothed themselves in animal skins, but for the increasing populations of the Neolithic villages, this was not adequate. Even after the domestication of animals, their slaughter to provide clothing was not economical. At any rate, the next step was the invention of the loom, a device which interweaves threads into cloth. Amazingly, the same series of inventions took place in both the old and the new worlds independently. Perhaps the most important single fiber, however, is wool. Its use did not appear until sometime later, perhaps around 3500 BCE. Interestingly, the first sheep domesticated did not produce wool but were used for meat, milk, and hides. Breeding sheep for wool was a human innovation, an example of how domesticated animals were modified by selection from an early time.

Religion was not a product of the Neolithic revolution, it had existed earlier, but it was surely an important aspect of the life of the inhabitants of the first farming villages. Early farmers were quite naturally concerned about fertility, weather, and the turn of the seasons, forces of nature beyond their control. It was also natural for them to personify the impersonal forces of nature, both benign and malignant, into beings or "divinities" with which they could interact. Regardless of whether this urge to transform the impersonal into the personal is rational or not, it seems to be

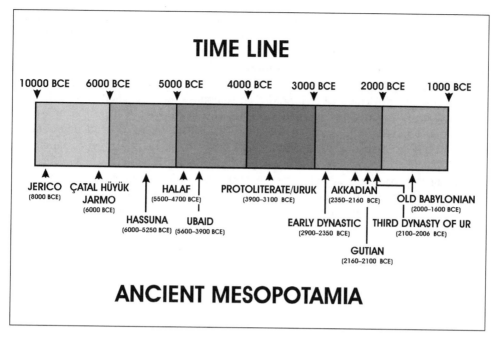

Figure 2.3

deeply embedded into what we can only describe as "human nature." The most important of these natural forces, at least to the early Neolithic humans, were the forces that drive the life cycles of the plants and animals upon which their existence depended, that basket of natural phenomena modern scholars call "fertility." The early agriculturalists, therefore, perceived these forces to be under the control of a divine being we call the "Mother Goddess." This term is derived from the countless statues of the obese female found in every Neolithic site (Fig. 2.3). Other deities were perceived to have a relationship with the central fertility power. Slowly, over the generations, ritual, ceremony, and custom grew up around these deities until the worship of the pantheon of gods and goddesses became the focus of daily life in the Neolithic societies.

The Settling of Mesopotamia

The rich alluvial plain of the Tigris-Euphrates river basin was not exploited during the first phase of the Neolithic revolution due to the lack of rainfall and the absence of plants a. .nimals suitable for domestication. However, once a diverse agricultural technology was acquired, a repertoire of domesticated plants and animals was established and a complex and stable social structure was developed, population pressure and the urge of adventure pushed groups of people into the Mesopotamian area. Only one more invention was necessary to open up the incredibly rich plain to exploitation: irrigation. Obviously, a vast investment of labor is required to construct and maintain the necessary irrigation canals, but once that investment is made, the rewards of farming the alluvial plain are far greater than farming the thin rocky soil of the highlands. It has been estimated that the return per man hour of labor for irrigation farming in Mesopotamia was at least 4 times greater than for dry farming in the surrounding mountains. Though rainfall was far from sufficient, the Tigris-Euphrates river system provided a plentiful supply of water. A series of cultures, each building on the accomplishments of its predecessors, settled and opened up the rich plain of Mesopotamia.

It is important to note, however, that the transition from Neolithic culture to urban civilization did not occur in a "Garden of Eden," but in one of the most unexpected and seemingly inhospitable environments imaginable. This "cradle of civilization" corresponds roughly to modern Iraq. There is very limited rainfall across the area—certainly not enough to support even the most primitive dry farming—and summer temperatures routinely exceed 110° F. The soil is arid and unproductive unless copiously irrigated. The land is flat and vulnerable to the frequent and irregular flooding of the Tigris and Euphrates rivers, which periodically produce floods of indescribable violence and destruction. The Tigris, in particular, is prone to settle back into a different course from one year to the next after a violent rampage. This could leave an entire city—which depended on the river for its very existence-isolated miles away from its water supply. Nevertheless, it was here where the first cities and the first civilization arose (Fig. 2.4).

Hassuna (6000–5250 BCE)

The first agricultural people to move into the Mesopotamian area were the Hassuna. They appeared about 6000 BCE along the west bank of the northern Euphrates, in the piedmont or foothill area where there was sufficient rainfall to allow dry farming in some places. They lived in small villages or hamlets ranging from two to eight acres in size. Obviously, dry farming here was much more tenuous than in the highlands. Even the largest Hussuna villages, which numbered 500 people at the most, were smaller than Çatal Hüyük, which was still occupied to the north in Anatolia. The earliest settlements may have been only semi-permanent, and the occupants may have moved elsewhere during bad crop years. There is no evidence of irrigation. They possessed domesticated cattle, sheep, and goats, but hunting, and probably foraging as well, were still very important to their subsistence. They constructed rectangular, multi-room dwellings around open courtyards out of packed mud. The houses contained small rooms with plastered floors, storage niches, and wall paintings. Both outdoor ovens and indoor ovens with chimneys were used. Other, larger buildings appear to be community or group storage facilities, which implies some kind of community economic cooperation. They developed their early crude earthenware into a sophisticated painted style of pottery. They utilized hand axes, sickles, and grinding stones. The female figurines found at their sites have been interpreted as the early fertility goddess worshiped throughout the Near East as the "Mother Goddess."

Halaf (5500–4700 BCE)

At the end of the Hassuna period a new culture appeared, named for the best known site at Tell Halaf on the Khabur River, a tributary of the Euphrates. The Halaf culture is characterized by a fine painted pottery with designs in black, red, and white on a buff background. Unfortunately, no Halaf settlement has been extensively excavated, although some buildings have been studied. They were circular buildings approached through long rectangular anterooms. The were constructed of mud brick, sometimes on stone foundations. The life of Halaf people was basically similar to that of the Hassuna. They practiced dry farming, cultivating emmer wheat, barley, and flax; they kept cattle, sheep, and goats. Analysis of the clay used in the pottery indicates that pots from a single clay source are found as much as 600 miles apart. Thus, some pots moved at least 300 miles, which indicates the existence of a complex long-distance trade. Halaf communities also produced baked clay

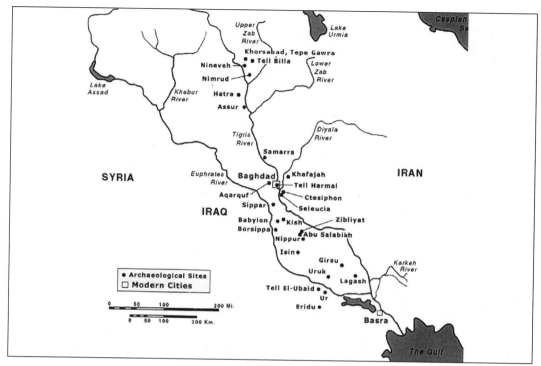

Figure 2.4: Archaeological sites of Mesopotamia.

female figurines and stamp seals of stone. The appearance of stamp seals has been interpreted to mark the appearance of the concept of personal property, because at a later date they were used to produce marks of ownership.

Ubaid (5600-3900 BCE)[13]

This culture, named after the site at Tell El-Ubaid (Fig. 2.4), represents the earliest settlers on the alluvial plain of southern Mesopotamia.[14] The early Ubaid period is contemporary with the late Halaf in the north. It eventually spread into northern Mesopotamia, however, and replaced the Halaf culture. Ubaid pottery is characterized by a buff or greenish background decorated with brown and black geometric designs.

The origin of the "Ubaidians" is obscure. Southern Mesopotamia may have been visited, or occupied, by a thin population of foragers and pastoralists earlier—the evidence is ambiguous. These earlier people (if they existed) may have settled down and become the Ubaid people, or they may have mixed with incoming settlers to create the new Ubaid culture. One problem is that the sea level is higher today than during the early and pre-Ubaid period (due to the melting of the

13. Archaeologists divide the Ubaid period into I, II, III, and IV sub-periods, and a few add a "0" period at the beginning. These sub-periods refer, in general, to the stratification, or layers, of settlement uncovered by the archaeologists as they excavate down to the bottom of a site. However, we need not concern ourselves here with niceties of this detailed classification. We will simply consider the general outline of this 1,700 year long period.

14. This is the area known as Sumer during the later, historical age.

retreating glaciers far to the north) and the coast may have been further out than it is today. Thus, the earliest sites may be under the sea, but there is nothing under the known Ubaid sites, indicating there were no earlier settlements in the region.

Lack of rain in the Mesopotamian plain required the development of irrigated agriculture, and the Ubaidians were the first to employ this new and revolutionary farming system. They grew wheat, barley, and lentils and they kept sheep, goats, and cattle. However, they also hunted gazelle and horses and took fish from the local rivers. Mineral resources, even stone, were very rare in southern Mesopotamia, but one thing the Ubaid people had in abundance: clay. Pottery was turned out on a "turnette," or slow wheel and it became simpler and more utilitarian over time. But they exploited clay for a wide range of other uses: clay sickles and other tools (amazingly!); clay figurines, both male and female; and mud bricks for construction. Building stone, precious stones, wood, metals, and many other materials all had to imported: thus the development of trade.

The Ubaid people built larger towns, developed a more complex social structure and more highly organized economy than any previous culture. The economy was driven by the exciting new irrigation agriculture and the need to import resources from neighboring areas—it can, in a sense, be described as the first "market economy." Procurement expeditions were mounted and trading posts were established, and this facilitated the spread of Ubaid culture to other areas. An expanding economy resulted in an expanding population. Ubaid culture expanded northward along the Tigris and Euphrates rivers as far north as modern Turkey and southward along the coast of the Persian Gulf into modern Saudi Arabia. Items were imported from as far away as India (amazonite, a semi-precious stone) and Anatolia (obsidian). Interestingly, much of this Ubaid expansion was not permanent. For example, the Ubaid sites in Saudi Arabia were occupied for long periods, but eventually abandoned and the local people reverted back to a hunting and foraging economy.

As the Ubaid settlements grew in size they increased in complexity. By 4500 BCE, there were a number of large urban cities ranging in population from 1,000 to 3,000 (and some archaeologists claim 5,000) inhabitants. These were surrounded by a network of small hamlets. The largest towns were comparable to Jericho and Çatal Hüyük in size, but unlike those earlier sites the Ubaid sites continued to expand and to get more complex. This was the dawn of the "urban revolution." These towns also began to exhibit the more stratified social structure which was developing. The best example is the site at Eridu, first occupied around 4750 BCE. The town was constructed around a large mud-brink temple, which was rebuilt no less than 13 times, each time larger and more elaborate, from about 2500 to 2000 BCE, a period of 500 years! The Ubaid temple form set the pattern for temples for the rest of ancient history in Mesopotamia: a central rectangular room, the "cella," with a recess at one end containing a pedestal, possibly an alter, and a second pedestal standing out in the main room with signs of burning on top. Later temples added more subsidiary rooms and were built on raised platforms approached by stairs. The final temple—built long after the Ubaid period—was atop a high platform measuring 35 × 65 feet with a stairway leading up the front of the platform to the temple entrance. Around the temple buildings were arranged in loose concentric zones: larger, elite houses closest to the temple, craft workshops further away, and farmers around the edges. This suggests a stratified social structure with the upper class people associated with the temple.

This was a new kind of society. The community centered around one, or a few, large shared religious structures that served not only the large town but also the inhabitants of the nearby hamlets, in contrast to the household shrines at Çatal Hüyük. These temples were places where labor and goods were concentrated to build and maintain the structure, to carry out rituals and other religious activities. The higher status individuals of the community were associated with the religious institution and probably exercised some kind of leadership and control over the community, as suggested by the fact that their houses, which were the largest and most elaborate, were situated near the temple. Again, the problem of cause or effect (the chicken or the egg dilemma); did the stratification of society cause the development of this new religion institution, the temple, or did the development of a new religious form produce a stratification of society?

The Emergence of Civilization

By the end of the Ubaid period, Mesopotamia was thinly inhabited by irrigation farming communities, and the area was poised for an explosive expansion and development into a more complex society. In other words, Mesopotamia was on the verge of civilization.

Protoliterate or Uruk (3900–3100 BCE)[15]

The Uruk *period* (the name preferred by archaeologists) should not be confused with the *site* of Uruk, which developed into an important city and was inhabited through several later periods. To avoid confusion, we will refer to this period, which marked the emergence of civilization, as the "protoliterate period."

One of the most striking aspects of the protoliterate period was the appearance of a dynamic new people, the Sumerians. Their origins are rather obscure. Some scholars believe their original homeland was somewhere around the Caspian Sea to the north.[16] In any event, by about 3800 BCE, the Sumerians had supplanted the Ubaidians in southern Mesopotamia and they gave their name to that area, which we today call "Sumer." Their influence was profound and they ushered in a period of accelerated change. They built vastly better canals for irrigating crops and opened up enormously productive new lands to cultivation. They introduced the plow, which also increased productivity. This brought about a large, sudden increase in the population. Sumerian towns sprang all over southern Mesopotamia.

The economy began to expand dramatically. The introduction of the true potter's wheel (in contrast with "tournette," or slow wheel) allowed mass production of ceramics. Interestingly, a side effect of this was the simplification of design and a decline of craftsmanship in the production of pottery. We are familiar with this phenomenon in the modern world. Whenever machines replace craftsmen, the resulting products almost always become more utilitarian, more efficient, but also less esthetically pleasing. The Sumerians also developed sophisticated copper casting techniques, using molds and the lost wax process. They introduced the wheeled cart, pulled by donkeys, and improved boat design, which contributed to the development of a greatly improved distribution system.

As the towns grew in size and prosperity they crossed over that vague, and admittedly arbitrary, line that distinguishes a village from a city. At least a dozen Sumerian cities arose in the shimmering sun along the banks of the southern Tigris and Euphrates rivers. Among them were Eridu, Ur,

---

15. Archaeologists divide this period into: Early Uruk, 3900–3600 BCE; Middle Uruk, 3600–3400 BCE; and Late Uruk, 3400–3100 BCE. As indicated from the rounded-off dates, this division is basically arbitrary and convenient. For purposes of a historical discussion, not centered around artifacts and layers at various site excavations, but on social, political, artistic, and religious matters, it seems more appropriate to refer to this area as the *protoliterate* period.

16. The unique form of the Sumerian ziggurat temple, basically a tower-like artificial mountain with a temple at the top, suggests that the Sumerians' original homeland was a mountainous area where they constructed temples at the top of certain mountains, which they considered sacred.

Uruk, Kish, and Lagash. These "cities," of course were not very impressive by modern standards. Eridu, for example, was one of the oldest, dating back into the Ubaid period to at least 4000 BCE. As you might expect, it was small in size compared to what we today think of as a city, the entire urban area was originally only about 3 1/2 acres. Its economy was based on irrigation farming, although gathering fish from the nearby river was also important. At the city's center was a mud brick temple dedicated to the worship of the city's patron deity, Ea, the god of the sweet waters. The homes of the people were rectangular and also constructed of sun-dried mud bricks. By the end of the protoliterate period it had expanded to about 10 acres and had a population of between 10,000 and 15,000 inhabitants.

But these were not just cities, they were city states. The protoliterate period is marked by the emergence of increasing social complexity and a much more rigid political organization, as compared with earlier Neolithic society. This did not just happen, it was produced by specific factors. One factor that pushed society toward more complexity was population pressure, the continuous increase in the number of humans as a result of the increased food supply. Another factor was the tenuous relationship between human existence in the Near East and the geographical environment. Life could, and often was, quite prosperous and pleasant in southern Mesopotamia, but that could all be wiped away suddenly and unexpectedly by a flood, an earthquake, or other natural disaster, in addition to the man-made disaster of war. Yet another factor was the heavy investment demanded for the construction and maintenance of the irrigation system that made habitation of Mesopotamia possible at all. All of these factors meant that society had to be highly organized and regulated in order to survive.

The city was at the center of Sumerian society. It was organized around a temple and ruled by a priesthood. This is one of the earliest and most enduring aspects of civilization: religion utilized as a method of control and regimentation of society. We will look at how religion accomplishes this in more detail later. Another social group—we can now begin calling these groups "classes"—was the craftsmen who basically produced items either for the temples or for the soldier class, whose function was to protect the city-state from the incursions of other city-states.[17] The vast majority of the population of the city-state, however, belonged to the peasant-farmer class. All the inhabitants of the Sumerian state were considered to be the slave-property of the city's patron deity. The city controlled surrounding territory large enough to make the entire state agriculturally self-sufficient. It was here, in the countryside, that the peasant-farmers toiled endlessly to produce the food and commodities to support the entire state. They did not labor for themselves, or even for the state, however, they were slaves of the god or goddess who owned the city.

This intricate social and political organization was made possible, in fact made necessary, by agricultural technology which allowed each farmer to produce a surplus of food beyond what was necessary for his own survival, and this surplus was made available to the community at large and controlled by the ruling priestly class. This was indeed something different from the earlier Neolithic village life of Çatal Hüyük. Now some members of the community could devote themselves to tasks other than growing food. Some could now be priests, administrators, craftsmen, soldiers, and scribes. This was another quantum leap in social complexity and political organization. It is referred to as the "urban revolution" by some and as the "dawn of civilization" by many.

---

17. Thus warfare and religious oppression are two of the first products of civilization and both have remained an integral part of civilization right down to the present time. This, of course, is not a pleasant observation.

The Invention of Writing: Cuneiform

One of the most important achievements of the Sumerians was the invention of writing, one of the most important intellectual tools ever discovered. Writing was invented independently by several peoples, including the Egyptians, Chinese, and the Maya, but Sumerian writing is the oldest full-fledged writing system ever discovered by archeologists. The earliest Sumerian texts date back to about 3000 BCE. This method of writing is called "cuneiform"[18] by modern scholars, because it employed a reed stylus with a wedged-shaped end to make impressions on a wet clay tablet, which was then baked to make it almost indestructible. Hundreds of thousands of these tablets have been recovered and countless more are still waiting to be recovered.

Was writing invented in order to record literature and preserve the thought of the present for posterity? Probably not. The driving force behind the development seems to have been economic. Very early, Sumerian traders and merchants began to experiment with clay tokens and seals as an aid to accounting. The tokens were symbols of the actual items and could be used for keeping track of inventories. But using a token for each item was cumbersome and inconvenient. Traders eventually created tokens which could represent the total number of similar items. The next step was to insert all the tokens representing a group or inventory of dissimilar items into a hollow clay ball, seal the ball, and inscribe the outside of the ball with the shapes of all the tokens it contained. This not only kept track of the exchange, it prevented dishonest middlemen from skimming off the top of the cargo.

By 3300 BCE the cumbersome token and ball system was replaced with flat, clay tablets on which the required information was inscribed with a sharp stick using pictographs that resembled the objects in question. Over time this system progressed to the point that the pictographs also represented abstract ideas. For example, the symbol for a bowl of food, *ninda*, came to also represent the abstract idea of "bread," or "sustenance." But this was still not true writing, because the symbols did not record the language itself. The final stage was to have a symbol represent not a *thing* but a *sound*. Thus whenever a scribe needed to record the sound *ninda* he would use the symbol for a bowl of food. The symbols now became *phonograms*.

By 3100 BCE scribes stopped scratching the symbols into the clay with sharp sticks and began to use a reed stylus which left wedge shaped impressions in the clay. This was faster and more efficient. However, this made it difficult to draw the pictographs, and as a result the symbols became more and more abstract until they often did not resemble the original pictograms at all. The symbols became only groups of wedge shaped impressions, they no longer represented things or even words, but sounds. Eventually symbols were invented to represent every possible syllable—that is, every vowel-consonant combination—in the Sumerian language. Several hundred different combinations of wedges were required to accomplish this. Cuneiform was a complex system, but it was a true system of writing, every sound and nuance of the language could be recorded on the clay tablets using nothing but wedge-shaped impressions.

It is important to note that cuneiform is not a language, but a system of writing. Cuneiform was later used to write many different languages, languages not related to Sumerian in any way. To say, "archaeologists uncovered a cash of cuneiform tablets," tells us nothing about the language recorded on those tablets. In fact cuneiform could be employed to write English if someone wished to do so.

---

18. From the Latin word cuneus, "*wedge*."

Early Mesopotamian History: Kingdoms and Empires

Samuel Kramer said "History begins at Sumer,"[19] and it is true that the Sumerians are the first people to leave us a record of their history. Of course the Sumerians are not the first people to have a history, but they are the first "historical" people, in the sense that they are the first people whose history we can know. The previous societies are classified as "prehistorical." By 2900 BCE the Sumerians were using cuneiform to write about a wide variety of religious, economic, and political subjects. They recorded the religious literature that had been passed down orally through the generations. Modern scholars, somewhat disingenuously, refer to this body of sacred literature as "mythology." While it was never intended to be a historical record, in the modern sense, mythology does record the folk memories of the prehistoric past.

Careful analysis of the earliest Sumerian texts and later texts that record myths which originated in the prehistorical period have caused some scholars to postulate that the prehistoric Sumerian cities governed themselves by a form of government known as "primitive democracy."[20] In each city-state the ultimate authority rested in an assembly of all the free members of the community. This assembly deliberated on important decisions of policy and chose administrative officials, such as the "*en*" (lord), a religious and economic manager, the "*ensi*" (governor), an administrative officer, and the "*lugal*" (literally, big man), the emergency war leader. Unfortunately, the city-states were almost constantly at war with each other, and since the very survival of the state depended on its effective defense, the lugal evolved into the king. Thus, by the time Sumer emerged into the light of written history, all the cities were ruled by permanent dynasties of kings, who claimed to be appointed by the city's patron deity. As one text states it: "kingship was lowered from heaven."[21] During historical times, the primitive democracy of the prehistoric age was remembered only in the myths describing the world of the gods.[22]

The Early Dynastic Period (2900–2350 BCE)

As each city-state grew larger, with populations ranging between 10,000 and 50,000 people, conflicts between them intensified and this tended to enhance the power and authority of the lugal, or king, in relation to the leaders of the priestly class. What were the conflicts all about? The expanding populations of the cities required ever larger territories to produce the necessary agricultural resources for survival. Inevitably, frontiers collided and disputes arose concerning precious water rights. Once the competitive process was set into motion, each city, each king, desired to become the most powerful and to achieve hegemony over the others. Driven by these circumstances, the power and authority of the king became supreme, but it is incorrect to think of him as a secular leader. The king was the leader of the army of the city's patron god and his power was religious as well as secular. In fact, the people of the ancient world would not have understood a discussion of

---

19. Kramer, Samuel Noah, *History Begins at Sumer* (1959), Doubleday, Garden City, N.Y.

20. Jacobsen, Thorkild, "Primitive Democracy in Ancient Mesopotamia," *Journal of Near Eastern Studies,* 2 (1943) 159–172. Reprinted in *Toward an Image of Tammuz* (1970), Harvard University Press, Cambridge, Massachusetts.

21. The first line of the Sumerian King List reads: "After the kingship descended from heaven, the kingship was Eridug, In Eridug, Alulim became king. . ."

22. One of the best descriptions of the world of the gods is given in the "Enuma Elish," the Mesopotamian story of the creation. See Cleve, Robert, "The Enuma Elish," Early Western Civilization, Source Readings (2002), Kendall/Hunt, Dubuque, pp. 34–41.

the secular versus the religious power. Such a thing never occurred to them. They perceived no difference between the power of the temple and the power of the palace—both were *equally* in the service of the god. This union of secular and religious power is clearly illustrated in such documents as the Sumerian King List and Epic of Gilgamesh.[23]

The city of Kish in the north of Sumer seems to have developed the institution of permanent kinship first, and this gave Kish a temporary advantage of the other cities. One of the early kings of Kish was Etana, who "stabilized all the lands and established the hegemony of Kish over all of Sumer." Although this unity was only temporary, it made a lasting impression on the Sumerians. For centuries afterward, the king of any city able to establish dominance over other cities took for himself the title "King of Kish." Around 2600 BCE we see Mesannepadda of Ur claiming this title. But the dynasty of Ur was unable to retain control over Sumer for long and most cities were able to assert their independence again. About 2450 BCE, the rulers of Lagash declared themselves "King of Kish," but failed to seriously control the region. Lugalzagesi of Umma razed Lagash, conquered Sumer, and in his turn declared himself "King of Kish." Unfortunately, all of this strife weakened Sumer and made it vulnerable to conquest from the outside.

The Akkadian Period (2350–2160 BCE)

During the Early Dynastic Period the fortunes of various cities rose and fell. Not only did the Sumerian cities struggle against each other, they also had to face an external threat. The open, flat Mesopotamian plain left the city-states vulnerable to invasion by the surrounding pre-civilized peoples. Among these were various Semitic[24] speaking peoples who inhabited the Arabian peninsula to the south. Among these, a people who spoke Akkadian infiltrated the area to the north of Sumer and settled there. They quickly came under the heavy influence of the culturally more advanced Sumerians, however. They adopted cuneiform to write their Semitic language and although they worshiped their own deities, they respected and revered the gods and religious practices of the Sumerians. Indeed, the Akkadians took on most of the Sumerian cultural traits and in turn influenced the Sumerians in a fundamental way to the extent that scholars recognize the result of this cultural blinding as "Sumero-Akkadian."

From among these Akkadians arose an unusual leader, whose origin and life is surrounded in legend. Sargon came from outside the aristocratic establishment and was not bound by the traditional conventions of his time. According to legend, he was the son of a priestess of the fertility goddess Ishtar, who set him adrift on the Euphrates river in a basket.[25] He was found by a gardener who raised him to adulthood. As a young man, Sargon attained the post of cupbearer in the court of the king of the city of Kish. How he attained supreme power there is obscure, but Sargon eventually subjected all the area of Sumer and Akkad. He is said to have campaigned from the "Upper

---

23. See Cleve, Robert, "The Epic of Gilgamesh," *Early Western Civilization, Source Readings* (2002), Kendall/Hunt, Dubuque, pp. 2–12.

24. The terms Semitic, Sumerian, Hamitic, Indo-European, etc., as used in this book, refer to languages and have nothing whatever to do with "race." The concept of race, as used in the modern world, was unknown in antiquity. Whenever a word is used in any of the ancient texts which is translated as "race," that term invariably refers to an ethnic group and has nothing to do with what people designated by the term may have looked like.

25. This is a common motif in ancient mythology: An important lady, a priestess, princess, etc., gives birth to a son by an unknown or divine father and sets him adrift in a basket on a river. The baby is found by member of the lower class, raised to adulthood, discovers his special identity, becomes a leader of his people, and founds a nation or empire. This story occurs again and again: Sargon, Moses, Romulus and Remus, etc.

to the Lower Sea" (from the Mediterranean Sea to the Persian Gulf), gaining control of all the trade routes so vital to the economic well being of the Sumerians. By 2350 BCE, Sargon had united all of Mesopotamia under his rule.

Sargon reorganized Mesopotamia into a centralized state and founded a new capital at Agade, just north of Kish. He appointed Akkadian speaking governors to rule the cities of Sumer, and thus for the first time the city was integrated into a larger political unit—the kingdom or empire. Sargon's empire prospered by collecting taxes from the cities and exploiting the network of trade routes that crisscrossed the Near East. He lavished most of the resources gleaned from his empire on his new capital city, making Agade the most splendid city in the world. Sargon ruled for 56 years over the world's first empire. He attributed his success to the goddess Ishtar, in whose honor Agade was erected. Two later Assyrian kings were named in his honor, and although his predecessor Lugalzagesi had already begun expansion beyond the Sumerian homeland, later Mesopotamians looked back to Sargon as the founder of the military tradition that runs through the history of the area.

Sargon appointed one of his daughters chief priestess of the moon god Nanna, patron deity of Ur. She took the name of Enheduanna and was succeeded in the same office by the daughter of Naram-Sin, the last king of the Sargonic dynasty. Enheduanna was a very gifted woman; two Sumerian hymns by her have been preserved, and she is also said to have been instrumental in starting a collection of songs dedicated to the temples of Babylonia.

Alas, the hard won unity established by Sargon did not last long. After his death the empire was fraught with rebellion. He was succeeded by his son, Rimush (2315–2306), but he immediately had to put down rebellions in Ur, Umma, and other cities. Palace intrigue led to his assassination, possibly by supporters of his brother. The texts tell us his head was bashed in by a clay tablet.

Manishtushu (2306–2291), either Rimush's older brother or his twin, became the third king of the Sargonic empire. We are told that he put down an uprising of a coalition of 32 rebel kings to retain control of Akkad and Sumer, but the power of the empire obviously continued to decline. Court documents record him buying land from private citizens, so the King's power was not absolute and he did not own all the land. An inscription informs us that he founded the famous temple of Ishtar in Nineveh. Like his brother, he also died in a palace revolt.

The last important king of the Sargonic dynasty was Naram-Sin (2291–2254), the son of Manishtushu. He also defeated a rebel coalition in Sumer to re-establish Akkadian power. He is said to have enlarged the boundaries of the empire into Syria and Lebanon as well as to the Taurus and Zagros mountains. He called himself "King of the Four Quarters" and "God of Agade," becoming the first Mesopotamian king to declare himself divine. Naram-Sin appointed his daughters as priestess' and his sons as governors, but even with all his military victories and glory, he continuously had to put down revolts against his rule, and the texts tell us his reign ended in disaster. The Gutians, who apparently came from the region between the Tigris River and the Zagros mountains to the east, invaded Sumer, wrecked destruction and caused the breakdown of communications. One text says the king was "bewildered, confused, sunk in gloom, sorrowful, exhausted" from the overwhelming invasion.

Shar-Kali-Sharri, the son of Naram-Sin, attempted to shore up the empire and undo the damage, but his efforts proved fruitless. The Sumerian King List gives the names of brief descriptions of a few more kings, but it is all too obvious that the power of the Sargonic empire was at an end.

The Gutian Interlude (2160–2100 BCE)

The Gutian period is an interlude, a digression, a dark age even, in the history of Mesopotamia. We don't really know who the Gutians were. The word in Akkadian means "snakes of the mountains," and could rather accurately be translated into English as "barbarian." The Akkadians and Sumerians obviously held them in contempt. Another factor complicates this period: the invasion and infiltration of Semitic nomads known as the Amorites into the area. However, these invasions were not necessarily the cause of the fall of the Sargonic empire, because in a sense they were provoked by Akkadian aggression and facilitated by the weakness of Akkad.

The Gutians are described in the texts as a ruthless, barbaric horde from the mountains of the east. The Sumerian King List describes the period as a state of anarchy: "Who is king, who is not king?" The period is one of confusion and can be described as a "dark age" in the sense that the events of the period are dark to historians. The Gutians' influence may not have extended far beyond Umma. We know that the neighboring state of Lagash enjoyed a century of independence after the reign of Shar-Kali-Sharri, during which time it had wide ranging trade connections. One of the rulers, Gudea, had the time, power, and means to carry out an extensive temple construction program. His statues, some almost life-size, bear long inscriptions recording his religious activities.

The Third Dynasty of Ur (2100–2006 BCE)

The Gutians were expelled from Sumer by Utuhegal, the king of Ur. However, one of his ambitious subordinates, Ur-Nammu (2111–2094 BCE), usurped the throne and established the last important Sumerian dynasty, known as the Third Dynasty of Ur, or simply Ur III. Ur-Nammu was a capable military leader and skillful administrator, who defeated the rival king of Lagash and soon gained control of all the Sumerian city-states. He promulgated the earliest known law code, which stated as its goal "to protect the weak from the strong," and provide equal justice for all. He established an effective, centralized government under which the cities of Sumer were administered by governors, known as ensis. One text tells us that "he straightened the highways from the lands below and the lands above." His efficient government brought internal peace and prosperity to Sumer for almost a century, indeed this period is often referred to as the "Sumerian Renaissance."

Ur-Nammu is perhaps best known for his grandiose building program, which made his capital city of Ur the largest and wealthiest city in the world. He constructed new temples in almost every city of his empire, but the most famous was the great ziggurat he constructed at Ur in honor of Enlil, the chief god of the Sumerian pantheon. It stood over 60 feet high and more than 200 feet wide. A figurine, which was buried in a foundation box beneath one of the temple towers, represents the king at the start of the building project, carrying on his head a basket containing the clay from which would be made the critically important first brick. The foundation deposit also contained an inscribed tablet, beads of frit, stone, and gold, chips of various stones, and four ancient date pits, which were placed atop the basket carried by the king. Ur-Nammu also constructed great new feeder canals to bring large new territories under cultivation, which substantially increased food production. But alas, Ur-Nammu was killed in a battle with the Gutians, who continued to harass Sumer throughout the Third Dynasty of Ur. A surviving text describes the return of Ur-Nammu's body to Ur for an extravagant burial and relates details of the Sumerian view of the world of the dead.

He was succeeded by his son, Shulgi (2094–2047 BCE), who enlarged and reorganized the empire. However, during his reign a new threat emerged from the Elamites from the west, who came to loot and pillage the land. Shulgi built a wall to protect the empire's boundaries. He was succeeded by two of his sons: Amar-Sin (2046–2038 BCE) and Shu-Suen (2037–2029 BCE).[26] Amar-Sin died of "the bite of a shoe," probably he was poisoned. During the reign of Shu-Suen, the Amorites, Semitic speaking nomads from the Arabian desert, began making major raids into Sumer.

Strangely, Shu-Suen's inscriptions predicted the disasters that were to befall his son and successor, Ibbi-Sin (2028–2006 BCE). But Ibbi-Sin's reign began well enough. He ascended the throne when Ur was at the height of its power and prosperity. Yet, there were ominous clouds already gathering on the horizon. Large stretches of the land were becoming unusable due to the salinity of the soil, caused by over irrigating, and finally a horde of Elamites descended into the Mesopotamian plain from the highlands to the west and besieged the city of Ur. The city was well protected by defensive walls and could not be taken by the Elamites, but after a long period of famine and suffering the defenders of the city simply opened the gates and the Elamites brutally slaughtered the population and destroyed the city. A surviving hymn, "Lamentation Over the Ruins of Ur," records the tragedy. After the demise of the Third Dynasty of Ur, Mesopotamia once again become divided into independent city-states under separate rulers.

Isin-Larsa and Old Babylonian Periods (2000–1600 BCE)

The Amorites first appeared as semi-nomads in the upper and middle Euphrates, but they became sedentary and adopted a dialect of the Akkadian language known as the Old Babylonian, which is written in cuneiform. The old Sumerian language was dying out as a spoken language by this time, but it was still used by intellectuals and it was the first type of writing learned by student scribes in school. Religious texts and diplomatic correspondence between rulers were mostly in Sumerian.

During the period after the fall of Ur in 2006, warfare between the cities once again raged throughout Mesopotamia, but this time the wars were fought between small kingdoms governed by Amorite kings. The cities of Isin and Larsa were rivals for the hegemony of Mesopotamia and they seem to have existed in a state of armed neutrality for more than a century. Some of these kings made significant contributions to the Western tradition. Lipit-Ishtar (1934–1924 BCE), king of Isin, developed a legal system in which the precedents set in past cases were used to formulate general legal principles for judging of future cases. Rim-Sin (1822–1763 BCE), king of Larsa, encouraged the arts and patronized the old Sumerian scribal schools.

In 1792 BCE, a young man named Hammurabi (1792–1750 BCE) became king of Babylon, a small kingdom in central Mesopotamia. Lacking a large army, he employed diplomacy, cunning, and deceit to trick his more powerful neighbors into armed conflict against each other. He pretended to be a friend to both sides and while they destroyed each other, Hammurabi quietly consolidated his own kingdom, and when the time was ripe, he fell upon his weakened neighbors and defeated them. In this way Hammurabi transformed his small kingdom into what is known to history as the Old Babylonian Empire, which ultimately stretched from the Persian Gulf to the northern reaches of Mesopotamia.

Hammurabi's Empire achieved an unprecedented degree of political and administrative centralization. The patron deity of the city of Babylon, Marduk, became the chief god of the

---

26. See "Love Song to King Shu-Suen," Cleve, Robert, *Early Western Civilization, Source Readings* (2002), Kendall/Hunt, Dubuque, pp. 22-23.

Mesopotamian pantheon, replacing the old Sumerian storm god Enlil in that position. Although Hammurabi, in keeping with his diplomatic approach, continued to observe the long-standing religious forms of the past by paying homage to the ancient gods of Sumer and Akkad, Marduk was now the king of the gods. The peoples of the empire could continue to worship their own local deities, but all owned their first allegiance to Marduk. This is one of history's first examples of the use of religion as a force to consolidate and unify the peoples of a diverse imperial state. It set a precedent that would be followed by other Near Eastern peoples-the Assyrians and the Israelites for example. It is a device that has frequently been employed throughout subsequent history down to the modern age and indeed is still employed in vast areas of the world today, a prime example being many of the modern Islamic nations.

The Religion of Ancient Mesopotamia

Mesopotamian religion reflects the world view of the peoples of the ancient Near East. The sacred literature of these ancient peoples, what we call their "mythology," represents the reality of their world as it appeared to them, just as the sacred writings of modern religions (Christianity, Islam, Buddhism, etc.) represent the world view to the adherents of modern religions, just as modern scientific literature represents reality as seen through a secular lens. We will survey, in the cursory manor necessitated by the limitations of our approach, the religions of the various ancient societies of Western Civilization, beginning here with early Mesopotamia. However, when studying ancient culture it is important to understand that religion is created by human beings to meet their human needs and desires. Only humans practice religion, and without humans there could be no religion. This fact is distasteful to many, but it is, nevertheless, an obvious observation of historical reality.

Consider the physical environment of ancient Mesopotamia. This is one of the most intolerable sites for human habitation to be found on the face of the earth. In the summer the temperature can reach 137°F. in the shade, while dust storms, so dense they hide the sun, envelop the land for weeks on end. As in all desert countries, winter is equally extreme. With no evaporation from the soil or vegetation to cool the air in the summer, and no blanket of humidity to preserve the sun's heat in the winter, the temperature fluctuates between extremes which are reminiscent of the surface of the moon. It almost never rains, but through this arid landscape run two rivers of life-giving water. A gift of the gods? Well, yes, but nevertheless at intervals, which no human could understand, great cloudbursts erupted in the far away mountains and transformed these placid rivers into destructive monsters, which leaped over their banks and devastated the countryside. Often, after a rampage, the rivers settled back into new riverbeds, leaving the cities built upon their banks by humans isolated and dry, tombs baking in the desert sun. Then there were the earthquakes, which periodically ripped through the land with unbelievable destructive force.

Consider the response to this environment by the humans who inhabited the area. How could they relate to, how could they cope with, how could they affect these forces? The most basic human response was to personalize the mysterious, incomprehensible powers of nature. Why does an unexpected storm occur? It is the divine act of the storm god. Everything that is vital in nature, every motion, every event, every manifestation of change is the result of a divine action. Since the ancient human's relationship to this environment was so tenuous and unsure, his assessment of his condition was necessarily gloomy and pessimistic. Yet, by employing the correct ritual and ceremony, the weak, powerless human might hope to have some interaction, to exert some small influence over these forces.

The Creation Story

The Sumerians developed several versions of the creation story, which was their basic explanation of the origin of the universe and of humanity. The most widely circulated version was the Enuma Elish.[27] The text revealed that out of the formless nothingness of non-existence before time the first gods appeared in male-female pairs. These early gods, with names like Apsu ("fresh water") and Tiamat ("salt water"), represented the inert, inactive forces of nature and they gave birth to more active generations of divine beings. Each generation of gods was more powerful and energetic. Eventually, the younger gods revolted against the older gods and took control of the destiny of the world. Thus the origin of the universe was violence and conflict. Once in control, the god Ea created humans as the slaves of heaven to work and labor for them for all time:

> After Ea, the Wise, had created humankind,
> He imposed upon it the service of the gods—
> That toil was beyond human comprehension.[28]

This pessimistic and gloomy image was suggested by the violence of their environment. It explained the meaning of human existence. A survey of the literature and mythology of ancient Mesopotamia confirms the underlying sense of futility and fatalism, which permeates their culture. The sacred writings of the Sumerians, that is, their mythological literature, give us a fairly clear picture of this relationship:

> The Sumerians and Akkadians pictured their gods as human in form, governed by human emotions, and living in the same type of world as did men. In almost every particular the world of the gods was a projection of terrestrial conditions. Since this process began relatively early, and since man is by nature conservative in religious matters, early features would, as a matter of course, be retained in the world of the gods long after the earthly counterpart had disappeared.[29]

During the third millennium BCE, the Sumerians developed religious and spiritual concepts which have influenced the West down to the present day. Sumerian intellectuals grappled with the basic problems of human existence: the origin of the universe (cosmology); the natural order of the universe (metaphysics); the relationship of humanity to the universe (philosophy). In the process they developed the theology which became the basic creed and dogma of the Near East for much of its latter history and is still deeply embedded in modern Judaism, Christianity, and Islam.

Personal Religion

On the practical daily level, the Sumerians felt themselves surrounded by a multitude of divine forces, both beneficial and malicious, and they responded with a host of incantations, rituals, magic formulas, and counter-incantations. Daily misfortunes, headaches, accidental bruises, even disagreements with one's neighbor, were attributed to demonic spirits, often vaguely conceived as inhabiting

---

27. See "The Enuma Elish," Cleve, Robert, *Early Western Civilization, Source Readings* (2002), Kendall/Hunt, Dubuque, pp. 34–41.

28. See "The Enuma Elish," Cleve, Robert, *Early Western Civilization, Source Readings* (2002), Kendall/Hunt, Dubuque, pp. 41.

29. Jacobsen, Thorkild, "Primitive Democracy in Ancient Mesopotamia," *Journal of Near Eastern Studies* 2 (1943) 166.

the "western horizon." Other spirits were more immediate and personified, such as Nantar, the demon of the "wasting disease" (tuberculosis?). Nightmares and other nocturnal menaces were the work of Lilitu ("Night-hag"). Figurines of Pazuzu (Fig. 2.5), the most popular demon in folk religion, represent him standing like a human, but with a scorpion's body, feathered wings projecting from his shoulders, talons for his hands and feet, and the face of a deformed lion. Pazuzu was the "king of the evil wind demons," but he was not entirely unfriendly toward humans, because he was the enemy of the dreaded Lamashtu, the bearer of sickness, especially to women and children. Pazuzu figurines almost always have a ring at the top of the head through which a string can be inserted so the figure can be worn around the neck as an amulet to ward off evil from the wearer's body.

Public Religion

The public, official religion of the city-states assumed that the city was an earthly copy or reflection of the world of the gods—though in reality the world of the gods was envisioned as an exact copy of the Sumerian city-state, except that the gods were super powerful and immortal. The state

Figure 2.5: Pazuzu, king of the Evil Wind Demons.

was intimately linked to heaven through the patronage of a god or goddess, who literally owned the city. Indeed, the overwhelming focus of earthly life was the temple, located atop a ziggurat set in a sacred area located near the center of the city. The city's divinity resided, symbolically, in his or her statue, which was ritually attended, cared for, and served by numerous priests, priestesses, and attendants. A large portion of the city's wealth and resources was devoted to the construction and upkeep of the temple and the living quarters of the priests and priestesses who served the god. The temple dominated the social, political, and economic life of the state. It was the direct and intimate link between earth and heaven, between the individual and the universe.

The ancient Sumerian believed that his universe consisted of the flat earth over which was superimposed a vast vaulted heaven. Between these two entities, however, existed a moving and undulating "atmosphere," which separated heaven and earth. The sun, moon, planets, and stars moved through this atmosphere on pre-determined courses. Operating, directing, and supervising this universe was a pantheon of living deities, humanlike in form and behavior, but super-powerful and immortal. They were invisible to human eyes, but the results of their activities were obvious for all to observe. They controlled the universe according to a divine plan, which was primarily structured to satisfy their own divine needs and selfish desires. As described by S. N. Kramer:

> The great realms of heaven, earth, sea and air; the major astral bodies, sun moon, and planets; such atmospheric forces as wind, storm, and tempest; and finally, on earth, such natural entities as river, mountain, and plain, such cultural entities as city and state, dike and ditch, field and farm, and even such implements as the pickax, brick mold, and plow—each was deemed to be under the charge of one or another anthropomorphic, but superhuman, being who guided its activities in accordance with established rules and regulations.[30]

The Mesopotamian Pantheon

The infinite sky was deified as Anu (also known as An), the supreme king of heaven and the fountain of the natural order and structure of heaven and earth. Human kingship was referred to as *anitu*, or "Anu-ship." Enlil was the deity of the wind and the storm. He was also thought of as king. While Anu was the divine sovereign and embodied the final heavenly authority, Enlil was his executive, his prime minister, so to speak. He was the divine reflection of the human king-exercising the royal authority derived from Anu. The human king's power was often described as *enlilitu*, or "Enlil-ship." But the actions of these gods were not always consistent or benevolent toward humans. The inhabitants of Mesopotamia were frequently exposed to the devastating floods of the Tigris and Euphrates, to dust storms and the hot parching winds of the desert (simooms), to locust swarms, to the marauding invaders from the Arabian peninsula to the south and the mountains to the north. The Mesopotamians attributed all of these occurrences to Enlil, the executive of Anu.

The earth itself was regarded as the living goddess Ninhursag, "Lady Mountain." An ancient Sumerian text explains that the origin of vegetation was the union of Ninhursag and Enki (also known as Ea), the god of the waters. This myth realistically recognizes the tension between earth and water and reflects the constant struggle between life and death in the physical environment of Mesopotamia. The initial union between Ninhursag and Enki produced life sustaining vegetation, but Enki was a fickle and unfaithful lover, who soon consummated unions with his own daughters. Insulted, Ninhursag cursed Enki and relegated him to the dark underground. This caused the

---

30. Kraner, Samuel Noah, *The Sumerians* (1963), University of Chicago Press, Chicago, pp 113–114.

earth to become barren, and the gods protested. Ninhursag was reluctantly persuaded to mitigate the curse, allowing Enki to appear both below and above the earth's surface. This is a recognition, in mythological terms, that water includes both destructive and beneficial qualities. Water, so necessary and beneficial to life, may also possess a "dark side." Astonishingly, Enki was also the god of wisdom. He had the power to impose and remove spells and curses.

Space does not permit us to catalog here the large number of Mesopotamian gods, both great and small—an entire book would not be large enough to inventory them all—but we should consider the major deities. Among the most active gods of the Babylonian period was Shamash, the sun god, who was given new prominence by emphasizing his dominion over justice. He is the all-seeing god who traverses the entire sky each day from east to west and accomplishes a similar nightly journey through the underworld each night to appear again in the east each morning. Shamash demands justice from the king and is the champion of the under-privileged. The stele on which Hammurabi's famous law code is recorded bears a bass-relief image of Hammurabi obediently receiving the law from the hand of Shamash. Thus law was first conceived as a divine command, a gift from heaven to humans.

Nanna (Sin in Akkadian) was the moon god, worshiped throughout Mesopotamia, but especially at Ur, where he was the city's patron—or from another point of view, Ur was the city sacred to him. Nanna held a mysterious sway over the world. He moved slowly through the night sky, forever changing, waxing and waning, opening the doors of heaven to pour out the days, months and years, but always returning to his starting point. For it was Nanna who measured out time, who governed the ebbing of the tides, the advance and retreat of spring. It was Nanna who regulated the growth sequence of green plants, and measured the monthly cycle of the sacred blood of womanhood. Nanna at the same time was both young and old. He brought rest to the land, repose to the living. He brought both sweet dreams and wild nightmares. Among his titles was "Prince of the gods."

The most important goddess in the Mesopotamian pantheon was called Inanna by the Sumerians and Ishtar by the Babylonians and Assyrians. Ishtar is the same "mother-goddess" figure we encountered at Çatal Hüyük. She was responsible for the fertility of nature in all its aspects. The practice of homeopathic, or imitative, magic to influence the gods was an intense component of the worship of Ishtar. The sacred marriage between god and goddess was an important rite in Mesopotamian religion, and it was re-enacted annually with the king representing the vegetation god Tammuz and a priestess from the temple of Ishtar representing the goddess. The act of consummation was believed to draw down from heaven the power of fertility necessary to germinate the crops in the spring. Ishtar was the great lover and mother. Her love was insatiable, consuming, even fatal. Ishtar searching for her lover Tammuz, the dying and rising vegetation god is a motif which occurs throughout the mythological cycles of the Near East and the eastern Mediterranean basin. In Canaan the goddess Anat searches for the dead Baal, in Egypt Isis searches for the dead Osiris, in Greece Demeter searches for Kore and Aphrodite searches for Adonis. Their union brings forth the fertility of spring, and the vegetation, dormant during the winter, springs to life again. Ishtar was also a warrior goddess, known in the texts as "perfect in courage" and in this guise she directed the warrior kings by her dream-oracles.

During the Babylonian period, Marduk, the city god of Babylonia, rose to prominence throughout Mesopotamia by assimilating the role of Enlil as the executive of the heavenly court and as storm god. In the Babylonian version of the *Enuma Elish* Marduk replaces Enlil as the subduer of Chaos, but this change of names does not alter the story itself in any fundamental way.

Two other deities in the vast pantheon of Mesopotamia deserve a mention. The strange story of the marriage of Nergal and Ereshkigal is a passionate love story that takes place in the dark and gloomy underworld. Ereshkigal, the sister of Ishtar, is the inflexible goddess of the Land of No

Return. She was probably once a sky goddess, but was consigned to the underworld after the separation of heaven and earth. She was dark and violent, as befits the goddess of the underworld and the ruler of the dead. She received the mortuary offerings made to the dead. Nergal, the son of Enlil and Ninlil,[31] was the god of war and plague. He was the "evil one" who brought war, pestilence, fever, and devastation. He was sometimes regarded as the sinister opposite of the sun god, Shamash.

One day Nergal was sent to her from heaven to the underworld with an offering of food for Ereshkigal. They fell in love with each other at first sight, and when Nergal had to leave the goddess was heartbroken. With tears streaming from her eyes, she threatened Anu that she would revive the dead, over whom she ruled, and send them back to earth, "so that they will outnumber the living," unless Nergal was sent back to her as her husband. Her minister, Namtar, was dispatched to heaven as her messenger. At last Nergal came storming down the stairs, broke violently through each of the seven gates guarding the underworld, and burst into the palace of Ereshkigal and straight into her passionate embrace, "to wipe away her tears."

A strange combination of good and evil, of masculine and feminine, of passion and resignation. Ereshkigal's surrender to Nergal is not, however, an act of passivity. Instead, she gives up separateness in order to be fulfilled by her beloved's essence without losing sight of her own uniqueness. After their union, they both ruled together over the underworld. Implicit in the marriage of Ereshkigal and Nergal is the redemption of the Mesopotamian underworld, in the sense that the Land of the Dead, is transformed into a place where passion and connectedness can be found.

The Sumerian view of the afterlife was the projection of the pessimism of the their existence in this world—only worse. After death there were neither punishment nor reward, simply a shadowy and temporary existence in a world of gloom, a world so distant that light could never reach it. There the soul wondered aimlessly for a time, but eventually faded away into oblivion and nothingness. This is a recognition of the fact that after a person dies, he lives on in the memory of loved ones and friends for a time, but eventually they die also and ultimately there is no one left on earth who can even conjure up in their minds an image of the departed and so, in the end, all is lost, all is returned to the nothingness from which it emerged.

Science and Technology

Surprisingly, the pessimistic fatalism of the Mesopotamians did not paralyze them intellectually, but actually seems to have instilled in them a high degree of self-reliance, fortitude, and ingenuity. They were first-rate inventors and resourceful innovators. We have already noted that they invented the first writing system. They also made great strides in metallurgy. Although Mesopotamia itself was devoid of mineral deposits, they imported copper from eastern Anatolia as early as the Uruk period and formed it into a variety of weapons, tools, and works of art. By adding tin they created bronze, which is superior to copper for most uses.

The wheel is one of the most important advances in human technology. The Sumerians employed the potter's wheel as early as 3500 BCE. Three hundred years later they were using two and four wheeled carts pulled by donkeys.[32] At first the cart was used principally in warfare, but their use eventually increased the productivity of the farmer and the tradesman to an extraordinary degree.

---

31. Ninlil was the goddess of grain and is called "queen wind." She is the consort of Enlil and shows compassion to the unfortunate.

32. Horses were unknown in Mesopotamia until they were introduced by eastern invaders sometime between 2000 and 1700 BCE.

The Sumerians also developed mathematics to the highest level of competence achieved before the age of the Greeks. Their numbering system was sexagesimal rather than decimal, that is it was based on sixty, not on ten, as ours is.[33] Remnants of this ancient counting system remain with us today. We still count units of time by the sexagesimal method: 24 hour days; 60 minute hours; 60 second minutes. We still divide the circumference of the circle into 360°. Even our calendar is a distant modification of the lunar calendar developed by the Sumerians, which contained twelve months, six with thirty days, and six with twenty-nine days. Since this produced a year with only 354 days the Sumerians had to add a month every four years to keep it in synchronization with the seasons.

The ancient Mesopotamians were also active in the field of medical science. Most of the surviving medical texts are in Akkadian, but these constantly refer to older Sumerian terms, so it is inferred that these writers drew upon a rich Sumerian medical tradition. The physician was known as the *a-zu*, literally the "water-knower," and medical treatment did often consist of cleansing with water. One of the most famous medical texts prescribes treatment for an infected wound:

> Having crushed turtle shell and. . .and having anointed the opening (of the sick organ, perhaps) with oil, you shall rub (with the crushed shell) the man lying prone (?). After rubbing with the crushed shell you shall rub (again) with fine beer; after rubbing with fine beer, you shall wash with water; after washing with water, you shall fill (the sick spot) with crushed fir wood. It is (a prescription) for someone afflicted by a disease in the *tun* and the *nu*.

The *tun* and the *nu* are probably two still unidentified parts of the sexual organs, and the treatment may therefore have been intended for some type of venereal disease.

---

33. Thus, while according the decimal system, the number 439 stands for $(4 \times 10^2) + (3 \times 10) + 9$, in the sexagesimal system the same number would stand for $(4 \times 60^2) + (3 \times 60) + 9$, or 14,589. The zero was unknown to the Mesopotamians.

3

Ancient Egypt

Land of Mystery

Egypt occupies a place of fantasy, mystery, and exotic escapism in the modern mind. Exhibitions of Egyptian art and artifacts invariably draw huge crowds into museums. Biographies of pharaohs, such Akhenaton or Ramesses II, and books about mummies and pyramids are always fast sellers. Television "documentaries" exposing the "secrets" of Egypt are common. And of course throngs of practitioners of the bizarre and the occult flock to the image of ancient Egypt. In a brilliant little article, "Dreaming of Egypt," Mary Prichard Poulter[1] discussed some of the individuals from all over the world who believe themselves to be reincarnations of famous Egyptians—Akhenaton, Nefertiti, and so on. All very mysterious and exotic. One woman, who believed she had once been Meritaton, the daughter of the pharaoh Akhenaton, described her meeting with someone who believed himself to be Akhenaton and "he recognized me at once."

Why does ancient Egypt elicit such response? This ancient land has always seemed an enigma and a mystery to outsiders. To the inhabitants of the 21st Century, the Greeks are thought of as "the ancients." Yet, when the ancient Greek historian Herodotus visited Egypt more than 2,500 years ago, Egypt was to him more ancient than Greece is to us—and just as unfathomable and out of the ordinary. He saw pyramids taller than any other man-made structure, but already scarred by incredible age. Then there were the avenues of sphinxes, half human and half animal; huge complex temples, grand beyond anything in Greece at the time; colossal statues of long dead pharaohs, staring out into eternity with a calm and serene attitude; and everywhere he saw examples of Egypt's sacred hieroglyphic writing. It was a civilization so old that its origins were shrouded in mystery. And so it remained throughout the history of the West, until only yesterday in historical terms. Even though we have now cracked the mysterious hieroglyphic code and reconstructed Egypt's history to an extraordinary extent—at least compared to what Herodotus knew—the aura of mystery and the enigma remains as strong as ever.

The Gift of the Nile

In the last chapter we saw that Mesopotamian society was greatly influenced by the environment of the Tigris-Euphrates river environment. The more one learns about Egypt the more it becomes clear that Egypt was literally the product of its environment. Herodotus, that ancient Greek historian

---

1. Poulter, Mary Prichard, "Dreaming of Egypt," *The Augustan Society Omnibus* 13 (1991) 26–29.

alluded to above, made a simple statement describing Egypt's relationship to the Nile river: "Egypt is the gift of the Nile," and that phrase has become something of a cliché over two and a half millennia later.

At first glance, the riverine environments of Egypt and Mesopotamia appear to be quite similar. Life in both regions is made possible by rivers which originate far outside their areas in highlands and mountains where there is an abundance of rain, and then flow through a desert area on their way to the sea. In both locations the rivers made life possible along their banks in the hot arid regions down stream. But there were fundamental differences also. While Mesopotamia had no natural boundaries and was open to constant harassment from the surrounding pre-civilized peoples of the Arabian peninsula to the south and the highlands to the north and east, Egypt was more isolated, with hot, dry deserts on the east and west, the sea on the north, a series of "cataracts" on the south. Egypt, in contrast to Mesopotamia, was rarely threatened from the outside.

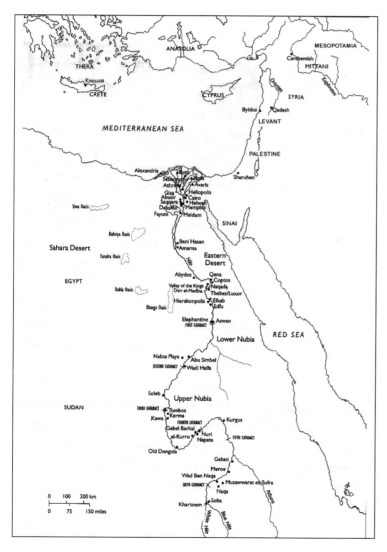

Figure 3.1: The Nile River.

Even more important was the behavior of the rivers themselves. The Tigris-Euphrates rivers flooded at irregular intervals, and the floods were destructive and they destroyed the irrigation systems upon which the very existence of the Mesopotamian Civilization depended. The Nile, on the other hand, flooded at regular, predictable intervals and the flood waters deposited a rich layer of organic soil on the river valley floor each year. The Egyptians welcomed the floods and perceived them as beneficial, not destructive. Thus, while the Mesopotamians had a love-hate relationship with their rivers, the Egyptians felt only love for their Nile.

The reasons for the Nile's consistent and benevolent behavior is to be found in its origins. The source of the world's longest river is in two areas of east-central Africa. The White Nile flows out of Lake Victoria, in modern Uganda, while both the Blue Nile and the Atbara rise in the Ethiopian highlands. The two Nile rivers converge near Khartoum, the Atbara joins some 200 miles to the south, in the modern Sudan. After a journey of some 3,400 miles the river reaches Egypt and then flows for 650 miles through the Nile Valley, which is known as Upper Egypt. The Nile Valley is very narrow and very long: it ranges between 1.2 and 13 miles in width (the average is less than 2 miles), but it is over 600 miles long! During the last 100 miles of its course the river fans out into the broad delta plain, known as lower Egypt, before flowing into the eastern Mediterranean Sea.

What sets the Nile apart from other rivers, especially the Tigris-Euphrates system, is the consistency and regularity of its flooding. The annual spring monsoons sweep in over central Africa from the Indian Ocean, and the spring melting of the snow in the high mountain ranges produce an annual flood far down river in Egypt during the summer. Herodotus thought this "contrary to the nature of all other rivers," which normally flood in the spring. The flood waters rushing down the slopes of mountains in far away central Africa dissolved large amounts of rich, organic laden soil and became a deep red in color. But when these waters reached the Nile Valley, they slowed down to a peaceful flow and the silt settled out, depositing a rich layer of new organic material on the valley's floor. Thus, the Nile Valley was self-fertilized by nature during the annual floods.

Another feature of the Nile, which had a far-reaching effect on Egyptian history, was the cataracts. As the river made its relentless journey toward the sea, it flowed over a series of geological plates, which interrupted the smooth flow of the river with steep white-water rapids. These were, of course, completely unsuitable for navigation. The ancient Egyptians knew six of these disturbances in the Nile. They numbered them, beginning with the first one they encountered looking up the river from Lower Egypt. Thus strangely, the "First Cataract" is the last one the river flows over on its journey to the sea. Not only did these cataracts interrupt navigation on the upper Nile, they served to isolate Egypt from the populations of central Africa. Without the cataracts, the river would have acted as a highway of communication with the interior, but because of their presence, ancient Egypt rarely had to worry about invasion from the south.

In contrast with Mesopotamia, natural resources along the Nile were abundant, although hardwood was somewhat scarce. Since most of the Nile valley possessed the same agricultural and mineral resources there was little need for internal trade up and down the river in agricultural commodities or locally available natural materials. However, eventually some places specialized in manufacturing certain items that were traded to other localities along the Nile, but this was based on social factors—more skilled craftsmen, larger workshops, "brand name" prestige, etc.—rather than any significant difference in resource location. The Nile provided efficient communication between the first cataract and the delta. To travel northward, a boat need only float along on the slow moving current. Since the prevailing winds in the valley were from north to south, hoisting a simple square sail would normally harness sufficient wind power to carry a boat upstream against the river's current. Archaeological evidence indicates that the population of Egypt was well below the area's support capacity in ancient times, and this suggests there was no population pressure. The temperature was pleasantly comfortable in the winter, but extremely hot in the summer: the average daytime temperature in January and February is about 75°, but in July and August it averages 104° and frequently reaches 115°. Annual rainfall is barely 1.5 inches in the delta and virtually 0 in upper Egypt.

Outline of the Political History of Egypt

The chronology of Egypt is traditionally divided into 30 dynasties, which are grouped into periods and labeled "kingdoms" and "intermediate periods." This organization of Egyptian history was first suggested by the ancient Egyptian writer, Manetho[2] (floruit c. 280–260 BCE), who wrote a history of Egypt in Greek. In addition, there were important periods of Egyptian history that occurred before and after the dynastic periods (See Figs. 3.2 & 3.3).

Predynastic Period (4500–3100 BCE)

The prehistoric period in Egypt (usually referred to as the predynastic period) differed from that of the Fertile Crescent in significant ways. Whereas the rising population of Mesopotamia forced the people to adopt a settled agricultural way of life early in the Neolithic Age, the increasing population

PREDYNASTIC	c. 5000–3200 BCE	Prehistoric
DYNASTIES 1–3	c. 3200–2680 BCE	Archaic Period
DYNASTIES 4–6	c. 2680–2135 BCE	Old Kingdom
DYNASTIES 7–10	c. 2135–2040 BCE	First Intermediate Period
DYNASTIES 11–12	c. 2040–1786 BCE	Middle Kingdom
DYNASTIES 13–17	c. 1786–1570 BCE	Second Intermediate Period
DYNASTIES 18–20	c. 1570–1085 BCE	New Kingdom
DYNASTIES 21–24	c. 1085–715 BCE	Third Intermediate Period
DYNASTIES 25–30	c. 715–332 BCE	Foreign Domination
PTOLEMIES	332–30 BCE	Greek Domination
ROMANS	30 BCE–642 CE	Roman/Byzantine Domination

Figure 3.2: Chronological table of Ancient Egypt

2. Manetho wrote the *Aegytiaca* in the 3rd Century BCE, a collection of three books about the history of ancient Egypt, commissioned by Ptolemy II as part of his efforts to unite the Egyptian and Hellenistic cultures. Manetho had access to the vast archives of the temple where he served as priest, which contained different kinds of materials ranging from mythological texts to official records. Thus it is not surprising to find myth mixed with fact in his history. It is to Manetho's writing that we own the division of the history of ancient Egypt into 30 dynasties, but unfortunately, this chronology is not always based on fact. For example, the 18th Dynasty begins with Ahmose, who was the brother of the last king of the 17th Dynasty. Conversely, the third king of the 18th Dynasty was probably not related to his predecessors, but yet he is still placed in the same dynasty. This seemingly arbitrary arrangement of the 18th Dynasty can be explained by the fact that the rule of Ahmose initiated a new era of prosperity for Egypt and thus the ancient record keepers, on whom Manetho relied, must have considered him the founder of a new dynasty.

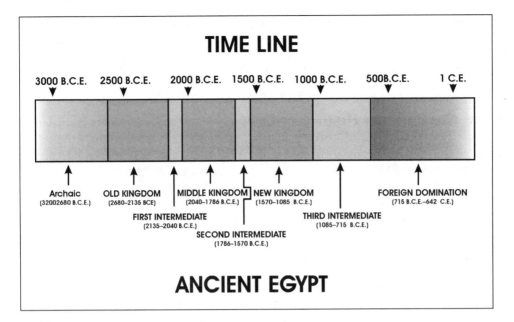

Figure 3.3

of Egypt was able to pursue the hunting and gathering life until the 5th millennium BCE. The early inhabitants of Egypt consisted of a combination of peoples who moved into the Nile Valley from North Africa, the Levant and the African interior. The largest contingent was probably from the Sahara Desert to the west.[3] Before about 10,000 BCE this now desolate land was a lushly watered environment, the home of a rich plant and animal life. Groups of human hunters and gatherers roamed the area, living off the plentiful herds of grazing animals. But when the glaciers of the last ice age retreated, the area was transformed into a desert and the people, as well as the animals, were forced to seek other locations to live. Many turned eastward toward the Nile Valley. Thus the later remarkable cultural unity of Egypt developed from an amazingly heterogeneous base.

The earliest settlement sites found so far are at Merimde on the western edge of the Delta and at villages in the Fayum region on the shores of Lake Qarun, which date back to c. 4750 BCE (compare to Jericho in the Levant, 8000 BCE). These early sites provide evidence of the cultivation of emmer wheat, barley, and flax, as well as the husbandry of cattle, goats, and pigs. All of these were domesticated at least 4,000 years earlier in the Near East, but this is not evidence that these peoples were Near Eastern in origin.

Why did the early migrants not settle in the valley along the river? The Nile river presented a far different appearance to these early settlers than it does to the modern eye. After the annual floods receded, the valley floor was dotted with swampy pools and the entire valley was overgrown with thickets of papyrus and reeds. The growth was even more dense and vigorous in the Delta. Land for cultivation had to be painstakingly developed little by little and at the same time cleared of wild animals. Poisonous snakes were a constant danger in the swampy areas and the river itself teemed with schools of dangerous crocodiles and herds of hippopotamuses—even encounters with elephants were not uncommon.

---

3. The ancient Egyptian language was Hamitic, a language which originated along the North African coast and in the northern Sahara.

The Predynastic period is divided into three sub-periods: the Badarian (5000–3500 BCE); the Amaratian (3800–3500 BCE); and the Gerzean (3500–3200 BCE). The great achievement of these prehistoric cultures was the control which they gained over the land. After developing an agricultural technology suited to the local environment and constructing a complex social and political organization in the villages along the western periphery of the Delta and in the Fayum, groups began to move into the Valley and the Delta themselves. The first settlements in the Valley were on stony outcroppings above the valley floor and along the edge of the desert, where they managed to clear land in their immediate neighborhood. Later they filled in the swamps and constructed dikes against the incursions of the annual floods. Gradually, they learned to use canals for irrigation. This work required social and political organization on a scale beyond that of the village and led to the growth of local political districts, known as "nomes." These nomes may be thought of as principalities or even provinces, though we know little about their specific organizational structure. Eventually there emerged 42 of these political divisions: 20 in Lower Egypt (the Delta); and 22 in Upper Egypt (the Nile Valley). At an early time the nomes of the Delta and the Valley coalesced into separate coalitions. The worship of Horus as the chief god appears first in the delta and then spreads into Upper Egypt. This used to be taken as evidence for the conquest of Upper Egypt by Lower Egypt during the Gerzean period, but this theory can no longer be supported. What is clear is that by the late Predynastic period, there were two separate kingdoms worshiping the falcon god Horus, with Nekheb (called Hierakopolis, "city of the falcon" by the Greeks) as the capital of Upper Egypt and Nekhen (called Buto by the Greeks) the capital of Lower Egypt.

The Archaic/Early Dynastic Period, Dynasties I–III (3200–2680 BCE)

The problem with the history of the Archaic Period is that so little dependable information about it survives. The kings of the first three dynasties are shadowy figures and the events of their reigns are obscure and colored by legend at best. Archaeological evidence indicates that between 3900 and 3100 BCE the villages along the Nile grew in size and prosperity. Two of these villages, Nekheb in the Delta, and Nekhen in Upper Egypt, developed into cities and became the administrative centers for Lower and Upper Egypt, respectively. Around 3000 BCE rivalry between them erupted into war. Upper Egypt emerged victorious and unified all of Egypt under the rule of a single king.

According to Manetho, this warrior-king was Menes, the Greek name for Narmer. Yet of all the kings of Egypt, Narmer is among the most legendary, because archaeological evidence indicates that several generations were required to unify Egypt. Nevertheless, the history of Egypt begins with Narmer, the first king of the "Two Lands, Upper and Lower Egypt." The unification was the most important single event in Egyptian history.

The kings of the Archaic Period were so successful that they became the overpowering focus of earthly life and were able to undertake enormous construction projects: large-scale irrigation systems; massive distribution of food and resources; regulation of trade. The wealth thus produced made possible the building of expensive tombs for themselves. The type of tomb they employed is called a Mastaba and it consisted of a shaft grave below ground covered by a large, solid rectangular building. Nothing like it had ever been seen before. The kings of the 3rd Dynasty began to stack these Mastaba structures on top of one another to form "step pyramids," the first stage in the development of the true pyramids. The step pyramid of Djoser at Saqqara is the most famous example. Abydos, "the city of Osiris" in Upper Egypt was the capital during the Archaic Period.

Old Kingdom, Dynasties IV–VI (2680–2135 BCE)

No break in the continuity of Egyptian civilization occurred between the Archaic Period and the Old Kingdom. Indeed, the kings of the 4th Dynasty appear to be descendants of Huni, the last king of the 3rd Dynasty. But from the historical point of view, the 4th Dynasty represents drastic changes in the culture, political structure, and religion of Egypt, which make the beginning of a golden age of Egyptian history. Although many of the aspects of this age are familiar to us—the great pyramids, for example—no detailed records of the events of the Old Kingdom have survived. There is archaeological evidence, however, and we can compile lists of the names of kings and other people, we can even learn a little about their private lives and know an outline of their public lives, but we can learn almost nothing about the important events of the period. It is all extremely frustrating for scholars.

The capital was moved to Memphis, just south of the Delta, a more centralized location. The government was now organized into a highly centralized institution, and the pharaoh possessed absolute power over the Egyptian people and the country's resources. The religious and political structure of Egypt were completely united and the king was now a living god. An Old Kingdom text describes the pharaoh: "The king of Upper and Lower Egypt is a god by whose dealings one lives, the father and the mother of all men, alone by himself, without equal." During the 24 year reign of Seneferu, the first king of the 4th Dynasty, military expeditions were sent east into the Sinai peninsula to put down local Bedouin chiefs. Other military forces were sent southward against the Nubians, probably to protect the diorite mines there, which were operated by the Egyptians. There is also evidence for trading expeditions to the coast of the Levant by sea to obtain cedar wood from Lebanon.

Seneferu built the first true pyramid, but it was not easy. In fact, he constructed no less than three massive tombs, all within site of each other. His first attempt was a complete disaster. Huni, the last king of the 3rd Dynasty, had constructed a large step Pyramid and Seneferu filled in the steps to form a true pyramid with smooth sides. Why he did this is an unanswered question, but it did not work. The structure was unstable and the outer parts collapsed, leaving the famous "Collapsed Pyramid at Meidum." He then attempted to build a true pyramid from scratch, but it too had structural problems. The angle of ascent for the sides was much too steep and the structure began to crack. The architects tried to fix it by changing the stone laying technique, but further cracking occurred and they had to change the angle of ascent in mid-construction, producing the "Bent Pyramid at Dahshur." Another failure. Learning from their mistakes, the third attempt employed a good foundation and larger blocks. It is very large, in fact, the footprint of Seneferu's third pyramid is almost as large as the Great Pyramid of Giza, but the sides are not as steep. It was successful and is known as the "Northern Pyramid of Dahshur." It should be noted that in building his two pyramids at Dahshur, Seneferu moved more stone than any other pharaoh, before or after. He was not only the *first* to build a true pyramid, but in total mass, he was the *biggest* builder of all time. Thus the whole technique of constructing the massive true pyramid was evolved in just one reign. A remarkable accomplishment. What a shame he did not leave us an account of it (Fig. 3.4).

When Seneferu's son, Khufu (called Cheops by the Greeks), came to the throne, everything was in place to accomplish something spectacular: the proven technology, the resources, the social and political structure, and, finally, the religious motivation. Khufu chose Giza as the location for his pyramid. At the time it was just an empty desert plateau. To put Khufu's accomplishment into perspective: the largest and artistically the most perfect pyramid ever constructed—counted as one

1. Step Pyramid of Djoser

2. Collapsed Pyramid of Seneferu

3. Bent Pyramid of Seneferu

4. Great Pyramid of Khufu

Figure 3.4: The evolution of the pyramid.

of the Seven Wonders of the World by the ancients—was completed in less than 100 years after the first step pyramid was begun. Seven massive burial projects had been constructed during a single century. During the average 30 to 40 year lifetime, a 4th Dynasty Egyptian witnessed the beginning of at least three massive royal pyramid projects. Khufu's accomplishment was never repeated. This is perhaps comparable the 20th Century accomplishment of a man walking on the moon only 66 years after the first powered flight. Like the building of the great pyramid, the moon walk may well be the culmination of an effort that may never be repeated. One of the fascinating aspects of history is the way human societies set a goal, marshal their resources to accomplish it, and then turn away toward other pursuits.

Khufu's Great Pyramid at Giza is the largest ever built—yet only the 7th attempted in the history of the world. At 756 feet on each side it has only a slightly larger footprint then Seneferu's Northern Pyramid at Dahshur (722 feet), but it is 475 feet high (vs. 340 feet for Seneferu's pyramid), because it is quite a bit steeper than his father's. The interior of the pyramid consists of 2.3 million cut sandstone blocks, weighing 2.5 tons each, quarried nearby. How was this possible? According to one statistical estimate, 84,000 laborers worked for 80 days a year (mostly during the annual floods). Assuming a twelve hour work day, one 2.5 ton block was set into place every 30 seconds for 20 years! All together this required about 370,000 man-years of labor. Realistically, if several blocks were put into place at the same time, it still would mean that only a few minutes were spent on each block. What an incredible engineering feat! The outside of the pyramid was covered with 16 ton limestone blocks quarried several miles up the Nile on the opposite side. These were fit together with amazing accuracy and gave the pyramid a glowing, almost shiny, appearance. Granite was used to line the interior corridors and chambers. This was brought from far up the Nile near Aswan. No one has ever been able to explain adequately how all this was accomplished. Why, oh why didn't just one architect or engineer who worked on this project leave us his memoirs?

Khufu's successors enjoyed varying success emulating his accomplishments. His immediate successor (his son?), Djedefre, reigned for only eight years, and left a smaller pyramid unfinished at another location. Two of Khufu's descendants, however, did manage to construct "great pyramids." Djedefre's successor, Khafre, also Khufu's son, built a pyramid almost a large as his father's. But he had a tough act to follow, and his structure was destined from the beginning to be referred to as the "second pyramid" of Giza. However, Khafre added some original touches of his own. He built his pyramid on higher ground, so that from a distance it looks like it is the largest, and he carved a colossal sphinx from an outcropping of local bedrock nearby. It is in the form of the head of Khafre with paws, body, and tail partially formed with stone bricks. Khafre's grandson (Mycerinus), added a third, smaller pyramid at Giza. These three "Great Pyramids" have fascinated people throughout the centuries and continue to do so today.[4]

The 5th Dynasty was an era of less grandiose building projects. Although the pyramids became smaller, the mortuary temples associated with them became more important and elaborate. Private tombs of the court aristocrats began to appear and inscriptions on their walls began to tell the stories of their occupants, which give us a glimpse into the everyday life of the period. Then the burial chambers of the pyramids themselves began to be adorned with the "Pyramid Texts," which relate the perils the deceased will encounter on his journey into the afterlife. These texts provide a kind of passport or guide for the soul, as well as the magical formula to ensure a safe and successful passage into the world of the gods.

The Old Kingdom ended with the rule of Pepi II, who appears to have the longest reign in world history: 94 years! He left a collection of texts that give us our most vivid picture of what life was like in the Old Kingdom. One letter to the leader of an expedition far into central Africa—how far we do not know—urging him to take special care of the pigmy or dwarf he was bringing back so that the king could enjoy seeing him. But the kingdom was in already decline and after Pepi II's reign the country broke up into warring principalities.

---

4. For further reading on the pyramids, see: Edwards, I.E.S., *The Pyramids of Egypt* (1961), Penguin Books, New York; Mendelssohn, Kurt, The Riddle of the Pyramids (1974), Thames and Hudson, London; Clayton, Peter A., *Chronicle of the Pharaohs* (1994), Thames and Hudson, London; Lehner, Mark, *The Complete Pyramids* (1997), Thames and Hudson, London.

First Intermediate Period, Dynasties VII–X (2135–2040 BCE)

It is difficult to know anything substantial about the First Intermediate Period. All are agreed that it was a era of strife, chaos, and anarchy. But there the agreement ends. Indeed, Egyptologists cannot even agree about such basic problems as how long the period lasted.[5] The most likely scenario for the breakdown of the Old Kingdom is pharaonic inertia and inability to cope with a series of problems caused—or at least exaggerated by—climatic changes. Many years of insufficient inundations of the Nile resulted in famine, shortages, and confusion.[6] The last king of the Old Kingdom, Pepi II, lost more and more power to the provincial governors. Since the central government was unable to cope with the results of the climatic change, it fell to local rulers to cope with the problems. Thus these local rulers began to assert their independence and often even to claim the status of king for themselves. This process of disintegration was perhaps intensified by the unnaturally long reign of Pepi II. He became king in early childhood and reigned well into his nineties. The last 30 years or so of his reign may well have been less than effective in coping with serious and unique crises.

A group of rulers based at Henen-Nesw (Herakleopolis) established control over Lower Egypt. They claimed to be the rightful heirs to Egypt's throne. They repaired canals, fortified the borders, and opened trade with Byblos in the Levant. The Herakleopolitan kings also had a reputation for cruelty, but they brought order to the Delta during a time of chaos. To the south the ruling family of Thebes united Upper Egypt into a loose coalition. Intef I was first ruler of this dynasty, and he assumed the title of "Great Chief of Upper Egypt," but unlike his Herakleopolitan rivals he did not claim the title of king. However, Intef I's successors tightened their hold on Upper Egypt and eventually claimed the title of pharaoh. Once they had a firm control of southern Egypt they moved against the Delta. Under Mentuhotep II, full scale civil war broke out between Upper and Lower Egypt, and in 2040 he captured Herakleopolis and re-united Egypt. Thus Mentuhotep II is counted as both the last king of the 10th Dynasty and first king of the 11th Dynasty. He was the founder of the Middle Kingdom.

Middle Kingdom, Dynasties XI–XII (2040–1786 BCE)

The king of Egypt was again the very center of religious and political life in ancient Egypt, but his position was now changed from what it had been during the Old Kingdom. The "nomarchs,"[7] or regional leaders, retained some of their power, in fact, some of them were allowed to maintain

---

5. James Henry Breasted, for example (*A History of Egypt* (1905) Bantam classic, 1994, p. 500), estimated the length of the period at 315 years, as opposed to 141 years for Peter A. Clayton (see note 4 above), and 110 years for Mark Lehner (see note 4 above). Manetho, whose figures are often wild exaggerations, allotted 409 years for the 9th Dynasty and 185 years for the 10th Dynasty. On the other hand he assigned "70 kings in 70 days" or in another version, "5 kings in 75 days" to the 7th Dynasty. For the 9th Dynasty Manetho assigns either "4 kings in 100 years" or "19 kings in 409 years," not a very dependable chronology. In fact, no historical kings have yet been discovered for either the 7th or the 9th Dynasties. The dates given for the First Intermediate Period in the chorological table in Figure 2 are really arbitrary and basically follow those worked out by William Stevenson Smith, *Ancient Egypt as Represented in the Museum of Fine Arts*, Boston (1960), Museum of Fine Arts, Boston, p. 197. The only thing certain is that the First Intermediate Period separates dynasties VI and XII.

6. Climatic changes have occurred periodically throughout the existence of the earth. Several changes have occurred during the short time known as "recorded history," always producing far-reaching and unforeseen consequences. The earth appears to be in the first stages of another periodic climatic change in the 21st Century. The ancients believed the gods were responsible for these changes, but in our modern, secular world the responsibility seems to rest squarely on the shoulders of humanity itself. In the long-term context of history, the assertion that humans are changing the earth's climate through the use, or misuse, of their own power, seems rather arrogant, even a bit like hubris.

7. Nomarch: the chief magistrate or governor of a nome. During the Middle Kingdom some "regional leaders" could compel the loyalty of several nomes.

standing armies on their own, as long as they could be called into the king's service in time of need. After the reunification of Egypt, Mentuhotep II and his successors of the 11th Dynasty ruled Egypt for about 70 years. The pharaoh was now more of a military leader than he had ever been, and whenever military power is available it is usually used. Expeditions were sent in every direction, into the Levant, Nubia and Libya to suppress enemies and exploit local natural resources. The kings of the 11th Dynasty also renewed trade relations with foreign countries. Mentuhotep III dispatched a trade mission to Punt to obtain Myrrh.[8] Both Mentuhotep II and III built elaborate mortuary complexes near Thebes and temples throughout Egypt. Mentuhotep II initiated a new type of funerary monument which combined the elements of a pillared, or colonnaded, hall and the pyramid complex. It was a terraced structure supported by pillars with a pyramid set in the center of the hall on the upper level. The new Kingdom queen Hatshepsut patterned her great mortuary temple after Mentuhotep's (it is located just adjacent to his), although it was built over 550 years later.

About 1919 BCE, Amenemhet I, some say by violence, others say through peaceful means, became king and founded the 12th Dynasty, which ruled Egypt for over 200 years to 1786 BCE. The 12th Dynasty pharaohs wanted to identify themselves with the Old Kingdom and revived the pyramid style of royal tomb, but added subterranean elements to invoke the cult of Osisis, the god of the netherworld, who had died and resurrected. Twelfth Dynasty pyramids are scattered up and down the west bank of the Nile. Most of them were built of mud bricks with limestone casings. One exception is Amenemhet II's "Black Pyramid," built in part of basalt.

Amenemhet I implemented three measures which became the general policy of the 12th Dynasty. First, he established a new capital at Ith-tawe, just south of Memphis, where he could better control both Upper and Lower Egypt. Second, to avoid the palace conspiracies that had plagued the 11th Dynasty, he initiated the practice of installing his son beside him on the throne as co-regent. Finally, he subdued Nubia and established fortified trading posts further south than had ever been attempted before. These military campaigns were continued by his successors who extended Egyptian control far beyond the Second Cataract into modern Sudan. Trade relations were also expanded with Syria, Lebanon, and Palestine. Middle Kingdom artifacts have been found as far east as the Aegean islands, probably taken there by traders from the Phoenician cities of Lebanon.

The end of the 12th Dynasty marked the end of the Middle Kingdom. The event was in some ways similar to the end of the Old Kingdom. The long 45 year reign of Amenemhet IV coincided with another climatic change. This time annual floods of the Nile were exceptionally high and lasted longer than normal, which shortened the growing season. The crisis was not as bleak as the end of the Old Kingdom, but the difficulties weakened the king's authority. The 13th Dynasty kings moved the capital back to Memphis and their reigns were short and ineffectual. Without a strong ruler, Egypt again dissolved into Upper and Lower Kingdoms.

Second Intermediate Period, Dynasties XIII–XVII (1786–1570)

The Second Intermediate Period lasted over two centuries, but is shrouded in obscurity and confusion. Sadly, there does not seem to be much that modern scholarship can do to cast light upon this dark age, even though it produced important and profound changes in Egyptian society. We know less about the events of Egypt during these two centuries than about those of any other time. It is possible to draw up a list of the names of kings, but their order and duration is disputed and

---

8. Myrrh is the resin, or sap, of the commiphora tree which is common in Somaliland. Cutting the tree's bark causes the sap to ooze out of the cut, which is allowed to dry on the tree and collected as hardened lumps. It was most commonly used to create insense.

they left few monuments. All efforts to reconstruct the events of this period with any accuracy have floundered on the paucity and unreliability of the evidence. Ironically, many of the most important events of history are surrounded with mystery and obscurity.

After the end of the 12th Dynasty, Egypt lost much of its political structure and social cohesion. The garrisons of the fortresses in Nubia became more independent—some of the soldiers seem to have settled there permanently. The fortifications guarding the eastern border of the Delta were abandoned and peoples from the Levant began moving into the Lower Egypt. Within a generation or two the Delta was populated mostly by "Asiatics." Here the history of the age descends into shadowy obscurity. It appears the immigrants took control over most of Lower Egypt without much difficulty.

Who were these intruders? Like most aspects of this period, the question of their origin has not been, and perhaps never will be, answered satisfactorily. Their arrival in Egypt corresponds with upheavals in western Asia involving problems not directly concerned with Egyptian history.[9] They were Semitic in language and culture, probably Canaanite or Amorite, and the evidence indicates they had hitherto pursued a nomadic lifestyle. Greek writers, beginning with Manetho, called them "Hyksos." This word was derived from the Egyptian word *hega-khasut* ("rulers of foreign lands"), but the Egyptians also referred to them as *amu* ("Asiatics"), or *shamu* ("sand-dwellers"), not very complementary terms.

After a rather peaceful 14th Dynasty, the Hyksos set up contemporaneous 15th and 16th Dynasties. The duration and sequence of these kings are impossible to sort out. They adopted Egyptian manners and laws. They maintained, and even expanded, the Egyptian trade relationships with the Levant and extended trade as far as Crete and Babylon. These kings claimed the status of pharaoh, with all the regalia and traditions attached to that title. In this way they ruled Egypt for more than a hundred years. But the Hyksos also had a deep influence on Egyptian society. They introduced new, improved weapons and the horse, an animal new to the Egyptians. They eventually gained control of the northern part of Upper Egypt, but never managed to penetrate further south than the town of Hermopolis.

What few records there are for this period are mostly concerned with the war of liberation fought by the kings of the 17th Dynasty, based on Thebes. It was a long and bitter struggle. In the end, the Thebans forced the Hyksos king Apepi II to negotiate the withdrawal of the Hyksos army from most of the Delta. But the Theban kings did not abide by the agreement and war soon broke out again. Eventually Ahmose I, the first king of the 18th Dynasty (successor to the 17th Dynasty at Thebes), a great general, drove the Hyksos out of Egypt and by 1570 established the New Kingdom. The Hyksos were pushed back into the Levant, where they were defeated and disappeared from history.

New Kingdom, Dynasties XVIII–XX (1570–1085 BCE)

In stark contrast with the preceding period, the history of the New Kingdom is better known than any other period of ancient Egypt, and it is the most popular with modern writers and the media. During the New Kingdom Egypt reached its zenith of power, wealth, and territorial expansion. This was the age of empire. The kings of this period were no longer content to live in isolation from the rest of the world, but actively projected Egyptian influence in every direction. This, of course, was partly a reaction to the humiliating experience of foreign rule during the Second

---

9. For example, this was the period of the movement of the Amorites into Mesopotamia (see Time Line Fig. 2.3).

Intermediate Period. The Egyptians were now determined never to be ruled by foreigners again. Ahmose I was honored by later generations as the founder of a new royal line, the 18th Dynasty, even though his brother, Kahmose, and his father, Taa II, were the last two kings of the 17th Dynasty.

During the 18th Dynasty the government was reorganized into a military state with the administration centralized directly into the hands of the pharaoh and his chief minister. The empire in the Levant was extended as far as the northern banks of the Euphrates River. This Egyptian influence brought peace, stability, and prosperity to the Levant for one of the longest periods of its entire history. Yet, the Egyptian Empire was not an overly oppressive régime. It was not even what we usually think of when we hear the word "empire." The Egyptians did not install bureaucrats to micro-manage the conquered territories. Instead the territories were still ruled by their own kings and princes, who paid an annual tax, or tribute, to the pharaoh. So the Egyptian "empire" was actually a complicated system of diplomatic alliances, treaties, and client states. During the New Kingdom the immense wealth which was funneled into Egypt from its empire funded grandiose building programs, such as the great temple complex at Karnak, near Thebes, dedicated to the god Amun-Re.

One of the most famous and interesting rulers of the 18th Dynasty was Queen Hatshepsut, who ruled Egypt for 22 years (1504–1483), calling herself "pharaoh," and "son of Amun-Re." There were female rulers before her, and there would be others after her, but Hatshepsut was in several ways unique. Even though ancient Egypt was a male-oriented society, women had an advantage over women in other ancient societies, such as Mesopotamia and Greece, because they were allowed to own and inherit property. In addition, Egyptian women were able to defend their legal rights in court—in contrast with Greece, for example, where women had no legal rights and were always under the control of a male "guardian." This gave Egyptian women the ability to function independently in public.

A glance at the stemma of Hatshepsut (Fig. 3.5) reveals the nature of her frustration. She was directly descended from Kamose and Ahmose I, the brothers who mark the end of the 17th and the beginning of the 18th Dynasties. She had two brothers who died in their youth, leaving her as the only heir of her father, Thutmose I. But her father had a son, Thutmose II, by his commoner concubine, Moutnofrit. Hatshepsut was married to her half brother, to keep it all in the family, so to speak. So Thutmose II became pharaoh upon his father's death and Hatshepsut became his queen. But Thutmose II died after a reign of only four years. Hatshepsut had no children by Thutmose II, but he had a son

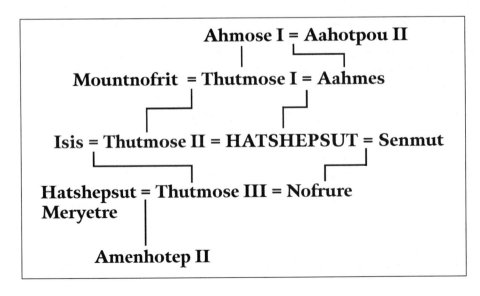

Figure 3.5:
The family of
Hatshepsut.

by Isis, his commoner concubine, who became pharaoh as Thutmose III, while still a very young child. This left Hatshepsut in a strong position as the most powerful representative of the dynasty and she took control of the throne, with the strong backing of the priesthood and most of the royal court.

As a female ruler, Hatshepsut always lived under the threat of revolt. Especially from her embittered nephew, Thutmose III. A more ruthless ruler would have simply eliminated the threat, but she countered it with political skill and elegant statesmanship. In her propaganda she became a "king" and appears so in all of her statuary, even dressed in the traditional male regalia and ceremonial beard. She constructed a large and beautiful temple/tomb at Deir el Bahri, in the Valley of the Kings. It is modeled after the mortuary temple of Mentuhotep II and was constructed adjacent to that 11th Dynasty structure. But Hatshepsut's temple is much larger. It lies within the mountainside and has rows of colonnades that reflect the vertical patters of the cliff backdrop. Two ramps connect the three levels of the structure and on either side there were large papyrus pools. On the ground level were rows of sphinxes with the heads representing Hatshepsut. The temple was dedicated to Amun and Hathor, but there were chapels throughout in honor of other gods. Another of her achievements was the erection of two enormous obelisks at the temple to Amun-Re at Karnak, each cut from a single block of granite transported from Aswan, far up the Nile.

In foreign affairs Hatshepsut avoided war and instead projected Egyptian influence through trade expeditions to far off lands, the most interesting of which was Punt, modern Somalia. These expeditions are documented in the inscriptions on the walls of her temple. The missions brought back ivory, animals, spices, gold, and aromatic trees. The representation of the Queen of Punt shows a short, obese figure with folds of fat hanging from her knees and elbows. Quite a contrast with the slim and beautiful Egyptian queen.

But Hatshepsut disappeared suddenly and mysteriously in 1483 when Thutmose III gained control of the throne. Her mummy was later stolen and her tomb destroyed. Thutmose III had her name erased from all her monuments, including her temple at Deir el Bahri. Her consort Senmut's name was also removed. Her daughter Nofrure by Senmut is not heard of again. Did Thutmose kill Hatshepsut, Sunmut, and Nofrure? There is no direct proof, but the circumstantial evidence is overwhelming. Certainly he showed only contempt for Hatshepsut's memory, and it is probable that he paid even less respect for her in life. It is ironic that had Hatshepsut been as ruthless and heartless as her nephew she would not have spared his life and she would have been safe on the throne.

The Hyksos had taught the Egyptians the bitter lesson that their eastern borders could now be made safe only through the conquest and domination of the Levant region. Thus, Thutmose III turned immediately to the military projects for which he was so well suited by both training and temperament. He is, in fact, the most effective military leader Egypt ever produced. A coalition of anti-Egyptian forces had been assembled in Palestine and Thutmose III advanced to meet them. In a brilliant maneuver, he moved his army through a narrow and little-used pass, outflanked and defeated the enemy. When the defeated chieftains took refuge in the fortress at Megiddo, he laid siege to it and forced its surrender, which gave him control of the Levant as far east as Lebanon. In subsequent campaigns he moved the boundary of the Egyptian Empire east to the Euphrates River.

The three succeeding pharaohs of the 18th Dynasty—Amenhotep II, Thutmose IV[10] and Amenhotep III—maintained and enhanced these holdings. However, the next king, Amenhotep IV

---

10. Thutmose IV erected a stela at Giza on which he recounts how, on a hunting trip, in the heat of the day he fell asleep in the shadow of the Sphinx. The sun god appeared to him in a dream and revealed to him that he would one day ascend to the throne of Egypt and asked him to clear away the sand that had accumulated around the Sphinx. When he became king he carried out the instructions and his pious act was recorded on the stela which still stands between the paws of the Sphinx today.

plunged the dynasty into crisis by pursuing unpopular religious reforms. He was a fanatical supporter of the cult of the sun god Aten and attempted to make his god the exclusive religion of the state. He changed his name to Akhenaten ("Aten is satisfied") in honor of his god and constructed a new capital at Tell el Amarna, called Akhetaten ("The place where Aten becomes effective"), which was intended to be a city uncontaminated by the worship of the other gods. The religious aspects of his reform will be discussed below in the section of this chapter devoted to Egyptian religion, but Akhenaten's reign also had deep political and social repercussions. First of all, the attempt to destroy the worship of the ancient gods was deeply divisive and destructive to Egyptian society. In fact, the evidence indicates that most of the people of Egypt simply ignored the government and continued to worship the gods in private. Secondly, Akhenaten's foreign policy (or some would say, lack of a foreign policy) abandoned the maintenance of the empire, and consequently Egyptian influence in the Levant immediately began to wane. Chaos spread through Syria and Palestine, where the principalities and petty kingdoms began to assert their independence and the rising Hittite Empire took advantage of the situation to win large territories for itself. At the same time a powerful wave of opposition to Akhenaten's policies swept across Egypt, led by the defrocked priests of the ancient gods.

Akhenaten died after only fifteen years of rule, almost certainly assassinated. His successors Semenkhkare and Tutankhamon immediately reversed the religious reforms of Akhenaton, and his reign had little if any influence on subsequent Egyptian history, except in the sphere of art. However, permanent damage was done to the 18th Dynasty. It never recovered its former glory and its last kings all disappeared mysteriously, probably falling victim to court intrigues. The last king of the 18th Dynasty, Haremhab, was not of the royal family. He was a general under Tutankhamon and after the short reign of Ay he became king. The length of his reign is still not determined, but his influence was lasting. The demolition of Akhenaten's city at Amarna, which was still inhabited, began under Haremhab, who had the temples of Aten dismantled. His own building projects included additions to the temple of Amun at Karnak and his own mortuary temple at Thebes. Haremhab also initiated a series of reforms to correct the laxness and political corruption which had grown up since the beginning of Akhenaten's reign.

The persecution of the Aten heresy was motivated by his desire to rid Egypt of the religious friction created by Akhenaten's experiment. Ramesses I, the founder of the 19th Dynasty, was an army officer under Haremhab and he was already an old man when he came to the throne. He reigned for only two years. His descendants, Seti I, Ramesses II, and Merenptah, were three of the most successful rulers in Egyptian history. But it should be remembered that their success was made possible, in large measure, by the wise domestic reforms of Haremhab.

Perhaps the most interesting of the 19th Dynasty pharaohs was Ramesses II, called Ramesses the Great, who reigned for 67 years (Fig. 3.6). He lived to be 97 years old, had 200 wives and concubines, who bore him 96 sons and 60 daughters.[11] When Ramesses came to the throne in 1290 BCE at the age of 25, Egyptian influence in the Levant was in sharp decline. The Akhenaten episode and its aftermath had presented the Hittites a golden opportunity and they had expanded their empire deep into Palestine. Ramesses II was determined to set things right again and led an army into Syria. However, at Qadesh on the Orontes River, near the modern Lebanese-Syria border, the Hittites

---

11. Consider for a moment what life would be like if you had 155 siblings! Ramesses positioned members of his family in important posts throughout the government. One son, Khaemwese, was high priest of Ptah and governor of Memphis. He was also in charge of the restoration of the pyramid of Unas, the last king of the 5th Dynasty. Thus, Ramesses II was not only a great builder, he was also a restorer and preserver of monuments of the past.

Figure 3.6: Ramesses II, Temple of Amun, Luxor.

caught him by surprise and he faced a humiliating defeat until the arrival of reinforcements saved the day. Nevertheless, the carnage and bloodshed of the inconclusive war seems to have stunned both sides, because eventually a treaty was concluded, which essentially divided the Levant between the two powers.[12]

Ramesses II reigned long enough to populate Egypt with hundreds of building projects, which include the Hypostyle Hall at the Temple of Amun-Re at Karnak, a mortuary complex at Abydos, a vast tomb for his family at Thebes, additions to the Luxor Temple, and, of course, the famous temples to himself and his favorite wife, Nefertari, at Abu Simbel. The mummy of Ramesses II is now

---

12. For the text of this treaty see "An Egyptian-Hittite Treaty," Cleve, Robert, *Early Western Civilization, Source Readings* (2002), Kendall/Hunt, Dubuque, pp. 107–108.

in the National Museum in Cairo, Egypt, but the story of its survival is quite amazing. He was originally buried in his tomb in the Valley of the Kings. Because widespread looting of tombs occurred during the 21ˢᵗ Dynasty, the priests removed Ramesses body and took it to a "holding area" where the valuable materials, such as gold-leaf and semi precious inlays, were removed. The bodies of Ramesses I and Seti I and several others were treated in the same fashion. Seventy-two hours later, all of the bodies were again removed, this time to the Royal Cache inside the tomb of the High Priest Pindjem II. The priests documented all of this on the linen that covered the bodies. This systematic looting by the priests was done in the guise of protecting the bodies from the "common" thieves.

Ramesses II's reign was so long, almost three generations by ancient standards, that by the time that he died at age 97, after 67 years on the throne, there was hardly anyone alive in Egypt who could remember being ruled by any other pharaoh. Many people had come to believe that Ramesses was indeed a living god and would rule Egypt forever. Understandably, his death was a shock that produced unease and even panic throughout the populace. But fortunately, these types of crises almost always pass with little or no lasting damage to society and such situations tend to re-enforce the old adage, "no one is indispensable."

Ramesses II outlived his 12 eldest sons. His middle-aged 13ᵗʰ son, Merenptah, had long lost his youthful vigor when he ascended the throne to reign for 12 years, and after him the events of the 19ᵗʰ Dynasty are obscure and confused. Ramesses III of the 20ᵗʰ Dynasty is the last well-known king of Egyptian History. A fundamental change occurs during this period throughout the ancient Near East. Old powers, like the Hittites, fade and disappear from history, to be replaced by the new empires of the Assyrians and the Persians, who will dominate history down to the Greek period. Ramesses III did not have to go to Syria to meet his enemies, they came to him. A wave of Indo-Europeans, whom the Egyptians called the "Peoples of the Sea," attempted to invade Egypt through the mouth of the Nile River, but were beaten back by Ramesses III. A remnant of these peoples settled on the coast of the Levant. These were the Philistines, and they gave their name to the area, which is still called Palestine to this day. It is strange that an area so completely identified with the Semitic peoples throughout its long history should be known as an Indo-European name.

After the 20ᵗʰ Dynasty Egypt entered a long period of decline and for all practical purposes its ancient history came to an end. In 671 BCE it became a part of the Assyrian Empire and it passed to their successors, the Persian Empire, in 525 BCE. Egypt was ruled by the Persians until it was conquered by Alexander the Great in 332 BCE. The Greek-Macedonian Ptolemaic Dynasty then ruled Egypt until it became a province of the Roman Empire in 30 BCE and remained so until conquered by the Arabs in 640.

Egyptian Religion

There was no word in the ancient Egyptian language for religion, as we understand that term. To the Egyptians, Egypt was an integral part of the universal order, the pharaoh was a divine king, one of the gods himself, who was responsible for maintaining the stability of Egypt's place in the cosmic order. It was as simple as that.

From the earliest Pre-Dynastic Period there is evidence of a belief in the afterlife. The annual cycle of the seasons, in which planting time and harvest time alternated in endless succession, driven by the timeless struggle between the Nile floods and the desert, between the life-giving water and the death dealing-sands, suggested to the Egyptians that the natural order of the world was one of endless cycles. All these aspects of nature were personified into various gods. When Egypt was unified, during the early Archaic Period, the more important of the local deities assumed a regional role. Horus and Seth became the patrons of kings. Ptah became the principle deity of Memphis, the first capital of unified Egypt. The worship of Re, the sun god, became an important cult at Heliopolis (the Greek name for *Iunu* or *Iunet Mehet*). Osiris, Thoth, Anubis, and dozens of other gods were all accepted as part of the Egyptian pantheon. The Egyptians had no problem with these multitudes of gods. The cult of the divine king, as an intermediary between the gods and humans, was an aspect of Egyptian religion from the beginning of Egyptian history. In the earliest texts the pharaoh was identified with Horus, the sky god, but by the 5th Dynasty the king was addressed as "the son of Re," the sun god. After their death, pharaohs were identified with Osiris.

Ancient Egyptians never attempted to develop a system of logical theology, indeed, the possibility or even the desirability of a logical framework for their spiritual life never occurred to them (as indeed it never occurs to most individuals today). Dogmas and doctrines did not concern them—in fact, they were uncomfortable with spiritual concepts that demanded logical or reasonable development. While the state priests observed the rites and ceremonies of the official cults necessary to maintain the divine order of the world, the individual Egyptians were free to practice whatever religious regimen they deemed correct or desirable for themselves. This led to the development of a spiritual ideal of cosmic harmony, justice, order, and peace, personified as the goddess Ma'at. Each new king claimed to restore the spirit of Ma'at upon his accession to the throne, no matter how benevolent the reign of his predecessor had been (much as each new U.S. president claims to restore the "old values" of our society upon taking office). Ma'at was the model for human behavior, for the universal order of the heavens, the cosmic balance here on earth and the essence of celestial beauty.

Cosmogony: Egyptian Creation Stories

Several different, and sometimes conflicting, creation myths were current in ancient Egypt and this did not offend the Egyptians at all. They are found in the texts of all the cults, on the walls of temples and embedded in the religious literature of every period, but four major stories were the most important and wide spread.

1. The creation story of the sun god cult was part of the Pyramid Texts of the Old Kingdom. Atum, the creator god, emerged from the watery chaos called *nun* ("void") on a hill or "creation mound" that became the great temple of Re at Heliopolis. Atum became Atum-Re and created the other gods. Shu, god of the air, and Tefnut, his consort, were spit out of his mouth. Shu and Tefnut gave birth to Geb, the earth, and Nut, the sky. They in turn gave birth to Osiris, Isis, Nephthys, and Seth. Osiris and Isis gave birth to Horus. All these divine beings formed the ennead, the first nine gods.
2. The creation myth from the city of Hermopolis held that the original gods were formed as an ogdoad (group of eight), four male/female pairs: Nun (water) and his consort Naunet, Huh (eternity) and Hauhet, Kuk (darkness) and Kaukrt, and Amon (air) and Amaunet. These gods produced a golden age before humans inhabited the Nile Valley. Amon became popular because of his role in stirring the waters to create life. This story included the laying of a cosmic egg by a celestial ibis. The Hermopolis ogdoad was concerned with the rising of the sun and flooding of the Nile, both vital to Egyptian society.
3. The Memphis cosmogony was old and complex. Ptah was the creator of the entire universe and the ennead of Heliopolis and the other gods were manifestations of Ptah. It does not refute the Heliopoliton story in any way but asserts that the creator god Atum was a concept in the mind of Ptah who created the world at Ptah's command. The *Theology of*

Memphis[13] included a rather sophisticated attempt to deal with what Aristotle will later call the "first principle." Ptah is seen as that creative first principle, responsible for not only the creation of the material world but for the creation of the moral, spiritual, and ethical order of the cosmos.

4. The Theban story of creation came into being during the New Kingdom to provide a rank above the other gods of Egypt for Amun. The priests of Amun used the concept of Amun as the god of air as at Hermopolis. Thebes became the site of the appearance of the original creation mound. Amun created himself in Thebes and all other gods were simply manifestations of him. He was Ptah and the ogdoad. Thebes also assumed Osiris into its domain, claiming that god also was born in the New Kingdom capital.

Strangely, the Egyptian creation myths did not include a description of the origin of humanity. The major concern of the Egyptians was the origin of life itself. Once the cycle of life was established, it could be repeated endlessly. There were, however, a number of folk stories accounting for the origin of humans. One story was that Atum created the first human beings from his own tears. The Egyptians words for human and tear had a rhyming sound, and the ancients believed that any words that sounded alike must be connected in some way. Another story was that Atum made the first humans out of clay on his potter's wheel. An important aspect cosmogony is that there is no hint of humankind being inherently evil or in any way displeasing to the gods, in stark contrast to the creation mythology of Mesopotamia or the "fall from grace" of Adam and Eve in the Hebrew story of creation.

Osiris: Death and Resurrection

At the very heart of Egyptian religion was the cult[14] of Osiris. The story of this god had great significance to the Egyptians and it requires a brief examination. Osiris was the son of Geb (the earth) and Nut (the sky). He had two sisters and a brother. Together these four gods formed two male/female pairs. Isis was the sister-wife of Osiris, while Nephthys was the sister-wife of his brother Seth. In due course Osiris became king of Egypt and taught men agriculture, how to worship the gods, and established the rule of law. However, his younger brother Seth (also Set) was jealous of Osiris's position and power and he plotted to destroy him. This is a variation of the war between the older and the younger gods that is so common in the mythological cycles of the eastern Mediterranean, but this story plays out the rivalry that often occurs between the eldest son and his younger sibling. In antiquity, the oldest son often inherited all the family estate and title while the younger sons got nothing. This naturally bred resentment.

One night while Osiris slept, Seth secretly measured his body and built a beautiful box—obviously a mummy case—exactly the size of his body. Seth brought this box to a feast where all the gods were present and offered to make a present of it to anyone who would fit it exactly. Of course all the gods lined up to try, but they were all either too large, too small, too tall, or too short. When Osiris got into the box, however, he fit perfectly and suddenly Seth shut it tightly and threw it into the Nile, which carried it out to sea. When Isis heard about this, being a faithful and loving wife,

---

13. For the text of "The Theology of Memphis," see Cleve, Robert, *Early Western Civilization, Source Readings* (2002), Kendall/Hunt, Dubuque, pp. 42–45.

14. The term *cult* as used in the context of ancient religion has a far different meaning than when used by the modern media. As used here it means "a formal religious veneration; a system of religious beliefs and ritual; also its body of adherents." As used by the modern media it means, "a religion regarded as unorthodox or spurious."

she set out to find her husband's body. After a long search, she finely traced it to the Phoenician city of Byblos, on the coast of present day Lebanon, where the chest had washed ashore and become entangled in the roots of a tamarisk tree. The tree had grown to a gigantic size and enclosed the box within its trunk. The king of Phoenicia had cut the tree and made it a pillar to hold up the roof of his palace. Isis went undercover and obtained the position of wet nurse to the king's infant son. But instead of nursing him in the ordinary way, Isis gave him her finger to suck. From her finger the child gradually ingested the goddess' immortality and each night she put him into the fire to burn away his mortal parts. But alas, before the process was completed, one night the queen came into the room and saw her son in the flames and cried out, thus depriving him of immortality. It is unclear exactly what all of this has to do with the main plot of the story, but the Egyptians loved to tell stories. At any rate, the Isis now went to the king and gained position of the chest containing the body of Osiris and departed for Egypt with her husband's body. She hid the box in the delta and made preparations to perform a ceremony to resurrect Osiris. This would require the assistance of her son Horus, Anubis, the god of the dead and patron of embalmers, and Thoth, the god of magic and the scribe of the gods.

Figure 3.7: Osiris, as king of the other world.

However, while these preparations were being made, Seth, one night while out hunting by the light of the full moon, found the body of Osiris and in rage he tore it to pieces and scattered it throughout Egypt. Isis now made a river boat of papyrus reads and sailed up and down the Nile until she had gathered all the fragments of her husbands body. In the meantime, Horus, now grown up, fought his father's murderer in a fierce battle that lasted many days, and eventually Seth was defeated and destroyed.

Now Isis reunited the fragments of her husband's body and it was carefully embalmed and she and the three others gods performed the ceremonies and rituals over Osiris's mummy which brought about a mysterious change that allowed the body he had possessed on earth to also serve as his body in the world beyond the grave, where he became the king of heaven.

This story of the death and resurrection of Osiris was very important to the Egyptians, and it formed the nucleus of belief around which the cult of Osiris developed. The Egyptians come to believe that these same four gods, Isis, Horace, Thoth, and Anubis, could, and under the right circumstances, would, perform the same magical life-restoring ceremonies for human beings as they performed for Osiris. This would allow them to share in Osiris's conquest of death and enjoy an afterlife. This was a revolutionary departure from the sun-god cult of the pharaoh which was the basis of the pharaoh's immortality. The cult of Osiris gave the ordinary Egyptian hope of eternal life.

The Democratization of the Afterlife

This spread of the access to the next world down through Egyptian society, from top to bottom, is sometimes called the "democratization of the afterlife." The obtaining of an afterlife can be understood as a process of association, of the sharing in the conquest of death by Osiris, and the Egyptians believed that the critical act was the journey of the soul between this world and the world of the gods. This journey was fraught with danger and difficulty and could only be successfully accomplished with the aid and assistance of magic and help from the gods.

Originally, back at the beginning of the Old Kingdom, only the pharaoh enjoyed immortality, because of his special relationship to the gods: his father was Amun-Re, one of the most important of the gods. When he died and received a proper burial in a pyramid, the magic formulae known as the Pyramid Texts were inscribed on the walls of his burial chamber. These texts acted as a guide, a kind of passport, for his soul through the perils of the journey into the land of the gods, where he was privileged to take his rightful place among his fellow gods.

But the hope of immortality was too wonderful and powerful to be kept forever behind the walls of the palace. Indeed, very soon the highest nobles and attendants of the pharaoh began to share his afterlife by virtue of their special relationship with the pharaoh. The Egyptians envisioned heaven as very much like this world, and if the pharaoh were going to be happy and successful there, he would require their services and assistance, just as he had in this world. So those officials and family members who were close to the pharaoh here on earth got the idea that they could share in his conquest of death, that they could ride along on his coat tails, as it were. So they began to build their own tombs in the vicinity of the king's pyramid and to inscribe the same pyramid texts, involving the sun-god cult, on the walls of their burial chambers. This broke the pharaoh's monopoly on immortality.

After the collapse of the Old Kingdom, access to the next world spread even further down through the social strata. During the Middle Kingdom the Cult of Osiris—based on the story of his death and resurrection—gained popularity among the upper classes and gave hope that anyone who could afford a proper tomb and the mummification of his body could attain immortality, through association with the god Osiris. The association with Osiris was accomplished by the proper worship of the god at his temple, living an ethical life and participating in the rituals and festivals of the Osiris cult. The tombs of these socially lower ranking individuals were much less elaborate than the pharaoh's and the magic formulae, now based on the Osiris myth in contrast to the pharaoh's formulae based on the sun-god mythology, were placed directly on the mummy cases and are known as the "coffin texts."

Finally, during the New Kingdom, the next world became accessible to everyone, through the use of a much cheaper method of recording the magic formulae known as the "Book of the Dead." The Book of the Dead is a kind of official passport into the next world written on papyrus, which guaranteed the bearer, whose name was written therein, entrance into the presence of Osiris. Although much cheaper than pyramids or even mummy cases, papyrus still cost money, and the more elaborate editions were quite expensive. Yet, there was no reason why a person could not write his own Book of the Dead, or use the services of a scribe to produce a shorter, more affordable, version. In fact, it became the practice of many scribes to stock mass produced and rather shabby copies of the Book of the Dead and to insert the customer's name in the proper places at the time of purchase. Even the lowliest peasant could afford one of these copies.

Akhenaten

One hardly knows what to think of Akhenaten. He has been lauded by some scholars as the "world's first monotheist" and dismissed by others as "a sexual deviate who used the cloak of religion to begat children by his own mother and daughters." The ancient Egyptians also seem to have had very definite opinions about him.

Akhenaten was the son of Amenhotep III and was raised in the traditional religion of Amun, the god of Thebes. As he grew older he turned to the worship of Aten, known in earlier Egypt only as a minor sun god. Soon after becoming pharaoh as Amenhotep IV ("Amun Is Satisfied"), he changed his name to Akhenaten ("Servant of Aten"). His wife, Nefertiti, changed her name to Nerer-Nefer-Aten ("Beautiful Is the Beauty of Aten"). The royal couple abandoned Thebes and began building a new capital at Tell el Amarna, which they named Akhetaten ("Horizon of Aten"), in the face of strong opposition from the priests of Amun. Perhaps part of Akhenaten's motive was to counter the rising power of Amun's priests over the office of the pharaoh.

The new city at Tell el Amarna displayed new modes and methods of artistic expression, termed "naturalistic," which depict Akhenaten and his family with strange deformities and peculiar physical traits. The god Aten, which was originally depicted as a form of Re, now took the form of a rayed solar disk with the rays ending in human hands. Whether this new style is a more "naturalistic" depiction of reality or an exaggerated caricature of reality is open to debate, to say the least.

But exalting the god Aten was not enough for Akhenaten. In the manner of intolerant religious fanatics throughout history, he attempted to destroy the cults of the other Egyptian gods—everyone must now conform to his concept of divine truth. This was an insult to the most fundamental beliefs of the mainstream of Egyptian society. Akhenaten dispatched teams of agents to demolish the statues of the ancient gods and to desecrate their temples. Worship of all other gods was forbidden. Actually, the Egyptian people were not to worship Aten, but to worship Akhenaten, and Akhenaten and his family were to worship Aten. The names of the other gods were erased from their inscriptions. Akhenaten even had his father's name, Amenhotep III, erased from monuments, because it contained the name of Amun. The great temples of Thebes, Memphis, and

Heliopolis were closed down and deprived of their estates, which became the property of Akhenaten. Not surprisingly, such a sudden and momentous change allowed considerable mismanagement and corruption to creep into the process. This display of intolerance and radical change produced a sharp and equally fanatical reaction. Unrest and anger spread through Egypt.

All was not so peaceful and serine even in the new capital as Akhenaten wanted observers to believe. About the twelfth year of the reign, Nefertiti disappeared. Whether she died or fell from favor is unclear. She was replaced by her daughter, Merytaten, who assumed the queen's duties and residence. Another queen, Kiya, bore Akhenaten a daughter and two sons. However, Akhenaten did not live long after his assault on the ancient gods. Whether he died of natural causes or was murdered we cannot know. His mummy was probably destroyed along with his holy city by his enemies in an attempt to abolish all memory of his reign. Haremhab, the last king of the 18th Dynasty, even claimed that his reign extended back to the time of Amenhotep III. The Egyptians so hated the heretic Akhenaten that they attempted to write him out of their history! He who tried to erase the others was himself erased.

Egyptian Culture

Most accounts of ancient Egypt dwell almost exclusively on pyramids, mummies, and the "mysteries" of Egyptian religion. However, other aspects of Egyptian culture are more interesting and important than is generally realized. They were the envy of the Greeks in applied science and mathematics. The need to re-establish property lines in the silt deposits after the Nile floods forced them to master the complex principles of surveying. In the field of medicine, the Egyptians largely depended on magic to drive out the evil spirits to which they attributed most disease. But medical treatment was not all based on magic. Many medical texts classify the patient's complaints according to the various parts of the body, or other criteria, and then suggest the proper treatment for each problem.

Egyptian Writing: Hieroglyphics

Ancient Egyptian occupies a special position among the languages of the world. It is not only one of the very oldest recorded languages (probably only Sumerian is older) but it also has a documented history longer by far than that of any other. It was first written down towards the end of the fourth millennium BC and thereafter remained in continuous recorded use down to about the eleventh century AD, a period of over 4,000 years. Egyptian, or Coptic (as the last stage of the language is called), expired as a spoken tongue during the Middle Ages, when it was superseded by Arabic. It is now, strictly, a dead language, though it continues to 'live on', albeit in a fossilized form, in the liturgy of the Coptic church in Egypt. Although it can only be a minute fraction of what was actually produced, the body of written material to have survived in Egyptian is, nevertheless, enormous. It consists, in large part, of religious and funerary texts, but it also includes secular documents of many different types—administrative, business, legal, literary and scientific—as well as private and official biographical and historical inscriptions. This record is our most important single source of evidence on ancient Egyptian society.[15]

---

15. Davis, W.V., *Egyptian Hieroglyphs* (1987), University of California Press, Berkeley, p. 6.

Three distinct scripts were used to write ancient Egyptian: hieroglyphics, hieratic, and demotic, respectively. The first hieroglyphs appeared in the late Predynastic Period around 3000 BCE. Hieroglyphic symbols are mostly pictographic in character, but the script is not a primitive form of "picture writing," as popularly supposed. Hieroglyphs communicate the same linguistic information as does our alphabetic method of writing. However, the Egyptian script is a "mixed system," which means that some of the symbols convey meaning while others convey sounds. Throughout its history new symbols were added and some old ones dropped out of use. Altogether, some 6,000 hieroglyphs have been documented. This is misleading, however, because the standard repertoire of symbols in use at any one time was fewer than 1,000, and only a small number of these occur frequently.

Hieratic, an adoption of hieroglyphic script, was Egypt's administrative and business script and also used to record literary, scientific, and religious documents in non-monumental contexts. It is most commonly found on papyrus, usually written in black or red ink. During the New Kingdom a cursive script, called demotic, developed from the hieratic. By the 26th Dynasty demotic had completely replaced hieratic script, and it remained the only script in day-to-day use for the rest of Egyptian history. It is barely recognizable as a descendant of the hieroglyphic form.

Literature

Egyptian literature comprises such a wide variety of genre and covers such a vast expanse of time that it is normally approached either chronologically or topically. The brief discussion offered here is organized by distinct category.

Religious Texts

The oldest examples of religious literature are the Pyramid Texts, preserved on the walls of the various chambers of the pyramids of the 5th and 6th Dynasties. These texts were designed to ensure the king's safe passage to the world of the gods and his ability to assume his rightful place among his fellow divinities. Soon the higher nobles claimed the same benefits of an afterlife and began to place the Pyramid Texts on their coffins. Increasingly these Coffin Texts, as they are called, were based on the cult of Osiris—in contrast to the pharaoh's texts which were based on the sun-god cult—and included spells and magic formula to instruct the soul of the dead how to successfully overcome all obstacles it might encounter on its perilous journey into the next world. The earliest forms of the Book on the Dead date from this period, but continued to evolve over the next centuries, reaching its mature form during the New Kingdom.

Other religious texts include theological documents like "The Theology of Memphis"[16] and hymns to various deities. Hymns to the gods Amun and Aten are the most numerous. At Abydos mortuary stelae were erected as part of the cult of Osiris and these provide valuable historical information regarding their owners. Yet another form of religious literature were letters written to the dead. These not only informed the deceased about contemporary issues but often enlisted their assistance to remedy problems here on earth.

---

16. See the "The Theology of Memphis," Cleve, Robert, *Early Western Civilization, Source Readings* (2002), Kendall/Hunt, Dubuque, pp. 42–44.

Scientific Texts

Scientific texts focus on solving the practical problems of life, not through magic and divine inter-cession, but through reason and rational action. Medical texts, such as the Edwin Smith Papyrus, reveal the extent of the anatomical knowledge and diagnostic techniques of the ancient Egyptians. Much of the treatment prescribed seems to reflect a primitive search for medical knowledge.[17]

There are also texts treating a wide range of subjects, including mathematics, agricultural crops, birds, animals geography, astronomy, and husbandry. Other texts record military campaigns, trade missions, and diplomatic relations with foreign lands. An example of this genre is "The Report of Wenamon". Near the end of the 20th Dynasty, Wenamon was sent on an expedition to the coast of Lebanon to acquire timber. After his return he reported to the king on the difficulties he encoun-tered, because of the loss of Egyptian prestige and power in the Levant. Some scholars believe this account is fiction, but it nevertheless provides an interesting insight into Egyptian life.

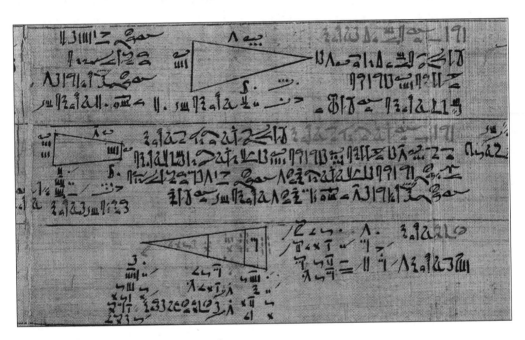

Figure 3.8: Rhind Mathematical Papyrus, 15th Dynasty.

Legal Tests

Wills, court records, edicts of the pharaohs (laws), and administrative records make up this category. Deeds of sale, inventories, and records of the other legal activities have also been found. The Abbott Papyrus, now in the British Museum, is a report of an investigation into tomb robberies under Ramesses IX, during the late 20th Dynasty. High ranking officials were implicated and a trial was held. It is couched in legal jargon that would warm the heart of any modern lawyer.

---

17. See the Old Kingdom text, "The Edwin Smith Surgical Papyrus," Cleve, Robert, *Early Western Civilization, Source Readings* (2002), Kendall/Hunt, Dubuque, pp. 104–106.

The Edict of Haremhab is the propagation of anti-corruption laws by the last king of the 18th Dynasty. The document states, "His majesty took counsel with his heart [how he might. . . . expel] evil and suppress lying. The plans of his majesty were an excellent refuge, repelling violence. . . . [and delivering the Egyptians from the oppressions] which were among them." There are specific laws against such crimes as "robbing the poor of wood due the pharaoh," "connivance of dishonest inspectors with thievish tax-collectors," and "stealing vegetables under the pretense of collecting taxes." The fact that these laws were necessary speaks volumes about the corruption that was rampant in Egypt after the reign of Akhenaten.

Government administrative records have survived as tomb inscriptions, because royal appointees often recorded the instructions given to them by the pharaoh at the time of appointment. Administrative texts have also survived from the Elephantine, an administrative center near the southern border of Egypt. They date from many eras and provide a fascinating record of governmental activities.

Fantasy and Adventure Tales

These stories relate magical events and adventures in imaginary lands with the same originality and imagination as modern fantasy novels. Some of these stories were written as early as the Middle Kingdom and remained popular until the end of Egyptian history.

The Story of Khufu and the Magicians describes the builder of the Great Pyramid being entertained by magicians performing tricks of magic such as severing the heads of animals and then rejoining them again—much like the acts of modern magicians—and spending idle hours on a pleasure boat among a harem of beautiful young maidens clothed only in fish nets.[18] Most modern fantasy writers would be hard pressed to come up with a more appealing scene.

"The Tale of the Shipwrecked Sailor," also from the Middle Kingdom, relates the adventures of a sailor who was the only survivor of a ship that was sunk in a storm. The sailor swam to a nearby island which was ruled by a enormous hooded snake. But the serpent was benevolent and befriended the sailor. The snake taught the sailor patience and valor. Later, when a ship came within sight of the island, the snake restored the sailor to his people with gifts of ointment, mirth, and precious objects, all of which the sailor gave to the king.

The Middle Kingdom adventure tale, "Story of Sinuhe,"[19] may have been the most popular piece of literature in ancient Egypt, as numerous copies of it have been found. Sinuhe was a minor official in the service of Sesostris I (12th Dynasty) at the time of the murder of his father, Amenemhet I. He overheard some kind of state secret, not revealed in the story, and fearing for his life, he fled Egypt. This began a series of adventures. He fought against a giant, reminiscent of the story of "David and Goliath," became successful and wealthy in foreign lands, but as he grew older he yearned to return to his beloved Egypt. Finally, he received a pardon from the king and was received by a forgiving pharaoh and his family.

---

18. "Indeed I shall go rowing! Have brought to me twenty ebony oars worked in gold with handles of skeb wood worked in fine gold. Have brought to me twenty women with beautiful bodies and breasts and hair who have not given birth. And have brought to me twenty nets and give these nets to these women in place of their cloths."

19. See "The Story of Sinuhe," Cleve, Robert, *Early Western Civilization, Source Readings* (2002), Kendall/Hunt, Dubuque, pp. 95–103.

Didactic Texts: Instructions in Wisdom

Often called "Instruction in Wisdom" (the Egyptians called them simply "Instructions"), these texts reflect the ethical standards of ancient Egyptian society. Egyptian thinkers (what the Greeks will call "philosophers") believed human society was a mirror image of the order that governed the universe. Just as the sun-god provided order for the universe, the divine pharaoh assured order for human society. This was an immensely popular genre, useful, enlightening, and entertaining. Originally these Instructions expressed primarily the aristocratic view, but by the New Kingdom they became "middle class." The best preserved and most famous was the "Instruction of Ptahhotep."[20]

Poetry

Egyptian poetry is primarily lyric, that is, it was normally accompanied by music. Thus, since we know almost nothing about the sounds of ancient Egyptian music, a major element of the poetry is missing. The joys of feasting, music, and love were an integral part of Egyptian life and promoted the genre of lyric love poetry. These poems reveal the directness and sensitivity of the Egyptians. A young girl tells her lover, "It is pleasant to go down to the pond that I may let you see my beauty in my tunic of finest royal linen, when it is wet." They often recount the bittersweet sadness of separated lovers, the delight of lovers pledging their eternal devotion to each other, and the heartbreak of broken love. This genre of literature appears first in the late Middle Kingdom and reached the height of development in the New Kingdom.[21]

Egyptian Art

There are no direct links between our own art of the 21st Century and that of the caves of France, the shrines of Çatal Hüyük, or the temples and royal palaces of Sumer, Babylon, and Assyria. However, there is a direct link, passed down through the centuries, between our art and the art of the Nile Valley of at least five thousand years ago. As we shall see, the Greek masters learned their craft from the Egyptians, and we are all students of the Greeks. Thus Egyptian art is of immense significance to the history of Western art.

The Egyptian art that is most familiar to us is the reliefs and paintings which adorned the walls of their tombs. It is seldom pointed out, however, that this art was meant to be seen only by the soul of the deceased—it was not intended to be enjoyed by us, rather it was intended to keep the soul alive. How strange that much of the most beautiful and powerful art produced by the Egyptians was never meant to be viewed by human eyes! The purpose of the scenes found in Egyptian tombs was to provide the servants and material objects for the soul to enjoy life in the next world. For us, however, the tomb art provides a vivid picture of life as it was lived in ancient Egypt—at least life as it was idealized by the ancient Egyptians, because these scenes represented the best possible life they could imagine, and life is seldom so joyful.

The most important thing to the Egyptian artist was not to create prettiness or exactness, but to represent everything as clearly and as completely as possible, to provide as much information as possible. In other words, the approach was more like that of a map-maker than of a painter. Every

---

20. See "The Instructions of Ptahhotep," Cleve, Robert, *Early Western Civilization, Source Readings* (2002), Kendall/Hunt, Dubuque, pp. 72–80.

21. See "Love Poems," Cleve, Robert, *Early Western Civilization, Source Readings* (2002), Kendall/Hunt, Dubuque, pp. 89–94.

object was drawn from the point of view that represents it most completely. This approach is often seen in children's art, but Egyptian art is not childish. It is a mature artistic style that obeys a set of specific conventions and rules which produce an art that adheres to what may be thought of as an "internal necessity." For example, the human form was almost always painted utilizing the same rigid rules: Since the head is most conveniently viewed from the side it is shown in profile, but we usually think of the eye as seen from the front, so a full-face eye is placed on the side view of the face; the top half of the body is best represented from the front, in order to see how the arms are hinged to the body; yet the arms, legs, and feet are best seen from the side and since we almost always view our feet from the inside, the artist drew both feet from the inside as if the body had two left feet! Egyptian art is not based on what the artist could see at a given moment but on what he knew belonged in the scene to make it complete. This is the attitude that gives these forms their monumentality, because while they appear contorted and two dimensional, they also appear permanent and unchanging. Furthermore, the components of a scene were joined together following similar rules of what was known to be true rather than what appeared to be reality. For example, we some times speak of the "big boss." The Egyptian artist drew the boss larger than his servants, larger even than his wife. Everything adds to the Egyptian sense of order and permanence. And the Egyptians were extremely conservative. What was considered good and beautiful in the Old Kingdom was also believed to be good and beautiful 1,500 years later during the New Kingdom.

Figure 3.9: The Pharaoh performs a sacrifice to Amun-Re.

Egyptian Architecture

The most distinctive and spectacular achievement of Egyptian architecture, the pyramids, has already been discussed. The Old Kingdom was primarily the age of pyramid building while Middle and New Kingdoms were the age of temple building, which was the second most distinctive achievement of Egyptian architecture. This was not because burials required less elaborate care during these latter periods, but because tomb robbery and plunder demonstrated the need for more security for the tombs. The burial sites moved to the desolate desert valley now known as the Valley of the Kings, where the burial chambers were cut deep into the stone cliffs and were reached by long corridors with carefully concealed entrances. The mortuary temple now became the only visible aspect of the burial site. The most notable achievement in this genre is the Temple of Hatshepsut at Deir el Bahri (the modern Arabic name of the site), also discussed above.

The Middle Kingdom saw the inauguration of the great temple building programs. These temples included large columned courts, halls, and ritual chambers. The two largest temple complexes grew up near Thebes. Karnak, dedicated to the god Amun, eventually became the largest religious complex in the history of the world. The nearby temple of Luxor, also dedicated to Amun, was later linked to Karnak by the famous Avenue of Ram-Headed Sphinxes. During the New Kingdom the focus of building decisively shifted from tomb construction to temple building, especially those honoring Amun. The temples at Karnak and Luxor were enlarged and elaborated by every New Kingdom pharaoh, but through the many stages of construction the architects successfully integrated the old and the new in a way that preserves the essential integrity of the temples.

The most famous of the Ramessid monuments is the great mortuary temple of Ramesses II at Abu Simbel (the Arab name for the site), south of Aswan. The main temple was cut out of the pink limestone cliff in honor of Amun and Ramesses II. Four colossal statues of Ramesses and

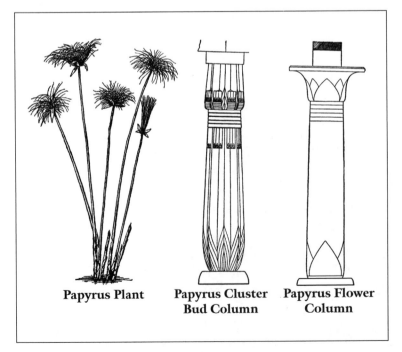

Papyrus Plant   **Papyrus Cluster Bud Column**   **Papyrus Flower Column**

Figure 3.10: Types of Egyptian columns derived from the papyrus plant.

some smaller figures comprise the striking façade to the this temple. A smaller temple was dedicated the goddess Hathor and Ramesses' favorite wife, Nefertari. The construction of the Aswan High Dam flooded the original site, but the temples were removed to higher ground in 1968 at the cost of $40 million.

One of the most appealing aspects of Egyptian temple architecture is the rows of majestic columns, reminiscent of groves of trees. The columns themselves were, in a sense, sacred symbols of the forests, which once covered the land before climatic change replaced them with the desert. The soaring temple columns also symbolized the connection between humanity and heaven. Originally, in the Old Kingdom, the first columns were part of temple walls and were not free standing. But by the 4th Dynasty the column emerged as an independent architectural element. By the New Kingdom columns became part of the splendor of the great temples of Thebes. Columns were normally modeled after the papyrus reed with the capital representing the bud or the flower. There were endless variations on this theme (Fig. 3.10).

4

The Ancient Levant
and the Later Near Eastern Empires

Outside the riverine environments of Mesopotamia and Egypt, where urban civilization first appeared, there was also important activity, beginning early in the second millennium before the Common Era. This phase of history involves the development of urban civilization along the coast of the Levant and the emergence of great empires, based in Mesopotamia, which attempted to unite all the urban civilizations into one world order. These attempts proved to be temporary at best, but seem to embody a kind of basic human urge toward unity, which will manifest itself again and again as the history of the West unfolds.

The Hittites

The Indo-Europeans Arrive

While the Mesopotamian and Egyptian civilizations were reaching their zenith of glory and power, something remarkable was taking place in the desolate steppes north of the Black and Caspian Seas. This was the original home of the Proto-Indo-European language, the mother of all Indo-European tongues.[1] What happened to that original Indo-European community has never been *explained* by scholars, although they have *described* it with fair accuracy. The most popular current theory is the horse-riding, war-like Indo-Europeans migrated into Europe and gave rise to the Celtic, Germanic, Balto-Slavic, Greek and other European branches, while migrations to the south and to the east produced the various Indo-European languages of India, Persia, Asia Minor, etc. Before the coming of the Indo-Europeans, Europe was inhabited by matriarchal tribes who worshiped the Mother Goddess. The patriarchal Indo-Europeans introduced their own pantheon of nature gods, the chief of whom was the sky god.

---

1. There are an estimated 6,000 languages spoken on the earth today, and hundreds of others which are no longer spoken but are known through written records. Historical linguistics classifies languages into "families" based on their common historical origins. The mother language of a family is known as a proto-language. For example, the common ancestor of the Romance languages (French, Spanish, Italian, Portuguese, and Romanian) is Latin, and likewise, the Indic languages (Hindi, Bengali) derive from Classical Sanskrit. The Indo-European family of languages is the largest of about 225 language families spoken in the world today and is comprised of 300 to 400 living languages plus numerous dead languages known only from written records. Approximately half of the world's population speaks an Indo-European language.

A Civilization Re-Discovered

Until the beginning of the 20th Century, the Hittites were a mysterious people known only from a few obscure accounts of the Egyptians and the Bible. They were a forgotten people, even the location of their homeland was unknown. As early as 1834 a French architect named Texier noted some ancient ruins near the modern Turkish city of Bogazkale, but this was largely ignored because it was generally believed that no ancient civilization existed in such a place. It was not until 1905 that a German archaeological team began excavations at the site and discovered the ancient Hittite state archive containing over 10,000 clay tablets written in a hitherto unknown language, but using the cuneiform script of Mesopotamia. Because the language proved to be Indo-European, it was eventually deciphered and revealed the lost history of the Hittites. These tablets are the oldest examples of a written Indo-European language found to date.

Today the Hittites do not seem so mysterious. We now know they arrived in the Anatolian peninsula, from north of the Black Sea, sometime before 2000 BCE and found the area already inhabited by a people known as the Hatti, whose origins are still unclear. The newcomers intermingled with the indigenous people, even taking their name from them, but imposing their language, and as early as 1900 BCE they took control of the Hatti city of Hattusas, which became the Hittite capital. By 1800 BCE they controlled most of the Anatolian plateau and enjoyed a thriving trade with the Assyrians, then based in northern Mesopotamia. By 1650 BCE they had crossed the Taurus mountains and established a presence in northern Syria. In 1595 BCE King Mursilis led a Hittite army deep into Mesopotamia and captured Babylon, which he plundered to such an extent that the Old Babylonian Empire, established back in the 18th Century BCE by Hammurabi, soon collapsed. However, the Hittites did not attempt to permanently occupy territory so far from their home base.

The Hurrians, a Semitic people, inhabited the land between the Hittites and the Assyrians. They accepted an Indo-European ruling aristocracy and built up a powerful state known as the Mitanni Kingdom. At the peak of their power the Mitanni kings sent their daughters to be married into the Egyptian royal family. They were tenacious rivals of the Hittites during the 15th Century BCE, but the Hittites were resurgent under King Suppiluliumas I (1344–1322). He was a near contemporary of the Egyptian pharaoh Akhenaten (1372–1355) and he took advantage of Egypt's preoccupation with internal religious quarrels to conquer most of the Levant. The ensuing conflict between Egypt and the Hittites has been discussed in the last chapter in the context of Egyptian history.

Hittite Religion and Society

The Hittites brought with them into Asia Minor their own Indo-European gods, but they recognized all gods as legitimate and readily incorporated into their pantheon the Sumerian and Babylonian gods of the older civilizations of Mesopotamia. This kind of tolerance was not uncommon in the ancient world, at least down to the emergence of the monotheistic religions. The Hittites themselves referred to their religion as the "1000 gods of Hatti," and the understanding was that their pantheon could always be extended. However, there was more than altruistic humanism behind this tolerance. By incorporating the gods of the conquered peoples into their pantheon, the Hittites secured control over them. As the defeated people became a part of the Hittite kingdom, their gods became the gods of their new rulers and a similar kinship was established with the conquered people—but always under Hittite power.

These numerous gods were arranged and classified according to their strength, function, and genealogy. At the center was a triad consisting of a male storm god (corresponding to the Sumerian Enlil or the Babylonian Marduk), his wife the sun goddess, and their daughter a fertility goddess similar to Ishtar. The gods, for the most part, had human characteristics. They experienced the human emotions of love, happiness, and anger, but they were more powerful and were immortal. Some gods took non-human form: the storm god was a bull, Ishtar was a lion, etc. The gods could also be represented as things, such as weapons or stones.

Strangely, in the Hittite religion we hear nothing concerning the creation of humanity. The concept of an afterlife is as vague as it is in Mesopotamian religion. The king and the more important members of the royal family were believed to ascend into the world of the gods after death, but the ordinary people descended into a gloomy underworld where they wondered around aimlessly for awhile but soon faded into non-existence. From Hittite hymns we learn that in general the human relationship to the gods is one of servant to master, but the gods could be influenced through sacrifice and ritual. For this purpose monthly and annual religious festivals were a regular part of Hittite life.

Most of the stories, such as the Gilgamesh Epic, found in Sumerian, Babylonian, and Akkadian literature have their counterpart in Hittite literature. Hittite mythology also includes several stories of the "disappearing god." The god is away from his temple doing something, like enjoying a pastime of leisure or hunting, and this causes a crop failure or natural other disaster. He must be found and convinced to forsake his pastime and attend to events in the land of the mortals. One story tells of a bee sent to find the missing god and there is a happy ending when the deity returns and the prosperity is restored to the world.[2]

Hittite law was patterned after the Babylonian code of Hammurabi, but was much more humane. Even slaves were guaranteed legal rights and women were treated with much more humanity than under the old Mesopotamian models, but it would be a stretch to say that they had equality with men. Capital punishment was restricted to a few serious offenses. Most crimes were punished with a fine of money or silver. As in Egypt, the king owned everything. The people were tenants on his land, but after paying a share of the crop as a tax to the king the remainder was theirs. The king was also the chief priest and judge. He was responsible to the gods for carrying out many of the rituals and ceremonies necessary for the benevolence of heaven toward the Hittite state.[3]

The Hittites were a diverse people who settled among the indigenous peoples of Anatolia and dominated them as a ruling class. They were predominantly a warrior class, but had among them a highly respected class of skilled craftsmen as well. The Hittites were the first to discover the use of iron, one of the cheapest and most plentiful resources on earth. They kept secret the smelting process for centuries but when its use was acquired by others the Hittite Empire went into a

---

2. "The Bee went away and searched . . . the streaming rivers, and searched the murmuring springs. The honey within it gave out, [the wax within it] gave out. [Then it found] him in a meadow in the grove at Lihzina. It stung him on his hands and his feet. It brought him to his feet, it took wax and wiped his eyes (and) his feet, [it purified him] and . . ." Eventually the god returned home: "Telepinus came home to his house and cared (again) for his land. The mist let go of the windows, the vapor let go of the house. The altars were set right for the gods, the hearth let go of the log. He let the sheep go to the fold, he let the cattle go to the pen. The mother tended her child, the ewe tended her lamb, the cow tended her calf. Also Telepinus tended the king and the queen and provided them with enduring life and vigor." Pritchard, James B., "The Telepinus Myth," *The Ancient Near East, An Anthology of Texts and Pictures* (1978), Princeton University Press, pp. 87–91.

3. If the king allowed events, such as war, to cause him to neglect his religious duties, he endangered the entire Hittite Empire. There survives the text of a prayer recited by King Mursilis asking the gods for forgiveness for such a slight to the gods, which had caused plague and epidemic among the Hittites. The king pleaded with the gods not to punish the innocent people for the sins of himself and his father.

period of steep decline. The capital city of Hattusas was sacked and burned around 1200 BCE and the Hittites quickly faded from history. They are mentioned in the Old Testament, but by the time the Israelites were first moving into Palestine the Hittites were in rapid decline. Their real history and importance to Western Civilization were not realized until the mid 20th Century.

The Sea Peoples, Philistines, Phoenicians

Around 1200 BCE the Aegean, Asia Minor, and the Near East experienced a far reaching and fundamental ethnic upheaval. Old societies declined and many disappeared. New peoples, such as the Iranians, Israelites, Philistines, and Phoenicians made their appearance upon the historical stage. This cataclysm was produced by two unconnected migrations of Indo-Europeans from the north. One came by sea, through the Aegean, and wrecked havoc throughout the eastern Mediterranean. They were called the "Sea Peoples" by the Egyptians. The other, known as the Iranians, came by land and settled north of Mesopotamia in the area of modern Iran.

The Sea Peoples and the Philistines

Around 1200 BCE the Indo-European "Sea Peoples" enter history. We know less about them than we know about almost any other important people. They may have come from as far as northern Europe, but probably from the Black Sea region. Armed with iron weapons, they crossed the Aegean, invaded the coastal Levant, and defeated the regional powers. They were composed of a coalition of numerous tribes, including Libyans, Lukka (ancestors of the Lycians?), Shekelesh (Sicilians?), Danuna (Danaai of the Iliad?), Shardana (Sardinians?), and Peleset (Philistines), who gave their name to Palestine. Their migrations across the Aegean stimulated the decline of the Mycenaean Greeks and created a power vacuum in the eastern Mediterranean. They posed such a threat to both the Egyptians and the Hittites that they may well have influenced those two powers to conclude their famous peace treaty. Some of them were mercenaries in the Egyptian army of Ramesses II.

Eventually the Sea People brought about the collapse of the Hittite Kingdom. The demise of the old economic and political powers of the region opened the way for many new groups, mostly of Semitic origin, to establish small states in the Levant, among them the Israelites. The Sea Peoples attacked Egypt through the Levant but were defeated before they could enter the country. Their navy then attempted to sail up the Nile, but was intercepted. The Egyptians were inferior as sailors and their ships were technologically less advanced, but they were powered by both sails and oars, which made them more maneuverable in the river than the larger sea-going ships of the Sea Peoples. Bowmen prevented the invaders from landing. The Egyptians showered the attackers with arrows for which they, being armed with swords and spears, had no answer. The ramming technique of naval warfare had not yet been developed, but the Egyptians succeeded in capsizing many enemy ships with grappling hooks. Thus, the power of the Sea Peoples was broken in the Nile delta,[4] but some of them, including the Philistines, settled along the coast of the Levant.

---

4. "Those who reached my frontier, their seed is not, their heart and their soul are finished forever and ever. Those who came forward together on the sea, the full flame was in front of them at the river-mouths, while a stockade of lances surrounded them on the shore. They were dragged in, enclosed, and prostrated on the beach, killed, and made into heaps from tail to head. Their ships and their goods were as if fallen into the water." From the inscription on the mortuary temple of Ramesses III at Medinet Habu, Thebes. "The War Against the Peoples of the Sea," *The Ancient Near East, An Anthology of Texts and Pictures* (1978), Princeton University Press, pp. 185–186.

The Phoenicians

Phoenician is the name given by the Greeks to the Semitic people who lived along the coast of the Levant during the period between 1200 and 900 BCE. They never formed a unified nation, but were organized into small city-states, the most prominent being Sidon, Tyre, Biblos, and Arvad. The Phoenicians drew the main elements of their culture from both Mesopotamia and Egypt, but they were innovators in several important spheres, especially economic.

Before the Phoenicians the only two forms of writing were Sumerian cuneiform and Egyptian hieroglyphics. Although these scripts were invented independently, both used pictures, or symbols derived from pictures, to represent words or syllables. But they were still complex and required a

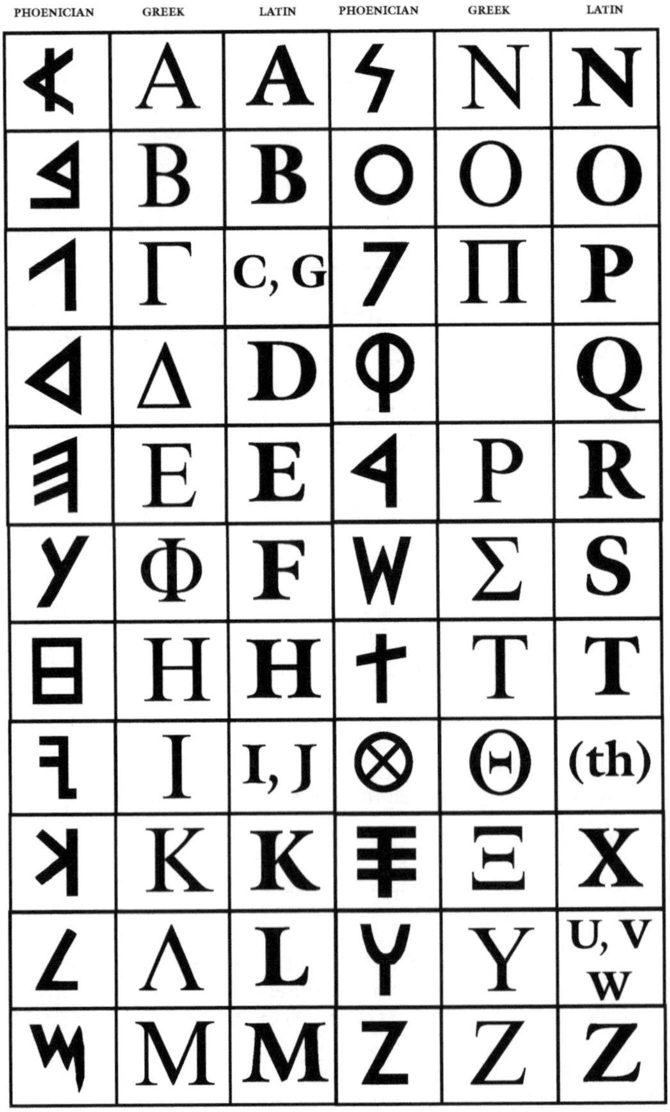

PHOENICIAN	GREEK	LATIN	PHOENICIAN	GREEK	LATIN
⏃	A	A	↯	N	N
◿	B	B	O	O	O
↿	Γ	C, G	↗	Π	P
◁	Δ	D	φ		Q
≣	E	E	◀	P	R
Y	Φ	F	W	Σ	S
⊟	H	H	†	T	T
⇂	I	I, J	⊗	Θ	(th)
⋇	K	K	≢	Ξ	X
∠	Λ	L	Y	Y	U, V W
⋔	M	M	Z	Z	Z

Figure 4.1: The evolution of the alphabet.

great deal of time to learn. About 1200 BCE the Phoenicians developed a true alphabet consisting of 22 letters, each representing a different sound. All modern European alphabets are descended from this Phoenician alphabet (Fig. 4.1).

The geographic location of Phoenicia had a number of advantages. The Phoenician cities were located at the end of the caravan routes arriving from the east and the beginning of the sea routes leading to the west. There were also the rich local resources of the cedar forests of Lebanon and an abundant supply of a small snail from which they extracted a marvelous purple dye. They imported cloth from abroad, dyed it purple and sold it throughout the Mediterranean basin. They also traded in ivory and ebony from India. Gold, silver, and precious stones from Yemen and Anatolia were manufactured into jewelry, ornamental objects, and fine furniture for export. Eventually, wine, olive oil, glass, and silk were added to the list of traded items. They became the most skilled and experienced sailors of the ancient world, pioneering trade routes all over the Mediterranean and into the Atlantic. They established trading posts in Britain and northward along the west coast of Europe, as well as southward along the west coast of Africa, at least as far as Sierra Leone. In fact, there is some evidence the Phoenicians circumnavigated the continent of Africa and returned to their homeland via the Red Sea. In addition the Phoenicians were great colonizers. They settled most of the coast of North Africa west of Egypt and placed colonies on Sicily and the Mediterranean coast of Spain.

The Israelites

Employing sacred writings as a historical source is always a difficult proposition. At times historians have no other alternative, however. We saw in chapter 2 how a careful analysis of the sacred writings of the Sumerians, which we called mythology, provided glimpses into their pre-history and revealed information about their early political institutions, which we labeled "primitive democracy." The religious traditions—verifiable or not—of any society contain valuable cultural information. When discussing the history of the Israelites, historians have no choice but to rely heavily on the Hebrew Bible as a source, regardless of the very difficult problems involved.

For more than a century a debate has raged among Biblical scholars concerning the "historicity" of the Old Testament, especially the first five books (called the Pentateuch by the Christians and the Torah by the Jews). Not only is it impossible to reconcile the chronological and factual contradictions contained in them, but much of the material appears to have been lifted from other New Eastern cultures.[5] Nevertheless, it is possible to relate a tradition—not a history, but more a legend—of the origins of the Israelites.

The Bible relates the tradition that the founder of the Israelite people was the patriarch Abraham, who led his clan out from the Sumerian city of Ur in a westward direction, between 1800 and 1700 BCE. This would have been two or three hundred years after the destruction of Ur by the Elamites in 2006 and after the establishment of the Old Babylonian Empire by Hammurabi.

---

5. Methuselah, for example, is said to have lived for more than 900 years. The story of the great flood is clearly adopted from a much older Sumerian myth (see "The Babylonian Story of the Flood," Cleve, Robert, *Early Western Civilization, Source Readings* (2002), Kendall/Hunt Publishing, Dubuque, pp. 6–12) and the description of Moses's childhood is almost identical to the legend of Sargon. The account of the Israelites' exodus from Egypt contains problems that cannot be resolved historically. Although the book of Joshua relates that the Israelites who returned from Egypt conquered and expelled the Canaanites, the archaeological and linguistic evidence indicates that they were continuously resident in Canaan for centuries. Thus, critical analysis indicates that the first five books of the Bible are a retrospective extrapolation and not an accurate historical narrative.

By 1800 BCE the city was rebuilt. As we learned earlier, from time to time groups of nomads came in from the desert and set up market fairs to exchange products with the townspeople. During the frequent periods of desert drought, families and sometimes whole tribes would seek refuge and even settle in the urban areas of Mesopotamia. Most of the time these small groups would, after several generations, assimilate into the general population and become part of the mainstream history of the area. However, sometimes, this settling down did not become permanent. After a generation or two, the urge to resume the freedom of the old wondering, nomadic lifestyle was too great, and these people would forsake their urban way of life and resume the nomadic lifestyle. This is what happened to Abraham's group. As the population of the clan increased, Abraham's grandson, Jacob, organized the growing people into 12 tribes, each tribe under one of his 12 sons. Thus, Israel was a tribal nation, in contrast to the urban societies of Sumer and Egypt.

As these tribes wondered in a vaguely westward direction along the periphery of the urban area, still practicing the symbiotic relationship with the urbanites, they passed along an inland route through the Levant and some of them settled in Canaan, while the rest of them eventually migrated to Egypt, where they became the subjects of the pharaohs. However, even if this phase of the legend is historical (which many scholars doubt), the Israelites could not have been a very numerous or important component of the Egyptian population. At any rate, no Egyptian records of the Israelite stay in Egypt have been discovered. Of course, this kind of thing was very familiar to the Egyptians and would not have been of particular note: groups of nomads continuously moved into Egypt from the surrounding deserts and settled among the Egyptians. After a few generations they became "Egyptized" and merged into the mainstream of Egyptian society. But for the Israelites the settling down once again was not permanent and around 1300 BCE, probably during the reign of Ramses II, or his successor Merenptah, the Israelites left Egypt, led by a man with a very Egyptian name, Moses.[6]

This time they migrated in an easterly direction across the Sinai peninsula, during a period of general unrest in the Near East. We are told that Moses organized the tribes of Israel and some of the neighboring Canaanites into a confederation bound by a covenant, a contract or treaty, to the god Yahweh, or Jehovah. According to the book of Exodus, Moses proclaimed the covenant between God and men on Mount Sinai and received his instructions directly from Yahweh.[7] Part of the covenant was the famous Ten Commandments, one of which ordered, "You"—this means the Israelites—"You shall have no other gods before me." Note the Yahweh does not assert that no other gods exist, but only that the Israelites shall not worship other gods. And the Old Testament states that this was very difficult for the Israelites to obey and in fact they did at times worship other gods, and we are told they were severely punished for their violation of the law. This is not yet pure monotheism, but a form of national monotheism, called monolatry.

Moses laid down a complex code of laws, only part of which has survived. This code was similar to the earlier codes of Mesopotamia, like that of Hammurabi, except that it emphasized ethically correct conduct over ritually correct conduct. This set the Israelite religion on a different course from the other Near Eastern and Egyptian religions, which stressed purity of ritual and ceremony above ethical conduct. The Israelites had traveled the same road as the other peoples of the Near East up to this point, but now there is a fork in the road and the Israelites took a different road from the other Near Eastern peoples. All religions have two components: ethical and ritual.

---

6. "Moses" is part of the name of several New Kingdom pharaohs: Kamose of the 17th Dynasty; Ahmose and Thutmose I-IV, of the 18th Dynasty.

7. This is in the tradition of the great law givers of the past in the Near East. For example Hammurabi is shown on the famous stela on which his code of laws is recorded, receiving his laws directly from Shamash, the god of justice.

However, each religion stresses these components in its own individual way. As history unfolded, the Israelites and the other peoples of the Near East diverged further and further from each other in this regard. As time passed the polytheistic religions put more and more stress upon correct ritual, while the Israelites put more stress on ethical behavior. Simultaneously, monotheism emerged as a contrast to polytheism. The tragedy is that both of these points of view cannot be correct—they are mutually exclusive—and thus intolerance was born.

By a series of attacks on Canaanite cities and treaties with other tribes, the Israelites managed to establish themselves in the Levant. About 1200 BCE, the Israelites invaded the fertile, hilly Canaanite territory overlooking the Mediterranean Sea, which was occupied by the Philistines. As they developed a more settled, urban way of life, the traditional tribal organization that had served them so well over the centuries as a wondering nomadic people was no longer sufficient and the Israelite nation now organized itself under a centralized monarchy. Saul became the first king about 1020 BCE. He was not very effective, but under his successor, David (1010?–960?), the Israelites conquered the Canaanite city of Jerusalem and made it their capital, and the entire nation now took the name Israel. The third king, Solomon (960?–920?), who was David's son, was famous for his wisdom and skillful administration. He is purported to be the author of some of the books of the Old Testament—Proverbs, Ecclesiastes, and the Song of Solomon—but these books were actually composed considerably later.

During this period the neighboring states were weak, and Solomon maintained peace by increasing the size of his standing army and equipping it with chariots. He made alliances with other rulers who sent him their daughters in marriage as a token of good faith. Solomon built up a large harem of these princesses. The harem was a political device often used in the Near East before and since. Solomon did not invent the harem, but he is purported to have had an unusually large one. Solomon was also a renowned builder. He constructed a temple in Jerusalem, which symbolized the faith of Israel. But the temple could not compare in size and magnificence with the great palace he built for himself. An indication of its immense size is the tradition that his stables housed 12,000 horses.

Solomon's extravagance caused resentment among the people, who were heavily taxed to pay for his palace and army. After his death the kingdom of Israel split into two parts. The northern half, consisting of ten of the ancient twelve tribes, was based on the ancient town of Shechem and it retained the name of Israel. The southern section was called Judah and retained Jerusalem as its capital. Judah continued under the rule of the house of David. This division denied Israel the chance for further political expansion and led to a long period of tragedy for its people. It had serious religious consequences also. The first king of the northern state of Israel, Jeroboam I, attempted to establish independent temples at Dan and Bethel in order to prevent his people from making pilgrimages to Jerusalem, which drained the country's resources. This caused further dissention between the two kingdoms. Although Israel and Judah existed independently for several centuries, Israel was weakened by internal quarrels and was easily conquered in 722 by the Assyrians, who deported all its leaders and a large part of its population into other Assyrian territories, where they soon disappeared from history. The scattered Israelites became known in biblical literature as the "ten lost tribes of Israel."

Judah was now the only Israelite kingdom, and from this point on the remaining Israelites are known as Jews. Although the Jews managed to negotiate an agreement with the Assyrians that allowed them to govern themselves as an autonomous region of the Assyrian Empire, in 586, Judah fell to the invading army of the New Babylonian Empire, the successor of the Assyrians. Many of the inhabitants of Judah were deported to Babylon—the so-called Babylonian captivity of biblical literature—but they were allowed to trickle back into Judah later in the century, especially after Babylonians were conquered by the Persians. There were occasional revivals of an independent Jewish kingdom in later times, most notably under the protection of the Romans, but in general terms the Jews became the pawns of the various outside forces that ruled Palestine from this point onward: the Persians, Macedonians, Romans, Arabs, and Turks. Only in the 20th Century did a revived Jewish state regain its sovereignty.

In the military and political history of the Near East the Jews made no memorable contributions, but in the intellectual history of Western Civilization their contributions cannot be ignored. For the Israelites Yahweh was the only god of Israel, but many, including the kings, worshiped other gods as well. It was among the Babylonian exiles during the 6th Century BCE that Yahweh came to be conceived as the only god, and their point of view became the pure monotheistic attitude of all Jews after their return. Then the gods of others come to be thought of as "idols." Yahweh was transcendent. He created the universe, but he was not a part of it. All peoples were his servants— even though they were not aware of it.

Yahweh was a jealous god, he judged the Jews sternly and he punished severely. But he was also forgiving—to those who sincerely repented of their wrongdoing.[8] The Israelites believed that Yahweh sent certain religious leaders, called prophets, to serve as his voice to the people. The great age of prophecy was between the 8th to the 5th centuries, when the Assyrian and New Babylonian Empires threatened to annihilate Israel and Judah. The general message of these holy men was that the people had failed to obey Yahweh's law and they will be punished. The prophet Amos, for example, prophesized the fall of Israel to Assyria, and twenty years later Isaiah predicted the fall of Judah. However, these prophets also preached that someday all nations would worship the God of Israel.[9] In addition, the prophets took a stand against social injustice, luxury, and promiscuity. They threatened dire punishments for these sins. In order to obey the law of Yahweh, the Jews had to remain separate from their neighbors. Unlike other peoples of the New East they did not simply melt into the community of the conquerors by accepting their gods. Through the centuries the Jews have remained rigidly faithful to their culture and religion all the way down to the modern area.

The Later Empires

By the second millennium BCE, a powerful tendency toward centralized control over ever larger territories was evident. Empire has many advantages, including more efficient use of resources. Until about 1200 BCE, bronze was the metal of choice for making agricultural tools and weapons. Bronze is made by adding tin to copper, which in its pure form is too soft to produce tools and weapons. But the disruptions caused by the Indo-European migrations caused a severe shortage of

---

8. Psalms 145.8–9: "The Lord is gracious, and full of compassion: slow to anger, and of great mercy. The Lord is good to all: and his tender mercies are over all his works."

9. Isaiah, 2.2–4: "And it shall come to pass in the last days, that the mountain of the Lord's house shall be established in the top of the mountains, and shall be exalted above the hills; and all nations shall flow unto it. And many people shall go and say, Come ye and let us go up to the mountain of the Lord, to the house of the God of Jacob; and he will teach us of his ways, and we will walk in his paths: for out of Zion shall go forth the law, and the word of the Lord from Jerusalem. And he shall judge among the nations, and shall rebuke many people: and they shall beat their swords into plowshares, and their spears into pruninghooks: nation shall not lift up the sword against nation, neither shall they learn war any more."

tin. The Hittites discovered iron about this time, but un-forged iron is not much harder than copper. However, if the iron is repeatedly heated in a charcoal furnace, carbon molecules combine with iron molecules to form carbon steal, which is many times stronger than bronze. This technology spread rapidly through the Near East and by about 1000 BCE ushered in what historians call the "Iron Age." Weapons were now cheaper and, consequently, armies became larger and more ruthless. It seems that every advance in military technology creates ever more totalitarian régimes. The first result of the new iron age weapons was a rule of terror, the Assyrian Empire (911–612 BCE).

The Assyrians (c. 2500–612 BCE)

The Assyrians have an unfavorable reputation in most history textbooks today. They are often described as the most totalitarian régime ever achieved in the ancient world. Most people remember them only for destroying the kingdom of Israel and taking the so-called "ten lost tribes" into oblivion and attacking Jerusalem a generation later. But this Biblical incident is only a small detail of the entire picture. For most of their history of over seven centuries, they were the defenders of civilization, not its brutal destroyers.

Although at its height, the Assyrian Empire was vast indeed, the original Assyrian homeland was only about the size of the state of Connecticut. It was located along the northern Tigress River. The Assyrians were originally Semitic nomads who founded the city of Assur (also known as Ashur) about 2500 BCE. Assur was the name of their chief god, and the Assyrian people also derived their name from this god. They took advantage of their unique location on the upper Tigress to establish trade relations with the inhabitants throughout the Anatolian plateau. In this capacity they influenced the spread of urban society into the area. However, they were eclipsed for a long period by the Old Babylonian Empire. While they managed to maintain their cultural identity throughout the Babylonian period, the struggles between the Hittites and the Egyptians and the confusion resulting from the incursions of the Sea Peoples into the Near East produced a weakening of the surrounding Mesopotamian powers. This presented the Assyrians with new possibilities. However, during the long period of foreign domination the spirit and outlook of the Assyrians underwent a profound change. For reasons that are not altogether clear to modern scholars, the Assyrians transformed themselves, rather suddenly, from a commercial and trading people into the ancient world's most ruthless and efficient military power.

The decline of the Hittite power gave the Assyrians the opportunity to establish themselves as an independent kingdom. The first to take the title "King of Assyria" was Assur-uballit I (1362–1327). Assur-uballit and his successors became very conscious of the antiquity of their culture and successfully defended Assyrian independence against the Kassite Babylonians, who they considered to be their cultural inferiors and relative newcomers to Mesopotamia. Yet, in spite of their claim to be the true heirs of Mesopotamian culture, the early kings were careful not to practice religious intolerance. But that changed abruptly with the accession of Tukuli-Ninurta I (1244–1208 BCE) in 1244 BCE. He captured the city of Babylon and carried both its king and its god Marduk off into captivity and proclaimed himself king of Babylon. However, this sacrilegious treatment of the great god Marduk even alienated his own people to the extent that they murdered him about 1208 BCE. Tukuli-Ninurta's act of narrow-mindedness aroused the vengeance of Assyria's neighbors, and Assyria was almost destroyed more than once during the next century. These wars for survival forged Assyria into a tightly organized and militaristic people. King Tiglathpileser I (1115–1077 BCE) led his people on a campaign of conquest that reached the shores of the Mediterranean, but so overextended Assyrian resources that his gains were lost soon after his death. Adadnirari II (911–891 BCE) finally established

Assyrian power on a permanent basis and the Assyrian Empire (911–612 BCE) is usually dated from his reign. His grandson, Assurnasirpal II (883–859 BCE), spread Assyrian power into the Levant. He began to practice annual aggressive campaigns, which forced the victims of these campaigns either to pay tribute or face the full might of the Assyrian military machine. It was under Assurnasirpal II that Assyria earned the reputation for vicious brutality and terror.

Tiglathpileser III (744–727 BCE) extended Assyrian territory even further westward. Among those submitting to him in 742 BCE was Menahem, king of Israel. But the next Israelite king, Hosea, rebelled and thousands of Israelites—the Ten Lost Tribes—were deported to other parts of the empire and replaced with other people deported from their homes. When Tiglathpileser III died in 727 BCE there was an uprising of some of the newer acquisitions, but this revolt was brutally suppressed by his son Shalmeneser V (727–722 BCE). Shalmeneser died in battle and was replaced by Sargon II (722–705 BCE), an army commander who founded a new dynasty. By taking the name Sargon he was claiming to be the cultural heir of the first Sargon who had founded the Akkadian Empire almost fifteen hundred years earlier. The Assyrians had a very keen sense of history. This "Sargonid" dynasty ruled the Assyria Empire for the next century, during which they expanded it to include all of Mesopotamia, the Levant, and Egypt.

Figure 4.2: King Assurbanipal killing lion.

The Assyrians organized their conquered territories into provinces ruled by Assyrian governors directly responsible to the king. The Assyrian government itself was reorganized to improve centralized control. An efficient communication system was developed, using messengers to carry reports from the provincial governors to the central government and orders back out to the provinces. At the center of this organization was the king, the god Assur's representative on earth. The king was not only head of state and the supreme military commander, he was the empire's chief priest, responsible for the elaborate sacrifices and rituals necessary to propitiate the great god Assur. And it was the king who discerned and communicated the will of Assur. Assyria was the ancient world's most centralized and totalitarian state. It was supported and nurtured by the state religion. Throughout its history, humanity has never discovered a force more powerful than the union of religion and politics.

Warfare is never pleasant, but as practiced by the Assyrians it was unusually and unnecessarily savage. Prisoner mutilations, wholesale decapitations, rape, deportations, and mass enslavements were relished and celebrated by the Assyrians with an intensity exhibited by no other ancient people. Assyrian art records scenes of unparalleled torture and inflected suffering. Smiling Assyrians archers shoot fleeing enemies in the back; soldiers throw a city's inhabitants from the walls onto impaling stakes below; captives are decapitated by the thousands. One scene even shows the Assyrians grinding up the bones of their enemies so that the dust may be blown away by the wind.

Assyrian religious, political, and military ideology is reminiscent in some aspects to the modern Islamic belief system. The roots of intolerance run deep in the Near East. The Assyrians viewed their military campaigns as holy wars. They were not monotheists, but they believed that their god, Assur, demanded that his worship be spread through military conquest, and while they did not deny the existence of other gods, they often performed ritual humiliation of defeated gods by deporting them to Assur's "court" where they were held as hostages. The defeated god's image was replaced by that of Assur, which the defeated people were forced to worship. Over time, however, Assur grew remote and aloof, a state god whom everyone was forced to serve out of fear, but none did so from affection or respect.

To the end of its history Assyria bathed its empire in blood. When the ancient city of Babylon revolted in 689 BCE, it was ruthlessly destroyed by Sennacherib (704–681 BCE). However, Sennacherib was a great builder as well as a destroyer. He constructed a magnificent new imperial capital at Nineveh, north of Assur, and fortified it with a nine mile long wall, which enclosed an enormous palace set on a high platform and decorated with marble, ivory, and rare woods. A thirty-nine mile long aqueduct supplied the city with fresh water. Sennacherib's son Esarhaddon (681–669 BCE) attempted to assuage the hatred of the empire's inhabitants by allowing the return of religious objects to the conquered peoples. He also rebuilt the city of Babylon and became a patron of the arts.

Assyria reached its peak under the reign of Esarhaddon's son, Assurbanipal (699–627 BCE). He attempted a series of reforms and saw himself as an enlightened ruler who tried to govern the empire without employing military terror and religious intolerance. He constructed a great library at Nineveh to house copies of all the great literature of the past. It also served as the state archive. After Nineveh's destruction, this library remained buried through the millennia until the city was excavated in the 19th Century and some 25,000 tablets were recovered. The modern editions of most ancient Mesopotamian texts, such as the Epic of Gilgamesh, came to us from these Assyrian tablets. On one of these tablets, Assurbanipal himself brags that he can read and understand "that ancient and obscure language" of the Sumerians, though by then it had been a dead language for more than a millennium.

The fall of Assyria was swift and dramatic. Within fifteen years of Assurbanipal's death Nineveh lay in ruins, and a few years later the Assyrian state itself ceased to exist. In spite of the reforms of the Sargonid kings, the hatred by the oppressed peoples of the empire, the legacy of centuries of savagery and terror, was too deep to be muted. A coalition of Indo-European Medes from the Iranian plateau led by Cyaxares (625–585 BCE) and Semitic Chaldeans from the Babylonian area led by Nabopolasser (625–605 BCE) brought down the mighty Assyrian Empire. Nineveh fell in 612 BCE and its temples and palaces were reduced to rubble. The prophet Nahum described the final assault on the city:

> Woe to the bloody city! It is all full of lies and robbery; the prey departeth not. The noise of the whip, and the noise of the rattling of the wheels, and of the pransing horses, and of the jumping chariots. The horseman lifteth up both the bright sword and the glittering spear: and there is a multitude of slain, and a great multitude of carcases; and there in none end of their corpses; they stumble over their corpses. . . . Thy shepherds slumber. O king of Assyria: thy nobles shall dwell in the dust: thy people is scattered upon the mountains, and no man gathereth them. There is no healing of thy bruise; thy wound is grievous: all that hear the bruit of thee shall clap the hands over thee: for upon whom hath not thy wickedness passed continually?[10]

So far as is known, no one wrote a lament over its ruins and, unlike Ur, Nineveh was never rebuilt.

The Neo-Babylonian Empire (612–550 BCE)

After the destruction of Nineveh the Medes retired to the Iranian plateau and the Chaldeans, also known as the Neo-Babylonians, inherited Assyria's position in Mesopotamia and the Levant. The Chaldeans, however, resorted to many of the same cruelties the Assyrians had employed to rule their empire. Although Nabopolasser established the Chaldean dynasty, it was his son, Nebuchadnezzar II (605–562 BCE), of Biblical fame, who accomplished the final defeat of the Assyrians and gained control of the Levant. Although Judah quickly submitted to Nebuchadnezzar, it revolted after the his army withdrew. In 597 BCE Judah was captured again, its king and many of its leaders were deported to Babylon and Jerusalem was plundered. But in 589 BCE, with the promise of aid from Egypt, it revolted again. Egyptian help never arrived and in 587 BCE Jerusalem was captured and burned and its walls were raised. Solomon's Temple was reduced to rubble. Most of the population was deported to Babylon (the "Babylonian Captivity" of Biblical literature). All that was left of Judah was a few rural peasants who were now leaderless. The House of David was defunct and the history of Israel seemed to be at an end.

Nebuchadnezzar restored Babylon to prosperity and it once again became the center of a far-flung empire. The Babylonian god Marduk was restored to his former position in the Mesopotamian pantheon. Magnificent temples and palaces again adorned the city. The most famous structure was the Hanging Gardens, which was counted as one of the Seven Wonders of the World by the ancients. It consisted of a series of terraces which led to a plateau and then to an artificial mountain upon which grew lush gardens irrigated by water piped up from the Euphrates River. From a distance the gardens seemed to be suspended in the air. It was said that Nebuchadnezzar built the Hanging Gardens to please his wife, a princess from Media who was homesick for the mountains of her homeland.

---

10. Old Testament (King James Translation), Naham 3.1–3; 18–19.

The Neo-Babylonian Empire was short lived, however. Nabonidus (555–539 BCE), the last king of the Chaldean dynasty, was a patron of the history and literature. Like the last Assyrian king, Assurbanipal, he had many of the old Sumerian texts collected into his library. But his religious policy was his undoing. He favored the moon god, Sin, over the traditional Babylonian god, Marduk, and this caused such internal descent among his people that when Babylon fell to the Persian king Cyrus in 539, he was welcomed as a liberator.

The Persian Empire (550–330 BCE)

The Persians were an Indo-European speaking people who migrated into the Iranian plateau north of the Persian Gulf as part of the great movement of Indo-European peoples of the early 2nd millennium BCE. Their homeland was desolate and mountainous and the seacoast possessed no harbors. At the time they emerged into history, they were organized into tribes, some still nomadic, others leading a more or less settled lifestyle, and all were vassals of the Medes, a closely related people.

Around 650 BCE a new religion appeared among the Persians, which transformed Persian society. It was invented by Zarathustra (called Zoroaster by the Greeks). Zoroastrianism was a dualistic religion, in which the cosmos was ruled by two opposing gods: Ahura-Mazda, the god of light and good; and Ahriman, the god of darkness and evil. The two gods were evenly matched in an epic struggle for control of the universe. The outcome of the struggle was certain, however. At the end of time, Ahura-Mazda will emerge victorious, and those who followed him will abide forever in a glorious paradise. Ahriman and all those who adhere to him will be vanquished and consigned to eternal punishment in a dark and foreboding place. This is the first appearance of the concept of heaven and hell as places of eternal reward and punishment. According to the Zoroastrian belief system, all the events of the human world must be understood as part of this epic struggle between good and evil, between light and darkness. Zoroastrianism is thus the world's first eschatological religion which relates the meaning of human existence to the great spiritual struggle between good and evil. It postulates that all human values and meaning are oriented toward the end of time and the final defeat of those gods, humans, and forces which adhere to the god of darkness. Therefore, the world of human history must also be understood as part of the struggle between good and evil, and the role of the Persians, as the enlightened people was clear. The harnessing of Zoroastrianism for political purposes was accomplished by Cyrus (559–530 BCE). And this new religion gave Cyrus a role in the struggle between good and evil. That role was to conquer the world.

In 559 BCE, Cyrus became the chief of an obscure Persian tribe. He was deeply devoted to Zoroastrianism and believed it was his duty to assist his god in the struggle against the forces of darkness. He was determined to bring the benefits of Zoroastrianism to the peoples of the world through conquest. Yet, there was an element of toleration in this new religion, because Zoroastrians believed in the existence of other gods, they were not monotheists. They believed that some of the gods were in the service of Ahura-Mazda, while others were in alliance with Ahriman. Cyrus assumed it to be his mission to destroy the religions of the evil gods and to shore up the worship of the gods allied with Ahura-Mazda. Throughout history whenever a political or religious leader has been able to harness the energy of a people to pursue a mission from god, he has been able to accomplish extraordinary things.

Between 559 and 549 BCE, Cyrus seized control of Persia and Media and took the title of "King of Persia." Media was relegated to a province of his empire, but the Medes always held a high place in the Persian state. He then advanced into Asia Minor as far as the Halys River. This brought him into contact with the kingdom of Lydia, another Indo-European people who were one of the successors to the Hittites. It was the most powerful and prosperous state in Anatolia at the time. The Lydians had grown wealthy through commerce, trade, and the exploitation of local gold mines. They invented the use of gold coinage as a medium of exchange. The present Lydian king, Croesus, reigned over all of Asia Minor west of the Halys River including the Greek city-states along the Anatolian coast. He was so fabulously rich that he gave us the simile "rich as Croesus."[11] Croesus did not trust Cyrus and in 546 BCE, he decided to initiate a preventive war against Persia in order to preserve his own kingdom. Herodotus, the Greek historian, tells us the Croesus consulted the oracle of Apollo at Delphi concerning the wisdom of his decision and was told that if he crossed the Halys River (the border between Lydia and Persia) he would destroy a great nation. Croesus interpreted this to mean that his invasion of Persia would be successful. When he attacked Cyrus, however, it was his own nation that was destroyed, thus fulfilling the oracle.

The demise of Croesus was swift indeed and was due to a combination of the unconventional tactics of Cyrus coupled Croesus's dependence of the traditional military wisdom. The first battle was hard fought but indecisive. Seeing that he was outnumbered and that the end of the campaigning season was approaching, Croesus returned to Sardis, his capital, and dismissed most of his troops, with the intention of assembling a much larger army in the spring. Ancient armies did not ordinarily campaign in the winter. However, Cyrus followed him into Lydia and won a decisive victory and captured Sardis in fourteen days. Croesus was taken prisoner and Asia Minor became a satrapy, or province, of the Persian Empire.

However, Cyrus did not spend much time in Asia Minor. He immediately turned eastward and brought the eastern Iranian plateau under his control and then conquered Parthia, Bactria, Sogdiana, and western India up to the Indus river. In 539 BCE, he invaded Mesopotamia and took Babylonia without a fight, as its inhabitants, tired of the oppression of the Chaldeans, greeted him as a liberator. Now the entire Neo-Babylonian Empire came under his rule. His treatment of the Babylonians reveals the wisdom and tolerance of this great empire builder. Although he made Babylonia into a Persian satrapy, most of the government officials kept their jobs. Cyrus allowed the Hebrews, who had been kept captive in Babylon since the reign of Nebuchadnezzar, to return to

---

11. According to the legend, the fame of the splendid court of Croesus at Sardis attracted many visitors. One of these, according to Herodotus, was the Athenian statesman and lawgiver Solon. The king proudly displayed his treasures and asked Solon who was the happiest man that he had met. Solon named two or three obscure men who had lived and died happily. Croesus was surprised and angry and said: "Man of Athens, do you count my happiness as nothing?" "In truth," replied Solon, "I count no man happy until his death, for no man can know what the gods may have in store for him."

There was indeed great misfortune in store for Croesus. Cyrus was soon threatening the kingdom of Lydia. Croesus consulted the oracle of Delphi in Greece. The oracle replied: "If Croesus goes to war he will destroy a great empire." So Croesus went out to meet the army of Cyrus and was utterly defeated. Thus he destroyed his own great empire.

Cyrus ordered Croesus to be burned alive. When Croesus saw the flames creeping upward to consume him, he remembered the words of the wise Solon and cried out, "O Solon! Solon! Solon!" Supposedly Cyrus was so moved by the story of how Solon had warned the proud king that he ordered Croesus to be released. Cyrus then asked Croesus why he shouted Solon's name, and Croesus asked him another question "What are your soldiers doing now?", pointing to the Persian soldiers taking all the treasures and destroying everything; Cyrus replied "They are plundering your city:" then Croesus said "They are not plundering my city, it's your city now and your soldiers are destroying your city." After that short conversation Cyrus the Great stopped his soldiers.

Judah and set up an autonomous state within the Persian Empire.[12] He also allowed other conquered peoples considerable self-government, which made Persian rule a welcome change from the oppression and totalitarian rule of the Assyrians and Chaldeans.

Cyrus now ruled an empire that stretched from the Indus River to the Levant coast and to the narrow waterway that separates Europe and Asia. He constructed the greatest empire the world had yet seen. His title had grown to include "Cyrus, King of the All, Great King, Mighty King, King of Babylonia, King of the Land of Sumer and Akkad, King of the Four Rims (of the Earth), the Son of Cambyses the Great King, King of Anshan."[13] The next eight years were spent consolidating his empire. He constructed defenses around the periphery of his territories, especially in the northeast to keep out the incursions of nomads. In 530 BCE, while campaigning near the Aral Sea, he died of wounds received in a battle against barbarian tribes.

Cambyses (530–521 BCE) inherited his father's empire and continued the policy of expansion. However, Cambyses possessed a far different personality than Cyrus. In order to make his throne secure, he had his brother Smerdis killed. Then he invaded Egypt and by the summer of 525 BCE he controlled all of it, but he was unable to conquer the kingdom of Meroë,[14] or modern Sudan, to the south of Egypt. But there was trouble back in the heartland of Persia. In 522 BCE a pretender named Gaumata seized the Persian throne and claimed to be the dead Smerdis. Cambyses rushed back to deal with the revolt, but died during the journey.

The death of Cambyses triggered other revolts in Babylonia and the eastern provinces. A short civil war resulted in a collateral member of the royal family, Darius I (521–486 BCE), coming to the throne. He continued the expansionary policies of his predecessors by adding the Indus Valley, in the east, and Libya, in the west, to the empire's holdings. However, during his thirty-five year reign, Darius's main concern was to consolidate the conquests of his predecessors. He reorganized the Persian Empire into satrapies (provinces), each administered by a satrap. These governors exercised surprisingly independent administrative and political authority. Some areas of the empire, like Judah, received an autonomous status which allowed their inhabitants to live under their own rulers and laws. However, all these units had to pay the central government a fixed annual tax and demonstrate their absolute loyalty to the Persian king.

Compared to the harsh and oppressive domination of the Assyrians and the Chaldeans, Persian rule was amazingly tolerant. The non-Persian peoples retained most of their local institutions, religions, and customs. Everyone benefited from the standardized currency and system of weights and measures. The taxes paid to the central government were not unreasonable and they were offset by the peace, security, and prosperity provided by that government. It was generally recognized by most

---

12. The prophet Isaiah even believed Cyrus was "anointed" by God: "That saith of Cyrus, he is my shepherd, and shall perform all my pleasure; even saying to Jerusalem, Thou shalt be built; and to the temple, Thy foundation shall be laid. Thus saith the Lord to his anointed, to Cyrus, whose right hand I have holden, to subue nations before him; and I will loose the loins of kings, to open before him the two leaved gates; and the gates shall not be shut." Isaiah, 44.28; 45.1

13. Cook, J.M., *The Persian Empire* (1983), Schocken Books, New York, pp. 32.

14. About 600 BCE., the rulers of the Nubian state moved their capital from Napata far upstream to Meroë, on a fertile floodplain between the Nile and Atbara Rivers in what is now the Sudan. This state flourished for nine centuries, ruled by African kings who imitated many of the customs of Egyptian pharaohs. Their capital lay at a strategic point on the Nile, where desert trading routes from the Red Sea to the east intersected with trails leading west along the southern margins of the Sahara and upstream along the Nile. Meroë maintained at least sporadic contacts with the Near Eastern and Mediterranean empires. He never conquered any of them, because the strategic obstacles separating the southern Nile region from Egypt were too great.

of the inhabitants as a fair and reasonable exchange. History provides no examples in which peace simply "happened." Peace does not naturally "break out," in the words of a popular cliché. History illustrates that peace must be achieved, it must be enforced by political and military power. Left to their own innate inclinations, human beings will always resort to violent and destructive behavior. This is not a pleasant thought, but it is a lesson of history that cannot be ignored. Even the so-called peace demonstrations so popular in the modern world invariably degenerate into violence if the

Figure 4.3: Darius I, relief from Persepolis.

participants are not controlled by their own leaders or outside crowd control. All the successful societies throughout history understood this fundamental trait of human nature and developed institutions to channel this energy into creative activity before it can become destructive.

Darius I was also a great builder. Most prominent among his projects was the construction of a new capital at Persepolis (the Greek name of Parsa), which included majestic audience halls and residential Palaces.[15] There were also royal residences at Susa, Ecbatanna, and Babylon. Darius enlarged and improved the irrigation systems throughout Mesopotamia to increase food production. He constructed the famous Royal Road from Susa to Sardis, a distance of 1,600 miles. Couriers passed messages along this road in a series of relays, or "posts," which comprised the world's first postal system. Each relay post was separated from the next by the distance that could be covered in one day on horseback. Darius also established an intelligence system to keep him informed concerning the events throughout his enormous empire.

Toward the end of his reign, Darius was forced to deal with the revolt of the Greek city-states located along the west coast of Asia Minor. These cities formed an alliance and, with the aid of Athens from the mainland, fought a war for independence between 499 and 494 BCE. Although Darius managed to put down this revolt, his invasion of mainland Greece was defeated at Marathon in 490 BCE. The Battle of Marathon is one of the most important battles in the history of Western Civilization. Had the Athenians lost, the Persians would have installed a Persian government and culture in Greece long before the classical period of Greek history. All the subsequent influences on succeeding Western societies would have been Persian rather than Greek. However, this clash of civilizations will be discussed in much more detail in succeeding chapters.

---

15. Darius proudly proclaimed his achievement in a foundation inscription which reads, "And Ahura-Mazda was of such a mind, together with the other gods, that this fortress (should) be built. And (so) I built it. And I built it secure and beautiful and adequate, just as I was intending to." Schmidt, Erich F., *Persepolis I: Structures, Reliefs, Inscriptions*, OIP LXVIII (1953), University of Chicago Press, Chicago, p. 63.

CHAPTER
5

Greek Origins

"No man is an island,"[1] according to the famous quote, but the ancient Greeks are often viewed in isolation. Many textbooks treat them as the starting point of the survey of Western Civilization, and most textbooks effectively begin with the history of Greek society as it already existed in the 5th Century BCE. This is a serious injustice to the peoples of the ancient Near East, the Levant and Egypt upon whose achievements the glories of Greek civilization are based. This view is also historically inaccurate. To understand the influences of these earlier civilizations on Greek society, we must digress several centuries back into the Aegean Bronze Age and look at the earliest origins of Classical Greece.

In contrast to the ancient Near East, the Levant and Egypt, the ancient Greek homeland was extremely small, measuring barely more than 300 miles on each side. It consisted of three distinctive regions: mainland Greece; the Aegean Islands; and the western coast of Asia Minor. These three areas have several distinguishing features which contributed to the diversity of Greek society.

Mainland Greece is a peninsula, projecting southward into the eastern Mediterranean Sea, from that part of Europe known as the Balkans. Mountains cover fully 80% of this peninsula, which is only about 45,000 square miles in area. Thus, only about 9,000 square miles of the mainland is inhabitable. On the other hand, even though Greece may be a very small country, it has an extremely long seacoast, formed by many inlets and bays. This coast contains countless harbors, which were more than adequate for the small boats of antiquity. There were also flat and hilly plains, some of them, such as the one around Athens, of considerable size, but most were hemmed in by mountain ranges, which are one of the two dominant characteristics of Greek geography. Mountain passes were not common and to travel from one plain or valley to the next was difficult, which caused the pockets of population located in them to form politically—though not culturally—independent states.

The second dominant feature of Greece is the sea, which seems to be everywhere. Between the eastern coast of the mainland and the western coast of Asia Minor is the Aegean Sea, which forms the second major geographical division of ancient Greece. The Aegean is a sea of contrasts. At one moment it can be incredibly beautiful and at the very next moment terrifyingly dangerous. It contains almost countless islands. Indeed, the current official Greek catalog of the Aegean islands lists more than 750 of them. In antiquity these islands were like stepping stones between Greece and Asia Minor, because one can sail almost anywhere in the area without loosing site of land for very long.

---

1. John Donne, *Meditation* 17 (1684): "No man is an island, entire of itself; every man is a piece of the continent, a part of the main. If a clod be washed away by the sea, Europe is the less, as well as if a promontory were, as well as if a manor of thy friend's or of thin own were: any man's death diminishes me, because I am involved in mankind, and therefore never send to know for whom the bell tolls, it tolls for thee."

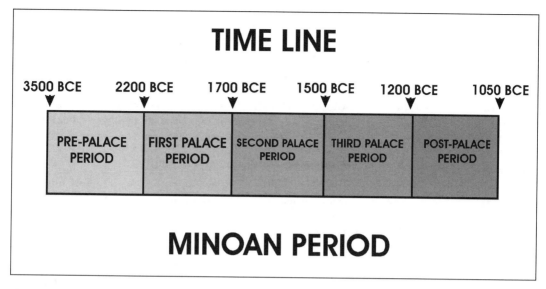

TIME LINE

3500 BCE	2200 BCE	1700 BCE	1500 BCE	1200 BCE	1050 BCE
PRE-PALACE PERIOD	FIRST PALACE PERIOD	SECOND PALACE PERIOD	THIRD PALACE PERIOD	POST-PALACE PERIOD

MINOAN PERIOD

Figure 5.1

These islands were also the home of a sizable population. The Cyclades island group contained important trading centers from an early period, though some of the islands, like Delos, are uninhabited today, mainly due to the lack of a fresh water source. During the classical period, the larger islands along the coast of Asia Minor—Lesbos, Chios, Samos, and Rhodes—were more significant. The 160 mile long island of Crete lies like a barricade across the southern end of the Aegean. It was the home of the pre-Greek Minoan civilization, which played an important economic and cultural role in the eastern Mediterranean sea before Greece emerged as the dominant civilization.

The west coast of Asia Minor, sometimes called Ionia, forms the third part of the ancient Greek homeland. The coastline is dotted with harbors and indeed has many of the same features as the coast of the mainland. A coastal plain stretches back to the foothills of the steep mountain range which rises to form the plateau of Asia Minor. This plain is wide and lush in some places but non-existent in other places, were the mountains come all the way down to the coast and confront the sea with jagged cliffs. These coastal plains are traversed by several rivers, which plunge down from the mountains through rocky canyons onto the plains, where they then flow slowly to the sea. The largest and most famous of these rivers is the Meander, which has become an English word meaning "to wander about aimlessly or casually without an urgent destination"—exactly the behavior of these rivers as they flowed across the coastal plain.

The Minoans

In 1900, the British archaeologist Sir Arthur Evans discovered an ancient site of an unknown people at Knossos on the island of Crete. Subsequent excavation revealed the site to be the ruins of a large and magnificent palace. It was built by a civilization that existed many centuries before the beginning of Greek history, a civilization that was, up to 1900, completely unknown to modern scholarship. Evans named the site "The Palace of Minos," because the network of walls revealed by the excavations resembled a labyrinth and brought to mind the Greek myth of King Minos.[2] From this naming—which to historians seems a bit whimsical—the civilization has come to be known as Minoan and the people as Minoans.

Over a century after its discovery, what we think we know about the Minoans we know only from excavated ruins and artifacts. We do not even know what name they called themselves. They have left us no history and no literature. They are silent. Even if by some miracle their language is someday deciphered, the mysterious clay tablets they left us will not reveal their history or relate the stories they told each other or even give us an insight into their religion, because we know that these tablets record only one thing: commercial accounts, records, and inventories. The sole purpose of Minoan writing was to keep records, it is the "paper-work" of a far flung commercial activity.

Only this much is certain. Shortly before 3000 BCE, groups of people, probably migrating from Anatolia, settled on the island of Crete and began to develop it agriculturally. By 2000 BCE the island was well populated and the Cretans were carrying on a multifaceted trade with all areas of the eastern Mediterranean basin. Very early on they adapted a hieroglyphic system of writing, probably derived from the Egyptians, and this soon evolved into a linear script. They constructed large and magnificent palaces at Knossos, Phaistos, and Kato Zakros, which were certainly centers of government. They spoke a language that seems to be unrelated to any other known language. Beyond this, all our "knowledge" about the Minoans is an educated guess.

Archaeologists divide the Minoan Bronze Age (3500–1100 BCE) into three major periods: Early Minoan (EM), Middle Minoan (MM), and Late Minoan (LM). Each of these periods is divided into several phases (Fig. 5.2) Historians prefer to divide Minoan history into four "palace periods" (Fig 5.1). Little is known about the "Pre-Palace" period (3300–2200 BCE), other than the cold facts provided by ruins and artifacts: they built sturdy houses from brick and stone; they left many

---

2. The story of Theseus and the Minotaur is a classical Greek myth. It was recorded by Homer, Hesiod, Thucydides, Plutarch, and others. Zeus was attracted to Europa, the daughter of the king of Phoenicia, and appeared to her as a bull. The princess who at the time was picking flowers climbed on to the back of this beautiful bull. Zeus quickly carried her off to Crete. They gave birth to a son, Minos. Europa became princess of Phoenicia and later married Asterios who was the king of Crete, and Minos eventually became the king of Crete. King Minos lived in the Palace of Knossos with Queen Pasiphae, daughter of Helios the sun god. His claim to the throne came into question among his brothers, so he prayed to Poseidon to send him a bull as a sign that the throne belonged to him alone. He promised Poseidon that he would sacrifice the bull. A majestic bull appeared from the sea as the requested sign, but the bull was so magnificent that Minos could not bring himself to sacrifice it. Instead, he chose another bull as an offering in its place.

Poseidon was angry, and as an act of revenge he caused the Queen to have an uncontrollable passion for the bull. The Queen had Daedalos, the ingenious craftsman, build a model of a cow, into which she climbed and orchestrated a union with the bull from which a son was born with the body of a man and the head and tail of a bull. In order to hide this shame, King Minos had Daedalos build a tremendous labyrinth where the Minotaur was placed. After winning a war against Athens, King Minos demanded as tribute that the Athenian king send seven boys and seven girls every year to be sacrificed to the Minotaur. Theseus, the son of the King of Athens, volunteered to be one of the fourteen youth sent to Crete. He was determined to kill the Minotaur and forever end this sacrifice of Athenian youth. King Minos's daughter, Ariadne, fell in love with Theseus and gave him a skein of golden thread from Daedalos, the craftsman, which Theseus tied to the entrance of the labyrinth—unwinding it as he penetrated the labyrinth to find the Minotaur. After a long and difficult journey he finally reached the heart of the labyrinth and succeeded in killing the Minotaur. He then found his way back out of the labyrinth by rewinding the ball of golden thread. Theseus, taking Ariadne with him, escaped from Crete to return to Athens. They had an overnight stop on the island of Naxos where, for some unknown reason, he sailed away leaving her asleep on the beach. But the story has a happy ending. The god Dionysus happened to come by, fell in love with and married Ariadne and together they had three sons.

3500 or 3300 BCE	Pre-palace period 3300–2200 BCE	EM I	Hand-made pottery, but more skillfully fired. Patterned, burnished Beak Spouted Jug
2900 BCE		EM II	Mottled red, orange, and black Vasilikiware. Myrtos is from this period. Vasiliki is a communal type ruin-forerunner of the later palaces?
2300 BCE	First palace period 2200–1700 BCE	EM III	Pottery of white spirals on a dark background develops into thin, polychrome Kamaresware. Use of potter's wheel to do this. Production of fine bronze daggers and weapons. Beginning of foreign contact.
1900 BCE		MM IB/IIA Old-Palace Period	Great strides in bronzework and other metal work. Superb goldwork being done. Harder seal stones being used. Extensive foreign contacts. Egyptian scarabs found on Crete.
1750 BCE		MM IIB	Seal cutters workshop found at Mallia. 7,000 seals found in a deposit at Phaestos. Hieroglypic deposit at Knossos.
1700 BCE	Second palace period 1700–1500 BCE	MM IIIA New Palace Period	Great palatial destruction via earthquake. Huge blocks at Knossos hurled from south facade into 'House of Fallen Blocks. All palaces rebuilt. Most ruins seen today are from this period. Efficient plumbing and drainage systems. Marine style pottery and other excellent pottery (later pottery with more repetitive patterns). Prosperous, with many large pithoi magazines. Linear A in use.
1600 BCE	1628 Thera Blows!	MM IIIB	
1550 BCE		LM IA	Increasing influence on mainland Greece.
1500 BCE	Third palace period 1500–1200 BCE	LM IB	Knossos less affected by destruction and repaired. Mycanaean influence increases. Knossos flourishes for several more generations.
1450 BCE		LM II Post Palatial Period	Widespread destruction at the end of LMI period. Most sites never reoccupied. Shrines have snake tubes and clay female figures with upraised arms and cylindrical skirts (see Knossos). Larnake burials in chest introduced. Linear B used. Heavy Mycanaean Influence.
1400 BCE		LM IIIA	Some evidence for a further destruction at Knossos but parts of the palace are still used.
1300 BCE		LM IIIB	
1220 BCE	Post-palace period 1200–1050 BCE	LM IIIC	
1050	Sub-Minoan period 1100–1000 BCE	Early Iron Age	Geometric. Mycanaeans and Minoans lose dominance. Dorians enter the picture. The 'Polis' or city-state appears.

Figure 5.2: Minoan Bronze Age (3500–1100 BCE). EM=Early Minoan, MM=Middle Minoan, LM=Late Minoan.

tombs behind, which provide us with a variety of artifacts. The development of Minoan arts and crafts made extraordinary progress during this period, witnessed by the appearance of polychrome pottery of striking decoration, produced by a sophisticated firing process. Exquisite jewelry was made from gold, ivory, and steatite (soapstone).

First Palace Period (2200–1700 BCE)

It was the good fortune of the Minoans that Crete was situated at the junction of the sea routes between the three continents of Africa, Asia, and Europe. This made it possible for them to dominate the trade of the eastern Mediterranean basin. From about 2200 BCE, the beginning of the First Palace period, political power began to center in the kings, who constructed large palaces at Knossos, Phaestos, and Zakros. However, we know little about these structures because their ruins are buried beneath later palaces built on the same locations. In order to excavate the early palaces it would be necessary to destroy the later Minoan sites that are so familiar to us today. Nevertheless, we know the essentials. The first palaces were arranged around a central court and constructed of closely fitted stone blocks. They were multi-storied and contained workshops, storage rooms, and religious shrines. The religion centered around the "Mother Goddess" and the two great symbols of Minoan religion, the sacred horns and the double axe, made their appearance. These palaces were reduced to ruins about 1700 BCE, probably by a series of earthquakes.

The Second Palace Period (1700–1500 BCE)

The zenith of Minoan civilization occurred during the Second Palace period, when magnificent new palaces were built on the ruins of the old ones and residential areas grew up around them. These palaces consisted of a complex array of rooms arranged around large courtyards. The palace at Knossos employed a kind of natural air conditioning provided by an ingenious system of movable door partitions and open stairwells which faced the Aegean sea and conducted cool sea air throughout the building. There were numerous skylights in the roof to provide light for all levels of the structure. A system of clay pipes brought fresh water into the palace for bathrooms and a sewage system carried off the waste. Sections of the palace were reserved for the royal quarters, shrines, audience, and banquet halls. But the largest area of the place was set aside for workshops and storage areas. Beautiful fresco paintings decorated the walls throughout the palace with landscapes, seascapes, and scenes from religious and social life.

Large rural villas appeared in the countryside which seems to indicate the development of landed "lords" reminiscent of the European Middle Ages, or more likely they may have been the country estates of wealthy commercial families. The main deity was still the Mother Goddess, now usually associated with snakes (thus sometimes called the "Snake Goddess"). The rituals and ceremonies of worship took place in the palace or residential shrines, open air altars, and in sacred caves. Most tombs of the period were cut from rock and had square burial chambers. Linear A script was now in use.

All the palace centers on Crete were destroyed by a cataclysmic event around 1450 BCE. What was the cause? That is still the subject of controversy, but one of the largest volcanic explosions known to have occurred anywhere on earth during the past fifteen or twenty millennia happened on the nearby island of Thera (modern Santorini), and this event certainly had a direct and dramatic impact on Crete. This volcanic event was accompanied by major earthquakes, but there is controversy among scholars as to weather it was responsible for the extensive destruction of the

Figure 5.3: Throne Room, Palace of Minos, Knossos.

palace centers across the island. In any event, only the palace at Knossos was subsequently rebuilt and the island immediately came under the rule of the Mycenaeans from the Greek mainland. Tablets written in the Linear B script now become plentiful. Unlike Linear A, this later writing system has been deciphered, and it turns out to be an archaic form of the Greek language. Unfortunately for modern researchers, Linear B was used exclusively for commercial records. No literature or other types of texts have been found.

The Third Palace Period (1500–1200 BCE)

After the destruction of the palaces in 1450 BCE, palace life resumed only at Knossos, which was partially rebuilt and served as the residence of the new Mycenaean rulers. The Mycenaeans made fundamental changes in the arrangement of the palace and erected new frescos, like the griffin motif in the throne room (Fig. 5.3). Many of the surviving frescoes date from this period and are in fact more Mycenaean than Minoan. The palace was destroyed again about 1380 BCE and was never rebuilt. The urban area around the palace remained alive and active, however. Mycenaean settlements spread throughout Crete and existed down to the Classical Greek period. Though this new society is still called Minoan, it is in fact now Mycenaean and its character is archaic Greek. Yet there was no substantial change in religion. From 1200 to 1050 BCE there was a steady decline and increasing disorder apparent across the island, and after 1100 BCE Crete entered the purely Greek era of its history.

What Was the True Function of the Palaces? A Controversy

During the final decades of the 20th Century, a controversy arose among archaeologists concerning the actual purpose of the Minoan sites that we have referred to as palaces. Some archaeologists now believe that they were not palaces at all but elaborate temples.[3] The problem is that we actually know so little about the political and governmental structure of Minoan civilization that any interpretation of the evidence is actually an educated guess. The history of archaeology demonstrates the futility of attempting to reconstruct a society's social and political history if the sources consist only of architectural ruins and disassociated artifacts. Archaeologists and pseudo-archaeologists have been able to develop extremely fantastic theories and scenarios based on such sparse evidence.[4]

As noted at the beginning of this discussion, what we think we know about the Minoans is not very extensive. Archaeological remains of the major sites on Crete indicate they served as residential, religious, and economic centers. The possibility that these structures were centers of tightly knit theocratic communities analogous to the early Sumerian city-states, ruled by kings-priests (or even by queens-priestesses), or that the government was administered by a priesthood resident in the palace-temple, cannot be totally dismissed, based on the evidence available. On the other hand, no large cult images have been found, and the shrine area of the palace at Knossos is a minor part of the structure compared to the areas devoted to residential quarters, banquet halls, workshops, storage areas, etc. Of course religious objects, such as small figurines of the Mother Goddess (Fig. 5.4) and small religious symbols, were found in all parts of the palace. But this does not indicate that all those areas were devoted to religious functions any more than the presence of a cross on a Medieval tomb indicates the burial of a priest. The preponderance of the evidence, when analyzed reasonably, indicates the function of these structures was primarily administrative, economic, and bureaucratic, with certain areas set aside for religious worship and ritual, like the chapels in Medieval castles.

One notable aspect of the Minoan sites that should be mentioned is the total lack of fortifications. This must certainly indicate that the Minoans did not practice warfare, at least between themselves on the island of Crete. Their isolation from the major powers of the Near East must have made the construction of defensive walls unnecessary. But there is evidence they possessed a powerful navy which controlled wide areas of the Aegean Sea, and until the rise of the Mycenaeans on the mainland of Greece, they probably had no need of land fortifications.

Minoan Religion and Culture

The most striking characteristic of Minoan religion is that it was matriarchal. Although the bull's horns, which suggests a male centered cult, was an important symbol of the religion, no male Minoan god has been identified until later periods. The specific pantheon of the Minoans, however, is vague, but the fact that it centered around a goddess can be explained by the female power of fertility. It is not clear whether the Minoans believed in one goddess who took many forms or if they believed in several goddess. The three most popular forms were: "The Goddess of Animals," "the Lady of the Beasts," or the "Huntress," represented as mastering and overcoming animals; "The Mountain Mother," who stands on a mountain and protects the animals and the natural world; and "The Snake Goddess," the most popu-

---

3. Castleden, Rodney, *The Knossos Labyrinth, A New View of the 'Palace of Minoa' at Knossos* (1990), Routledge, London.

4. The media often reports the silliest fantasies with the same veracity and seriousness it reports valid scholarship. Several "documentaries" reporting that the pyramids were constructed by aliens from outer space have been aired on the History Channel in recent years.

Figure 5.4: The Snake Goddess.

lar of all, who has snakes entwined about her body or in her hands. The figurines of the Snake goddess (Fig. 5.4) are found almost exclusively in houses and in small shrines in the palaces, which cause many to believe that she was a domestic goddess, a protectress of the house. Most scholars also believe that the goddesses of later Greek religion, such as Hera and Artemis, were derived from the Minoan goddess.

The evidence of Minoan art indicates that the priesthood was exclusively female and archaeological evidence as a whole suggests that women played an important role in public life. Crete appears not to be a class-oriented or a gender-based society. Women served as priestesses, functionaries, and administrators and participated in all the sports that men practiced, including boxing and bull-jumping. Women also performed every occupation and trade available to men. Although the palace kings were male, the society itself does not seem to have been patriarchal. In fact, the evidence implies that Minoan society was matrilineal, that is, the descent was traced through the mother and families took their name from the mother, not the father.

One of the most popular subjects of Minoan art is the extraordinary activity of bull-jumping (Fig. 5.5). The question of whether this activity was a religious ritual or an entertainment sport cannot be answered conclusively. Almost all sports events in antiquity had their origin in religious festivals. Bull-jumping probably began as a religious ritual and later became a spectator sport, but retained its links to religion. Bull-jumping was a test of courage and skill. The bull charged the jumper, or a line of jumpers, and the jumper grabbed the bull's horns and, as the bull naturally jerked its head, the jumper used that energy to spring up over the bull in a half summersault, coming down head first on the bull's back and then springing with his or her hands back up into the air again in another half somersault,

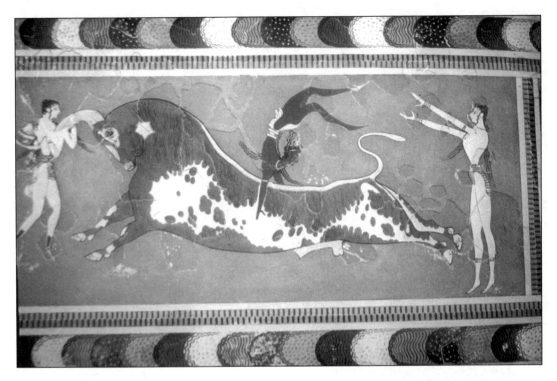

Figure 5.5: Bull-jumping.

coming down behind the bull on his or her feet. The bull was not harmed in this activity and thus bull-jumping had more in common with gymnastics than with bull-fighting. Both men and women participated in bull-jumping, though women dressed in male costume. How often were the young athletes maimed or even killed in this activity? We cannot know, but it was obviously extremely dangerous, and there are many illustrations of bull-jumpers being gored and tossed about violently.

The Mycenaeans

The first inhabitants of Greece were not the Greeks.[5] In historical times the Greeks called the original inhabitants "Pelasgians." Between 2200 and 1600 BCE, waves of Indo-European speaking peoples migrated southward into the Greek peninsula from Europe and perhaps, to a lesser extent, from Anatolia as well. These new arrivals are referred to as Mycenaeans, a term derived from Mycenae, the most important archaeological site of this culture. Mycenae was the home of the legendary King Agamemnon, who in Homer's Iliad was the leader of the Greek expedition to Troy. Homer called the Mycenaeans "Achaeans." With the addition of vocabulary from the language of the Pelasgians, the language of the invaders developed into classical Greek.

---

5. Our English word Greek has a strange history: it comes from the Latin, "*Graeci*," which is from the Greek "*Grakoi*," which was the name originally used by the Illyrians (modern Yugoslavia) for the name of the Dorians of Epirus (modern Albania). The Greeks called themselves "Hellenes," and their country "Hellas."

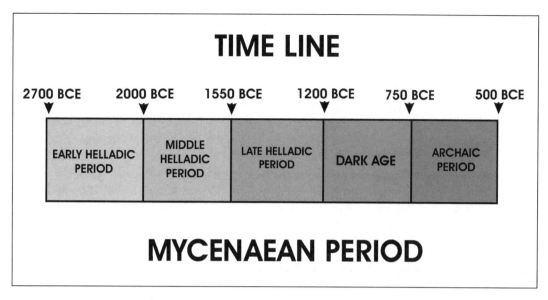

Figure 5.6

The Mycenaeans brought with them the Indo-European male sky-god religion. Archaeological evidence reveals that their pantheon included many of the gods of classical times, such as Poseidon, Zeus, Hera, Athena, and Apollo. At an early period the influence of Minoan religion and culture is evident. They borrowed the techniques of wall painting, pottery decoration, and seal making from the Minoans, and contact between the two cultures led to extensive trade and eventually to competition.

In the political and social spheres, however, the Mycenaeans retained many of their Indo-European traits. Tribal chieftains, or kings, established hereditary monarchies and attempted to gain authority over other kings. But in keeping with their Indo-European traditions, the Mycenaean kings did not have absolute power over their states as Egyptians and Mesopotamian monarchs had. In the Iliad, Homer describes Agamemnon frequently consulting the assembly of the army before making decisions. The members of the assembly speak freely and frankly to the king and their advice is taken seriously. Unlike the nations of the East, within Indo-European societies political power was derived ultimately from the members of the community, not from the gods, although political power was supported by religion.

In the words of John V. A. Fine:

At the head of these highly organized states stood the king, *wanax*, whose powers, civil, military, and religious, must have been very extensive, if not absolute. Beneath him, but not necessarily next in rank, was the *lawagetas*—literally, the leader of the people. Many scholars have argued that he was an army leader, which is quite possible, but his connection with the military has not yet been proved. Then there were various other officials, some of them clearly important, but it is rather rash to equate them with barons, counts, and the like, and the *lawagetas* with duke, for by introducing the terminology of feudalism with all its associations, the impression is given that much more is known about Mycenaean society than actually is the case. One other title should be mentioned, *basileus*, which in historical Greece came to mean king but in the Linear b tablets referred to a minor official, possibly the ruler of a village.[6]

6. Fine, John V. A., *The Ancient Greeks: A Critical History* (1983), Harvard University Press, Cambridge, p. 25.

Nor did women have the high status in Mycenaean society that they had in Minoan society. In Homer, women are consistently viewed as property, although he suggests that there was a time when aristocratic women had a higher status and considerable freedom. Andormache offered Hector advice on military strategy, but he reminded her that war was men's work and urged her to go back to her house and work on the loom. Royal women and female slaves engaged in similar work, though royal women worked of their own choice.

The Mycenaean Age is divided into three periods: Early, Middle, and Late Helladic Periods.

Early Helladic Period (2750–2000 BCE)

During this period, the Greek lands were settled by a metal-using people who spoke a non-Indo-European language. These were the people the Greeks later called Pelasgians and some of the place names they gave their villages, for example those ending in "ssos," are preserved. The Early Helladic seems to have been a period of relative peace and quite, but beginning around 2000 BCE their villages were suddenly destroyed by fire and abandoned.

Middle Helladic Period (2000–1550 BCE)

This is the period of the migrations of the Indo-European Mycenaeans into Greece. They settled among the former population, intermarried with them but imposed their language, an archaic form of Greek. The result of this blending was the early Mycenaean culture. This new society was primarily based on warfare with communities led by chieftains who were essentially military leaders. The Greek climate is hot and dry, the soil is thin and rocky, which make agriculture difficult, though some crops, such as grapes and olives are quite well adapted to this environment. These are crops, however, which require a long period between first planting and the onset of harvest cycles, which means that a stable and ordered community life is necessary. The coastal settlements relied heavily on fishing, and these communities also began trading with the Minoans. Contact with this much older, more sophisticated civilization brought about instant and fundamental influences which led to the urbanization of the Mycenaean settlements and pushed the Mycenaeans across that line that separates a culture from a civilization.

Figure 5.7:
The Lion Gate
Pediment, Mycenae.

Late Helladic Period (1550–1150 BCE)

The date for the Late Helladic and the emergence of Mycenaean civilization is arbitrary, because the Mycenaeans had begun building the elements of civilization earlier. Around 1600, however, the settlements began to emerge as true cities and a new era of cultural creative activity began. The line drawn by historians between a culture and a civilization is always arbitrary and approximate, which is the reason the dates for historical periods usually end in zero. As the cities grew larger, the surrounding rural territories they control became more stable and secure and agriculture thrived as never before. The new prosperity is reflected in the opulence of their graves and the creativity of their art. The leaders of these new cities also began to exert military power throughout the Aegean area. Thus the Late Helladic Period is often referred to as simply the Mycenaean Period (1550–1150 BCE).

The Mycenaean civilization thrived for four centuries, but left us only ruined cities and plundered tombs that tell us very little about their life. When their day in the sun was complete, they disappeared into the silence and emptiness of the past. For two thousand years the Mycenaeans were known only through the epic poetry of Homer and mythological legend. Indeed, scholars dismissed the entire Mycenaean civilization as simply a mythological invention of the classical Greeks, until the amateur German archaeologist Heinrich Schliemann[7] excavated the sites at Troy, Mycenae,[8] and Tiryns.

The Mycenaeans derived much of their culture from the Minoans, but there were dramatic differences. Mycenaean civilization was composed of numerous small kingdoms centered around fortress-like cities, protected by thick walls. Unlike the Minoans their society was class and gender

---

7. Heinrich Schliemann was one of the most colorful figures in the history of archaeology. He was born on January 6, 1822 in the small village of Neu Buckow, Germany. He was largely self-educated. His family was so poor that he had to leave school at the age of 14 to earn a living. He continued studying on his own, however, showing an exceptional ability to master foreign languages. At one point he taught himself Dutch, English, French, Spanish, Italian, and Portuguese in two years. Soon he began to exploit his remarkable aptitude for business dealings, which enabled him to amass a large fortune early in life and to retire at the age of 41. From then on, he devoted himself to archaeology. He began to dig at Troy, his most famous excavation, in 1870, and later also made extraordinary discoveries at Mycenae, the legendary home of Agamemnon, leader of the Greeks in the Trojan War. His discoveries later established a historical background for the stories and legends told by Homer and Vergil that had fascinated Schliemann from childhood. Schliemann has been criticized for using methods that seem crude by comparison with the highly developed techniques of today. He deserves great credit, however, for creating method where none had existed and for demonstrating that excavation can be more than the mere treasure hunt it had been up until his time—that it can, in fact, restore a knowledge of lost civilizations. Schliemann's work led to continuing investigations that are still today revealing the wonders of pre-classical Greece (6000–1000 BCE). Before Schliemann, this civilization was not even known to have existed.

In his later life, Schliemann built a house for himself in Athens, where he ruled like a Homeric king—messages had to be sent to him in ancient Greek, he insisted that Greek be spoken at the dinner table, and he renamed all his servants after characters in Greek mythology and history. He wrote about his excavations in a work titled *Ilios*. When he died while on a trip to Naples on December 26, 1890, his body was returned to Athens. His funeral took place on January 4, 1891 and he was buried in a great Mausoleum he had built for himself. The inscription above the entrance is a powerful declaration of how he wanted to be remembered: "For the hero Schliemann."

For further reading:

Deuel, Leo, *The Memoirs of Heinrich Schliemann* (1977), Harper and Row, New York.
King, Wellington, *Heinrich Schliemann: Heros & Mythos* (1997), University of Texas.
Payne, Robert, *The Gold of Troy: The Story of Heinrich Schliemann and the Buried Cities of Ancient Greece* (1959), Funk & Wagnall, New York.
Poole, Gary and Lynn, *One Passion, Two loves: The Story of Heinrich and Sophie Schliemann, Discoverers of Troy* (1966), Thomas Y Crowell, New York.

8. The site which gives this age its name. Homer called these early Greeks the Achaeans.

based. The rulers were called *wanax* and they accumulated vast wealth, in the form of treasure, but their prosperity was not shared with the rest of society, as was the case in the Minoan civilization. The *wanax* was primarily a war lord and Mycenaean civilization was primarily a warrior society. They were quite aggressive and constantly engaged in warfare both between themselves and others. They also engaged in trade, exchanging raw materials, such as olive oil and animal skins for luxury items such as jewelry, with Crete, Asia Minor, the Levant, and Egypt. However, the Mycenaeans made little distinction between trade and piracy. If they could take what they wanted by force they did so, if not, then they were ready to negotiate a trade. There are Hittite and Egyptian records of their trading expedition, pirate raids and invasions.

Through these methods, the Mycenaean rulers amassed great wealth. Much of it was spent on defense and warfare, but a large part was spent on magnificent palaces and expensive burials. Originally the Mycenaean rulers and higher aristocrats were buried in deep shaft graves, like the ones excavated by Schliemann at Mycenae in 1876. However, around 1500 BCE, they began to bury the most prominent members of society in tholos tombs—large chambers cut into the sides of hills.

Because the Minoan influence on Mycenaean civilization was so strong and obvious, it is often assumed the Mycenaean religion was almost identical to the Minoan. However, recent studies indicate that this is misleading. It is true, however, that there are many outward similarities. As presented by the archeological evidence, divinity is usually personified as a goddess, with a male god playing an inferior role. At times a mystical union is suggested between male and female divinities and between

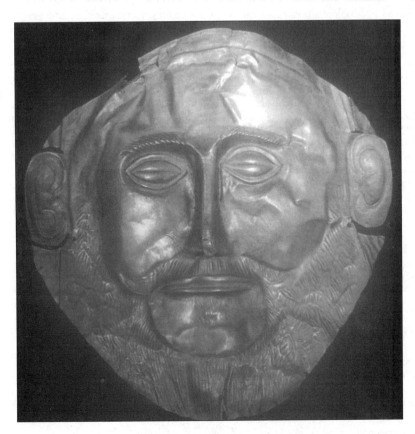

Figure 5.8: The "Mask of Agamemnon." The Gold Death Mask from Mycenae, believed by Schliemann to be that of Agamemnon.

the worshiper and the divinity. The goddess is worshiped through fertility rites and tree cults are frequently evident. Yet the religion presented by Homer is in stark contrast. Zeus is the sky god and supreme ruler. The gods and goddesses are exactly like humans in every way except they are infinitely more powerful and they are immortal. They stand apart as exalted beings, but there is little mystery surrounding them. The same emotions and motives drive their actions that propel human affairs.

In reality, elements of both of these contrasting pictures of Mycenaean religion are present. From the Linear B tablets we learn that Poseidon, the brother of Zeus, was an important deity. He is called the "Earth-Shaker" by Homer. His classical identification with the sea is a later development. But there is no evidence whatever during the Mycenaean period of the large temples later associated with classical Greek religion. As in Crete, Mycenaean religious activity centered around small shrines, either in the palaces or in the open air. This is very similar to the Minoan practice. In the end, however, we must recognize that we cannot construct Mycenaean religion in any detail. It remains a vague and intriguing mystery to us.

We know the Mycenaeans invaded and occupied the island of Crete soon after the disastrous earthquakes destroyed the palaces there around 1400 BCE. They established themselves as rulers—and exploiters—of the civilization that had exerted such a deep influence on their own civilization. However, the details and circumstances of this episode are unclear. Was it the result of the action of a single Mycenaean state or did a combination of allied states accomplish this feat? The ruins are silent regarding this and other questions of detail.

The only time the Mycenaean kingdoms are known to have united into a league for a common purpose was during the war against Troy, which was a prosperous city guarding the narrow waterway connecting the Back Sea to the Aegean Sea—if indeed the Trojan War is historical.[9] Apparently the Trojans were rich and offered a tempting prospect of loot, which was probably the real cause of the war. However, much later, the Greeks explained the origins of the war by the romantic story in Homer's Iliad. According to this legend, Paris, a Trojan prince, seduced Helen, the beautiful wife of King Menelaus of Sparta and carried her off to Troy. The kings of Greece then united and Agamemnon, the brother of Menelaus, led an expedition which, after a ten-year siege, destroyed Troy. The excavations of Schliemann at Hissarlik in turkey seem to indicate that Troy was destroyed about 1250 BCE and that Homer's account of the war contains at least a kernel of truth.

But if it is historical, the Trojan War was the last feat of the Mycenaeans. Beginning about 1200 BCE or a little later, the marauders that we met in the context of Egyptians as the "sea peoples" swept into the Aegean Sea and made trading impossible. These Indo-European invaders brought chaos and confusion to the entire eastern Mediterranean and Mycenaean civilization suffered a deep economic decline.

---

9. Is the Trojan War historical? Until the 19th Century it was widely believed that Troy and the Trojan war were imaginary. Then, in 1871, the German-born amateur archaeologist Heinrich Schliemann (see note 7) began excavating an ancient city in Turkey at a site named Hissarlik. Nine cities have been found at the site, one on top of the other. The seventh city was destroyed around 1250 BCE and appears to be the Troy of legend. The ruins of its towers and its walls, which were sixteen feet thick, are still visible. Schliemann identified Troy's location through clues he found in the Iliad, the epic attributed to the Greek poet Homer. Little is known about Homer except that he was blind. In ancient times it was believed that he had lived during the Trojan War, but modern scholars think that he lived in the 8th or 9th Century BCE. His poems were oral epics, transmitted orally for several centuries. Some scholars suspect that the poems were actually the work of successive generations of poets, and that Homer did not exist.
But Schliemann's discoveries seemed to prove that Homer's writings were historical, not mythological, and for a generation or so afterward the Trojan War was accepted as historical. However, with closer analysis of the evidence, doubts began to creep in and today opinion is mixed among scholars. The Trojan War is not now universally believed to be historical. For a discussion of this controversy see Wood, Michael, *In Search of the Trojan War* (1983), University of California Press, Berkeley.

The Greek Dark Age (1200–750 BCE)

Between 1200 and 1100 BCE life on mainland Greece reverted to a level of pre-civilization. The cities were abandoned and destroyed. The major crafts declined to the extent that all types of permanent buildings ceased to be constructed. One of the most basic elements of any civilization, writing, disappeared completely, leaving Greece literally in the dark for almost five centuries, from 1200 to 750 BCE. This period is, in fact, known as the Greek Dark Age. The Greeks of the later historical period believed this cultural decline was caused by the influx of a new people who spoke a primitive Greek dialect, known as Dorians. They supposedly rushed down from central Europe and wrested control of the Greek peninsula. These primitive and barbaric Dorians destroyed the Mycenaean civilization.

This version of events was accepted as historical during the 19th and early 20th centuries. There are, however, problems with this scenario. For one thing, there is an absence of supporting archaeological evidence. Also it is difficult to understand how a primitive, nomadic, tribal group could so easily overcome a highly efficient and war-centered society like the Mycenaeans. Yet, there is no logical reason to disbelieve the Greeks. This is another of those controversies of ancient history that may never be solved completely.[10] The best explanation seems to be that a combination of economic decline, caused by the marauding sea people, and the invasion of a migrant people from the north caused the collapse of the Mycenaean society, in which most of the prosperity and wealth was concentrated at the very top of the social hierarchy. And some unseen disaster, such as a plague, or severe drought, which could account for the sudden decline in population, cannot be ruled out as a contributing factor.

The Greek Dark Age was a period of apathy and stagnation. Most of the promising elements of Mycenaean civilization were lost forever. The cities and even the agricultural villages were abandoned, and urbanized culture, including writing, vanished. The great trading system began by the Minoans and inherited by the Mycenaeans was destroyed and contact with Asia Minor, the Near East and Egypt stopped entirely. The lifestyle of Greece shifted from an urban setting to a sedentary and drab agricultural existence. No longer did powerful rulers preside over tightly organized territories from magnificent stone fortresses. No longer did Greek ships filled with adventurers, raiders, and traders ply the Mediterranean. Now the people eked out a miserable existence as herders, shepherds, and subsistence farmers, huddled in tiny settlements as small as twenty people in most cases. Indeed the entire population of Greece was a mere fraction of what it had been during the Mycenaean period, and the decreased food production encouraged a further decrease in population in a spiraling process of decline into abject poverty. An increasing number of Greeks turned away from agriculture to a wandering, pastoral way of life. People became more mobile. In fact, the population of the dark age became a wandering, rootless, disorganized hoard of chaotic humanity. No permanent buildings were constructed. Artists no longer depicted people and animals, but decorated their crude ceramics with abstract geometric designs.

A New Beginning?

But some historians see a positive aspect to this catastrophe. As Nels M. Bailkey says:

> While the Dorian invasion was an undoubted catastrophe, it was also vital to the ultimate rise of a unique Greek civilization that was not largely an offshoot of the Near East, as was the Mycenaean civilization.[11]

---

10. For a cogent discussion of the "Dorian problem," see Fine, John V.A., *The Ancient Greeks: A Critical History* (1983), Harvard University Press, Cambridge, pp. 12–17; 30–33.

11. Wallbank, T. Walter, Taylor, Bailkey, *Civilization, Past and Present* (1976), Scott, Foresman and Co., Glenview, IL., p. 96.

Figure 5.9: Geometric Amphora, Mid-7th Century.

Another historian, Mortimer Chambers, puts it this way:

> The shattering of the monarchic pattern in the Mycenaean Age can be viewed as a liberating and constructive event. We cannot show that the kings and dynasties in Greece were dependant on or were imitating the kings in the ancient Near East, but the two systems of monarchy resembled each other. If the Mycenaean kings had survived, mainland Greece might have developed as Anatolia did, with strong monarchies and priests who interpreted and refined religious thought in ways that would justify the divine right of kings. Self-government within the Greek states might not have emerged for centuries if it appeared at all.[12]

In this view, it was necessary to "wipe the slate clean," so to speak, of all Near Eastern influences in order to develop a truly "Western" civilization. The classicists of the 19th and 20th centuries tended to view Greece as the birthplace of European civilization and of Western democracy and therefore unique and "untainted" by the corrupt cultures of the "Orient." Today, however, most historians realize that important contributions were made to Greek culture by the societies of the Near East, the Levant, and Egypt. That is why the first four chapters of this book are devoted to an understanding of the histories of those peoples. However, that having been stated, it is still important to recognize the significance of the discontinuity of the Greek Dark Age to the history of Greece. This break with the past did, in fact, facilitate a new start, so to speak.

---

12. Chambers, Motimer, et al., *The Western Experience,* 3rd ed. (1974), Alfred A. Knopf, New York, p. 41.

The universal level of poverty during the Dark Age meant that the communities were basically egalitarian—all its members were poor. The prime indicator of this is the burial customs of the time. However, as early as 1050 BCE a reformation of the social hierarchy was beginning to take shape. Again, the burials are the chief evidence for this. At a site known as Lefkandi on the island of Euboea, a richly furnished burial of a man and a woman who died about 950 BCE has been found. The woman wore elaborate gold jewelry and the couple was buried under a building more than 150 feet long, which suggests they enjoyed a high social status during their life. This was a rare exception during the Dark Age, but it illustrates that social differentiation was once again emerging in the Greek world.

The Beginning of Recovery

Around 900 BCE there is archaeological evidence of economic improvement, but recovery was long and slow. Not until around 750 BCE did political states begin to form and these were a new kind of political organization. Unfortunately, it was during the obscurity of the Dark Age that the social, political, and intellectual foundations were laid for the emergence of a unique new kind of state—the *polis,* or Greek city-state. Renewed commercial and intellectual contact with the Near East greatly influenced Greece, introducing new technology, such as iron working, and new ideas, which made their way into Greek mythology and religion.

About 900 BCE, burials of males begin to contain iron weapons, indicating a transition from the use of bronze to the use of iron. The Greeks probably learned the use of iron from the Near East. Thus, the Dark Age is sometimes thought of as the Early Iron Age in Greece. Iron is obviously superior to bronze for making tools and weapons, but the Greeks appear to have turned to iron because they could no longer obtain the tin necessary to mix with copper to make bronze. Iron, by contrast, was available locally. However, bronze continued in use for shields and armor. Since iron is cheaper than bronze and could be afforded by more people, armies became larger and warfare became more bloody.

The use of iron also meant more plentiful agricultural tools and helped to increase the production of food. Agriculture thus began a recovery from the devastation of the Dark Age, and grain production became as important as hoarding. Indeed, an increase in food production was accompanied by an increase in population. From about 850 BCE onward, the burials of the wealthier members of the community begin to contain objects, such as jewelry from Egypt and Syria, which indicates the beginnings of a revival of trade. An increase in population and prosperity in turn led to an increase in social complexity. Some members of the community were now wealthy enough to form an aristocratic class. The term "aristocracy" means "the rule of the best," and in the ancient Greek context it refers to a social elite, whose status was the result of a combination of wealth, birth, and public conduct. The aristocrats of ancient Greece did possess more wealth than others but birth was also a criterion. We cannot know precisely how families originally gained the aristocratic status, but once they did, the status was passed on to their heirs. Possibly some families of the Dark Age inherited their aristocratic status as descendants of important families of the preceding Mycenaean period. More likely, most of the aristocratic families of the Dark Age earned their status by first attaining wealth and then befriending less fortunate members of the community, who then were willing to acknowledge their superior status in exchange for material help. Still others may have gained aristocratic status through the control of sacred locations and religious ritual.

The Archaic Age (750–500 BCE)

The term "archaic" is derived from the Greek word *archaikos,* which means "old fashioned," or even more basically from *arche*, which means "beginning." It was first applied to pre-classical Greek art, which seemed to modern scholars to be primitive and less refined than classical art. In fact, the art produced between 750 and 500 BCE appeared to imitate the old fashioned Egyptian style. The Archaic Age was a period of great change in the political, economic, and social spheres as well as the artistic area. The developments of the Archaic Age were fundamental, and the achievements of the later classical period cannot be understood except by reference to accomplishments of the Archaic Age.

The Emergence of Self-Government

During the Dark Age, as we have seen, Greek life centered around small tribal units—some of them sedentary, most of them nomadic. At the beginning of the archaic age, these tribes slowly grew, or assembled, into larger units. First villages, then even larger urban settlements appeared, usually centered around a high hill, called an *acropolis*, and a central market area, called an *agora*, and surrounded by defensive fortifications. Independent and sovereign political units emerged, based on these cities but including the surrounding agricultural territory. This unit is called the *polis* (plural = *poleis*)—a term often translated as "city-state." The polis is central to the history of ancient Greece.

About 750 BCE, the Greeks adopted a modified form of the Phoenician alphabet to write their own language. This was a result of their renewed contacts with the literate civilizations of the Near East. The Greek version of the Phoenician alphabet was later adopted and further modified by the Romans to write their Latin language and eventually became the alphabet used to write modern English. The Greeks first employed the new alphabet to write down the oral literature of the Dark Age, most notably the epic poems of Homer, the *Iliad*[13] and the *Odyssey*,[14] and the writings of Hesiod, *Works and Days*[15] and the *Theogony*.[16]

---

13. The Iliad is the epic of the Wrath of Achilles during the siege of Troy. It begins with the quarrel between Agamemnon and Achilles, as a result of which the latter withdraws from the fight. He refuses to return even when an embassy promises him fabulous rewards, and only when his friend Patroclus is killed does he re-enter the war, using the glorious new armor that Hephaestus, the god of craftsmen, has made for him. The Iliad ends with the single combat between Achilles and Hector, the prince of Troy, and the latter's death and funeral. The noble, dignified, but always moving language, the sharp characterizations, the vivid similes and epithets, the almost overbearing detail, the universality of emotions, the compassion and sympathy, the love of nature—these are some of the reasons for the Iliad's position of pre-eminence in Greek literature.

14. The Odyssey is the story of the wanderings, homecoming, and vengeance of Odysseus. It begins *in medias res* (i.e.,"in or into the middle of a narrative or plot"), with Telemachus, the son of Odysseus, going to look for his father. The scene shifts to the island of Calypso, where Odysseus has been for seven years, after the destruction of his ship and comrades. Calypso lets him go (on Zeus's order), he makes a raft and departs, but is shipwrecked, and he swims ashore at Scheria, where he is met by Nausicaa, daughter of Alcinous. At a banquet given by King Alcinous, he tells the story of his previous adventures and wanderings, including the Laestrygonians, Cyclopes, Scylla and Charybdis, the Sirens, the Lotus-Eaters, Circe, the descent to Hades, etc. Alcinous then gives Odysseus a ship to take him home. The second half of the Odyssey tells of his homecoming, recognition by Eumaeus, and the tremendous slaughter of the Suitors. The style, language, characterizations, etc. are consistent with the Iliad.

15. Hesiod is the earliest poet whose works are extant, except for Homer. *Works and Days* is a didactic poem dealing with farm life, moral precepts, mythology, description of a year's work on a farm, folk-lore, and miscellaneous advice and superstitions.

16. Theogony deals with the universe and the genealogy of the gods.

Unfortunately, by the time that Greece emerged into the light of full history, it was already organized politically into small self-governing poleis, with constitutional governments. Today, of course, we take constitutional government for granted, as if it were a normal way of life, but we should understand that constitutional or self-government is an extremely rare and temporary condition. It has occurred only on very few occasions throughout all of human history. Historically, it is an aberration, a rare and unnatural event. In the words of the American statesman Adlai Stevenson: "The natural government of man is servitude. Tyranny is the normal pattern of human government." What is so frustrating to historians is that this momentous step from monarchy to constitutional government in ancient Greece occurred in the darkness, out of view of history. Consequently, all we really have to study is the result, not the process, of this crucial event. Thus, we are consigned by fate to toil in the darkness and to duel with shadows in order to develop even a vague understanding of the development of constitutional government, and any knowledge we think we acquire concerning the process will always be open to doubt and controversy.

The emergence of constitutional government and the organization of the Greek people into numerous small poleis are two inseparable elements of the political history of ancient Greece. In fact, the polis, a uniquely Greek institution, was the vehicle of constitutional government. The greatest philosophers of Greece, thinkers like Plato and Aristotle, took it for granted that all truly civilized people would live in a polis. Plato's most famous and important work was a book called *The Republic.* This was history's first attempt to describe utopia, the ideal state of perfection, the best possible environment for human beings to exist and live the "good life." The utopia Plato described was the polis. Aristotle wrote a book called On *Politics* and in it he stated: "Man is by nature an animal intended to live in a polis." In other words the Greeks believed that civilized people would live in a polis just as naturally as bees live in a beehive or ants live in an anthill. Therefore, any evaluation of Greek culture, any analysis of Greek history, must be made in the context of the polis.

The emergence of the polis in Greece was the result of the settling down of the nomadic tribes of the Dark Age. One contributing factor was certainly the renewal of trade and the growth of the population during the 8th Century BCE. In their early state of development all poleis were monarchies, ruled by a *basileus*, or hereditary king, with the aid of a small aristocratic class. Many of the men who acquired wealth through successful farming or commerce were outside the aristocracy and they gradually came to demand a greater role in the political process of the polis. This caused social conflict. The 6th Century poet Theognis of Megara records the distress of the hereditary aristocrats at the emergence of this new social group and the threat it posed to their social position.[17] But the other side of the issue was the growing number of poor citizens who viewed as unaccept-

---

17. Theonis of Megara, *The Theonidea,* (7. 183-192)
Among rams and asses and horses, Kyrnos, we look for those
Of noble breeding, and a man wants them to mate
From worthy stock. Yet a noble man does not mind marrying
A base woman of base birth if she brings him money in abundance,
Nor does a woman shrink from becoming the wife of a base man
With wealth; she prefers a rich husband to a worthy one.
Money is what they honor; the noble weds a base man's daughter,
The base a worthy man's: wealth mixes stock.
Thus do not be amazed, son of Polypaos, that the citizen's stock
Is growing feeble, for what is noble is being mixed with what is base.

able the inequity of the aristocrats. Hesiod decried the "crooked" justice these aristocrats dispensed to the poorer citizens as unfair and immoral.[18]

The invention of the concept of citizenship was a response to this unrest. Citizenship included non-aristocrats and it involved a catalog of rights and responsibilities. The rights included: access to the courts; protection from enslavement; participation in the religious and cultural life of the state; and participation in the political process. Citizen status distinguished free men and women from slaves and resident aliens. But citizenship did not imply equality. Social inequality persisted and of course economic inequality can never be eliminated. However, the most striking example of inequality among citizens was the difference between the sexes. Women were granted citizenship, as made clear by certain religious cults which were reserved for citizen women, and they had local rights denied aliens and slaves, such as protection against being sold into slavery, but they could not represent themselves in court and must have men speak for them. Thus, every citizen woman had to have a male guardian to protect her physically and legally. If there were no males available from her own family—as in the case of an orphan—then a guardian was assigned by the state. And of course, women could play no role in the political process.

Beginning in the 8th Century BCE, the *basileus* was replaced by an oligarchy ("rule of the few") of the leading families of the polis. In most cases the power of the king was assumed by the oligarchs, and from the point of view of the common citizens there was little change in their own status. Indeed the rule of the oligarchs was often even more totalitarian than rule of the king, because the old *basileus* had often sought the support of the lower classes as a balance against the aristocracy and this had given them some small political leverage, whereas the oligarchs often ignored the interests of the common people entirely. Thus, eventually most of the oligarchic governments were overthrown by "tyrants," with the support of the lower classes of the citizens. The tyrant was an illegitimate usurper of power and ruled through naked force and fear. Ironically, however, the fact that most of these tyrants gained their power through support of the lower classes represents, in a sense, an exercise of political power on the part of the masses. Unfortunately, once in power, the tyrant usually attempted to rule like a king and to make his status hereditary. Since they were illegitimate and ruled by force, their régime was unstable. Nevertheless, tyrannies became a widespread political phenomenon during the Archaic Age.

---

18. Hesiod, *Works and Days,* (ll. 238–247) But for those who practice violence and cruel deeds far-seeing Zeus, the son of Cronos, ordains a punishment. Often even a whole city suffers for a bad man who sins and devises presumptuous deeds, and the son of Cronos lays great trouble upon the people, famine and plague together, so that the men perish away, and their women do not bear children, and their houses become few, through the contriving of Olympian Zeus. And again, at another time, the son of Cronos either destroys their wide army, or their walls, or else makes an end of their ships on the sea.

(ll. 248–264) You princes, mark well this punishment you also; for the deathless gods are near among men and mark all those who oppress their fellows with crooked judgments, and worry not the anger of the gods. For upon the bounteous earth Zeus has thrice ten thousand spirits, watchers of mortal men, and these keep watch on judgments and deeds of wrong as they roam, clothed in mist, all over the earth. And there is virgin Justice, the daughter of Zeus, who is honored and reverenced among the gods who dwell on Olympus, and whenever anyone hurts her with lying slander, she sits beside her father, Zeus the son of Cronos, and tells him of men's wicked heart, until the people pay for the mad folly of their princes who, evilly minded, pervert judgment and give sentence crookedly. Keep watch against this, you princes, and make straight your judgments, you who devour bribes; put crooked judgments altogether from your thoughts.

Although tyrannies never entirely disappeared and occurred in every age of Greek history, by the 6th Century BCE most tyrannies were replaced by either a return to a somewhat more broad-based oligarchy, or by a new form of government known as democracy, the "rule of the *demos*," the Greek word for "people." It should be clearly understood that ancient Greek democracy really *was* the rule of the people—or at least the rule of the male citizens. Our modern term democracy actually means *representative government*, because the people elect representatives to rule, they do not rule directly themselves. However, in ancient Greek democracy, the people ruled themselves directly through an assembly composed of all citizens. We will look at this form of direct democracy in more detail in the next chapter.

Slavery

According to the writings of Homer and Hesiod, the only consistent source for slavery during the Dark Age was prisoners of war. Other dependant people were simply inferior members of the owner's household. By the Archaic Period, however, slaves were being imported from outside Greece. A slave trade developed when the tribes to the north and east of Greece began capturing each other and selling the captives to slave dealers for a profit. The 5th Century BCE historian Herodotus says that some Thracians even sold their own children into slavery. The Greeks, like other slave owning peoples, found it easier to enslave those whom they considered different from themselves. But the Greeks did enslave other Greeks. Rich families even utilized educated Greek slaves as tutors for their children.

By the 5th Century BCE the population of many poleis were one third slaves. Still, much of the common labor had to be done by free workers. While high born Greeks considered manual labor disgraceful, the common citizens and slaves preformed the same kinds of jobs. There was no kind of work in ancient Greece reserved specifically for slaves. Household slaves, usually female, preformed all the domestic chores normally performed by women, and they shared this work with the free women of the household. In addition, they were often used for sexual purposes by the master of the house. Slaves might be appointed as supervisors of other slaves in the fields. The worst job of the slave was work in the mines, but even here some free labor was found also.

Some slaves were owned by the polis and were known as public slaves. They performed specialized services and some even served as a kind of police force in 5th Century BCE Athens, by assisting citizen magistrates in the arrest and punishment of criminals. The state executioner was a public slave. A few slaves were owned by temples and considered the property of the god. Female slaves served as sacred prostitutes at the temple of Aphrodite in Corinth and their earnings helped support the temple.

The life of the ancient slave was miserable and degraded beyond even the most disgusting horror movie produced by Hollywood. It is near impossible to understand how the great philosophers, like Socrates, Plato, and Aristotle, could wax so elegant about the rights and dignity of humanity, and at the same time support the disgusting system of slavery. The only explanation is that once a human being became a slave, that individual was no longer thought of as a human being but became a mere "thing." Indeed the word "chattel" is closely related to the word "cattle." Slaves were without family, without property, without any legal or political rights whatsoever. Although their endless toil helped to maintain the Greek economy, it never benefited the slave. One of the great mysteries of Greek history is that there were no widespread slave revolts. They were so utterly oppressed that no hope was left to them. Without hope, resistance is unthinkable. In rare cases slaves were freed voluntarily—usually when they were no longer of any economic value—but even then they remained at the bottom of the social scale. Freed slaves melted into the population of resident aliens and were still expected to work for their former masters when called upon.

Women's Life

The life of ancient Greek women was almost completely confined to the household. "Respectable" women were never seen in public without a male escort from her family. Yet, the institution of slavery placed important responsibilities on free women, especially those of rich families, to manage their households. Wives were expected to bear and raise the children (males if possible), supervise the operation of the household, manage the family's financial affairs, weave cloth and make clothing, and direct the work of the family slaves. Women performed the tasks which freed the male members of the family to participate in the public life of the polis. In a very real sense, the culture and life of the ancient Greek polis rested on the toil and dedication of its women.

But her life was private. The 5th Century BCE Athenian statesman Pericles said to the women of Athens: "Great is your glory if you fall not below the standard which nature has set for your sex, and great also is hers of whom there is least talk among men whether in praise or in blame."[19] The only public role allowed to women was participation in funerals, certain state festivals, and religious rituals. Some festivals, such as the cult of Demeter (goddess of agriculture), were reserved for women only. In fact, women participated in more than forty cults in Athens during the 5th Century BCE. These responsibilities provided a few women with considerable prestige and a greater freedom to move about in public. Very poor citizen women sometimes worked outside the home as small shop keepers in the market, but this was not considered respectable or proper.

Marriage was arranged by men and basically consisted of the transfer of legal wardship of the woman from the father to the husband. In this sense women were very close to being chattel property. A woman's father (or uncle or brother if the father was dead) normally betrothed her to another man's son while she was still a very young child. The marriage itself took place soon after puberty when the girl was in her early teens. Hesiod advised a man to marry in his thirtieth year to a virgin in her fifth year of puberty. The power imbalance inherent in such an age difference was obvious and intentional. The woman's father provided her with a dowry, which was her contribution to the new household. The dowry could be inherited by her children and was intended to provide her with a livelihood in case of divorce. Thus the husband, although he took possession of the dowry, was legally responsible to preserve its value. If the woman was from a rich family, the dowry might consist of income-earning property.

Divorce was almost completely under the control of the husband. He could evict his wife from his house on any whim. While the wife could—in theory—leave her husband's guardianship and return to her male relatives, the husband could prevent this by keeping her confined to his house. Adultery was basically a female crime and carried a harsh penalty, although male adulterers were also punished. Men, on the other hand, had a great deal of sexual freedom. They could have sexual relations with slaves, concubines, prostitutes, and willing pre-adult male citizens. Strangely, in Sparta adultery was permitted when a woman was childless if the aim of the liaison was to produce children and the husband gave his consent.

On the surface, then, Greek paternalism appears to be a system to control human reproduction and the distribution of property. However, beneath the surface of Greek culture there lurked a deep-seated fear of women and their power of fertility. Hesiod revealed this fear when he related

---

19. See Cleve, *Early Western Civilization Source Readings* (2002), Kendall/Hunt, Dubuque, p. 134.

the myth of Pandora,[20] the first woman, who brought all manner of evil to mankind. But man cannot avoid the "beautiful evil," because if he refuses to marry in order to avoid the "troublesome deeds of women," he will reach old age without children to care for him, and after he dies his property will be divided among his relatives.

Greek Colonization

During the Archaic Age the Greeks colonized the coast of Anatolia, Cyprus, parts of the coast of Africa west of Egypt (they even planted a trading post in the Nile Delta), southern Italy, most of Sicily, parts of Corsica and Sardinia, parts of the coasts of Spain and southern France, and about 90%

---

20. To punish mankind for accepting fire from Prometheus, Zeus ordered Hephaestus to create the first woman. She was named "Pandora," to mean "All Gifted One" because each of the gods left her with something. Athena gave her intelligence, talent, manners, and clothed her in fine garments. Aphrodite gave her the grace and beauty of a goddess. Other gods gave her gold and crowned her head with flowers. But Hermes, the last to go, added her speech, and put in a shameless mind and a deceitful nature. And so she was given a trait no other mortal had ever possessed: Curiosity.

Before sending Pandora to Earth, Zeus asked Epimethus, lord of Earth's creatures, if he would accept a new mortal named Pandora to help with mankind's work. Epimethus had been warned by his brother Prometheus to accept no gifts from Zeus. But Epimethus gave the warning no heed once he saw Pandora, and agreed to accept her.

And so Pandora and her virtues and vices were sent to Earth. Once there, the messenger gods Iris and Hermes brought to Pandora a large box. Pandora was asked to watch it until they returned and warned sternly against opening the box under any circumstances.

But Pandora's curiosity got the best of her. She fretted for days, but finally gave in to temptation, and thought it would not hurt to take a peek. As soon as she cracked open the box, out flew evil, disease, death, sickness, hatred, war, crime, sorrow, and all other ills that afflict people. With his usual good hindsight, Epimethus told Pandora to close the box, and she obeyed, trapping hope within.

Before Pandora opened the box, Civilization had passed through two ages: the Golden Age (a time of peace) when laws, judges, and the plow were not needed; and the Silver Age (a time of plenty) when Zeus made winter and mortals began to plow the earth and plant their food. After Pandora's box was opened, the Bronze Age (a time of crime) began. Mortals made weapons and property was divided up between people. Some got more, some got less, and inequality and injustice were widespread. During the Bronze Age, crime became so terrible that Zeus decided to walk the Earth to see what motivated humans to commit crimes against other humans. Zeus went in the guise of a mortal, but gave a sign that a god had come to Earth.

The Arcadian King Lycaon mocked Zeus, laughed at prayers and all those who made sacrifices to the gods. To insult Zeus all the more, Lycaon killed a fellow human, cooked him in a stew and planned to feed him to Zeus. Lycaon was angry with Zeus because his daughter, the Arcadian nymph Callisto, had been turned into a bear by Zeus' wife Hera (Hera was in turn angered that the nymph had given birth to Zeus' son). While on Earth, Zeus was so distressed by Lycaon that he condemned him to roam the world with wolves. He then asked the other gods on Mount Olympus for permission to destroy the rest of humankind for their evil ways, and the gods agreed. The world would be destroyed by flood.

Two good people, Deucalion, son of Prometheus, and Pyrrha, the red-haired daughter of Pandora, were spared by the gods and put on a boat. After the flood, their boat came to rest on the twin peaks of Mount Parnassus—The center of the earth. There they consulted the oracle of Themis, daughter of Heaven and Earth (Uranus and Gaea), keeper of the scales of justice and protector of oppressed people. Themis told them: "Cover your heads and throw your mother's bones behind you."

Deucalion and Pyrrha were befuddled. They prayed. They thought. Then Deucalion realized that their mother was the Earth. Her bones were stones. So they threw stones over their shoulders, and the stones lost their hardness and took on the form of humans. The stones Deucalion threw turned into men, while the stones thrown by Pyrrha turned into women. In this way, the population was replenished. From their own son Hellen, all Greek tribes descended.

Pyrrha also found Pandora's Box. She opened it and let hope out of the box. Once again, there was hope for humankind.

of the coast of the Black Sea. The Greeks did not venture very far inland in most of these areas—Sicily and Italy are exceptions—but confined their settlements to the coastal area. By the time this movement ran its course, more Greeks lived outside the Greek homeland than inside. This had a permanent and fundamental effect on the cultural patterns of the Mediterranean and Black Sea basins.

The motives for sending out colonies were numerous and complex. The earliest colonies were planted by Greeks migrating across the Aegean escaping from the invading Dorians. These refugees were some of the wealthiest and best educated of the mainland Greeks. This, in some measure, accounts for the fact that for several centuries the Anatolian area, known as Ionia, was the most progressive and cultured area of Greece. For example, Ionia was the birthplace of philosophy. Beginning around 750 BCE, however, the Greeks ventured further afield. One motive for this new wave of migration was the increasing population pressure within the mainland poleis, due to the limited amount of arable land. Greece is not agriculturally rich. The soil is thin and rocky. Over 80% of the land is mountainous and unsuitable for agriculture, so when the population increased, as it did consistently during the Archaic Age, one answer to the problem is to export the surplus population. The revival of trade was yet another stimulus to migration. Some Greeks with commercial interests became residents of foreign countries quite early. The colony of Naucratis in the Nile Delta was primarily a trading post. In fact most of the coastal colonies were active traders with the native peoples among whom they settled. In addition to the demographic and commercial motives, much of the impetus to migrate was driven by the Greek love of adventure, which is reflected in the stories and mythology of the Archaic Age.

The temptation to analogize Greek colonialism with the colonial empires of modern Europe must be rejected. Greek colonies from their inception were politically sovereign and economically independent. It is true, however, that colonies normally retained cultural and emotional ties with the "mother city" (metropolis in Greek), and on a larger scale the Greek peninsula was considered the ancient homeland of all Greeks.

Very little is known about the actual process by which the new cities were established. At the beginning of the enterprise a leader was selected who became known as the ktistes, or "founder." Homer described the process: "So the founder led them away, settling them in a place called Scheria, far from the bustle of men. He has a wall constructed around the town center, built houses, erected temples for the gods, and divided the land." Often the colonizers were able to settle on vacant land, but sometimes had to fight for the land for their new polis. Since the expeditions were apparently made up of males only, they had to send back to the metropolis later for wives or more often acquired wives from the locals through negotiation or violent kidnapping.

One important document does survive, an inscription from Cyrene, a colony on the North African coast, called the "Pact of the founders." It indicates that population pressure caused at least some Greek cities to coerce a portion of the people to set out on colonizing expeditions. The Pact is a decree of the assembly of Thera which authorizes the establishment of Cyrene on the north coast of Africa:

> Since Apollo has given a spontaneous prophesy to Battus and the Theraeans ordering them to colonize Cyrene, the Theraeans resolve that Battus be sent to Libya as leader and king: that the Theraeans sail as his companions: that they sail on fair and equal terms, according to family; that one son be conscripted from each family; that those who sail be in the prime of life; and that, of the rest of the Theraeans, any free man who wishes may sail. If the colonists establish a settlement, any of their fellow citizens who later sails to Libya shall have a share in citizenship and honors and shall be allowed a portion of the unoccupied land. But if they do not establish

the settlement and the Theraeans are unable to help them and they suffer inescapable troubles up to five years, let them return from that land without fear to Thera, to their possessions and to be citizens. But he who is unwilling to sail when the city sends him shall be liable to punishment by death and his goods shall be confiscated. And he who receives or protects another, even it be his own son or brother, shall suffer the same penalty as the man unwilling to sail.[21]

Archaic Art

The art of the Dark Age was based on abstract geometric shapes. Around the end of the 8th Century BCE, human and animal figures were introduced—the first glimmer of the humanism which would sweep through Greek culture during the Classical Age. There was an enthusiasm for hybrid monsters, like sphinxes and griffins, chimaeras and centaurs, as well as plant ornamentation based on the lotus bud, the tree, and the palmette. Much of this was due to the influence from the East, a result of the trading and colonizing activities of the period.

Figure 5.10: Left, "Kouros from Anavysos," National Archaeological Museum, Athens; Right, "Peplos Kore," Acropolis Museum, Athens.

21. Crawford, C. and Whitehead, D., *Archaic and Classical Greece: A Selection of Ancient Sources in Translation* (1983), Cambridge, No. 16B.

Cities like Corinth grew rich from trading in art-objects, especially painted vases, which flooded the markets of the Mediterranean basin. It was the Corinthian artists who invented the black figured style, consisting of painted figures, usually in black pigment, against the natural clay background. This style gained tremendous vogue throughout the ancient world. Athens came later to the art scene, but developed techniques and skills that allowed it to dominate the market within a generation.

By the end of the 7th Century BCE, marble sculpture began to appear in two major motifs: the *kouros* (the "youth"), and the *kore* (the "maiden"). The sculpture of the Archaic Age represents state sponsored subjects designed to decorate temples or other religious buildings or memorials to the memory of deceased individuals. Obviously the memorials represent only the aristocrats who could afford such displays. In creating a statue the Archaic artist followed a rigid formula governing the relationship between the different parts of the body—almost transforming the human form into a geometric pattern. The frontal pose, the arms close to the body with hands at the hips, the special attention to the detail of the hair, the mysterious "archaic smile" are all easily recognizable characteristics of the Archaic style. Archaic Greek art was obviously influenced by ancient Egyptian art, as a result of commercial contact between the two cultures, but there is also a strong influence of the geometric style of the preceding Dark Age. But Archaic art also looked forward. Although it was produced primarily in the service of religion, there was a underlying secular influence, because the Greeks did not concern themselves with the afterlife, but gave their attention to living the "good life" here on earth. The humanism that would sweep through the Greek culture of the Classical Age was already an influence in Archaic art. It is true that the *kouros* and the *kore* statues are not humanistic in their fundamental conception—their monumental stance seems anchored in eternity—but that archaic smile seems to reveal the potential of the coming golden age of humanism. When we see the wonderfully humanistic achievements of Classical art, we are not surprised that it all began with these Archaic statues.

6

The Classical Age

The Classical Age (500–323 BCE) was the apex of ancient Greek civilization. Suddenly, at the beginning of the 5th Century BCE, Greek culture exploded in an outburst of creativity. In every field of human endeavor the Greeks made far reaching and fundamental contributions. Philosophers developed the formal tools of logic and reason that are still used today to probe and seek understanding of our physical universe. The first tentative movement toward a true science occurred during this period—especially in the field of medicine and at the Lyceum, the academy established by Aristotle at Athens. At the same time, these philosophers came more closely to grips with the ethical problems of human life. In the field of literature, playwrights wrote dramas that still speak to us today and historians set the standards for that genre that modern historians still strive toward. In addition, the great triumphs of Classical art, for which the Greeks are so famous, were the products of this period. Greek painting, sculpture, and architecture enshrined the standards of harmony, proportion, and beauty that are the envy of all subsequent ages. Thus, the term "golden age" is perhaps an understatement when applied to Classical Greece. Every society experiences its golden age, but of the Greeks, during this short time of less than two centuries, it can truly be said: nothing like them ever was or is ever likely to be again. The Greek Classical Age is simply unique in the history of Western Civilization.

The Political Structure of the Polis

The emergence of the polis during the Archaic Period as the vehicle of self-government was discussed in chapter 5. Originally the poleis was ruled by kings, but by the end of the Archaic period most Greek states were self-governing. The constitutional structure of the polis typically consisted of three major elements: an assembly of all male citizens; a board of elected administrative magistrates; and an advisory council of community elders. However, the Greeks developed almost endless variations of this structure and each polis was, in a sense, a unique interpretation of this basic model. Unlike the large bureaucratic monarchies of the East, each polis was a small state ruled by its male citizen class, ranging from a few hundred to tens of thousands, which was tied to a specific territory. Most poleis were tiny indeed when compared to modern states. Recent estimates are that there were over one thousand poleis in the ancient Greek world, after the colonization of the Archaic Period had run its course. This means that there were far more sovereign states in ancient Greece than in all of the world today. We do not even know the names of the vast majority, and their histories are, of course, lost forever.

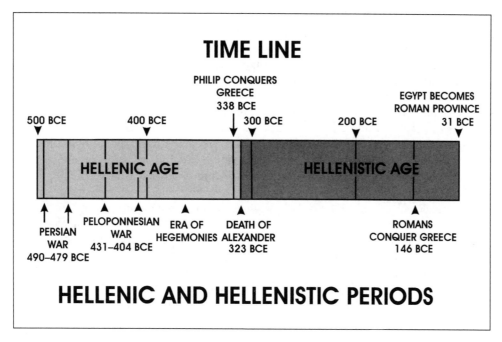

TIME LINE

HELLENIC AND HELLENISTIC PERIODS

Figure 6.1

The citizens of the polis assembled periodically to vote on major issues and to elect officials. The role of the assembly tended to grow as the city states developed, and by 600 BCE, steering committees, or councils, appeared, whose job it was to prepare the agenda of items to be considered at assembly meetings. Usually, the early councils represented the aristocracy and in many cases acted as the administrative branch of the government between meetings of the assembly. The members of the councils were normally chosen for life. Also, in the early polis, membership in the assembly was limited to landholders or otherwise restricted. In reality it was almost always the aristocracy that replaced the monarchy, and consequently the reigns of the government fell naturally into their hands.

Gradually, the monarchal power of the king was broken down and split into separate responsibilities which ordinary citizens could perform on a temporary basis. In most cases these elected officials served for one-year terms. However, one of these elected officials bore the title of "king" in order that he might properly conduct the religious rites on behalf of the state. In other words, the title of king became a religious title and by historical times it really meant little more than the chief priest of the state religion. Another of these officials commanded the army. Yet another conducted the civil affairs of the government, while others directed the judicial machinery and supervised economic regulations, such as the inspection of the scales used by merchants, to ensure honest measurements.

In the earliest stages of this evolution from kingship to constitutional government, the Greek polis was not a democracy, and indeed many poleis never became full democracies, but nevertheless the Greeks held political ideals which are of great significance. Aristotle stated these ideals most clearly when he said; "A state aims at being, as far as possible, a society composed of equals and peers."[1] This is quite startling when compared to the class structure of other ancient societies. This

---

1. See, Aristotle, "Politics," in Cleve, Robert, *Early Western Civilization, Source Reading* (2002), Kendall/Hunt Publishing Company, pp. 275–309.

kind of an attitude has prevailed in only very rare circumstances during the entire history of humanity. Historically speaking, it is abnormal, it is a kind of temporary aberration. Will the modern era of democracy and self-government, which actually prevails in only a small minority of the modern world's states, be more permanent? It is impossible to know, but a careful reading of history does not provide much confidence for an affirmative answer.

A contributing factor to this attitude was the fact that the Greek world, by comparison to the other societies we have studied, was a simple world. It has been observed that if rocks and clay were valuable substances, Greece would be wealthy beyond the imagination, but they are not valuable and Greece is a land poor in resources. The rich and the poor were not sharply distinguished, and both the lower and the upper classes felt themselves bound together by an overwhelming sense of community. While this goes a long way to explain the feeling of equality among the population of the polis, keep in mind that all these statements about equality and democracy are made concerning only the male citizens of the polis. At least one half of the free population was made up of women, who were considered politically incompetent. Every polis included in its population a percentage of aliens, who were immigrants or descendents of immigrants, and had no political rights. Somewhere between 1/4 and 1/3 of the people were slaves, who had no rights of any kind. At best, then, only a small percentage, probably less than a quarter of the population of the average polis were male citizens who participated in its political life. Still, even considering all these qualifications, what the Greeks accomplished was unprecedented and nothing like it had been seen before in the entire history of humanity—or, with very rare exceptions, since.

Another element central to the polis was justice, and this meant the rule of law over the arbitrary actions of the state officials. By the middle of the 7th Century BCE the Greek city-states were beginning to commit their law codes to writing and to place them on public display, so that all citizens could see exactly what their rights and duties were.

Finally, there were two more qualities necessary for the system of Greek city-states to function. One was local patriotism, which expressed itself in the worship of state heroes and the veneration of one great god or goddess as the patron of the polis. The most prominent example of this is the worship of the goddess Athena at Athens. The other quality was the burden laid on the citizen to defend and maintain their local city-state. As Aristotle put it: "We must regard every citizen as belonging to the state." This statement has the ring of modern nationalism to it. However, today we turn that idea over, and say "The state belongs to every citizen." But whichever side of the coin you view, the ideal is the same, and as the city-state system developed in ancient Greece, the family, clan, and other social groups lost much of their power to the state. In the ancient polis, just as in the modern nation-state, the ties that bind the individual to the state are more basic than the ties that bind him to his family or friends.

There is another aspect of Greek culture that made the polis system possible. When we think of ancient Greece, we tend to think first of philosophy, art, poetry, and beautiful architecture. Surely the Greeks made priceless contributions to all these fields, but Greece was also the birthplace of the Western art, or science, of warfare—a factor that has been at least as important as philosophy and art in shaping the history of Western Civilization. Before the Greeks, armies consisted of individual hordes of soldiers, and when these hordes met in battles the soldiers engaged in individual duels. If the Greeks had depended on this form of defense, they almost certainly would not have survived. In the 8th Century BCE the Greeks abandoned single chaotic combat and adopted an organized formation of infantry known as the phalanx. The phalanx was designed to operate as a disciplined, cohesive unit. It was composed of heavily armored soldiers known as hoplites. Each hoplite carried a long iron-tipped spear and a shield. The shield was large enough to partially protect the man to his left. As the phalanx advanced the hoplites would maintain a steady pace and slowly begin to quicken their pace as they approached the enemy line. The momentum they gained would turn the phalanx into a battering ram as they crashed into the enemy. As men in the front rank fell those from the rear would take their places.

To make it possible for a large group of soldiers to operate as one disciplined unit, close order drill was employed. Close order drill may seem like a small invention, but the difference between a mob and a disciplined military unit is a difference in power of many magnitude. In fact close order drill and military discipline eventually allowed the Greeks to defeat Persian armies that outnumbered them by as much as ten to one. It should also be noted that in many coastal states, the navy became an important part of the military establishment. The Greeks made great contributions to the development of warships, which were rowed by members of the lower class of citizens, who need not be wealthy enough to own the expensive armor necessary to serve as a hoplite in the army.

Sparta and Athens

So far we have discussed the polis only in general terms. The problem with a generalization is that because it must be constructed in a way to include all possible situations, it can never completely describe any specific situation. And so when put to a practical test, generalizations don't always work very well. For that reason, it has been said: "all generalizations are false, including this one."

The traditional method for introducing the student to Greek political history and political science is to compare and contrast the constitutions of Sparta and Athens. This method has some drawbacks, however. One thing that must be kept in mind, is that these two states, Sparta and Athens, were not typical. Indeed, an important reason that they are studied so intently is that they represent the two extreme poles of Greek political ideals and development. There were more than a thousand city-states in ancient Greece, but of them all, Sparta and Athens were the most atypical, the most extreme examples of militarism and democracy that the Greeks were able to achieve. Furthermore, they were the two superpowers of the Greek world. They possessed the largest populations, fielded the most powerful military organizations, and wielded the greatest economic power of all the Greek states. And finally, they were bitter enemies almost from the beginning to the end of their history. All the other poleis, in size, power, social structure, and political organization, fell somewhere between the extremes of Spartan militarism and Athenian democracy.

Sparta

Sparta was the leader of the Dorian states of the Peloponnesus, the peninsula which forms the western half of the Greek mainland. Sparta achieved greatness by imposing upon itself a rigid communistic political system that made every citizen the unflinching servant of the state.

Sparta set the military standard for all of Greece. Its militarism was deeply rooted in its history, an outgrowth of a problem common to all the Greek poleis: overpopulation. Instead of sending out colonies to relieve the population pressure, however, Sparta resorted to imperialism and conquered their neighbors to their west, the Messenians, and divided their land among the Spartan warriors. The Messenians became state slaves, called helots, and were forced to work the land to support their Spartan masters. Since the helots outnumbered the Spartans by about ten to one, every able-bodied Spartan was required to spend his life in constant military training and activity in order to maintain control over them.

At the conclusion of the Messenian conquest, the Spartans dispatched a group of malcontents to southern Italy to found the colony of Tarentum. This was the only colony they ever sent out. Thus, the Messenian conquest meant that, in the long run, Sparta was denied the enlarged intellectual horizons which came from contact with the outside world through colonization. But Sparta was not yet isolationist. In fact, at the beginning of the 7th Century BCE Sparta was in some ways the cultural leader of Greece. Poets from all over Greece came to Laconia[2] to sing their songs, and their poetry gives us glimpse of the contentment, peace, and love of pleasure that marked Spartan life of the time. Laconian pottery also illustrates the fine taste of the early Spartans. Sparta even had commercial relations with the Greeks of Asia Minor.

At this point there was no real reason why Sparta should not develop much as the other Greek states did. To be sure, the helot system and the withdrawal from colonization set it somewhat apart, but every Greek state had a certain individuality. Then in the second half of the 7th Century BCE, a serious, though ultimately unsuccessful, revolt of the Messenians changed the whole course of Sparta's history. Their near defeat frightened the Spartans into accepting far reaching reforms in the government of their state. In order to maintain control over a subjugated people at least ten times their size, they adopted an extremely strict constitution, which was later attributed to a legendary lawgiver named Lycurgus.[3] This constitution established a government that was in reality an oligarchy, that is rule by a small aristocratic group, but was tempered by a measure of democracy. Basically, there were four major elements of the Lycurgan constitution: the kings, the council, the assembly, and the magistrates.

Sparta always retained two kings, a survival from prehistoric times and an indication of the depth of Spartan conservatism. Although the duel kingship was retained, by historical times their role was mostly ceremonial. They did have certain minor religious and judicial roles, but their most important function was to command the army when it was dispatched outside Spartan territory. The origin of the duel kingship, unique to Sparta, is unknown. Of course, the most logical explanation is that in unrecorded pre-history, the Spartan state was created by the union of two independent states, and the new state retained both royal families. But this is pure speculation and no evidence exists to either support or refute it.

The ruling circle also included a board of five magistrates, called *ephors* ("supervisors"), who were elected annually by the citizen assembly. In theory, any Spartan male citizen could become a candidate for the office of ephor, but as in any society, they almost always came from the upper class. The ephors formed an executive body which administered domestic affairs and also had considerable influence over foreign policy as well. They initiated legislation, summoned the assembly and the council into session and wielded both police and judicial powers. The *gerousia*, or council of elders, consisted of the two kings as permanent members and twenty eight other men chosen for life by the assembly. Theoretically any citizen over the age of sixty qualified for election to the council. The *gerousia* prepared the agenda for the assembly, tried criminal cases and assisted the magistrates in the conduct of public affairs. Finally, the fourth element of the government was the assembly, or the *appella,* and it was made up of all male citizens over the age of 30. The assembly elected magistrates, decided questions concerning the succession of kings, and accepted or rejected measures put before it by the magistrates or the council. But the assembly

---

2. The territory of the Spartan state is called Laconia or Lacedaemon and in ancient texts the Spartans are often called "Lacedaemonians" or "Laconians."

3. Described by Plutarch, "Lycurgus," in Cleve, Robert, *Early Western Civilization, Source Reading* (2002), Kendall/Hunt Publishing Company, pp. 154–167.

had no right to initiate proposals or to debate any question, its function was strictly to listen and to vote. Furthermore, Plutarch tells us that the council could change the vote of the assembly "if it voted crookedly."

In foreign affairs, Sparta very early tried to dominate the entire Peloponnesus through conquest. Now that Sparta had turned its back on commerce and given its entire attention to the perfection of its army, there was no reason why the army should not be used to obtain more territory. But although they could always win victories on the battlefield, the Spartans did not have the manpower and resources to sustain control over all of the Peloponnesus. So they had to content themselves with a permanent alliance. About 530 BCE Sparta established an alliance system, called the Peloponnesian League, made up of all the Peloponnesian states, except Argos—something analogous to NATO during the Cold War of the late 20th Century. Sparta did not actually dominate the league but was unquestionably its leader. Each state signed a separate treaty with Sparta, in which both states promised "to have the same friends and enemies."

The Peloponnesian League had no formal constitution. In its role as the central and leading member of the league, Sparta called meetings at its own convenience. Obviously a meeting would be called to gain the support of their allies before embarking on a war. On such occasions an important ally might veto the Spartan proposal and thwart Sparta's will. Usually, however, the Spartans were strong enough to have their way and often they entered a war and called upon their allies for troops without even holding a meeting. The league was not an empire and no tribute was assessed, but in wartime, financial contributions might sometimes be "requested." In theory Sparta did not manage the internal affairs of its allies, but it usually insisted on oligarchic regimes with which it felt comfortable. Sparta did not trust either tyrannies or democracies.

Domestically, Sparta was a military state to its very core, indeed it was a permanently mobilized army. Every Spartan male devoted most of his life to military service. Training began in childhood at the age of seven. From that time until he was an old man, the Spartan male lived and ate in the military barracks. Military training and discipline were severe. Young boys were required to go without food and shelter for long periods and received floggings for even a minor breach of discipline—sometimes so severe that they proved fatal. The severe training produced soldiers who possessed strength, agility, and endurance. It also fashioned a quiet, modest personality that has no counterpart in modern life.

Spartan girls were also given rigorous training so that they would bear healthy children and be able to manage their husbands' affairs while they were off on military duty—which was most of the time. Because of this, Spartan women were far more independent and held a far more responsible position in society than women of any other polis. They played an important role in many religious festivals. Through dowries and inheritances they gradually accumulated property, and by the late 5th Century BCE they owned about two fifths of the land, according to Aristotle. While the land which each Spartan received from the state was inalienable, other lands could be bought and sold. Nevertheless, differences in wealth were of little importance in Sparta because everyone lived in a socialistic community that sacrificed the individual to the interests of the state.

Spartan men were not permitted to marry until late in their twenties and even then they could not live at home. In Sparta there was nothing resembling what we would call a "normal" family life. The family was almost totally surrendered to the state. Since spending time with their wives was considered unmanly, a man saw his wife only by going through an elaborate and silly ritual of sneaking away from the barracks late at night and returning in the morning before the other soldiers were awake. In fact, the Spartan citizen never had the enjoyment of a home but spent his entire life on drill and living in the barracks. He joined a *syssition* (military mess) of about fifteen members. Each member contributed his share of barley, wine, cheese, figs, and meat, which made up the "Spartan" diet of the soldier. At age thirty he became eligible for membership in the assembly and to fill the elected offices that did not require a higher age. The citizen passed the remainder of his life living in the barracks and eating in the mess. Indeed, military campaigns seemed a relief from the labors of peace. One is forced to contemplate who was actually more oppressed, the helot or the Spartan citizen. Sparta will stand forever as an example of the terrible price exacted upon the master as well as the slave in such societies.

One might expect that Spartan women would be alienated by all of this. Their children were torn from them at an early age and they lived their lives without male companionship. But the Spartan women, we are told, enthusiastically supported this military system. It is said that as their men marched off to war, the women would gather along the streets or lean out of the upper story windows and shout, "Return victorious or return on your shield!" Then there is the story of the young boy who asked his mother why the Spartan sword was so short and his mother replied that the Spartan man adds length to his sword by taking two steps forward. However, it is important to remember that we have no testimony whatever directly from the women themselves. All we know about Spartan women is written by the men. We have not one utterance directly from an ancient Spartan woman. And we know, when men write about women, much of what they say is pure fantasy.

In the final analysis, whatever one may think of this rigidly militaristic regime of Sparta, it was successful in preserving itself—it changed little throughout its history. And it was greatly admired by other Greeks, though not quite enough, it seems, for them to imitate it. Philosophers like Plato admired the stability and patriotism of the Spartans. Plato's *Republic*, which attempts to define the perfect polis, is patterned to a large extent after the Spartan constitution. But the admiration of Plato must be balanced by the reality that citizens comprised only about seven percent of the population. For every "free" Spartan, ten to fifteen helots lived in utter subjugation. And consider the life of the Spartan citizen: was he really less subjugated than those he oppressed? Did the toil of all those helots really enrich his life in any significant way, either materially or spiritually? History does not answer these questions, history simply describes and records the events and circumstances. Each student must answer these questions for him or herself.

Athens

Athens became the most radical democracy[4] of ancient Greece, or indeed, of any age. Why Athens became a democracy is as important as why Sparta became a military state, but more complicated. The evolution from monarchy to democracy was a long process, and the Athenians set out along that road with no conscious knowledge of their ultimate destination. One basic factor determining the early direction of Athenian development was certainly the fact that Athens, unlike Sparta, did not inherit the curse of serfdom, with all its hatred and fear. The horizons of the Athenians were, from the beginning, more open and tolerant. The route from monarchy to democracy led Athens through aristocracy, then a period of lawgivers who attempted to avert revolution, and ultimately through revolution and tyranny, before they reached their final destination of democracy. There was a definite reason why the Athenians advanced to each new stage in the journey. The initiating motive in each case was the failure of the existing regime. The Athenians pressed on until they finally reached an objective which they had not originally envisioned.

---

4. Democracy, from the Greek *demokratia*, from *demos* (the people) + *kratia* (to rule, to be strong). The form of government in which the sovereign power resides in the people as a whole and is exercised by them either directly or by officers elected by them.

Athens entered the Archaic Period as a typical polis, ruled by a basileus, or king. Unlike Sparta, however, its early history was not dominated by aggression against its neighbors. The peninsula of Attica is large, at least by Greek standards, and forms a natural unit. But this alone did not guarantee unity in ancient Greece. For example, just north of Attica lies the large and lush plain of Boeotia, which would also seem to form a single natural unit, yet it was divided into dozens of poleis. Therefore, one of the critical aspects of Athenian pre-history is the gradual growth of sense of community among the inhabitants of Attica between 1000 and 700 BCE. For some unexplainable reason, the people of the entire Attica peninsula were willing to transfer their allegiance to the city of Athens—even though they remained in their villages, they came to think of themselves as Athenians. There was never any such thing as an "Attican." Unification on this scale is unprecedented anywhere else in ancient Greece. This extraordinary feat is attributed to the hero Theseus, the legendary king of archaic Athens.

Like other Greek states in the archaic Period, Athens had a king, a council of elders (*Areopagus*), and an assembly of the people (*ecclesia*). We know the king completed the process of unification of Attica by 700 BCE, but the process is obscure to us. Sometime after this, the power of the king gradually faded and Athens entered a period of rule by the aristocracy. Again the process is obscure, but it was certainly evolutionary, not violently revolutionary. During the 8th Century BCE, the leading families became wealthy from the cash crops of wine and olive oil—products which require wealth and large estates to get started. As their wealth increased the aristocrats stripped the king of power until the Athenian government became an oligarchy.[5] The king's power was first reduced by appointment of a *polemarch*, or commander-in-chief of the army. In the early 7th Century BCE, the office of archon was created and this left the kingship so little power that the office became elective: the *archon basileus*, or king archon, was concerned only with religious matters. In other words, the office of the king was reduced to the high priest of the state religion, who was elected for a one-year term. Eventually, nine archons ("rulers") were elected annually to perform the functions of the king. But the archons were always under the authority of the Council of the Areopagus, the aristocratic council of elders. It became the practice for the archons to become members of the Areopagus after completion of their one-year term in office and to serve in that capacity for life. During this period the *ecclesia*, or the assembly of the citizens, had few powers. It did elect the archons, an important function, but only from those men "suited" for the office by birth and wealth, and the Areopagus had the right to scrutinize the candidates. Although the assembly was consulted on important matters, such as war and peace, public policy lay with the archons and the Areopagus. The assembly met infrequently at best and had only a minor influence on the conduct of the government. Nevertheless, the very existence of the assembly was a vague recognition of the people's sovereignty.

Aristocratic rule, however, was inherently unstable because while it produced great wealth for the aristocrats it created unbearable poverty and suffering for the common people. The poor farmers, who possessed only small plots of land, could produce only grain. But their land was poorly managed—crops were not rotated to allow fields to lay fallow—and the soil began to deplete. At the same time wheat began to be imported and the price dropped dramatically. The big landowners became even wealthier due to exports on wine and oil, while the small farmers

---

5. Oligarchy, from the Greek *oligarchia*, "government in the hands of the few." A form of government in which the power is confined to a few persons or families; also the body of persons composing such a government.

sank ever deeper into debt. Farmers began to sell their children, their wives, even themselves into slavery. Athens thus became a powder keg ready to explode. The population was ready to support a tyranny[6] if it promised to alleviate their suffering.

The first attempt at tyranny was a failure. In 632 BCE, a high ranking aristocrat named Cylon seized the Acropolis and attempted to make himself tyrant. It is possible that he had radical tendencies that appealed to the poor farmers and he must have counted on their support. But the government brought in the army and besieged the conspirators, who took refuge on the alter of Athena. The government promised the conspirators their lives if they would surrender. However, as they were descending from the Acropolis, the archon Megacles and his supporters suddenly fell upon them and slaughtered them. Megacles belonged to the famous Alcmaeonidae family and for this grave sacrilege the entire family was cursed[7] and exiled. The most important aspect of this event was that it profoundly increased the mistrust of the people for the aristocrats. The average farmer was now radicalized and ready to support revolution.

The privileged few had been making all the decisions for too long. By 621 BCE the people were no longer willing to accept the arbitrary, oral rules of the aristocrats. Draco was therefore commissioned to codify and write down the laws. Almost nothing is known about Draco and he may in fact be only a legend. The laws of Draco were uncompromisingly harsh. Indeed, the death penalty was proscribed for almost every criminal offense. When asked why he specified death as the penalty for most offenses, he replied that small offenses deserved death and he knew of no severer penalty for the great offenses. The 4th Century BCE orator Demades remarked that Draco wrote his laws in blood instead of ink. Hence the modern term "draconian" for excessively severe punishments.

A harsh law code, operating in the interests of the landowners, seemed like the final provocation to the common Athenian people. Violent revolution or civil war seemed inevitable. But history is unpredictable. In 594 BCE, the Areopagus and the people of Athens recognized the danger and agreed to hand over all power to a single individual, Solon (Fig. 6.2), to reform the government and restore justice and harmony to the state. In effect Solon became a tyrant with the mission to prevent tyranny. He was a moderately wealthy aristocrat, a merchant, poet and sage. He was already a

---

6. Tyranny (*tyrannos*, 'tyrant', was perhaps a Lydian word) is the name given to the form of monarchy set up by usurpers in many Greek states in the 7th and 6th centuries BCE. Tyranny was not a special form of constitution, or necessarily a reign of terror; the tyrant might either rule directly or retain the existing political institutions but exercise a preponderant influence over their working, and his rule might be benevolent or malevolent. Tyranny was given a bad sense especially by Plato and Aristotle, for whom it was the worst possible form of constitution.

7. The "Curse of the Alcmaeonidae." The Alcmaeonidae were a noble Athenian family, claiming descent from Alcmaeon, the great-grandson of Nestor, who emigrated from Pylos to Athens at the time of the Dorian invasion of Peloponnesus. During the archonship of the Alcmaeonid Megacles, Cylon, who had unsuccessfully attempted to make himself "tyrant," was treacherously murdered with his followers. The curse or pollution thus incurred was frequently in later years used by their enemies for political reasons. The Spartans even demanded that Pericles should be expelled as accursed at the beginning of the Peloponnesian war. After the murder of Cylon, all the members of the family went into exile, and returned in the time of Solon (594), were again exiled (538) by Peisistratus. Their great wealth enabled them during their exile to enhance their reputation and secure the favor of the Delphian oracle by rebuilding the temple of Apollo at Delphi after its destruction by fire in 548. Their importance is shown by the fact that Cleisthenes, tyrant of Sicyon, gave his daughter Agariste in marriage to the Alcmaeonid Megacles in preference to all the assembled suitors after. Under the statesman Cleisthenes, the issue of this union, the Alcmaeonids became supreme in Athens about 510 BCE. To them was generally attributed (though Herodotus disbelieves the story) the treacherous raising of the shield as a signal to the Persians at Marathon, but, whatever the truth of this may be, there can be little doubt that they were not the only one of the great Athenian families to make treasonable overtures to Persia. Pericles and Alcibiades were both connected with the Alcmaeonidae. Nothing is heard of them after the Peloponnesian war.

Figure 6.2: Solon.

successful political leader who had commanded the army in a victory over the neighboring polis of Megara. Most important, he was trusted by all segments of the population, both rich and poor. But could the divergent interests of the large landowners and the poor farmers be reconciled? Could long-standing enmities be resolved? Could harmony and stability be restored? An extraordinary act of statesmanship was required.

Solon's first act was the *seisachtheia*, the "shaking off of burdens," whereby he canceled all outstanding non-commercial debts, freed those who had fallen into slavery, and banned all future loans secured by promise of slavery. Of course some slaves had been sold abroad and he tried to repatriate as many of these as he could. However, he resisted the demand of the poor for the redistribution of the land. The cancellation of debts did not apply to commercial loans, but he initiated monetary reforms that made the loans easier to pay. His economic policy encouraged industrial development. To this end he offered citizenship to induce artisans to immigrate to Athens from other poleis. This seems natural to us in the modern world, but remember that citizenship in ancient Greece was a right of birth, and Solon's grant of citizenship to outsiders was quite innovative and controversial.

Solon's reform of the law and the constitution was also far reaching and innovative. Draco's laws regarding homicide were left substantially untouched, but other excessive penalties were lightened. He decreed an amnesty on all who had been exiled under the old laws, except those convicted of homicide and attempted tyranny. His constitutional reforms transformed Athens from an aristocracy to a timocracy.[8] He divided the Athenian population into four classes based on

---

8. Timocracy, from the Greek *timokratia* (*tim* = price, value, honor + *-kratia* = rule); government in which a certain amount of property is necessary for office.

wealth. The two wealthiest classes were allowed to serve on the Areopagus. The third class was allowed to serve on a new council of four hundred, which he created. This council was organized according to the traditional four tribes of the Athenian people; each tribe was allowed to elect one hundred representatives from this third class. The council of four hundred served as a kind of balance or check to the power of the Areopagus. The fourth class, comprised of the poorest citizens, was allowed to participate in the assembly, which voted on affairs brought before it by the council of four hundred and elected magistrates. This class also participated in a new judicial court that gradually drew civil and criminal cases out of the hands of the Areopagus. Although Solon's reforms were not intended to be democratic, they nevertheless set Athenian society on the path toward democracy.

Upon completion of his reforms Solon left Athens for ten years to allow his new system to take root and bare results. But it soon became evident that Solon's reforms were only a compromise between the powerful competing interests of the various elements of Athenian society and, like most compromises, it tried to go far enough to assuage the demands of all parties but did not go far enough to really satisfy anyone, especially the poorest citizens who had lost their land to the creditors. While they had regained their freedom they were still trapped in poverty and without land. Attica now fractured into three contending political parties, named for the regions of the country, although their interests and goals were not strictly regional. The "Coast" was made up mainly of fishermen and city craftsmen who were the newer citizens. The Coast was inclined to support Solon's arrangements. The "Plain" represented the interests of the landed aristocracy. These two parties more or less balanced each other—democratic and oligarchic. The danger to public order came from the "Hill," composed of the shepherds and the poor citizens who had lost their land. They had been bitterly disappointed in Solon's reforms, because they had expected a redistribution of land. The leadership of the Hill fell to an ambitious aristocrat named Peisistratus, a distant relative of Solon.

Peisistratus claimed his political enemies were trying to assassinate him and the assembly granted him a personal body guard. In antiquity this was always recognized as the first step toward tyranny. Sure enough, Peisistratus employed this band of armed men in 560 BCE to seize the Acropolis and make himself tyrant. Ironically, the tyranny of Peisistratus was another stage on the journey toward democracy, because it dealt a blow to the power of the aristocracy. Those old-guard aristocrats who were too proud to submit to him were forced into exile and their lands were distributed among the landless citizens. Peisistratus instituted a ten percent tax (later reduced to five percent) on all produce and used the revenue to promote both expanded commerce and improved agriculture. However, he did not change the Solon constitution in any significant way, but simply secured control of the political machinery to ensure the election of his relatives and supporters to the chief offices, through which he controlled the state. He did make important religious and cultural changes in Athenian society for the benefit of the poorest classes. The spring festival to the god Dionysus (Dionysia), which nurtured the birth of drama, and the great Panathenaic festival in honor of Athena were founded during his régime. He also invited poets and artists from all over Greece to come to Athens and thereby created a more sophisticated and dynamic society.

At the time of his death in 527 BCE, then, the tyranny of Peisistratus could have been viewed by the Athenians as a positive, even a progressive, event in their history. But unfortunately tyrants of any age have a dirty little attitude that tends to diminish any positive aspect of their regime: dynastic ambition. If Peisistratus had not attempted to perpetuate a dynasty and simply allowed Athens to revert to its established constitution, he may have been remembered as a statesman on the level of Solon, who also ruled like a tyrant but without dynastic ambitions. One of the reasons tyranny later became so distasteful to the Greeks was the fact that its power was illegitimate and only the illegitimate use of violence could dislodge it.

Thus, upon Peisistratus's death his two sons, Hippias and Hipparchus, assumed the power of the tyranny. Hippias was the elder and he managed the political affairs of the regime while Hipparchus acted as a patron of the arts. The first 13 years of their rule went well, but in 514 BCE, the assassination of Hipparchus changed the whole character of the tyranny. The murder was carried out by two aristocrats, named Harmodius and Aristogeiton, for purely personal reasons. Later, however, the murderers were celebrated in song and art as "tyrannicides" and the founders of Athenian freedom. Alas, false heroes flourish in every age. Hippias now became suspicious and vindictive—a tyrant in the worst sense of the word. The Alcmaeonidae were exiled again, and they allied themselves with the Spartans and with them they invaded Attica and besieged the tyrant on the Acropolis. Hippias agreed to go into exile in 510 BCE, thus ending the tyranny.

Athens, after two generations under the tyranny of the Peisistratidae, as the dynasty was called, was changed, politically, economically, and socially. The citizens of the Coast, artisans and fishermen, were now strong and prosperous. The people of the Hill had won their land and under the economic policy of Peisistratus had become prosperous, producing money crops like olive oil and wine for export—most grain was now imported from the Black Sea region. These elements of the population, by now the vast majority of the citizen body, had greatly benefited from the tyranny and were ready for full democracy. The question was, what the aristocracy of the Plain would do. The removal of Hippias was a victory for the exiled aristocrats, who now resumed power and began to rule with their traditional short-sighted arrogance. In 508 BCE the leader of the Plain, Isagoras, was elected to the archonship with Spartan backing, but he had not reckoned with the city population. Many of these were descendants of the new citizens who had been enfranchised under Solon and Peisistratus, and Isagoras attempted to "purify" the citizen lists by removing these people. This simply would not do and the state again seemed to be on the brink of conflict and civil war.

At this point a new leader of the people arose, strangely a member of the old-guard aristocratic Alcmaeonid family. His name was Cleisthenes and he understood clearly the necessity of preventing the majority of the people from supporting another tyranny, under which they had benefited so much in the past. A democratic government in which the people would rule themselves was the answer. Cleisthenes, a great aristocrat himself, rose above the interests and limitations of his own class and became a great statesman and the founder of Athenian democracy.

The task of bringing order and equity to the state required a radical change to the constitution. Between 508 and 502 BCE, Cleisthenes accomplished a complete reorganization of the Athenian state. He replaced the four old tribes with ten new ones. In order to assure that each tribe was representative of the national interest and not a special or regional interest, he based the membership of the tribes on residence in a local *deme*. Henceforth the deme was the unit of local self-government. The demes were the wards or townships of Attica and Athens itself. Each deme had an office where an official list of its citizens was maintained. Only registration in a deme provided citizenship, and that registration, once established, became hereditary. Even if a citizen moved away from his deme, his descendants must return there to register their citizenship when they became adults. There were about 140 demes (the exact number is uncertain). All the demes were grouped into 30 *trittyes*, a word which simply means "thirds." A *trittys* was not a political organization in itself, but only a grouping of demes. Each of the new tribes was composed of three trittyes, one from each of the three major regions of the state: the city, the plain, and the coast. Thus each tribe was a cross section of the population and represented the national interest, not a regional or other special interest group. Among other benefits, this made it impossible for any particular element, such as the aristocracy, to gain control of the state.

The old Council of Four Hundred was abolished and a new Council of Five Hundred, called the boulè was instituted in its place. The members of boulè were chosen by lot, fifty from each tribe. They served for one year. The tribe's fifty members were thus distributed randomly among its demes and were a proportional representation of the population. The boulè was the deliberative and governing body of the state. It was responsible for both domestic and foreign affairs and prepared the agenda of items to be brought before the assembly. Since a committee of five hundred is much too large to accomplish the day-to-day operation of the government, the year was divided into ten equal periods,[9] and the boulè was formed into ten committees, each consisting of the fifty members of each tribe. Each tribe's committee presided over the state during one tenth of the year and conducted the public business for that period. The sequence in which the tribes rotated each year was determined by lot. The presiding tribe was called the prytaneis, or "presidents," and the committee was called the prytany. The chairmanship of the prytany, who was in effect the head of state, was rotated among its members every twenty-four hours and the selection was determined by lot. The entire system operated by lottery. Election by lottery is the most democratic form of election that can be devised, because each citizen has an equal opportunity of being elected. Selection does not depend on wealth or birth or even on charisma or intelligence. Would any society in the world today dare to be so purely democratic?

The assembly, or *ecclesia*, met every ten days and was composed of all adult male citizens. The ecclesia was the sovereign body of the state and passed laws, declared war and peace, and made major decisions. Voting was by strict majority.

In order to ensure that no one individual would ever again gain enough power to become a tyrant, a curious device was instituted, called ostracism.[10] The ostracism was simply a method of removing from the state those politicians considered too powerful or in some other way dangerous to the state. Once a year the assembly voted on weather to hold an ostracism. It the vote was affirmative, a special session of the assembly was scheduled at which each citizen placed an ostracon (Fig. 6.3) into an urn, or ballot box, as he entered the assembly. On this ostracon, which served as a secret ballot, the citizen could inscribe the name of a person he wished to be "ostracized." The winner of this election was exiled for ten years. There was no criminal stigma attached, and the ostracized person did not loose his property or citizenship, he simply enjoyed an enforced and extended vacation. Of course, over time, the ostracism became an instrument of party warfare and intrigue. It would be interesting to observe how the popular politicians of the modern world would thrive under such a system. How many voters today would not derive great pleasure from inscribing the name of a contemporary politician on such a ballot?

What about the older elements of government? Cleisthenes did not destroy the old institutions. The Areopagus remained, but was stripped of almost all its powers and it soon faded into the background. The archons continued as the executive officials of the government, but lost most of their important functions. Eventually they too were chosen by lot and thus ceased to be the basis of political power. There was one office, however, that could not be chosen by lot. The commander of the military forces of the state must be an individual of experience, intelligence, and possess

---

9. Actually slightly unequal. It works out to five periods of thirty-six days and five periods of thirty-seven days.

10. The voting was done on *ostraca*, or potsherds, which were fragments of broken pottery.

Figure 6.3: Ostraca, or potsherds, on which voters cast their ballots for an ostracism. Seen here are votes for "Aristides," "Cimon," and "Themistocles."

leadership qualities. So a board of ten strategoi, or generals, was formed. Every year each of the ten tribes elected one of its members to this board, not by lot but by the usual election process. Whenever the army or navy were dispatched on campaign, the commanders were chosen by the assembly or the boulè from this board of ten strategoi.

The judicial process was also very democratic. The court was called the *heliaea*. Trials were held before juries numbering two hundred, five hundred, or even more, depending on the importance of the case. These juries were chosen by lot, and guilt or innocence was determined by a majority vote. Defendants in ancient Athens did not have the privilege of interviewing their prospective jurors and choosing those they believed would be favorable to their case. The student can decide for himself if the ancient or the modern system is more "fair."

This Athenian constitution was not very popular with Greek intellectuals. Plato and Socrates especially found it distasteful and deplored the state in the hands of the unlearned masses. Plato believed, quite logically, that the power of the state should be exercised by the intelligent and the well educated. How could a baker or a potter effectively rule a nation? But the constitution of Cleisthenes was extremely popular with the people and it endured to the end of Greek history as one of the most stable and successful governments of the ancient world.

The Persian Wars

When the public thinks of ancient Greece, it almost always thinks of the 5th Century BCE. When the modern media evokes an image of the ancient Greeks, it is usually the image of Socrates, Herodotus, Thucydides, or the great playwrights of the 5th Century BCE. This is the age of Greek democracy, the age of extraordinary artistic monuments, the greatest age of human achievement, the age that is proudly known as "Classical." However, like most ages of human history, the Classical Period was an age of war and conflict. Indeed the entire period can be defined by two great wars:

the Persian Wars and the Peloponnesian War. These conflicts more or less form the background or the canvas upon which this extraordinary age unfolds and they had drastically different effects on the history of Greece. The Athenians, who were the cultural and political leaders of Greece during the 5th Century BCE and part of the 4th, regarded the Persian Wars as their greatest and most characteristic moment.

In the late 6th Century BCE, the westward expansion of the mighty Persian Empire brought its armies and navies into Greece. If a disinterested observer from another world had been asked to predict the outcome of this contest between the huge, wealthy, and powerful Persian Empire and the tiny, disunited city-states of Greece, he would have said that a Greek victory was impossible. Yet in the end it was the gigantic Persian Empire that went down to defeat, and this amazing victory gave the Greeks the supreme self-confidence—some would say the overbearing arrogance—which was an important element of the spirit of classical Greece. That was the result of the first great war. But as the decades of the 5th Century wore on, the two largest states in Greece, Athens and Sparta, stood more and more at odds, until their rivalry culminated in a long and bitter conflict, called the Peloponnesian War, which ended in a devastating defeat for Athens and the disarray and discredit of the entire poleis system. By the end of the 5th Century BCE, then, somber shadows were falling across the bright glow of classical Greece.

The Revolt of the Ionians

The initial causes of the conflict between East and West can be traced back to around 560 BCE, when the Greek city-states of Asia Minor—the Ionians—were conquered by the Lydians under King Croesus. These possessions were claimed by the Persian king Cyrus when he defeated Croesus in 547 BCE. The Persians ruled the Greek cities by installing Tyrants. This made it easy to collect taxes since a single person was responsible and any hint of an uprising could be crushed quickly by force. In this way the Greeks were ruled by their own rulers and the only way the Persians would loose control was if the ruling tyrant himself rebelled. It was assumed that the tyrants had no reason to revolt since that would result in the forfeiture of their comfortable life. In other parts of the empire the Persians had had great success in ruling conquered peoples by appointing native governors. And in truth, the Greek tyrants of Asia Minor were simply viewed as governors by the Persians.

All seemed to be going well for the Persians. About 512 BCE king Darius crossed the Bosporus and subdued Thrace. This gave Persia a beachhead in Europe. Suggestions were made that the Persians invade Greece proper. Hippias, the deposed Athenian tyrant of Athens, had fled to the Persian court and he sought Persian aid to restore his régime in Athens. In reality, an invasion of Greece was a natural policy for the Persians to pursue and almost certainly would have occurred at some point. The Persian Empire lived on expansion and its ideology viewed the Persian king as the rightful ruler of the world. Greece was an urban area on the western periphery of the empire and it was only natural for the Persians to annex it.

However, the specific event that touched off the conflict was the revolt of Miletus, one of the leading Greek cities of Asia Minor. In 499 BCE, Aristagoras, the tyrant of Miletus, attempted to improve his standing with the king by persuading the Persians to conquer the Aegean island of Naxos. Unfortunately, Aristagoras quarreled with the Persian admiral and the plan failed. He now feared his Persian superiors would replace him, or worse yet put him to death, and he instigated a revolt of the Ionians, encouraging them to overthrow their tyrants and replace them with democracies. He sought aid from the mainland. First he turned to the Spartans, because they were the most powerful Greek state, but they, being basically isolationist and mistrustful of both tyrants and democracies, declined to get involved. Next he asked the Athenians for help. Since they were the first to establish settlements in Asia Minor they felt a special kinship for the Ionians, and they agreed to send a small navel force of twenty ships.

At first the rebellion seemed to go well. The Greeks marched inland in 498 BCE and burned Sardis, the old capital of Lydia and now the seat of the Persian governor (satrap) of Asia Minor. After all, the Persian Empire was large and ponderous and required time to react, but once the Empire assembled and marshaled its resources the rebellion was crushed. The Athenians seemed to have lost interest and abandoned the campaign early. The decisive battle was a navel clash fought off the coast of Miletus in 494. Herodotus says the Ionian fleet numbered 353 ships against a Persian fleet numbering 600. The Greeks might have won except that the city of Samos deserted at the critical moment. Thus, the Ionian navy was defeated and Miletus was captured and sacked. Most of its population was deported to the mouth of the Tigris River and by 493 BCE the entire rebellion was suppressed. The Greek cities of the Asia Minor coast returned to Persian control. This event is significant. For centuries the Ionians had been the standard bearers of Greek civilization. Miletus was a great city of commerce and industry and of the arts, poetry, and science. It was perhaps the most brilliant city of Greece at the time and it was suddenly blotted out of existence.

The Battle of Marathon

Now Darius wanted revenge. According to Herodotus, when he was told the Athenians had helped to burn Sardis, he said, "Who are they?" Afterward he had a slave tell him three times a day, "Remember the Athenians." The Persians also had Hippias, the former Athenian tyrant, who wanted the Persians to restore him to power. So in the summer of 490 BCE, Darius dispatched a large fleet westward across the Aegean Sea, conveying a force of infantry, cavalry, and Hippias, and waited confidently for news of the fall of Athens. Most of the islands along the way submitted. The mission was to subdue Eretria[11] and Athens and restore Hippias as the tyrant of Athens, to act as a Persian governor in the tradition of Asia Minor.

A Persian army of over 20,000 men landed on the east coast of Attica near the little village of Marathon, because Hippias believed he still had supporters in that area. The Athenians met this invasion almost entirely alone and their army numbered less than 10,000. The Spartans had promised to send aid, but not until after they completed the celebration of an important religious festival.[12] The only polis that joined the Athenians was the small state of Plataea, located just north of Attica, which sent its entire infantry force of 500 hoplites to fight beside the Athenians. It was a gesture the Athenians never forgot, and Plataea remained one of the closest friends of Athens for the rest of their history. The Greek historian Herodotus described the battle:

---

11. Back in 499 BCE, Eretria, a polis on the northern end of the island of Euboea, joined Athens and sent a small force of five ships with the Athenian expedition to aid the Ionians. Thus in 490 BCE, after a siege of six days, Eretria was betrayed by two of its people and the city was sacked and its population taken captive. The Persian fleet then proceeded to Attica.

12. Herodotus, 6.106: ". . .the Lacedaemonians resolved to send help to the Athenians; but they could not do this immediately, being loath to break their law; for it was the ninth day of the first part of the month, and they would make no expedition (they said) on the ninth day, when the moon was not full. So they waited for the full moon."

. . .the Athenians arrayed for battle as I shall show the right wing was commanded by Callimachus the polemarch; for it was then the Athenian custom, that the holder of that office should have the right wing. He being their captain, next to him came the tribes one after another in the order of their numbers; last of all the Plataeans were posted on the left wing. Ever since that fight, when the Athenians bring sacrifices to the assemblies that are held at the five-yearly festivals, the Athenian herald prays that all blessings may be granted to Athenians and Plataeans alike. But now, when the Athenians were arraying at Marathon, it so fell out that their line being equal in length to the Median [Persian], the middle part of it was but a few ranks deep, and here the line was weakest, each wing being strong in numbers.

Their battle being arrayed and the omens of sacrifice favoring, straightway the Athenians were let go and charged the Persians at a run. There was between the armies a space of not less than eight furlongs [a little less than a mile]. When the Persians saw them come running they prepared to receive them, deeming the Athenians frenzied to their utter destruction, who being (as they saw) so few were yet charging them at speed, albeit they had no horsemen nor archers. Such was the imagination of the foreigners; but the Athenians, closing all together with the Persians, fought in memorable fashion; for they were the first Greeks, within my knowledge, who charged their enemies at a run, and the first who endured the sight of Median garments and men clad therein; till then, the Greeks were frightened by the very name of the Medes.

For a long time they fought at Marathon; and the foreigners overcame the middle part of the line, against which the Persians themselves and the Sacae were arrayed; here the foreigners prevailed and broke the Greeks, pursuing them inland. But on either wing the Athenians and Plataeans were victorious; and being so, they defeated their enemies, and drew their wings together to fight against those that had broken the middle of their line; and here the Athenians had the victory, and followed after the Persians in their flight, hewing them down, till they came to the sea. There they called for fire and laid hands on the ships.

. . .In this fight at Marathon there were slain of the foreigners about 6,400 men, and of the Athenians a 192. These are the numbers of them that fell on both sides.

. . .After the full moon 2,000 Lacedaemonians came to Athens. So eager had they been to arrive in time, that they took but three days to reach Attica from Sparta. They came, however, too late for battle; yet, as they had a longing to see the Medes, they continued their march to Marathon and there viewed the slain. Then, after giving the Athenians all praise for their achievement, they departed and returned home.[13]

The Athenian commander at Marathon dispatched a runner to carry the news of victory back to Athens and, more importantly, to warn the city of the approach of the Persian fleet. The runner in fact reached Athens[14] before the Persians and when the Persian commander learned that the element of surprise had been lost, the attack was called off and the fleet returned to Persia. The moral effect of this victory can hardly be underestimated, because it demonstrated that the Greek warrior was superior to the Persian. The westward advance of the Persian Empire was halted and Greeks everywhere were infused with hope and confidence.

Intermission: Political Strife in Persia and Athens

While Marathon was seen as a great achievement by the Greeks, it was more like a mosquito bite on the skin of the empire to the Persians—just an minor irritation. After all, the Persians were the masters of most of the world. King Darius immediately began preparations for a second invasion

---

13. Herodotus, 6.112–120.

14. This event was the inspiration for the modern Marathon race which covers the exact distance from ancient Marathon to Athens.

and this time he intended to bring to bare the full resources and might of his empire against the upstart Greeks who dared to challenge the power of the Great King. However, preparations were suspended by the death of Darius in 486 BCE and some time was required for the new king, his son Xerxes, to consolidate his hold on the throne. The Persian Empire was large and ponderous and the ascension to the throne of a new king often led to rebellions and uprisings. A major rebellion in Egypt had to be put down and there was unrest in other parts of the empire. This gave Greece some time to prepare for the onslaught.

At Athens there was also a period of political strife as the aristocrats once again attempted to gain power. This resulted in further democratic reforms. At this time the archonship became an office chosen by lot, and the board of strategoi, which now became the focus of a political power at Athens, was instituted. A politician named Themistocles took advantage of this new situation to become the leader of Athens. He was a man of boundless energy, a statesman of great vision, but he was vain and jealous of the fame of others. But above all, Themistocles was a great strategist. He realized that in the present context of the Aegean area a small state like Athens could defeat a much larger land power through control of the sea. It so happened that at this time a rich vain of silver was discovered in the mines at Laurium in southern Attica. Employing his considerable skill as an orator in the assembly, he convinced the Athenians to use this new revenue to construct the largest and best trained fleet in the eastern Mediterranean Sea. This naval policy further strengthened the democratic tendencies of Athens, because it was members of the lower classes who rowed the warships and they were paid for their services. As the navy became bulwark of Athenian defense, the importance of the sailors increased and with increased importance came new political leverage and influence. The growth of the Athenian navy and the Athenian democracy fed on each other. One would not have been possible without the other.

In Persia, preparations for the conquest of Greece slowly matured. The plan was to overwhelm Greece by the force of numbers. Engineers and workmen bridged the Hellespont with boats and cut a canal across the isthmus of Mount Athos. Huge depots of food and supplies were established along the projected invasion route. Persian heralds were sent throughout Greece demanding submission, and they found many states ready to purchase safety at the price of freedom. It became clear that the responsibility for the defense of Greece would fall to the Peloponnesian League, Athens, and a few other small states. Everywhere the prevailing sentiment was a feeling of despair. Spies sent to the Persians were captured, conducted through the camp, and then released with the expectation that their report of the immense size of the Persian army would induce the Greeks to surrender without resistance. On the initiative of Themistocles, a meeting of those states willing to fight was held at Corinth in 481 BCE to discuss the common defense. Command of the joint forces on land and sea was conferred on Sparta, who was viewed as the leading military power. The coalition decided to attempt to defeat the Persian navy, because the invading army required the fleet for support, as it would be impossible for such a large force to live off the land. This strategy was undoubtedly due to the influence of Themistocles. The Spartans suggested making a stand at the Isthmus, but this was unacceptable to Athens and the other states outside the Peloponnesus, and the decision was thus made to defend Thermopylae.

The Battle of Thermopylae

Finally, early in 480 BCE, Xerxes assembled the vast resources of his empire and began his long march from central Persia across Asia Minor toward Greece. Herodotus says that this Persian army numbered 2,317,610 soldiers and that including logistics personal and camp followers it numbered more than five million. This is obviously an exaggeration. A horde of five million people marching across Asia Minor simply could not have been accomplished with ancient logistical technology-indeed, it is doubtful that such a thing would be possible even today. How large was the Persian army then? Scholars have made estimates that range from a high of one million down to a low of under one hundred thousand. The fact is that no one knows how large this army really was, but one thing is certain: it was the largest and most grandiose invasion of Europe that has ever occurred in all of history, down to the invasion of Europe across the English Channel in the Second World War. After crossing into Europe at the Hellespont on a pontoon bridge consisting of planks laid across a row of ships, the huge army marched southward along the coast of northern Greece accompanied by a large fleet of supply and war ships numbering at least seven hundred.[15]

Meanwhile, the Greeks were preparing to make their stand at Thermopylae, which means "hot gates" from its nearby sulfur springs. It was a strategic pass on the main route from northern to central Greece. Here the road passed for a distance of two miles between steep cliffs and the sea, and at one point the pass was so narrow that only four men could march through it at once. It was, therefore, an excellent place for a small army to make a stand against a larger army. There was a weakness in the plan, however, because there were other little known ways around the pass using the high ground "along the spine of the mountain," but this was not evident to an invader. The Greeks planned to delay the Persian army at Thermopylae while the Greek fleet of 300 hundred ships took up a station at Artemisium to block the Persian fleet. If the pass could be held and the vast Persian army be denied supplies, then it could not survive more than a few days because so large an army could not live off the surrounding countryside. Therefore, a force of about five thousand Greeks, including about 300 Spartans, under the command of the Spartan king Leonidas, occupied the pass to hold the enemy in check until the sea battle could be fought.

At first the plan seemed to be working. Herodotus described how day after day the Persians were repulsed from the pass with great losses, which greatly frustrated Xerxes. However, after a time, a Greek traitor, a local shepherd, informed the Persians of the little known path around the pass and led a Persian force through the hills to the rear of the Greek position and the Greeks were surrounded. There is some confusion about exactly what happened next, but all of the Greeks, except the Spartans, Thespians, and Thebans, either escaped of their own accord or were ordered to leave by Leonidas before it was too late. However, there was never any thought of surrender on the part of the Spartans. When one of the Spartans was told that on the day of the final battle the Persians would launch such a massive barrage of arrows against them that they would blot out the sun, he replied: "Good news! Then we shall have our fight in the shade." On the night before the battle, a Persian patrol observed the Greek soldiers down in the pass setting around a huge fire combing out their long hair. When the Persian commander asked his Greek guide what the soldiers were doing, he was told, "They are preparing to die tomorrow." And die they did, to the very last man. The Spartans were buried in a massive grave mound and later a grave marker was erected which read: "Traveler, when you pass Sparta, stop there for a moment and tell them, we lie here obedient to their command." This was the indomitable spirit of the ancient Greeks when they fought for their freedom over 2,400 years ago.

Meanwhile, the Greek navy at Artemisium was meeting with some early success. The Persian fleet was damaged in a storm and the Greeks were successful in some minor skirmishes. However, when they learned that the Persians had forced the pass at Thermopylae, they withdrew without fighting a decisive battle. The net result of these conflicts was a victory for the Persians but renewed hope and

---

15. Again, Herodotus exaggerates and gives us the number 1,207, which is not accepted by modern scholars.

confidence for the Greeks. As at Marathon, the Persians were revealed not to be invincible, and under more favorable circumstances the struggle might yet be successful. However, the Persians still did not realize that a strategy of depending on overwhelming numbers alone might not necessarily prevail.

The Battles of Salamis and Plataea

The Persian victory at Thermopylae was a costly one for the Persians as well as the Greeks, but now all of southern Greece lay open to the advancing army of King Xerxes and the Persian navy waited off the coast of Attica. Athens was the immediate target of the king's rage and at this moment it seemed to many that there was no chance that the Athenian people could escape total annihilation.

The Greek fleet retired to Salamis and Themistocles returned to Athens and found it full of gloom. But now an extraordinary thing happened, which demonstrates again the leadership and foresight of Themistocles. The Athenians had asked the Oracle of Apollo at Delphi for guidance and received this advice: "Trust your fate to the wooden wall." There was considerable debate about what this oracle meant. Some interpreted it to mean they should defend the Acropolis. After all there had at one time been a wooden palisade around the Acropolis. But Themistocles persuaded most Athenians that "wooden wall" referred to the wooden hulls of the ships. The Athenians abandoned their beloved city and utilized their new navy to transport the entire population of Attica to the island of Salamis and the west coast of the Peloponnesus. Now Athens was totally dependant on its navy.

The Persians laid waste to Greek countryside as they advanced toward Athens, but they found little more than a ghost town when they arrived. In a rage of revenge, Xerxes ordered the city burned to the ground. From the island of Salamis, the Athenians could see their city in flames. There was now some talk of evacuating the entire population to a new home in Italy. But Themistocles had a plan. He wanted to draw the huge Persian fleet into the narrow strait between the Attic mainland and the island of Salamis, where superior numbers would not count for much. To this end Themistocles devised a clever stratagem which lured the Persian navy to its destruction. He sent a message to King Xerxes wherein he pretended to be a traitor. He wished the king well and advised him to strike the Greeks on Salamis immediately in order to prevent them from escaping to the west.

The king was taken in by this ruse—after all he had won the Battle of Thermopylae only weeks before by relying on Greek traitors and he thought he now knew the Greeks pretty well. He ordered the large, lumbering ships of the Persian fleet into the narrow channel between Attica and Salamis. This put the Persians at a distinct disadvantage against the smaller, faster Greek ships, but Xerxes was not aware of this and he was supremely confident of victory. The Great King contemptuously arranged for a sumptuous feast to be served to him and his court on the shore of Attica overlooking the channel. Tents were set up and an elegant picnic was served, the equivalent, perhaps, of a modern tail-gate party. He expected the naval battle to provide an afternoon's entertainment for him and his court. The Greeks thought of this kind of behavior as hubris, or overblown pride, and they believed it was offensive to the gods.

The Greek sailors were now as determined to fight for their freedom as those Spartan hoplites had been at Thermopylae a few weeks earlier. The famous playwright Aeschylus fought at Salamis. Later in his life he wrote a drama about this battle, called *The Persians*, which is the only surviving Greek tragedy based on historical material. In this drama Aeschylus put the following words into the mouth of the Greek course:

Go, O sons of Greeks, set free your fatherland, your wives, your children, temples of your gods, ancestral tombs. . . Go, for now all is at stake!

Figure 6.4: The Battle of Salamis.

And so, on that faithful day of September 20th, of the year 480 BCE, the huge, ponderous, and proud Persian fleet lumbered into the narrows between Salamis and Attica and lined up along the Attic shore—from where king Xerxes watched confidently. The much smaller line of Greek ships faced them and for a while both fleets lay almost motionless in the water. Then suddenly the two fleets lunged at each other. But the large Persian ships had difficulty maneuvering in the narrow waters. The faster Greek ships skirted along the side of the Persian ships and ripped off their oars, leaving them floating helplessly in the water. Then, as panic spread through the Persian fleet, they began to ram their own ships as much as those of the enemy in their attempts to escape. Greek ships began to pull along side the floundering Persian warships and parties of Greek hoplites boarded them and slaughtered their crews. The king, from his command post on the shore, ordered his fleet to retreat, but it was too late, the victorious Greeks cut it pieces. Herodotus describes the final chaos of battle:

> When the rout of the barbarians began, and they sought to make their escape to Phaleron, the Aeginetans, waiting for them in the channel, performed exploits worthy to be recorded. Through the whole of the confused struggle the Athenians employed themselves in destroying such ships as either made resistance or fled to shore, while the Aeginetans dealt with those which endeavored to escape down the straits; so that the Persian vessels were no sooner clear of the Athenians than straightway they fell into the hands of the Aeginetan squadron.[16]

Soon the wrecks and debris of Persian ships drifted along the coast of Attica and the bloated bodies of Persian sailors became food of the Aegean fish. The battle lasted all day and long into the night. The Greeks, who had themselves suffered heavy losses, nevertheless regrouped and prepared

16. Herodotus, 8.91.

Figure 6.5: Themistocles.

to fight again the next day, but sunrise revealed that their victory was complete. The few crippled Persian ships that did escape limped back toward Asia. A dejected king Xerxes, turned over command of his army to his general, Mardonius, and made his way overland back to Persia—a Persian king had walked upon the soil of Europe for the last time.

Themistocles, always counseling action rather than reaction, urged the Greeks to sail immediately to the Hellespont and destroy Xerxes' bridge and thereby cut off the Persians' supplies. If this action had been taken it probably would have ended the war, but the idea seemed too risky for the allies, and thus the war dragged on for another year. The Persian commander, Mardonius, spent the winter in Thessaly. His plan was to divide the Greeks by making a separate peace with Athens and then crushing Sparta, but the Athenians refused to desert their allies. For their part, the Spartans abandoned their insistence that a stand be made at the isthmus and marched north with their main army to join other allied contingents at Plataea, in Boeotia, just north of Attica. The combined Greek army, commanded by the Spartan Pausanias, the regent for the young son of Leonidas, was only slightly smaller than the Persian army. For almost two weeks the two armies maneuvered and counter-maneuvered until Mardonius took the opportunity to attack the Greeks while they were changing positions. The main attack was against the Spartans, but the heavy infantry of Sparta turned the tables on the Persians and charged their center line. Mardonius and all those around him were destroyed immediately. That decided the battle. Of the more than 50,000 Persian soldiers who went into battle that day, fewer than 3,000 survived to live out their lives as Greek slaves.

From this point the tide of Greek victory could not be stopped. Even before the Battle of Plataea, a joint fleet of Athens, Chios, and Samos crossed over to Asia Minor and landed at Mycale. During the ensuing battle the Greek mercenaries employed by the Persians deserted, the Persian army was destroyed and its ships were burned. According to legend, the battle at Mycale was fought on the same day as the one at Plataea, in late August of 479 BCE. Within a short time all of Greece, including the Asia Minor coast, was cleared of Persian influence. After the Battle of Mycale, the Spartans returned home. The Athenians, to their credit, remained to help complete the job. The essential difference between Athens and Sparta was thus revealed and inevitably it led to rivalry and conflict. Even though the Persian Wars were over, the final reckoning with the Persians would not occur until the time of Alexander the Great, some one hundred and fifty years later.

No name was given to the alliance of Greek states which repelled the Persian invasion. Historians usually refer to it as "The Hellenic League of 481." After the Battle of Plataea the victors dedicated an offering to Apollo at Delphi, consisting of a gold tripod with a bronze column in the shape of three intertwined serpents. On this column was inscribed, under the heading "These fought the war," a list of 31 states, even though some of these states were not formal members of the alliance. Centuries later the column was removed to Constantinople by the emperor Constantine. It survives today in Istanbul.

Warfare and military history are not very popular subjects for Western Civilization textbooks today and most scholars attempt to avoid discussion of them when possible. Nevertheless, one of the important lessons of history is that violent battles and brutal wars have time and time again determined the course of our past, and thus have determined our present, and certainly will determine our future. In spite of all the peaceful intentions and wistful ideology, there is no denying this simple fact. It is the reality of history. All the dreaming in the world cannot change reality. If the Greeks had lost the Battle of Salamis over 2,000 years ago, how vastly different would be the world we live in today. There is no basis in this observation for knowing if the world would be better or worse, only the certainty that it would be different. In all probability we would not even have a Western Civilization to study had the Greeks not successfully defended their freedom against overwhelming odds, almost 2,500 years ago. Warfare is surely not the most noble aspect of human history, but the simple reality is that no other human activity has had a more decisive influence on the development of civilizations. Neither philosophy, art, nor religion, as important as they are, will effect our future more than warfare. To deny this, as many historians today attempt to do, is simply an attempt to deny reality. Ideology and reality are rarely synonyms.

The Delian League and the Athenian Empire

After the Persian invasion of the Greek mainland was turned back, the leadership of Greece fell to the Athenians, more or less from default. The Persians still controlled many strong points in Asia Minor and still maintained a presence in Thrace. Sparta had exercised the command in the important land battles of the war but victory was made possible by the Athenian navy. Although Sparta was still recognized as the premier military power in Greece, the Spartans did not want to accept responsibility for distant expeditions—the constant threat of a helot uprising at home was always an important drag on Sparta's foreign policy decisions. The Athenians, on the other hand, considered the liberation of the Ionians, whom they felt were their kinsmen, to be in their long-term interests and there was a great groundswell of enthusiasm for action in Athens. Once the Athenians committed their future to the sea, nothing seemed impossible. No one could foresee the result but the expulsion of Persia and the eclipse of Sparta meant that Athens would be at the center of the Greek world. The character of Athenian society was demonstrated by the fact that they did not hesitate to meet the challenge. Sparta's failure to seize leadership at this moment allowed the reigns of power to fall to Athens. From Athen's decision to act developed the confederacy of Aegean states known as the Delian League, which in time became the mighty Athenian Empire.

Persia, however, remained powerful and revenge was always a threat. The next phase of Greek history, the Classical Age, was played out under the shadow of a possible Persian return. Vigilance and a strong defense were necessary. Accordingly, in 478 BCE, one year after the defeat of the Persians at Plataea, representatives from the Greek poleis in the Aegean area met with the Athenians on the island of Delos to discuss the formation of a defensive alliance against the Persians. Delos was chosen because it was a sacred island believed to be the birthplace of Artemis and Apollo. Thus this alliance was known as the Delian League. It was a free confederation (*symmachia*) of autonomous city-states. Athens automatically assumed the leadership (*hegemon*) of the League because of its naval supremacy and because the allies were annoyed with the tyrannical behavior of the Spartan commander Pausanias, who had been the leader of the Greeks during the Persian invasion. The organization of the League was mainly the work of the Athenian Aristides, because he was trusted by all parties. The governing body consisted of a council of representatives of the member states, an admiral and treasurers appointed by Athens. The League treasury was deposited in the temple of Artemis and Apollo on Delos. Initially the allies were assessed 460 talents a year, to be paid either in cash or in ships to serve in the joint fleet, commanded by Athens.

The Delian League had several goals in addition to defense, including a campaign to free all Greek cities still under Persian domination. For ten years the Delian League's fleet sailed around the Aegean Sea, sweeping it clean of Persian influence. Along the coast of Asia Minor, city after city was freed, all of which joined the League—either voluntarily or under pressure or even threat of destruction. Although the League was essentially democratic, its members believed that the safety of the entire Aegean basin would be seriously compromised by independent states. Athens during this critical period was led by a brilliant statesman named Cimon, who was the son of Miltiades, the hero of Marathon. Under his leadership the Delian League aggressively campaigned against the Persians. As the power of the League increased, the power of Athens, as its leader, grew proportionally.

Relations between Sparta and Athens were already strained. After the defeat of the Persians at Plataea, the Spartans had requested (more accurately, commanded) the Athenians not to rebuild their walls and to join Sparta in razing the fortifications of all the cities of Greece outside of the Peloponnesus. Of course this would have made Sparta supreme and would have been fatal to Athens, politically and culturally. Themistocles persuaded the Athenians to send him as an envoy to Sparta where he managed to conceal the truth from the Spartans while the Athenians feverishly rebuilt their walls. In the end, Sparta was presented with a *fait accompli* and had to accept Athenian independence. The next year (478 BCE) Themistocles persuaded the people to build dockyards at Piraeus and surround the entire port with a massive seven-mile long wall. Later the road between Piraeus and Athens was enclosed by a set of walls, known as the "Long Walls." This was of great significance for the history of Athens, because it meant that in times of danger, Athens could pull its entire population back behind the walls, and so long as it controlled the sea, it was safe. This was the culmination of the naval policy of Themistocles. It meant that the future of Athens was inevitably tied to its navy. Thus, as Sparta and Athens emerged as the two super powers of the Greek world, Sparta was supreme on land while Athens ruled the sea.

Athens became very wealthy and prosperous during this time and its power began to be felt throughout the Greek world. The original agreement for establishing the Delian League provided that part of the League's income should go to Athens to pay for maintaining the fleet. Gradually, Athens began to demand that all allies provide annual cash payments instead of providing ships, so that the fleet slowly became a purely Athenian fleet. In 454 BCE the League treasury was arbitrarily moved from the temple of Apollo on the island of Delos to the temple of Athena in Athens. From this point the Delian League was the Athenian Empire, as Athens would not permit the formally free allies to secede and the annual "contributions" became enforced tribute payments.

Athens enjoyed its greatest success during the two decades between 450 and 430 BCE, a period which was so completely dominated by the statesman Pericles that it is often known as the "Age of Pericles." He was born into a distinguished family, given the best education available and rapidly rose to become the leader of the Athenian democracy. Although he was an aristocrat, Pericles secured many advantages for the common people and as a result won their total support. His policies diminished the influence of the aristocracy from which he came, but as the historian Thucydides pointed out, "he controlled the masses, rather than letting them control him." Pericles was a particularly outstanding orator, an absolute necessity for success in the Athenian assembly. When he came to power Athenian foreign policy was devoted toward two goals: the continuation of the war with Persia, and maintaining cordial relations with Sparta. Pericles set Athens on a different course. He convinced the assembly that the war with Persia was in the past and to direct its

Figure 6.6: Pericles.

attention toward Sparta, which he believed was a direct threat to the prosperity of the Athenian Empire. Pericles was eventually proven to be correct. Even though Sparta practiced a policy of isolation from the affairs of the rest of Greece, it was the only other power that could resist Athenian expansion. In any event, the two powers were destined to become enemies.

Internally, Pericles pursued a policy of rebuilding the city, which had been ravished by the Persians, as a worthy capital of a great empire. He used the public money from the Delian League to build some of the greatest masterpieces of ancient Greek architecture, such as the Parthenon and the Propylaea on the Acropolis. Most of the great works of Greek tragedy and comedy, the plays of Aeschylus, Sophocles, Euripides, and Aristophanes, were written during this time in the city of Athens. Industry and commerce also flourished. Under Pericles, Athens embarked on a program of aggressive imperialism. He put down rebellions and colonized other areas of the Aegean and Asia Minor. He used the Athenian navy to force many of the poleis even along the Black Sea coast into the "alliance." As the annual tribute payments mounted, the wealth of Athens grew at an amazing rate. Pericles used some of the money to pay poor citizens to serve as jurors and magistrates, so that no one could be barred by poverty from serving the state, and his popularity with the people soared to ever new heights. But there were problems on the not-too-distant horizon.

The Peloponnesian War (431–404 BCE)

The Delian League was no longer at war with Persia, but the money kept rolling in. It was no longer used for the common defense but to glorify the city of Athens and to run the democratic government. In this case, democracy and imperialism fed upon each other. As Athens grew more powerful and opulent, discontent grew among the tribute states. On the other hand, Sparta and its allies grew increasingly resentful of Athenian power and wealth. As time went on, war increasingly seemed inevitable, but no one really wanted a conflagration that would involve almost all of Greece on one side or the other, and repeated attempts were made to avoid it. In 446 BCE a non-aggression treaty was negotiated which was supposed to last for thirty years—an ancient form of détente, so to speak. The forces of conflict were too powerful to control, however. Corinth, one of the most important allies of Sparta, got into a quarrel with Corcyra, a commercial rival and naval power of northwestern Greece. In 433 BCE Corcyra appealed to Athens for an alliance. Such an alliance would upset the balance of power and make war inevitable. In that same year, the Athenians demanded that the city of Potidaea dismantle its defensive walls and exile its magistrates, which further outraged the Corinthians. When Potidaea rejected the ultimatum, Athens besieged the city. In a meeting of the assembly of the Peloponnesian League, Corinth managed to get Sparta to declare war.

Both sides believed that their strategy would wear down the other and force a surrender. The Spartans, of course, wanted to fight a land war, in which they outnumbered the Athenians by two to one. No one had ever defeated the full Spartan army in a pitched battle. The elite Spartan hoplites would guarantee victory in battle, and if the Athenians chose to stay behind their walls, the Peloponnesian army would ravage and plunder Attica. Eventually Athens would either sue for peace or be forced to fight to defend its land. The Spartans had good reason for confidence in this strategy: it had worked against all its enemies for centuries.

But fifth century Athens was unlike any polis Greece had ever seen, and as a result the Peloponnesian War was far longer and bloodier than either side had expected. The combination of its naval supremacy and its far-flung empire meant that Athens could not be forced to surrender or fight a land battle with the Spartan army by an invasion of its territory. The Athenians merely

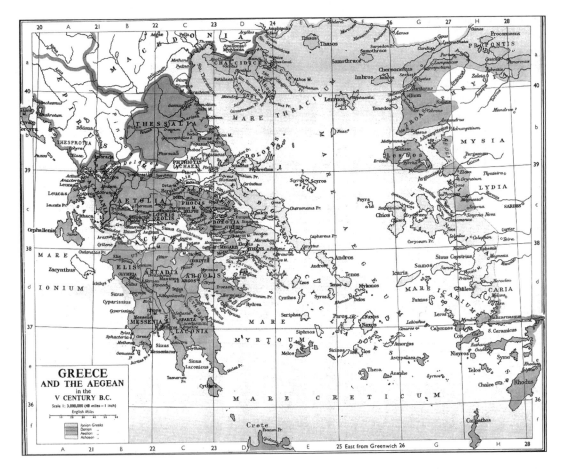

Figure 6.7: Greece during the Peloponnesian War.

retreated behind their Long Walls until the Spartan army retired at the end of the campaigning season. Tribute from the empire allowed Athens to import all necessary food and supplies for its population and to maintain its fleet. The Long Walls between Athens and Piraeus guaranteed Athens access to the sea and so as long as the grain supply from the Black Sea was not cut off, Athens was relatively invulnerable.

The strategy of Pericles was based on this unique circumstance. While the Peloponnesian army was camped ineffectually outside the walls of Athens, the Athenian fleet was dispatched to raid the coastline of the Peloponnesus. Because of its vast treasury and yearly tribute, Athens could carry on the war year-round. The Peloponnesians, by contrast, had to return home for the harvest, and they were also much more vulnerable to the effects of having their lands ravaged—if they lost their crops they would starve. Pericles was confident that eventually the Spartans would loose their patience with the war and agree to leave Athens in peace with its empire.

However, war never unfolds as expected. Even the best war plans cannot be crafted to deal with the unexpected and the unpredictable. Both strategies relied on winning the war by attrition of the enemy's will rather than by direct annihilation of his military forces. Would ravaging the enemy's territory cause them to tire of war, or would it embitter them and make an end to the war without complete victory more difficult? The length of the war and the depths of savagery to which it sunk suggest that the latter effect far overshadowed any war-weariness produced by these strategies.

In the first year of the war, 431 BCE, both sides proceeded as planned and the year ended without either side having gained any significant advantage, but with some disillusionment already becoming evident. According to Thucydides, enthusiasm for the war was high at first. Large numbers of young men on both sides, who had no experience of war, saw it as an adventure, somewhat like the generation of young men who crowed naively into the trenches between France and Germany at the beginning of the First World War in the 20th Century. But the war quickly brought losses and hardship to the Athenians that began to sap the people's moral. The following winter a public funeral was held for the men who had fallen in battle during the course of the year and Pericles gave his famous funeral oration that is so often quoted as summing up the idealism of the Athenian democracy:[17]

> We live under a form of government which does not emulate the institutions of our neighbors; on the contrary, we are ourselves a model which some follow, rather than the imitators of other peoples. It is true that our government is called a democracy, because its administration is in the hands, not of the few, but of the many; yet while as regards the law all men are on an equality for the settlement of their private disputes, as regards the value set on them it is as each man is in any way distinguished that he is preferred to public honors, not because he belongs to a particular class, but because of personal merits; nor, again, on the ground of poverty is a man barred from a public career by obscurity of rank if he but has it in him to do the state a service. And not only in our public life are we liberal, but also as regards our freedom from suspicion of one another in the pursuits of every-day life; for we do not feel resentment at our neighbor if he does as he likes, nor yet do we put on sour looks which, though harmless, are painful to behold. But while we thus avoid giving offence in our private intercourse, in our public life we are restrained from lawlessness chiefly through reverent fear, for we render obedience to those in authority and to the laws, and especially to those laws which are ordained for the succor of the oppressed and those which, though unwritten, bring upon the transgressor a disgrace which all men recognize.[18]

The next summer, the Peloponnesians again invaded, and Pericles again restrained the Athenians from marching out to battle. A few days after the Peloponnesians arrived, however, unforeseen disaster struck Athens: a virulent plague broke out in the city crowded with refugees from the countryside, eventually killing at least one-third of the population.[19] Meanwhile, a large

---

17. See, Thucydides, "Pericles' Funeral Oration," in Cleve, Robert, *Early Western Civilization, Source Reading* (2002), Kendall/Hunt Publishing Company, pp. 129–134.

18. Thucydides, 2.37

19. Ironically, despite Thucydides' detailed description, modern scholars are still not able to agree on the identity of the disease. It was clearly not the bubonic plague of the Black Death which occurred in the 14th Century, for the characteristic symptom of the bubo (inflammatory swelling of a lymph gland especially in the groin) is not found in Thucydides' description. Other candidates that have been suggested are measles, typhus, ergotism, and even toxic shock syndrome as a complication of influenza. The case for typhus seems strongest both epidemiologically-the age group is similar-and from the standpoint of the symptoms. Typhus is characterized by fever and a rash, gangrene of the extremities occurs, it is known as a "doctors' disease" from its frequent incidence among care-givers, it confers immunity. But the fit is not exact. The rash is difficult to identify on the basis of Thucydides' description (modern medical texts often employ pictures to differentiate rashes), and the state of mental confusion may not fit Thucydides' description. In the long run, all such attempts at identification may be futile. Diseases develop and change over time, and it may be that the plague of the 5th Century BCE no longer exists today in a recognizable form.

force sent to reinforce the siege of Potidaea succeeded only in carrying the plague to the troops already there, and returned after a loss of 1,000 out of 4,000 men. Nevertheless, Potidaea finally surrendered in the winter of 430/429 BCE, after a siege of over two years.

By 429 BCE, the Spartans had begun to realize that simply invading Attica every year was not going to end the war, at least not soon. So far so good for Pericles' strategy. But the Spartans were no more ready to give up than the Athenians. Instead, they began a long trial-and-error process to find a new way to destroy Athenian power. In September 429 BCE, Pericles died, possibly from the plague. The impact that his loss had on the future course of the war is unclear. Pericles' original strategy was almost completely defensive. It is at least debatable whether the Spartans could have been induced to make peace without the Athenians demonstrating an ability to seriously hurt them. Thus, if Pericles had lived, he may have actually hindered Athenian attempts to find some way out of the stalemated war.

The war now descended into savagery and revenge. Plataea was captured by the Spartans in 427 BCE and each Plataean was forced to answer "yes" or "no" to the question, "Have you done anything to help the Spartans and their allies in the present war?" All the Plataeans answered "no," of course, and were all executed. The Thebans later razed the city to the ground. Mytilene, an ally of Athens, revolted and after a long siege narrowly avoided the same fate. The vengeful Athenian assembly voted to kill all the men and sell the rest of the population into slavery, but repented the next day. A trireme dispatched with news of the reprieve of the city arrived as the executions were about to be carried out.[20]

The Peace of Nicias

Ten years of this kind of fighting resulted in disastrous events and senseless losses on both sides, but the power balance between the two states was no different than at the beginning of the war. Both sides were exhausted and tired of war:

> It so happened, too, that directly after the battle at Amphipolis and the withdrawal of Rhamphias from Thessaly neither side undertook any further military operations, and both were more inclined to peace. The Athenians were so inclined because they had been beaten at Delium, and again at Amphipolis a little later, and consequently had no longer that confidence in their strength in reliance upon which they had earlier refused to accept the truce, as they then thought that with their existing good luck they would prove superior. They were afraid, too, of their allies, lest, elated over these failures of theirs, the revolt among them might spread, and they repented that they had not come to terms when a good opportunity offered after the affair at Pylos. The Lacedaemonians, on the other hand, favored peace because the war was turning out contrary to their hopes. They had expected that in a few years, if they should ravage their territory, they could pull down the power of the Athenians; whereas they had met with the calamity on the island of Sphacteria, such had never before befallen Sparta; their territory was ravaged from Pylos and Cythera; the Helots were deserting, and always there was apprehension that those who remained, relying on those beyond the border, might revolt in the present state of affairs, just as they had done before [the great revolt of the Helots, known as the Third Messenian War]. It happened also that the thirty years' truce with the Argives was on the point of expiring, and the Argives were unwilling to make another treaty unless the territory of Cynuria were restored to them; and it seemed impossible to carry on the war with the Argives and the Athenians at the same time. Besides, they suspected that some of the cities in the Peloponnesus would revolt to the Argives, as indeed did happen.[21]

---

20. See, Thucydides, "The Revolt of Mitylene," in Cleve, Robert, *Early Western Civilization, Source Reading* (2002), Kendall/Hunt Publishing Company, pp. 134–137.

21. Thucydides, 5.14.

After a series of negotiations, led by Nicias on the Athenian side (who gave his name to the "peace" that followed), Sparta and Athens signed a fifty-year peace treaty in the spring of 421 BCE. Essentially similar in view and ability to Pericles, Nicias was a brilliant and cautious man who managed to pull off an effective truce. Everyone was allowed to go home, and the territorial status as it stood at the time of the peace was allowed to remain in place.

The so-called Peace of Nicias was never much of a peace, but more like a lull in the ongoing war. As Thucydides explained:

> For six years and ten months the two powers abstained from invading each other's territory; in other regions, however, there was only an unstable cessation of arms and they kept on doing each other the greatest possible damage. But at last they were forced to break the treaty which had been concluded after the first ten years, and again engaged in open war.[22]

Nicias, however, had rivals in the assembly. The most important of them was a young politician named Alcibiades. He was handsome, brilliant, daring, vain, highly educated, a pupil of the philosopher Socrates, and socially outrageous. He was clever, well-spoken, and he threw the best parties in town. Even more fortunate for his political career, he was the nephew of Pericles. But he was also politically amoral—well, admittedly most politicians are, but Alcibiades was scandalously unscrupulous. He was not really a hawk; rather, he chose the war party because he wanted to be a leader and the position was open. It was easy for him to lampoon Nicias and his followers. He loved to mock authority and to rile the conservatives.

The Sicilian Expedition

Alcibiades became strategos in 420 BCE and immediately began maneuvering for war. The politics of all this is most complex, but in the end Alcibiades was able to get what he wanted: a renewal of the war effort, with a new plan under his leadership. The plan was daring, outrageous, but had the potential for brilliant victory. His uncle, Pericles, had figured out how to defend Athens but not how to defeat Sparta. Alcibiades had solved the other half of the equation. Athens had been unable to make large gains anywhere in Greece. Sparta was secure from direct invasion, but it depended on getting supplies from Greek cities of Sicily and southern Italy. And its most important ally, Corinth, was heavily dependant on trade from the area and, indeed, considered the Greek poleis in southern Italy and Sicily its closed sphere of economic operations. Syracuse was the chief city of Sicily and was one of the largest Greek cities anywhere. Take Syracuse and the rest of Sicily would follow. Take Sicily, and both Corinth and Sparta would be cut off from their supplies and wealth. Victory for Athens would soon follow.

Nicias opposed the expedition from the start. As the architect of the 30-year truce, he thought Alcibiades little short of mad. But Alcibiades knew how to use his oratory skills to win over the assembly, and Nicias soon found himself out-maneuvered. Nicias tried to be clever by proposing a fleet of unprecedented size, hoping the assembly vote against it because of its cost. Instead, the assembly granted all he asked. In fine Athenian tradition, the assembly named both Nicias and Alcibiades as co-commanders of the expedition. Thus, neither political faction in Athens could claim that its leader was undermining the efforts of the other. To mediate between the two, the Athenians even named a third commander, Lamachus. Now the expedition had three co-commanders! But there was little doubt that the expedition belonged to Alcibiades.

---

22. Thucydides, 5.25.

Figure 6.8: Alcibiades.

The expeditionary force dispatched to Sicily consisted of 134 triremes and 27,000 men, the largest Athens had ever fielded. It all but exhausted the Athenian treasury, which represented the income of its entire empire and employed an entire generation of young Athenian men. But it would all be worth it to bring Sparta to its knees. On the eve of the departure of the fleet, however, an event occurred that seemed to cast a foreboding atmosphere over the entire project. Many of the Herms,[23] which protected the intersections of the city, were mutilated and it was widely said that the deed had been done by Alcibiades and his buddies during a drunken party. Certainly it was the sort of thing Alcibiades was infamous for: outrageous, impious, more than a little loony. But also it was just the sort of story that would be manufactured by his enemies to discredit him. As soon as the fleet had sailed, charges were brought against Alcibiades in court, and a state ship was sent after the fleet to bring him back. The ship caught up with the fleet, Alcibiades was duly arrested and accused of sacrilege. It was an Athenian madness to gamble on such an expedition in the first place and then to arrest the man who had conceived it is beyond rational explanation. But it was plain bad policing to let the man get away during the return to Athens. As the state ship rounded the Peloponnesus Alcibiades gave his captors the slip, dove over the side and swam to shore, whereupon he went directly to Sparta and proceeded to tell the enemy every detail of the expedition. A defector extraordinaire.

---

23. Hermes, the messenger of the gods, was also the god of every kind of prosperity, as well as the protector of the traveler. His stylized statue, called a "herm," was a quadrangular pillar topped with a head, with tenons on its sides and a phallus on the front. It guaranteed the success of undertakings. Herms were found at the threshold of houses, at street intersections in the city and at crossroads in the countryside. Their mutilation was considered to be an omen of bad luck.

Lamachus was killed in the early fighting, leaving Nicias in sole command. Nicias was not a dynamic or resourceful commander—he procrastinated and hesitated, and his forces were killed off slowly. The army became demoralized, for everyone understood that the key was a rapid victory. Of course, it didn't help that the chief architect of the plan had gone over to the enemy and its chief opponent was now in command. Nicias reported the situation to the assembly as hopeless, expecting to be ordered to come home. Instead, Athens sent him 15,000 more men, under Demosthenes, creating thereby the largest army ever assembled in Greece. Demosthenes was a dynamic general and tried an immediate offensive. But Syracuse was well defended and the attack failed. After this failure, all the commanders began thinking of ways to withdraw the army safely.

The one thing that the expedition had to do was to keep the fleet safe, for those ships were their only way home again. But Nicias himself was the expedition's main obstacle. Even as the commanders at last recognized the hopelessness of ever defeating Syracuse, even after they had given the orders to sail, even indeed the very night before they were to depart, Nicias hesitated. The Athenians were caught by surprise, the fleet was bottled up in the harbor and destroyed by fire in 413 BCE. There was now no way home. The only possible hope was to try to cross the interior of Sicily and reach a port friendly to Athens, where some ships might be had. This demoralized and defeated army of thirty-five thousand Athenians (and allies) set out across Sicily. The soldiers were already suffering from diseases contracted in the swamps outside Syracuse. They suffered further from lack of supplies, particularly the lack of water, as they crossed the arid interior of Sicily. For eight days the army struggled under constant attack by the Syracusan cavalry. Demosthenes surrendered the main body of the army after it was surrounded in an olive grove. The vanguard, under Nicias, kept on marching for two more days. When it was almost out of water and despair was at its height, scouts reported a river ahead, the army dissolved into a mob and ran toward it. It was a trap. The Syracusans were waiting on the opposite bank, and as the Athenians scrambled into the small river, they attacked. The Athenians were slaughtered as they trampled over each other trying to get to the water. Those who were captured were imprisoned in an abandoned quarry and perished almost to a man in great misery. Only a handful ever made it back to Athens.

The news of the destruction of the Sicilian Expedition stunned Athens. Never had a single Greek city mobilized such an army, and never had a single Greek city suffered such terrible losses. The expedition against Syracuse consumed nearly all of Athens' resources and took the lives of an entire generation of its young men. Athenian power since the Persian War had depended solely on its navy and the Sicilian disaster left Athens almost powerless. The government of Athens had made enormous demands on its citizens and on its empire. The issue now was not how to win the war but how to avoid defeat.

The Ionian War

Yet, Athens was not defeated. It still controlled the substantial resources of its empire and much wealth still flowed into their city. It was a measure of Athenian tenacity and determination that Athens now raised yet another fleet and was able to continue the war. However, three serious problems now confronted Athens: it still had no means of defeating its enemies, other than holding on and hoping for a settlement; it now lacked a great leader such as Pericles or even Alcibiades; finally, the ancient conflict between the aristocrats and the democrats kept interfering with the war. The last part of the war was a grim time for Athens. Sparta was now demanding virtual surrender. Eventually, the Athenians went so far as to forgive and recall Alcibiades in 411 BCE. He gave Athens four years of victories before he again fell from favor. But the victories brought no permanent results and served merely to put off the inevitable.

Finally, the Spartans realized that they would never defeat the Athenians unless they could gain control of the sea. Sparta had entered the war in the first place as the defender of Greek freedom against the aggression of Athens, but the realities of war often change a state's original motives. Thus, the Spartans entered into negotiations with the Persians and in exchange for a large amount of gold to build a fleet, Sparta promised Persia that after Athens was defeated, the Greek cities of Asia Minor would be returned to Persian control. So much for Greek freedom!

The Spartans constructed a fleet and sailed boldly out into the Aegean to do battle with the Athenian navy, but although they possessed the most powerful army in Greece, they had no experience with naval warfare. In the very first battle—off the coast of Asia Minor—the entire Peloponnesian fleet was destroyed. So the war resumed its usual pattern of annual invasions of Attica, which resolved nothing. Eventually the Spartans decided to try again and they secured more money from Persia and built another fleet. This time they were more careful. The key to the whole war was really the narrow waterway at the Hellespont which connects the Black and Aegean seas. It was through this waterway that Athens imported grain from the Black Sea area. If Athens did not control this vital waterway, it would starve.

The Peloponnesian fleet, under the command of Lysander, moved up toward the entrance to the Hellespont, but cautiously refused to give battle immediately. The Athenian fleet used the village of Aegospotami as a base from which to watch for an opportunity to attack Lysander's fleet. Aegospotami had no harbor, forcing the Athenians to pull their ships up on the beach every day. After five days of waiting, the Athenians grew careless. In a surprise attack, Lysander caught almost the entire fleet on the beach. Only ten Athenian ships escaped this "battle" of Aegospotami; 170 were captured or destroyed. Lysander executed all 3,000 Athenians captured in the battle.

And so the war ended in 404 BCE. After so many years of sacrifice and bloodshed and destruction, the war ended in a fluke, almost an accident! Back in Athens the people realized they now had only two choices open to them: to starve to death, or to surrender. After some agonizing debate in the assembly, they chose the last alternative and surrendered to the Spartans. The Spartans proceeded to pull down the Long Walls with great ceremony and celebration and they cynically declared the "freedom of the Greeks"—but they also returned the Greek cities of Asia Minor to Persian rule.

Aftermath

Considering the circumstances, the peace terms offered (or enforced) by the Spartans were surprisingly lenient. After all the bitterness and savagery between the two powers, one would expect the Spartans to destroy Athens completely, but such was not the case. Of course the Athenian empire was dismantled and the Long Walls as well as the walls around Piraeus were razed. The Athenian's were allowed to keep only ten warships. Athens was also required to join the Spartan alliance and adhere to Sparta's foreign policy. Nevertheless, Athens remained independent and retained its homeland intact. This was far more than the Athenians could have expected and certainly more than most Spartan allies wished.

What was the effect of the Peloponnesian War on Greece as a whole? This is a more difficult question. The violence and divisiveness was a severe blow to Greek pride and self-confidence, because it exposed the dark side of Greek culture. The same Greeks who produced the great classical masterpieces of sculpture and architecture and gave birth to philosophy, also senselessly slaughtered thousands of prisoners of war and enslaved the whole populations of other Greek cities. These atrocities were difficult to reconcile with the high humanistic ideals of the Greek intellectuals.

The long-term effects on Greek civilization can be interpreted in two contrasting ways. First, the outcome of the war can be seen as detrimental because only Athens could have united the Greeks and only a united Greece could have withstood, first Alexander and, later, Rome. For this reason some scholars see Athens's defeat as Greece's defeat. But other historians make the second argument that Sparta's victory was Greece's victory. A united Greece was never a real possibility, because it was not what the Greeks themselves wanted. Greek civilization was a world of independent city-states, and Athenian victory would have destroyed that world. In this view, Sparta's victory preserved Greek liberty—as the Greeks themselves understood that word—for another 250 years.

CHAPTER

7

The Cultural and Intellectual Life of Ancient Greece

"Ancient Greece was the cradle of Western Civilization," has become something of a cliché. For more than two thousand years, one age after another looked back to Classical Greece to discover its origins, to recover the meaning of its present, to find inspiration for its future. For the past five hundred years or so, this tendency was especially strong for the scholars, artists, intellectuals, philosophers, and scientists of the modern Western world. In Classical Greece they came into direct confrontation with the foundations of the Western intellectual, artistic, and cultural tradition. In short, they found themselves. Recently, however, it has become fashionable in intellectual circles, as well as the media at large, to demean and negate all things Western as the meaningless, irrelevant, and futile study of "dead white men." Nevertheless, a serious examination of ancient Greek culture reveals wondrous and beautiful aspects of the heritage of Western Civilization. There is little for which the West needs to apologize and there is much for which it should be proud.

Greek Religion

The diversity of Greek culture is aptly expressed in the universality and inclusiveness of Hellenic religion. The Classical Greeks did not, in reality, possess "a religion" in the modern sense of a specific set of beliefs and practices advocated by its devotees as a matter of conscious choice, to the exclusion of other beliefs. That concept was not applied to the Greek system until the advent of Christianity. However, they did perceive of a vague and ill-defined boundary between Greek and non-Greek religious practice, which can be characterized as "Greekness," but without a formal dogma or orthodoxy.

The Greeks, like the other peoples of the ancient Mediterranean, were polytheists. Greek deities were anthropomorphic, that is, they were exactly like human beings in every way, except that they were more powerful and they were immortal. The vast, almost uncountable, number of gods and goddesses were headed up by the twelve Olympian gods who lived on Mount Olympus. The other gods lived on and beneath the earth and the sea. Greek gods were the personifications of either abstract concepts, like love (Aphrodite) and wisdom (Athena), or of natural phenomena, like rivers (Scamander in the *Iliad*) or the sea (Poseidon). The individual gods assumed different aspects, however. Apollo was the god of prophecy, the arts, and among other things, both the sender and the healer of plague. This involved him in medicine and Asclepius, the god of medicine and healing, is said to be his son. At the head of the Olympian gods was Zeus, the father and the king of the gods.

The major function of the gods was to hold Chaos at bay and to ensure that order prevailed. They were not engaged in a struggle between righteousness and evil—they possessed human traits like envy and jealousy—and there was no "Satan." Greek religion embodied no concept of sin or guilt or even of reward and punishment after death. Their religion was not about creed or doctrine or enforcement of a systematic pattern of behavior. The gods themselves were part of the natural order and structure of the universe. That structure was a hierarchy with the gods at the top, followed by humans and below them the animals. Piety for the Greeks consisted of knowing one's proper place in this scheme of things. For an individual to think of himself as better, to act in a manner above his station, was a sacrilege and an insult to the gods known as *hubris*.[1] Hubris always resulted in destruction and tragedy. It was the closest thing in ancient Greek religion to the modern concept of "sin." Morality was public (as was most aspects of Greek culture). A person must be seen to do the right thing, to be honest and sincere—in short, a person must be seen to be honorable. Fear of punishment after death was not a part of the ancient Greek psyche.

One important aspect sets Greek religion apart from the other ancient belief systems; it supported no separate priesthood.[2] The priests were simply members of the society, usually drawn from the ranks of the aristocracy. Thus, the priesthood was never able—indeed, was never motivated—to impose its own will on the rest of society in the rigid and totalitarian pattern of the societies of the Near East and Egypt. Contact between the human and the divine world occurred at the temple, the alter, the sanctuary, or other cult site. The relationship between gods and humans was consummated by sacrifice, which was a gift to the gods. The sacrifice could be vegetable (first fruits of the harvest), wine, oil, or an animal. The concept of the sacrifice was founded in reciprocity: a gift to the gods would solicit something in return. The slave-master relationship between heaven and earth, so much a part of the religions of the ancient Near East, seems totally absent from Greek religious practice.

An even more extravagant form of worship was the festival, a celebration in honor of a local or a major deity. A national celebration was called a Panhellenic festival. The Olympian Games, held every four years at Olympia, in Elis in the Peloponnesus, is the most famous example. It drew official ambassadors, as well as numerous visitors, from all over Greece. Some festivals were local, such as

---

1. The best ancient discussion of *hubris* is found in Aristotle's *Rhetoric*: his definition is that *hubris* is "doing and saying things at which the victim incurs shame, not in order that one may achieve anything other than what is done, but simply to get pleasure from it. For those who act in return for something do not commit *hubris*, they avenge themselves. The cause of the pleasure for those committing *hubris* is that by harming people, they think themselves superior; that is why the young and the rich are hubristic, as they think they are superior when they commit *hubris*" (*Rhetoric* 137.23–30). This account, locating *hubris* within a framework of ideas concerned with the honor and shame of the individual, which took a central place in the value-systems of the ancient Greeks, fits very well the vast majority of ancient texts, from Homer till well after Aristotle's own time. While it primarily denotes gratuitous dishonoring by those who are, or think they are, powerful and superior, it can also at times denote the insolence of accepted "inferiors," such as women, children, or slaves, who disobey or claim independence; or it may be used to emphasize the degree of humiliation actually inflicted on a victim, regardless of the agent's intention; some cases, especially applied to verbal insults, may be humorously exaggerated; and revenge taken to excessive or brutal lengths can be condemned as constituting fresh *hubris*. Hornblower, Simon and Spawforth, Anthony, *The Oxford Companion to Classical Civilization* (1998), Oxford University Press, Oxford, pp. 362–363.

2. The Minoan religion of Bronze Age Crete appears to be an exception. There is no evidence of a professional priesthood in Minoan religion, indeed no large temples or cult statues have been found.

Figure 7.1: Procession of worshipers carrying sacrifices with woman at right pouring libation on the altar.

the Dionysia at Athens, which featured contests between dramatic playwrights. The prize awarded to the winner of these festivals was a simple olive wreath. The purpose of the events was not to distribute valuable prizes, but to honor the gods.

Another feature of worship was the oracle. The most famous oracle was at Delphi, where a priestess sitting on a tripod in the temple of Apollo went into a trance and delivered cryptic messages from Apollo, which were then deciphered and put into final form by an officiating priest. Sick and infirm Greeks of every social station, aristocrat and commoner alike, crowded into the temples of Asclepius, the god of healing, where they slept in the hope of a visitation from the god (via a dream) with advice for the cure of their illness. There were also mystical cults that offered worshipers direct, personal connection with specific deities through secret initiation rites. The penalty for revealing the secret of these rituals to the uninitiated was severe. These "mystery cults" provided individual worshipers with a personal religious experience not available in the public rituals and ceremonies of the public state religion.

The Olympian Creation Myth

It is not possible for the modern scholar to relate the ancient Greek creation myth, because there were many different, often conflicting, creation stories explaining the origin of the universe. However, in the 8th Century BCE, the poet Hesiod, in his book Theogony, complied an account that was accepted by most Greeks during the Classical Age. According to Hesiod, it all began with Chaos, an empty void of formless nothingness. From Chaos evolved five elements: (1) Gaea, the earth; (2) Tartarus, the underworld, located deep within the earth; (3) Erebus, the darkness of Tartarus; (4) Eros, the power of love; and (5) Night, the darkness.

Gaea produced a son, Uranus, who was the sky. Together Gaea and Uranus had many children. This was not seen as inappropriate, since they were the first male/female beings in existence. In fact, two of their children and two of their grandchildren married.[3] Rain fell from the sky onto the earth, plants and animals appeared, rivers and oceans formed. Then the union of Uranus and Gaea

---

3. Another version: In the beginning there was only an empty darkness. The one thing existing in this void was Nyx, a bird with black wings. Nyx laid a golden egg, set upon it for many ages until life began to stir and out of the egg rose Eros. One half of the shell rose into the air and became the sky, Uranus, and the other became the earth, Gaea. Eros caused Uranus and Gaea to fall in love and they had many children together.

produced many strange monsters and giants. Among these were three Cyclops, each with one huge eye in his forehead. Uranus loathed these monsters and banished them to the Underworld. Later, a group of human-shaped giants, called Titans, were born and they became the first gods and goddess. Gaea could not forgive Uranus for his treatment of her first offspring and enlisted the aid of Titans, led by Cronos, to rebel against their father. Gaea fashioned a sickle, with which Cronos overpowered Uranus and castrated him, throwing his testicles into the sea. From this terrible wound black blood dropped onto the earth which gave birth to the furies and tree nymphs. The furies had a dog's head and bat's wings and they were the spirits of revenge and justice. They hounded murderers, especially those who had killed a relative. The debris that floated to the surface of the sea became a white foam from which Aphrodite, the goddess of love, was born.

Cronos married his sister Rhea and became king of the Titans. They had five children, but Cronos had been warned that one of them would kill him, so he swallowed each one of them as they were born. Overcome by grief, Rhea traveled to Crete and sought the advice of her own parents, Uranus and Gaea. There she gave birth to her sixth child, a son, in a deep cavern in the forests of Mount Ageun. Gaea looked after the child while Rhea wrapped a stone in baby's cloths and gave it to Cronos to swallow. This child was Zeus. When Zeus grew up he returned home in disguise and deceived Cronos into drinking a potion which made him choke. The five children he had swallowed were coughed out safe and sound. They were the three goddesses Hestia, Demeter, and Hera, and the two gods, Hades,[4] and Poseidon.

Figure 7.2: The Zeus (or Poseidon?) of Artemisium.

---

4. Occasionally referred to as Pluto in the texts. Pluto is simply a ritual title of Hades.

A fierce battle now took place between the Titans and the younger gods—the rift between the generations that appears in almost all the creation myths of the Mediterranean and Near East. Zeus freed the Cyclops who made thunderbolts for him to hurl. They also made a forked trident for Poseidon, and a helmet for Hades that made the wearer invisible. After a heroic struggle the younger gods were victorious. The Titans were banished and one of them, Atlas, was condemned to hold up the heavens as punishment.

Now began the Olympian period. Zeus became ruler of the sky and the king of the gods. Poseidon was made king of the sea and Hades the ruler of the Underworld. The home of the gods was Mount Olympus, which was located in an inaccessible region of northern Greece, but eventually Olympus come to be conceived as a place high above the earth, like the later concept of heaven.

An Abbreviated Roster of Greek Deities

Zeus is the archetypal patriarch, father, ruler, and king. He rules the sky and commands all the atmospheric phenomena. Despite the fact that he is married to Hera, he fathered children by many other unions. He was the great womanizer of the gods, a Don Juan with divine powers. What girl could resist? He turned himself into bulls, serpents, swans, and showers of gold dust in order to seduce numerous goddesses, nymphs, and even pretty young human lasses. This promiscuous behavior can be explained by the fact that as the early Greeks moved into the valleys and islands of Greece there were many local earth goddesses already in place with whom he, as the patriarchal ruler of the world, must subdue.

Poseidon is the ruler of the Sea, the second realm of the world. Also the god of earthquakes, he was represented in art as a mature man holding a trident and sometimes a fish. He was not always on friendly terms with Zeus and once joined Hera and Athena in the gods' conspiracy to put Zeus in chains, which never materialized. He married Amphitrite and she bore him six sons and a daughter, Rhodus, on the island of Rhodes, which took its name form Poseidon's daughter.

Hades (the Invisible), the second brother of Zeus and third of the three "overlords" who shared the empire of the universe between them, was the god of the Underworld and of the dead. He was a pitiless master over the dead and allowed none of his subjects to return to the world of the living. Hades fell in love with Persephone, the daughter of Zeus and Demeter, the goddess of agriculture, but her father would not agree to the marriage, because Demeter did not want her daughter imprisoned for all eternity in the land of the dead. Hades therefore abducted her. Demeter was so distressed that she withdrew her energies from the earth and nothing would grow. Zeus ordered Hades to return Persephone to her mother, but Hades had given her a pomegranate seed to eat. Whoever visits the land of the dead and eats anything there can never return and dwell among the living. Persephone was thus obliged to spend part of each year in the Underworld. Thus, when Persephone is in the Underworld by the side of her husband, nothing grows on the earth and winter is with us, but when she returns to her mother, Demeter restores her gifts to the earth, and spring returns. This explains the passage of the seasons.

Ares, the God of war, was the son of Zeus and Hera. He is the spirit of battle, delighting in slaughter and blood, but with little regard for the justice of the cause. He is attended by the demons Deimos (Fear) and Phobos (Terror). But Ares was not always the victor. One day on the battlefield before Troy, he was fighting alongside Hector when he found himself confronting Diomedes. He at once attacked him, but Athena, rendered invisible by the magic helmet of Hades, deflected Ares's spear and he was wounded by Diomedes. The god uttered a terrible cry that was heard throughout the whole battlefield and fled back to Olympus, where Zeus had his wound dressed.

Apollo, the greatest of the gods after Zeus, was the son of Zeus and Leto and the twin brother of Artemis. He was the god of prophecy, of music, poetry, and elegance, but he was also the bringer of plague, as well as the healer. Apollo may be thought of as the god of the intellect, the god of those aspects of human nature which set humans apart from the other animals. In this respect, he is the opposite of Dionysus.

Dionysus was the god of wine and mystic ecstasy, the god of the emotions, representing those aspects of human nature that humans have in common with the other animals. The Greeks realized that there are two sides to human nature: the intellect and the emotions. Both must be satisfied. Thus, in a sense, the two gods Apollo and Dionysus compliment each other. Dionysus was the son of Zeus and the human Semele, who asked Zeus to revel himself to her, but she was unable to endure the lightening which flashed around her lover and was struck dead. Zeus plucked the child she was carrying in her womb, which was only in the sixth month, and sewed it into his thigh. When it was full term it emerged as the infant Dionysus, the "twice born." He was given to the nymphs to raise. There are many legends and stories told about him. His annual festival at Athens was the origin of tragic drama.

Hermes, the son of Zeus and the nymph Maia (daughter of Atlas), was the messenger of the gods. He was the god of commerce and the guardian of the traveler. His statue, in the form of a pillar with only a human bust, known as Herms, was set up at intersections and crossroads.

Hephaestus, god of fire and metalworking, the son of Zeus and Hera, was the lame god. Homer says that when Hera was quarreling with Zeus about Heracles, Hephaestus took his mother's side. Zeus grabbed him by the foot and threw him down from Olympus. His fall lasted for a whole day. He hit the ground in the island of Lemnos and remained lame forever afterward. He ranks as a major Olympian god, however, and was married to Aphrodite.

Hera, the greatest of the Olympian goddesses, was the daughter of Cronos and Rhea, and hence the sister of Zeus. Hera appears in many legends in which she is usually portrayed as the vengeful and jealous wife, who regards Zeus's infidelities as insults. She visited her hatred not only on Zeus's mistresses, but on the children he sired by them as well. Heracles was the most frequent victim of her wrath. She was the goddess of weddings and marriage. The worship of Hera was ancient and her temple at Olympus predated that of Zeus, which may indicate that her worship in Greece predates the arrival of the Greeks. The marriage, which was celebrated in festivals throughout Greece, was arranged in order to explain the fusion of two cults that had first been distinct.

Artemis, the goddess of wild animals and the hunt, was the twin sister of Apollo. She was always a virgin and eternally young, an untamed girl with no interests beyond hunting—the archetypical "tomboy." She was vindictive and many suffered from her anger. For example, Actaeon, while hunting in the forest, inadvertently came upon Artemis bathing in a spring. Outraged at being seen naked, the goddess cast a spell upon Actaeon's fifty hounds and they, mistaking their master for a stag, tore him to pieces. Paradoxically, Artemis was the goddess of both unmarried girls and mothers in childbirth. This is an expression of the ambivalence at reaching a turning point in life. Young girls considering marriage came to dance at her festivals and then the night before marriage consecrated their tunics to the goddess—a rite of passage from childhood to adulthood.[5]

---

5. The bear was the animal sacred to her. At her festivals young girls danced while wearing bear masks and costumes and were called *arktoi,* or "she bears." Even today, in modern Crete, Mary is still worshipped in her role as "Virgin Mary of the Bear."

Figure 7.3: The birth of Athena, who springs from the head of Zeus, fully grown and armed. She is greeted by Eileithyia, the goddess of birth, Ares (right) and Poseidon (left).

Athena, was the daughter of Zeus and Metis. When Metis was about to give birth to a daughter, Zeus swallowed it, because Uranus and Gaea informed him that she would have a son who would dethrone him. When the time came for the child to be born, Zeus had Hephaestus split open his head with a blow from his axe and the goddess Athena, in full armor, sprang forth from his head. Thus Athena was born of Zeus, not Metis, and the prophecy was invalid. In classical art there are two different images of Athena. The more familier one is the severe, helmeted, goddess with spear and shield, the guardian of the city of Athens. The old image of a wild goddess with head gear wreathed in snakes seems to be the direct descendant of the Minoan Snake Goddess of a thousand years earlier. Even in classical times she was depicted with the head of Gorgon,[6] hissing with snakes on her shield. She was the goddess of wisdom and tactical warfare, and patroness of the urban arts. The olive and the owl were sacred to her.

Aphrodite, goddess of love and fertility, was (as related above) born from the sea foam. She was the archetypical beautiful, seductive love goddess. She was married to Hephaestus and gave birth to Eros, known today as Cupid. Aphrodite was often attended by the three Charites (three Graces in Latin): joyous, brilliance, and flowers. Wherever she goes, animals and humans are filled with longing for each other—not even the gods can resist her power.

---

6. The name gorgon was generally applied to Medusa, one of the three sister (Gorgons) who were the daughters of the sea divinities Phorcys and Ceto. Medusa's hair consisted of hissing snakes, she had huge tusks, like a wild bore, and her eyes flashed with such a penetrating gaze that anyone who looked at her was turned into stone. Perseus, a hero, on the advice of Athena, found Medusa's lair and, using his polished breastplate as a mirror to avoid looking at her, he managed to cut off her head. When he presented Medusa's head to Athena she affixed it to the center of her shield and her enemies were turned to stone by simply looking at her shield.

The Cult of the Hero

The worship of heroes was an important aspect of ancient Greek religion. The worship of mortal human beings may seem totally out of step with modern sensibilities, but the Greek hero occupied approximately the same position in their religion as the prophet occupies in the Judeo-Christian tradition: a go-between, or point of interface between this world and the world of the gods (or God).[7] A hero was usually, though not always, half divine, in that he had one divine parent.[8] The hero was invariably tested with extraordinary challenges, which prompted super-human deeds, resulting in the hero achieving divine status. The heroic path is the way of the individual, although he often received assistance from a divine source. Ultimately, however, the hero stands alone and must face and cope with his challenges—in addition to his mental weaknesses and spiritual short-comings—alone. The hero, then, was a human who rose above his human limitations to achieve super-human results.

Heracles

Heracles is the perfect example of the hero. Zeus, in order to gain sexual access to Alcmena, disguised himself as her husband, Amphytrion. Both Zeus and Amphytrion had intercourse with Alcmena and she bore twin sons by two different fathers: Iphides by Amphytrion and Heracles by Zeus. Heracles's paternity was a source of never-ending pain during his life, because he had to suffer the continuous hatred and jealousy of Hera, the wife of Zeus. Heracles's original name was Alacides. Heracles, which means "Hera's Glory," was given to him by Apollo when he became Hera's bond-servant and committed himself to the Twelve Labors imposed upon him by her. These were tasks assigned to him by his cousin Eurystheus. Hercules's most distinctive weapon was his club, which he fashioned himself. His other weapons were of divine origin: a sword given to him by Hermes; a bow and arrows given by Apollo; a gilded breastplate presented by Hephaestus; a peplum added by Athena; and finally, his horses were a gift from Poseidon.

A brief description of the twelve labors:

1. Kill the **Nemean Lion,** a monster that ravaged the region of Nemea, a valley in the Argolis. In true heroic style, Heracles cornered and strangled the lion with his bare hands! Then he clad himself in its skin and the lion's head served as a helmet. Thus, he is usually depicted in art.
2. Kill the **Lernaean Hydra,** a monster snake with several heads. When a head was cut off it immediately grew back, but Heracles used burning torches to sear the neck-stumps after he cut off the heads, preventing them from growing back again.
3. Bring back alive the monstrous **Erymanthian Boar,** which lived on Mount Erymanthus. Heracles chased it through the deep snow that covered the mountain side until it was exhausted and brought it back across his shoulders.
4. Capture the enormous **Hind of Ceryneia** that ravaged the crops of Oenoe. The animal was larger than a bull and had golden horns. After hunting it for a year, he wounded it slightly with an arrow, caught it and carried it back on his shoulders.

---

7. Be careful not to take such analogies too far. Remember, an analogy is not proof or evidence of fact. An analogy does not validate an argument, statement or conclusion; it merely explains the argument or statement and makes it more understandable. The student must always be on guard to never be fooled into accepting an argument or statement of fact based solely on analogy.

8. For example: Heracles (Latin, Hercules), son of Zeus and the human Alcmena; Achilles, son of Peleus and the goddess Thetis; and Aeneas, son of Anchises and Aphrodite.

5. Destroy the **Stymphalian Birds** that plagued the shores of Lake Stymphyalus in Arcadia. To drive them out of the dense thickets where they took refuge, Heracles used bronze castanets fashioned by Hephaestus and given to him by Athena. Frightened by the noise the birds broke cover and the hero killed them with his arrows.

6. Clean the **Stables of Augias.** The king of Elis in the Peloponnesus had been given great herds of cattle by his father, Helios, the Sun, but he had made no attempt to clear the dung out of the cattle sheds. Eurystheus wished to humiliate Heracles by ordering him to do manual labor. However, Heracles diverted the flow of the Alpheus and Peneus rivers through the stables and cleaned them out in one day.

7. Bring the **Cretan Bull** to Eurystheus alive. Heracles captured the bull and returned to Greece riding on the beast's back as it swam across the sea.

8. Bring back the four **Mares of Diomedes** alive. King Diomedes of Thrace had four mares which fed on human flesh. Heracles gave the mares Diomedes to eat, after which they became calm and allowed themselves to be led back to Greece.

9. Bring back the **Girdle of Hippolyta,** the queen of the Amazons. Heracles set sail in one ship manned by a crew of volunteers and arrived in the land of the Amazons after many adventures. Hippolyta agreed to give Heracles the belt, but Hera disguised herself as an Amazon and provoked a quarrel between the Amazons and the followers of Heracles. In the ensuing battle Heracles killed Hippolyta.

10. Bring back the of **Cattle of Geryon,** an immense herd which grazed on the island of Erythia. Though owned by Geryon, the cattle were attended by the herdsman, Eurytion, and the enormous dog, Orthrus. The island was located in the extreme west. To cross the sea, the hero borrowed the Cup of the Sun, a large vessel used by Helios to cross the ocean each night back to the east after he reached the west. At Erythia Heracles killed the dog Orthrus and Eurytion with a single blows of his club. He then set off toward Greece with the cattle, but was met by Geryon, at the banks of the river Anthemus, whom he killed with his arrows. He then returned to Greece. This may seem like outright robbery, but evidently it was justified because he had been ordered to take the cattle by his taskmaster. During this labor Heracles also had several unrelated adventures.

11. Bring back the terrible three headed dog **Cerberus** that guards the entrance to the Underworld. Heracles was first initiated into the Mysteries of Eleusis, which taught him how to safely cross over to the world of the dead. After many adventures he reached the presence of Hades and asked permission to take Cerberus away. Hades granted permission provided that Heracles subdue the dog without using his normal weapons. Heracles grasped the dog and did not let go until it was subdued. He returned with it to earth, but Eurystheus was so frightened that he did not know what to do with Cerberus, and Heracles returned the dog to his master.

12. Bring back the Golden Apples of the Hesperides. When Hera married Zeus, Gaea gave her golden apples as a wedding present. Hera planted the apples in her garden near Mount Atlas, where they were guarded by an immortal dragon with a hundred heads. After many adventures, Heracles found his way to the land of the Hesperides. Though his route is unclear, it led him northward through Macedonia and beyond. As he was climbing the Caucasus, he met Prometheus, who was chained to a rock and his liver was eaten away each day by an eagle, but always grew back again. This was the punishment decreed by Zeus because Prometheus has stolen fire from the gods and given it to humanity. Heracles freed Prometheus and in gratitude he told Heracles that he would not be able to collect the golden apples himself but that only Atlas could do it. After more adventures, Heracles found Atlas, who had been condemned to hold up the weight of the sky on his shoulders because he fought on the side of the Titans against the young gods during the epic battle of creation. Heracles offered to relieve Atlas of his burden if he would retrieve the golden apples from the garden of the Hesperides. Atlas

Figure 7.4: Heracles bringing Cerberus to Eurystheus.

agreed to this but upon his return with the apples he insisted on taking them to Eurystheus himself. Heracles pretended to agree to this but asked Atlas to take the weight of the sky for only a moment while he put a cushion on his shoulders. Atlas agreed, but once he resumed his burden, Heracles picked up the golden apples and fled. Heroes must not only exhibit super-human strength but super-human wisdom and cleverness!

There are many other stories of Hercules's adventures, but the most important is the account of his deification. His marriage to Deianeira was arranged by her deceased brother when he visited the underworld, but he had to fight the river god Achelous to obtain her hand. The couple was happy for a time, but when Heracles took a mistress, Deianeira gave Heracles a poison tunic (she thought it contained a love potion) and when he put it on it stuck to his skin and caused such intense pain that the hero climbed onto a huge funeral pyre and ordered it to be set on fire. But as the flames grew higher there was a clap of thunder and Heracles was lifted up into the sky on a cloud. Once among the gods Heracles was reconciled with Hera. He married Hebe, the goddess of youth, and became one of the immortals. Truly, Heracles is a hero for all time!

Ancient Greek Literature

The history of Greek literature begins with the oral, epic poetry of the Greek Dark Age. For more than a millennium the Greeks created a literature that has rarely been equaled and never surpassed. The masterworks of poetry, tragic and comedic drama, history, and philosophy fashioned by the ancient Greeks have inspired and influenced every succeeding age of Western Civilization down to the 21st Century. One is hard pressed to site a single idea or concept that concerns us today which was not discussed and debated by the ancient Greek writers. Of the four broad periods of Greek literature, Pre-Classical, Classical, Hellenistic, and Byzantine, only the first two concern us here. Hellenistic and Byzantine literature will be discussed in later chapters.

Pre-Classical

Homer

During the Greek Dark Age, the emphasis was on epic poetry. Two monumental works by Homer, the *Iliad* and the *Odyssey*, stand unchallenged as the greatest masterpieces of Western literature. The *Iliad* tells the story of only a single episode in the ten year long siege of Troy, and it centers around the hero Achilles, who embodies the very essence of the Greek heroic ideal. The *Odyssey* tells of the return of one of the heroes, Odysseus, from Troy to his home on the island of Ithaca, a ten-year journey back to his faithful wife and family.

Although the Homeric poems were a product of the Dark Age, they describe legendary events that occurred during the preceding Mycenaean Period. Throughout the bleak Dark Age the memories of the heroes of the by-gone age were kept alive, embellished, and made relevant to each succeeding generation by nameless bards who traveled from place to place celebrating ancient heroes and the heroic ideal. This was accomplished without a written language through an oral tradition of epic

Figure 7.5: Achilles and Ajax playing game.

poetry. Finally, the greatest of these bards, Homer, pulled together a cycle of stories into a single grand epic, known as the *Iliad*. It is centered around the wrath of the hero Achilles, who quarreled with Agamemnon, the king of Mycenae and the leader of the expedition against Troy. Homer lived long after the events he records. Indeed, he himself informs us that he is of an age of lesser men. He probably lived during the 8th Century BCE. Thus he gives us a picture of a time as remote from his own day as Shakespeare is from our own.

Homer by no means invented the epic style, indeed he drew from a long tradition and he assumes that his listeners are familier with that tradition. The language of Homer is not the ordinary speech of everyday communication, but a special language invented for use in poetry. This is evident even in translation:

> Sing goddess of the anger of Achilles, son of Peleus,
> Of the ruinous wrath that brought upon the Achaeans woes innumerable
> And hurled down into Hades many strong souls of Heroes,
> And gave their bodies to the pray of dogs and winged fowls
> And so the counsel of Zeus wrought out its accomplishment
> From that day when first strife parted Agamemnon
> King of men and the noble Achilles.[9]

The *Iliad* is a double story, two tightly organized sagas wound together like a fugue. One is the Tale of Troy, which forms a kind of canvas upon which the other story, the Tragedy of Achilles, is painted in vivid colors. Both stories retain an absorbing yet mutually dependant interest. Achilles's story is a typical Greek moral tragedy in which a great and noble character is caught in the grip of circumstances that cause him to suffer from a defect in his own high qualities.

> We are shown how one great soul, privately and in relation to other great souls, confronted large problems and overcame them, and his victory communicates a vicarious satisfaction to hearers whose souls are less great. Nothing in the story nor in its characters is puny, and the manner of its telling is rich and full; there is no exaggeration, no theatricals, no moral falsetto.[10]

Achilles is a true hero, he possesses a greatness that sets him apart from ordinary humans. Yet, in the end, he is all too human, and like all humans he is not perfect. Achilles possesses a human defect–not a vice–but a tragic flaw, which leads to his moral corrosion. The human flaw is his temper. He quarrels with Agamemnon and though his cause is just, his moral balance is destroyed when he rejects Agamemnon's bid for reconciliation. To understand the depth of Achilles's tragedy, however, one must grasp the enormity of what is at stake. Achilles was the son of Peleus, the king of the Myrmidons in Thessaly, a direct descendant of Zeus, and the goddess Thetis, daughter of Oceanus. When he decided to participate in the Trojan War, his mother warned him of his fate: if he went to Troy he would win great fame but his life would be short, whereas if he stayed home his life would be long but inglorious. Achilles did not hesitate to choose the short life full of glory. Thus, it was doubly tragic for Achilles when Agamemnon deprived him of the prize he had won

---

9. The first lines of the Iliad. "Sing goddess. . ." addressed to Calliope, the muse of epic poetry. "Achaeans . . ." the Greeks.

10. Hadas, Moses, *A History of Greek Literature* (1950), Columbia University Press, New York, p. 17.

on the field of battle: he had chosen glory over a long life and now, even though he was destined to die at Troy, Agamemnon had deprived him of his fame. This was the source of the anger Achilles could not control.

After many trials and much suffering, "He rehabilitates himself and asserts the victory of civilization when he overcomes his own passionate impulse to abuse the body of Hector and returns that body to Priam." The Iliad became the model and the guide by which the ancient Greeks defined the moral and upright life. "Throughout their history the Greeks were as closely familiar with its text as Puritans with the text of the Bible." And what was the moral teaching of the Iliad?

> Glory is the driving force and the object of existence, and honor is the paramount code. Birth, wealth, and prowess in arms confirm a man's title and give him the right to whatever his strength, qualified by a feeling of *noblesse oblige*, can win him. There is no other law, human or divine.[11]

It is an aristocratic code, "but Homer was read and venerated, not only under aristocracies, but under democracies and tyrannies as well."

Homer's other work, the *Odyssey*, is about 12,000 lines long, compared with the 15,600 lines of the Iliad. Both poems are organized into 24 books. The plot of the *Odyssey*, like the *Iliad*, involves two story lines which are brought together and resolved at the end. The *Odyssey* opens with the events of Odysseus's home on the island of Ithaca, where ten years after the end of the Trojan War his faithful wife Penelope has been resisting the advances of the suitors who have gathered to offer their "services" and his son Telemachus, who now journeys to Pylos and Sparta to inquire of Nestor and Menelaus what news they have of his father. The other story is the long and detailed account of the sufferings and adventures of Odysseus, as he is swept off course during his return and wanders for ten years around the Mediterranean trying to return home. Finally, the two stories come together as Odysseus returns home to face still more dangers from the suitors. After the suitors are slaughtered, Telemachus returns from Sparta and the family is reunited and begins to enjoy the bliss of a secure family life after twenty years of separation. The Odyssey is a romance that can be enjoyed of many different levels.

Hesiod

The other great poet of the Pre-Classical Period was Hesiod. Although little is known about him, he is more clearly a historical person than Homer. He lived and worked about 800 BCE in Boeotia in central Greece. His two surviving works are *Theogony* and *Works and Days*. While Homer describes the world of heroes and aristocratic honor, Hesiod writes about the dull and poverty-stricken country life of the farmers. Hesiod lays out a plan of moral behavior and law that makes human society possible. As Moses Hadas says, Homer describes "the world which Don Quixote tried to create," while Hesiod wrote about "the world Sancho Panza lived in."[12]

Theogony deals with the origin and genealogies of the divinities and the events that led to the kingship of Zeus. Hesiod describes the beginning of the world and how some 300 gods descended from Chaos and Earth. He maps out the complex family relationships of these divine beings. The poem ends with the marriage of Zeus and the other Olympians and a list of goddesses who lay with mortal men.

---

11. Hadas, Moses, *A History of Greek Literature* (1950), Columbia University Press, New York, p. 23.

12. Hadas, Moses, *A History of Greek Literature* (1950), Columbia University Press, New York, p. 34.

Works and Days provides advice for living a life of honest work, a subject that needs to be revisited by every generation, including our own. Hesiod is outraged by the dishonesty and idleness of his contemporary society. He gives both moral advice and practical instruction, especially for proper social and religious conduct. The final section is an almanac which lists the favorable and unfavorable days of the month for various activities. *Works and Days* is our most important source for the life of Archaic Greece.

Classical Age

Poetry

Toward the end of the Archaic Period there was a shift from epic to a more personal type of poetry, known as lyric poetry. Unfortunately for us, almost all of it has perished. Early Greek poetry actually went through three stages, which mirrored the changes that occurred in society. We have discussed the early epic style which was public in nature. It was composed to be recited before an assembled audience. Honor was the most important aspect of epic poetry. In contrast, lyric poetry is private and intimate in nature. It expresses the personal emotions and feelings that had no place in the public poetry of the bards. Homer's heroes would rather die a gory death on the battlefield than loose their shield to the enemy. Far better death than dishonor. Lyric poetry is a different world. About 650 BCE, for example, Archilochus wrote:

> Some Thracian struts about with my shield,
> For, being somewhat flurried,
> I left if by a wayside bush,
> when from the field I hurried:
>
> A right good skirmish, but I got away,
> The duce man take my shield;
> I'll get another just as good
> when next I take the field.

Who can imagine a Homeric hero speaking such words? Even if a hero thought of throwing down his shield and running from the battle, he would never admit it, much less brag about it in song! But here the poet confides in the reader his most intimate secrets, almost like a confession.

The most renowned lyric poet was Sappho, who has been described as "the greatest poetess of whom the world has knowledge."[13] In antiquity she was hailed as "the tenth muse." We know very little about her, however. She lived on the island of Lesbos in the second half of the 7th Century BCE. Her works were collected into nine books by the scholars at Alexandria, but only one complete poem and a few fragments survive. These have been gathered by scholars from quotations in other writers and from papyrus finds. Many of her poems refer to love between women and girls and have a distinctly homosexual tone. The constant references to partings and absences suggest that her circle shared their lives for only a limited period before marriage. In ancient Greece homoeroticism was institutionalized among both women and men due to the segregation between the sexes. All of this has been assumed to be evidence that Sappho was a headmistress of

---

13. Hadas, Moses, *A History of Greek Literature* (1950), Columbia University Press, New York, p. 51.

a kind of "finishing school for girls." Almost everything about her is speculation, however. What comes through all of this is her poetry. Even in translation her images evoke deep emotions in the reader.[14] For example:

> Six birthdays of mine had passed
> When the bones of my parent,
> Gathered from the pyre,
> Drank before their time my tears.

Or:

> The silver moon is set
> And the Pleiades are gone;
> Half the night is spent, and yet
> I lie alone.

Grief, loneliness. Very personal and private feelings.

During the Classical Period, poetry changed once again. It was now composed not to express personal, private feelings, but public celebrations and festivals. In other words, poetry changed from private back to public, and this was right in step with the spirit of the Classical Age, with its starkly public lifestyle. The second most notable characteristic of this new poetry is that religion permeates its very fabric. The ode, which is the most prominent form of classical poetry, originated as a celebration of victory at the athletic games, which were part of religious festivals, and it celebrated the victory by recounting myths in order to state moral lessons, or even sometimes to make political and social comments. This poetry was usually produced on commission for a patron. Pindar was the most famous of these poets. Since he almost always worked for tyrants and wealthy aristocrats, it is no wonder that his poetry reflects more of the traditional values of the old aristocracy than it does of the emerging democracy of the new poleis.

Even in our age of celebrity-worship, we have nothing to compare with the glory accorded to a victor in the athletic games of ancient Greece. The prime event of the ancient Olympic Games was the chariot races. The winner was as celebrated as a modern rock star, champion athlete, and a Nobel Laureate combined into one. When the victor returned to his native polis, he was received with great celebration. His entry was accompanied with the singing of "Hail the conquering hero," and a chorus performed a lyric ode, which was composed by a professional poet especially for the occasion. He remained an important member of the community as long as he lived and he dinned at the state hall at public expense. Nothing that he would ever accomplish during his entire life would ever be as important as winning an event at the Olympic Games. Pindar made his living composing poems, on commission, for such occasions.

The public quality of the ode and its use of religious allegory are illustrated in the opening lines of an ode composed by Pindar to celebrate the victory of Arkesilas, King of Cyrene, in an Olympian chariot race. Pindar compares the young athlete to the god Apollo and to the hero Battos, who was the founder of the athlete's home city of Cyrene in North Africa:

---

14. For selections from Sappho and other lyric poets, see "Three Greek Poets" in Cleve, Robert, *Early Western Civilization, Source Readings* (2002), Kendall/Hunt Publishing Company, Dubuque, pp. 310-317.

Today, muse, you must stand by the side of a friend,
By the king of Kyrene, the land of good horses:
And when Arkessilas holds his triumph,
Swell the gale of your songs,
Paying your debt to Lato's twins,[15] and to the Pytho,[16]
Where once, when Apollo was in his land,
The priestess, she who sits by god's gold eagles,[17]
Ordained Battos a leader of men
Into fruitful Libya.

What a contrast between this pompous, public verse and the tender and personal images of
Sappho. In language, in attitude, in tone, this seems much more akin to the epic poetry of Homer
than to the private poetry of the preceding age.

Drama

Greek tragic drama must be counted among humanity's highest achievements. It was the outcome
of the conjunction of artistic elements which came together in 5th Century BCE Athens: a democratic society eager to accept artistic innovation; a group of poets with profound insight into the
nature and fundamental problems of humanity; and the mature development of an epic tradition.
But of the elements that made up Greek tragedy, music and dance are missing today. It was a true
spectacle and what we have is only the words. It may be that we can only read libretti instead of
witness the operas. Yet, in spite of this, the modern reader needs no commentary to grasp the meaning of Greek tragedy, and it still touches the base of the human soul.

We know in fact that tragic drama originated in Athens, the leading democracy of ancient
Greece, but its actual origins are quite obscure. When one thinks about it, there seems no logical
reason to explain why people would even attempt to tell a story through a dramatic representation
on a stage utilizing a chorus and actors. Of course, we take all of it for granted today, but there is
nothing self-evident about the idea of theater, about plays and players, through whom private individuals—that is, the playwrights—lacking priestly or other authority, publicly examine humanity's
fate through the action of dramatic characters and through the moods, images, and comments of
actors on a stage. If "necessity is the mother of invention," what necessity inspired the origin of this
strange contrivance? This coupling of tragedy, epic poetry, music, and the plastic arts was a bold and
revolutionary step which has long outlasted the society which produced it.

Although tragic drama was not in itself a religious ritual, it nevertheless retained close ties to
religion for a long time. It originated as part of the "Great Dionysia," the annual spring festival of
Dionysus at Athens, established sometime near the beginning of the 5th Century BCE by the tyrant
Peisistratus. The festival lasted for five days and was celebrated at the end of March, when the city
was full of visitors after the winter. The first day was given over to a colorful procession in which
the image of Dionysus was brought to the theater on the south slope of the Acropolis and a ceremonial sacrifice of a bull to the god took place. At some point the sons of citizens killed in battle

---

15. Apollo and Artemis were the twin children of Leto and Zeus.

16. The priestess of the oracle of Apollo at Delphi.

17. Zeus released a gold eagle on each side of the world and they flew toward each other. They met at Delphi which
is thus the center of the earth-the Greeks called it literally "the navel" of the earth. The "Navel Stone" which marked
that spot is now in the Delphi Museum. It was originally surmounted by two gold eagles. Battos was directed by
an oracle of Apollo to found Cyrene.

Figure 7.6: Tragic actor holding mask.

were paraded in full armor in the theater, and so was the tribute brought in by the Athenian allies. Then there was a contest of odes, involving 10 choruses—5 of men and 5 of young boys—each containing 50 members and accompanied by flutes.

On the second day, five comedies were produced. Athens was also the birthplace of comic drama. Finally, there came the competition in tragedy, extending over three days. On each day one playwright presented three tragedies, which might be connected to form a trilogy, but need not be, and in fact usually were not. The highest official of the state, the eponymous archon,[18] presided over the proceedings and he selected a panel of five citizens to act as judges to select the winner of the competition. The effort required at least a thousand men and boys and it was repeated every year, even during the Peloponnesian War, and always only new works were presented—no re-runs.

The three most famous playwrights are Aeschylus, Sophocles, and Euripides. Between them they wrote approximately 300 plays, of which only 32 survive today. On the other hand, we do not possess a single play from any of the other 150 writers whose names we know—and how many other playwrights must there have been whose names are lost? However, it is almost certain that the 32 plays we have are not simply the result of random survival. In this case, the filter of time has given us the very best examples of what the ancient Greeks produced.

Aeschylus

Aeschylus was the most popular playwright of his day, winning no less than 13 victories at Athens. He also visited Sicily to produce his plays for Hieron, the tyrant of Syracuse. He was also an active citizen who fought at the Battles of Marathon—where his brother died a heroic death—and

---

18. By the end of the 5th Century BCE it became the common practice to identify the year by the name of the archon basileus ("king archon"), and he is usually referred to as eponymous archon (eponymous: a person whose name is or is thought to be the source of the name of something, such as a city, country, or the years of the colander), but that expression is not found in Greek texts until the Roman Period.

Salamis. In spite of his great celebrity throughout Greece as a playwright, the epithet he left for himself makes no mention of his art but records only what he considered most important in his life: his loyal service to his polis, Athens.[19]

The number of his plays is believed to be at least ninety, of which the titles of eighty-two are known, but only seven have survived. Among them are: *The Persians*, which treats the defeat of the Persians at Salamis; *Prometheus Bound*, the second part of a trilogy (the first and last parts do not survive), which depicts the punishment of Prometheus for stealing fire from the gods and giving it to humans; and The *Oresteia*, the only one of his trilogies that survives, consisting of *Agamemnon*, dealing with the murder of that hero on his return home from the Trojan War, The *Choephoroe* (*Libation Bearers*) in which Orestes avenges the murder of his father by killing his mother, Clytemnestra, and the *Eumenides* (*Furies*), in which Orestes is pursued by the Furies for the murder of his mother, but is eventually acquitted by the court of the Areopagus in Athens.

Aeschylus's style is marked by sublimity and majesty. His view of the universe reveals a profoundly philosophical mind, but at the same time he exhibits a heartfelt piety towards the gods, whom he sees as the upholders of morality. He introduced a long list of innovations into Greek theater, including scenic apparatus, masks for the players, and rich costumes. In keep with the custom of the time, he acted in his own plays, rehearsed the chorus, and choreographed dances.

Sophocles

Sophocles had an extraordinarily productive career. He was born in 496 BCE into a wealthy family and received the best education available. He won first prize with his very first play in 468 BCE at the age of 28, even though he was competing against Aeschylus. He was still active and creating masterpieces well into his eighties. He is known to have written 123 plays, of which we know the titles of 110, and he never placed third in the competitions. Like Aeschylus, only seven of his plays survive.

Every play of Sophocles presents a sequence of events carefully held together by case and effect and human motivation. They involve an oracle or prophecy being fulfilled in an unexpected way, but prophesy does not limit the freedom of choice of the characters. Each of his plays depict extreme suffering and an abrupt change in fortune. *Oedipus Tyrannus* is perhaps the best example. King Larius of Thebes received an oracle from Apollo that his son would kill him, so he ordered a shepherd to expose the infant Oedipus. The shepherd, however, took pity on the baby and took it to Corinth where it was raised by the king as his own son. When he grew older, an oracle warned him that he would kill his father and marry his mother, so he fled from Corinth. At a junction of three roads he became involved in a quarrel with a group of strangers and killed Larius, unaware that it was his father. He then traveled on to Thebes, where he answered the riddle of the sphinx and married Larius's widow Jocasta (not knowing she was his mother) and became king. The play begins at this point with the city of Thebes ravaged by a plague, caused, an oracle reveals, by the polluting presence of the murderer of Larius. Since Oedipus is a just and benevolent king, he begins an investigation, which eventually exposes the horrible truth. Jocasta hangs herself and Oedipus blinds himself with the pins from her dress. Here the play ends, but toward the end of his life Sophocles wrote *Oedipus at Colonus*. Here Oedipus, led by his daughter Antigone, comes to the grove of the Furies at Colonus near Athens, where he knows he will die. Protected by Theseus, the king of Athens, he resists the attempts of the Thebans to bring him back to Thebes for their own selfish purposes and

---

19. The geographer Pausanias, 1.14.5, says that the epithet of Aeschylus contained only his name, his father's name, the name of his city and that the Persians had witnessed his valor at Marathon.

finally dies mysteriously at a spot known only to Theseus, where his angry corpse will protect Athens against Theban attack. What a contrast between the stark hopelessness of his characters and the long successful life and career of Sophocles himself.

Euripides

Of the three Greek tragic playwrights, Euripides had the most artistic temperament. He was as eccentric as any modern artist and of course this caused stories concerning his lifestyle to circulate widely- some of them may actually be true. He is said to have written his plays in a lonely, book-filled cave on the island of Salamis. He was not a socialite and did not actively participate in the political life of his city as Aeschylus and Sophocles did. And also unlike them he only won a few prizes in the competitions. Thus, in modern accounts at least, there is the aura about him of a "man born before his time." His origins were said to be lowly, the gossips even said his mother was a green-grocer.[20]

Euripides's date of birth is uncertain, but he must have been born during the 480s BCE. He wrote at least 92 plays and we know the titles of about 80 of them. However, more of his plays— nineteen—survive than of any other ancient Greek Tragic playwright. He competed twenty-two times in the Great Dionysia at Athens, but won only four first prizes during his lifetime and one after his death. Thus, Euripides fits perfectly with the modern image of the misunderstood artist who did not receive full recognition until after his death. The modern media would have loved him.

He was an innovator in both form and content. He injected realism into his plays in a way that made his characters seem like contemporaries to the audience—as they do even today. The sufferings of Jason, Orestes, Electra, Medea, and Helen seem as real and relevant now as when they were first pinned by Euripides almost 2,500 years ago. He used reason to inveigh against social, political, and religious abuses, but he offered no consistent program of reform to correct them. Thus, his plays do not come across as preachy or as promoting a narrow political agenda.

Euripides's darkly tragic play, *The Trojan Women,* for example, seems to have been produced as a protest against the Melian massacre of the previous year.[21] Yet, *The Trojan Women* is not really an "anti-war protest" in the modern sense of that term. To the Greeks war was an expected fact of life and it was normally very bad for the losers. *The Trojan Women* goes deeper than anti-war protest, it deals with the sufferings of the conquered and was a reminder that those sufferings, which the Athenians inflicted on others, might also be inflicted on them. It reminded the audience how easy it is to disassociate themselves from the sufferings of others when those others can be placed in the category of "them;" but the realism of Euripides made those sufferings real in the minds of the audience. Now the suffers became "us," not "them." That is the genius of Euripides. And that, perhaps, is why he was not so popular with the panels of judges who awarded the prizes as was Aeschylus and Sophocles.

The Trojan Women takes place during the time between the defeat of Troy and return home of the Greeks. The main characters are the mothers, widows, and children of the dead Trojans, as they wait to be allotted to their future masters. The main characters are four Trojan women: Hecuba, the Queen of Troy; Cassandra, daughter of Hecuba and priestess of Apollo; Andromache, the widow of Hector; and Helen, the wife of Menelaus, king of Sparta (her seduction by the Trojan prince Paris

---

20. The ancients always believed manual labor was humiliating and intellectually debilitating. The story is almost certainly false.

21. After a six month siege, the island of Melos was captured. All the men were slaughtered and the woman and children were sold into slavery. See "Thucydides, The Melian Dialog" in Cleve, Robert, *Early Western Civilization, Source Readings* (2002), Kendall/Hunt Publishing Company, Dubuque, pp. 140–146.

was the cause of the Trojan War). The women's fate is decided by lot: Cassandra goes to Agamemnon; Andromache to Pyrrhus, the son of Achilles; and Hecuba will be the slave of Odysseus. Polyxena, another daughter of Hecuba, will be sacrificed on the tomb of Achilles. The young child Astyanax, the son of Andromache and Hector, is the only living male member of the royal family of Troy. The child is torn out of his mother's arms and thrown from the walls of Troy to his death, to prevent his growing up to avenge the destruction of Troy. Menelaus confronts Helen and is won over by her beauty. He intended to kill her, but she calmly proclaims her innocence, blaming her crime on Paris and the goddess Aphrodite. She claims she tried to escape from Troy but was held prisoner. Menelaus relents and takes her back to Sparta with him. The tragic irony of the play is that the Trojan women retain a courage and dignity which their Greek conquers have lost.

Comedy

Comedy was also an Athenian invention. The actors in comedy plays wore exaggerated and grotesque costumes, engaged in slapstick, and were often flagrantly obscene by modern standards. These plays dealt with the contemporary scene, and the comic playwrights poured out a stream of ridicule and verbal abuse on both popular personalities and ideas—indeed, not even the gods escaped their humor.

Only the plays of one writer of 5th Century BCE comedy—usually called "Old Comedy"—survives: Aristophanes. His plays demonstrate the amazing depth of freedom of speech and thought that existed in democratic Athens. For example, one of his most famous plays is Lysistrata, in which the women of Greece become so tired of the Peloponnesian War that they organize and go on a sex strike until their husbands are forced to make peace. This obviously anti-war play was produced at the very height of the Peloponnesian War in 411 BCE. No where else in the ancient world—and only a few places in the modern world—would such freedom be allowed.

By the middle of the 4th Century, however, this type of comedy gave way to a new type, the so-called "New Comedy," which was a comedy of errors. The characters and situations are still drawn from contemporary life, but the plots involve domestic problems and conflicts, such as love, marriage, and rediscovered offspring. The characters are mostly stereotypes: the wealthy young man; the difficult father; the wronged woman, and the endings are always happy. The most famous new Comedy playwright was Menander (342–293 BCE). His plots involve fictitious characters and fantastically complex plots, but he exhibits a sympathy and tolerance for the follies of humanity. New Comedy was funny, everyone could have a good laugh, and it did not offend any of the powerful members of society, as Old Comedy often did. Although none of Menander's plays survive, he was imitated by the Latin playwrights Plautus and Terence, so we know what they were like.

History

The Greeks invented history. About 300 years after Homer composed the epic Iliad, Herodotus of Halicarnassus (c. 484–425 BCE), a city on the coast of Asia Minor, wrote the first history.[22] It was Herodotus who first recognized a distinction between the "West" and the "East." He wrote an account of the most critical event his time, in which a few Greek cities opposed the great Persian Empire. Persian armies twice crossed the barrier of the Aegean Sea that separates Europe from Asia

---

22. History, from the Greek *historia*, an inquiry or investigation. The recent feminist etymology of the word as a combination of the two English words "his" and "story" is a pure invention and has no bases in reality.

and were twice repulsed by the Greeks. With that event, the West triumphed over the East. It was, in the view of Herodotus, a war between two competing visions of human society, between free men and men under the yoke of slavery.

Herodotus tried to control the mass of accumulated data concerning his subject through personal investigation and rational analysis. He traveled to all the areas about which he wrote and personally consulted the royal archives of Assyria, Persia, and Egypt for at least the previous 150 years or so. He also drew on the memories of those who had participated in the war. Importantly, Herodotus displays the attitude which distinguishes the study of history from a mere recording of events: skepticism. He dutifully reports everything he believed to be relevant to the events he investigates, including even the supernatural explanations, but he leaves no doubt about his own opinion. For example, when he records the report that in the upper room of the highest tower (ziggurat) of Babylon a god had sexual relations with a woman provided for his pleasure, he remarks "I do not believe it." Herodotus can, without hesitation, be awarded the title "father of history."

The next great historian was the Athenian Thucydides (c. 460–c. 400 BCE), who wrote a history of the Peloponnesian War. He was a member of a prominent Athenian family and fought in the war himself until 426 BCE, when he was ostracized. From exile he was able to describe the war objectively. He improved on the method of Herodotus by a more intense concentration on factual accuracy, by the elimination of all romance and myth from his account, by narrowing his focus to the war itself and the politics surrounding it and by a closer analysis of the causes of the events. He was the first to make the clear distinction between the cause and the beginning of an important event. For example, an uncritical reporter would refer to the Battle of Corcyra in 431 BCE, the first clash between the Athenians and the Spartan ally Corinth, as the cause of the Peloponnesian War, but Thucydides pointed out that the battle was only the beginning of the war. The cause was more subtle and complicated. An analysis revealed that "love of power, operating through greed and personal ambition, was the cause of all these events." For Thucydides, human nature is the motivation that drives history. History, he believed, is the study of the causes and effects of human actions, of the events of humanity's past, not an account of the will of the gods or a dissertation on the relationship between earth and heaven. For Herodotus the Persian War was an epic confrontation between freedom and slavery. For Thucydides the Peloponnesian War was a catastrophe of major proportions for all of Greece, which unfolds in a series of dramatic disasters.

Xenophon wrote a history called *Anabasis*, or *The March of the Ten Thousand*, also an event in which he participated. He was among the 10,000 Greek mercenaries involved in the rebellion and defeat of Cyrus at Cunaxa in 401 BCE. After the murder of the Greek generals by the Persians, he emerged as a replacement and led the survivors back to Greece. The *Anabasis* was more or less a memoir or journal of his adventure and it had a far reaching influence on the history of his times. However, after this, history grew in popularity and many writers tried their hand at it, but none managed to achieve the quality of Herodotus and Thucydides. History became either a dry list of facts or degenerated into a vehicle of political propaganda—as it sometimes does today.

Philosophy

For hundreds of thousands of years of humanity's early existence, human beings did not know the world the way we know it. Before philosophy the world was conceived as a collection of living beings. Why did the sun rise in the east and move across the sky each day to set in the west? Because the sun-god pulled it across the sky in his chariot. Why did the Nile River flood each year, providing the Nile Valley with a fresh coating of rich soil? Because the Pharaoh commanded it to do so. The living world often confronted the human being in ways he could not understand. So the human acquired knowledge of this living thing in the same way he got to know another person, by living with him and acquiring a feel for his moods and learning what he can be expected to do. Before philosophy, human life was dominated by these creatures who where not very well understood. The Greeks liberated the human mind, at least in the West, from these shackles.

Philosophy was rigorously pursued by the Greeks from the beginning of their history down to the end of the ancient world. Ancient Greek philosophy grappled with very basic questions, like "what is this world?" "What is a human being?" These were certainly not new questions, but previous answers had all been mythical and poetic, and the Greeks had their mythical explanation also: for example, the earth gave birth to the sky; Zeus, Poseidon and Hades were three brothers who overthrew the titans and divided the universe among themselves into three realms: the earth to Zeus, the Sea to Poseidon and the underworld to Hades. In this way, mythology explains both natural and human phenomena by reference to primeval events, which in themselves are unaccountable, not susceptible to verification. No one can actually prove that the statements above are not true, just as no one can prove they are true. In mythology, that is in religion, everything is defined in relation to, and in the context of, the divine world. The earth is seen simply as a reflection—and a dim reflection at that—of heaven or that unseen world of the spirit.

Philosophy, on the other hand, proposes rational, impersonal answers to such questions. To be sure, the first attempts to accomplish this were extremely naïve and speculative—such as "the earth remains in place by floating like a log." This was the solution of Thales (early 6th Century BCE), who has been given the title "the first philosopher." He was a 6th Century Ionian from Miletus, a city on the coast of Asia Minor. Now, his idea that the earth floats on water does not advance science very far in itself. Yet, his effort to explain the earth's existence through rational analysis rather than through mythological interpretation is a pivotal event in the history of human intellectual development. To put it quite simply, Thales invented philosophy and philosophy is the mother of science.

The Pre-Socratic Philosophers

The Greeks called Thales a physicist. The Greek word *physis* means "nature." Thus, Thales was literally a naturalist. He introduced a tradition based on theories about the fundamental nature of the physical world. Soon other individuals advanced along the path opened by Thales. In the next generation, Anaximenes (mid 6th Century BCE) suggested that air is the principle element. He thought this because by rarefaction or condensation, air can alter its appearance without undergoing a change in its nature.

A third Ionian, Anaximander (mid 6th Century BCE), actually proposed the first theory of evolution, when he wrote:

> In the beginning man was born from creatures of a different kind; because other creatures are soon self-supporting, but man alone needs prolonged nursing. For this reason he would not have survived if this had been his original form.

Anaximander suggested that these progenitors of the human species were "either fish or creatures very like fish." Certainly parts of this theory are very naïve, but how different it is from the traditional mythological explanation that human beings were created from the blood of an evil god.

Philosophy did not reject religion, however. Pythagoras (late 6th Century BCE), for example, was deeply religious. He and his followers formed a secretive mystery cult devoted to the purification of the soul through the attainment of wisdom. To them the cosmos was a well ordered material expression of numbers and numerical relations, based on the same principle of the harmonies of a tuned lyre. The Pythagoreans are distinguished from other Pre-Socratic philosophers by their mystical attitude, but they share with them the belief that a rational unity and order underlie the universe and are thus a part of the same philosophic and scientific tradition. We possess only fragments of the original works of the philosophers of this period, but even the bits and pieces we do possess are enlightening.

Socrates and Plato

A revolution occurred in philosophy during the second half of the 5th Century. This change is so completely identified with Socrates (c. 469–399 BCE) that all his predecessors are called "Pre-Socratic." Socrates devoted himself entirely to the study of humanity, not to physical nature, but it is incorrect to think that the earlier philosophers ignored humanity completely for a concentration on nature and the cosmos-Pythagoras, as we have seen, was very much concerned with the nature of humanity. It would also be wrong to overlook the contributions of Socrates's contemporaries, the much maligned sophists, those professional intellectuals that Socrates so detested. But having said all of this, it is true that Socrates was without rival in placing humanity at the center of philosophical inquiry.

He was mainly interested in obtaining a clear insight into the moral concepts guiding our lives and in the method by which we come to know the truth about them and about anything else. His method of inquiry involved getting together a group of young men to discuss such questions as "What is courage?" or "What is justice?" Someone would propose an answer which would then be subjected to a searching process of question and answer that would expose its contradictions. This process would continue until an answer was found that would survive critical scrutiny. This came to be called the "Socratic method."

His ultimate formula reads: knowledge = virtue = happiness. Socrates believed that only a fool would take actions against his own interests, if only he were wise enough to know what those interests really are. Thus, his philosophical system included a number of seminal ideas: One of them is that a human being is capable of knowing himself by rigorous, rational thought, by the dialectical method of analysis, described above, which weighs alternative hypotheses or explanations against each other; another Socratic idea is that true knowledge cannot, strictly speaking, be taught, but must be apprehended from within oneself; and finally, a person's knowledge of himself, of his own nature, is the true end of all knowledge and therefore, "a life unexamined is not worth living."

These are all generalizations, but beyond this we know almost nothing about him for certain, because Socrates, like Jesus, never wrote anything himself and because he became a legendary figure soon after his death. The only Socrates that we really know is the figure who was the protagonist in Plato's dialogues. How much of this Platonic Socrates is an invention of Plato (c. 429–347 BCE) and how much is the actual historical Socrates is certainly open to debate. There is good reason to believe that the Platonic Socrates and the historical Socrates are not altogether the same person, but nevertheless, it is the Platonic Socrates who has had such a strong and enduring impact on Western Philosophy.

Socrates believed that the soul, a term that was never fully defined in Greek philosophy, is the seat of the rational facility, and the soul is the essential factor which distinguishes humans from other animals. But the soul, unfortunately, is a mixture of the rational and the irrational, and to be truly human is to allow the rational element to dominate and control the irrational. However, all this has meaning only within the context of the society of the Greek polis, for it was that environment that produced Socratic philosophy. Therefore, love, friendship, piety, and immortality were among the subjects of the Socratic dialogues—but above all, justice. Justice is what Socratic philosophy is really about. And any inquiry into justice leads into politics. This is where Socrates got into trouble.[23]

The Socratic approach to politics was radical, because it went to the very root of the matter and attempted to deal with the nature of man.[24] Here we have to rely completely on Plato. It was a fundamental assumption of Plato that human beings are created unequal, not only in terms of their physique, wealth, or social position, but unequal in terms of their souls, that is they are morally and intellectually unequal. In Plato's judgment, that is, in the judgment of the Platonic Socrates, only a few people are potentially capable of completely rational behavior, that is, of correct moral judgment. Most are not. Therefore, the government of society ought to be placed in the hands of the morally superior few, that is, the philosophers. This is only logical and rational. And that authority should be total and final. This is the theme of Plato's most famous work, *The Republic*: a dictatorship of the morally superior.

Why did he believe this? According to Plato/Socrates, all of the visible, tangible things of this world are unreal and transitory, they are merely imperfect copies of the perfect and universal "forms" or "ideas" that exist somewhere else—in a non-natural, non-temporal world, or in the mind of god, perhaps.[25] Plato was never very clear or certain were this world of the ideas might be, but he was certain that world really did exist somewhere. Why did he think that these perfect ideas actually exist? Because the mind perceives them. For example, we know a chair when we see one, because the mind perceives what Plato called "chairness," that is, the mind perceives the ideal of chair and recognizes the similarity of this imperfect copy. But none of the chairs we see in this world are perfect, because they are simply corrupted copies of the ideal, of the absolute chair that exists in that other world.

This led Plato/Socrates to assert that there are also absolute forms for concepts such as truth, love, justice, etc., and that they are knowable to some people only, to those individuals who possess the morally superior souls, the philosophers. And it follows by simple logic that once these individuals are known, it is in the interest of everyone that they be placed in charge of society, in order that they may cause society to live by the standards of these absolute truths that only they can perceive. Who does not want to be ruled by those individuals who know the absolute truth? It is all very neat, and rational, and logical. . . and also very dangerous. How many disasters have been brought to fruition in Western Civilization by those who believe they perceive the absolute truth? Yet the existence of absolute truth and perfection has never been proven. It must be accepted on faith in order for the argument to be valid.

---

23. See note 26 below.

24. Today it is quite fashionable to deny the existence of the human nature. Many modern intellectuals and social critics have still not moved beyond the simplistic dichotomy between heredity and environment to acknowledge that all behavior comes out of an interaction between the two. See Pinker, Steven, *The Blank Slate, The Modern Denial of Human Nature* (2002), Viking Press, New York.

25. This was, in fact, a point the Platonists were never able to explain and here is where their philosophy comes to resemble a religion more than a rational philosophy: the basic premise on which all else is based is not rational at all, but must be accepted on faith. See "Plato, The Allegory of the Cave" in Cleve, Robert, *Early Western Civilization, Source Readings* (2002), Kendall/Hunt Publishing Company, Dubuque, pp. 251-256.

Aristotle and Greek Science

Aristotle (384–322 BCE) was born in Stagira, a city in Macedonia, the son of a physician. At age 17 he was sent to Athens to complete his education and he studied at Plato's Academy for some twenty years until Plato's death in 347 BCE. He then spent time in Asia Minor and at Pella in Macedonia where he served as Alexander's tutor for three years. In 355 BCE he returned to Athens and established his famous school, the Lyceum. After Alexander's death in 323 BCE, Aristotle was charged with "impiety" and withdrew to Euboea, saying that he was leaving to prevent Athens from "sinning twice against philosophy," where he died in 322 BCE.

Although profoundly influenced by Plato's ideas, Aristotle never accepted Plato's basic tenet that there is some other, non-natural world. For him, only the world we live in exists—and he had a passionate love for it, believing that every part of it had a beauty of its own, from the heavenly bodies to the lowliest grub. According to him, knowledge of this world is acquired by allowing our five senses to perceive it, and by then letting our intelligence go to work on the material provided by the operation of our senses—defining it, analyzing it, and systematizing it. Our intelligence, or reason, is our highest power, and our possession of this power distinguishes us from all other creatures and makes us human. The aim of every individual should be to become as fully human as possible. More than anything, that means pursuing knowledge as diligently as we can, contemplating it once we have it, and always, so far as humanly possible, letting our actions be guided by it.

All of this seems to be the basis for the development of a modern experimental science, but to the ancient Greeks, including Aristotle, science meant a "knowledge of causes and first principles." This knowledge produced *Sophia*, or wisdom. The word philosopher means literally "lover of wisdom." With the increasing accumulation of knowledge, however, specialists appeared. Philosophers like Socrates dismissed science as an inferior concern, and there were men who studied medicine or astronomy and showed little interest in metaphysics or ethics. But no real breach between philosophy and science ever appeared in the ancient world.

There was, however, an increasingly severe block to scientific progress, and this difficulty was the growing divorce between theory and practice. The ancients believed that knowledge was the highest good, but the aim of philosophy was to know, not to do. The goal of philosophy was to understand nature, not to conquer it, not to increase efficiency or improve production. Actually, astronomy, theoretical physics and mathematics prospered long after the applied sciences came to a virtual standstill.

Nevertheless, there were great scientists in ancient Greece. The most famous one, of course, was Aristotle and he rejected Plato's method of speculation and mental exercise and embraced empiricism totally. To him experience was the basis of all knowledge. According to Aristotle, all the speculation in the world cannot substitute for the observation of a single fact. His most intense interest was in biology. About a third of his writings were dedicated to this subject, and his successors at the Lyceum continued his biological researches. Because of the growing appreciation of experimentation, within two or three generations after Aristotle, Greek science had reached the very threshold of becoming a modern experimental science—but it lingered on that threshold for more than three centuries, failed to cross over it, and eventually turned away altogether.

Why? What was missing? Well, many scholars have attempted to answer this question, but no one has come up with a solution that seems convincing. These scholars speak of many factors, such as the presence of slavery, which they claim obviated the need to seek ways of improving production. But the simple fact is, the spark that turns speculation into research and research into practical application was simply not a part of the Greek psyche. For example, Aristotle and his followers collected extensive data on animal breeding and plant yields, but no one ever drew the conclusions from this knowledge which would lead to selective breeding in agriculture and animal husbandry. One more example; Democritus (c. 460–c. 370 BCE) proposed an atomic theory of matter. But although the Greeks speculated for centuries about atoms, this never led to empirical observation, never led to more advanced scientific investigation of the nature of matter. It is all very mystifying.

But the fate of Greek science was not shared by philosophy. One reason that philosophy was such a strong force in Greek intellectual development was that Greek religion lacked a dogma or a systematic theology. Its public rituals were emotionally stimulating, but its explanations were intellectually unsatisfying. Because Greek religion was not organized into an institutionalized church and there was no strong class of professional priests, philosophers had unusual freedom to speculate. Unlike other societies, such speculation, no matter how outrageous, did not threaten any class or institution. For example, Aristarchus of Samos (fl. c. 270 BCE) put forth the hypothesis that the earth rotates on its axis and revolves around the sun. This no doubt annoyed the gods and offended pious men, but neither the gods nor the men raised any great outcry. Certainly there was never any thought of burning Aristarchus at the stake, as the Christians burned scientists during the Middle Ages. His theory, however, failed to win support on quite different grounds: other astronomers put forward what to the Greek mind seemed to be a simpler hypothesis, the geocentric model of the universe, in which the sun revolves around the earth. The geocentric universe, with the earth at its center, was more in keeping with the Greek humanistic mind-set: "Man is the measure of all things."

Of course, at least one philosopher was put to death, ostensibly for his beliefs. The trial and execution of Socrates comes immediately to mind—indeed it comes to mind too readily and too often, because it was not typical.[26] It was, in fact, an aberration. One cannot name another example. And so one example does not prove a rule and it serves no purpose to dwell on it. This is not the way the Greeks normally dealt with dissention and original thought.

Art

Classical Greek art was one of the most brilliant achievements of the West. The standards of style and harmony established during the brief period dating roughly from 480 to 323 BCE have largely dominated the art of the Western world to the day. During a period of barely a century and a half, the Greeks in general, and the Athenians in particular, achieved near perfection in vase painting, sculpture, and architecture. The one word that best describes the Classical style is idealism. It was based on the ideals of reason, moderation, symmetry, balance, and harmony. Classical Greek art was not concerned with experimentation but with expressing eternally true ideals.

---

26. In 399 BCE, during the aftermath of the Peloponnesian War, Socrates was charged with "not recognizing the gods that the state recognizes and introducing other new divinities" and with "corrupting the young." The fact that the aristocrat Critias, who administered the reign of terror in Athens during the Spartan occupation of the city after the Peloponnesian War, was a student of Socrates and proclaimed that he was putting the political principles of Socrates into effect, did not help Socrates's case. See "Plato, The Apology: The Defense of Socrates at His Trial" in Cleve, Robert, *Early Western Civilization, Source Readings* (2002), Kendall/Hunt Publishing Company, Dubuque, pp. 251–256.

Vase Painting

> When old age shall this generation waste,
>   Thou shalt remain, in midst of other woe
> Than ours, a friend to man, to whom tho say'st,
>   "Beauty is truth, truth beauty—that is all
>   Ye know on earth, and all ye need to know."

Thus a moment of beauty captured by an ancient Greek artist over 2,000 years ago inspired the Romantic poet John Keats—and is preserved long after both the artist and poet are gone. The Classical Greek artists covered their pottery with detailed illustrations of figures living in a complex and beautiful world:

> Thou still unravish'd bride of quietness,
>   Thou foster-child of silence and slow time,
> Sylvan historian, who canst thus express
>   A flowery tale more sweetly than our rhyme:
> What leaf-fring'd legend haunts about thy shape
>   Of deities or mortals, or of both,
>   In Tempe or the dales of Arcady?
>   What men or gods are these? What maidens loth?
> What mad pursuit? What struggle to escape?
>   What pipes and timbrels? What wild ecstasy?[27]

One of the joys of a visit to any major art museum is the section devoted to Greek vases, displayed reverently in their glass cases. However, in ancient Greece, pottery played an important role in every home. Vases were used as storage vessels for wine and oil, for bringing water from the community well, and for many other utilitarian purposes. What distinguishes Greek vases from all other pottery is that their decoration, both in content and technique, rises above the level of decoration and deserves the special term "vase painting."

Beginning about the middle of the 6th Century BCE, pottery produced in Athens, known as the Attic style, became supreme in Greece and held that position until the end of the Peloponnesian War in 404 BCE, when Athens lost its profitable markets. Afterward, Attic pottery went into decline.

The archaic style, known as geometric, consisted of strict, orderly patterns applied with dark paint on the natural clay background. Human and animal figures appeared by the 8th Century BCE, but they were highly stylized and subordinated to an element of the geometric design. Beginning about 700 BCE, the Greeks came under increasing influence of the Near Eastern tradition of floral ornaments, exotic beasts, and strange monsters. This is known as the "Orientalizing" style. During this period, the "black figure" technique was developed in Corinth. Figures are shown in black silhouette against a red clay background, with details carefully etched into the black paint. The focus is now on the main subject which covers the belly of the vessel. The rest is painted black, giving the style a simplified and elegant feel. This style is a revolutionary break with the past.[28]

---

27. John Keats (1795–1821), Ode to a Grecian Urn.

28. While the black figure technique was abandoned in the late 5th Century BCE, the "Panathenaic amphorae" were still decorated with the old technique. These amphorae, filled with olive oil taken from the trees at Akademia, were prizes for winners of the athletic games held at the Great Panathenaia held every four years at Athens.

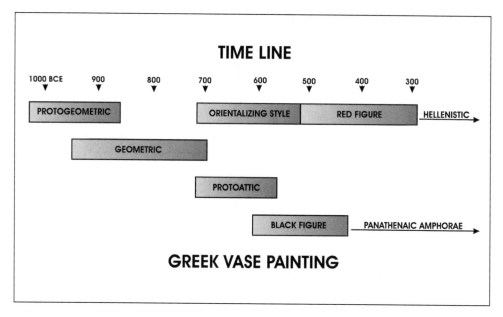

Figure 7.7

About the time Cleisthenes was developing democracy in Athens around 500 BCE, a new technique, the red figure style, developed, which in effect was a reversal of the black figure style. Now the background is painted black and the figures are left in red clay. Bodies overlap and the detail of muscles, hair, dress, etc., are drawn with the use of thin, delicate black lines. Even facial expressions now appear on the figures.

Both these styles exploit the natural redness of the Athenian clay, which is rich in iron oxides. A third technique outlines figures on a background which is made using a white clay slip applied over the reddish clay. This "white ground" technique has quite a long history but is most common in 5th Century Athens. It provides a more realistic effect than the black and red figure styles. A wide verity of colors, including yellow, pink, red, violent, and blue, can be added. The drawing technique, however, is the same as black and red figure.

Pottery shapes were remarkably standardized. There were some thirty different shapes employed but only about fifteen were common. The painting itself continued to develop during the entire period. Until about 520 BCE the human form was depicted as it had been in earlier styles, as two-dimensional profile, or in combination of profile and frontal views. Then, towards the end of the 6th Century BCE, more realistic poses appeared, showing the human body as it appears in life, not stylized as it had been. The artists also attempted to show the body in motion. An artist named Kimon from the town of Kleonai, is credited[29] with inventing three-quarter views, showing human figures in various poses with body parts clearly articulated and drapery with folds and creases. Similar advances can be seen in sculpture and bass-relief at roughly the same time. About the end of the 5th Century BCE the greatest painters of their time, Parrhasios and Zeuxis, introduced new techniques, which used outline and shading in new ways to achieve greater realism. These technical advances are as fundamental to Western painting as the earlier abandonment of the rigid profile at the beginning of the century.

29. Pliny, Natural History, 35.55–56.

BLACK FIGURE   **RED FIGURE**   **WHITE GROUND**

Figure 7.8: The three major types of Greek vase painting.

The subjects of Greek vase painting include every conceivable aspect of ancient life: weddings, funerals, scenes from the market and work place, and much more. A large percentage of vases depict stories from mythology. Even the most intimate and erotic scenes are common. Homosexual activity, sexual relationships between an older man and a young boy, the ideal type of sexual and romantic relationship according to philosophers such as Plato—which in our society is called "child molesting"—as well heterosexual, even group sex, is common in Greek vase painting. Thus, above and beyond its great artistic value, Greek vase painting is a prime historical source for the modern scholar. For example, the information it provides concerning everyday life can be found in no other source.[30]

Sculpture

The sculpture produced during the Classical period is some of the most beautiful the world has ever seen. Classical Greek sculpture is the very essence of humanism, characterized by a freedom of movement and expression never seen before. The stylized Archaic kouros and kore gave way to realistic figures which radiated the illusion of moving through space. Strict asymmetry was replaced with a free flowing form more true to life. The static archaic sculptures were transformed into dynamic masterpieces bursting with potential energy. For the first time in history, the human anatomy was deemed worthy of being immortalized in stone or bronze.

---

30. For an overview of Greek vase painting see: Boardman, John, *The History of Greek Vases* (2001), Thames & Hudson, London; Buschor, Ernst, *Greek Vase Painting* (1978), Hacker Art Books, New York; Cook, R.M., *Greek Painted Pottery* (1966), Methuen, London.

MYRON, DISCUS THROWER   LYSIPPUS, YOUNG ATHLETE

Figure 7.9: Left, Roman marble copy of Greek bronze; Right, Greek bronze recovered from ship wreck in 20th Century.

Why, among the ancient civilizations, only the Greeks celebrate the naked human body is a mystery. The amount of skin visible in Classical Chinese art, for example, is limited to faces, arms, hands, and occasionally a leg or foot. India is much the same, except for a late, brief, outburst of erotic art. But the Greek artist celebrated the human body as a thing of beauty. Even today museums are inhibited about showing it all: the Vatican Museum has, in a childish display of prudishness, ruined countless ancient masterpieces by placing fig leaves over parts of the human body considered by the Church fathers to be offensive.[31] Another mystery: what happened to the women? In Classical Greek art, the ratio of male to female subjects is roughly twenty to one.

Above all, Classical art was humanistic. Throughout history the human figure had been used by other civilizations as a mere object which signified metaphysical preoccupation. The Greek artist reversed thousands of years of artistic tradition by shifting the focus of art from the supernatural and unknown to more earthly matters. While Classical Greek sculpture often depicts deities, the human body clearly becomes the subject of study. The gods were used as a mere excuse to celebrate humans.

During the Classical period the Archaic smile was replaced by a solemn facial expression. Even in sculptures which depict violent and passionate scenes the faces betray no expression of any kind. However, this was the case only for Greeks because barbarians were always depicted with dramatic facial expressions. The Greeks believed that suppression of the emotions was a noble characteristic of civilized men (i.e. Greeks), while the public display of emotion was a sign of barbarism. Thus, logic and reason must dominate human expression even during the most dramatic situations.

---

31. The scholar Kenneth Clark even managed to turn his priggish little book (*The Nude, a Study in Ideal Form* (1959), Doubleday, New York), in which he convinced himself that there was a profound esthetic difference between nudity and nakedness, into a PBS series.

Classical Greek sculpture was also harmonious. During this period the Greeks came to understand the world as a series of opposing forces that created a synthesis and maintained a balance. In sculpture the human figure was also composed of opposing forces which created a perfect aesthetic entity the moment they achieved balance. As the weight of the upper body shifted towards one side, the corresponding leg muscles stiffened and the bones straightened in order to support it, while another group of muscles and bones on the other side relaxed and moved to retain the physical balance and harmony. It was clear to a Classical artist that the beauty of the whole depends on the harmony of the parts which comprise it, and that each part depends on the others in order to create a harmonious whole.

Thus, the primary focus of Classical sculptures shifted away from metaphysical subjects toward the formal problems of creating an art which represented the real world by creating a harmonious balance of opposing forces. They searched for this balance in astronomy, in philosophy, in politics, in science, in architecture, and in art, and they expressed it in mathematical formulas which could be applied in nature.

Although the vast majority of the surviving Classical Greek sculpture we see in museums today is marble, in antiquity probably more bronze statuary was produced than marble. However, very little bronze art survived through the Middle Ages. During those dark times, metal became so valuable that almost all of the great bronze art from the past was melted down to obtain metal for weapons and tools. Almost all of the Greek bronze on display in museums today was recovered during the past century or two by archaeologists. The most famous bronze statues, like the Zeus (or Poseidon) of Artemisium and the Getty Bronze, were retrieved from ancient ship wrecks. Another invaluable source of Classical Greek sculpture is Roman copies. The later Romans were great admirers of Greek culture and art. They made many splendid copies of the great Greek masterpieces, which are now lost. Fortunately, some of the Roman copies survived and give us a good idea of what the originals were like.

Architecture

For the Greeks, as for the Mesopotamians and the Egyptians before them, architecture began in the service of the gods. By the Classical Period they had developed a series of well-defined standards of relationships and proportions, which were accepted as the norm for temple design. These norms were codified into three "orders:" Doric, Ionic, and Corinthian.

Greek temple design seems to have derived from the Mycenaean megaron, or house of the chief, and were constructed of wood. After adopting stone as the building material the Greeks retained the basic temple form, which explains certain features of the classical temple, such as the triglyph and metope sequence of the Doric frieze. The development of the classical temple design resulted from an endless quest for perfection. By the 5th Century BCE distinct styles, or "orders," had emerged, each with its own form of entablature. The Doric style reached its maturity at the end of the 6th Century BCE, when a set of almost universally accepted proportions was adopted. The formula was repeated all over western Greece, but the most famous and perfect example of the Doric style is the Parthenon in Athens.

The architecture of the Greeks who settled in Asia Minor exhibits the influence of the older civilizations of the Near East. A succession of colossal temples at Ephesus, Samos, and Didyma reflected the influence of the gigantic Egyptian architecture. From the Middle East the Ionians acquired the idea that columns should have bases and capitals. They developed the volute, or scroll shape, into the Ionic capital, which is one of the most enduring decorative forms ever devised. Although some of the temples constructed in Ionia, among them the temple of Artemis at Ephesus,

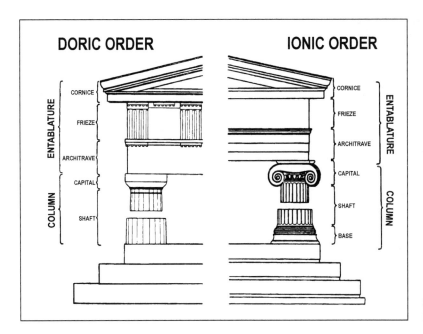

Figure 7.10: The Doric and Ionic Orders.

counted as one of the Seven Wonders of the World,[32] were the largest temples ever built by the Greeks, only traces of them remain today. By the 5th Century BCE, the Ionic order was being used even in Athens. The most famous example is the little temple of Athena Nike at the gateway to the Acropolis.

The ancient writer Vitruvius says the Corinthian capital was invented by the Corinthian Callimachus[33] in the late 5th Century BCE, but this is disputed by some modern scholars. The Corinthian Order is essentially the Ionic Order with a different type of capital, shaped like an inverted bell with the Ionic volutes reduced and placed at the corners and surrounded by acanthus leaves. Thus, the Corinthian capital was designed to be viewed only from the front. The Corinthian Order made little impact in Greece, however, perhaps because it was considered to be too ostentatious, but later it became immensely popular in Rome. It was modified by the Romans to become the Composite Order used by the Romans for their imperial buildings constructed throughout their empire.

---

32. The other six: the pyramids; the hanging gardens of Babylon; the statue of Zeus at Olympia; the Mausoleum of Halicarnassus; the Colossus of Rhodes; the lighthouse on the island of Pharos in Alexandria, Egypt.

33. *Vitruvius, On Architecture,* 4.1.7–10. "Now the first invention of that capital is related to have happened thus. A girl, a native of Corinth, already of age to be married, was attacked by disease and died. After her funeral, the goblets which delighted her when living, were put together in a basket by her nurse, carried to the monument, and placed on the top. That they might remain longer, exposed as they were to the weather, she covered the basket with a tile. As it happened the basket was placed upon the root of an acanthus. Meanwhile about spring time, the root of the acanthus, being pressed down in the middle by the weight, put forth leaves and shoots. The shoots grew up the sides of the basket, and, being pressed down at the angles by the force of the weight of the tile, were compelled to form the curves of volutes at the extreme parts. Then Callimachus, who for the elegance and refinement of his marble carving was nick-named *catatechnos* by the Athenians, was passing the monument, perceived the basket and the young leaves growing up. Pleased with the style and novelty of the grouping, he made columns for the Corinthians on this model and fixed the proportions. Thence he distributed the details of the Corinthian order throughout the work."

Figure 7.11: Corinthian Capital.

Civil and domestic architecture was almost completely ignored during the Archaic and even the early Classical periods. It was not until the 4th Century BCE that Greek architects turned their attention to public buildings and private houses. Public buildings took two major forms: the stoa, which was a covered hall open on one side by a colonnade; and the hypostyle, a covered room with internal columns supporting the roof. These hypostyle rooms were known as gymnasia, or *plalstrae*, when they housed sporting or cultural activities. Vitruvius described these buildings as containing conference rooms in which philosophers, orators, and all those interested in learned discussion could sit and talk.

Public theaters were originally required for certain religious festivals and celebrations and they were thus built near sanctuaries. Theaters were in the shape of shells and were normally cut out of hillsides. They were open to the sky, but were enclosed by a wall, which later developed into a complex building, which housed shops, shrines, etc.

Private Life

What can we know about the private, everyday life of ancient Greece? Probably less than we think we know. The attempt to recover a knowledge and understanding of the daily life of ordinary people in the ancient world has become something of a growth industry in recent decades. But all the resources and energy that have been devoted to the effort have not measurably increased the available evidence, which is surprisingly sparse. It is far easier to analyze documents and texts concerning the affairs of state or the structure of government than it is, for example, to learn anything substantial about the private and intimate affairs which occurred behind the "closed doors" of the ancient household. That task is daunting enough even for the contemporary world. Thus, the large number of learned books, articles, surveys, etc. that have been published recently are overwhelmingly based on a

Figure 7.12: A woman's lot. The drunken husband comes home after a party and hammers on the door with butt end of his torch. Inside, his young wife, lamp in hand, trembles in fear.

rehash and reinterpretation of former writings and pure speculation. Invariably, speculation projects the attitudes and biases of the modern world back into the past. So this is really yet another case of a generation rewriting history in its own image. Nevertheless, we should try to understand as much as we can about how the people of the ancient Greece actually lived.

The Status of Women

In ancient Greece the sexes were rigidly segregated, and upper class citizen women, especially, were only a small, barely distinguishable step above the status of slave. In many ways her life was quite similar to that of a modern Islamic woman in societies like Saudi Arabia. Two rooms in the Greek house, the *andron*, or "men's apartment," and the *gynaikonitis*, or "women's quarters," reveal much about the status of the sexes in Greek society. Women were normally secluded in the *gynaikonitis*, usually located on the second floor and out of the way of male visitors the husband might be entertaining in the *andron*. This was in keeping with the Greek belief that men and women occupy two different spheres of activity in life. As Xenophon put it:

> It is more honorable for a woman to remain indoors rather than to be outside, but for the man it is more shameful to remain indoors than to take care of affairs outside the house.[34]

34. Xenophon, *Oeconomicus*, 7.30.6.

The husband lived a public life out in the agora, the assembly or the gymnasium, or on the battlefield in time of war, while the wife was confined to the house. She was rarely allowed outside unless accompanied by her husband or another male member of the family. Even the shopping was done by the husband or a slave. The only time a respectable woman could be seen outside the house was at weddings, funerals, or certain religious festivals. Of course, seclusion was somewhat less rigid in poor families. If the family did not own slaves, for example, the wife would have to fetch water from the local public well herself. This is one of the reasons poor families were considered less "respectable" than wealthy families.

A woman could not live independently, but must always be under the guardianship of a man. She was under the control of her father until she married at the age of 14 or 15. Marriage was arranged between the father and the groom. The bride and groom would hardly know each other because respectable women were not allowed any contact with males outside the family. Even after marriage the husband and wife did not have a very personal and intimate relationship, because purpose of marriage was not love or emotional satisfaction (the man satisfied those needs outside the house), but the production of healthy children. After the wedding, control of the woman passed to the husband and remained with him until his death or divorce.

From a man's point of view—we have almost no evidence at all for the woman's point of view, because all ancient Greek texts were written by men—the ideal status was invisibility. This is stated very clearly in Pericles's Funeral Oration:

> If I am to speak also of womanly virtues, referring to those of you who will henceforth be in widowhood, I will sum up all in a brief admonition: Great is your glory if you fall not below the standard which nature has set for your sex, and great is it hers of whom there is least talk among men whether in praise or in blame.[35]

What is this "standard which nature has set?" According to Aristotle:

> In comparison to a man a woman is more jealous and complaining of her lot, more given to verbal and physical abuse. The female is more melancholy than the male and more dependant, also more shameless, more given to lying, and more disposed to cheat. . .[36]

The ideal of invisibility expressed by Pericles is in stark contrast with the ideal of public visibility of Greek males, who cherished the glory and fame of military achievement and public service.

Slavery

The existence of slavery in a society so admired for its enlightened humanism is disturbing to many scholars, but it should not be surprising. Until very recently, historically speaking, no complex civilization has been able to function without some form of involuntary servitude, whatever name is given to it. Only the advent of the machine has made civilization possible without enforced servitude. In any event, as the ancients were well aware, servitude is relative. Many forms of servitude have existed throughout history, slavery being only one of those forms. It is far from clear, for example, that the ordinary serf of the early Middle Ages was more "free" than the household slave of

---

35. Thucydides, 2.45. See "Thucydides, Pericles' Oration" in Cleve, Robert, *Early Western Civilization, Source Readings* (2002), Kendall/Hunt Publishing Company, Dubuque, p. 134.

36. Aristotle, *Historia Animalium,* 608b.8–12.

Figure 7.13: Funerary preparations. The young woman who died before being married, wears a bride's crown. Left, a relative with loose hair laments. Right, her nurse/slave offers last services.

ancient Athens. Conversely, it is entirely possible that the members of some utopian society centuries hence—served by armies of sophisticated robots—may look back at the 21st Century and interpret the necessity of individuals in our society to "work for a living" as a form of involuntary servitude as distasteful to them as the slavery of past societies is to us.

The origins of slavery in Greek society are unclear. In Homer and other early texts, most slaves were the result of piracy, kidnapping, and warfare. In historical times it was the general practice to enslave the women and children of a captured city—the men were more difficult to control and were normally killed. Some slaves, though this seems to be the exception rather than the rule, were bred in captivity. Xenophon states:

> As a general rule, if good slaves are permitted to breed, their loyalty increases, whereas when bad slaves lie together as husband and wife they are more liable to cause trouble.[37]

By the 7th Century BCE, the institution of slavery was firmly established throughout Greece, even among the poorest classes. Hesiod expressed the opinion that the ox and the slave were essential to successful farming. None of the great philosophers, even the Stoics who believed in the brotherhood of humanity, ever seriously questioned slavery. Even Aristotle regarded slavery as part of the natural order of existence.

---

37. Xenophon, *Oeconomicus,* 9.5.

Figure 7.14: Homosexual activity between man and young boy. This was a highly idealized romantic relationship in Classical Greece.

However, it is important to recognize that slavery in the ancient world was not an absolute condition. There was a wide range of different statuses just as there were a range of statuses for free individuals. The ancients did not recognize either absolute slavery or absolute liberty. They knew that the slave working in the horrible conditions of the silver mine was not in the same status of servitude as the domestic slave entrusted with the care of the family's children.

In cities like Athens, the possession of at least one slave was considered necessary. Most citizens probably owned two or three slaves and the wealthy citizens possessed ten or twenty. In the 5th Century BCE, Nicias, the wealthiest man in Athens, owned 1,000 slaves, which he employed in a rent-a-slave business for one obol per slave per day. Slaves were imported from Thrace, Scythia, Illyria, and Asia Minor. The price of a slave depended on the slave's skills and looks. An educated slave was most valuable and one with management skills was extremely expensive. A pretty girl, of course, cost more than an ugly old hag. Handsome young boys also fetched a high price.

The most privileged Athenian slaves were those owned by the state. As strange as it sounds to modern ears, the Athenian civil service was composed of slaves, including accountants, jury clerks, and even a unit of Scythians who acted as the city's police force. On one occasion, it is even recorded that these Scythian slaves were sent out to forcibly round up citizens to attend an emergency meeting of the assembly. A large number of state-owned slaves were kept busy maintaining the roads and public buildings, and slaves often worked alongside Athenian citizens on building projects like the Parthenon. In fact, slaves could be found performing almost every job in Greek society, except politician. A few slaves even became wealthy. These were the managers of shops and factories, bankers, captains of commercial ships, and artisans. One 5th Century BCE slave, who was a banker, became one of the wealthiest men in Athens and was eventually granted Athenian citizenship because he made a generous contribution to the state in a time of crisis. This was a rare exception, however. Greeks were much more niggardly than the Romans in granting freedom to their slaves, even after they had served them loyally all their lives. On the other end of the scale, the most dangerous and exhausting work was performed by the mine slaves. Work in the dark, unhealthy mines continued uninterrupted twenty-four hours a day, on ten hour shifts.

Domestic slaves served in every household function imaginable, including cook, cleaner, tutor, escort, messenger, nurse, and companion. They were in fact very much like members of the family. Whether slaves were also employed in large numbers as agricultural workers in the countryside is not known, but the assumption that they were is reasonable. Upon entering a household a new slave underwent an initiation ceremony similar to that required of a bride upon entering a household. This placed the slave under the protection of Hestia, the goddess of the hearth and tended to bond the slave to the family. On Odysseus's return home after an absence of twenty years, his faithful slaves threw their arms around him and kissed him. Scenes of mistresses and their slaves are prominent on Athenian grave monuments, and slaves were occasionally buried in the family plots of their master or mistress.

The treatment of slaves varied, of course, from one household to another, depending on the predisposition of the owners. Athenian slaves were protected by law against violent abuse, but in practice it was almost impossible for them to lodge a complaint with the authorities, since only a citizen could represent them in court. Starvation and beatings were the normal punishments for bad behavior and runaway slaves were branded with a hot iron upon capture. If a slave was required to be a witness in court, their testimony could only be accepted under torture. We have no accounts written by slaves to tell us how they felt about their conditions. Thus, all of our attempts to understand this aspect of slavery in ancient Greece are, in the end, based on hearsay and speculation, and every image we reconstruct is tainted by our own biases and attitudes.

Everyday Life

Ancient Greek children played with many toys, including rattles, little clay animals, horses on wheels that could be pulled on a string, yo-yos, and dolls. The family might have several different kinds of pets, including dogs, birds, goats, tortoises, and mice-but not cats. Dogs especially were popular and were trained to perform various functions such as hunting and guarding.

The ancient Greek diet consisted of wheat, barley, vegetables, breads, and cakes. Of course, New World vegetables like tomatoes and potatoes were unknown, and sweetening was accomplished with honey, not sugar. Fish and various varieties of seafood were an important part of the diet, but red meat was eaten rarely, normally only as part of a religious sacrifice. A lot of wine was consumed. Most ordinary meals were prepared and eaten in the courtyard.

Clothing was very simple. Linen was worn in the summer and wool in the winter. Cloth and clothes could be purchased in the agora, but that was expensive. Most cloth was woven at home by the women and female slaves. The women of the family dyed the cloth a bright color or bleached it white and constructed simple tunics and warm cloaks. Pants were not worn by the Greeks and, in fact, were considered a mark of barbarism. Jewelry could be purchased in the agora or from traveling peddlers. Both men and women used perfume made from boiling flowers and herbs. A broad-brimmed hat was worn for traveling to protect the head and face from the sun.

The Greeks admired the blonde look, though blonde hair was rare, so women sometimes attempted to bleach their hair. Men cut their hair short and wore beards, unless they were soldiers. Barber shops were a popular part of men's social life. They gathered there frequently to exchange news and gossip. However, women had to care for their personal needs at home, attended by their maid servants.

Dance and music were an important part of life. Dancing was believed to improve both the physical and the emotional health. But men and women did not dance together. We know of over 200 different dances for weddings, funerals, and religious ceremonies. Music was provided by lyres, flutes, and a wide variety of percussion instruments, such as tambourines, cymbals, castanets, and drums.

8

The Hellenistic Age

The tragedy of Greek history was the Greeks' inability to solve the problem of inter-state warfare. For two centuries the cities of Greece—Athens, Sparta, Thebes, Corinth, the island states of the Aegean Sea, and the Greek cities of Asia Minor—engaged in violent wars that spilled the blood of generation after generation. The long and bitter Peloponnesian War eventually involved almost the entire Greek world and it seriously undermined the Greek spirit and brought discredit to the entire Poleis system. A desire, almost a yearning, for peace and unity, known as Pan-Hellenism, spread throughout Greece. Nevertheless, during the decades after the war, the poleis continued to quarrel among themselves. Continuous warfare further weakened Greece and left it vulnerable to the advance of the emerging kingdom of Macedonia. But the Macedonian conquest of Greece was not the end of Greek history; in fact, it opened a new period marked by the outward explosion of Greek civilization which spread Greek culture throughout the entire Mediterranean basin.

The Era of the Hegemonies

The beginning of the 4th Century BCE is usually called the "Era of the Hegemonies," because there was a continuous struggle for power in which first one polis and then another gained hegemony, or dominance, over a group of allies. This was the last act of the Greek city-state drama, which had begun more than 400 years ago at the end of the Greek Dark Age.

The Occupation of Athens

After the defeat of Athens at the end of the Peloponnesian War, the Spartans, who had billed themselves as the defenders of Greek freedom, might have been expected to retire once more within their Peloponnesian stronghold. After all, their most pressing problem remained, as it had always been, to maintain their position of mastery over the helots at home. But the long war convinced the Spartan leaders—as successful war often does—that only imperialism could now guarantee their security, and so Sparta, in its turn, determined to exert control over all of Greece. The general moral support which Sparta had enjoyed in its war against what was seen by most of Greece as Athenian aggression, may have misled it to believe that the task of dominating the rest of Greece would be easy.

Whereas Athens had ruled its empire by encouraging and allying itself with the democratic elements of its subject states, Sparta encouraged the conservative factions. Sparta never trusted either democracies nor tyrannies, and after the war it basically adopted the same policy Athens had employed to build and maintain its empire, that is, to exert influence and control over other poleis by transforming them into states as much like itself as possible. In the modern world this kind of policy is sometimes known by the vague term "nation building." In a few states, Sparta resorted to old-fashioned imperialism and installed a governor with an occupying garrison and attempted to administer them directly. However, Sparta did not have the manpower and resources to govern all of Greece in this manner, and this is where the more subtle policy of nation building came into play. Most often Sparta worked with the conservative factions of the polis—which basically meant the aristocracy—and installed a governing board of pro-Spartan conservative oligarchs to act as a kind of "puppet" government. Since this government owed its existence to Spartan support, it could be counted on to pursue a pro-Spartan foreign policy, and Sparta thus dominated these states as the "leader" of an alliance of like-minded states. This, at least, was the theory and the expectation, but the policy did not always work the way the Spartans intended.

Athens will serve as an example of how this policy usually worked out in practice. That city was placed under a government of thirty (later known as the "Thirty Tyrants") of the most conservative leaders the Spartans could find and they were maintained in power by a small garrison of Spartan hoplites stationed on the Acropolis.[1] However, before very long, an extreme right wing faction, led by the aristocrat Critias, gained power and proceeded to reshape Athenian society in the image of its own ideology. Critias was a nephew of Plato, a long-time associate of Socrates, and a friend of Alcibiades (see chapter 6). He was implicated in the mutilation of the herms in 415 BCE, but was later cleared of the charges. Critias proposed the recall of Alcibiades in the assembly in 408 BCE and was himself exiled soon after Alcibiades's second fall from grace. He was a great admirer of the Spartan system and wrote several works praising the Spartans. Upon the defeat of Athens in 404 BCE, Critias returned with the Spartan occupation forces and was selected as one of the thirty oligarchs to rule Athens.

Critias seems to have attempted to put the philosophy of Plato/Socrates—government should be the dictatorship of the morally superior—into practice. The Thirty appointed a Council of Five Hundred to exercise the judicial functions formally belonging to all the citizens. A Board of Ten was appointed to rule the Piraeus. Three thousand citizens were granted the right to be tried by the new judicial system and to bear arms, while all others could be condemned without trial by the Thirty, effectively transforming them into non-citizens. The result of these actions was nothing less than a reign of terror. The Thirty began a campaign to remove their democratic opponents, and it soon turned into a purge which included respected citizens and even metics. When Theramenes, the leader of the moderate faction of the Thirty, proposed to broaden the franchise beyond the three thousand citizens initially approved, Critias had him executed. He then proceeded to execute some 1,500 democrats and to exile over 5,000 others. Eventually, greed became the guiding motivation, and many Athenians were condemned simply because those in power wanted to confiscate their property.

Socrates got into trouble with the democrats during this time. Several of his close associates, including Critias and Alcibiades, had turned against the democracy, and Socrates himself was in some way allied with the Thirty. However, his association could not have lasted long, because when the régime insisted that he arrest a prominent foreign resident, he refused on legal grounds, and there is no real evidence to support the claim by some scholars that he was actually a member of the Thirty. Nevertheless, by associating with the Thirty Tyrants, Socrates made himself appear to be an enemy of democracy, and later, when the democracy was restored, he became one of their first scapegoats.

---

1. It would be a mistake to assume that all Athenians were unhappy with the new oligarchic constitution. There were still many who favored an oligarchy over a democracy and, in fact, the democratic government later had to be restored by force.

These events resulted, as such extremes measures always do, in a strong shift of public opinion, even among the conservative aristocrats. The exiled democrats fled mostly north into the territory of the rising state of Thebes. The Thebans were eager to play Athens and Sparta off against each other to their own advantage. Thus, with the help of arms and money supplied by Thebes, the exiled Athenians, led by Thrasybulus, invaded Attica in 401 BCE. Almost the entire population of Attica rose up in their support, and the government of the Thirty Tyrants was overthrown. That, for all practical purposes, was the end of Spartan occupation of Athens, because the Spartans realized they were in an untenable situation and the occupying garrison withdrew. Soon afterward the democratic constitution was restored.

The March of the Ten Thousand

An interesting episode occurred during this period, which, although of minor importance itself, had a far-reaching influence on the future of Greece. During the Peloponnesian War the Spartans had entered into a secret agreement with the Persians to turn over the Greek cities of Asia Minor to them in exchange for financial backing in its war with Athens. At the end of the war, the Spartans were as good as their word and the Asian Greeks once again fell under the rule of the Persian king. But these cities almost immediately revolted against the renewed Persian rule and supported a usurper to the Persian throne, named Cyrus, who was the brother of the legitimate king, Artaxerxes II (404–359/8 BCE). Cyrus was the governor of Asia Minor and thus already commanded a Persian army. In addition, he raised a force of 13,000 Greek mercenaries from the Ionian cities under his rule to help him secure the Persian throne by force. In return for their support he promised to free the Greek cities once he gained the throne. In 401 BCE, this combined Persian/Greek army marched off deep into Persia. Unfortunately, in the critical battle against the king's army, the Persian soldiers of Cyrus's army deserted him and he was killed, even though the Greeks scored a victory on the left wing of the battlefield.

The Greek mercenary unit was still in tact and, in fact, little diminished by the defeat of Cyrus, so the Persians were forced to negotiate with them. But when the Greek officers were isolated from their troops during the negotiations, the Persians treacherously killed them. Now, this might appear to be a hopeless situation for the Greeks: isolated thousands of miles inside a hostile country, without supplies or friends and without leadership. But the Greeks were not dismayed. The surviving 10,000 mercenaries simply held an assembly and elected new officers, including the Athenian Xenophon, who later wrote an account of the event. The Greek army then marched hundreds of miles northward through hostile Persian territory, through deserts and over mountains, almost constantly under attack, to the Black Sea, where they confiscated ships and made their way back to their home cities in Greece.

This famous exploit became known as the "March of the Ten Thousand," and it suggested to Greeks everywhere that they were vastly superior to the Persians in military ability, and that if only they were united, they could conquer the whole Persian Empire, which in the words of the Athenian orator Isocrates (436–388 BCE), "is a country so vast and so rich that it will easily accommodate all the people among us who are in want of the necessities of life." This may sound strange to modern ears. After all, those "necessities" belonged to someone else. But this was by no means the first time that the civilizations of the Near East were regarded by outsiders as a kind of natural resource simply to be harvested by conquest. This argument that if only Greece was united it could accomplish great things is part of the Pan-Hellenism movement that became popular after the Peloponnesian War.

The Spartan Empire

When the Spartans, as the victors of the Peloponnesian War, found themselves the leaders of Greece, and had the opportunity to unite the country, they could come up with no higher policy than to simply hold on to what they had gained. They attempted to simply substitute Sparta for Athens as the head of an empire, much of which they had already sacrificed to Persia at the price of their victory. The transformation from an Athenian to a Spartan empire was a severe deterioration in the state of affairs for the subject poleis, because the Spartans had no talent or experience in governing an empire. Sparta did not possess the necessary resources to govern far flung territories or administer the complex financial and judicial affairs of the subject states. But the problems of empire paled in comparison with the troubles Sparta faced at home. For many generations, the Spartan citizens, due to their rigidly exclusive attitude, had failed to reproduce themselves.[2] By the end of the Peloponnesian War, the number of full Spartan citizens had shrunk to perhaps two thousand, and the Spartans had difficulties even keeping their helots in subjugation. The addition of the duties of governing an empire increased the burdens of citizenship to the breaking point. It was the great misfortune of Spartan history that no reform or revolution ever extended citizenship to the *perioikoi*[3] or emancipated the helots, because Sparta's rigid system of state slavery was now so obsolete that it hung like a heavy weight around Sparta's neck—a burden that had to be born by Spartan citizens from the cradle to the grave. The sudden influx of imperial wealth and the loosening of their traditional isolation during the war now began to take a toll on the old Spartan discipline. One of the most ignored lessons of history is the cruel price a society must pay for sudden success. Great good fortune often contains the seeds of a society's destruction. We have seen this principle work its way through the Assyrian and the Persian empires. We witnessed how success weakened the Athenians and was a factor leading to their demise. We now see the effects of success cut down the Spartans almost immediately. And we shall see how sudden success came very close to destroying the Roman civilization near the close of the 1st Century BCE. History has illustrated many times over that determination and fortitude are required for a society to survive sudden and spectacular success. Sparta was simply not up to the challenge.

At the end of the war the Spartan leader Lysander reorganized the governments of the cities taken over from Athens under "*decarchies*," or boards of ten members drawn from the most conservative aristocratic elements of their poleis, which were maintained in power by a small Spartan occupying garrison whose commander, in effect, acted as the Spartan governor. The result in most of the cities was similar to the reign of terror in Athens described above. At about the time the democracy was restored in Athens, however, most of these *decarchies* were abolished, and the Spartan garrisons were called home. The Spartans allowed this to happen because they disapproved of the ambition and insolence of Lysander and by the fact that Sparta did not possess the manpower resources to maintain permanently the occupation of so many cities in the face of the determined

---

2. A common problem. Demographers have long ago noted that the upper classes of all societies invariably fail to reproduce themselves and must constantly be replenished by the "vertical mobility" of members of the lower classes rising up to take their places at the top. If a rigid exclusiveness of the upper class prevents this, the numbers of that class will always decline.

3. *Perioikoi*, "dwellers round about," was a term employed to describe groups of subjects or half-citizens. In Sparta, perioikoi served in the Spartan army—after 450 BCE, in the same regiments with Spartan citizens—but they played no role in the political process of making Spartan policy and seem to have been subject to a special taxation. So they can be considered at best only half-citizens or second class citizens of Sparta. Thus, by excluding them from full citizenship, what could have been a great strength to the state became a divisive weakness.

opposition of their populations. With his policies discredited, Lysander retired into exile. For all practical purposes, this marked the end of the Spartan Empire, though Sparta remained, for the time being, the most powerful and influential state in Greece.

Most Greeks viewed Sparta's policy as narrow and self-serving, and anti-Spartan resentment began to grow. To make matters worse, Sparta seemed to make one blunder after another. When Sparta began to interfere in the internal affairs of its two most important allies, Corinth and Thebes—already irritated at being excluded from the advantages of the victory over Athens—they declared war. They were joined by Argos and Athens in what is known to history as the Corinthian War (395–387 BCE). The Spartan navy was destroyed in 394 BCE by a Persian fleet commanded by an Athenian admiral and manned by Greek mercenaries. The next year the Persian fleet sailed into the Piraeus and the Persians and Thebans helped Athens rebuild its fortification, including the Long Walls. Then in 390 BCE a Spartan army unit of 600 hoplites was annihilated near Corinth. This was a terrible blow to Sparta because it could now muster no more than six such units.

But fortunately for Sparta, Persia switched sides and negotiated a settlement known as the King's Peace in 387 BCE. This agreement required the return of Asia Minor to Persia and Athens to give up its navel allies. The King's Peace restored Sparta to its position of leadership, but it learned nothing from this war and renewed its policy of insolence and brutality. Thus, over the next decade the King's Peace slowly fell apart and the Athenian alliance began to reform for the protection of the small states against Sparta, and in 377 BCE the Second Athenian Confederacy was born. This time, however, there were built-in protections against Athenian imperialism. All members were autonomous and sent representatives to a confederate congress in Athens, but the Athenians took no part in its deliberations. To be binding, a resolution had to be passed by both the confederate congress and the Athenian assembly.

The Rise of Thebes

Meanwhile, Thebes was busy building the Boeotian League, a group of allies under Theban supremacy. There were more conflicts and more peace agreements, which were immediately breached by more warfare. In 371 BCE, a great peace conference was held at Sparta to address all the issues of Greece and beyond. It was attended by representatives from all the Greek states including those of Sicily and Macedonia. Even the Persians sent representatives. It was the largest and most representative peace congress yet assembled. An elaborate scheme for peace was developed, complete with voluntary enforcement of sanctions. But disputes broke out between Sparta and Thebes, and the agreement was never signed.

Under the leadership of Epaminondas, Thebes had developed its infantry and cavalry into the largest and best military organization in the Greek world. As the peace conference of 371 BCE dissolved, Thebes was ready. Sparta immediately invaded Boeotia with an army of 10,000 men commanded by the Spartan King Cleombrotus. The Theban army, led by Epaminondas, numbered 6,000 hoplites and 1,000 cavalry. The two armies met at Leuctra. It was a great and stunning victory for Thebes that marked the end of Spartan supremacy forever. The shock reverberated throughout Greece, because until the Battle of Leuctra, no one believed that the full Spartan army could ever be defeated. Of the 700 Spartans who entered the battle, 400, including the king, lost their lives. Now barely 1,000 Spartan citizens remained who were capable of bearing arms and, more important, their military prestige had vanished.

A wave of democratic reform swept across the Peloponnesus as Sparta's allies deserted en mass and Sparta was helpless to stop it. Thebes invaded and ravaged the Spartan homeland for the first time in history, but was unable to capture the city of Sparta itself. But Messenia was librated from its long slavery and organized into a new state. Thebes temporarily forced its hegemony on the Peloponnesus, Thessaly, and Macedonia, but nowhere was it able to maintain the peace or establish its firm and permanent control. Several more peace conferences were held but achieved nothing. The real impediment to Theban supremacy was the Athenian navy, an obstacle Thebes was never able to overcome.

Revolts in the Peloponnesus forced Epaminondas to invade again, but at the Battle of Mantinea in 362 BCE, the great commander was killed and the power of Thebes went into a steep decline. For some thirty years after the Battle of Leuctra, Thebes, a democracy, held sway over most of the Greek mainland. But as it turned out, the Thebans were as narrow in their vision as the Spartans and could think of no other method than terror to control Greece—and terror could never win the loyalty of the other Greeks. Their sudden decline after the Battle of Mantinea indicates that their ascendancy was largely due to one man, Epaminondas, who was a great commander, but fell far short of what Greece really needed at this time: a great statesman.

Philip II (c. 382–336 BCE) and the Rise of Macedonia

This era of the hegemonies was the final act in the city-state drama that began over 400 years earlier, during the late Dark Age. Constant warfare weakened Greece and made it vulnerable to outside conquest. In the end, the polis system was replaced by a reversion to monarchy, or rather by the spread of the influence of the kingdom of Macedonia over the entire Greek mainland.

Macedonia, or Macedon as it is often called, was a large, somewhat backward, although very ancient kingdom in northern Greece. It was essentially a tribal kingdom, but so loosely organized, and so troubled by even more barbarian peoples to the north and east, that it had never played an important role in the affairs of Greece. In fact, the Greeks were never quite sure whether the Macedonians were Greek or barbarian. The kings of Macedonia patronized Greek culture at their court and they were accepted as Greek by the officials of the Olympic Games;[4] but the peasantry and even the lesser nobility were considered to be little more than barbarians by the Greeks living in the cultured and urbane poleis to the south. The emergence of Macedonia as a Hellenic power was the accomplishment of King Philip II, the father of Alexander the Great. Because of the fame of his son, the considerable achievements of Philip have been unjustly overshadowed.

Philip was born about 382 BCE in Pella, the capital of Macedonia, the third son of King Amyntas II. During his early childhood he witnessed the disintegration of Macedonia as his elder brothers, Alexander II and Perdiccas III, struggled against their own nobles, the invasions of the Illyrians, and the continuous attacks of Thebes. Philip was a hostage in Thebes from about 368 to 365 BCE. We know almost nothing about his life during these years or even why he was a hostage. The exchange of political hostages was a common diplomatic practice during this period, and Philip was probably held to guarantee the performance of a treaty or agreement between Thebes and Macedonia. At any rate, political hostages were treated as honored guests and, since these were his formative years, he received an education in Greek culture, political practice, and military strategy. From this time onward he considered himself to be a Greek and exhibited an undying love for all things Greek.

---

4. Only "Greeks" were accepted as participants in the various games associated with religious festivals, of which the Olympic Games were the most famous. Exactly what established an individual's "Greekness" is unclear.

In 359 BCE, his brother, King Perdiccas III, was killed while on a military expedition against the invading Illyrians, and Philip became the regent for his brother's infant son. At the time, Macedonia was caught up in a crisis that threatened its very existence, and Philip persuaded the aristocrats to recognize him as king in place of his infant nephew, in order to provide a more stable government. Philip was only 23-years old, but he moved swiftly to secure the safety of his kingdom. He quickly reorganized the army into Theban style phalanx formations, but he armed them with a new weapon, the heavy fourteen-foot long spear, called the sarissa, which the soldiers held with both hands. The Macedonian phalanx bristled with a menacing array of lethal spears which could run through enemy soldiers from 15 feet away. The cavalry, called the King's Companions, composed of Macedonian aristocrats, was used as a strike force to soften up the enemy and protect the phalanx's flanks. During his first two years of rule, Philip brought about a dramatic turnaround in Macedonia's fortunes. He bought off the Thracians, obtained a treaty with Athens by ceding Amphipolis, and firmly established himself on the throne. In 358 BCE he defeated the Illyrians and secured the kingdom's borders.

Philip pursued a policy of urbanization by founding new cities all over Macedonia. However, these new cities were under the king's tight control rather than being independent city-states in the traditional Greek manner. Philip built up a strong economy and increased his revenues through the growth of trade, control of the seacoast, and the development of major gold mines at Mt. Pangaeus. He was the first European to imitate the Persian king by issuing gold coins. Philip used some of this money for bribery, and he boasted that he could take any fortress in Greece without shedding a drop of blood, provided there was a road leading up to it wide enough to drive a donkey load of gold. Much of the money, however, was also spent on the Macedonian military, which he transformed into a standing, professional army.

Philip's policies toward the Greeks were as brilliant as they were unscrupulous, and his influence spread steadily southward. He utilized both aggression and diplomacy to equal advantage. If fighting were necessary he led his army in person and indeed he was wounded several times, including the loss of his right eye, and a deep cut in his leg that gave him a permanent limp. But Philip understood that fighting left a residue of lasting hatred, and he preferred to use flattery, bribery, and promises to contract alliances, on his own terms, of course. By 352 BCE, Philip had annexed his northern neighbor, Thrace, subdued the Illyrians to the west, and conquered the territory of Thessaly to the south.

But Philip was not completely Greek: he practiced polygamy, principally as a political device to create alliances and strengthen loyalties. He first married the Illyrian princess Audata, in order to seal an alliance with the Illyrians. Next he married Phila, a member of a noble family from Elimea, to strengthen internal unity. In 357 BCE, Philip married Olympias, a princess of the neighboring kingdom of Epirus, modern Albania. She became his principle wife. A year later Olympias gave birth to a son, named Alexander.

The disunited and demoralized poleis to the south, which were still expending their energies and resources on rivalries among themselves, had little chance against such a strong and persistent adversary as Philip. One hundred and fifty years earlier when these same city-states had faced the Persians, they had done so with a youthful vigor, but now the Greek poleis system seemed old and outdated and senile. Their citizens were far less willing now than of old to sacrifice their lives and property for the common good. Internal politics seemed more important now than external threats. In Athens, for example, the citizens and their leaders were preoccupied with a raging debate over the use of state funds to pay the poor citizens to attend the assembly, sit on juries, and participate in religious festivals—in other words, a debate over what we today call welfare assistance. And this time, the Greek city-states did not face the Persian Empire, which fielded a mob and called it an army. They were now up against a large quasi-Greek state, which intelligently exploited the very same Greek military science and superior technology that had made the difference at Marathon, Salamis, and Plataea.

Nevertheless, Athens built up its navy and attempted to rally the other poleis to form a united front against the growing power of Macedonia. Demosthenes, the greatest orator of ancient Greece, flourished during this time, and he delivered a series of stinging speeches, known to history as "Philippics," which branded Philip as a public enemy of all Greece and aroused at least some Greeks to action. These speeches are still studied today as masterpieces of political rhetoric. But it was too late. The great era of the Greek polis was over.

As Philip expanded southward there were intermittent skirmishes and peace agreements between him and the Athenians. And all the time Macedonian money was trickling into the Greek poleis, where it created friends for Philip among various groups of politicians. He also used what we have come to call propaganda. And Philip's propaganda carried a message: It was, said Philip, Greek destiny to conquer Persia as revenge for the crimes committed against Greek freedom over a hundred and fifty years ago, and it was his mission to lead a united Greek army on that conquest—but first the quarreling Greeks must be united. Athens, Thebes and a few other states joined forces against Philip, but the Peloponnesian League remained neutral—what a different response than the Greeks had made against Persia over a century before.

In 339 BCE, the Scythians crossed the Danube River into Macedonian territory with a large army. Philip won a stunning victory in which the Scythian king was killed and 20,000 women and children were taken as slaves. But on his return to Macedonia, the Thracians attacked the convoy and the Macedonians lost all their booty, and Philip suffered a severe injury which left him with a permanent limp. The army returned empty-handed. Thus, while the Greek coalition, led by Thebes and Athens, assembled a large army, Philip spent the next months recovering from his injury.

As soon as he recovered, Philip organized the largest Macedonian army yet assembled and marched southward into Greece. The decisive battle took place at Chaeronea, on August 2, 338 BCE. Each army was approximately 30,000 strong. The Macedonian army, with the right wing under the command of Philip himself and the left wing under the command of his young son Alexander, was completely victorious. The remnants of the Athenian army fell back on Athens, and the Athenians prepared to stand off a siege, but Philip, who was a great admirer of Athenian culture, did not want to crush the city. He wanted its cooperation and if he could not have that, at least he wanted Athenian neutrality. Besides, Philip did not have a navy, and the Athenians had proven many times in the past that they could not be defeated so long as they controlled the sea. So Philip offered the Athenians very favorable peace terms and they accepted them. Thebes, on the other hand, was stripped of all power and garrisoned by a Macedonian occupation force.

Philip was now the master of all Greece. The polis system of government would continue to be important in the domestic affairs of the Aegean area, but henceforth the real power of Greece would be in other hands—first Philip and Alexander, then of the Hellenistic monarchies, and after them the Romans, and finally the Turks. Not until the 19th Century CE would Greece regain its freedom from foreign occupation. But the city governments of Athens, Sparta, and others continued to operate and to control their domestic affairs down into the late Roman period. Although the poleis system may not be in step with our modern sensibilities, accustomed as we are to live in the large, impersonal, national state, few political systems in the history of the world have persisted as long—and anyone who has ever attended a town meeting can attest to its attraction.

The year after the Battle of Chaeronea (337 BCE), Philip convened a meeting of the Greek states at Corinth and formed a league which included all the mainland states except Sparta. This organization was called the League of Corinth. Philip contracted a formal alliance with the League of Corinth and took the title Hegemon of Greece—which means leader or executive of Greece. The league now formally declared war on Persia to avenge the devastation of the Greek temples by Xerxes a hundred and fifty years ago, and commissioned Philip to lead the joint Greek-Macedonian army.

Thus, in 336 BCE, Philip dispatched the advanced guard of his army across the Hellespont to begin the invasion of Persia, but he stayed behind for a few days to attend a religious festival and the wedding of one of his daughters. During a procession to make a sacrifice, Philip was suddenly assassinated by someone from the crowd of onlookers. Who was responsible? Well, there were many who had a motive. Earlier, Philip had taken a new queen, whereupon his first wife, Olympias, and their son, Alexander, had left the court in anger.[5] Alexander soon returned, however, and was present at the court when the assassination took place. It was officially reported that the assassin was in the pay of the Persians, but he was cut down immediately by Alexander and the royal body guards and unfortunately never lived to tell his own story. No historian today believes the official explanation. But if the assassin was not working for the Persians, who *was* he working for? Olympias, the cast off queen? Alexander, who might have been disinherited by the new queen son? Some other unhappy member of Philip's court? The possibilities are almost endless. An abundance of conflicting evidence has survived, and over the centuries much scholarly time and effort has been devoted to this problem, but the riddle remains unsolved.

Alexander the Great (356–323 BCE)

The powerful empire built by Philip now passed to his son, Alexander III, known to history as Alexander the Great.[6] He was only 20 years of age when he became king. And although he would die only 13 years later, Alexander has always been regarded as one of the greatest individuals in all of human history.

---

5. Cleopatra, a young girl from the high Macedonian nobility, was Philip's seventh wife. The ancients say he married her "out of love," but the marriage led to a break with Olympias and his son Alexander. At the wedding banquet, Cleopatra's uncle, the general Attalus, made a remark about Philip fathering a "legitimate" heir, that is one that was of pure Macedonian blood. Alexander threw his cup at the man, for calling him a "bastard child." Philip stood up, drew his sward, and charged toward Alexander, only to trip and fall on his face in a drunken stupor, at which Alexander shouted, "Here is the man who was ready to cross from Europe to Asia, and who cannot even cross from one table to another without losing his balance." Alexander and Olympias then fled to Epirus. Although Alexander was later allowed to return to the court, he remained isolated and insecure. Meanwhile, Cleopatra gave birth to a son, which was named Caranus, in honor of the founder of the Macedonian royal dynasty.

6. See Cleve, Robert, "Alexander," *Early Western Civilization, Source Readings* (2002), Kendall/Hunt Publishing Company, Dubuque, pp. 218–237.

Figure 8.1: Alexander the Great.

Alexander was born on (or around) July 20, 356 BCE,[7] the same day that the famous temple of Artemis at Ephesus was destroyed by fire. Even as a young boy, Alexander was fearless and strong. At the age of twelve, he tamed a beautiful and high-spirited horse that no one else could ride. His father was so impressed that he said: "My son, seek out a kingdom equal to yourself; Macedonia has not room for you." Later the famous horse, named Bucephalus, carried Alexander all the way to India, where it died. There he built a city and named it Bucephala in the horse's honor.

Alexander grew up and was educated in the court of Philip at a time when great things were being accomplished by the Macedonians. Macedonia was in the process of achieving what no other power had ever accomplished: the unification of Greece. He was provided with a number of teachers, the most famous being Aristotle, who came to Pella in 343 BCE and taught Alexander from age 13 to 16. The great Greek philosopher introduced the young prince to the arts and sciences. Alexander developed a life-long love of Homer's *Iliad* and, according to legend, he always slept with a copy under his pillow. He consciously patterned his life after the hero Achilles. Later, Alexander would say that he loved the philosopher more than his father, "for the one had given him life, but the other had taught him the noble life."

---

7. This date may have been created after the fact to coincide exactly with the burning of the temple. The legend also asserts that Philip heard the news of the birth of Alexander on the same day he received the news of the success of his army, commanded by Parmenio, in Illyria and the victory of his horse at the Olympic games. Furthermore, according to tradition his mother, Olympias, was descended from Achilles and his father, Philip II, descended from Heracles, the son of Zeus. A later legend relates that on the night Alexander was conceived Olympias was visited in her bed chamber by Zeus, and that actually Alexander's father was really Zeus, not Philip. This would put Alexander on an equal footing with the Heracles.

Figure 8.2: Olympias.

During Philip's expedition against Byzantium in 340 BCE, Alexander, at age sixteen, was left in Pella as regent. He put his time to good use: he put down a rebellion in Thrace and established a new city which he called Alexandroupolis. This brief taste of power must have been tremendously exhilarating for Alexander, and it was only a small indication of things to come.

When Philip was assassinated in 336 BCE, Alexander was not the only contender to the throne thus vacated, but he was immediately recognized as king by the army, and this gave him the power to sweep all rivals from his path. He led a drive to execute all those alleged to be in the conspiracy that murdered Philip, and this actually became a swift purge that eliminated all his rivals. Even Philip's last wife, Cleopatra, and her infant daughter was killed—Olympias may have been responsible for this act. Then he turned his attention to consolidating his rule of Macedonia's empire. He marched south, pacified Thessaly, and had the assembly of the league of Corinth confirm him as *hegemon* of Greece and Supreme Commander (*strategos autocrator*) of the Greek forces against Persia, the same titles his father had held. Alexander then undertook a series of lightening campaigns to put down rebellious tribes in Illyria and Thrace, which took him across the Danube. In the spring of 335 BCE, he struck deep into the Balkans to pacify the restive Celtic tribes. A rumor of Alexander's death in Illyria led to a revolt of Thebes and some other Greek poleis. By a forced march of 14 days he took the Thebans completely by surprise and in a few days had won back the leadership of Greece. Thebes, which refused to surrender, was wiped out of existence—only the temples and house of the poet Pindar were spared. Six thousand people were killed and 30,000 survivors were sold into slavery. Greece remained quietly obedient for the rest of Alexander's reign.

Alexander inherited from Philip not only a powerful kingdom with a well trained and efficient military machine but a major policy as well, the invasion of the Persian Empire. It was a tremendous task. Persia was a vast empire that could swallow whole armies and still not be subdued, and

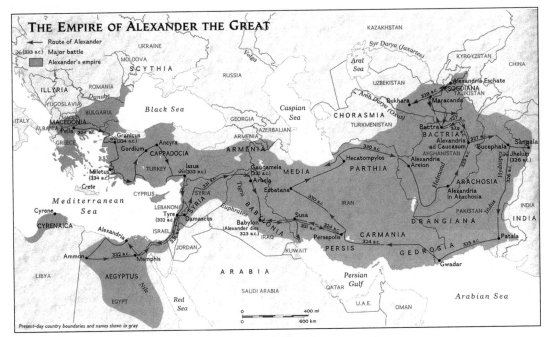

©National Geographic Image Collection

Figure 8.3: The conquests of Alexander.

it now controlled most of the Aegean Sea with a large navy commanded by a Greek admiral. But the Persia that Alexander attacked in 334 BCE was much weaker than the empire Xerxes led against the Greeks back in 480 BCE. Court intrigue and the disloyalty of the Persian nobles had weakened the administration. The present king, Darius III, depended heavily on Greek mercenaries as the disciplined element of his army, because his native troops were mainly untrained peasants. These facts help to explain Alexander's success, but they in no way diminish his reputation as one of the supreme military leaders of all time. His physical courage, strategic cleverness, and superb generalship are not to be encountered anywhere else in the annals of history. And he is the first general whom we can actually follow in his thinking out of the tactical and strategic problems he faced and then watch him doggedly executing his plans.

Alexander seems to have been very much aware of the historic role he was playing. This sense of history is also a first with Alexander. As soon as he crossed the Hellespont, he dramatically threw his spear into the soil of Asia in a symbolic gesture indicating that he intended to conquer the land of the enemy. Then he went to Troy and offered sacrifices to Achilles and the other Greek heroes who had fought there in the epic legends. He also took with him on his campaign a cadre of philosophers and historians to record his exploits for history. Today we take this historical point of view for granted. We expect our political and military leaders to "play to history."[8]

---

8. For example, when the president makes his annual State of the Union Address, we understand that he is not really speaking to the assembled members of congress, not even to the American public through the television camera, but to history. He does this by evoking great leaders of the past, such as FDR and Lincoln, just as Alexander evoked the heroes of Homer by sacrificing at Achilles's tomb.

Alexander crossed the Hellespont into Asia with an army of only 30,000 infantry plus about 5,000 cavalry—quite a mark of his confidence to invade an empire that could easily field armies numbering in the hundreds of thousands. His army was made up not only of Macedonians, but Illyrians, Thracians and the contingents of the Greeks states of the League of Corinth. About 14,000 of these were Macedonians and about 7,000 were Greek allies. The army possessed an excellent variety of arms: lightly armed Cretan and Macedonian archers; Thracians and Agrianians armed with Javelins; a strong cavalry; and of course the infantry phalanx, armed with the sarissa. This army was accompanied by explorers, engineers, architects, scientists, court officials, and historians. Alexander's second in command was Parmenio, who had secured a foothold in Asia Minor before Philip's assassination.

The Persians had a permanent army stationed in Asia Minor that was quite a bit larger than Alexander's, but even more seriously the Persians controlled the Aegean Sea. Therefore, Alexander could communicate with his base in Macedonia only through a narrow line across the Hellespont and ran the risk of being cut off and isolated if he ventured too far from it. The correct strategy for the Persians was to draw Alexander deep into Persia before giving battle, but the Persians were never sophisticated about strategy, and Alexander found the Persian Army of Asia Minor waiting for him on the banks of the Granicus River.

The Persian plan was to tempt Alexander to cross the river and destroy his army before it could re-form. It almost succeeded, but the Persian line broke and Alexander was victorious in the first major battle, but he was wounded as a result of his over zealous participation in the combat. The first three years of the war were spent neutralizing the Persian navy by capturing all the ports along the coast from Asia Minor to Egypt and thereby denying the enemy fleet a base from which to operate. This task required two major battles and many sieges. The Macedonians, with the help of Greek engineers, had developed siege machines that could breach almost any defensive wall, and most cities could not withstand Alexander's attack for more than a few days.[9] This is another example of the continuing superiority of Greek military technology.

The tyrants of the Greek cities of Asia Minor, installed by the Persians, were expelled, and in contrast with the Macedonian policy in Europe, democracies were installed in them. To confirm his Pan-Hellenic policy, Alexander sent three hundred sets of armor taken at the Battle of Granicus River to Athens to be dedicated to Athena with the announcement: "Alexander the son of Philip, and of the Hellenes, except for the Lacedaemonians, won these from the barbarians who inhabit Asia." This is what the Pan-Hellenes had clamored for decades. He now took possession of the old Lydian capital of Sardis without a fight. It was the headquarters of the Persian government west of the Taurus. When the city of Miletus, encouraged by the presence of Persian fleet, refused to open its gates, Alexander took it by assault, thus beginning the defeat of the Persian navy without fighting a navel battle, by occupying all the coastal cities and thus depriving the fleet of its bases. He conquered western Asia Minor by subduing the hill tribes during the winter of 334–333 BCE.

---

9. Military history involves a constant development of technology which produces an alternation or swing between an advantage for the two modes of warfare: offensive and defensive. A century before Alexander's invasion of Persia, during the Peloponnesian War, the advantage was with the defensive mode of warfare. The Greeks possessed the technology to construct massive defensive walls, and so long as a city could supply itself with food (as Athens did through the control of the sea), there was not much an enemy could do to defeat it. But by Alexander's time the advantage had swung almost completely over to the offensive mode of warfare. The Greeks had now developed the technology to breach and overcome defensive walls. Now a city must either defeat the invading army—most effectively accomplished by confrontation on an open battlefield before the city was put under siege—or it would be destroyed.

At Gordium in Phrygia there was exhibited a "Gordian Knot," a intricate entanglement of rope that according to tradition could be loosened only by the man destined to conquer Asia. When shown the knot, Alexander simply drew his sword and cut through it with a single stroke. A puzzle, no matter how clever, was not apt to deter this man. He moved on through Cappadocia toward the Cilician Gates, then passed into northern Syria. Meanwhile, the Grand Army of Persia, under the command of King Darius himself, was advancing into Syria. In 333 BCE, Alexander descended through the Cilician Gates into northern Syria and defeated Darius and the main Persian army at Issus. He captured the royal camp and most of the Persian royal family, but Darius himself escaped into the interior to raise another army. After the battle, Alexander, who was known for sharing in the Spartan living conditions of his own soldiers, entered the royal tent of Darius and observed the golden bath, silk carpets, and other luxuries. He is reported to have said, "So this is what it means to be king." The treasure captured at Issus amounted to 3,000 talents. The courteous treatment he accorded to the royal captives, "due to their station," became a favorite theme of later writers, and an interesting fact is that later when Sisygambis, the mother of Darius, had the opportunity to return to the Persians, she refused.

The victory at Issus did not change Alexander's strategy. He continued to move along the coast of the eastern Mediterranean Sea, capturing the coast cities to deny them as bases for the Persian navy. When Darius offered terms which included a ransom of 10,000 talents for his family and to cede all his lands west of the Euphrates, Alexander refused and demanded the unconditional surrender to himself as the lord of Asia. His general Parmenio said, "If I were Alexander, I would accept," to which Alexander replied, "I too would accept, if I were Parmenio!"

The Phoenician cities of Marathus and Aradus surrendered to Alexander without opposition, Byblos and Sidon were taken with little trouble, but Alexander met serious resistance at Tyre. That city was located on an off-shore island which was also walled on all four sides. Since Alexander could not bypass the city for fear it would attack his rear and could not attack via the sea, he decided to build a causeway to bridge the island to the mainland. That causeway still exists (Fig. 8.4). A long and fero-

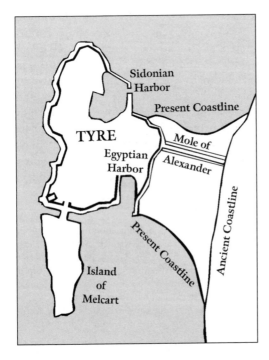

Figure 8.4: Island city of Tyre.

cious battle ensued. Once within reach of the walls, he was able to use his siege engines to breach the fortifications and the city fell after seven months. The city's 30,000 inhabitants were sold into slavery.

Alexander continued capturing the ports along the Mediterranean coast, and in 332 BCE he entered Egypt, which received him as a liberator. He was crowned Pharaoh, and the traditional religion, which had been oppressed by the Persians, was protected and encouraged. He reorganized Egypt, assigning the civil administration to native Egyptian governors, but keeping the command of the army under Macedonian generals. He founded the city of Alexandria in the east Nile delta. Alexandria soon became the largest and wealthiest city in the ancient world, and it is even today the second largest city in Egypt. Then Alexander marched through the burning desert to an isolated temple of the Egyptian god Amun-Re, whom the Greeks equated with Zeus, to receive an oracle. He was greeted by the priests as the son of Amun-Re—after all he was now Pharaoh—and he then disappeared into the inner sanctum of the temple where only the high priest and the pharaoh were allowed. He never divulged to anyone what happened to him there at the high alter, but from this time onward Alexander began to behave as if he believed himself to be a hero, that is semi-divine. Indeed the ancient world was full of stories that his mother, Olympias, had been visited by Zeus, just as the mother of Hercules had been—and Olympias was not the kind of woman to deny these rumors. Whatever actually happened in the temple changed his life forever. Even his closest associates and friends noted a remarkable alteration in his personality.

In 331 BCE, what was left of the Persian fleet surrendered, which gave Alexander the command of the sea without having fought a single significant naval battle. His strategy of occupying the coastal cities had worked magnificently. Now he could turn his attention toward Mesopotamia and the heart of the Persian Empire. Alexander returned to Phoenicia and appointed a Macedonian satrap, or governor, for Syria. He received reinforcements from Macedonia—during the entire campaign he regularly received reinforcements to replace the garrisons he left behind in the conquered territories—and then marched off into the vastness of Persia in pursuit of Darius. This was the supreme test of leadership: to lead an army of no more than 47,000 men into the heart of an empire so vast, against a king who could easily field an army 5 times the size of his force; thousands of miles from home, facing an army fighting deep inside its own borders and defending its own homeland. What superb leadership that required!

By July of 331 BCE Alexander had arrived at Thapsacus on the Euphrates River. He crossed the river and advanced eastward across northern Mesopotamia toward the Tigress, while the Persian army marched northward along the Tigress to meet him. When the time came for the final showdown in the plain of Gaugamela,[10] Alexander confined himself in his tent for 4 days with only his closest advisors, while his men prepared for battle. Finally, he emerged from his tent and gave his plan of battle to his officers and men in a firm speech, went back into the tent and slept so soundly that his aid had to awaken him on the morning of the battle.

The Battle of Gaugamela on October 1, 330 BCE,[11] was the first battle in history in which a major infantry unit was stationed in the rear to be used as a reserve. This is another example of Alexander's genius—today, this is one of the cardinal principles of military science that no commander would even think of violating. The Greeks and Macedonians were completely victorious over the larger Persian

---

10. Near the modern Iraqi city of Mosul. There is some confusion over the name of this battle. Archaeological excavations confirm the existence of a Persian garrison at the nearby Assyrian town of Arbela in the 4th Century BCE. Darius III used Arbela as a base before marching to the plain of Gaugamela, between Nineveh and Arbela, to meet Alexander. Thus, the battle is often called the Battle of Arbela.

11. This is one of those rare ancient events that we can date precisely and confidently because of the lucky coincidence of a lunar eclipse, which is also recorded in the ancient texts.

army, but Darius managed to escape into Media with his Bactrian cavalry and some Greek mercenaries before the battle was over. Nevertheless, the Battle of Gaugamela sealed the fate of the Persian Empire.

Alexander followed the course of the Tigress River southward into Babylonia, where the ancient city of Babylon welcomed him as the "King of Asia." Mazaeus, the Persian governor of Babylon, was appointed by Alexander as his satrap of Babylonia as a reward for his peaceful surrender of the city. Alexander also wisely followed the same policy he had instituted in Egypt and encouraged the local religion and priesthood. Because of these tolerant policies, Alexander was more often than not seen as a liberator rather than a conqueror by the local people.

He moved on to Susa, the winter residence of the Persian kings, which also surrendered without resistance. Here Alexander came into possession of the fabulous personal treasure the Persian kings has amassed, equivalent to 120,000 talents of gold.[12] From here he crossed over the Zagros mountain range, ascended onto the plateau of Iran, reducing to obedience the fierce mountain tribes along the way. These tribes were accustomed to exert blackmail even from the king's train, but they quickly learned that a stronger hand now ruled the empire. He entered the main Persian capital of Persepolis and took possession of treasure even larger than that of Susa. Surely, Alexander's budget was no longer in the red. He remained in Persepolis for several months to give his army a rest. During his stay, the palace was burned to the ground. How this happened is still a source of controversy. Some accounts say it was set as a symbol of revenge for the Persian destruction of the Greek temples in 490 BCE. Other accounts say the fire was set at the suggestion of an Athenian woman, Thais, at one of Alexander's drinking parties.[13] Then, there is the possibility that the fire was an actually an accident, but since that is no fun, few historians subscribe to that theory.

Early in 330 BCE, allegations were brought against some of Alexander's officers of a plot to murder him. Several were executed and during an evening of heavy drinking and feasting, an argument broke out between Alexander and his life-long friend, Cleitus. After a period of taunting by Cleitus, Alexander ran him through with a spear. Although he mourned his friend and almost committed suicide when he realized what he had done, this incident contributed to his growing paranoia and promoted a fear of his temper among his associates.

The year 330 BCE also marked the end of the Pan-Hellenic phase of his campaign. Alexander received more reinforcements from Macedonia and sent home the Greek allies, and reorganized his army to pursue a purely personal war from this point onward. He prepared to march further east, into areas hitherto unknown to the Greeks. He fully intended to march to the ends of the world,

---

12. There is no way to accurately translate the value of ancient money into modern numbers. However, a rough estimate of the value of 120,000 talents of gold would be in the neighborhood of $50 billion. Whatever the actual value, it was an unbelievably large treasure.

13. Immortalized in a poem by John Dryden (1631–1700): Alexander's Feast; the Power of Music. An Ode in Honor of St. Cecillia's Day: 1697.

'Twas at the royal feast, for Persia won
By Philip's warlike son:
Aloft, in awful state
The godlike hero sate
On his imperial throne;
His valiant peers were plac'd around;
Their brows with roses and with myrtles bound:
(So should desert in arms be crown'd.)
The lovely Thaïs, by his side,
Sate like a blooming Eastern bride
In flow'r of youth and beauty's pride.

to the shores of what the Greeks called Ocean, that great expanse of water they believed surrounded the entire land mass of the earth.

Alexander now moved northward into Ecbatana in pursuit of Darius, who fled ahead of him into Bactria. At Ecbatana, however, he came into possession of large new masses of treasure. He appointed Harpalus as his chief treasurer and also left Parmenio at Ecbatana with a strong garrison to guard his line of communications. Then, with his fastest troops, Alexander pursued Darius for twelve days. The king's army had been reduced to 6,000 infantry and 3,000 cavalry. Finally, one morning he overtook the broken royal convoy in which Darius had been murdered by his guards. Alexander was not pleased. He organized a state funeral with all possible honors for the last Persian king. Later he captured and executed the perpetrators of the crime.

The Macedonians marched through Parthia, Bactria, Arachosia, and in 327 BCE he conquered Sogdiana. This area is today known as Afghanistan. Alexander had to devise completely new tactics to deal with what we today would call guerrilla warfare. So he divided his army into small independent units and spread out across the country and brought the whole area under control in less than a year. One of the princes, Oxyartes, ruled from a fortress situated on Sogdian Rock. Oxyartes felt quite secure in his fortress because of the vertical cliffs on all sides. He taunted Alexander to send up men with wings to take his fortress. Alexander sent 300 hundred experienced climbers up the cliffs during the night, and the next morning Oxyartes was so astonished see these men "with wings" waving down at him that he surrendered without resistance. Alexander and Oxyartes became friends, and Alexander married his sister (in some accounts his daughter), Roxane.

Then he reformed his army and, in the summer of 327 BCE, descended through the Khyber pass down into northern India. These areas had never been part of the Persian Empire. And again Alexander faced a type of warfare completely new to the Greeks—armies equipped with elephants. However, Alexander never lost a battle. But in July of 326 BCE, when the monsoon rains began, his soldiers refused to go any further. Alexander's response to this was the same as the hero Achilles in Homer's epic, he went into his tent and pouted. However, his soldiers would not relent. They had marched so many thousands of miles, all the way from Greece and they were tired and worn out. They wanted to go home. At last Alexander yielded to his men and agreed to lead them back to the West. However, he persuaded them to travel down the Hydaspes and Indus rivers to the reach the ocean. On the Hydaspes he erected twelve altars to the twelve Olympian gods and constructed a fleet of 800 ships. He divided his forces and proceeded down the river, with half of the men aboard ships and half marching down the two river banks. The march encountered heavy fighting. During the siege of the town of Malli, Alexander was badly wounded, but as usual he survived. During the journey Alexander sought out Indian philosophers noted for their wisdom and debated them on philosophical issues. For centuries afterwards, he became legendary for being both a courageous conqueror and a wise philosopher. Alexander and his army reached the mouth of the Indus in July of 325 BCE. He left the conquered portion of India east of the Indus to be governed by native princes and the country west of the river under Macedonian governors.

The plan was for Alexander, with the main body of the army, to march along the coast of the Gedrosia Desert and for a fleet of supply ships to sail simultaneously off the coast with water and provisions. However, Alexander was soon forced by the mountainous country to turn inland, and he was separated from the supply ships. He lost nearly three quarters of his army because of the severe conditions of the desert. Many of them died while encamped in a wadi when an unexpected monsoon flooded their camp. Finally the survivors reached the region called Carmania, and their fortune changed radically as they were welcomed into the prosperous country. Alexander and his men celebrated their success and traveled in comfort to Babylon.

By the spring of 324 BCE, he was back in Susa, the Persian administrative capital, and spent a year reorganizing his empire. He began to put grandiose plans into effect, which were intended to unite the Persian and Greek cultures. He began the training of Persian troops in the Greek art of warfare. He adopted a modified form of Persian royal dress, he insisted that his officers take Persian wives. He himself had earlier married Roxane, a Persian princess. In the spring of 323 BCE, he moved to Babylon, now making plans for the conquest of the western Mediterranean and creation of a universal monarchy. He also developed plans for the exploration of Arabia and the Caspian and for opening a water route from the Persian Gulf to the Indus.

But it was not to be. Suddenly, Alexander was taken sick with a fever. His suffering increased and no one was able to do anything to help him. His friends asked: "To whom do you leave the kingdom?" Alexander replied, "To the best (the strongest)." These were his last words. At sundown on the 10th of June, 323 BCE, Alexander the Great died in the palace of Nebuchadnezzar, at the age of 33. He had reigned for twelve years and eight months. A few weeks after his death, Roxane gave birth to his son, who was named Alexander IV. However, both the boy and his mother became pawns of the ensuing struggle for power among his generals and a few years later both were murdered. His empire disintegrated into several kingdoms that almost immediately began fighting among themselves.

Alexander possessed the imagination of a genius combined with the drive of an iron will and a gift of charismatic leadership ability. The success of his ambition spread a veneer of Greek culture into central Asia, which remained his legacy throughout the succeeding Hellenistic Period. Alexander founded over 70 new cities (some 23 of them named Alexandria), and the process of settlement and colonization was continued by his successors, but his plans for ethnic fusion were not successful. The Macedonians rejected the idea of ethnic unity and in the Hellenistic kingdoms Greek culture was dominant. After his death, nearly all the noble marriages between Persians and Macedonians were dissolved. As a conqueror Alexander has never been surpassed in all of history. He constantly adapted new tactics and created innovative forms of warfare. His strategy was ingenious to the point of disbelief. He could always "think outside the box."

Yet, "the verdict of posterity" has been both kind and unkind to Alexander the Great, and the controversy surrounding his character and his policy are as varied today as they were in antiquity. His enormous physical courage, impulsive energy, and fervid imagination stand out clearly, but beyond that disagreement reigns. The traditional view is that he aimed at conquering the whole world and demanded to be worshipped as a god, but the best ancient authority, Arrian, fails to substantiate this view satisfactorily. The policy of fusing the Greek and Oriental cultures can be judged in various ways. On the one hand it can be viewed as the dream of human brotherhood, the plan for a world empire in which all races and cultures would live together in mutual peace and respect. Thus, the dreamy-eyed romantics. The ancients, for the most part, viewed it as evidence of Alexander's ambition taken to the point of madness. "He's gone native," they said, he thinks he is an Oriental potentate, he has forgotten that he is a Greek. All of this is part of the almost mystical fascination that kept Alexander the Great at the forefront of historical interest for over two thousand years. That fascination shows no signs of ebbing even today.

The Hellenistic Kingdoms

"Hellenistic" refers to the spread of Greek culture and civilization throughout the Middle East and the Mediterranean after Alexander's death. The Hellenistic Age is dated between 323 BCE, the death of Alexander and 31 BCE, the year in which Egypt, the last of the Hellenistic kingdoms, became part of the Roman Empire. But this date for the end of the Hellenistic Age is arbitrary and ignores the fact that the Roman period was, in a very real sense, a continuation of the spread of Greek cultural influence. In fact, the centuries of Greek and Roman history are most accurately thought of together as the "Greco-Roman" Age, because neither of these great civilizations can be understood without reference to the other. But that is getting far ahead of our story.

When Alexander died in 323 BCE, he left behind one of the greatest empires ever assembled in the history of the world. But it was not yet adequately organized or unified. Who could fill the shoes of the great conqueror? Alexander had an older brother, Philip IV Arrhidaeus, who was mentally incompetent, and a few weeks after Alexander's death, Roxane gave birth to his son, Alexander IV. Neither of these could rule, so Alexander's generals appointed themselves as satraps of the large regions of the empire and attempted to rule as a kind of regency committee. But obviously this was not a workable solution. Within three years, suspicion and antagonism grew between the generals to the extent that the empire broke up into three major kingdoms and several smaller states. The year 321 BCE marked the beginning of about forty years of conflict among the generals—and their descendants. By 301 BCE, the basic structure of the Hellenistic world was set. Macedonia and the Greek mainland were ruled by Antigonus. Egypt was ruled by Ptolemy, and the Ptolemaic dynasty continued in Egypt down to the death of Cleopatra VII in 30 BCE. Most of the central area of Alexander's empire came under the control of Seleucus and his descendants. This state is usually known as the Seleucid Kingdom or Empire, but is often referred to simply as Syria. Of the smaller states to emerge from the empire, the kingdom of Pergamum in western Asia Minor, ruled by a dynasty founded by Philstaerus, was the most important.

The Hellenistic rulers did not share Alexander's vision of multiculturalism and staffed their administrations with Macedonians and Greeks. The new regimes were not purely Greek, however. The rulers of Egypt and the Seleucid Kingdom transformed themselves into eastern style monarchs. The inhabitants of Egypt had always been accustomed to worship their rulers as semi-divine beings, and the new Greek rulers passed themselves off as saviors[14] and received the benefits of their subject's worship. These Hellenistic kings ruled their non-Greek subjects through the use of Greek armies and bureaucracies, which were, for the most part, still recruited in Greece, and this facilitated a steady stream of Greek immigration into the conquered areas. In fact, the Hellenistic Age was the second great outward migration of Greek people—the first had been the colonization movement toward the end of the Dark Age.

The Hellenistic Age ushered in a period of intense economic expansion. One factor contributing to this new prosperity was the increased money supply. When Alexander seized the Persian treasuries at Susa, Persepolis, and elsewhere, he restored vast quantities of money into circulation. The Persians liked to accumulate their treasure, which removed money from circulation. In the modern world, whenever the government has a surplus of funds it is deposited in banks, which invest the money and it becomes a stimulant to economic activity. But in the ancient world surplus money was often hoarded in treasuries, which removed the money from circulation and put a drag on the economy. Alexander, on the other hand, believed that the only good use for money was to spend it, which he did on grandiose, and often wasteful, projects, but it trickled down through the economy of the Middle East, providing a tremendous economic stimulus.

One of the sharpest contrasts between the Hellenic and the Hellenistic worlds was the difference in the size of the economic operations. In classical Greece farmers worked small plots of land while industry and commerce was carried on either by families or small entrepreneurs. But in

---

14. *Soter*, a title of honor accorded to some deities and rulers, expressing their power to save people from danger. Christian ideas of a Savior must not be projected back onto pre-Christian usage.

Hellenistic Egypt and the Seleucid Kingdom vast estates were the general rule. The Greeks introduced new crops and agricultural techniques. In Egypt they introduced the cultivation of grapes for wine and improved the irrigation system. They also developed huge sheep and horse ranches which provided leather, cloth, and cavalry horses. Industry and trade operated on the largest scale yet seen and required the services of sophisticated banking and financial systems. During the Hellenistic Age, for example, you could make a deposit in a banking house in Antioch and then travel to Alexandria and make a withdrawal. You did not have to carry around a large bag of coins when you traveled.

Great prosperity resulted from this economic growth, but the wealth derived from it was confined, for the most part, to the upper classes, which were usually Greek. The increasing disparity between the rich and poor was a new feature to the Greek culture and it led to social conflict. For one thing, the old Greek homeland did not share in a significant way in the new prosperity. Athens became little more than a back-water university town, because the center of trade shifted to Alexandria and the coast of the Levant. All of mainland Greece suffered both a population and an economic decline, due to the large numbers of Greeks emigrating to Egypt and the Near East.

This new Hellenistic civilization, like the old Hellenic one, was predominately urban, but with a difference. Many new Greek cities were founded by Alexander and his successors. Alexander himself founded about seventy cities during his conquest, at least twenty-three of them named Alexandria. Antioch was named for the son of Seleucus, the founder of the Seleucid dynasty, and it became the capital of Syria. These cities were the centers of government, commerce and culture. They were extremely large by Hellenic standards. Most of them had populations many times larger than the average Greek polis. Alexandria, the largest of them, grew to almost a million inhabitants at its peak. The Greeks built many of the same features in these new cities as in the ones they left at home: temples, theaters, gymnasia, and other public buildings.

The upper classes of the native populations copied Greek culture and gave their children a Greek education in order to take their place among the upper classes. A form of the Greek language called Koiné, a simplified version of the Attic dialect, became the international language. During the Hellenistic Age, for the first time, a person could travel to any city in the known civilized world and make himself understood with one language. This process by which the native populations of the Near East acquired at least a veneer of Greek culture is called Hellenization. For example, the Jewish historian Josephus wrote his famous history of the Jewish people in Koiné Greek, not Hebrew. The Christian missionary St. Paul was also a Hellenized Jew, and the letters he wrote to the various early churches throughout the Roman Empire and which were collected into the several books of the New Testament, were written in Koiné, not Hebrew.

But unlike the old Greek poleis, these new Hellenistic cities were very cosmopolitan, that is, they contained peoples of many different cultures and nationalities. This too was something new to Greek culture. In the old Greek polis the population was basically homogeneous. A citizen walking along the street could bid those passing by "good morning" and be reasonably secure as to what their response would be. In the new Hellenistic cities, the citizen could not be sure that those passing him in the street could even understand his greeting. Alexandria, for example, had groups of Jews, Palestinians, Greeks, representative from just about every ethnic group of the Middle East, as well as the native Egyptians, all living together, all rubbing shoulders in the busy streets. The Ptolemaic dynasty cultivated Greek culture by building a huge museum and library in Alexandria, with research facilities, which attracted scholars from all over the Greek world. But at best, the "Greekness" of Alexandria was a thin and in some aspects an artificial veneer. Athens continued its leadership in the field of philosophy, but Alexandria became the most renowned center in the Hellenistic world for the study of literature, history, and science.

After the initial conflicts between the successor kingdoms to Alexander's empire, the Hellenistic Age was also a period of relative peace. One contributing factor to this was the fact that soldiers were drawn from Greece and Macedonia, to the exclusion of native manpower. Since the supply of soldiers was limited, the size of armies was also limited and this forced the kings to solve their disputes by diplomatic means, rather than risk their limited armies in combat. During the Hellenistic Age—at least until the advent of the Romans, who possessed almost unlimited manpower—losing a battle meant losing the war. Thus, it was far better to negotiate.

However, the Hellenistic Age was also a period of personal crisis. Because these new cities were so large and because they were now governed by appointed agents of the king, their citizens did not participate in an active and vigorous political life as they had in the old Greek polis. Therefore, they began to withdraw from community life into the privacy of their families and private clubs. In religion, they abandoned the public ceremonies of the state religion for private cults. This contrast between the public lifestyle of the Classical Period and the private lifestyle of the Hellenistic Age, is one of the fundamental differences between the two ages, and it is reflected in every cultural, political, social, and religious aspect of life.

Hellenistic Philosophies

There were important changes in both religion and philosophy during the Hellenistic period. The radical change from the security and small-town intimacy of life in the Greek city-state to the new sophistication, variety, and even loneliness of life in the big Hellenistic city, produced corresponding changes in philosophy and religion. After all, Greek culture had developed for hundreds of years in its mainland setting of the small independent polis and now almost overnight that culture was transferred into a new and unfamiliar environment. Classical philosophers, like Socrates/Plato and Aristotle, had been concerned with the citizen's relationship to, and his role in, the polis. But now the state had been transformed from a small polis into a large kingdom, ruled by a remote king through a huge professional bureaucracy. Individual men and women seemed no longer to be capable of influencing the policies of this new state, but they were still caught up in the state's wars, as well its changes in economic fortune. The problems of the individual's relationship to this new kind of state were quite different than his relationship to the old polis, and the Hellenistic schools of philosophy attempted to deal with these new problems.

Stoicism

There were three major schools of Hellenistic philosophy. The most popular of them, Stoicism, was founded by Zeno (335–262 BCE), who began teaching on the porch, or stoa, of a public building in Athens, and thus the name of his philosophy is derived from that fact. Zeno taught that a single divine plan governs the universe, and that to find happiness, the individual must act in harmony with that plan. For example, we should be patient in adversity, for adversity is a necessary part of the divine plan and, in any event, we can do nothing to change it. If the individual will simply accept his fate, he will then become immune to earthly anxieties and will achieve thereby an inner freedom and tranquility. But the stoics did not carry this principle to extremes, because they did not advocate complete withdrawal from the world. They believed that all civilized people, as rational beings, are members of one great human family. We are all brothers and sisters. Therefore, we should be tolerant of one another. Moreover, it is the duty of rational individuals to engage in public affairs in order to advance the common good.

The Stoic system is holistic, that is, all of its parts are necessary to the whole: there are no fundamental parts upon which the entire system rests, as in Socratic philosophy. Thus, Stoicism must be understood as a whole, not as a structure derived from a few fundamental principles. However, Stoicism includes—but is not limited to—three distinguishable parts: logic, physics, and ethics. To understand anything about Stoicism, logic, in its technical sense, must be employed, and the Stoics developed the logic of propositions to a higher degree than any of the other philosophies. Stoicism is radically empiricist: knowledge is that which makes an impact on the human mind from the outside world, not what is apprehended from within the mind itself. Stoic physics involves the concept of a determinist world made up of material objects and their interactions, which are governed by "natural" laws called "fate." However, within this determinist system, human action is free and each individual is responsible for his own fate. Thus, Stoic ethics is the product of a set of uncompromising principles: virtue (the skill of putting things to correct use) produces happiness; only virtue is good; emotions (illogical actions) are always bad. These principles are not easily defended in isolation and only seem valid when fit into the holistic view of the Stoics. Humans should live in accordance with human nature. Because the human is a rational animal, this means living in accordance with human reason, that is, in accordance with "nature."

The ideas advanced by the Stoics have influenced Western Civilization down to the present day. The Stoic concept of the brotherhood of all humanity was, in reality, an adjustment of Greek life to the new cosmopolitan lifestyle of the Hellenistic cities. In the old polis, non-Greeks were called "barbarians," not brothers. And of course, the Greeks had accepted the institution of slavery as a "natural" social phenomenon. But the Stoics believed that the practice of exploiting others corrupted the master as well as the slave. These are ideals that, of course, have never been fully realized. Nevertheless, Stoicism became the most influential philosophy among the educated people of the Hellenistic age and later achieved great influence among the later Romans.

Epicureanism

Epicurus (341–270 BCE), the founder of Epicureanism, also believed that people should strive for inner tranquility, but he differed with the Stoics on how this should be achieved. He addressed himself to the anxieties and fears of his contemporaries toward the gods and, above all, toward death. Epicurus decided that the gods were basically indifferent to humankind, and thus not to be feared. Concerning death, he said: "Good and bad exist only when they are perceived by the mind and death deprives us of all perception—while we are, death is not, and when death is, we are not." Another way of saying it: Death does not exist in reality because it can only be perceived by a mind while it is living; after a mind ceases to live, it can perceive nothing, neither life nor death, pain nor pleasure. Therefore, people should have no fear of death and concern themselves only with leading pleasurable lives. Epicureanism has a bad reputation among later ages, especially among the Christians, because of its perceived atheism. However, the epicureans were not really atheists and by seeking pleasure Epicurus did not mean self-indulgence but rather the avoidance of physical and mental pain. Indeed, self-indulgence almost always leads to physical and emotional pain. The epicureans believed that people should avoid entanglements of any kind. Falling in love, for example, may be quite enjoyable in the short term, but it almost always leads to a broken heart, not a pleasant experience. And since political and emotional involvement can cause pain, the wise person will withdraw from the active world to a quite life of study and the companionship of a few friends.

Epicurus adopted the atomic theory of Democritus, to which he made some minor changes, evidently to answer Aristotle's criticisms. The atoms themselves are indestructible, and change in the physical world is explained by the rearrangement of atoms. The cosmos came into existence through the random collisions of atoms and will someday dissolve again into the individual atoms. All atoms move naturally downward and at a constant and equal speed. If some of them did not sway form their original path and collide with others, there would be no world as we know it. Thus, the internal cosmic order of Aristotle is rejected. The natural movement of atoms explains the origin and development of everything in our world. The soul, or mind, is composed of atoms and at death all the component atoms are dispersed and the individual ceases to exist. From all of this, it is easy to understand the fundamental principle of Epicureanism: "pleasure is naturally the only object of human life." But as usual, it is not that simple. Some pleasures are temporary and partial and involve pain. It is necessary to distinguish between different pleasures and pursue only those which are not outweighed by pain. Pain is caused by unsatisfied desire. Pleasure is not the process of satisfying desire, but the state of having desires satisfied. The pleasure of the soul (mind) consists mainly of contemplation which is more valuable than physical pleasure. Thus, Epicureanism finds room for most of the traditional Greek virtues and its moral philosophy was much less selfish than its statements make it appear. Even the enemies of Epicureanism were impressed with the friendship and loyalty which bound Epicureans together and the virtues displayed by epicurean communities.

Cynicism

Diogenes (c. 404–323 BCE) was not the founder of the Cynic philosophy, but he was its chief propagandist. (Antisthenes, c. 444–366 BCE, a student of Socrates, was the founder.) Diogenes was one of the most eccentric individuals of the ancient world. He professed to believe in naturalism, but he seemed to spend most of his time simply being unnecessarily obnoxious. The main principles of his

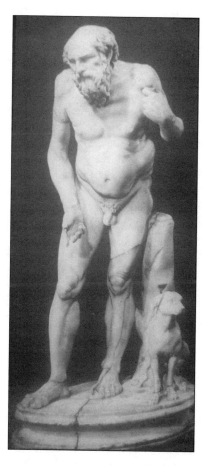

Figure 8.5: Diogenes.

philosophy were: happiness is attained by satisfying only one's natural needs and doing so in the cheapest and easiest way possible. What is natural cannot be indecent or shameful. It sounds logical enough, but the practical application of these principles resulted in the discarding of all inhibitions which make it possible for human beings to live together in social groups. For this reason a practitioner of this philosophy was called in Greek *kynikos*, "like a dog," from which the English word cynic is derived.

Diogenes adapted the clothes of a beggar and for a time even made his home in a tub in the courtyard of the temple of Cybele in Athens. He slept on the ground, ate food whenever and wherever he found it, and performed the duties of nature as well as the rites of love in full public view. He traveled leisurely about Greece and on one of his journeys he was captured by pirates and sold as a slave. When his master asked him what he could do, he answered: "Govern men." He was made the tutor of his master's sons and manager of the household. He later regained his freedom and became famous for his cynical humor. He once rebuked a woman who knelt with her head on the ground in front of a sacred altar, saying, "Are you not afraid to be in so indecent an attitude, when some god may be behind you, for they say the gods are everywhere." When he saw a prostitute throwing a stone into a crowd during a riot, he said, "Take care lest you hit your father." He is said to have been greatly admired by the ancients for these eccentric tendencies. Then there is the story, probably an invention, that Alexander came upon Diogenes one day sitting in the street and when he approached the philosopher he was told, "Get out of my sunshine." Alexander is reported to have responded: "If I was not Alexander I would want to be Diogenes."

Cynicism, like the "hippy" movement of the 20th Century, was never a formal school of philosophy, but rather a way of life grounded in the principle of "living according to nature." After Diogenes discovered the "true way," there was little development of original thought in the movement. Nevertheless, Cynicism had a far reaching influence on later Greek and Roman philosophy, rulership ideology, literature, and religion. Zeno, the founder of Stoicism, was originally a follower of the Cynic Crates, and stoic ethics are essentially those of the Cynics reworked slightly: for example, from the Cynic concept of "nature" Zeno developed the Stoic notion of "divine plan." Even later, Cynic ethics had a strong and obvious influence on Christian ethics. The very extremism of Cynic positions on ethical and political questions determined the definition of these categories in other philosophies. Throughout the ancient period, for example, the debate on the ethics of wealth and poverty—the fact that some people possess far more material possessions than is necessary for the "good life," while others are deprived of even the bare essentials—was more or less controlled by the cynical definition of this problem. The Stoic and Epicurean philosophers, and even the early Christian theologians, found it impossible to discuss ethics of these problems without beginning with the definitions set up by the Cynics.

Obviously, the answer of these new philosophies to the problems of life in the Hellenistic environment was a turning inward. The classical philosophers believed the good life was found through public service and participation in the political life of the polis. In contrast, the thinkers of the Hellenistic age believed happiness was to be found within one's self. These contrasting points of view are yet another reflection of the contrast between the public lifestyle of the Hellenic and the private lifestyles of the Hellenistic Age.

Hellenistic Religion

But, in the end, philosophy is for the intellectual elite and the wealthy. The ordinary person, as always, turned to religion. The old Greek state religions declined along with the decline of the polis. Greek religion was never successfully transplanted into the Near East. Rather, in the field of religion, the cultural influence was quite the opposite: the religions of the East gradually dominated those of the West.

In fact, the religions of the East were not new to the Greeks, they began to borrow myth and cult practices from the East at least as early as 650 BCE. A group of so-called mystery religions originated in the East. All of them had certain features in common. For one thing, each cult centered around the worship of a *soter*, or savior, who had died and been resurrected and could share his or her conquest of death with his followers through rituals, ceremonies, and "mysteries." Unlike the state religion, these mystery cults were not separated from everyday life and indeed permeated every aspect of the believer's life. The rituals employed by these cults were usually extremely emotional and orgiastic and provided a direct connection, or confrontation, with the spiritual world. Another important aspect of the mystery cults was their promise of an afterlife of bliss to compensate for the miseries of this world. Among the most important of these mystery religions was the cult of Osiris and Isis, the Egyptian religion involving the Book of the Dead discussed earlier in chapter 3. During the Hellenistic age the goddess Isis slowly replaced Osiris as the central deity of this cult; after all, it was Isis who had achieved the resurrection of her husband and it was her benevolence that was necessary for the worshipers to attain life after death.

At the beginning of the Hellenistic Age, Greek religion spread quickly throughout the Near East, but it never achieved much depth of acceptance among the native populations, because the Oriental religions were so firmly established—and these belief systems catered to a deep-seated human need. Gradually, the Greeks who settled in the conquered areas began to turn to the Oriental religions to fill the emotional gap left by the failure of their own religious experience. Throughout history it can be observed that whenever a religion fails to adapt to new social conditions, fails to console its adherents, it becomes irrelevant and either changes to meet those needs or is replaced by other religious systems which do. The Greek philosophers like to think of the human being as a "rational animal," but that is only one aspect of human nature. The human being is also a "religious animal," and no amount of logic or rational contemplation can turn most human beings away from superstition, mythology, and religion. Buried somewhere deep within the human genome there must lurk a "religion" gene.

Representative of the fusion of Greek and Eastern religions is the appearance of the cult of Sarapis. In order to provide themselves with a divine Greco-Egyptian patron, the early Ptolemies founded a cult centered around the god Sarapis, a combination of Osiris and Pluto (Hades) and also including the attributes of several other Egyptian and Greek divinities. He was worshiped at Memphis essentially as the benevolent god of the underworld and resembled Osiris more than any Greek deity. However, at Alexandria, Sarapis was interpreted in accordance with political or individual requirements and was closely tied to the court. Beyond Egypt devotion to Sarapis took the form of membership in the cult, which met for worship and feasts. Sarapis was later adopted as the universal godhead by some Gnostic[15] cults.

However, the mystery religion that was destined to achieve the greatest acceptance and have the most far-reaching influence on Western Civilization was not born for another three centuries: that was, of course, Christianity. Although much of the development of Christianity was Jewish in origin, practices such as baptism, the confession of sins, partaking of sacrificial meals, the death and resurrection of the savior, and the general tone of mysticism, are only part of the heritage of the mystery religions of the Hellenistic Age. All this will be discussed in more detail later.

---

15. Gnosticism is a generic term primarily used for theosophical groups which broke with the 2nd Century Christian Church. A wider, more imprecise use of the term describes the syncretistic religiosity diffused in the Near East, contemporaneous with and independent of Christianity. The proliferation of Gnostic Web sites in recent years is evidence of a renewed interest in this form of religion in the modern world.

Hellenistic Literature

Hellenistic literature cannot, of course, compare with the golden age of the Classical Period. Writers now became far more concerned with style than with content. Poetry, for example, achieved a high degree of technical perfection and polish, but had little emotional depth. The most popular literature of the time is something called pastoral, or bucolic, poetry. The Greeks, now living in the congested urban setting of the large Hellenistic cities, much like the inhabitants of our modern cities, waned nostalgic over the dreamy beauty of an idealized country life that they had left behind.

The settings for these insufferably sentimental poems was always the same. First the poet would set the scene: the sweeping vista of a beautiful landscape, beside a river of peacefully flowing water, the foliage of the trees rustles in a gentle and cooling breeze and, to the sweet sound of singing birds and buzzing insects, the ephemeral images of woodland gods and dancing nymphs appear and disappear throughout this landscape in a hazy and vague rhythm. Throughout this idyllic scene, sun-tanned rustics, shepherds, reapers, and fresh, healthy, country girls with rosy checks, play and frolic the day away, while they converse, tease, sing love songs, relate old folk tales, and indulge in delight-fully delicate and erotic activities with an innocence and childish joy that no city slicker could ever match—after all, having lost our innocence, such things seem pornographic to us. Nevertheless, the best of these pastoral poets, writers like Theocritus (c. 316–c. 260 BCE), could weave a fugue of fantasy and myth in such a setting that it influenced later writers like Virgil, Spenser, and Milton and even some of the modern writers of science fiction and fantasy, like Ray Bradbury.

Once the idealized pastoral scene was set, a typical plot might involve a shepherd boy named Daphnis, who won the love of a beautiful woodland nymph, named Chloe, by promising to be faith-ful to her forever.[16] Of course, forever is a long, long time, and simply by making such a promise he aroused the jealousy of Aphrodite, the goddess of love, and she, with the assistance of her son Eros (we call him Cupid) put his promise to the test: the arrow of Eros inflicted Daphnis with a desper-ate passion for a beautiful princess, who just happened to be passing through the countryside. But rather then yield to this passion, he remained firmly true to his promise of faithfulness to his beloved Chloe, and thus wasted away and died of unrequited longing. He was mourned in poem and song by all the inhabitants of the countryside, both mortal and immortal. . . and the goddess herself regret-ted her deed and finally reunited the lovers, and they lived happily ever after in their idyllic country setting. If only country life was half as wonderful as we city dwellers imagine it to be—but alas, it is not. Those city-slickers who have actually ventured out there have, to their dismay, discovered an ugly secret: it is full of ants and mosquitoes and after about two weeks it gets BORING!

Hellenistic prose was dominated by history, theater, and the novel. The most successful writer of history was Polybius (c. 200–after 118 BCE). Indeed he ranks with Thucydides as one of the greatest historians of any age. Polybius believed that historical development passed inevitably through stages of growth and decay—somewhat analogous to human life—and that it is therefore possible to predict where a nation is headed by studying its past.[17] Polybius is one of our most important sources for the history of the Roman Republic, and we will meet him again in that context in a later chapter.

---

16. Theocritus's *The Daphnis Song* does not follow the precise plot outlined here. Rather, I have provided a "generic" plot that is typical of the pastoral poetry of the Hellenistic Age.

17. This concept of history has been propagated by such modern historians as Arnold J. Toynbee, *A Study of History* (Volumes I–III, 1934; IV–VI, 1939, VII–X, 1954), Oxford University Press, London; Oswald Spengler, *Der Untergang des Abendlandes* (1918), translated by Charles Frances Atkinson as *The Decline of the West* (1926–28), 2 volumes, Knopf, New York; Jacques Barzun, *From Dawn to Decadence* (2000), Harper Collins, New York; and others.

Theater was extremely popular with the Hellenistic urban populations. Although some tragedy was written during this period, almost all of it has been lost, but much Hellenistic comedy survives and it contrasts so strongly with the comedy of the Hellenic Period that it is called "New Comedy." This Hellenistic comedy does not deal at all with political or social problems, but instead focuses on the life of individuals. The best known New Comedy playwright is Menander (342–c.293 BCE), whose plots often involved young men who fell in love with women who were unattainable for some reason, such as a difference in station. Invariably the lovers overcome the many obstacles in their path and achieve final happiness. This, of course, is yet another reflection of the turning inward toward private concerns during the Hellenistic Age.

The Hellenistic novel, a new genre, also reflected this move toward the private lifestyle. The plots are similar to those of New Comedy and even to the modern romantic paperback novel: young men and women fall in love at first sight and must overcome circumstances which separate them. A surprising feature of these novels is the strong female character, a resourceful and outspoken woman who determines her own fate. Even more in contrast with classical literature is the ideal of affection and mutual love within marriage. The Stoic philosopher Antipater of Tarsus (2nd Century BCE) wrote, "The man who has had no experience of a married woman and children has not tasted true and noble happiness." Although most marriages were still arranged, some men and women began to follow their hearts in choosing a mate. The philosopher Hipparchia,[18] who rejected her father's wishes and selected her own husband, is an example of the "new woman" of the Hellenistic Age.

Hellenistic Science and Technology

The scientific capital of the Hellenistic world was also at Alexandria, in Egypt. By 200 BCE, the great library built by the ruling Ptolemies contained approximately one million books. A museum

---

18. Hipparchia was a near contemporary of Diogenes and a philosopher in her own right. She dared to defy the social norms of her times and to bravely assert equality of the sexes. According to Diogenes Laertius, *Lives of Eminent Philosophers*, volume 2, translated by R.D. Hicks (1925), William Heinemann, London:

Hipparchia too, sister of Metrocles, was captured by [the doctrines of the Cynics]. Both of them were born at Maronea. She fell in love with the words and life of Crates, and would not pay attention to any of her suitors, their wealth, their high birth or their good looks. But to her Crates was everything. She used even to threaten her parents that she would kill herself, unless she were given in marriage to him. Crates therefore was implored by her parents to dissuade the girl, and did all he could. Finally, failing to persuade her, got up, took off his clothes right in front of her and said: "This is your bridegroom, here are his possessions; make your choice accordingly; for you will be no partner of mine, unless you share my way of life."

The girl chose and, adopting the same dress, went about with her husband and consorted with him in public and went out to dinners with him. Accordingly she appeared at the banquet given by Lysimachus, and there put down Theodorus, known as the atheist, by means of the following argument:

Any action which would not be called wrong if done by Theodorus, would not be called wrong if done by Hipparchia. Now Theodorus does no wrong when he strikes himself. Therefore neither does Hipparchia do wrong when she strikes Theodorus.

He had no reply to this argument, but tried to strip her of her cloak. But Hipparchia showed no signs of alarm or of the kind of agitation natural to a woman. And when he said to her, "Is this she who left behind her comb and loom?" she replied, "It is I, Theodorus. But do you suppose that I have chosen incorrectly, if instead of wasting further time upon the loom I spent it in education?"

These tales and countless others are told of the female philosopher.

was attached to the library which housed literary and scientific research facilities and supported large numbers of resident scholars and scientists.

The knowledge and accomplishments of these Hellenistic scientists, separated from us as they are by the Christian Dark Ages, seem amazing and unreal to us today. The mathematician Euclid, around 300 BCE, complied a textbook of geometry that is basically the textbook still in use in high schools and colleges today. There is not much anyone can add to it. Almost nothing is known of his life except that he lived in Alexandria under Ptolemy I, to whom he said, when Ptolemy complained about the length of Euclid's proofs, "There is no royal road to geometry."

The most gifted engineer of the day was Archimedes (287–212 BCE). The story is told about him that while contemplating his own displacement in a bath, he suddenly realized how he could calculate the proportion of silver and gold in a crown made for his friend Hieron II (King of Syracuse c. 270–215 BCE). He shouted "Eureka," and absent-mindedly ran home naked.[19] Among his inventions was the "Archimedes screw," a device for lifting water that is still in use today in many parts of the world. He designed many types of lifting devises using pulleys and block and tackle techniques. He once said: "Give me a place upon which to stand and I will move the earth." He was killed by a Roman soldier in 212 BCE when his native city of Syracuse fell after a hard siege in which machines devised by him caused many Roman casualties.

Astronomy reached an apex of development in Alexandria not attained again until modern times. About 250 BCE, Aristarchus (c. first half of 3rd Century BCE) advanced the heliocentric theory of the solar system, that is, that the earth and planets move around the sun, which is fixed in its position like the stars. Unfortunately this theory was not generally accepted until the 16th Century. Another great astronomer, Hipparchus of Nicaea (fl. 146–127 BCE), by using trigonometry with extensive observations and old Babylonian records, discovered the precession of the equinoxes, calculated the size and distance of the moon and measured the length of the lunar month correctly to within one second. However, his rejection of the heliocentric solar system had a long-term detrimental effect on astronomy. And Eratosthenes (c. 276–194 BCE) measured the circumference of the earth to within 1.7% of its actual size. All of these achievements, of course, were achieved without the benefit of modern precision instruments, such as laser beams.

Hellenistic Art

We come now to the third and last period of Greek art, having already looked at the art of the Archaic and Classical ages. Hellenistic art differs from Classical art in several important attitudes and characteristics. Throughout history, most critics and observers have preferred Classical art. Pliny the Elder (23–78 CE), writing in the late roman Period, was no different:

> An almost innumerable multitude of artists have been rendered famous by statues and figures . . . [he names dozens of artists from 450 to 295 BCE]. . . and in the 121st [Olympiad, 295–292 BCE] Eutychides, Euthyerates, Laippus, Cephisodotus, Timarchus, and Pyromachus. After that the art languished, and it revived again in the 156th Olympiad [156–153 BCE], when there were the following, far inferior it is true to those mentioned above, but nevertheless, artists of repute: Antaeus, Callistratus, Polycles, of Athens, Callixenus, Pythicles, Pythias and Timocles.[20]

---

19. The tradition of the absent-minded professor, it seems, has a long history.

20. Pliny the Elder, *Natural History*, 34.51-52.

In other words, those artists working between 280 and 155 BCE, roughly the years we refer to as the High Hellenistic Period, were inferior to the Classical artists. Yet, Hellenistic art seems, in many ways, more compatible with modern tastes than classical art. Indeed, Hellenistic art often seems almost "modern." So what were the important differences between these two styles?

Hellenistic artists did not completely abandon classical concepts, but more accurately expanded its vocabulary and horizon through dramatic posing , sweeping lines, and high emotional contrast. The confining conventions and suffocating rules of the Classical Period gave way to fresh and liberating freedom that allowed the artist to express unique and personal points of view. Classical idealism gave way to realism. The quiet, sublime greatness of the Classical style was replaced by the bold energy and tension of real life. The subject matter of sculpture also changed. The Hellenistic artist was much less interested in deities and heroic figures and more preoccupied with the dramatic and psychological aspects of his subjects.

The Nike of Samothrace (Fig. 8.6), for example, depicts the winged goddess of victory at the precise moment that she alights on the prow of the Rhodian flagship to announce victory. This is a goddess. We might expect to view the sublime and the holy. But the artist has mastered the rigid stone

Figure 8.6: Nike of Samothrace.

upon which he works to such an extent that we immediately see (perhaps the word is experience) the soft, flowing cloth of her robe waving in the wind. The wind presses the soft material against her substantial body underneath, causing it to conform to the twists and curves of her nude body. The goddess appears to be suspended just above the ground, with the air rushing through the feathers of her wings, perhaps the wind is stronger than gravity, perhaps her feet will never rest firmly on the ground. We can feel the wind. Only later do we realize that we are looking at heavy, hard, cold marble. Nothing approaching this realism was ever accomplished—or indeed, attempted—in Classical art. The Nike of Samothrace occupies no place in the world of the gods, she is completely of this windy, human world in which we live.

The same cosmopolitanism we saw manifested in philosophy and literature is also boldly stated in Hellenistic art. In the Capitoline Museum in Rome is a life-size marble copy of one of the bronze statues dedicated at Pergamum by Attalus I in commemoration of his victories over the Gauls who invaded Asia Minor in 239 BCE. The mortally wounded Gaul (Figs. 8.7 & 8.8) is depicted at the moment of death. The moustache and matted hair and twisted collar identify him as a barbarian. He supports himself with one arm as his strength ebbs away. Blood oozes from the open wound. His skin appears dry and dirty. His eyes close as he drifts into unconsciousness forever. But there is no melodrama, no preaching or overstatement. Indeed the effect is one of overwhelming artistic restraint. In Classical art barbarians are sub-human beings incapable of exhibiting dignity, not deserving of sympathy. But here Greek chauvinism is replaced by the universalism of the Stoics and the Cynics.[21] There is no doubt here that realism is used by the Greek artist to express his compassion for the agony and despair of this warrior.

The Seated Boxer (Fig. 8.9) illustrates how far Hellenistic art departed from ideals of Classicism. This cast bronze piece dates from the 1st Century BCE. No attempt whatever is made by the artist to display beauty or nobility, rather, the treatment is ruthlessly blunt and realistic to the point of nauseam. This is real life, not life as it could be or should be, but as it really is, and we are forced to experience it even though we had rather not. This professional athlete is not a young man and he has obviously competed in the ring all his life. He has the muscle tone of a trained athlete who "works out" every day, but his body exhibits the marks of the utter brutality and cruelty of professional sports in any age. Bruises and deep scars cover his shoulders, arms, and thighs. His nose had been broken so many times that he must breathe with difficulty through his open mouth, which reveals broken and jagged teeth, the legacy of countless hits to his face. Repeated blows to his head have turned his ears into cauliflower like appendages. His hands are encased in the savage leather gloves of the professional boxer, which contain lead knuckles known as "killers" (caestus). Someone has spoken to him and he has looked up at them in a stupor, struggling to perceive the world through the ringing bells and throbbing buzz that cloud his brain—the result of a lifetime spent in the boxing ring. We like to be entertained by athletes, but most of us don't like to be reminded of the brutality and cruelty of professional sports. That is why old athletes are not heroes. They can be discarded like pieces of stale meat and replaced by young beautiful men—and we don't need see the evidence of the pain and suffering. This is the story of professional sports in all ages, certainly our own. But this Hellenistic artist—the sculpture is signed "Apollonius, son of Nestor"—forces us to look at reality.

In a sense, the Hellenistic Age seems very "modern" to us. Many aspects of Hellenistic culture resemble characteristics found in our own world of the 21st Century. The cosmopolitan tone and

---

21. When Diogenes was asked which polis he was from, he replied, "I am a citizen of the world." Diogenes Laertius, 6.62.

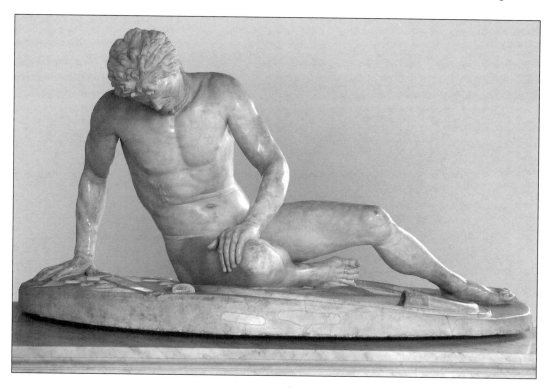

Figure 8.7 and 8.8:
The Dying Gaul.

Figure 8.9: The Seated Boxer.

private lifestyle[22] are obvious examples. The nostalgia for an imagined romanticized "simple life" of the past is another. And of course, the realism running through the art of the Hellenistic Age seems very familier to us. All of these factors, however, are even more evident in the next civilization we will study, the Romans. In fact, the Roman Period is a kind of culmination or extension of the Hellenistic Age, and many scholars indeed classify Roman Civilization as Hellenistic.

---

22. One of the great controversies in this "information age" is how the individual can maintain a degree of privacy. Those living in the Hellenistic Age had similar concerns of protecting themselves from the impersonal state bureaucracies.

CHAPTER

9

The Etruscans and the Origins of Rome

The Greek ascendancy in the eastern Mediterranean and the Near East, achieved by Alexander the Great, endured little more than two centuries before it was challenged by the rise of the young power from the West, the Romans. Although Rome developed a distinctive civilization in its own right, it also embraced the Hellenistic heritage and spread it westward to the Atlantic Ocean. The result is often referred to as the "Greco-Roman" civilization. The empire of the Romans, however, was built more slowly and more deliberately than that of the Greeks and was thus more enduring. The great strength of the Romans was that, in contrast to the Greeks, they were culturally and politically inclusive. They consistently sought to include others in their own system and in the end all the inhabitants of their far-flung empire became Roman citizens and came to think of themselves as Romans. Many of the later emperors came from the very people who had once been conquered by the Romans. Yet, while Greek civilization flourished in the East, the first four centuries of Roman history, for the most part, went unnoticed by the eastern powers.

The Roman Achievement

At its founding, around the mid 8th Century BCE, the state of Rome was confined to the few acres which comprise the Palatine Hill, yet by the 1st Century BCE, it ruled most of the known civilized world. There is something endlessly fascinating about the rise and fall of a great empire, but of all the empires that have come and gone across the face of our planet, none can hold so strong an appeal for us who inhabit the modern world as the empire of the Romans. Of all the peoples of the ancient world, the Romans are the most easily understood by us, because when we look at the Romans we are not looking only at the cold marble of dead ruins, or at the sterile beauty of pottery paintings displayed in museum showcases, but rather when we look at the Romans we see the conflicting loyalties of proud men, we see the unbridled ambition of unscrupulous politicians, we see the intimate emotions of close friendship and malicious enmities, we see the naked power of brutal aggression, and the inspiring strength, as well as the frustrating frailty, of the human spirit, as if it were laid out on a dissection table for us to inspect. When we study the Romans we find that they grappled with the same problems we face in the modern world: run-away pollution, over-crowded cities, out-of-control welfare programs, entrenched bureaucracies, and political corruption. These were people very much like us, and we can feel an empathy toward them that we feel toward no other ancient people.

The sheer scale of the Roman achievement is astounding. At its height, the Roman Empire extended for over 3,200 miles, from Armenia in the east to Britain in the west, and over 2,000 miles, from the Rhine-Danube frontier in the north, to the upper reaches of the Nile in the south. Never before and never since have the diverse and heterogeneous peoples of the Mediterranean Basin lived for so many centuries together in peace and prosperity as they did under the Roman Empire—during that era of history called the *Pax Romana,* the "Peace of Rome."

Like Caesar's Gaul,[1] Roman history is normally divided into three parts, the Kingdom (753–509 BCE), the Republic (509–27 BCE), and the Empire (27 BCE–476 CE). During the Kingdom, or the Royal Period, Rome was ruled by kings, but the period is shrouded in legend and myth and can only vaguely be dealt with in a historical sense. When the patricians, the aristocratic upper class of Roman society, overthrew the monarchy in 509 BCE, they established a republican form of government, under which Rome expanded to dominate first Italy and then the entire Mediterranean basin. But the effects of its success tore asunder the republic and almost destroyed Roman society as well. The deep crisis resulted in the demise of the Republic and the formation of a new governmental structure known as the Principate, or sometimes the "Empire," under an autocratic ruler known as the *imperator,* or emperor. This was the final Roman solution to ruling the unified Mediterranean basin, and it worked remarkably well for over two centuries.

The Italian Homeland

Rome began, of course, in Italy, and the first four centuries of its history was almost exclusively Italian. A brief examination of the geography of Italy is, therefore, appropriate. The peninsula of Italy is approximately 650 miles long, but nowhere more than 150 miles wide. The rocky Apennine Mountains run roughly down the center of the "boot" and then across the toe, where they dip under the sea for little more than a mile, to emerge again as the complex Sicilian Mountains of Sicily. Geologically, this is a single mountain system. Although fully three quarters of Italy is mountainous and uninhabitable, the plains here are more extensive than in the nearby peninsula of Greece, and the Italian peninsula has somewhat more abundant rainfall and can support a much larger population than Greece—or more importantly, in antiquity it supported a denser population. On the other hand, there are far fewer good harbors in Italy than in Greece. The best Italian ports are south of the Bay of Naples, and they were all settled by the Greeks during their colonial period. This is one of the factors that determined that Rome would develop primarily as land power: Roman armies conquered the Mediterranean basin by marching around its shores, rather than by first dominating the sea itself, as earlier Mediterranean powers had done.

Although at first glance Italy seems to be cut off from northern Europe by the very formidable Alpine mountains, it can in fact easily communicate with Europe along the coasts. Southern France is approached without difficulty to the west, and the Balkan area can be reached along the coastal plain to the east. And the Alps themselves could be traversed through several passes, at least during the summer. But it is true that Italy, especially in ancient times, faced the Mediterranean. It could easily be approached from Africa by way of Sicily from the south, and it was only a short distance from Greece and the Aegean, which served as a highway to the Middle East. So Italy, simply by virtue of its central location, was destined to play an important role in the history of the Mediterranean Basin.

---

1. The famous opening words of Julius Caesar's memoir *The Gallic War: Gallia est omnis divisa in partes tres. . .* "all of Gaul is divided into three parts. . ."

Italy has a wide variety of climate and topography. As one moves around the country, the scene constantly changes from evergreen plains to rocky wastes to rolling land which turns brown in the summer from lack of rain but blossoms into a lush and green landscape when the winter rains arrive. The climate of the peninsula of Italy, that is Italy south of the Po Valley, is the general climate of the Mediterranean basin. During the winter Italy lies in the path of the westerly winds, which bring periods of intense rainfall and sudden storms, although the winter cold is tempered by the warm Mediterranean Sea. In the spring, however, the westerlies, with their moisture, shift northward over the European continent and are replaced by the northeast winds devoid of rain. During the annual summer drought, the rivers, which were flooded by winter rain, dry up, and the fields and hills turn brown in the summer sun, which shines unerringly day after day from a cloudless sky. The rainless months in Italy, however, are not so long as in southern California, or even in Greece or Palestine. Sicily has four months each year without rain; Rome usually only two; whereas the Po Valley in the north, like the European continent to which it is more akin than to southern Italy, has no summer drought at all and can also depend upon the melting snows of the Alps to feed its rivers throughout the summer months.

The limestone mountains of Italy are rather devoid of valuable minerals. Some copper and lead could be found in Etruria and moderate though important iron deposits were discovered on the island of Elba. Although these deposits were not large by modern standards, they were quite valuable to the ancient economy. But tin, necessary for the making of bronze, and precious metals, such as gold and silver, which were more valuable to the ancient economy then to ours, were not to be found in Italy.

In antiquity, Italy was celebrated for its forests as well as its pastures and fields. At the dawn of history, heavy forests covered the Apennines, but alas, the ancients were at least as wasteful of natural resources as we are today. By the 1st Century BCE, most of the accessible forests in Italy had disappeared. In the main, destruction was accomplished by the harvesting of timber, but it was exasperated by the grazing of goats, who ate the tree seedlings as fast as they appeared. And once the rocky hills were stripped of their ground cover, the soil washed away entirely, so that today most slopes in Italy are bare, or at best support only an anemic, bushy growth.

The chief domestic animals raised on Italian pastures in antiquity were sheep and goats. They were small, they thrived on the local vegetation, and they could be moved easily. Since the lowland pastures dried up in summer, grazing involved an annual cycle of movement. The herds were pastured in the lowlands during the winter and during the summer were driven up into the mountains along regular paths which, incidentally, are still in use today. Cattle and horses were raised only where good pastures could be found all year round, that is, along the coast and in the Po Valley. Yet, even with this restriction, cattle were more common in Italy than in other areas of the Mediterranean. In fact, the name "Italia" means "cattle-land."

Agriculture was the chief occupation of the Italian population throughout the ancient period. The major growing season for most crops was the rainy winter months, not the summer. The ancient Italian farmer planted his barley and wheat in the fall, beginning in September, so that it could germinate with the fall rains, grow through the mild winter, and mature during the warm spring rains for harvest in May or June. Some crops, however, such as grapes and olives, which were very important to the ancient economy, were harvested in the fall. These were native plants of the Mediterranean climate and were long-rooted enough to survive through the summer drought.

Usually about half of a farmer's land was left fallow each year to regain its fertility. This seems very inefficient to us. Even so, the average farm was only two or three acres in size. Farming in this period was a hard life that produced little wealth, and it is worth remembering that the men who made Rome great, the soldiers who marched the length and breadth of the Mediterranean basin, were the product of the hard life of the Italian farm and that farming always remained their chief occupation. Wherever the Roman soldier found himself—in Asia, in Spain, or in Africa—it was always back to the Italian land that they yearned to return. And the rhythm of the Italian agricultural year underlies the history of early Rome.

Located further away from the center of the Near Eastern civilizations than Greece, Italy was quite naturally slower and later in developing the urban culture that had been native in the eastern Mediterranean for many centuries before it came to Italy. Today, we easily conceive of Italy as a country, as a unified cultural unit—but Italy, very much like the nearby Greek peninsula, is also naturally divided by its hills and mountains into sections that have always tended to develop independently of each other. The greatness of the Roman achievement in unifying the diverse peoples of Italy into a single political unit can be appreciated when one realizes that Italy has been unified only twice in its long history—after the passing of Rome, it was not again unified until the 19th Century. Even the glorious period of the Italian Renaissance was played out against a background on numerous states, principalities, and free cities.

Pre-Roman Italy

During the past century or so, archaeology has unraveled and revealed the chronology of the prehistory of Italy to an extraordinary extent. Most of this work has been accomplished by the Italians.

The Neolithic (c. 10,000–4,000 BCE)

During the Neolithic, or New Stone Age, Italy was only sparsely inhabited by peoples living in caves or in tiny villages of crude huts. They eked out a precarious existence principally from hunting and food gathering, but eventually learned to breed animals and practice elementary agriculture. They buried their dead without cremation and always placed the body on its right side with the legs drawn up, as if in repose. They manufactured specialized tools and weapons from polished flint and obsidian. Finally, these Neolithic peoples also made pottery, which evolved through several complex stages of decoration, and these changing pottery types are used by archaeologists to catalog and date the different Neolithic cultures.

The Bronze Age (c. 1300–1100 BCE)

A culture known as Palafitte appeared in northern Italy, just south of the Alps during the early Bronze Age. They built villages on the lakes supported by wooden piles, which continued to exist for several centuries. They manufactured a great variety of flint weapons and were the first to use metals, specifically bronze. Their pottery was mostly undecorated. The Palafitte introduced the practice of cremation into Italy.

The next important prehistoric culture appeared in the marshy lowlands of the Po Valley. They are called the Terramara, which means "rich earth," because the refuse mounds that they left around their villages were so rich in organic matter that the modern peasants traditionally dug them for compost. These Terramara people employed the older Palafitte principle of building their homes on piles, even though they were no longer lake dwellers. The reason for this was to provide a defense against the sudden floods and the rising of the marshes in the lowlands in which they lived. It was a local solution to a local problem, and it is found only in the Po Valley. Farming was the basis of the Terramara economy, and they made various types of farming tools from bronze. The pottery

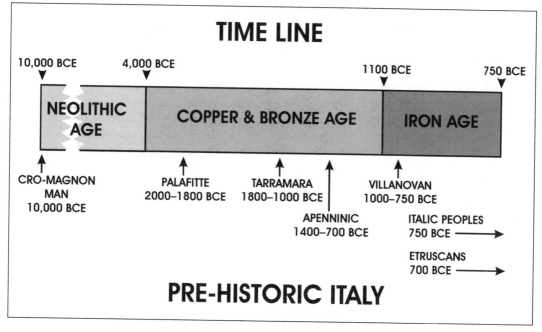

TIME LINE

10,000 BCE   4,000 BCE   1100 BCE   750 BCE

| NEOLITHIC AGE | COPPER & BRONZE AGE | IRON AGE |

CRO-MAGNON
MAN
10,000 BCE

PALAFITTE
2000–1800 BCE

TARRAMARA
1800–1000 BCE

APENNINIC
1400–700 BCE

VILLANOVAN
1000–750 BCE

ITALIC PEOPLES
750 BCE ⟶

ETRUSCANS
700 BCE ⟶

PRE-HISTORIC ITALY

Figure 9.1

of the Terramaras was decorated with incised grooves which bears no kingship to other Italian pottery. For this reason some archaeologists suggest that the Terramara came into Italy from central Europe. They, like the lake dwellers, practiced cremation. The Terramara culture existed from about 1500 BCE down to perhaps 700 BCE.

Another culture, which has been labeled "Apenninic" because it occupied the Apennine highlands, stretched along the backbone of Italy beginning about 1400 BCE. It was a semi-nomadic, patriarchal, and warlike culture of herdsmen, who drove their herds through the mountain passes in regular seasonal cycles. Unlike the other Bronze Age peoples of the region, they practiced inhumation.

The Iron Age (c. 1000–750 BCE)

Both the dating and the process by which Italy was transformed from the Bronze Age into the Iron Age are still obscure. Only the result is clear: sometime around 1,000 BCE, a culture which archaeologists have named Villanovan appeared and ultimately occupied all northern and central Italy as far south as Rome. The term Villanovan is derived from the name of a small town near Bologna where the first of many Iron Age cemeteries were discovered in 1853. The name is now used to denote the period and the people (or perhaps the peoples) represented by Iron Age cemeteries throughout the northern two thirds of Italy.

Though many archaeologists have argued that the Villanovans came into Italy from north of the Alps (as part of the Indo-European invasion?), their material culture seems to derive directly from a combination of the Terramara and Apennine cultures of Bronze Age Italy. Our knowledge of them is derived almost exclusively on the evidence of their cemeteries, which does not give us a very clear picture of their culture. At any rate, it seems safe to say that the

Villanovan economy was based on agriculture, stock-raising, and hunting, with an extensive use of the horse. The fine quality of their pottery and bronze implements indicates that the production of these items were now in the hands of professional craftsmen. This division of labor was an important new development and indicates that social structure had become more complex.

But all of this is pre-history and, as noted before, a detailed political and social history of a people cannot be developed from the style of pottery decorations or the shape of bronze axes. These cold artifacts do not provide us with the details of specific events upon which a history can be constructed. All of this classifying of artifacts into the patterns which the archaeologists call "cultures" does not come close to reflecting a true picture of the complexity and interaction between the various peoples who inhabited Italy during this period. Archaeologists describe a kind of uniform Iron Age culture, called Villanovan, which they say occupied most of prehistoric Italy, yet, at the dawn of history, say around the beginning of the 8th Century BCE, Italy was in fact not a uniform culture at all, but a mosaic of diverse and competing peoples. It does not make sense to say that this diversity is the legacy of a uniform pre-historic culture.

A Catalog of Italic Peoples

Some of the people who inhabited Italy at the beginning of history seem to have occupied very fixed and defined territories, while others were still on the move, that is, they still pursued a semi-nomadic life. To the north, the Ligurians inhabited the shores of the Gulf of Genoa extending inland into the maritime Alps, but not much is known about them before their conquest by the Romans. Indeed, the archaeological evidence is so inadequate that it is impossible to equate any archaeological culture with the historical Ligurians. However, the prehistoric Iron Age culture of this area shows the strong influences of the local Greek colonists, most notably, from Massilia, or modern Marseille, located at the mouth of the Rhone river.

The plain of the Po Valley was later colonized by the Etruscans, but the Po River delta always remained in the hands of the Veneti. The Greek historian Herodotus[2] tells us that they emigrated to Italy from Illyricum, but their surviving inscriptions do not appear to be related to any known Illyrian language. Archaeological evidence does indicate that they immigrated into northern Italy in the mid tenth Century BCE, but does not reveal where they came from. Even though they were not especially war-like, they successfully defended themselves against the incursions of the Etruscans and later the Gauls. Even though the Gallic invasions, which occurred around 400 BCE, turned the Po Valley into what the Romans called "Cisalpine Gaul," the Venetians maintained their independence. During historical times they became highly civilized, but they preferred horse breeding and commerce to war. For example, they organized the early amber trade with the Baltic area, which made them prosperous. They were allies of Rome from their first contacts, and they aided the Romans against the Gauls and against Hannibal. They retained their local autonomy until they became full Roman citizens in 49 BCE.

The most important of the pre-Roman peoples was the Etruscans. At the height of their civilization, they controlled most of Italy north of the Tiber River and extended their power southward as far as the Campanian plain around Naples and even into the Tyrrhenian Sea to include the

---

2. Herodotus, *Persian War,* 1.196.

eastern cost of Corsica and the islands between Corsica and Italy. Elba, because of its iron deposits, was the most important of these islands. The Etruscan homeland was the Etrurian plain north of Rome—that area of modern Italy called Tuscany today.

Then, south of the Tiber, was the area known as Latium, inhabited by the Latins, the group to whom the Romans themselves belonged. Many linguists group the Latins together with other closely-related peoples of central Italy under the term Italic. At any rate, Latium consisted of the plain bounded on the north by the Tiber River, on the east by the Alban Hills, and extending as far south as the Circaeian Promontory.

The other so-called Italic peoples were numerous and only the most important of them need be mentioned. Upstream from Rome, the Tiber divided the Etruscans from the Umbrians, who at an earlier time probably occupied Etruria as well. In fact, the term Umbrian has been used to denote a variety of linguistic, cultural, and geographical areas. Evidence of the language called Umbrian is found in the central part of Italy where the rites of cremation and inhumation overlapped. The language was written in a script derived from Greek by way of the Etruscan alphabet. To the east and south-east of Latium, the Apennines was the home of a semi-nomadic, pastoral population of interrelated tribes known as the Sabines.

The Samnites lived in the Apennine highlands from Latium southward and were divided into four tribal states (Caraceni, Caudini, Hirpini, Pentri) each administered by an official known as a *meddix*, but they were linked together into a confederation which had a federal assembly. The confederated army of the Samnites was led by a supreme commander in wartime. Other peoples, known as the Marsi and the Volscians, occupied inland villages in central Italy. The Campanians lived in the plain around Naples. These peoples, together with the Oscans, who lived further south, all spoke dialects of the Oscan language, another of the Indo-European Italic tongues. Still further south, lived the Lucani and the Bruttii.

Finally, there were the Greek colonies of *Magna Graecia*, planted in southern Italy and Sicily from the 8th Century BCE onwards. These will be discussed in more detail later. Pushed back into the central area of Sicily were the Sicels, who were the original inhabitants of the island. And we must at least mention the Apuli and the Iapagians, two peoples who inhabited the heel of Italy. All of these peoples spoke different languages, though many of them were closely enough related to each other to be classified as dialects.

Only three peoples of Ancient Italy spoke non Indo-European languages: the Ligurians, the Rhaetians, and the Etruscans. Presumably, this is because they were already present in Italy before the influx of the Indo-Europeans sometime around 2000 BCE. Many linguistic experts believe that these three languages go back to the ancient Mediterranean language stock that was spoken throughout the area before the Indo-European invasions. But this whole subject is controversial and need not be discussed in detail here.

The Etruscans

Ancient Etruria is the area of north-central Italy bounded by the Arnus River in the north, by the Apennine Mountains on the east, by the Tiber River on the south, and the Tyrrhenian Sea on the west. In this area, by the beginning of the 8th Century BCE, a wonderfully gifted and active people had established the first native Italian civilization. The Greeks called these people the Tyrrhenoi; the Romans called them the Etrusci or the Tusci; and today we call them the Etruscans.

Etruscan Origins

How this brilliant and sudden flowering of civilization occurred, on the west coast of Italy, so far removed from the ancient centers of civilization in the eastern Mediterranean, is a very controversial subject for which there is, at present, no definitive answer. In fact, this may be one of those problems of ancient history that cannot be solved, unless some dramatic new evidence is uncovered.[3]

There are two possibilities. Either the Etruscans were indigenous, that is, the Etruscan civilization developed independently in Italy itself, or they came to Italy from some other place and brought their civilized culture with them. This controversy over the origins of the Etruscans actually has its roots in antiquity. The Greek historian Herodotus,[4] writing in the 5th Century BCE, believed that the Etruscans were immigrants from Lydia, in Asia Minor, whereas, another Greek historian, Dionysius of Halicarnassus,[5] writing during the time of Augustus, maintained that they were indigenous. The modern archeological evidence also seems to be inconsistent. A growing body of archaeological information, gathered mainly by the Italians since the mid 20th Century, seems to indicate that most Etruscan cities were developments of older Villanovan sites. But there is also strong evidence for the immigration theory. For example, burial by inhumation was added rather abruptly in the 8th Century to the native practice of cremation in Etruria. And it cannot be denied that Etruscan culture, especially their religion, shows strong oriental and Greek influences. They worshiped many of the same gods and shared much of the same mythology as the Greeks. Even more important is an inscribed tombstone found on the island of Lemnos, just off the coast of Asia Minor. This inscription is in a language that has undeniable similarities to both Etruscan and to several languages of Asia Minor. And another Greek historian, Thucydides,[6] tells us that the pre-Greek population of Lemnos was Tyrrhenian—but where he got this information he does not say.

At any rate, Etruscan civilization did appear suddenly on Italian soil and it assimilated Greek and oriental influences to the realities of Italian life. Etruscan civilization, regardless of its origins, is rightly called the first native civilization of Italy. In the early 7th Century BCE, when the rest of the Italian peninsula, except the Greek colonies, still pursued a primitive village or semi-nomadic lifestyle, the Etruscans lived in cities, founded according to religious rites, which the Romans later adopted. These religious rites regulated the location of the city boundaries, the disposition of the gates, and the number and placement of the temples within the city. The Etruscans had a well deserved reputation for the depth of their piety and the quality of their religious ritual.

Etruscan Political and Social Structure

Very little is known about the Etruscans' political institutions. Later Roman historians tell us that the Etruscan civilization in its centuries of glory consisted of a federation of twelve city-states, and various lists of capitals are furnished, but for some unexplained reason these lists always have either more or less than twelve names. Since the available evidence is so inconsistent, it is not easy to reconstruct an outline of this system of federal government. It is certain, however, that each city operated as a fully independent state, and we know that each of these city-states was ruled by a king in the early

---

3. For a brief and recent discussion of the problem, see Briquel, Dominique, "The Origins of the Etruscans: a Controversy Handed Down from Antiquity," in Torelli, Mario, editor, *The Etruscans* (2001), Rizzoli International Publications, Inc., New York, pp. 43–52.

4. Herodotus, *Persian War,* 1.194

5. Dionysius of Halicarnassus, *Roman Antiquities,* 1.30

6. Thucydides, *Peloponnesian War,* 4.109.

stages of their history. During the 5th Century BCE the monarchy was replaced by a republic with a chief magistrate called the *zilath*, elected annually. He was the eponymous magistrate, that is, he gave his name to the year, in the tradition of the Athenian archons and as the later Roman consuls did. The *zilath* seems to have been assisted by a college of junior magistrates, each of whom had his own duties and responsibilities, rather like the cabinet ministers in the British government, for example. The *zilath* was probably entrusted with the supreme political and judicial power and the secondary magistrates with the day to day administrative responsibilities, but this is all rather unclear. The government was under the strict control of a small number of noble families and the chief magistrate was always elected from this class. There was also a council of elders, who had a consultative role, like the Roman Senate or the Athenian Areopagus. We shall see later that the early Roman republican government exhibited striking similarities to the Etruscan city-state, even though we are only able to construct this vague idea of its actual structure. This, of course, is but one of many examples of the tremendously important influence of the Etruscans upon Roman civilization.

Socially, the Etruscans were almost a feudalistic society. A small class of nobles, called the *principes*, lorded it over a much larger class of commoners. Everything that we learn from the surviving documents or the archaeological remains attests to the wealth and opulence of the *principes*, who were served by hosts of domestic slaves in their city palaces and gangs of peasants who worked their country estates, almost like serfs. Etruscan society never developed a middle class. Unlike Rome and Greece, however, Etruscan women enjoyed a high social position. At one time it was even believed that Etruscan society was matriarchal, but that idea can no longer be supported, although many of the highest ranking aristocratic families traced their ancestry through the female

Figure 9.2: Sarcophqagus lid of Etruscan man and wife.

line. Also Etruscan women, unlike Roman women, were given *praenomena*, or first names, in addition to their family names and the tomb paintings show Etruscan women taking part in state banquets and observing the athletic games alongside the men. The sarcophagi of women are often every bit as elaborate as those of men. All of this indicates that women played an important social and even a minor political role in Etruscan society.

The organization and the power of the Etruscan federation is even more vague to us. We know that the delegates of the twelve Etruscan states met each year to choose a common leader, but we know almost nothing of his function or power, which seems to have been mostly religious. The federal assembly convened in a sanctuary consecrated to the god Voltumna, which was probably located near Volsinii. This meeting was accompanied by elaborate religious ceremonies, athletic games, and a great commercial fair. During the early period, the delegates to this assembly consisted of the kings from each city, but after the kingship was abolished, in the 5th Century BCE, the meetings were attended by the city magistrates.

But, in fact, the federal organization of the Etruscans never overcame their inherent disunity, and the city-states always exercised their right of independent action. In this, they resembled the Greeks. The expansion of the Etruscan civilization into the Po Valley to the north and into Campania to the south was not carried out by a unified state, but rather was the work of various individual members of the Etruscan federation. Recent excavations in Campania confirm that there was an Etruscan presence there before 700 BCE. At first there were several villages that were really Villanovan in character, but contacts with the Greek colony at Cumae seems to have stimulated them to unite into a new city called Capua. Capua soon became a commercial and industrial center, especially known for its bronze art work. Contrary to earlier belief, then, the formation of Etruscan Campania took place at virtually the same time as the emergence of the Etruscan civilization in Etruria; indeed, it seems to have been part of the same process, not exactly what we would call a "conquest." However, the development of Campania did involve the migration of Etruscans from the homeland of Etruria, although clearly there was no "federal" colonization by the Etruscan League. And just as the Etruscan city-states in Etruria developed independently of one another, so did their expansion in Campania, where the new city-states also exercised political sovereignty.

The expansion into Campania required Etruscans to maintain an active presence in Latium, which lay between that territory and Etruria. Place names and archaeological remains demonstrate that Latin cities such as Alba Longa and Praeneste were Etruscan strong-holds in the Latin territory. The bridge between Etruria and Latium was provided by Rome. For part of the 7th Century and all of the 6th Century BCE, Rome was under the rule of the Etruscans. From the 6th Century onward, the Etruscan relations with the Greeks in southern Italy deteriorated and they were defeated by the Greeks more than once. Then, in the years following 430 BCE, not only the Etruscan but even the Greek settlements in Campania were destroyed by the conquests of the native Samnites from the hills in the center of the peninsula. Thus ended the Etruscan influence in southern Italy.

The Etruscan civilization also expanded into the Po Valley, that area of northern Italy which the Romans would later call Cisalpine Gaul, that is "Gaul on this side of the Alps." The earliest and most important Etruscan urban center was at Bononia, modern Bologna, which was already a prominent city by the year 700 BCE. Thus, Bologna is about a half century older than Rome. Another important Etruscan city in the north was Mantua, later the home of Virgil. The Etruscan port city of Atria, near the mouth of the Po, also was the home of a large Greek community. The Greeks and Etruscans at Atria cooperated peacefully and profitably in spite of the deterioration of Greco-Etruscan relations in southern Italy. The Etruscan civilization in northern Italy came to an end shortly after 400 BCE, when it was overrun by the Gauls.

Figure 9.3: Bronze model of sheep's liver.

Etruscan Religion

The Etruscan religion, unlike the religions of Greece and Rome, but like Judaism, Christianity, and Islam, was a revealed religion. Half-divine prophets were said to have imparted revelations from the divine world to their people, sometime in the distant past. The teachings of these prophets were collected into a series of books called the *Disciplina Etrusca*. They described in minute detail the ritual proceedings by which the will of the gods could be determined and followed. The Roman historian Livy says: "No people was ever more devoted to religious observances—the more so since they had unique gifts in this sphere."[7] *The Disciplina Etrusca* was divided into sections. The *libri rituales*, or ritual books, contained the rules for the founding of cities, consecration of altars and temples, and the placing of walls and gates.

The *libri fulgurales* dealt with thunder and lightning. The Etruscans believed each god had distinct kinds of thunderbolts at his disposal. The god Tin, or Jupiter, for example, either on his own accord or on the advice of his counselors, threw three different kinds of thunderbolts, while eight other gods had one kind each. A "brontoscopic calendar" has been preserved, which describes what each of these different thunder claps meant when they occurred on each day of the year (this means that with eleven different types of thunder possible on each of the 365 days of the year, there were almost 4,000 different meanings for thunder).

The *libri haruspicini* recorded the experience and knowledge gained by the Etruscans in the examining of the entrails of sacrificial victims. Their expertise in *haruspices* was so well known that the Roman senate used to appeal to them when a difficult portent had to be reported. Examination

7. Livy, *From the Founding of the City*, 5.1.6.

of the liver, called hepatoscopy, was also highly developed by the Etruscans. Several models of the liver in bronze exist. One of them divides the liver into 44 compartments, each one marked with the name of one or two gods (Fig. 9.3). It is laid out according to the points of the compass and is, in effect, an image, or map of heaven, showing the place occupied by each of the gods. Exactly how this sophisticated instrument was used to determine the will of the gods is not known.

We know the names of a fair number of Etruscan deities, but their functions and characteristics are not clear because their original significance has been lost or modified through being merged with Italic gods and contaminated by Greek and oriental influences. The chief god of the Etruscan pantheon was Tin, later identified with Jupiter. He formed a trinity with two female deities, Uni, or Juno, and Minerva, and they were worshiped in tripartite temples, that is, temples with three separate sanctuaries. However, at Volsinii, the god Voltumna was said to be the "foremost among gods." Other important deities were Turan, a fertility goddess often equated with Aphrodite or Venus; Fufluns, identified with Dionysus, and Turns identified with Hermes, or Mercury. The Greek god Charon, who in Greek mythology conveyed the spirits of the dead into the underworld, came to play an important role in the tomb paintings of the Etruscans.

Etruscan Language

The Etruscan language does not belong to the Indo-European language group, even though it is rich in borrowed words from Greek and the Italic dialects. Even though all Etruscan literature has been lost, we know the Etruscan language from some 10,000 inscriptions that still survive. Most of them are tombstones, which bear epitaphs, which are short and often contain only proper names, kinship information, and magistratical rank of the deceased. Only a few inscriptions are rich in content and go back to the 5th or 4th centuries BCE. We still cannot read them literally, but we can at least determine fairly accurately what they are talking about. The Etruscans, of course, derived their alphabet from the Greeks and we find it in two forms. Around the 6th Century BCE, an alphabet of 26 letters was drawn from the Greeks of southern Italy. About the 5th Century, the number of letters used was reduced to 20. In most Etruscan inscriptions the words are separated by dots, unlike the Greek method where there is no separation. The Etruscans spread the use of this alphabet among the Latins, Oscans, Umbrians, and Venetians and thereby brought literacy to most of Italy. This was perhaps their greatest legacy. And through the Romans, their alphabet was spread to the later Europeans and is, in fact, the same alphabet which is in use today to write English.

Etruscan Art

Etruscan art also displayed strong Greek influence. Many beautiful Etruscan paintings are preserved in their underground tombs and show fascinating scenes of daily life, as well as scenes from Greek mythology. Also, some of our best and most beautiful examples of Greek pottery were recovered from the tombs of wealthy Etruscans. The wealthy Etruscan aristocrats were great art collectors, and this means of course that they collected Greek art. When they die, Modern art collectors often leave their collections to museums, or if they are really wealthy sometimes endow a new museum to house their collections. The Etruscan collectors were a little more selfish and took their collections with them when they died—at least into the grave. Amazingly, many of these tombs survived the grave robbers down into the 18th and 19th centuries. However, apparently none have escaped the modern tomb robber, called an archaeologist. Indeed, it is in Etruscan tombs that many of the best examples of Greek pottery survived.

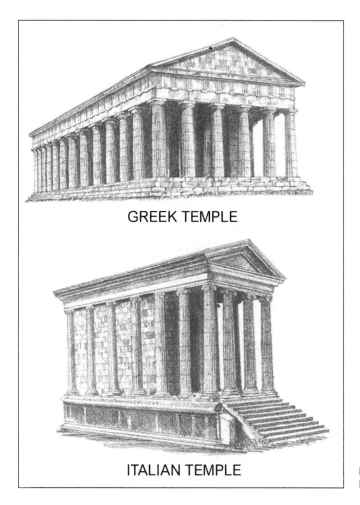

GREEK TEMPLE

ITALIAN TEMPLE

Figure 9.4: Comparison of Greek and Italian temple styles.

Etruscan architecture reveals an adaptation of Greek influences to the Italian setting. The gates in the walls of Etruscan cities utilized arches and vaults. Their temples were built in the Greek style, with columns and gabled roofs, but they were placed on high platforms, and the cella, the room which houses the cult statue, was expanded until the columns along the sides and rear of the building were embedded into its walls. Whereas the Greeks placed free standing columns on all four sides of their temples, the Italian temples have free standing columns only at the front of the building which forms a porch or entry area (Fig. 9.4). Italian temples were placed on a rather high podium and situated at the end of long enclosures, or sacred areas. A set of wide steps was added to the porch approach, imparting a formality and feeling of discipline which is often missing from the Greek temple plan. Art historians have invented a pretentious term, "frontality," to describe this aspect of Italian temples. All these Etruscan adaptations were later taken over by the Romans and spread throughout the empire, especially in the western Mediterranean.

Etruscan art follows the same development phases as Greek art from archaic to classical styles. The Etruscan artists were not simply copyists, however. Etruscan art has an originality and value all its own. They excelled in bronze and terracotta sculpture, and the fresco wall

Figure 9.5: Etruscan art (clockwise from top): The Sarcophagus of the Reclining Couple; Tomb of the Augurs; Tomb of the Dinning Couch; bronze figurine of Mars.

paintings in their tombs are unequaled in the ancient world. The Greeks greatly admired Etruscan bronze and imported large quantities of bronze cups, lamp stands, candlesticks, tripods, incense burners, mirrors, and toilet boxes. The extraordinary development of miniature design techniques allowed the Etruscans to craft some of the most beautiful and delicate gold jewelry found anywhere.

Etruscan Pessimism

On the darker side, toward the end of their civilization, the Etruscans developed a morbid infatuation with death and violence which is reflected in tomb paintings of the underworld populated with hideous daemons and monsters which menace and torture the soul of the deceased mortal. Human sacrifice was practiced in the form of duels to the death at the funeral games of the aristocrats. This was, in a sense, simply the logical extension of the Greek practice of celebrating funerals by holding games in which athletes competed for prizes. Homer describes this ritual in minute detail in the *Iliad*, when Achilles hosts sumptuous games at the funeral of his friend Patroclus. Unfortunately, this too was borrowed by the Romans, who developed it into the gladiatorial combats which were so popular in the later Roman Empire. Ironically, human sacrifice was anathema to the Romans and whenever they came across it during their conquests they immediately and ruthlessly stamped it out. Yet they unconsciously practiced human sacrifice in the gladiatorial games in their arenas.

All in all, the Etruscans remain the most peculiar element in early Italian history. In many ways, the Etruscan outlook of life seems far removed from that of the Greeks and the Romans. As noted above, women, for example, held so high a place in Etruscan society that family descent was often traced through the female line, and the lifestyle of the Etruscan aristocracy exhibited an unusually marked emphasis on physical pleasure and luxury. The stern old moralistic outlook of the early Romans was perhaps partly a reaction against the Etruscan access of hedonistic enjoyment.

Roman Origins

The origin of the Etruscans is shrouded in controversy. The origin of the Romans is clouded in legend and myth. The Romans, of course, like all peoples, told folk tales and fantastic stories about their earlier history, and the aristocratic families circulated bombastic accounts of their past deeds. As Rome grew in power and came into contact with the Greeks, however, they quite rightly wanted to take their place among the civilized nations of the Mediterranean and to do so they needed a foundation legend that was part of the eastern Mediterranean mythological cycle, a story that would make them part of the tradition of Homer. Thus, a cohesive legend began to develop. Not all elements of the story were Roman, many details were inserted by the Greeks and other peoples the Romans came into contact with, and some aspects of the tale were not very flattering. The chronicle reached its final form during the 1st Century BCE when it was transformed into a brilliant epic poem called the *Aeneid* by the great Latin poet Vergil. The saga was also recorded by the Latin historian Levy. According to the most developed form of the legend, Rome was founded by descendants of the survivors of Troy.

The Legend of Rome's Founding

In outline, the story runs like this. Aeneas was a Trojan prince, the son of Anchises and the goddess Aphrodite,[8] known to the Romans as Venus. Thus, Aeneas was himself half divine and therefore a proper Greek hero. The god Poseidon prophesied that his descendants would rule over Greece,[9]

---

8. Aphrodite saw Anchises looking after his flocks on Mount Ida, near Troy. She approached him pretending to be the daughter of Otreus, king of Phrygia, and to have been abducted by Hermes and carried off to the pastures of Ida. By this ruse she married him. Later, she told Anchises who she really was and she would bear him a son ("You will have a son, who will rule over the Trojans, and sons will be born to his sons, and so on for all eternity."), but begged him not to tell anyone the son was a child of a goddess, because if Zeus should hear of it he would strike the child with lightening. But Anchises drank too much wine at a feast and boasted of his love affair. Zeus punished him by making him lame with a blast from a thunderbolt.

9. It is not clear weather this detail was an original part of the mythology surrounding Troy or inserted later by the Romans.

which makes him an ideal candidate for the founder of Rome because it explains the subsequent history of Greece and Rome. After the fall of Troy, Aeneas escaped from the burning city with his aged father, his small son, and the images of his ancestral gods.

He wandered around the Mediterranean for many years, engaging in adventures and suffering hardships until he finally arrived at Carthage in North Africa. That city was still under the rule of its founder, Queen Dido.[10] Aeneas and Dido had an affair and Aeneas planned to marry Dido and settle in Carthage, but at the last minute, through divine intervention, he was ordered to leave Africa: "Your destiny is in Italy." Dido was so upset that she uttered a curse on Aeneas and his descendants and committed suicide by jumping onto a funeral pyre. This episode, of course, explains the later life and death struggle between the two peoples.

Finally Aeneas landed on the cost of central Italy, made an alliance with the king of Lavinium, and married his daughter. Aeneas's son, Iulus,[11] now a grown man, founded the city of Alba Longa, where his descendants ruled for 13 generations. The 13th king, named Numitor, was deposed by his younger brother, Amulius. Although Numitor had no sons, he did have a daughter, Rhea Silvia, and if she should have children they would have a more legitimate claim to the throne than the children of Amulius. To avoid this, Amulius appointed Rhea a Vestal Virgin, a priestess to the goddess Vesta. Vesta was the goddess of the hearth, and her temple in the Forum was the hearth of the state. The very important college of Vestal Virgins tended the sacred fire in this temple and they must remain virgins so long as they were priestesses.

These kinds of complex schemes are seldom successful, even in mythology. Sure enough, Rhea Silvia was visited even in the sacred House of the Vestals by the god Mars and she bore twin sons, Romulus and Remus. Of course, Amulius was furious, and he ordered the babies to be thrown into

---

10. The story of Dido, queen of Carthage, was in existence before Virgil, and relates the migrations of the Phoenicians to the western Mediterranean. Mutto, king of Tyre, had two children, a son Pygmalion, and a daughter Elissa (Elissa was Queen Dido's Phoenician name). When he died, he left his kingdom to his children, and the people recognized Pygmalion as their king, although he was still only an infant. Elissa married her uncle Sicharbas, the priest of Heracles and the second most important personage in the kingdom after the king himself. But Pygmalion had Sicharbas assassinated so that he could seize his treasure. However, Elissa was horrified by her brother's crime and had Sicharbas' treasure secretly loaded onto boats and fled, accompanied by some disaffected Tyrian nobles. After many adventures they reached North Africa, where they were warmly welcomed by the local inhabitants. When Dido asked these people for some land where she could settle they allowed her to take "as much as she could enclose in the hide of a bull." Dido had the hide cut up into the thinnest possible strips, obtaining a long leather thong which enabled her to surround a fairly large plot of land. The inhabitants kept their promise and gave her the land she had enclosed. Here she founded the city of Carthage. An influx of colonists from the motherland gave the city new strength, and a neighboring king, Larbas, expressed his wish to marry Dido, threatening to declare war upon the city if she refused.

This was the theme on which Virgil based the story of Aeneas, a story in which the hero was driven by a storm on to the shores of Africa and welcomed by the inhabitants of Carthage, the city founded by Dido. At a banquet given in his honor, Aeneas related his adventures and told of the fall of Troy. Then, while his companions were repairing the ships, he became the guest of the queen, who gradually began to fall in love with him. Finally, during a hunting party, they were brought together by a storm which forced them both to take shelter in the same cave, and she became his mistress, through the will of Venus and at Juno's instigation. But soon, King Larbas, aware of what had happened, and angered at seeing a stranger preferred to himself, asked Jupiter to send Aeneas on his way. Jupiter, aware of what the future held in store, and knowing that Rome must come into being far from the shores of Africa, commanded Aeneas to leave and end this transient relationship. Aeneas departed without seeing the queen again. When Dido learned that she had been abandoned she built a tall funeral pyre and sought death amid the flames.

11. The Julians traced their ancestry back to Iulus. Julius Caesar and, by adoption, Augustus belonged to this family.

Figure 9.6: Romulus and Remus with She-Wolf.

the Tiber and Rhea Silvia to be executed. However, the centurion given the responsibility for this obeyed the letter but not the spirit of the order and set the twins adrift on the river in a basket. They drifted ashore at the foot of the Palatine Hill and were suckled by a she-wolf (Fig. 9.6). This is symbolic, of course, since the wolf was sacred to Mars. They were eventually discovered by a shepherd and raised to adulthood. They eventually discovered their identity, went to Alba Longa and restored their grandfather to the throne.

Romulus and Remus had now become the leaders of the young men in the area and they founded a new city up on the Palatine Hill. But almost immediately a dispute arose between them over who was to give his name to the city. The twins decided to settle the argument by an augury, a very Etruscan custom. Each of the brothers was assigned a place to stand (*templum*) and an area of the sky to observe. Remus reported to the officiating priest that he saw 6 ravens flying across his area of the sky and was about to be declared the winner when Romulus came running up and reported that he saw 12 ravens flying across his area. So the city was named Rome. Romulus built a wall around the new city and Remus, jealous of his brother, belittled the wall by jumping over it, a violation of its sacredness. For this Romulus ordered him executed.

The Kings of Rome

To attract settlers, Romulus opened Rome to all fugitives, criminals, and run-away slaves and the population began to increase dramatically,[12] but most of the new inhabitants were men. To obtain wives for his new citizens he invited the nearby Sabines to a religious festival. Then, while everyone was enjoying a feast, at a pre-arranged signal, the Romans seized all the young unmarried Sabine women and carried them off to become their wives. This incident is known to Roman history as "The Rape of the Sabine Women"—the word "rape" here is derived from the Latin word *rapere*, "to carry away." When the Sabines, understandably upset at this breach of hospitality, invaded Rome, the Sabine women, who now had husbands in one army and fathers and brothers in the other, went out to the battlefield and put themselves between the two armies (Fig. 9.7). A battle was averted and eventually an agreement was reached for the two peoples to be united into one state, and the Sabine king, Titus Tatius, became co-king with Romulus.

Figure 9.7: "Sabine Women Enforcing Peace," painting by Jacques-Louis David, 1794–1799.

---

12. These kinds of details derogatory to the reputation of Rome were obviously slipped into the legend by some of Rome's enemies.

Five years later, however, associates of Tatius killed some ambassadors during a robbery. Tatius shielded the culprits from prosecution, so the victims' relatives attacked and killed him. After his death, Romulus enjoyed a long and prosperous reign. Instead of dying like an ordinary mortal, he mysteriously vanished during a thunderstorm (it was said he was carried off to heaven in a chariot), and was thereafter worshipped as the god Quirinus.

The next king of Rome, according to tradition, was Tatius's son-in-law, Numa Pompilius, a peaceable and pious man. After his death, the war-like Tullus Hostilius—who came from a prominent Roman family—was elected king. He reigned for more than three decades. Tullus was a military leader. He led the Roman army against the nearby city of Alba Longa, destroyed it, and moved its inhabitants to Rome. Then the Romans took over the sacred festivals of Latium and all the regional prestige and status that came with it. Tullus was succeeded by Numa's grandson Ancus Marcius. He extended Rome's power further by building the first bridge across the Tiber at Tiber Island and founding Ostia at the mouth of the river to serve as Rome's seaport.

Next came the Tarquin dynasty which was Etruscan. The first Tarquin king was a Greek noble who emigrated to Rome with his Etruscan wife and rose high in Roman society. He was called Lucius Tarquinius Priscus, or Tarquin the Elder. He became guardian of Ancus Marcius's sons and somehow seized the throne after the king's death in 616 BCE. He continued the policy of conquest and also improved the city by constructing the *Cloaca Maxima*, the main sewer, laid out the Circus Maximus, began the building of the temple to Jupiter on the Capitoline Hill. He reigned until 578 BCE, when he was murdered by Ancus Marcius's sons and was succeeded by his son-in-law, Servius Tullius.

Servius Tullius, the sixth king of Rome, is remembered as a monarch of great achievements. He organized the Roman people into tribes and classes, thus setting up social and political structure in which wealth, especially ownership of land, was the dominant consideration. He built a wall around the city five miles in circumference with nineteen gates, which embraced the traditional seven hills of Rome. He also accomplished various religious reforms and completed the temple to Jupiter on the Capitoline. He arranged for his daughters, both called Tullia,[13] to marry two brothers who were Priscus's sons or grandsons. The couples were mismatched, however, and one of the

Kings	Reign
ROMULUS	753–715
NUMA POMPILIUS	714–673
TULLUS HOSTILIUS	672–641
ANCUS MARCIUS	640–617
LUCIUS TARQUINIUS PRISCUS	616–579
SERVIUS TULLIUS	578–535
LUCIUS TARQUINIUS SUPERBUS	534–510

Figure 9.8: The seven kings of Rome.

---

13. Roman women did not have *praenomia*, or first names. They were known by their family names only. Thus, the two daughters of Servius Tullius would be known as simply Tullia the Elder and Tullia the Younger.

Tullias fell in love with her sister's husband, Lucius Tarquinius Superbus (Tarquin the Proud). Tullia and Tarquin killed their spouses, married each other, and then, to top it off, Tarquin killed old King Servius, and Tullia deliberately drove her chariot over her father's corpse.

Tarquinius Superbus was Rome's seventh and last king. He continued to extend Rome's power by founding colonies which mark the beginning of Rome's imperialism. But he was not very politically astute and irritated the people by the undue burdens he placed on them. This diabolical couple had an equally despicable son named Sextus who brought about the downfall of the Tarquin dynasty, but this will be discussed later in the context of the founding of the Republic.

Of course these legends of early Rome are unreliable in their historical details, but do they reflect any historical reality at all? What do the archaeologists say about the early history of the city? Well, they tell us that a small village of huts appeared on the Palatine Hill near the middle of the 8th Century BCE. Amazingly, this agrees extremely well with the date of 753 BCE given in the foundation legend. The 13 generations of kings at Alba Longa in the legend may be a device to reconcile the difference in time between the fall of Troy and the founding of Rome. The Romans knew their city was not as old as the fall of Troy and if they were going to claim Aeneas as their ancestor they must account for the time between the founding of Rome and the fall of Troy. From the earliest times Rome was a mixture of the peoples of western Italy and this is also reflected in the legend of its founding. By 700 BCE, Sabines from the central mountains had settled on the Esquiline, another of the 7 hills of Rome. The "Rape of the Sabine Women" may be a folk memory of the intermarriage between these two groups of people. And while the legend does not formally recognize the historical reality that Rome was under Etruscan rule during much of this early period, the Etruscan dynasty of the Tarquins is a less embarrassing way of acknowledging this fact. Yet, the legend is not overwhelmingly favorable to the Romans. It relates that the city was founded by a man who was descended from both Venus, the goddess of love, and Mars, the god of war. He was pious, in that he killed his own brother for violating the sacred law, yet he populated his new city with criminals who carried off women from another city in violation of the sacredness of a religious festival.

Early Roman Society

It is important to acquire at least a cursory familiarity with the structure of Roman society and the personal and social relationships and the religious and ethical framework within which they functioned in order to understand later Roman history. Most of the fundamental aspects of Roman society took shape during this very early period, characteristics which made Roman society different from the other societies of antiquity we have studied. First and foremost, hierarchy was the most important feature of all levels of Roman life. In Roman society, unlike our modern society, all relationships were vertical. That is, there were always higher authorities to whom those lower down in the hierarchy owed allegiance and obedience, in exchange for benefits due to them from above. In other words, inequality was the ideal condition of Roman life. Every individual had a niche into which he fit. Every individual knew where they fit in the scheme of things, they knew what their natural and proper relationship was to every other individual. For the Roman, this was natural and comfortable, and the source of security.

The Familia (Family)

Nowhere was this vertical aspect of life more clear or more important than in the *familia*, and it was the family, not the individual, which was the basis of Roman society. This is in contrast with Greek society, which was much more public in its structure than the Roman, and it is significant, for example, that the Greeks lived in a house, while the Romans lived in a home. The Greeks would say "the man belongs to the state," while the Romans would say "the man belongs first to his family and second to the state." From the very earliest time the family formed the basis of Roman society and it was the family that provided the individual both with his education and his grounding in public and private morality—tasks which in our society are, to a large extent, performed by public schools and the church. The *familia* included not only the father, the mother, and their children, but also all their dependants, such as the sons' wives and children and all the family members' slaves and even the farm animals.

The head of the *familia* was the *paterfamilias*, literally, "the father of the family." The *paterfamilias* exercised, in theory, absolute power over the members of the *familia*, including the power of life and death. The family members were said to be in his *manus*, or "hand," and his power was known as *patria potestas*, or "the father's power." Well, that was in theory. Actually, in practice the *paterfamilias*' power was limited to private affairs, since he could not, for example, control a son while he was holding a magistracy. His power was also limited by custom. There are almost no examples of the arbitrary or abusive use of the *patria potestas* and, indeed, the very fact that this institution survived as a legal principle for so many centuries is proof that it was seldom abused. But even though it was seldom used to its full extent, it was nevertheless a reality of Roman life. It is difficult for us in the modern age to understand this concept, but the evidence strongly indicates that the position of *patria potestas* was generally considered more of a responsibility than a right or privilege, and membership in the familia was always desired: expulsion from it was viewed not as a release or a freedom (as it often is in our society), but as a punishment. Important decisions were never taken before extensive advisory consultations were completed with family members. Indeed, the practice of seeking advice before making decisions permeates all of Roman social and political life—the Romans always took their responsibilities very seriously. When a *paterfamilias* died, there came into existence as many new *familia* as there had been male persons immediately under his *potestas*, that is, sons and grandsons whose fathers had already died. So, every male, not merely the eldest sons, could expect to become the head of their own family eventually.

Although women, of course, enjoyed nowhere near the freedom and rights that they do in the modern Western world, within the Roman household, women held dignified and influential positions. This was particularly true of *materfamilias*, literally "the mother of the family," or perhaps "the lady of the house." She was the wife of the *paterfamilias* and she played an important role in holding the family together. Unlike the women of Greece, the Roman lady pursued her daily life in the *atrium*, that is, the main living room of the house, not in oriental seclusion. Her chief responsibilities were: to bring up the children, including important areas of their education; to manage the household and supervise the slaves; and to make, or more often, to supervise the making of wool for the family clothes. Roman woman attended festivals and banquets and, in fact, had almost complete social liberty. This sounds like a small thing to us today, but in the history of civilizations up to this time, it is quite extraordinary. Of course, even in Rome women were in theory, if not always in practice, totally dependant upon their husbands, their fathers, or some other male guardian. In early Rome, as in Greece, a woman was not a legal person in that she had no standing in the courts—she must have a man take care of her business for her. When she married she simply passed from the *manus* (hand) of her father to the *manus*, of her husband.

However, the emancipation of women from this legal restraint began early. Even during the early Republic, women were allowed to hold property, within the context of Roman family. And when a woman can own property, she can attain at least a measure of personal independence. This new status of women was soon reflected in a change in marriage forms. In the earliest marriage rites, *confarreatio*, the husband gained complete authority over his wife, through a religious ceremony, just as if she were property. But very early on a different form of marriage, known as *coemtio* ("a private ceremony"), came into use, which took the form of a fictitious contract of sale of the woman by the father to the husband. This may not sound like much of a step forward but in actual practice the purpose was to free the arrangement of any religious obligations. And in fact, in spite of its form, *coemtio* came to imply a kind of partnership. Indeed, under the *coemtio* marriage the wife could say, *ubi tu Gaius, ego Gaia*, or "where you are master, I am mistress." Under this form of marriage, the husband's power over his wife was established by one year's uninterrupted cohabitation and the woman could thus avoid the legal control of her husband by passing three nights each year away from her husband's house. This kind of arrangement was possible because under Roman law, marriage was a private and personal affair and of no concern to the state—very different from our modern concept. The actual ceremonies which accompanied marriage had no legal character. All that was really necessary for a marriage to exist was the living together of a man and a woman with the intention of forming a lasting union. The function of ceremonies was to provide evidence of that intention. Moreover, the intention was not only necessary at the beginning of the marriage, but throughout its existence. Therefore, if the intention ceased, the marriage came to an end. Despite this, divorce, at least during the early republic, was not so frequent as you might expect. This was partly because the continuity of family life was of primary importance to the Romans, and although one hears a great deal about the loosening of family ties in later Roman society, research with tombstones and funeral monuments have demonstrated the prevalence of permanent and happy marriages throughout Roman history was the norm.

But the role of women in ancient Rome did not conform to our modern ideal: women had a specific and important place, but that place was not in the senate. The funeral inscription from the tomb of a *materfamilias* who died in the third century records that ideal:

> She loved her husband with her whole heart, she bore two sons, she was cheerful in conversation, dignified in manner, she administered the house, she made the wool, she was loved dearly by her husband.

Education

Roman education was a family concern, not a government responsibility. In the early period, the object of education was to form character rather than to promote culture; to make the child into a good and responsible citizen, not to prepare him to live a sophisticated life. Although Roman religion did not specifically promote morality, the daily religious ceremonies of the household produced in the child a sense of awe and respect toward the sacred. However, the most important influences in the building of character of the child were first the parents and second that uniquely Roman concept *mos majorum,* translated literally it means "the customs of our ancestors."

Figure 9.9: A Roman teacher with pupils.

The Roman education of the boys attempted to transform them into the ideal men, which in Roman eyes was of the *vir fortis et strenuus*, "the strong and active man." The essential qualities of such a man were: *gravitas* (seriousness); *continentia* (self-control); *industria* (industry); *deligentia* (diligence); *constantia* (constancy); *pietas* (piety, especially toward one's parents); *simplicitas* (frankness); and above all *virtus* (virtue, manliness).

The mother was responsible for the child's early training and her influence was great. There are numerous examples of Roman women who were left as widows with small children and who supervised their education into adulthood—ancient writers often praise these women for their good work. This in itself is proof that women—at least in the upper classes—were often well educated. When the boys were older they attended their father at his duties in the home and in public and also received instruction from him in the three Rs, as well as physical and military training. The girls continued their training under their mother in the skills of household administration, which obviously also required some training in the three Rs, and the making of wool. Both boys and girls were taught respect for the traditions of the family and for the *mos majorum*. The first public school is said to have been opened in Rome about 250 BCE. From that period onward, Greek influences increased, but the major responsibility for a child's education remained with the family.

The Gens

As the Roman state grew larger and the number of families increased, various families found themselves linked together by the use of a common name. It was probably in this way that another social body was formed, called the *gens*, or clan, which also played an important part in Rome's political life. In Rome, each man had three names. His *praenomen*, or what we call the first name, was his personal name. There were only about thirty *praenomia* used at all and only about fifteen were ever in common use. Next came the *nomen* which denoted the *gens*, and there were about a thousand of these. Finally came the *cognomen*, or family name, which denoted a group of families within the gens. Thus Gaius Julius Caesar tells us that Gaius was from the Julian clan and a member of the Caesar family. All the members of a gens traced their ancestry back to a single person—as the Julians traced theirs back to Iulus, the son of Aeneas. Women, however, had only one name, the *nomen*, or clan name. All the women of Caesar's family would be named Julia. If there were several of them they would be called Julia the Elder, Julia the Younger, etc. The family was the basic unit of Roman society and the gens was the basic unit of Roman politics. It was the gens and the blocks of clients that they controlled which formed the building blocks of the political factions of the Republic. These political factions served the same basic functions as political parties do in modern politics.

Early Roman society was sharply divided into two classes, called orders (*ordo,* pl. *ordinis)* by the Romans. These were the *patricii,* or patricians, who were aristocrats, and the *plebs,* or plebeians, who were the common people. By the time of the late Republic, a third order, called the *equites,* or the equestrians, had come into existence, as a kind of middle class, but we will not discuss them until later. The early social and political history of the Republic consists largely of the struggle of plebeians to attain complete political equality with the patricians. There were three major aspects to patrician exclusiveness: political, social, and religious. In the political sphere of the early Republic, they alone could be members of the Senate and hold public office. This, of course, gave them a virtual monopoly on the political life of the state and an absolute control of the government. Socially, the patricians maintained their exclusive position by avoiding intermarriage with the *plebs.* As late as 450 BCE, there was legislation enforcing this prohibition. They even practiced a different form of marriage, at which the *pontifex maximus,* the chief priest, officiated. The third aspect of patrician exclusiveness was their control of religious institutions. The two great priestly colleges, the pontiffs and the augurs, were exclusively in the hands of the patricians. The pontiffs were responsible for the *pax deorum,* literally, the "peace of the gods," and they were also the guardians of the *ius divinum,* or divine law. In this capacity they had control of the Roman calendar, which was of great significance. The Roman calendar was not divided into seven-day weeks, as ours is, and holy days did not come at regular intervals as our Sundays do. Instead, each day was marked either *fasti* or *nefasti.* On the days marked *fasti,* which literally means "days of speaking," the words formally necessary to transact legal business might be spoken—that is, the courts were open, public business could be transacted, and the day was not a festival. However, on days marked *nefasti,* literally "days of not speaking," for one reason or another public business could not be done. Now, it was the job of the college of pontiffs to interpret the prodigies and to formally designate each day of the month as *fasti* or *nefasti.* And since these priests were exclusively patricians, it is easy to see how this function could be used to exert considerable influence on the conduct of public business in the interest of the patrician order. The augurs, the other major priestly college, was also extremely influential. All state business required *auspicia,* which were signs or omens duly and officially observed which indicated the favor of heaven. Although the magistrates took the auspices, it was the augurs who interpreted them to determine the will of the gods, and they thus welded considerable political power. And the augurs were, of course, also exclusively patrician.

Finally, another group of priests, the *fetiales,* played an important role in the conduct of Rome's foreign policy. The *fetiales* were responsible for the religious rituals involved in the declaration of war and the swearing of treaties. Religious practice forbade Rome from engaging in "unjust wars," because to do so would disrupt the pax deorum and provoke the wrath of the gods upon the state. Therefore, a careful procedure was observed to ensure against involvement in unjust wars. When complaints of an act of aggression or the violation of a treaty by another state reached the Senate, the board of *fetiales* investigated the matter and, if necessary, dispatched one of its members to seek redress. If redress was not forthcoming, he spoke the formula, "if I unjustly demand that the aforesaid offenders be surrendered, then permit me not to return to my country." If restitution was not made during a thirty day interval, while Roman citizens where mustering for war and a special standard was flying on the Capitoline, the fetial priest then stood on Roman territory and hurled a charred spear into the enemy's territory and war was thus justly declared. This elaborate procedure demonstrates that Rome considered the normal status between itself and its neighbors to be one of peace, not war, and that Roman custom did not recognize territorial aggrandizement as a legitimate reason for war. These then were some of the privileges which the patricians reserved for themselves and through which they controlled the Roman state.

10

The Roman Republic

The Founding of the Roman Republic

The archaeological evidence indicates that by around 600 BCE the villages that had grown up on the various hills of Rome became united into a true city. We do not know the process of this unification, whether it was peaceful or through aggression, but there are no indications of a long or bitter struggle between the villages. Shortly after this unification, the low marshy area between the Palatine and Capitoline Hills was drained and leveled off to become the Roman Forum. The forum serves the same economic, social, and political function for Italian cities what the agora serves for Greek cities. The Roman Forum was a central public square or plaza, surrounded by public buildings, which served as a focus for Rome's political and economic life and indeed would one day become the center of the Roman Empire.

The king was first of all a military leader, and he was elected by the army. But he was also a religious leader responsible for the proper performance of the rituals of the state religion. The function of the state religion was to secure the support of the gods and thereby ensure the good fortune and prosperity of the state. This was carried out in the service of and for the benefit of all the state's citizens. The king also levied taxes and drafted men into the army. But the king's power was by no means absolute. Roman society, from the very beginning, was a patriarchal system. As noted above, many aspects of the law were in the hands of the *paterfamilias*. The king's power was also diluted by the institutions of the state. There was an advisory body, known as the senate, which was composed of the men of highest authority and reputation, the *paterfamilae* of the most important families. There was also an assembly of all the free citizens of Rome, originally an assembly of the army.

The Legend Continues

The history of the early republic, like the kingdom, is shrouded in legend and myth. According to the legend, the monarchy came to an end when the Romans could no longer endure the tyranny of King Tarquinius Superbus. The situation reached a boiling point when the Roman army was besieging a nearby town, and during a lull in the war. The king's son, Sextus Tarquinius, was entertaining some of the officers in his tent, when the subject of wives came up. Each man, of course, bragged that his own wife excelled all others in womanly virtue. Finally, one of the officers, Collatinus, proposed a wager. So they all rode back to Rome to look in on their wives unexpectedly and thereby settle the bet by determining whose wife was engaged in the most virtuous activity.

Figure 10.1: An archaic bust of Lucius Junius Brutus. It can hardly have been taken from life, but it represents the austerity of the early Romans.

They first visited the wife of the king's son and found her entertaining the neighborhood wives at a sumptuous banquet—not very virtuous in Roman eyes. The wives of the other officers also proved to be engaged in frivolous or luxurious activities. Finally the men arrived at the house of Collatinus and found his wife, the beautiful Lucretia, secluded in a back room with her servants busily weaving wool—one of the most virtuous activities in which a Roman matron could engage—and so Collatinus won the contest. The officers were invited in for the evening meal, which was served efficiently and modestly by the lady of the house, but during the dinner Sextus Tarquinius was seized by the wicked desire to debauch the virtuous Lucretia. So, a few days latter he returned under the cover of night and raped her at knife point. After he left, Lucretia sent messages to both her husband and her father to come at once because a terrible thing had happened. They came and her husband brought with him a close friend, Lucius Brutus. Lucretia explained to the men what had happened to her. With down-cast eyes she told her husband, "The imprint of a strange man is upon your bed." She made the men swear an oath to revenge her dishonor and then saying, "though I am not guilty of any wrong, I do not absolve myself from punishment," she suddenly plunged a knife into her own

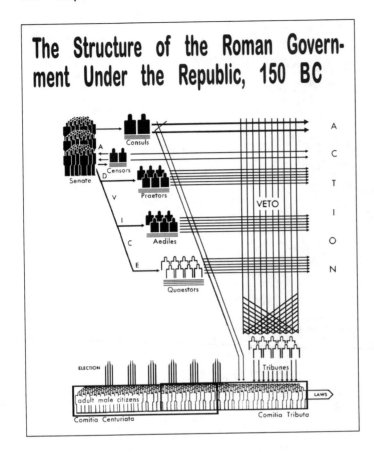

Figure 10.2: Diagram of the constitution of the Roman Republic.

heart and fell to the floor dead. The men carried Lucretia's body out into the forum and Brutus began to entreat the population to revolt. They soon raised a small band of armed citizens and Brutus led it against the king and drove the hated Tarquinius and his entire family out of Rome. The Romans swore that never again would a king rule over their city and in 509 BCE they established the Roman Republic with Brutus and Collatinus as the first consuls.

This is not entirely a romantic legend. The date of 509 BCE for the beginning of the Republic is accepted as historical—mainly because it is as good a guess as we can make—and the name of Brutus seems to be authentic. And so far as we can tell, the change from monarchy to republic was in fact revolutionary, not evolutionary as in the case of the Greek city-states. To prevent the rise of kingship ever again, the royal power, which the Romans called *imperium*, was divided between two elected magistrates known as consuls.

Constitution of the Roman Republic

Much of the history of the Roman Republic revolves around its constitution, which, like those of the Greek city-states, was not a written document, but rather a set of carefully observed procedures and customs. To the modern ear, the term "unwritten constitution" sounds strange and contradictory.

However, the written constitution is a very modern invention. The constitution of the United States, written in 1787, is the first such document and that was only yesterday in historical terms. Throughout the more than five thousand years of written human history, all governments operated under "unwritten" constitutions. Ancient Rome, like other ancient states, operated under a traditional constitution which was the product of precedent, consensus, and a series of compromises between the various power blocks and interest groups of the population. These compromises had been worked out over a long period of time and while they did not always seem absolutely just to the Romans in all circumstances, a deviation from them seemed even less just. Therefore, it was only with great reluctance that these procedures were altered.

Although the Roman constitution was not based on a written document, it was based on something very real and strong, something the Romans called their *mos majorum*, literally the "custom of our ancestors." The concept of *mos majorum* was at least as significant to the ancient Romans as the term constitution is to us. When a Roman politician charged that an act was "against the custom of our ancestors," that charge had the same force that "unconstitutional" has in the modern world.

Well, if the Roman constitution was not a document, then how can we study it? We must look not at a legal text but rather look at how the government itself was *constituted*, that is, we must look at the actual structure and machinery of the government. One of the most detailed and important sources for this is the description of the Greek historian Polybius[1] (c. 201–120 BCE), who wrote a history of Rome. His description is especially useful because he himself was not a Roman but a highly educated Greek who could observe aspects of the Roman political system that might go unnoticed or unreported by a Roman writing about his own history.

The structure of the Roman government was complex, to say the least. In essence, the government consisted of three components, which checked and balanced each other (Fig. 10.2). Polybius believed each of these three elements functioned like one of the three basic types of government: the senate represented the aristocracy (oligarchy), the elected magistrates wielded the administrative power of kings (monarchy), while the sovereignty of the state was vested in the assembly of the people (democracy). The Greeks believed that each of these forms of government had both advantages and disadvantages. For example, when a state is constituted as a monarchy, the very best individual in the community is chosen to be king. This person usually rules quite justly and in the common interest. However, as the generations pass, the members of the royal family become selfish and eventually come to think of the state as their private estate to be ruled for their own selfish benefit, not for the common good of the people. This is a fatal flaw of monarchy, it becomes oppressive. Much the same analysis can be made of an oligarchy, or the rule of a small upper class. As for democracy, its benefits appear to be overwhelming in the beginning, but the

---

1. See "Polybius, The Constitution of the Roman Republic" in Cleve, Robert, *Early Western Civilization, Source Readings* (2002), Kendall/Hunt Publishing Company, Dubuque, pp. 333–342.
Polybius was one of the Greeks who was deported to Rome in 167 BCE as part of the 1,000 Greeks taken to Italy as hostages to guarantee the good behavior of the states of the Peloponnesus. These hostages were held in a kind of house arrest in the homes of various aristocratic families in Rome. Polybius was lucky to be assigned to the Scipios, one of the most prominent political families of the day. He remained in Italy for over ten years. As he came to know the Romans he grew to greatly admire them and he became convinced they were destined to rule the Mediterranean world—and he thought that this might not be a bad idea, since the Greeks had never been able to rule themselves very well. However, at this time the Greeks still did not know much about the Romans, so Polybius decided to write a history of the Romans for the Greek audience. One of the great values of Polybius's history is that it is written by an outsider, from an outsider's point of view.

Greeks discovered that after a time a number of flaws emerged. One problem is that of demagogues, individuals who through the use of charisma and oratorical skills inflame the common people and lead them down the path to violence and self-destruction. Another problem with democracy is what the Greeks called the "tyranny of the majority," when the majority indulged in abusive and oppressive acts against the minority. All of these flaws, if not countered in some way, led to what the Greeks called "*stasis*," or the paralysis of government. Polybius attributed the great success of Rome to its constitution, which he perceived to be an almost perfect combination of the three types of government. This, he thought, had been accomplished through a complicated system of checks and balances.

The Senate

Let's look at these elements of the Roman government each in turn. First the senate. That body consisted of all present and past magistrates. Its members served for life, unless removed by the censors. In other words, any citizen elected to any public office became a permanent member of the senate. This kept the senate, during the late republic, at a strength of about 450 members, depending of course on how many new members were admitted and how many old members died each year.

In the strict constitutional sense, the Senate was only an advisory body to the elected magistrates, who had the responsibility of administrating the government. Indeed, the Senate could not even convene itself, it had to be called into session by a magistrate. When requested, however, it offered advice on matters of domestic and foreign policy, finance and religion, and made legislative proposals. Well, this was its strict constitutional function, an advisory council. But in practice and by custom, its functions and powers went much further. Gradually, the Senate assumed the power to perform six major functions of government. However, since in the final analysis the Senate's powers were only advisory, its performance of these functions could be overturned or assumed by the assembly or the magistrates at any time. To do so might result in severe political and social tension, but everyone recognized the assembly's inherent sovereignty and authority in all matters of state. Governing without the consent of the Senate was normally considered to be unwise and improper—and actually unconstitutional by some.

Specifically, the first of these six major functions of the Senate was the assignment of the duties of the elected magistrates, that is, the Senate marked out what the Romans called the magistrates' *provincia*, or "province." The Senate assigned the specific commands and duties to the consuls and praetors and, when necessary, extended the time of those commands beyond the limits of the magistrate's one year term of office. When a consul, for example, was given command of an army in the field and his term of office ran out before his mission was completed, the Senate could extend his command beyond the time of his consulship. He then became a "proconsul." His consular power was over at the end of his term, but the proconsul retained the power to complete his assignment. As you might expect, the Senate often used this authority for narrow political purposes.

Secondly, the Senate assumed the right to approve legislative proposals before they were submitted to the assembly. This right was not absolute and became controversial during times of social or political conflict. In fact, laws were sometimes passed by the assembly over the Senate's objections. But this was considered undesirable by everyone, and of course it was considered unconstitutional by the most conservative factions of the population. Most people believed that good laws were the product of the wisdom of the Senate, not the demoguery of the assembly.

The third major function of the Senate was to fix the number of citizens conscripted into the army each year. In other words, the Senate authorized the size of the army.

Fourth, the Senate controlled the state treasury and supervised both the rate of taxation and expenditure. It also regulated the coinage. It had control of the mints and in practice determined the size of the money supply.

Fifth, was the formulation of foreign policy. Although the formal declaration of war and the ratification of treaties belonged to the assembly, the Senate controlled the conduct of foreign affairs through its advice to the consuls, and when the Senate decided to go to war, the assembly usually had no choice but to follow the Senate's lead. Thus, while the assembly formally declared war, the actual decision to go to war almost always was made by the Senate.

Finally, after 121 BCE, the Senate assumed the authority to issue a *Senatus Consultum Ultimum* (SCU), "the final decree of the Senate." This was more or less a declaration of martial law which suspended the normal constitutional guarantees of civil rights and empowered the consuls to take extraordinary action against someone or some group designated the "enemies of the state." This sounds ominous. Who are these "enemies of the state?" In practice, they were political opponents and any faction of the Senate that could garner a majority could outlaw their opposition. However, since the SCU was a unilateral act of the Senate and not approved by the assembly, its legality was never accepted by some Romans. How could an act that was not accepted as constitutional be employed time and again? For example, in the year 63 BCE, the famous statesman Marcus Cicero was consul, and he discovered a conspiracy against the state led by a disgruntled aristocrat named Catiline. The Senate issued an SCU which ordered Cicero to put down the Catiline conspiracy. Under the authority of the SCU, Cicero put several Roman citizens to death without a trial. But under Roman law all citizens had the right to appeal a capital sentence directly to the assembly. However, it was also a principle of Roman law that no magistrate could be brought into court while in office. But later, after his term of office was over and he was a private citizen, Cicero was brought into court and found guilty of violating the law and sentenced to 10 years in exile. So weather or not the SCU was constitutional was never really settled. After the demise of the republic and the establishment of emperorship in 27 BCE, the question became mute.

And so by assuming these and other powers, the Senate was able to become the most important branch of the Roman Republic. In fact, laws and public policy were propagated under the authority of the *Senatus Populasque Romanus*, "the senate and the people of Rome." This phrase was often abbreviated SPQR. It is still a kind of logo for the municipal government of the city of Rome today and appears on government buildings and even manhole covers.

The Magistrates

The second element of the government was the elected magistrates. Roman magistrates were regarded as the representatives of the *populus Romanus*, the Roman people, because it was the people who elected them and invested them with *imperium*, or the executive power of the state. Although the two consuls exercised the ultimate *imperium*, there was a slate of six constitutional offices. Politicians normally ran for the most junior offices first and then worked their way up the ladder to the more senior offices. Those who were most successful culminated their career by attaining the consulship. All of the offices, except the censor, were held for one-year terms. This pattern of service progressing from junior to senior positions was known as the *cursus honorum*, literally "the course of honor." Politics was considered to be the most honorable of all occupations, but the politicians did not receive remuneration for their service, only honor. Indeed, the office holder had to meet the expense of service out of his own pocket. Thus, only the independently wealthy could pursue the honor of a public career.

The lowest ranking office, though by no means the least powerful, and usually the first office held by a plebeian politician, was the tribune. A board of ten tribunes was elected annually by the *plebs*, the common people. Their duty was to protect the common citizens from the abuse and oppression of the government. To accomplish this task, each tribune possessed the right of *veto* ("I forbid") against any and all actions of any government official, agent, or institution, except a *dictator* (a special magistracy which will be discussed below). They could even veto each other and the assembly which elected them. During the late republic the tribunes also acted as political leaders of the people and could call the assembly into session, and even the senate, in the absence of higher ranking magistrates. They sat as members of the senate.

The quaestor was the lowest rank of full government magistrate—the tribunes were considered to be magistrates of the *plebs* only. Quaestors were very junior civil officials who acted as supervisors of the archives and the treasury and served as assistants to consuls and provincial governors. Their number varied, but in the late republic 30 of them were elected annually.

The aediles were also junior officials who administered public buildings, supervised street maintenance, and provided public games. The games were financed out of their own pockets, and this was an opportunity for a young politician to gain popularity with the people. Julius Caesar first gained fame by putting on lavish games while he was aedile. Eight aediles were elected each year.

The praetors administered justice. Trials were held before juries, but the praetors presided over the courts much like a judge does today and adjudicated points of law. Praetors were also often extended in their powers beyond their year in office and appointed as governors of some of the less important provinces by the Senate. When this occurred, they were then called propraetors. They were the lowest ranking magistrates who held *imperium*.

The two consuls were the supreme civil and military magistrates of the Republic. Like the other officials, except the censors, they were elected to one year terms by the assembly and they gave their names to the year.[2] Both consuls possessed equal *imperium*, and could not only veto each other but all the lower ranking magistrates as well, except the tribunes. The idea behind this was to prevent a return of the kingship, while preserving the administrative power of the monarchy. When the Senate prolonged or extended a consul in his command in order to allow him to complete a military campaign or serve as a provincial governor, he became a proconsul. In such a case he retained his imperium, but it was a proconsular *imperium*, which gave him power only over his specific assignment and he could be overridden by a consul.

The Romans realized that in cases of extreme national emergencies, the state must have unified leadership. And in a crises one of the consuls could nominate a dictator who was then confirmed by the Senate. The dictator had supreme power, which was not even subject to the veto of the tribunes, but his office was limited to six months or the duration of the crises, whichever was shorter.

There is one more office to discuss, the censor, who did not posses *imperium*, but nevertheless had great authority. Two censors were elected every five years and served for a term of 18 months. Their job included the drawing up of a complete and official list of all citizens. This was called a census. From this list was chosen the names of those citizens who were drafted into military serv-

---

2. The Romans, like most ancient states, employed a system of naming the years after eponymous magistrates—in this case, the consuls. They maintained consul lists supposedly going back to the first year of the Republic. These lists were called the *fasti* and the ancient Roman and Greek historians attempted to correlate the *fasti* with various Greek chronological systems. Modern historians attempt to assign corresponding BCE and CE dates to these lists. For an overview of the complexities and problems involved in the accurate dating of antiquity, see Bickerman, E.J., *Chronology of the Ancient World* (1968), Thames and Hudson, London.

ice whenever an army was raised. The censors also supervised the leasing of public lands and buildings and were responsible for public morals. In this capacity they drew up an official list of the members of the senate and were authorized to leave off of that list any senators whose morals did not meet public standards. The Romans have been given a bad press by later Christian writers, and by modern media, who often pictured them as spending most of their time engaged in drunken orgies, but in fact the early Romans were insufferably moralistic.

The Assembly

Finally, we come to the third division of Roman government, the Assembly—or more accurately, the assemblies, because there were several different assemblies, or at least several different forms of assembly. The sovereignty of the Roman state was vested in the people, who expressed that sovereignty through their assembly, or *comitia*. However, the people of Rome did not vote directly as in Greece, but rather they voted in blocks, or districts, or wards. The Assembly could be organized in different configurations for different purposes and there were thus different types of assemblies. The two most important ones were the *comitia centuriata* and the *comitia tributa*.

The *comitia centuriata* was not, by our standards, a very democratic political body. Indeed, it was purposefully organized so that the votes of the wealthier citizens would carry more weight than those of the poorer citizens. But from the Roman point of view, there were sound reasons for this. During the early Republic, Roman society was simple, and the army was a direct reflection of that society. The Roman army was a citizen army, not a standing professional army. Furthermore, the soldier had to furnish his own equipment, provide for his own training, and even support himself while on campaign. This means that in order to serve in the army, a citizen had to be a property owner with sufficient income to maintain himself and his equipment in the field. Thus, it was considered only fair that those property-owning citizens, who had the most to lose, should contribute the most toward the defense of the state. And it also followed that the vote of those contributing the most to the state's defense should carry the most weight in the decisions of the assembly. This seemed only fair to the Romans.

Therefore, the citizens were divided into classes according to their wealth. The highest of these classes was the equites—actually the equites class was one step above what was called the "first class." Originally, the equites consisted of only 1,800 men whose horses were supplied and maintained by the state. For this they had to serve in ten campaigns. They were armed with lances in

Equites	18 centuries
1st class	80 centuries
2nd class	20 centuries
3rd class	20 centuries
4th class	20 centuries
5th class	30 centuries
Urban craftsman	4 centuries
Proletarii	1 century
TOTAL	193 centuries
MAJORITY	97 centuries

Figure 10.3: Composition of the *comitia centuriata.*

addition to the shields, swords, and the other armor of the foot soldiers. They did not form a cavalry so much as a mobile unit that could be dispatched quickly to trouble spots on the battlefield or to take advantage of a promising weakness in the enemy ranks. Before the invention of the stirrup, fighting from horseback was not really very effective and the equites seemed to normally dismount after reaching the point of combat and to then engage the enemy on foot.

The rest of the property-owning citizens were divided into five classes. The property qualifications for these classes does not seem very high and reflects the fact that there was not a very great separation between the rich and the poor in early Rome. Qualification for the equites class required ownership of only about 16 acres of land—not an inordinately large estate, either by modern or by later Roman standards. The first class requirement was about 12 acres; second class, 9 acres; fourth class, 3 acres; and the fifth and lowest class, about one acre. Below these five classes there were two other groups of citizens: the *proletarii* were those urban citizens who had no property at all. They could not have been very numerous during the earliest period of the republic when the *comitia centuriata* was established. But during the later history of the republic, the city of Rome teamed with the landless poor, and they became as serious a problem for Rome as our urban slums are for us today. There was one other group which included the skilled urban craftsmen—while they were landless, they were not really poor. The greater the wealth of the individual, the greater his contribution to the army, and the greater was his potential loss in a war, consequently, the greater was the weight of his vote in the *comitia centuriata*, whose function it was to deal with questions of war and peace.

How was this difference in voting weight in the *comitia centuriata* expressed? The *comitia centuriata* was made up of a of 193 centuries (*centuriae*), which cast one vote each. A simple majority, or 97 of the centuries, was required to pass a proposal. Figure 10.3 indicates how the 193 centuries were allotted to the different classes. Obviously, the citizens of the equites and the first class, voting together, could carry the day, because they controlled a total of 98 centuries. Yet, a century of equites consisted of only 100 citizens, while the one century of *prolatarii* contained many times that number. During the late Republic, it consisted of several thousand.

The *comitia centuriata* fell into disuse during the later Republic, and most of its functions were taken over by the more democratic tribal assembly. It continued, however, to elect consuls, praetors, and censors. This is another illustration of how, even though new elements were added to the Roman constitution from time to time, nothing was ever completely discarded.

There were actually two tribal assemblies: the *concilium plebis tributa*, or the plebeian tribal assembly; and the *comitia populi tributa*, or the tribal assembly of the people. They were both organized exactly alike, that is, they were both organized by tribes. The difference was that the patricians were excluded from the plebeian assembly.

The function of the *concilium plebis* was to elect tribunes and plebeian aediles, but during the late Republic it could conduct nearly every form of official business, including the passage of laws and the granting of special commands. The function of the *comitia populi tributa* was to elect quaestors and aediles, but it also was competent to pass laws and to transact other official business. The plebeian assembly could be convened by the tribunes, whereas the consuls and the praetors could convoke the popular assembly.

This assembly by tribes was much more democratic than the assembly by centuries, because the vote of a wealthy citizen counted for no more than the vote of the poorest citizen. The Roman tribe was simply a political division of the population of the state. Originally, there were only three tribes, but the number gradually grew to 35 by the year 241 BCE. Thereafter, new citizens were enrolled in one of the existing tribes and no new tribes were created. In the beginning the tribes were local in nature. There were four urban tribes and the rest were called "rustic," or rural tribes. With the extension of

Roman citizenship to all of Italy, there was an attempt to confine all of the influx of new citizens to a few tribes in order to check their influence in the tribal assembly, but this ultimately failed. In general, however, freedmen were admitted only to the four urban tribes so that in time these urban tribes became larger than the rustic ones. In the tribal assembly, a vote of the majority, or 18 tribes, carried the issue, no matter how many individual members of each tribe were present and voting.

In summery then, we can discern three branches, or elements, in the government of the Roman Republic, which tended to balance and check each other. The assembly of the people which, in theory at least, had the most power, did not meet very frequently and, in fact, during most of the Republic's history did not exercise its maximum power. The day-to-day operation of the government was managed by the magistrates, who, while advised by the Senate, possessed supreme executive power. And the third branch was the Senate, which was an aristocratic body of elder statesmen. All the higher magistrates had already served as members of the Senate for several years and after their one-year terms of office they would return to that body to serve the rest of their political lives among their equals. The magistrates were not likely, then, to disregard the Senate's advice. In contrast to the Assembly, the Senate met regularly and over the centuries acquired great prestige. A Greek statesman, who had conducted business with the Senate as a diplomat, called it "an assembly of kings." The Senate's importance to the structure of the government was so great that commands and government decrees were issued in the name of the *Senatus Populusque Romanus*, "the Senate and the people of Rome." This phrase, to the Romans, represented the basic authority of the state just as the first three words of our constitution, "we the people," does for us. Nothing illustrates better the enormous prestige and importance of the Senate than the fact that it was considered equal to the people themselves.

The legacy of the constitutions of ancient Greece and Rome are still present in our modern political system. The authors of our own constitution took the idea of the separation of powers into

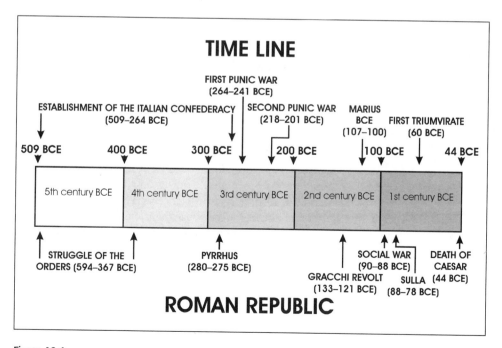

Figure 10.4

three branches which check and balance each other, from ancient political theory. Every member of the constitutional convention, which gathered in Philadelphia in 1878 to write that document, had what we today would call a classical education, that is they were fluent in Latin and ancient Greek and they were all familiar with the writing of Polybius. It is no accident that the upper house of our congress is called the Senate and that it was intended to be the conservative check on the more democratic House of Representatives. It is no accident the chief executive officer of our government is called the president, a word which has its roots in the ancient Greek word *prytaneis*, the presiding tribe of Athens. It is important for the modern citizen to be aware of how ancient these political principles are and how deep these concepts go back into one history. These principles of self-government are unique to Western Civilization.

The Early Republic

The constitution of the Roman Republic was the product of over three centuries of struggle and compromise between the various social and political factions of the Roman population. One of the first compromises that had to be worked out was between the aristocratic class, known as the patricians, and the common people, known as the plebeians. At the beginning of the Republic, in 509 BCE, the patricians controlled the government in every aspect. They alone could be elected to office or serve as priests of the state religion, and, thus, in the early days of the Republic, every member of the Senate was a patrician. This gave them a monopoly on political power and the political process. In fact, even the popular assembly was dominated by the approximately 50 patrician families, through a system of patronage, although they made up less than 5% of the citizen body. The patricians were able to control the assembly because under the Roman system of voting by blocks, or political unites, rather than directly, the votes of the few wealthy citizens carried more weight than the mass of common people. In addition, almost all of the plebeians were clients of the patrician families, who controlled their votes. Voting in the assembly was not by secret ballot, and a patron could easily determine if his client voted in the right way. Thus, during the early Republic the plebs was economically and politically oppressed by the aristocratic patricians. Two centuries of struggle were required for the plebeians to win an equal voice in their government.

The Struggle of the Orders

The fundamental reason for the eventual success of the plebeians was the fact that they were essential for Rome's ever widening wars. The regular draft quota for a year's campaign rose dramatically because Rome was almost constantly engaged in war. Since the Patricians only rarely admitted new families to their ranks, almost all of these additional soldiers were plebeians. This gave them a certain amount of political leverage. Another factor in their success was their ability to gain effective leaders. Most of these spokesmen came from the wealthier families of the *plebs*. They were men who were quite wealthy, often wealthier than many of the patricians, but who nevertheless were restricted in their political participation in the state due to their social standing as plebeians.

The first step in what the Romans called "struggle of the orders,"[3] was the creation of the tribal assembly and the office of the tribune of the people. The plebeians accomplished this revolutionary

---

3. The Latin word *ordo* in this context can be translated as "class." However, the origin of the division of Rome's population into the patrician and plebeian orders is disputed and controversial. Tradition assigned it to Romulus.

reform without violence or bloodshed by literally setting up a "state within the state." In 494 BCE, the *plebs* actually withdrew from the city to a place called the Sacred Mountain and refused further participation in any activity of the state. This event was called the "first secession of the *plebs*," by the Romans.

In most societies, such a revolutionary step would lead to a bloody conflict, but in these types of situations the Romans were remarkably tolerant and patient. After long negotiations, a compromise was reached, and the plebeians were persuaded to return to Rome, in exchange for the recognition of the tribal assembly and the office of tribune as legal and permanent institutions of the state.

The next step came in 450 BCE when the plebeians, by means of a second secession, forced the patricians to write down and codify the law.[4] The result was the famous Twelve Tables, which were drawn up by two successive boards of ten officials (*decemviri*) especially elected for that purpose. The law code set down in writing the rights as well as the duties of all citizens. It also covered such things as wills, contracts, and provisions for wives and children to secure legal emancipation from the power of the *paterfamilias*. So the Twelve Tables included what we today call both criminal and civil law. The Twelve Tables became the basis and foundation of the Roman civil law, perhaps the greatest legacy and gift of Rome to succeeding societies.[5]

Thereafter, the plebeians pressed for admittance to the elected magistracies. In 367 BCE, two tribunes (Licinius and Sextius) forced the additions of a new praetor and two new aedile offices which were reserved for the *plebs*. This broke, finally, the monopoly of the patricians on public office and began a long process by which the plebeians gradually obtained the right to hold any and all of the state magistracies.

But after the admission of the plebeians to the political process, the Roman government was still not conducted as democratically as, say, the government of classical Athens. For one thing, a new, unofficial class division of the citizen body occurred. During the 3rd Century BCE the old patrician families united with the leading plebeian families to form a "senatorial aristocracy." This new group was known as the *nobilitas*, or the nobility, and it was this new senatorial aristocracy that furnished almost all the nominations for public office. Those coming from outside this group had great difficulty running for office, but there were a few who were successful from time to time, and this provided some social mobility.[6] Yet, the eventual surrender

---

4. Up to this time the law had been under the control of the pontiffs, the priests of the state religion. The *pontifex maximus*, the chief priest, was judge and arbiter of "all things human and divine." Thus, the members of the college of pontiffs were the first Roman jurists. They functioned as legal consultants and interpreters of the law. Magistrates consulted the entire college on matters of religious and public law, and private disputes were referred to the pontiff appointed by the college to deal with such cases. The problem for the plebs was that all the pontiffs were patricians, and the plebeians believed, quite reasonably, that they were not immune from using their monopoly over the law for their own interests. Much better that the law be written.

5. It is easy to confuse these two different uses of the word "civil" when discussing Roman law. In the modern United States, the term "civil law" refers to that body of law which is concerned with civil or private rights including the private relationships between individuals. However, the common usage of the term "civil law" in the context of ancient Roman history refers to "the law established by a nation or state for its own jurisdiction." The "civil" in the term "Roman civil law" refers to *civitas* (citizenship, the state) and defines domestic law, that is, the law that pertains to Roman citizens, in contrast with the *ius gentium*, international law, or the law of nations. Eventually, Roman civil law became the basis of the law systems of all modern European nations (accept Britain) and the *ius gentium* became the basis of modern international law.

6. A person from outside the *nobilitas* who ran for the consulship was labeled a *novus homo*, or "new man." This was a rather derogatory term which had much the same connotations as our terms "upstart," and "nouveau riche," meaning an arrogant or presumptuous person who has risen to a higher status but has not gained the social skills appropriate for his new status and thus cannot gain the acceptance of others in that class.

by the patricians of their exclusive position without a bloody revolution attests to the political good sense of the Romans. It was the same good sense that would later keep the empire loyal to them for centuries.

Roman Expansion in Italy

While the Romans were culturally backward during their early history, as compared with the Greeks, and they themselves were aware of this, their great political and military skills were demonstrated by the fact that between 509 and 264 BCE, they conquered and unified the entire peninsula of Italy. This alone would have ensured their place in history.

Down to 340 BCE, the wars of the early Republic took place in a narrow strip of central western Italy known as Latium. Then by 290 BCE, the Romans had conquered both the Etruscans to the north and the Samnites to the south. The Romans throughout their history occasionally lost battles, but they never lost a war, because they simply refused to make peace with anyone, except on terms favorable to themselves.

The Italian Confederacy

However, the Romans did not simply conquer and exploit the peoples of Italy, in the same way, for example, that the Assyrians exploited the peoples of the Near East. The Romans were as astute at diplomacy as they were tenacious at warfare. Within Italy, Rome did not establish an empire, in the usual sense of that word, but rather formed the Italian peoples into a powerful confederation. When Rome defeated another state, they did not enslave or annex that state, but rather they signed a treaty of alliance and friendship with it. The goal of Rome's foreign policy was to transform its former enemies into supporters, into enthusiastic participants in its own expansion and prosperity, *not* into sullen exploited subjects, who would wait for any opportunity to rise up in revolt. The goal of Roman foreign policy was the security for their city, and they realized that surrounding themselves with hostile states, waiting for any opportunity to rise in revolt, would not achieve security. So in a very real sense, the Italian peoples were not conquered by Rome, but rather forced into a federation of allies, with Rome as its senior member and leader. Nevertheless, the word "force" is the operative word, because the unification of Italy was not a peaceful and voluntary process but accomplished by military force. It is the result, not the means, that is to Rome's credit.[7]

But alliance was only the first step, Rome went even further. Through a policy of establishing different degrees of privilege and responsibility among the Italians, they were gradually Romanized and became full Roman citizens. The result was that one language, Latin, and one culture, Greco-Roman, became standard throughout Italy by the late 1st Century BCE.

This was a long process, however. In the beginning, Rome set up a kind of hierarchy of privilege and responsibility by which the conquered peoples could work their way up into full Roman citizenship. The status of Italians fell into three main categories: at the top were the most favored communities, those who had been Rome's most loyal allies and most of them had never been enemies.

---

7. But looked at realistically, it is difficult to imagine how Italy could have been unified, or the city of Rome's security assured, without the use of military force. With historical hindsight, it is always easy, but never profound or learned, to apply the liberal ideology of the present ("give peace a chance") to the distant past and thereby self-righteously condemn past societies for not conforming to modern ethics—ethics which we ourselves are more than ready to abandon in the interests of "national security."

These were granted full Roman citizenship at an early date, which means they enjoyed the same protection of Roman law and the same right to hold public office as did all Roman citizens. Aristocratic families of these communities were admitted into the patrician order. Secondly, some communities became "citizens without suffrage" (*civitas sine suffragio*). These people enjoyed the full protection of Roman law and the right of intermarriage with Romans, but not the right to vote or hold office. They also had the responsibilities of citizenship and were subject to draft into the Roman army. This status seems to have been a temporary one for communities who had proven themselves loyal allies, but were still not fully Romanized or were located too far away from Rome to participate in the day-to-day political activity of the state. When the Romans became more comfortable with citizens living farther away from the city, these communities were granted full citizenship and this status disappeared. Finally, the lowest level of privilege were the *socii* (sg. *socius*) or allies. They received Rome's protection from attack by other peoples and were liable for service with Rome's army as auxiliaries.

Once they joined the Roman alliance system, none of these groups could pursue an independent foreign policy, but they were allowed to conduct their own domestic affairs without interference from Rome and they could progress upward into full Roman citizenship. What they could not do was withdraw from the alliance. Rome had an iron clad policy which can be summed up in the phrase: "Once a friend of Rome, always a friend of Rome." This system of confederation enabled the Romans to solve an administrative problem that had hampered earlier empires: how to control a large territory without having to station a large army of occupation in the conquered area. In the old style empires of Greece and the Near East, as the conquered territory increased, the demands on the manpower of the conquering army became ever more acute, because more and more soldiers were required to garrison the occupied territories as well as to defend the ever expanding borders of the empire. Yet the manpower pool remained the same, or even diminished, as the empire expanded. Under the Roman system, however, not only was there little or no requirement for occupying garrisons, but as the conquered territory increased, the available manpower for the army increased, not decreased, due to the constant admission of new citizens and allies. It is for reasons such as this that we must consider Rome's political and diplomatic skills at least as important to its success as its military skills.

This early period of expansion was interrupted by one major disaster. About 390 BCE, a large force of Gauls invaded Italy from the north and captured Rome itself. But the Gauls were still a semi-nomadic people and they were not so much interested in permanent conquest as they were in loot and plunder, and the Romans were able to buy them off with a payment of gold. A vindication of the Roman system of governing is that during this defeat, almost all of the allies remained loyal and after the Gauls withdrew, Rome renewed its policy of expansion with little difficulty. By 290 BCE, Rome dominated the Italian peninsula as far south as the Greek city-states. At this point Rome finally emerges into the clear light of history, with firm dates that we can substantiate and information basically unclouded by legendary decoration.

Pyrrhus

In 280 BCE, the Greek city of Tarentum, located inside the heel of the Italian boot, requested help from the Greek king of Epirus, modern Albania, against the Romans. The ambitious Pyrrhus, who was a distant relative of Alexander the Great, led an army of 25,000 men and 20 elephants into Southern Italy where he destroyed a Roman army at Heraclea. It was a terrible defeat for the Romans, but the victory was so costly for Pyrrhus that the term "Pyrrhic victory" has come into the English language to denote a victory in which the losses far outweighed the benefits of winning the battle. However, Pyrrhus, drawing on his previous experience, now believed that he had won the war and offered the Romans very favorable peace terms. The senate's reply was stunning: Rome only negotiates surrender and if Pyrrhus is not ready to surrender then there is nothing to negotiate. Pyrrhus marched northward toward Rome but discovered that he could not safely bring the city under siege because Rome's allies remained loyal. So another battle was fought at Asculum in 279 BCE, which resulted in another Pyrrhic victory for Pyrrhus. But he was still not able to bring the city of Rome under siege. Then, at the invitation of Syracuse, the largest Greek city of Sicily, he undertook a campaign to drive the Carthaginians from that island. He achieved great success there and returned to Italy and fought the Romans again at Beneventum in 275 BCE. This battle was a draw, as neither side could really claim a victory. Well, by this time Pyrrhus thought it best to withdraw back to Epirus. After two great victories and a draw against the Romans, he had barely one third of his expeditionary force left and he had nothing at all to show for his victorious campaign in Italy. Once again Rome's allies had remained loyal, even in defeat.

From this point onward, the history of Rome is merged with the history of Italy and when we speak of Rome, we mean not only the city of Rome but all the peoples of Italy allied with Rome and under its leadership. After unifying Italy, Rome began to intervene in the quarrels of the states outside Italy. Within little more than a century, from 264 to 133 BCE, Rome made itself the supreme Mediterranean power. This imperialism, we shall see, had a radical influence on everything in Roman life, from its government and society to its literature and art.

The Punic Wars

The three wars with Carthage—known as the Punic[8] wars—established the foundations of Roman imperialism. The city of Carthage located on the coast of North Africa near modern Tunis was founded about 700 BCE by Phoenician exiles from Tyre in Syria and during the next centuries established a large empire in the western Mediterranean which included the North African coast, Corsica, Sardinia, parts of Spain, and much of Sicily.

The Carthaginians

The Carthaginians were the ancient world's most successful commercial people. It can truly be said that the most important business of the Carthaginians was business. They maintained a virtual monopoly on the trade in the western Mediterranean by simply sinking the ships of other states which entered their closed economic sphere. The city itself became the richest in the ancient world and was surrounded by a massive wall 22 miles in length and a population of over half a million. This probably made it the second most populous city of its time, after Alexandria in Egypt.

The empire established by the Carthaginians was in stark contrast to the Italian Confederacy of the Romans. Unlike Rome, Carthage selfishly exploited the inhabitants of its empire. The other Phoenician colonies in the western Mediterranean were reduced to servitude. The natives of Sardinia and Spain were exploited commercially and forced to supply mercenary troops. In Sicily, where they came into competition with the Greeks, the Carthaginians had to be more careful to

---

8. From the Latin word *punicus,* "Phoenician." Since the Carthaginians were Phoenician in origin it was logical for the Romans to name these wars "Punic."

avoid driving the whole island into the arms of its old enemy, Syracuse, the largest Greek city on the island. But on the whole, the condition of the subjects of Carthage was far inferior to that of the allies of Rome.

The Phoenicians of Carthage did not model the government of their new city on the monarchical pattern of the mother country. Instead of a king as the head of state, we find two elected suffetes, whose original function was judicial, not military—a reflection of the fact that the early aims of Carthage were commercial, not imperial. However, the real conduct of state affairs rested with a Council of Thirty, which was a subcommittee of the senate of three hundred. There was also a popular assembly, which was consulted whenever there was a question of major importance or whenever the members of the council or the senate could not agree. Judicial power was vested in a Council of One Hundred and Four, chosen by the senate.

To maintain its empire, Carthage required money, soldiers, and ships. Money was derived from tribute and customs dues levied on the subject peoples. Because of the famous Carthaginian commercial skills and business acumen, Carthage never seemed to lack for money. Its army was originally formed of Carthaginian citizens, but as its empire expanded faster than its population, there were not enough citizens to fill the need and soon it became necessary to conscript Africans,

Figure 10.5: A Carthaginian priest carrying a child he is about to offer as sacrifice: a stele from Carthage, 4th Century BCE.

Sardinians, and Iberians and to employ mercenaries. Thus, by the 3rd Century BCE, her own citizens had grown successful and prosperous and no longer served in the Carthaginian army except as officers, or in wars fought in Africa itself. The Carthaginian navy was maintained by the tribute of the subject peoples. The skill and courage of the seamen and navigators of Carthage is well attested, from many sources.

The religion of the Carthaginians was a variation of Phoenician polytheism. They brought with them the ancient deities of Phoenicia. Their chief god was called Baal Hammon, "the Lord of the Furnace." The Carthaginians practiced a religious custom long since discontinued in their Phoenician homeland of Syria, which rightly horrified the Greeks and the Romans. In times of danger—whether it be war, drought, or famine—the Carthaginians sacrificed their children to Baal Hammon. The babies of even the highest ranking nobles were selected for this purpose and archaeological excavations suggest that these infant holocausts were quite frequent and extensive.

After every allowance has been made for the hostility of our sources, the resulting picture is not an attractive one. Carthage exploited the caravan routes of Egypt and Africa, sailed to Britain and Senegal, and became the richest state in the ancient world, but produced nothing of lasting value. Carthaginian industry aimed at mass-production and cheapness, rather than beauty. Its art was unoriginal and imitative of Egypt and Greece, and while we hear of Carthaginian books and libraries, there is no evidence to suggest that they ever produced any literature of value. Carthage was not admired by its contemporaries and the judgment of history has not been kind. In 1642, F. N. Psyche wrote:

> Bearded Orientals in loose robes, covered with gaudy trinkets, often with great rings of gold hanging from their nostrils, dripping with perfumes, cringing and salaaming, the Carthaginians inspired disgust as much by their personal appearance as by their sensual appetites, their treacherous cruelty, their blood-thirsty religion. To the end they remained hucksters, intent on personal gain, careless or incapable of winning the goodwill of their subjects.

Thus, at any rate, were they perceived by the Greeks, the Romans, and later historians, but after all, we can view the Carthaginians only though the eyes of their enemies, which is not the most objective source, to say the least.

The First Punic War (264–241 BCE)

The causes of the Punic Wars are not difficult to discern. It has rarely proven possible for two large, important, and expanding states to exist in close contact for very long without conflict. However, the earlier relations between the two Republics had been amicable enough to result in a series of treaties designed to prevent either party from interfering in the other's sphere of operations. The thrust of those treaties was to give Carthage a monopoly in the Western Mediterranean and to leave Italy as the preserve of the Romans. But the unification of Italy and the expansion of Carthage into Sicily made the former arrangements irrelevant. Put into simple terms, Rome and Carthage lived in peace with each other until their empires came into contact through mutual expansion and at that point, Sicily, the contact ignited into war.

As usual, the event that touched off the war was of minor importance. In 275 BCE, a group of unemployed mercenaries, who called themselves the Marmertines, seized the strategic town of Messana, which controls the Sicilian Straits. Carthage, which already controlled much of Sicily, intervened and inserted a garrison into the town. Rome, which now controlled the town of Rhegium, barely more than two miles across the straights on the toe of Italy, saw this as a threat to their security, or at least a threat to its newly acquired Greek allies in southern Italy. The prosperity of these Greek cities depended on trade with Sicily and the west coast of Italy through the Sicilian Straits, and the Carthaginian policy was to monopolize trade in the areas it controlled. Thus, when the Marmertines appealed to Rome for help in ejecting the Carthaginian garrison, Rome felt bound to respond, even though it had no love for the outlaw Marmertines. This complicated little local dispute resulted in a war that would last twenty years and result in unimaginable bloodshed and loss of resources for both powers.

The Romans rather quickly dislodged the Carthaginians from most of Sicily and acquired the Greek cities there as allies, but when they were unable to push the Carthaginians out of their strongholds on the western end of the island because the enemy controlled the sea around the island, the Romans realized that they would have to build a navy in order to attain victory. The Romans, of course, were a land power and knew nothing about ships or navel warfare. The account of what happened next is embellished by legend, but that cannot detract from their achievement. The Romans took a wrecked Punic vessel as their model and constructed a fleet of 160 ships within sixty days from the cutting of the first timber.[9] Meanwhile, crews were trained in rowing and seamanship on large wooden stages constructed on land. However, the Romans correctly understood that they would never be able to defeat the Carthaginians in a traditional sea battle, which involved ramming the enemy ships in their weak midsection, ripping a hole in it and thereby sinking it. The Carthaginians were masters of this type of warfare. Thus, the invention of the corvus,[10] which consisted of a long board mounted upright on a hinge in the bow of the ship and fitted with an iron spike on the underside of the upper end. When the Roman ship was maneuvered into close quarters with the enemy, the board was dropped onto the enemy's deck, the spike stuck into the deck and a unit of marines then rushed across it and slaughtered the crew of the enemy ship. The beauty of the corvus for the Romans was that, in effect, it converted a sea battle into a land battle and neutralized their inexperience at navel combat.

With their new fleet, the Romans scored an important victory in their very first navel battle off the northern coast of Sicily near Mylae: 50 of the 130 Carthaginian ships were sunk, including the flagship, and many others were captured. But Rome also suffered great losses, not so much from the Carthaginian navy as from their inexperience on the sea. On two occasions during the war Roman fleets were destroyed by storms. In 284 BCE a sudden storm wrecked 364 ships near Camarina in southern Sicily, resulting in the loss of 80,000 men. But the Romans built another fleet and finally prevailed in 241 BCE, when Carthage sued for peace. The terms of the peace treaty required Carthage to evacuate Sicily and the surrounding islands. The allies of both sides were to be free from attack and neither side was to form alliances with the allies of the other. Finally, Carthage was to pay an indemnity of 2,000 talents[11] over ten years. The city itself, however, remained unconquered and its merchant fleets continued to generate wealth.

---

9. This account omits the fact that the Romans almost certainly received valuable aid in this project from their new Greek allies of southern Italy, who had a long tradition of sea faring.

10. *Corvus*, literally "raven," refers to the iron spike on the boarding board, which resembled a raven's beak.

11. The talent was a unit of weight as well as a unit of money used in ancient Greece, Rome, and the Middle East. The term had different meanings when used as a unit of weight or as a monetary unit. There is no satisfactory way to equate the value of an ancient talent to modern monetary systems.

Interlude between Wars (241–218 BCE)

Rome learned some important lessons from the war. First of all it learned how to conduct war at sea. The Romans never became particularly good sailors and eventually began to hire Greek ship captains, but the invention of the corvus is proof of their adaptability to new situations. The Romans also learned how to conduct warfare on a massive scale. The senate learned how to finance large scale war, how to raise massive armies and build fleets, and how to conduct domestic policies in times of war. All of these lessons would be applied in future conflicts. Rome was now a major Mediterranean power, even though it did not seem to realize it yet. But the Romans still had no interest in commerce, although they had acquired allies who did and were now responsible for the protection of their commercial interests.

Carthage, on the other hand, was put in an impossible position by the peace treaty. It must regain its position of dominance in the western Mediterranean or wither away into insignificance. Moreover, Rome continued to be aggressive, occupying Sardinia in 237 BCE and imposing an extra indemnity of 1,200 talents on Carthage. But during this time of uneasy peace, Carthage was preparing its revenge. Hamilcar Barca conquered much of the southern Spanish coast, which gave Carthage access to vast resources, including quantities of gold and silver, as well as an ample supply of mercenaries. According to the Roman accounts, Hamilcar made his nine-year-old son, Hannibal, swear eternal hatred of Rome. The incident was known by the Romans as "the curse of the Barcas." In 221 BCE Hamilcar died and Hannibal assumed supreme command in Spain and immediately began preparing for war against Rome.

Hannibal is recognized by historians, both ancient and modern, as one of history's great generals. His tactical genius is unquestioned. Time and again he won battles against vastly larger armies. For 16 years he was invincible on the battlefield. But in spite of his victories, his strategy was fatally flawed, and this was his eventual undoing. A truly great and successful general must combine tactics and strategy in equal measure—the one is useless without the other. The problem for Hannibal was that he was never able to rise above the limitations of his own culture. He was very familiar with the Carthaginian empire and knew well that since it was based on the conquest and exploitation of the subject peoples, these oppressed peoples were waiting for any opportunity to revolt against their masters. Hannibal, against all the evidence to the contrary, assumed that the Roman empire was similar and he based his strategy on that incorrect assumption. His plan was to invade Italy itself and inflict a defeat on Rome's army, which he believed would induce the Italian allies to desert Rome and support the Carthaginian conquest of Italy. Why Hannibal believed the Italians were interested in exchanging Roman protection and leadership for Carthaginian oppression and enslavement is difficult for us to understand today, but of course we view the situation from the comfortable position of historical hindsight. The generals and statesmen of every age have always viewed their world from the flawed perspective of their own culture. Only the most brilliant generals, like Alexander the Great and Julius Caesar, have been able to rise above the limitations of their own culture, and Hannibal was not one of them.

The Second Punic War (218–201 BCE)

Like the first war, the Second Punic War also began with a relatively insignificant local incident. In 218 BCE a quarrel broke out over the city of Saguntum in Spain, which was located in the Carthaginian sphere of control but was a friend or ally of Rome. When the Carthaginians laid siege to the city, Rome sent Carthage an ultimatum which resulted in a declaration of war.

However, Hannibal's army was already on the march through the Alps toward northern Italy before the declaration was issued, which illustrates that Saguntum was not the actual cause of the war, but only its beginning.

Hannibal completely outfoxed the Romans, who had dispatched an army to Spain to prevent his passage into Italy by blocking the bridges at the Rhone River. But Hannibal slipped northward, crossed the river on pontoons, using bladders filled with air to float his elephants across without any loss. He crossed the Alps in a heroic effort, fighting against the savage mountain tribes. His losses were great. He arrived in Italy with only 26,000 men and about two dozen elephants—most of his elephants died in the Alps.

Hannibal reached northern Italy early in 217 BCE and proclaimed the freedom of the Gauls. Rome dispatched both consuls with a combined army of over 40,000 men, which outnumbered Hannibal's army almost two to one. However, Hannibal lured the Romans into an ambush at the Trebia River and scored an overwhelming victory. Barely 10,000 of the Romans escaped the carnage. The Romans quickly fielded another army and met Hannibal at Lake Trasimene later in the year. This army also was destroyed. Hannibal was proving himself almost invincible, but his strategy was not working as planned. A few Gauls deserted Rome, as they had only recently come under Roman rule, but none of the Italians came over to Hannibal's side. He had completely misjudged Rome's allies. Actually, the Italians were apt to see the Gauls, not the Romans, as their real enemy and the fact that Hannibal had championed their cause did not make him look much like a liberator.

The Senate now chose the course of caution and appointed Fabius Maximus as dictator. He avoided pitched battles and instead adopted a program of "scorched earth," which sought to deny Hannibal's army the supplies it needed to survive. This strategy began to take its toll on the invader, but it hardly aroused the admiration of the common people. In the next elections the winning consuls campaigned on the promise of taking decisive action. So in 216 BCE a Roman army of 70,000 men took the field with the expectation that overwhelming force would carry them to victory. Near Cannae in central Italy, Hannibal again inflicted a decisive defeat on the Romans, killing more than 48,000 men. A terrible setback. When the survivors staggered back to Rome they were met with utter disbelief and panic. Hannibal had now defeated no less than eight consular armies in two years. By all the ordinary rules of warfare, Hannibal had won the war. He had decisively defeated the Romans repeatedly. Almost any other nation would have sued for peace. But he was not fighting an ordinary foe, he was fighting the Romans.

Now the first of the allies, Capua, defected to Hannibal, but the others held firm, in large part due to the conduct of the Romans in this time of crisis. After Cannae, the Roman Senate went into continuous session to demonstrate that its leaders had not abandoned the city and the people settled into a posture of grime determination. Fabius Maximus was again given the dictatorship and again employed the tactics of delay and harassment. He used the much reduced army to protect the allied cities from Hannibal's attack. The Carthaginian army was too small to settle in for a long siege because they had always to fear that Fabius would arrive and disrupt their encampment. Thus, the allies came to believe that Rome could indeed protect them from the invader. Rome was slowly able to rebuild its strength and by 212 BCE it had twenty-five legions in the field. In reality, Hannibal's strategy was bankrupt when Rome did not collapse after Cannae. Although he gained Tarentum in 212 BCE, he lost Capua in 211.

Meanwhile, Rome had not been idle on other fronts. Its army in Spain, commanded by the brothers Gaius and Publius Scipio, met with varying success. First of all, it prevented reinforcements from reaching Hannibal and also gained navel supremacy off the Spanish coast. And when

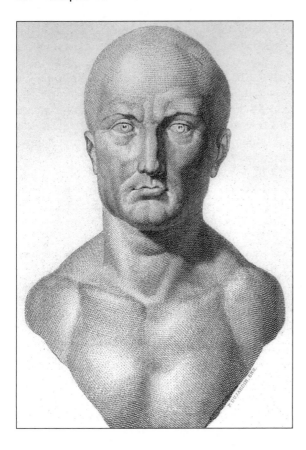

Figure 10.6: Scipio Aficanus.

Hannibal's brother Hasdrubal attempted to lead a reinforcing army into Italy, following the same route through the Alps that Hannibal had used, he was defeated and killed in 215 BCE, only a few days march from Hannibal's army. A few days after his death, Hasdrubal's severed head was thrown into Hannibal's camp. Finally in 206 BCE, the Carthaginians were driven completely out of Spain. Hannibal's days in Italy were now numbered.

When Publius Scipio (later Aficanus, Fig. 10.6) returned from Spain he was elected consul for 205 BCE. He went to Sicily and began to plan an invasion of Africa. The senate assigned him only the two legions made up of the survivors of the disaster at Cannae, but he managed to raise 7,000 more volunteers and the allies supplied a small fleet of thirty ships, which became the nucleus of his African expedition. Scipio had studied the tactics of Hannibal and made adjustments in his army and no longer feared a battle with him. He continued to build and train his force, and in 204 BCE a Roman expeditionary force of about 30,000 men set sail for Africa. Carthage was forced to recall Hannibal to defend the city. The fateful battle took place on the plain of Zama, near Carthage in 202 BCE. This time the outcome was different. After operating for sixteen years in enemy territory without suffering a defeat, Hannibal returned home and lost the only battle that really counts in any war: the last one.

Carthage now was totally defeated and the peace treaty it signed reduced it to a dependant ally of Rome. Carthage surrendered all overseas territory, but was allowed to retain the area around the city itself as well as its autonomy. But it had to pay an indemnity of 10,000 talents in 50 annual payments.

The Romans took no territory in Africa and after signing the peace treaty, the Roman army sailed for home, leaving no garrison anywhere in Africa. One wonders what would have been the fate of Rome if Carthage had won the war.

Aftermath

The outcome of the Second Punic War was a major turning point in ancient history, indeed in the history of Western Civilization. It had profound effects on the political, economic, and religious life of Italy, as well as the entire Mediterranean basin. Thereafter for many generations, no power could endanger or threaten the existence of Rome. Although the Hellenistic monarchies of the east, Egypt, Syria, and Macedonia, still flourished, they would soon, at Rome's very touch, collapse like a house of cards. Nevertheless, Italy suffered horribly in the war. Hannibal spent sixteen years in southern and central Italy. During much of that time, both sides ruthlessly burned fields and orchards, slaughtered livestock, and destroyed villages. As the years went by, the steep hillsides began to lose their topsoil. By the end of the war, southern Italy was permanently impoverished. Even today, 2,000 years later, the scars remain. The Italian government finally began a reclamation program in the 1960s that today is far from complete. The famous British historian Arnold Toynbee has called this devastation "Hannibal's Legacy."[12]

The Effects of Empire

After the two long wars with Carthage, there were a series of wars with Macedonia and the Seleucid Kingdom (Syria) that resulted in Macedonia, Greece, Asia Minor, and most of the Levant coming under Roman domination. And in 133 BCE, the King Attalus III of Pergamum, located in western Asia Minor just across the Bosphorus from Europe, died and bequeathed his kingdom to the Roman people. By doing so he recognized that it was now impossible for any independent state to exist in the Mediterranean basin without Roman protection. Thus, the year, 133 BCE, is a watershed date in the history of the Roman Empire.

Social Changes

These new territories outside Italy did not immediately receive the same status of federation with Rome that the Italians received. For one thing, they were not considered to be Romanized enough for such a status. Instead, the overseas territories were organized into provinces. Governors were appointed by the Senate from the ranks of ex-consuls and ex-praetors. These governors possessed full *imperium,* or executive power, to rule these territories, except they could not violate Roman law. Most of the time the provinces were ruled efficiently and justly, though some suffered occasionally under corrupt governors. The Romans always assumed that the administration of these territories was a responsibility, not a privilege. On the whole, the system worked remarkably well. Rebellions were few, and the Romans did not normally resort to massacres or massive deportations to maintain control. Most importantly, the benefits of peace spread across the Mediterranean basin. The advantages of Roman rule gradually became clear to everyone, and after a few generations the peoples of the provinces slowly came to believe that it was a privilege to belong to the Roman

---

12. Toynbee, Arnold J., *Hannibal's Legacy, the Hannibalic War's Effects on Roman Life* (1965), 2 volumes, Oxford University Press, London.

Empire, and eventually they began to think of themselves as Romans and were even willing to risk their own lives in its defense. In the end, even the Roman ruling class was more and more drawn from the ranks of the formally conquered peoples.

By 133 BCE then, the Roman state had overcome all its adversaries and was now rich and proud and powerful. But its success overseas was not without severe social and political cost at home. Expansion created power blocks and pressure groups within the Roman population which eventually tore apart the very fabric of the Republic. Overseas conquest funneled sudden and unprecedented wealth into Italy and created a whole new class of wealthy citizens known as *equites* (sometimes translated "equestrians" or less appropriately "knights").

The *equites* are usually thought of as the business or middle class of ancient Rome, because socially they ranked below the senatorial class. In fact, they did conduct almost all of the commercial activity of Rome, since the senators were forbidden by law to engage in business—all of their wealth must, in theory at least, be derived from land ownership. But in practice the *equites* were members of the upper class and many of them were members of senatorial or noble families. When the Romans who had made their fortunes overseas in the provinces returned home to Italy, they invested their new capital in land, because land was the most honorable form of wealth, and land ownership allowed them to work their way up into the senatorial class.

Hannibal's Legacy

During Hannibal's invasion of Italy large numbers of small farmers were forced to desert their farms and migrate to the cities for protection. After the war, the rising equites and senatorial classes bought up this vacant land, especially in central and southern Italy, and formed it into large estates, called *latifundia*, which they worked with gangs of slaves. Huge numbers of slaves were imported from overseas as a result of Rome's imperialism, because prisoners of war were the chief source of slavery in the ancient world. Since cheap slave labor naturally drives out more expensive free labor, Rome's success overseas exacerbated the plight of the small farmers and forced increasing numbers of them off the land and into the cities, especially Rome.

These landless, unemployed citizens formed yet another new class, of the *proletarii*. During the period after the Second Punic War, the *proletarii* began to increase dramatically as more and more small farmers were driven off their land and large, teaming slum areas spread through Rome. Since the small farmer was the mainstay of the Republic and the backbone of the army, this produced an alarming and harmful change in Roman society. The small farmers, in fact, formed the manpower pool from which the Roman army was drawn and they had made the Roman expansion possible. Without them all the gains of imperialism would be lost. Yet this class, that had borne the brunt of the fighting that made Rome great, received none of the rewards. This situation of rapid social change and distorting economic displacement among Italy's population put such a severe strain on the body politic of the Roman Republic that it was eventually ripped asunder.

The Gracchi Revolt

By 133 BCE then, the decline of the small farmer class threatened to seriously impede the recruitment of soldiers, and at that time two ambitious young Roman aristocrats, the brothers Tiberius and Gaius Gracchus, attempted to solve this problem—and in the process, to also carve out lucrative political careers for themselves. Historians, especially modern liberal historians, have tended to perceive these two men almost as altruistic saints, who had only the interests of the poor *proletarii* in mind when they injected the disorder and violence into the Roman political process known as the "Gracchi Revolt." But our study of history so far should demonstrate that few individuals or events are totally good or evil. The Gracchi brothers were, of course, politicians, and their motives were complex. They were no more altruistic than their contemporaries, or indeed, the politicians of any age, including our own. They attempted to solve the problem of the disappearing small farmer class, but at the same time they were attempting to exploit an explosive situation for their own political advantage. Their goal was much the same as the goal of all politicians of all ages: power.[13] The other politicians who were already in control of the state did not acquiesce to the agenda of the Gracchi brothers and so they were ultimately unsuccessful.

The short careers of the Gracchi brothers, Tiberius and Gaius, sent shockwaves through the entire structure of the Roman state, which affected the Roman political system for generations. Around this time the people of Rome began to divide into two warring political factions: the conservative *optimates* (the "best"), who based their power in the Senate; and the *populares* ("popular"), who based their power in the Assembly. But this was not a simple contest between the Senate and the assembly, because the politicians of both factions were senators and members of the aristocracy. The Gracchi became the leaders of the *populares* and took up the cause of the *proletarii*, even though they themselves were from one of Rome's most elite families. Their father was a consul and their mother was from the distinguished patrician Scipio family.

Tiberius Gracchus

When Tiberius Gracchus was elected tribune in 133 BCE, Rome faced a grave problem that threatened its continued prosperity. Traditionally, the Roman army was recruited from the land-owning citizens whose property was sufficient to allow them to provide for themselves the weapons and equipment necessary for military campaigning. In spite of successive lowering of the minimum qualification, by 133 BCE there were not enough citizens available for service and it was becoming increasing difficult to recruit legions to protect Rome's far-flung international responsibilities. The problem was not a shortage of land, but an unequal distribution of land. There was a great deal of land throughout Italy owned by the Roman state, known as *ager publicus*, or "public land." This was land that had been confiscated from Italian states due to war or rebellion. Some of it had been used to found Roman or Latin colonies, but vast stretches of *ager publicus* had been rented to wealthy Roman landowners. Over the generations, the families living on this rented *ager publicus* came to think of it as their own property.

---

13. See the famous biographies of the Gracchi brothers by Plutarch in Cleve, Robert, *Early Western Civilization, Source Readings* (2002), Kendall/Hunt Publishing Company, Dubuque, pp. 352–370.

There may be a lesson here, but it is not that politicians are more honest and morally upright in some societies or historical situations than others, but rather that the political structure of a society is the determining factor. Politicians of all ages and situations will always seek power and wealth, that seems to be a basic and fundamental aspect of human nature. However, if the political institutions of a society are so structured that a politician must produce programs and projects which promote justice, equity, and the common good in order to attain that power and success, then that is a just society. But if the society is so structured that the politician attains success and power through serving his own selfish interests or the interests of a special group, then that is an unjust society. During the time of the Gracchi, the Roman Republic seemed to be tottering on the line between a just and an unjust society and the failure of the Gracchi pushed it into the status of an unjust society, which caused it to eventually break up and reform as a monarchy.

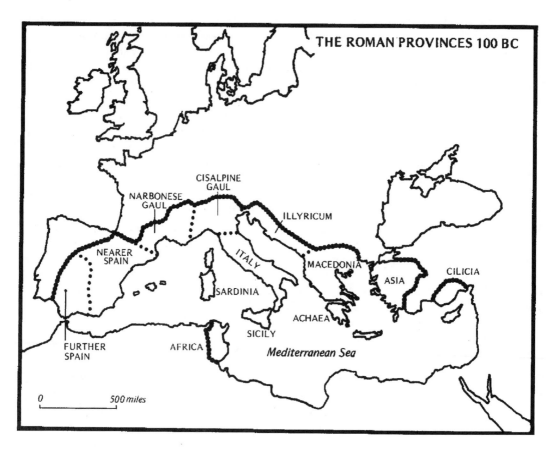

Figure 10.7: Roman Provinces in 100 BCE. (Source: Grant, Michael, History of Rome (1978), Charles Scribneis Sons, New York, page 180.)

The Licino-Sextian laws, passed back in 367 BCE, limited an individual to 500 iugera (about 320 acres) of public land, but in succeeding generations this limit was ignored, and some landowners now occupied huge estates on the *ager publicus*. Tiberius, without consulting the Senate, submitted an agrarian reform bill to the assembly designed to break up these illegal estates and distribute the land into small allotments to the landless Roman citizens. This action was supported by some powerful politicians, including Appius Claudius Pulcher, the senior senator (*princeps senatus*). But Tiberius attempted to placate the large landowners. The bill allowed the present occupiers of the land to retain not only the 500 *iugera* permitted under the old law, but to keep an additional allowance of 250 *iugera* (160 acres) for each of two sons. These owners were now to receive clear title to the land in the amounts allotted, unencumbered by taxes or rents. But all other *ager publicus* was to be repossessed by the state and distributed to the landless citizens.

When the bill was passed by the Assembly, however, it was vetoed by another tribune, Marcus Octavius, who was a political ally of the *optimates*. After a second attempt to pass his bill, which was also vetoed by Octavius, Tiberius persuaded the Assembly to remove Octavius from office, and then the agrarian bill was voted on once again and became law. The problem here was that the impeachment of tribunes was not within the Roman constitution and this further inflamed the opposition against Tiberius.

Nevertheless, the agrarian reform program went forward. The assembly appointed three commissioners, Tiberius, his younger brother, Gaius, and his father-in-law, Appius Claudius Pulcher, to administer the project. Some 75,000 parcels of land were distributed and, when the commission ran out of money, Tiberius convinced the Assembly to divert the taxes from the new province of Asia[14] to the commission's use. This was another infringement on the powers of the Senate and the *optimates* began to view Tiberius's actions as a revolution or even a coup d'état. Tiberius was now in danger of being prosecuted in court or even assassinated and to protect himself he sought to run for a second term as tribune, a step that was contrary to custom and precedent, but not illegal.[15] However, his refusal to abide by traditional political protocol and custom convinced his enemies that he was determined to set himself up as a tyrant. During the Assembly meeting in which the vote was going strongly in Tiberius's favor, a mob of *optimates* and their supporters, led by Scipio Nasica, rushed toward Tiberius and clubbed him and some three hundred of his followers to death. They threw the bodies into the Tiber. This was the first time that the Roman political process resulted in bloodshed. It set a precedent that would degenerate into social strife and civil war until the Republic was reduced to shambles.

Gaius Gracchus

After the violent death of Tiberius Gracchus, his younger brother, Gaius, who was a flamboyant and powerful public speaker, became an even more formidable political force. The land commission, of which Gaius was still a member, continued to administer the agrarian reform law which was the legacy of Tiberius. The land redistribution may have played itself out in relative peace, but soon a fresh grievance arose, this time among the Italian allies, who were becoming restless because of the slowdown in the granting of Roman citizenship and the confiscation of some of their land by commission. M. Fulvius Flaccus, one of the political supporters of Tiberius, introduced the "Italian problem" into Roman politics when he proposed a grant of Roman citizenship as compensation for any disadvantages the Italians should suffer from agrarian reform. For different reasons both the *optimates* and the *populares* opposed this move. The *optimates* feared that the new citizens would overwhelm the Assembly and vote primarily with their opponents, the *populares*. On the other hand, the leaders of the *populares* convinced the people that a large influx of new citizens would dilute the advantages of citizenship, and so the proposal was unpopular with both factions. Although Flaccus gained election to the consulship on his program in 125 BCE, the Senate sent him off as commander in Gaul to protect the Roman allies of Massilia, who had appealed for help against the aggressive Celtic tribes.

But while Flaccus was absent, Gaius Gracchus, having finished his term of office as quaestor in Sardinia, returned to Rome to take the place of his brother. He was elected to the tribunate in 123 BCE. Flaccus now also returned in triumph from his Gallic victories. The program initiated by the younger Gracchus was wider in scope than that of his brother and designed to appeal to wider interests, including the equites. He carried the "Sempronian Laws" through the Assembly, which reaffirmed his brother's land laws and created new Roman colonies overseas. One of these new colonies was to be on the old site of the destroyed city of Carthage.

---

14. Asia was the new province formed from the kingdom of Pergamum which was bequeathed to the Roman people by King Attalus III in 133 BCE.

15. Under Roman law a magistrate, while in office, could not be prosecuted in court. The assembly was sovereign and could reelect Tiberius in spite of law or custom, as they had elected his grandfather, Scipio Africanus, to the supreme command during the Second Punic war.

Reminiscent of modern political maneuvers, Gaius now enacted legislation to repay various special interests for their support. The first pay off was to the urban unemployed, in the form of grain provided to them at half price. This soon became the basis of Rome's ancient welfare program, the outright distribution of free grain to poor citizens, and it would be grossly abused by later generations. The next measure struck at the heart of the Senate's power. The equestrian class was given the exclusive right to sit on the juries of extortion courts, created primarily to hear cases of corruption against provincial governors. This was an important concession to the equestrians because the ancient Roman government had no civil service. Taxes in the provinces, for example, were collected by private companies who bid on government contracts. This is often called tax farming. The company (or individual) who bid the highest was awarded the contract and it paid the government the amount it had bid. The company's agents (called *publicani*, or publicans) then collected the taxes, and all the money they could collect above what had been paid for the contract was their profit. The new exclusive privilege of the equestrians to serve on the extortion court juries assured them that the provincial governors would not interfere in their tax collections (no matter how oppressive it became) since the governors could be brought into court on trumped-up charges by the equestrians when they returned home. Gaius also forced through huge increased expenditure on public works, such as roads and harbors, which once more mainly benefited the equestrian business community.

In 122 BCE Gaius Gracchus was re-elected tribune. Moreover, Flaccus was also elected tribune, granting the two political allies almost absolute power over Rome. However, their bill granting citizenship to the Italian allies failed to pass the assembly. When Gaius Gracchus stood for yet another term as tribune in 121 BCE, the optimates in the Senate decided they had to take action against what they now considered to be a full fledged tyranny. A group of senators put forward their own candidate, M. Livius Drusus, with an entirely false program which was by its very nature simply designed to be yet more lavish than anything Gracchus proposed.

This assault on Gaius Gracchus's standing as the champion of the people, together with the loss of popularity resulting from the failed proposal to extend Roman citizenship and wild rumors and superstitions of curses circulating after a visit to Carthage by Gaius, led to his losing the vote for his third term in office. Gaius's supporters, led by Flaccus, held an angry mass demonstration on the Aventine Hill, but some of them made the fatal mistake of carrying weapons. The Senate issued a *senatus consultum ultimum*, authorizing the consul Lucius Opimius to restore order. The bearing of weapons by some of Gracchus's supporters was all the excuse Opimius needed. And there was little doubt that Opimius sought to bring about the end of Gaius Gracchus, for he was in fact the most prominent and most bitter rival of Gracchus and Flaccus. What followed was in effect a massacre. Gaius, realizing the situation hopeless, ordered his personal slave to stab him to death. Following the massacre, another 3,000 of Gracchus's supporters are believed to have been arrested, taken to jail, and strangled.

Gaius Marius: The Army Politicized

The brief emergence and demise of the Gracchi brothers on the scene of Roman politics sent shockwaves through the entire structure of the Roman state, and their effects would be felt for generations. Rome was now irrevocably divided into two factions: the *optimates* and the *populares*. Now there seemed no alternative to those on either side of the divide but to battle it out to the end, regardless of the bloodshed and the resulting destruction of the republican institutions.

The Jugurthine War

In 118 BCE Micipsa, the king of Numidia, died, leaving the throne to his two young sons, Hiempsal and Adherbal, jointly with a much older nephew, Jugurtha, who was an experienced soldier. Jugurtha was obviously supposed to act as the guardian of the two young brothers, but such arrangements, although they seem wise in theory, rarely work out in practice. Jugurtha arranged the assassination of Hiempsal, whereupon Adherbal fled for his life to Rome and appealed to the Senate. Adhering to its usual practice of compromise when arbitrating between Rome's allies, the Senate decided to send a commission to Numidia to divide the kingdom between the two claimants. Jugurtha appeared to bribe the commission's leader, Opimius, who returned to Rome a richer man, after awarding the greater and wealthier part of Numidia to Jugurtha. But this was not enough for the ambitious Jugurtha, who then marched into the territory of Adherbal and murdered him too. This was an outrage and an insult to Rome. The Senate dispatched the consul L Calpurnius Bestia with an army to Numidia to deal with the usurper, but the campaign was ineffective from the start, because Jugurtha resorted to guerrilla-style warfare, and the Roman heavy infantry could not be brought to bear effectively. Eventually, the Assembly summoned Jugurtha to Rome to give evidence against any senators who were alleged to have accepted bribes from him. For this he was given "safe-conduct," meaning he would not be charged or in any way harmed himself. But, once Jugurtha had arrived in Rome, these legal proceedings were vetoed by a tribune in the service of the senate who sought to avoid a political scandal. However, Jugurtha, stupidly and arrogantly, had another of his cousins murdered in Rome. This was too much, and he was ordered to depart.[16] A commission of inquiry was held, which revealed such widespread scandals of bribery and corruption that three ex-consuls, one being Opimius, retired into exile.

In 109 BCE, Quintus Metellus, known for being virtually incorruptible, was sent out to Africa to take command of the campaign against Jugurtha. Metellus was a good soldier, but Jugurtha managed to hold out against him. Serving as a legate (a junior field officer) in Metellus's army was a very ambitious young man named Gaius Marius (Fig. 10.8), who was a non-noble and felt that he was being ignored and held back from advancement by the proud old patrician, Metellus. So Marius took leave, returned to Rome and stood for the consulship, claiming that if the command were given to him the war would be ended at once. With *populares* support he won the consulship and, ignoring the prerogatives of the Senate, a special law was passed through the Assembly transferring the command in Africa to him. In fact, by the time he returned to Africa as consul to supersede Metellus, it appeared that Jugurtha was already beaten and Metellus went home bitterly disappointed at having had his victory snatched from him. But Marius could not catch Jugurtha because he fled to neighboring Mauretania and sought asylum from king Bocchus. Finally it was the diplomatic skill of the quaestor Lucius Cornelius Sulla that induced Bocchus to betray Jugurtha to the Romans and to a miserable death at Rome. But the victory was credited to Marius and this strengthened the resolve of the *populares* in the Assembly to take control of foreign affairs away from the Senate, and they re-elected Marius to a second consulship in 104 BCE even before he returned to Rome.[17]

---

16. Jugurtha is said to have muttered contemptuously as he left, "A city for sale!"

17. Under Roman law a candidate was required to be present in Rome in order to be elected to office. Thus, Marius's absence was a violation of the law.

Reform of the Army

The impetus for the Assembly's action was a serious crisis now facing Rome, a crisis far more threatening than the war in Africa. Two German tribes, Teutones and the Cimbri, had defeated the consul Silanus in 109 BCE and in 107 BCE another consul, Cassius, lost his army and his life. In 105 BCE the forces of the proconsul Caepio and the consul Mallius were annihilated by the Cimbri at the Battle of Arausio. Ancient sources estimate the losses in the battles amounted to 80,000 or even 100,000 men. Then for no apparent reason there was a temporary pause in the German advance. Since the senate seemed incapable of dealing with this menace, the Assembly turned to Marius and elected him consul year after year. And Marius met the challenge with energy and originality: he reorganized the Roman Army.

Gracchi reforms failed to stem the vicious cycle of economic derangement described above as "Hannibal's legacy." Small farms continued to fall into disuse and ruin because their occupants were constantly away at war. As Roman conquests spread through the Mediterranean basin, even more men were required, and wealth and cheap grain poured into Rome. Most of the wealth, however, flowed into the hands of equites and senators, who carved out vast estates, known as *latifundia*, for vines, olives, and sheep farming, all managed by slave labor. The dispossessed rural poor became the urban poor, ineligible for military service because they were no longer property holders. Not only was there a growing shortage of recruits, but the soldiers had nothing to return to at the end of their service.

A solution to this problem was finally devised by Gaius Marius. Rather than conscripting soldiers from Roman landowners, he recruited volunteers from the urban poor and thus transformed the Roman army from a conscript citizen militia into volunteer professional army. In order to induce these *proletarii* to enlist, Marius promised the soldiers allotments of farmland and bonuses after completing their term of service. But whereas in the old army, the citizens had reported for service already trained, bearing their own arms and ready to be formed into legions, the recruits for this new professional army reported for duty with nothing except their bodies. The government had to train them and provide arms for them, as well as pay them.

Figure 10.8: Gaius Marius.

Marius's reform of the army came only just in time. In 103 BCE the Germans were preparing to invade Italy by crossing the Alps in two different places, because their combined army was too large to live off the land if they marched together. The Teutones crossed the mountains in the West, the Cimbri did so in the East. In 102 BCE Marius, consul for the fourth time, annihilated the Teutones at Aquae Sextiae beyond the Alps, while his colleague, Quintus Lutatius Catulus stood guard behind him. Next in 101 BCE the Cimbri poured through the eastern mountain passes into the Po River plain and were, in their turn, annihilated by the combined forces of Marius and Catulus at Campi Raudii. Marius reaped the benefit of his joint victory with Catulus, by being elected to his sixth consulship.

The *optimates*, however, had become jealous of Marius's immense popularity and power, and the Senate opposed Marius's land bill as a way to undercut his popularity with the soldiers. It was a selfish and short-sighted policy, especially because the optimates were not opposed to land grants to the veterans who had saved the state from destruction, but were only using the soldiers as political pawns. We often see this same kind of political rivalry at work in our own society: each party automatically opposing the initiatives of the other as a method of undercutting the other's popularity with the voters. Taken to the extreme, it undermines even the most fundamental institutions of the state. After some hesitation, Marius believed that he had no choice, so he brought his army into the Assembly and with the soldiers standing around leaning on their spears, the land bill was voted into law without the Senate's approval. For the first time the army was used as a political instrument—and once this professional army had been publicized it would be used by one general after another until the republic was torn asunder.

The Social War (90–88 BCE)

During this period, the Roman policy of gradually granting citizenship to the Italian allies had slowed down, indeed had almost halted because it, like the veterans benefits, had become a hostage of the struggle between the two political factions. To make matters worse, Roman magistrates and even ordinary Roman citizens had taken to behaving like arrogant conquers toward the allies. By 91 BCE, the pressure from the Italians for redress of their grievances became so explosive that Marcus Livius Drusus the Younger—the son of the Livius Drusus who had helped bring down the Gracchi—used the office of tribune to propose granting citizenship to all allies. However, before he was able to bring the law to a vote he was murdered by an unknown assassin.

With this, the Italians finally lost all hope of achieving their rights and the freedom of citizenship through peaceful means, and many, though not all, of the allies, or socii, revolted against Rome. The allies did not plan the uprising, it was a spontaneous outburst of frustration, but they hastily formed a confederation with its capital at Corfinium—renamed Italia—about 75 miles east of Rome and raised an army of 100,000 men, many of them seasoned veterans of Roman campaigns. The first months of the war went badly for the Romans as they suffered one defeat after another. When Marius came out of retirement and volunteered for service, the senate merely assigned him as a legate to an incompetent commander.

Actually, the allies had a strong party of sympathizers in the Senate, and in 89 BCE it managed to pass a *lex Julia*, or Julian Law, which granted Roman citizenship to all allies who had remained loyal to Rome. At the same time the Romans put two strong armies in the field, one under the command of Lucius Cornelius Sulla and another under Pompeius Strabo, and the rebellious allies began to be defeated on the battlefield. Finally, the senate brought an end to the fighting with *lex Plautia-Papiria*, which granted citizenship to all who laid down their arms within sixty days. Most allies simply put down their arms and claimed citizenship, and by the beginning of 88 BC the Social War was at an end.

Lucius Cornelius Sulla

In 88 BCE the activities of king Mithridates of Pontus called for urgent action. He had invaded the province of Asia and massacred 80,000 Romans, mostly civilians, and brought pressure against all Roman interests in the East. Sulla (Fig. 10.9), fresh from his success in the Social War, was elected consul and the senate appointed him to the command of the force preparing to embark against Mithridates, but rivalry and infighting between the optimates and the *populares* continued to tear at the institutions of the republic. The tribune Sulpicius Rufus, a political ally of Marius, passed a bill through the assembly transferring the command to Marius—a very foolish act—and Sulla was in no mood to submit to such an order. At the head of six Roman legions, veterans of the Social War, Sulla marched on Rome and seized the city. Sulpicius was killed and Marius, now 70 years old, fled to Africa, pursued by Sulla's agents. Sulla installed his associates in power before he departed in 87 BCE with his forces to fight Mithridates in the east.

Since Rome did not maintain a large occupying force in the East, Mithridates had scored quite spectacular gains because he was virtually unopposed. His forces had overrun Asia Minor, sacked Delos, and invaded the Greek mainland. When Sulla arrived on the scene he could do little more than restore the status quo and punish the cities that had deserted Rome.

Figure 10.9: Lucius Cornelius Sulla.

Meanwhile, back in Rome, Lucius Cornelius Cinna was elected consul for the year 87 BCE with populares support. When he tried to rescind the legislation of Sulla, his colleague in the consulship, Gnaeus Octavius, an optimate and supporter of Sulla, drove him out of Rome and illegally deposed him. However, Cinna collected a force and, as Sulla had done the year before, marched on Rome and occupied it. Marius returned from exile and joined him, though he appeared more intent on revenge than on anything else. In a reign of terror, Marius wreaked revenge on his enemies. At the head of a body of armed slaves he massacred everyone who had ever offended him, including some leading senators, before Cinna finally put a stop to the butchery. The Romans, who had settled their political differences for four centuries without bloodshed, had now descended to the level of murdering each other in the streets with gangs of slaves. Marius (for the seventh time) and Cinna (for the second time) were elected consuls for the year 86 BCE, but Marius died soon afterward. Cinna remained the master and consul of Rome until he was killed in a mutiny in 84 BCE. The power then fell to Gnaeus Carbo, an ally of Cinna.

Out in the East, in 85 BCE, Sulla opened negotiations with Mithridates and arranged a treaty by which the king surrendered his conquests to Rome and retreated behind the borders he had held before the war. Therefore, in 84 BCE, his campaigns a success, Sulla could start making his way back to Rome, but Mithridates, though reigned in, was not beaten and would haunt Rome for some time to come.

When Sulla arrived back in Italy in the spring of 83 BCE the stage was set for civil war. His army numbered between thirty and forty thousand veterans, and he was joined by two young nobles, Gnaeus Pompey and Marcus Crassus, who brought with them detachments of their own. However, Carbo commanded a slightly larger force and both sides were cautious and continued to recruit soldiers. The final showdown did not occur until August of 82 BCE outside Rome at the Battle of the Colline Gate. The fighting, which cost some fifty thousand Romans their lives, lasted all day and throughout the night, before Sulla emerged victorious. Civil conflicts always seem to be the bloodiest battles of all.

Sulla was now the master of Rome, but he faced two immediate problems: first, to put an end to the rule of the *populares* and, second, to provide for his own veterans and political supporters. He shrewdly conceived how the solution to these two problems could compliment each other. He would kill or exile his opponents, confiscate their lands and property and use it to reward his followers. Sulla applied this simple formula on a gigantic scale. He issued a series of proscription lists and a general reign of terror ensued in which of some forty senators and at least 1,600 wealthy equestrians were murdered. The lives of the people of Rome were entirely in Sulla's hands. He could have them killed or he could spare them. One that he chose to spare, probably on a mere whim, was a young patrician, whose father's sister had been the wife of Marius, and who himself was the husband of Cinna's daughter—Gaius Julius Caesar.

After he destroyed his enemies, Sulla turned to his long-term objective, the reform of the constitution in order to establish the power of the aristocratic oligarchy on a lasting and unchangeable basis. For this purpose he revived the obsolete office of dictator, but this new dictatorship had little in common with the old office, which was appointed only to meet an external danger and had a maximum duration of only six months. The office assumed by Sulla in 82 BCE could be terminated only by his death or abdication. Under his constitutional reforms, all the power of the state would henceforth lay in the hands of the Senate. The power of the tribunes and the Assembly was reduced to insignificance. Persons elected to the tribunate were barred from ever holding another office, and the Assembly was deprived of the power of initiating any legislation. The senatorial control of the courts was restored at the expense of the equestrians. Repeated consulships, like those of Marius and Cinna, were henceforth unlawful. He set up a rigid order of age and qualifications for election to the various magistracies. First a politician must hold the quaestorship, then the praetorship and finally the consulship, with a minimum of at least two years between each office. The minimum age qualifications were 30 years for the quaestorship, 40 for the praetorship, and 43 for the consulship.

Then unexpectedly in 79 BCE Sulla appeared before the people and ceremoniously laid down his dictatorship, dismissed his lectors and bodyguard, and returned to his home as a private citizen. He settled on his country estate in Campania, where he spent his time in leisure, writing his autobiography, which unfortunately does not survive, and raising cabbages (well, Churchill liked to lay bricks for relaxation!). The very next year, in 78 BCE, Sulla died suddenly at the age of 60, although he had seemingly been in excellent health.

Although the Roman Republic would technically last for another fifty years, Sulla pretty much sealed its demise. He stood as an example to future generals that is was possible to take Rome by force and rule it, if only one was strong and ruthlessness enough to do what ever deeds were required.

Pompey, Crassus, and Cicero

During the two decades following the death of Sulla, four men dominated the political life of ancient Rome: Gnaeus Pompeius Magnus (106–47 BCE), known to history as Pompey the Great (Fig. 10.10); Marcus Licinius Crassus (c. 112–53 BCE), the richest man in Rome; Marcus Tullius Cicero (106–43 BCE), generally recognized as the greatest orator in the entire history of Rome (Fig. 10.11); and Gaius Julius Caesar (102–44 BCE), the most famous Roman of all (Fig. 10.12). These four men played the leading roles in the tragic drama of the final demise of the Roman Republic. All of them met violent deaths within ten years of each other.

Pompey, "the Great"

Pompey moves across the pages of history as a strangely familiar image to the modern reader. He was a man of uneven ability, but he understood just as clearly and keenly as modern politicians do that talent and accomplishment are not so important to political success as image—and Pompey was a master at projecting the correct image, regardless of what the actual situation might be. In this sense he was the most "modern" of all Roman politicians.

Pompey rose to prominence as the supporter of Sulla. During the Social War, the young 17-year old Pompey served as an officer in the army of his father, Pompey Strabo. When his father died suddenly in 89 BCE, he assumed control of the vast family estates and clientage. Only six years later Sulla returned from the East with his battle-hardened veterans to face a hostile regime in Rome. Pompey raised three legions from his father's veterans and presented himself to the general, not so much as an ally but as a partner. Sulla found the 23-year Pompey useful and dispatched him to Sicily to recover the island from forces loyal to the old regime. Then he moved on to Africa. Although he faced only the rag-tag remnants of the old units of Marius, he proclaimed his activity as an unprecedented string of great victories and at some point added *Magnus*, "the Great," to his name. Although many of his contemporaries laughed behind his back, the public accepted the image at face value and began to idolize the young Pompey.

After the death of Sulla, Pompey refused to disband his legions and demanded that the Senate grant him proconsular *imperium* and send him to Spain to fight against the brilliant Marian general Sertorius, even though he was still legally too young to hold even the most junior magistracy, let alone the consulship. Sertorius had retreated to Spain when Sulla returned to Italy and had built up a substantial following there, partially by rallying the Spanish tribes to join him as their leader. He proved to be more than a match for the generals sent against him by the Senate. Pompey fared no better than his predecessors, indeed at one point he was saved from a humiliating defeat only by the timely arrival of another army commanded by Metellus Pius. It is significant that the war was finally won only because rivals in his own camp murdered Sertorius, not because either Pompey or Metellus was able to achieve a victory on the battlefield. But nevertheless, Pompey's reputation grew by leaps and bounds.

Spartacus

Meanwhile, in Italy there had been a dangerous slave revolt led by the Thracian gladiator Spartacus.[18] Eventually the slave army numbered 70,000. For months the slave army plundered and pillaged southern Italy and repeatedly defeated Roman forces sent against it. In desperation the Senate turned to the praetor Marcus Crassus, who raised an army of six legions and shattered the slave army in 71 BCE. It is believed that Spartacus died in the battle, but his body was never found. The historian Appian reports that 6,000 slaves were captured and crucified along the Appian Way from Capua to Rome as an example to other slaves who might think of rebellion. As many as 5,000 slaves escaped and fled northward, but there they ran into Pompey's army marching back from Spain. True to form, Pompey mopped up the miserable remnants of the once proud slave army and claimed credit for putting down the slave revolt, although in reality the credit was due to Crassus.

Marcus Crassus

Crassus used his enormous wealth to gain power and influence in Roman politics. He acquired his enormous wealth through the traffic in slaves, the working of silver mines, and the judicious purchase of real estate, especially the estates of those on Sulla's proscription lists.

---

18. Most aptly played by Kirk Douglas in the 1960 film of the same name. Directed by Stanley Kubrick, and with a cast of over 10,000, it was the most expensive film ever made up to that time. It was a great success, turning a profit in the first year of its release and winning the Golden Globe Award for the Best Picture. The film was re-released in 1967 and 1991 to great acclaim. But as usual with Hollywood productions, the movie was historically inaccurate and was employed more as a vehicle for modern liberal ideology and the self-righteous demeaning of ancient Roman society than a serious attempt to present an important historical event. See Gruen, Erich, *The Last Generation of the Roman Republic* (1974), University of California Press, p. 20.

It was not the governing class alone that would react in horror to the prospect of a slave insurrection. Whatever the grievances of men disenfranchised and dispossessed by Sulla, they would have found unthinkable any common enterprise with Thracian or Gallic slaves. It causes no surprise that Marxist historians and writers have idealized Spartacus as a champion of the masses and leader of the one genuine social revolution in Roman history. That, however, is excessive. Spartacus and his companions sought to break the bonds of their own grievous oppression. There is no sign that they were motivated by ideological considerations to overturn the social structure. The sources make clear that Spartacus endeavored to bring his forces out of Italy toward freedom rather than to reform or reverse Roman society. The achievements of Spartacus are no less formidable for that. The courage, tenacity, and ability of the Thracian gladiator who held Roman forces at bay for some two years and built a handful of followers into an assemblage of over 70,000 men can only inspire admiration.

Figure 10.10: Gnaeus Pompey "the Great."

In 71 BCE, as soon as the slave revolt was put down, both victorious generals marched to Rome and camped their armies outside the gates. Both expected military honors, both wanted the consulship for 70 BCE. The Senate tried to play the two men—who were indeed natural rivals—off against each other. Pompey was permitted to celebrate a triumph for his "victory" in Spain, while Crassus was only allowed an ovation,[19] since his victory was only over a slave revolt. Again image proved more important than substance. But instead of playing the senate's game, which could have led to a civil war, the two generals formed a temporary political alliance and demanded that they both stand for the consulship. Although this was unconstitutional on the face of it,[20] since two large armies were camped around Rome the Senate considered it wise to make an exception in this case. Pompey and Crassus were elected to the consulship for the year 70 BCE. During their

---

19. A triumph was a solemn procession of a victorious commander with his army and spoils into Rome. He entered the city in a chariot drawn by four white horses, dressed in purple, a golden wreath on his head. The ovation was a much less prestigious affair: the commander rode on horseback or went on foot and wore a wreath of myrtle instead of laurel.

20. Neither man was qualified to stand for the consulship in 71 BCE under the Sullan constitutional reforms, which required at least a two-year hiatus between the praetorship and the consulship and a minimum age of 45 for the consulship. Crassus had been praetor the year before and Pompey had never held any elective office and was only 34 years old.

joint consulship they repealed the last of the Sullan constitutional reforms. This was a severe defeat for the optimates, because it meant that the *populares* could again push their programs through the assembly against senatorial opposition. At the end of their consulship, both Pompey and Crassus disbanded their armies and returned to private life. For the time being, the Roman political scene was quiet and peaceful.

Mithridates and the Pirates

Unfortunately, out in the East, Mithridates IV, the king of Pontus, was again on the rampage. In fact, Mithridates managed to challenge the power of Rome for twenty-five years (88–63 BCE) and tested the skills of three of Rome's most famous generals: Sulla, Lucullus, and Pompey.[21] To make matters worse, during Rome's preoccupation with the slave revolt and other internal problems, piracy had become the scourge of the Mediterranean. Indeed, ship owners refused to put to sea and the cities of Italy, particularly Rome, were on the verge of famine. The optimates in the senate had dispatched several of their own members[22] to bring the pirates under control, but they had made little progress. So in 67 BCE, one of the tribunes, taking advantage of the tribunate's restored powers, carried a bill through the assembly awarding Pompey a special command over all the waters of the Mediterranean, with almost unlimited forces, for the purpose of clearing the sea of piracy.

Finally, Pompey managed an accomplishment worthy of his image. He spread the Roman fleet systematically across the Mediterranean and swept the sea clean from the Pillars of Hercules (Straights of Gibraltar) to the eastern shores. The pirates were destroyed. Amazingly, even though the special command was for three years, he accomplished all of this in just three months. While Pompey was not an original or resourceful general, not even a particularly adroit politician (in spite of his PR genius), he did possess extraordinary organizational and administrative skills.

---

21. It is said that to guard himself from being poisoned by his enemies, he consumed small doses of various kinds of poisons for many years in order to build up an immunity to them. This story prompted the English poet A. E. Houseman to compose the following lines (from Epilogue, The Shropshire Lad):

There was a king who reigned in the East:
There, when kings will sit and feast,
They get their fill before they think
With poisoned meat and poisoned drink.
He gathered all that springs to birth
From the many-venomed earth;
First a little, thence to more,
He sampled all their killing store;
And easy, smiling, seasoned sound,
Sat the king when healths went round.
They put arsenic in his meat
And stared aghast to watch him eat;
They poured strychnine in his cup
And shook to see him drink it up:
They shook, they stared as white's their shirt:
Them it was their poison hurt.
—I tell the tale I heard told. Mithridates, he died old.

22. Including Marcus Antonius, the father of famous Mark Antony, in 74 BCE, but his attempts ended in dismal failure. In 69 BCE Quintus Metellus, a member of one of the most distinguished patrician families, was assigned the same task, but again matters did not improve and his mission was cut short by appointment of Pompey in 67 BCE.

Of course the triumph over the pirates made Pompey the unquestioned darling of the people, although many optimates became even more deeply suspicious of his intentions. So now the assembly gave him another unprecedented command: unlimited and absolute authority over the entire East. His wildest dreams had come true! Between 65 and 62 BCE, Pompey marched and strutted around the East like a latter-day Alexander the Great, conquering, annexing, and organizing. Asia Minor was brought firmly into the empire. He not only destroyed Mithridates,[23] but defeated King Tigranes of Armenia, conquered Antiochus XIII of Syria and captured Jerusalem. He annexed Syria as a Roman province and set up Judea as a client state.[24] He imposed complex and far-reaching settlements on the client kings, protectorate states, and new eastern provinces, which established a stable and peaceful eastern frontier for Rome in the East that largely was unchanged until the fall of Rome. The arrangements were so just and fair that the peoples of the East were transformed from enemies into friends of Rome. At the same time, the amount of tribute and booty brought back to Rome by Pompey was almost incalculable: at least 20,000 talents of gold and silver and an increase in the annual tax revenue from 50 million to 85 million drachmas.

Marcus Tullius Cicero

During Pompey's absence from Rome for over five years, a new star appeared on the political stage. The figure of Cicero represents the ultimate politician caught in an impossible historical position. More writings of Cicero survive that of any other ancient author. His speeches became the primary teaching sources for the Middle Ages and the Renaissance. His personal letters reveal the whole man, "warts and all." He sought to restore consensus and reason in an age gone mad. For all of his brilliance he seems never to have realized that his beloved republic was already old, decrepit, and senile, and would have to be replaced by a new order. But to his everlasting credit he did see clearly that violence in politics does not solve but only exacerbates problems:

> I know that your heart was always as heavy as mine. Not only did we foresee the destruction of one of the two armies and its leader, a vast disaster, but we realized that victory in civil war is the worst of all calamities. I dreaded the prospect, even if victory should fall to those we had joined. . . we live, it may be said, in a state that has been turned upside down.[25]

Cicero came from the town of Arpinum, about seventy miles east of Rome. He was a "new man," not a member of the exclusive noble class, and this was the salient fact of his life. His father moved to Rome when he was ten and he received a good education. As a teenager he served briefly

---

23. Actually Mithridates was already defeated by the previous commander in the East, Lucullus, and faced with Pompey's overwhelming forces, committed suicide. After attempting unsuccessfully to poison himself, he had one of his servants dispatch him with a sword. Again, of course, Pompey received all the credit.

24. When Pompey arrived in Judea he found the Jews engaged in a struggle between the two major religious factions led by the two brothers Hyrcanus, supported by the Pharisees, and Aristobulus, the leader of the Sadducees. Both sought Pompey's favor. Strictly on the basis of Roman interests, Pompey sided with Hyrcanus and unwittingly contributed to the ultimate triumph of the Pharisees over the Sadducees. Ironically, Pompey knew or cared nothing about Jewish theology. The Sadducees were mainly a conservative aristocratic and priestly caste who accepted the Torah (the first five books of the Bible) literally as the Written Law. The Pharisees also accepted the Written Law but included a mass of interpretations and oral traditions handed down by the scribes. The Pharisees later produced the great commentaries on the law known as the Mishna and the Talmud. Thus, Pompey, driven purely by political motive, may have set the future course of Judaism.

25. Cicero, Letter to Varro, 46 BCE.

Figure 10.11: Marcus Tullius Cicero.

on the staff of Pompeius Strabo during the Social War and became acquainted with his son, Gnaeus Pompey, with whom he maintained a friendship until their deaths. Cicero began his career as a lawyer in 80 BCE, successfully defending a man charged with murder by one of Sulla's associates. From 79 to 76 BCE he traveled in Greece and Asia Minor, studying Greek philosophy and oratory. Upon returning to Rome he began the *cursus honorum*, achieving each successive office at the minimum allowable age, including the consulship in 63 BCE, an incredible accomplishment for a new man.

However, the man that Cicero defeated in the consular elections was a proud patrician named Lucius Sergius Catilina, known to history as Catiline. Defeat at the polls by an upstart new man was something Catiline's dignity simply could not bear and he planned a conspiracy to seize the government as the leader of a group of bankrupt veterans, dissolute aristocrats, and dispossessed citizens. Cicero discovered the plot and delivered a speech in the Senate so devastating to Catiline that he left Rome to join his forces in the north. Shortly afterward some Gallic envoys, in Rome on other business, were approached by the agents of Catiline and invited to join the conspiracy but instead reported the incident to Cicero. This was the smoking gun he needed and the Senate authorized him to take action. Cicero arrested the conspirators, several of them prominent Romans, and put them to death without a trial, a serious violation of the constitution. However, the plot against the government was put down and Cicero was proclaimed the savior of the state.

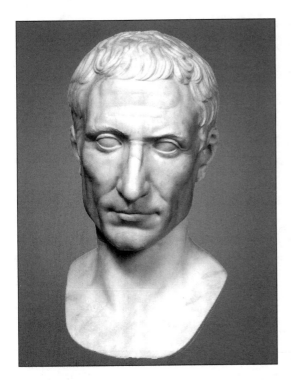

Figure 10.12: Gaius Julius Caesar.

Gaius Julius Caesar

Caesar was descended from an impoverished patrician family, but his immediate forebears had fallen from prominence, and no Caesars had graced the consul list for several generations. His father died when Caesar was only 15, having only reached the praetorship, and he was raised by his mother. From the beginning he associated himself with the *populares*, perhaps influenced by the fact that—unusual even for an impoverished patrician family—he grew up in *Subura,* an area of Rome known for its poor multicultural neighborhoods and by family connections to Gaius Marius.[26] It may also be significant that from the time of the Gracchi, some thirty years before his birth, Rome had slipped step-by-step into riot and chaos, and the young Caesar never knew a time when his world was stable or safe.[27]

---

26. His father's sister, Julia, married Gaius Marius.

27. In what could almost pass as a description of the gang infested neighborhoods of our 21st Century cities, the 2nd Century CE historian, Appian, *The Civil Wars,* 1.2–3, describes life in the Rome in which Caesar spent his childhood:

Repeatedly the factions came into open conflict, often carrying daggers; and from time to time in the temples, or the assemblies, or the forum, some tribune, or praetor, or consul, or candidate for those offices, or some person otherwise distinguished, would be slain. Unseemly violence prevailed almost constantly, together with the shameful contempt for law and justice. As the evil gained in magnitude open insurrections against the government and large warlike expeditions against their country were undertaken by exiles, or criminals, or persons contending against each other for some office or military command. There arose chiefs of factions quite frequently, aspiring to supreme power, some of them refusing to disband the troops entrusted to them by the people, others even hiring forces against each other on their own account, without public authority. Whenever either side first got possession of the city, the opposition party made war nominally against their own adversaries, but actually against their country. They assailed it like an enemy's capital, and ruthless and indiscriminate massacres of citizens were perpetrated. Some were proscribed, others banished, property was confiscated, and, prisoners were even subjected to excruciating tortures.

Indeed Caesar came dangerously close to not achieving adulthood. In 84 BCE he married Cornelia, the daughter of Cinna, Sulla's bitter enemy. When the dictator ordered Caesar to divorce his wife, he refused and it was only with great difficulty that his friends managed to keep his name off the proscription list. In sparing his life, Sulla is said to have warned that the world would later find him as dangerous as Gaius Marius. Prudently, Caesar embarked on an extended trip in Greece and Asia to round off his education and did not return until after Sulla's death in 78 BCE. These horrors must have permanently effected his conception of the Roman state.

He returned to Rome in his twenties and began his career as a lawyer, gaining fame by tenacious though unsuccessful prosecution of the ex-consul Cornelius Dolabella for extortion during his governorship of Macedonia. In 75 BCE he then left Rome again on a second journey to the East, this time Rhodes, to study rhetoric. It was during this trip that he was captured by pirates. The story is famous, as it reveals the character of Caesar. He was held captive for 40 days. While waiting for his ransom to arrive, his biographer Suetonius says "he often smilingly sworn, while still in their power, that he would soon capture and crucify them; and this is exactly what he did."

Back in Rome, Caesar began his military career by successfully standing for the quaestorship for 69 BCE, which earned him admission to the Senate. There he gained political capital by supporting Pompey's command against the pirates and then against Mithridates in the East. In 65 BCE he was elected aedile. While serving in that office, which includes the responsibility of providing public entertainment, he borrowed heavily from Crassus and provided such spectacular and lavish games that he became wildly popular with the people. During the senatorial debate on the Catiline affair, Caesar opposed Cicero and almost persuaded the Senate towards the more moderate punishment of exile, instead of execution, which was violation of Roman law.[28] This was the beginning of his open opposition to the optimates, and Cicero later wrote that he knew from this time that Caesar was capable of destroying the Republic. Then, after serving as praetor for the year 62 BCE, he was sent to Spain as propraetor, where he won a considerable military reputation with victories against the war-like Lusitanians (modern Portugal). He was now, at age 39, in possession of the fame and political capital to seek the consulship.

The First Triumvirate

As Pompey's mission in the East neared completion and he prepared to return to Rome, great anxiety began to develop among the political leaders there. The conqueror of the East had under his command the largest, best trained, and most experienced army Rome had ever fielded. His veterans had marched the length and breadth of the eastern Mediterranean and imposed the will of Rome on all the nations they encountered. Now the glorious conqueror was coming home, and no one, least of all Crassus or Caesar or Cicero, doubted that if he wished he could dominate the Roman state. And if he decided to destroy his political rivals, Crassus and Caesar knew that their names would be near the top of his proscription list. Both men had worked hard during Pompey's absence to build up their influence and power by backing friendly candidates for office, thereby storing up political obligations for the future, while Crassus had used his money to secure political

---

28. Under Roman law, every Roman citizen had the right to appeal a sentence of capital punishment directly to the Assembly. These citizens were being executed without even having a trial.

influence. Cicero had let no opportunity go by to draw attention to his services to the state. Nevertheless, everyone knew that Pompey could sweep all before him if he decided, like Sulla, to march on Rome with his veterans. And everyone knew that Pompey had unfinished business, unrealized political goals. First there were his tens of thousands of veterans who were entitled to bonuses for their service to the state, and second, there were treaties, agreements, and settlements with the many peoples of the eastern Mediterranean to be ratified. These goals, of course, would be easy to obtain if Pompey marched on Rome with his army. So, toward the end of 62 BCE, all eyes were on Pompey the Great, conqueror of the East, as he landed at Brundisium. But Pompey surprised everyone. He immediately disbanded his powerful army and entered Rome as a private citizen.

The Short Sightedness of the Senate

Thus, at the beginning of the year 61 BCE there seemed reason for optimism. Cicero's policy of *concordia ordinum*, "harmony of the orders," seemed to be working. But it was not to be. The jealously of Crassus, the political ineptness of Pompey, the ambition of Caesar, Cicero's incredible vanity, and above all, the short-sighted stupidity of the optimates in the senate, all but ensured the demise of the Republic. The Senate, during this critical time, should have sought the cooperation and support of at least one of these powerful leaders—after all they were natural rivals. But the Senate seemed determined to alienate every important politician in the populares faction and to drive them into a coalition with each other. Just how the optimates hoped to dominate the state without an army loyal to it is a mystery.

At any rate, the Senate refused to approve Pompey's bonuses for his veterans and continued to delay and obstruct the ratification of his eastern settlements. Pompey quite reasonably began to look around for other ways to attain his goals. At the same time, Crassus was having some financial problems with the tax contract for Asia, on which he and his associates had been the high bidder.[29] He was discovering that he had bid too high and was not making a sufficient profit, but the senate refused to re-negotiate the contract, and Crassus also began to look for other methods to attain his objectives. Then in 60 BCE Caesar returned from Spain, enriched by the spoils of successful military campaigns. He expected to celebrate a triumph and then stand for the consulship for the next year. The senate refused to allow his triumph until after the elections and since Caesar would not be a private citizen until after his triumph, this disqualified him from the elections.

For some time Caesar had maneuvered himself closer to Pompey but at the same time been supportive of the aims of Crassus. Late in 60 BCE, he persuaded both of these men, several years his elder, to join him in a private political alliance, which later came to be known as the First Triumvirate. To cement his alliance with Pompey, Caesar married his only child, his teenage daughter Julia, to the middle-aged Pompey, which tied him firmly to Caesar's policies for the next critical years. While no one of these three men was powerful enough at this point to dominate the state by himself, by pooling their political resources they could easily overcome all opposition. With the backing of Pompey and Crassus, Caesar was elected to the consulship for the year 59 BCE, but the optimate opposition managed to elect his enemy Bibulus as his colleague.

---

29. During the republic Rome had no civil service and all governmental functions were carried out by contract with private individuals or companies. The collection of taxes in the provinces was accomplished by tax collectors, called "publicans" (*publicani*), under contract. The contract was awarded to the highest bidder, who paid the government what he had bid for the contract and then collected the taxes. All the money the contractor could collect above what he paid for the contract was his profit. This system has sometimes been called "tax farming."

The strategy of Bibulus was to neutralize Caesar with his veto or failing that to push him into the illegality for which he could be put on trial once he completed his term of office. Caesar's methods were controversial to say the least. In order to enact the Triumvirate's program he did not take the traditional step of seeking senatorial approval but convened the popular assembly and forced through measures to grant the land and bonuses for Pompey's veterans, to formally ratify the eastern arrangements, and to re-negotiate Crassus's tax contracts. Early in the year Bibulus attempted to invalidate Caesar's efforts by withdrawing to his home and observing the sky for hostile omens. Theoretically, no laws could be passed under such circumstances. But the passive inaction of Bibulus was no match for the aggressive action of Caesar. So many laws were passed that it was jokingly referred to as the "consulship of Julius and Caesar" instead of the "consulship of Caesar and Bibulus." Toward the end of his consulship, Caesar obtained from the assembly a special command in Gaul for a term of five years. He was now 40 years of age and, though he had received the highest honors the Roman state could offer, his career was just beginning.

Caesar in Gaul

Caesar now embarked upon a perilous path. Because he left behind him a mass of enemies in Rome, he must perform glorious deeds in Gaul, for inactivity meant ruin. Only if he returned far stronger than when he left would he be able to prevail. Yet, while he was in far away Gaul he must maintain his support in Rome or his enemies would cut his feet from under him. Between the years 58 and 50 BCE, Caesar led a series of campaigns that brought all of modern France, Belgium, and parts of Germany under Roman rule. A constant stream of progress reports flowed back to Rome and were nailed up in the forum for the people to read. He also wrote a detailed account of his campaigns in *The Gallic Wars*, still to this day one of the most popular war memoirs of all time. In the year 56 BCE the triumvirs met at Luca in northern Italy and renewed the Triumvirate. Caesar's command in Gaul was extended another five years. Crassus and Pompey were elected to the consulship in 55 BCE. Pompey was given a command in Spain, but remained in Rome and exercised his authority through a legate. Crassus was given a command in the East, where he led an army against the Parthian empire (which had now replaced the old Seleucid Empire) and there, in 53 BCE, was killed in one of the worst defeats ever suffered by a Roman army.

After the conference of Luca, Caesar conquered the whole of Gaul in three campaigns. In 55 BCE invasions by the Germans across the Rhine were completely defeated, and this was then followed by Caesar's invasion of Germany that convinced him that the Rhine River should be the northern frontier of Roman Territory. Then he led an expedition to Britain, a land thus far almost unknown to the Romans. Another expedition was conducted the next year but Caesar decided that a conquest of the island was not worth the trouble. The following year was occupied putting down various revolts in northeastern Gaul. The year 51 BCE was taken up organizing the conquered land and establishing garrisons to retain control.

The End of the Republic

With the elimination of Crassus the final breakdown of the Republic began to play itself out. In 52 BCE Pompey was elected sole consul and in effect became the virtual dictator of Rome. His growing jealousy of Caesar caused him to have a law passed to cut short Caesar's command in Gaul by almost a year. Finally, Pompey demanded the resignation of Caesar. As a counter move, Caesar offered a joint resignation of both himself and Pompey. Negotiations continued in Rome for several months. In January of 49 BCE, the Senate evidently resigned itself to civil war and issued a *Senatus Consultum Ultimum* authorizing Pompey to "defend the Republic against its enemies," and ordered Caesar to give up his command. Several of the tribunes were political allies of Caesar and attempted to impose a veto on this unilateral action of the Senate, but the *optimates* threatened their lives if they interfered. This of course handed Caesar a propaganda victory, because he could now claim he was defending the prerogatives of the people's tribunes. Caesar, who was still in Gaul, decided that he had no choice but to fight for his own dignity and the rights of the tribunes of the people. So on January 11, 49 BCE he crossed the Rubicon (a small river that separated Italy from Cisalpine Gaul) and thus invaded his own country at the head of his legions. As he moved southward through Italy, the cities and people joined his cause. Pompey, in panic, fled from Rome to Greece and raised an army. Caesar first went to Spain[30] and defeated Pompey's forces there and then moved to Greece and defeated Pompey at Pharsalus in Thessaly. Pompey fled to Egypt, where he was murdered by renegades who realized Caesar would be victorious.

Caesar Triumphant

Caesar was not yet the master of the empire. The Pompeians still controlled the sea and Africa, and parts of the East sided with them. Caesar arrived in Egypt with a small force shortly after Pompey's assassination and was asked to arbitrate between the young king Ptolemy XII and his sister Cleopatra. After Ptolemy XII lost his life in a revolt against Caesar, his younger brother Ptolemy XIII and Cleopatra were proclaimed joint rulers, but Cleopatra as regent was the effective ruler of

Figure 10.13: Julius Caesar from a silver denarius minted in 44 BCE. The reverse shows Venus holding Victoria in her right hand.

---

30. He left Italy with the words, "I go to Spain to fight an army without a general and will return to fight a general without an army."

Egypt. Caesar spent several months in Egypt with the young Cleopatra, but it is not certain that he fathered a son by her, as she herself claimed. Then he moved on to mop up the remnants of Pompey's forces in Asia Minor[31] and Africa before returning to Rome in 46 BCE.

In the manor of Sulla, Caesar assumed the office of dictator and also like Sulla, he extended the term of that office beyond the constitutional limit of six months. In fact, in 44 BCE, he had himself named dictator for life and thus swept aside all the constitutional restraints on his power. But unlike Sulla, he did not perpetrate a reign of terror; instead, he practiced a policy of magnanimity and reconciliation toward his political enemies—a policy that would eventually be his undoing.

As dictator, he had complete authority to pass laws, declare war, and appoint men to office. He was, in fact, already a monarch and the Republic was, in fact, already dead, even though no one seemed to realize it yet. In his capacity of absolute master of Rome, Caesar instituted a series of rapid and far-reaching reforms intended to alleviate some of the serious problems plaguing the state. He raised the number of praetors and quaestors elected each year in order to reward his supporters. He also increased the size of the Senate from its traditional size of about 450 to around 900, by admitting many of his veteran officers. The Senate thus became a mere rubber stamp for any measure he put before it. This was the last blow to the Senate's prestige as the bulwark of the state. He also created many colonies for his veteran soldiers throughout the Roman provinces and extended Roman citizenship into some provinces, most notably Gaul. His most lasting reform, however, was to establish a new calendar based on the Egyptian system of 365 days to the year, with one day added every 4th year to keep it in step with the seasons.[32] Since, as it turns out, the actual length of the year is a few minutes longer than 365 1/4 days, the Julian Calendar slowly began to drift out of synchronization with the seasons and had to be revised slightly in 1582 by Pope Gregory XIII to become our present calendar. Gregory added an extra leap year every 400 years (i.e., one additional day every 400 years). Our month of July still bears Julius Caesar's name.

Caesar Assassinated

But Caesar's open autocratic rule and his trampling underfoot of the Republic was a grave and unforgivable insult to Rome's upper class, and they turned against him and committed the most famous political assassination of ancient times. The conspiracy against Caesar began to form after the incident at the festival of the Lupercalia in February 44 BCE, when Mark Antony offered the crown of kingship to Caesar and he dramatically rejected it—some said with reluctance. Actually, the episode was probably staged by Caesar himself in an effort to allay rumors that he planned to make himself king, but of course nothing can stop rumors from circulating. The

---

31. It was after his lightning campaign in Asia Minor that Caesar sent the famous message to the senate: "veni, vidi, vici" ("I came, I saw, I conquered").

32. The original Roman calendar consisted of ten months only—the present March to December—and must have had an uncounted gap in the winter between the years. In the Republican calendar January, named for Janus, the god of the gates and of beginnings and endings, was introduced as the first month of the year. The official year of the magistrates began on January 1. To keep the calendar in synchronization with the seasons an "intercalary" month was inserted by the pontifex maximus, but was so clumsily done that by the time of Caesar the civic calendar was about three months ahead of the solar year. Caesar inserted days into the year 46 BCE to make a total of 446 days. From the next year onward the Egyptian calendar was used. Thus, the procedure for providing the exact dates for events which occurred before 45 BCE is a historian's nightmare.

organizers of the plot were pardoned Pompeians, but the majority of their accomplices were former officers of Caesar. Caesar never took precautions for his personal safety. He was scheduled to attend a meeting of the Senate in the Theater of Pompey on March 15 of 44 BCE, because the Senate house was being renovated. As he entered the door someone in the crowd handed him a note warning him of the conspiracy, but he put it into his toga to read later. Inside the theater he was immediately surrounded by a throng of senators, but he had no reason to fear them, as many of them were his own friends and supporters, including two of his most trusted aids, Marcus Brutus and Gaius Cassius. However, at a prearranged signal some 30 senators suddenly drew daggers from their togas and began to stab Caesar. At first he drew up his heavy woolen toga as protection, but when he saw his dear friend Brutus, whom he had treated almost as his son, among those with drawn daggers, he uttered those famous words, *et tu Brutae,* "You too Brutus? Then fall Caesar." And fall he did, at the foot of a statue of Pompey, with over 30 wounds in his body. This was undoubtedly the most famous political assassination of antiquity and has been portrayed again and again in Western literature to this day. It was the subject of one of Shakespeare's most famous plays.

Caesar's Legacy

Opinions concerning Caesar's career varied widely even among his own contemporaries and continue to be controversial today, but his greatness and his influence on Roman history, and indeed, on Western Civilization, cannot be doubted. In the field of statesmanship he was not particularly original, but then that statesman is most effective who can find a solution for the problems of his time while keeping within the bounds of common ideas. However, Caesar's real greatness was in his clear perception of reality and in the boldness with which he used each opportunity to the limits of what was possible. While he often seemed to display great daring, the outcome of the event always proved that he was not reckless but rather had the ability to see the reality of the situation clearly, and this is surely the greatest ability a leader can possess.

As to his character, it is necessary to guard against both the exaggerations of his supporters and the falsehoods of his enemies, but it is difficult not to admire aspects of his personality. He seems to have had little inclination toward the common Roman vice of cruelty and revenge, and he displayed extraordinary forbearance and generosity toward his fellow citizens, friend and enemy alike. The chief charge against Caesar is that in order to gratify his own personal ambition, he overthrew the Republic and introduced a military monarchy. But to say that Caesar destroyed the Republic is a superficial view and reveals a basic lack of understanding of the event. Caesar's crossing of the Rubicon on January 11th of 49 BCE was the beginning of the civil war that brought with it the demise of the Roman Republic; it was not the cause of that demise. The causes were multiple and complex and they reach far back into the history of Rome, at least as far back as the period of the Gracchi, and logically as far back as the invasion of Hannibal. Rome had, in fact, already been dominated by the army for many years before Caesar came upon the scene. The real difference between Caesar and Pompey or Sulla was that he used his power intelligently to promote the welfare of the world, instead of laying it down as soon as his narrow personal demands were satisfied. When all the scholarly study and analysis is done, the fact remains that Caesar did not willingly seek to overthrow the Republic. He operated within the bounds of the Republic as long as he could, but when the narrow and selfish faction of the nobility, who called themselves the *optimates,* the "best," deliberately and recklessly forced Caesar to draw the sword, they themselves, destroyed their own supremacy forever.

In regard to his person, Caesar was described as tall and fair, with keen black eyes. He is uniformly said to have been a man of courteous manors and great personal charm. He was a versatile and many-sided man: not only a soldier, but a writer, an orator, even a wit and a poet of sorts. About the worst thing that Suetonius (who recorded every piece of gossip he could dig up) could say about him personally was that "he bore the deformity of boldness very badly." In Caesar alone were found the insight and the daring which, if he had lived longer, might have found real solutions for the evils of his society. What he would have done, we of course cannot say, but it was unquestionably a great misfortune that a handful of Roman nobles deprived Rome of the services of one of the greatest men it ever produced. And that act could not possibly produce anything more than another round of civil conflict and bloodshed.

11

The Roman Empire

The term "Roman Empire" is normally applied to that period of Roman history during which the state was ruled by a monarch bearing the title of emperor. This system of government was established by the adopted son of Julius Caesar, known as Gaius Octavius, or Octavian, until the year 27 BCE, when the Senate awarded him the title "Augustus," which marked the beginning of his rule as "*imperator*," or emperor. This monarchy survived until 476 of the Common Era (CE), which is the date usually cited as the "fall" of the Roman Empire, although the office of Roman emperor continued in the eastern part of the empire, with its capital at Byzantium (modern Istanbul), until 1453. The later Roman Empire is usually referred to as the Byzantine Empire.

Aftermath of Caesar's Assassination

The demise of the Roman Republic occurred against a background of strange and bizarre misjudgment of reality by the players involved. Although the republic had been dying for several generations before Julius Caesar made himself dictator for life in 44 BCE, no one seemed to realize it. Everyone behaved as if the ancient institutions were perfectly healthy and would endure forever. The conspirators against Caesar seemed to believe that the complex machinery of the Roman government was driven by the force of nature and that Caesar the tyrant was simply a cog stuck in the gears of the great machine and if he was removed the ponderous machine would somehow of its own inertia began to operate again. Thus, no action was taken against Caesar's associates or his party organization. Furthermore, the conspirators actually expected their act to be received with great joy and celebration by the Roman people. It was a monumental misreading of reality!

The immediate effect of Caesar's assassination was complete paralysis. It left his partisans in command of the armies throughout the Roman world and they were not men who would meekly lay down their powers at the feet of the Senate. One of these men was Marcus Antonius, known to history as Mark Antony, who was the favored lieutenant of the murdered dictator. He immediately attempted to secure control of Gaul, Caesar's old power base. Another was Marcus Aemilius Lepidus, whose command of a large army in nearby Cisalpine Gaul, gave him important influence in the post-Caesar era. Then another name was added to the equation. The reading of Caesar's will revealed that the childless dictator had posthumously adopted his eighteen year old nephew Gaius Octavius (Octavian) and designated him his heir. In accordance with Roman custom, Octavian's official name became Gaius Julius Caesar Octavianus, which meant as "Caesar" he could command the loyalty of the dead Julius Caesar's soldiers and veterans.

Antony secured Caesar's papers and the ratification of Caesar's acts by the senate and prepared a state funeral, at which he gave a fiery speech[1] that produced a violent popular reaction against the self-styled "liberators." Under the threat from the angry mob, the conspirators hastily left Rome. This seemed to leave Antony in control of the situation. But Octavian, who had been in Illyricum training with Caesar's army in preparation for the campaign in the East when the dictator was murdered, appeared in Italy at the head of several legions of veterans and the likelihood that other legions under Antony and Lepidus would transfer their allegiance to him. This changed everything.

At first Octavian played the part of the discreet young supporter of the senate against Antony and Lepidus. Again, however, the optimates attempted to pursue the bankrupt policy of playing their opponents off against each other, but it was as foolish to try it with Octavian and Antony as it had been with Pompey and Caesar. In 43 BCE, the year after Caesar's death, Octavian, Antony, and Lepidus formed the Second Triumvirate. Then with their combined armies, they marched on Rome and forced a law through the assembly which gave them supreme

---

1. Made famous by Shakespeare in Julius Caesar, Act III, Scene II:
I come to bury Caesar not to praise him.
The evil that men do lives after them;
The good is oft interred with their bones;
So let it be with Caesar. The noble Brutus
Hath told you Caesar was ambitious:
If it were so, it was a grievous fault;
And grievously hath Caesar answer'd it.
Here, under leave of Brutus and the rest,—
For Brutus is an honourable man;
So are they all, all honourable men,—
Come I to speak in Caesar's funeral.
He was my friend, faithful and just to me:
But Brutus says he was ambitious;
And Brutus is an honourable man.
He hath brought many captives home to Rome,
Whose ransoms did the general coffers fill:
Did this in Caesar seem ambitious?
When that the poor have cried, Caesar hath wept:
Ambition should be made of sterner stuff:
Yet Brutus says he was ambitious;
And Brutus is an honourable man.
You all did see that on the Lupercal
I thrice presented him a kingly crown,
Which he did thrice refuse: was this ambition?
Yet Brutus says he was ambitious;
And, sure, he is an honourable man.
I speak not to disprove what Brutus spoke,
But here I am to speak what I do know.
You all did love him once,—not without cause:
What cause withholds you, then, to mourn for him?
O judgment, thou art fled to brutish beasts,
And men have lost their reason!—Bear with me;
My heart is in the coffin there with Caesar,
And I must pause till it come back to me...

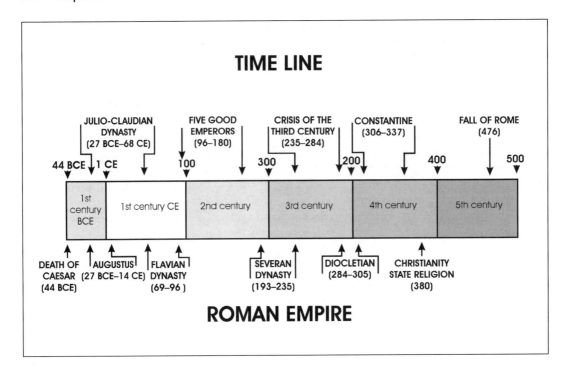

TIME LINE

JULIO-CLAUDIAN DYNASTY (27 BCE–68 CE)

FIVE GOOD EMPERORS (96–180)

CRISIS OF THE THIRD CENTURY (235–284)

CONSTANTINE (306–337)

FALL OF ROME (476)

44 BCE   1 CE   100   300   200   400   500

| 1st century BCE | 1st century CE | 2nd century | 3rd century | 4th century | 5th century |

DEATH OF CAESAR (44 BCE)

AUGUSTUS (27 BCE–14 CE)

FLAVIAN DYNASTY (69–96)

SEVERAN DYNASTY (193–235)

DIOCLETIAN (284–305)

CHRISTIANITY STATE RELIGION (380)

ROMAN EMPIRE

Figure 11.1

power for a period of five years "to provide for the order and security of the state." Their power was later renewed for five more years. Thus, within a year of Caesar's death, the dictator was replaced with a board of three dictators—although the term "dictator" was never used again by the Romans.

Brutus, Cassius, and the other leaders of the conspiracy against Caesar fled to the East and managed to gain control of Macedonia and Syria and raised at least nineteen legions, maintaining them by robbing cities and extorting money from the client states. In Rome, Octavian's prestige rose dramatically because the Senate recognized Julius Caesar as a god, which made Octavian *divi filius,* or "the son of a god." He and Antony now took twenty-eight of the forty-five legions controlled by the triumvirs and marched east, where they defeated the republicans at the Battle of Philippi (42 BCE). Both Cassius and Brutus took their own lives after this battle and the republican cause was irretrievably lost, and the murder of Julius Caesar was avenged.

There followed then a brutal purge in Rome, in which the three leaders, Antony, Lepidus, and Octavian, ruthlessly destroyed their enemies in a series of proscriptions and mass murders. Octavian cannot be exonerated of guilt for this reign of terror simply because he was at this time the junior member of the Triumvirate. One of those killed in this purge was Marcus Cicero, who became a symbol of the now dead Republic. The lands and property confiscated from those people unfortunate enough to be on the losing side of this conflict were redistributed among those fortunate enough to be on the winning side. This is usually called a "revolution:" the names at the top of society sink down to the bottom and those on the bottom rise up to the top. Otherwise, very little is changed by even the most radical revolutions.

The Struggle between Antony and Octavian

The empire was now divided between the triumvirs: Octavian took Italy, including Cisalpine Gaul which now became part of Italy; Antony was given the rest of Gaul; while Lepidus was allotted Africa. New problems now beset the empire. Antony remained in the East to restore order there and raise funds for the some 100,000 veterans who now had to be satisfied. The next few years were spent by both Antony and Octavian consolidating their positions. When Antony attempted to return to Italy in 40 BCE to take care of some business, as he had every right to do, he was at first denied permission and a civil war almost broke out before an agreement was reached. This agreement is known as the Treaty of Brundisium, under which Antony retained his holdings in the East while Octavian took over all of the West, except Africa, which was left to Lepidus, who now definitely became the junior member of the triumvirate—the odd man out, so to speak. The pact was sealed by the marriage of Antony to Octavian's sister, Octavia. But there was still much consolidation to be accomplished by both leaders before either would be ready for the final showdown.

In order to strengthen his position, Octavian had to deal with Sextus Pompeius, the son of Pompey, who was now occupying Sicily and Sardinia and commanded a 1arge fleet of ships, which he used to interfere with Rome's overseas grain supply. Octavian agreed to recognize the command of Sextus Pompeius over the islands for five years and married Scribonia, a relative of Pompeius, to seal the pact. However, a year later, on the same day that she bore him a daughter, Julia (destined to be his only child), he divorced her. Octavian had fallen in love with Livia, the wife of Tiberius Claudius Nero. Livia had already born her first husband a son, who was to become the future emperor Tiberius, but now Claudius Nero complacently divorced the nineteen year old Livia, so that she could marry Octavian. She was also several months pregnant with her second son, Claudius Drusus, when she married Octavian. To modern sensibilities, this seems like a strange way to begin a romance, yet Livia and Octavian lived together happily and affectionately for the next fifty years, although they never had the children they longed for so intensely.

Now that Octavian had divorced Scribonia, his pact with Sextus Pompeius collapsed. Octavian was short of ships and had to request help from Antony in order to deal with Sextus. Antony loaned Octavian a large fleet, but over half of it was lost in an engagement with Sextus off the coast of Italy, even though the outcome of the battle was indecisive. Finally, Octavian had his very competent general, Agrippa, construct a new fleet, and with some additional ships acquired from Antony, Sextus was at last completely defeated in a sea battle near the Sicilian Straits in 36 BCE.

Then Lepidus, who had quietly acquired the command of no less than twenty-two legions, claimed Sicily for himself, but when the time came for battle, his troops deserted him to Octavian, who thus won Africa without bloodshed. The legions simply refused to fight against Caesar. Under the circumstances, Octavian graciously spared Lepidus's life and even allowed him to retain the title *Pontifex Maximus*, although he stripped him of all other powers. At this point Lepidus, in effect, disappears from history. We hear no more of him until his death in 13 or 12 BCE. Octavian now found himself in command of some forty legions, far more than he could maintain, so he discharged about 20,000 veterans, which he settled in Sicily and then he returned to Rome. Now the entire western part of the empire was united behind him.

But what about Antony in the East? After the Battle of Philippi, which saw the demise of republican cause, Antony remained in the eastern provinces to raise money. When he reached Tarsus, in Cilicia, in Asia Minor, he summoned Cleopatra, the Queen of Egypt, to meet him there. His excuse was that she had given help to Cassius and the republicans, but the real reason was that he needed the vast wealth of Egypt for his planned campaign against Octavian. Antony had most likely

Figure 11.2: Antony and Cleopatra, from a 1st Century BCE Alexandrian coin.

known Cleopatra as a girl of fourteen when he visited Alexandria in Caesar's army back in 48 BCE, and again in Rome when she was living there as Caesar's mistress. After Caesar's death, she had gone back to Alexandria and killed her young brother and consort, Ptolemy XIV, and she was now the sole ruler of Egypt. Her arrival at Tarsus was immortalized by Shakespeare in the following words:[2]

> The barge she sat in, like a burnish'd throne,
> Burn'd on the water: the poop was beaten gold;
> Purple the sails, and so perfumed that
> The winds were love-sick with them; the oars were silver,
> Which to the tune of flutes kept stroke, and made
> The water, which they beat, to follow faster,
> As amorous of their strokes. For her own person,
> It beggar'd all description: she did lie
> In her pavilion,—cloth-of-gold of tissue,—
> O'er-picturing that of Venus where we see
> The fancy outwork of nature: on each side of her
> Stood pretty dimpled boys, like smiling cupids,
> With divers-colored fans, whose wind did seem
> To glow the delicate cheeks which they did cool,
> And what they undid did.

So. . .after their meeting at Tarsus, Cleopatra became the mistress of Antony, but their relationship was far more than simply a steamy romance—it made good sense politically. Cleopatra needed Antony's support to strengthen her rule in Egypt while Antony needed her money to finance his coming struggle with Octavian. However, the tradition that the relationship between Antony and

---

2. Shakespeare, *Antony and Cleopatra*, Act II, Scene II

Cleopatra was one of uncontrollable lust and passion has a long history. It first appears, in fact, as part of Octavian's propaganda to paint Antony as a man driven by passion, not reason, and to instill the fear in the Italians that if Antony should win the struggle, Rome would be ruled by an "oriental queen."

The couple spent the winter in Egypt, but Antony had to leave in the spring of 40 BCE to visit Italy and did not see her again for four years, nor did he see the twins, a boy and a girl, that she bore him soon after his departure. During these four years he had to fight wars against the Parthians, who were invading Syria, and a barbarian tribe which was threatening Macedonia, as well as negotiate the Treaty of Brundisium with Octavian—at which time he married Octavia—as described above. But relations between Antony and Octavian steadily deteriorated and in 37 BCE Antony sent Octavia, who was pregnant, back to Italy and joined Cleopatra in Antioch. Whether he married her now or later under Egyptian law is uncertain: at any rate, the marriage was not legal under Roman law, since Cleopatra was not a Roman citizen. He recognized the children that she had born him and named them Alexander Helios (the Sun) and Cleopatra Selene (the Moon). He also gave them client kingdoms in Asia Minor which he carved out of Roman provinces—a move which provided Octavian with more material for his propaganda mill.

In 36 BCE, Antony sent Cleopatra, now pregnant again, back to Egypt and invaded Parthia with an army of 60,000 men (Antony always seemed to be getting women pregnant and then sending them home!). This expedition met with disaster, and he lost some 22,000 soldiers. However, he reorganized his army, and two years later, in 34 BCE, he successfully invaded Armenia, which he made a province, but Parthia was still undefeated and still a threat to the Roman Empire. Antony then returned to Egypt and celebrated a triumph of sorts. This episode is known as the "Donations of Alexandria" and furnished still more material for Octavian's propaganda against him. Antony and Cleopatra sat on high golden thrones with their children. Cleopatra was dressed as the goddess Isis. To the assembled people of Alexandria, Antony proclaimed that Caesarian was the legitimate son of Julius Caesar, thus by implication the adopted son, Octavian, was a usurper. This boy was proclaimed Ptolemy Caesar, King of Kings, and his mother Cleopatra was proclaimed Queen of Kings, and they were hailed as the joint rulers of Egypt and Cyprus. Although Antony did not take any royal title for himself, this partition of Rome's eastern provinces under the new Queen of Kings aroused considerable mistrust in Rome and played into Octavian's hands.

After two more years spent in a campaign of mutual slander, the two rivals were ready for the final showdown. In the year 31 BCE, Antony and Cleopatra crossed over to Greece with their forces. Thereupon, Octavian formally proclaimed a war against Cleopatra and, holding his third consulship, he also crossed into Greece. On the 2nd of September, 31 BCE, the battle finally took place, and it was a very strange contest. For the first time since the First Punic War, a naval battle decided a major war: Octavian was completely victorious at Actium, off the west coast of Greece. Antony and Cleopatra managed to escape with some forty ships and sailed back to Egypt. In the summer of 30 BCE, after a leisurely trip overland, Octavian reached Egypt and occupied Alexandria, which Antony could not defend because his remaining troops deserted. When Antony heard a false rumor that Cleopatra was dead, he stabbed himself but survived long enough to die in her arms. Cleopatra was taken prisoner. She attempted to negotiate with Octavian, as she had with Caesar and Antony, to keep her kingdom (she had, by now, a lot of experience negotiating with Roman generals), but Octavian would have none of it. When she finally realized that she was destined to grace Octavian's triumph in Rome, she had an asp smuggled into her room and died by its bite. The ancient Egyptians believed that the bite of the asp deified its victim, that is, it transported the soul directly into paradise. The fact that Cleopatra chose this method of suicide indicates how Egyptized the Ptolemaic dynasty had become.

The treasure of the Ptolemies, as well as Egypt itself became the personal property of Octavian. Towards Antony's followers he was lenient: he could afford to be lenient now, because he had no enemies left in power. Towards the children of Antony and Cleopatra he was merciful, and they were brought back to Italy and raised by Octavia: Selene later married king Juba II of Mauritania. But Octavian killed Caesarian because he could not allow a potential rival to survive. Egypt itself was annexed, but not as an ordinary province: rather this richest single unit in the entire empire became the private possession of the Roman emperor, administered by his personal agent.

Octavian Triumphant

In the summer of 29 BCE, Octavian returned to Rome as the master of the world. On three successive days he celebrated three triumphs: for the conquest of Illyricum, Actium, and the annexation of Egypt. For more than three generations, all the warring factions had fought for peace, and peace, as always, once attained, became the spoils and the prerogative of the victor. In the Roman forum, not far from the senate house, there was a small but important temple dedicated to the god Janus, the god of beginnings and endings. It was the custom of the Romans to leave the doors of this temple open during times of war and to close them during periods of peace. And so, in 29 BCE, with great ceremony the doors of the temple of Janus were closed, symbolizing that the world was at peace. According to Livy[3] this was only the third time since the birth of the Roman state, more than 700 years before, that the doors of the temple had been closed.

Octavian had seduced the armies of all his adversaries and he found himself in the embarrassing possession of no less than seventy legions: costly to maintain and, in themselves, a threat to internal peace. He decided that twenty-six were necessary for the defense of the empire and he disbanded the rest, settling the thousands of veterans both in Italy and the provinces. As for the remaining legions, it seemed as clear to Octavian's contemporaries as it does to us today: the only guarantee for the good behavior of the army was the continuing undivided control of Octavian, as the heir of Caesar. Simply put, the army had become the client of the Julian house, which now meant Octavian. For him to step down from command now, as Sulla had done, would have the same effect: civil war. It would mean that ambitious generals would again turn the soldiers against each other and, in another orgy of violence, fight yet another round of civil war until another victor would emerge. Rome had been through it all already. . .so many times. It was obvious that the army must have a patron. There had been a time during the history of the Republic when far-sighted statesmanship might have welded the loyalty of the soldiers to the state and not to their generals, but that opportunity had been lost long ago, and now the very fabric of Roman society demanded that the relationship between the army and its commander be a personal client-patron relationship.

Octavian was indeed now the master of the Roman world. He could count on the support of the army: it was his client. He could depend on the support of the people: they were also his clients. They, like the army, had sworn an oath of allegiance to him personally. But alas, Octavian, for all of this support, could not rule and administer the vast Roman empire without the help of the aristocratic oligarchy of the Senate. Caesar had tried, and Caesar had failed. Yes, of course the men of Octavian's own inner faction—perhaps party is now a better term—would stand by him: they owed their careers to him and they had been rewarded well. But among the consulars—that small oligarchy of ex-consuls

---

3. Livy, *Ab Urbe Condita*, 1.19.3

who determined the sentiment and direction of the senate—there was hardly a man who did not have a republican or an Antonian past. Unless Octavian could reach a tolerable compromise with these eminent persons, his position would remain as vulnerable and precarious as Caesar's had been, and he would not ever dare to walk unguarded across the Senate floor. Furthermore, the administration of the great empire required the expertise and cooperation of these men: Octavian could issue decrees and orders, but without loyal governors and skilled administrators to carry them out, the empire would again disintegrate into chaos. This put Octavian in the mood for compromise.

Over in the senate, the mood was also one of compromise. The great noble families who formed the ruling class of the Roman Republic had been decimated by the long civil wars. There was no one living who could remember when there was civil peace in Rome. Many of the most famous and important families—the Scipios, the Catos, and more—had now been killed off completely. Just as Octavian knew well that he could not rule the empire without the cooperation of the Senate, the senators now realized that they could not survive without a strong hand in control of the administration of the state and the army.

Therefore, Octavian carefully and slowly worked his way toward a compromise between the old and the new. The results of these compromises, know as "constitutional settlements," institutionalized the Augustan revolution and established the form of government known as the Principate, or Empire. The actual construction of this new government took place slowly over a period of many years.

Back in 36 BCE, when Lepidus was stripped of his command, Octavian had vowed to restore the Republic and he now began that task by restoring the Senate, if not to its former power, at least to its former exclusiveness. In the year 28 BCE, Octavian and Agrippa, his most important advisor and confidant, held the censorship, and they reduced the Senate's membership from 1,000 to 800. Later, the number was reduced still further to 600, which was closer to its traditional size of 450. The list of the Senate drawn up by Octavian and Agrippa listed Octavian as *princeps senatus*, literally "the first senator," but more accurately translated as the "senior senator." Octavian was seeking to present an image of himself not as an autocrat but simply as a very successful politician within the republican mold, and *princeps senatus* had good republican associations: it had long been the custom to designate the senior senator as "*princeps*," and Octavian was, after all, serving his sixth consulship and was beyond doubt the senior consular.

Also, during the year 28 BCE, the groundwork was carefully prepared behind the scenes for the formal "restoration" of the Republic. Almost nothing is known about these secret consultations between the ruler and his political allies and, perhaps, even with other politicians outside his own circle, but judging from what happened later, it is obvious that nothing was left to chance.

Finally, in the session of the Senate on January 13th 27 BCE, the process came to a dramatic culmination. Gaius Julius Caesar Octavianus solemnly resigned all powers and all provinces to the free disposal of the Senate and the people of Rome. Acclamation and protest filled the senate chamber! The senators pleaded with him not to abandon the state which he had saved. And so reluctantly, the master of the whole world relented and, out of a feeling of patriotism and a sense of duty, Octavian assumed a special command which granted him Proconsular *imperium* for a period of ten years over the provinces of Spain, Gaul, and Syria, but he would except nothing more. For the rest of the empire, proconsuls were to govern as before, under the direction of the Senate. The Senate, the people, and the magistrates were to resume the exercise of their rightful functions as of old. Three days later, the senate met again, eager to confer honors upon the savior of Rome. In the words of Octavian himself:[4]

---

4. Augustus, *Res Gestae Divi Augusti* (The Achievements of the Divine Augustus), 34

In my 6th and 7th consulships, after I had extinguished civil wars, and with universal consent, I was in complete control of affairs, I transferred the Republic from my power to the domination of the Senate and the people of Rome. For this service of mine I was named Augustus by decree of the Senate, and the door-posts of my house were publicly wreathed with bay leaves and a civil crown was fixed over my door and a golden shield was set in the Curia Julia, which as attested by the inscription thereon, was given to me by the senate and the people of Rome on account on my courage, justice and piety. After this time I excelled all others in *auctoritas*, although I possessed no more *potestas* than others who where my colleagues in the several magistracies.

From this day onward, Octavian is known as Augustus, and historians designate the year 27 BCE as the beginning of his reign as the first emperor of the Roman Empire.

So the Republic was restored: but what does this really mean? First of all this action established two types of provinces. Imperial provinces were governed directly by Caesar Augustus, by virtue of his proconsular *imperium*. As a proconsul he was technically no more than equal to any other proconsul. True, the provinces assigned to him did include the majority of the legions, but there were also legions stationed in three senatorial provinces as well: Illyricum, Macedonia, and Africa. These, like all the senatorial provinces, were now governed by proconsuls under the direction of the Senate. And this provided opportunities for members of the nobility to pursue political careers as in the old days. Egypt, however, the richest province of all, stood outside this arrangement. It was not even mentioned in the deliberations of the Senate, because it was now and remained forever the personal estate of the emperor. Before the law, then, Augustus was no longer commander-in-chief of the whole army but simply a Roman magistrate invested with special powers for a term of ten years. And for such a mandate as this, there was plenty of precedent. It was not a gross violation of the ancient constitution. His provinces did require special attention. Spain, even now after so many generations, was still not completely pacified. Gaul, only recently added to the empire, required proper organization. Out in the East, Syria was exposed to the resurgent Parthians. And as for precedent, special commands were neither new nor revolutionary: such arrangements no longer made republicans feel uncomfortable. True, Augustus did remain consul in Rome while governing his provinces through legates, and his consular *imperium* did give him supervising power over the other proconsuls, but there was also precedent for this: Pompey had been consul in Rome (52 BCE) for the third time while he exercised his proconsular *imperium* in Spain through a legate. Nothing unprecedented or unconstitutional here. But there was another element that made Augustus's control over the Empire more secure than all of these constitutional powers. Above all, Augustus claimed preeminence for himself by virtue of his *auctoritas* (authority): "after this time I excelled all others in *auctoritas*, although I possessed no more *potestas* (power) than others." In the final analysis, it was upon his personal influence, his authority, that Augustus depended on in order to rule the empire. This arrangement of 27 BCE is known to history as the First Constitutional Settlement of Augustus.

In the summer following the settlement, Augustus left Rome to tour Gaul and Spain and was away from Rome until 24 BCE, staying out of the public eye while the new arrangements took effect. During his absence, his aids Agrippa and Maecenas supervised affairs in Rome. After his return, the Second Constitutional Settlement was staged. Augustus now relinquished the consulship, which he had monopolized since 31 BCE, in order to give himself supervising power over the other magistrates. This was necessary to allow the members of the old noble class to pursue their political careers and maintain their *dignitas* (dignity). Nobles cut off from the consular honor were still resentful and bitter: the Republic must have consuls. So Augustus let the consulship go and he took it up on only two other occasions for the rest of his life and those were for dynastic reasons. His vacant consular office was taken up Lucius Sestius, who had once been a quaestor under Marcus Brutus, one

Figure 11.3: The Augustus Prima Porta in the Vatican Museum.

of Caesar's assassins and who worshiped the memory of the murderers of Augustus's father. The other vacancy was filled by Gnaeus Calpurnius Piso, another proud and unrepentant republican. The readiness of these men to accept the position of consul within the framework of the Principate demonstrates that the old nobility was at last ready to make peace with the new regime. Their motives, of course, were patriotism, ambition, and profit—not necessarily in that order.

To compensate for the loss of the consular *imperium*, Augustus was granted *imperium proconsulare maius* ("greater" proconsular power), which extended over the entire empire and, unlike other proconsuls, he was also given dispensation to retain his power within the city of Rome itself. In addition, Augustus was granted the *tribunicia potestas*, or tribunician power, which gave him the prerogatives of the people's tribune without actually holding the office. With both his proconsular and tribunician powers, Augustus had the ability to direct and control every aspect of the domestic and foreign affairs of the state. These two powers remained the twin pillars of the emperor's constitutional position to the end of Roman history.

While the settlements of 27 and 23 BCE established the framework of the office of the emperor, further refinements were necessary. Over the coming years, he received, piecemeal, more significant privileges and honors. In 23 BCE, for instance, he was given the right to convene the Senate whenever he saw fit. In 22 BCE, he was appointed to oversee Rome's grain supply. In 19 BCE, when he had returned from the East, he was given censorial powers for five years. When Lepidus finally died in 13 or 12 BCE, Augustus became chief priest (*pontifex maximus*). Finally, in 2 BCE, he was granted the title "Father of His Country" (*pater patriae*), which placed Augustus in a relationship with the Roman people analogous to that of a *paterfamilias* over his family. In addition, there was his *auctoritas*. Augustus's *auctoritas* allowed him get the business of the state done without constantly invoking his legally-conferred powers. Augustus simply had to make known his preferences for matters to transpire accordingly, so that, for instance, candidates for office whom he favored invariably got elected. No wonder he was proud to boast that he "surpassed all in *auctoritas*."

In this sense, the Principate can be viewed as a constitutional monarchy, but it was, at heart, a sham. Yet, like all successful shams, it was one that people could believe in. Above all, there was political genius in Augustus's slow and careful acquisition of overarching authority in every area of public life. At every step of the way the "constitutional settlements" as well as the honors and privileges conferred upon him piecemeal were accomplished voluntarily and legally. He was no dictator. Indeed, he often expressed reluctance to accept offices and honors that struck him as excessive, and occasionally he refused them outright. He never attempted to project the image of an absolute ruler (which in fact he was). The title by which he most wanted to be known was *princeps*, the "leading citizen," the most successful politician of the Republic, not an autocrat. Throw into the equation his modest lifestyle, affable approachability, routine consultation with the Senate, and genuinely impressive work ethic, and we have in Augustus one of the greatest and most skillfully manipulative politicians of any nation in any age.

And so order came to the Roman world at last. There was something more important than political liberty: after all, political rights are a means, not an end in themselves. The old republican constitution had been devised to secure the liberty and the property of the Roman people. But in the end, the people, broken by civil war and disorder, willingly exchanged the ruinous burden of freedom for the security and peace provided by a strict government. The Republic, in fact, had died long ago. Marius and Sulla had overthrown liberty by force of arms and Pompey had been no better. But even before the Republic had begun to self-destruct, it had been little more than a sham, a mere façade behind which twenty to thirty men from a dozen noble families held a virtual monopoly of office and of power. Now, the survivors of that old oligarchy, decimated in numbers and shattered in spirit, willingly acquiesced to the new regime and even actively shared in its administration. This was possible because Augustus, both for the security of his own position and in order to obtain the necessary manpower to govern the empire, had devised an ingenious formula, which revealed to the members of the governing class how they could cooperate in maintaining the new regime ostensibly as servants of the Republic, not as mere lieutenants of a military leader, not as subservient agents of an arbitrary ruler. But, in fact, all this elaborate republican form was nothing but a shame, a mere façade behind which Augustus held all the power. The people of every age and time are forced, or choose, to play little mental games of self-deception in order to reconcile reality with ideology, and the ancient Romans were no more immune from this than we are in the modern world.

Although the Principate was absolute, it was not completely arbitrary. In theory, it was derived from the consent and delegation of powers by the people, it was founded upon the law, it was a "constitutional monarchy." To the very end of its history, the Principate theoretically derived its sovereignty from the people. This, at least, was something different from the monarchies of the East, which derived their power from heaven. The Romans had not sunk so low as that. Complete freedom might be unworkable, but total enslavement was intolerable. The Principate provided a middle way between these two extremes: this, after all, was the purpose of the elaborate façade of republican forms, created by Augustus.

Nevertheless, everyone knew that behind the benign mask of the law, the basis of the *princeps'* position was the naked power of the army. The happy outcome of the Principate might lead one to an indulgent estimate of the person and the acts of Augustus. All are agreed that Octavian was one of the most despicable opportunists ever to grace the pages of history. It was his avowed purpose to suggest and to demonstrate a sharp line of division between the careers of Octavian on the one hand and of Augustus on the other: the first of deplorable but necessary illegalities, the second of constitutional government. So well did he succeed in this deception that Augustus, in contrast to Octavian, ranks among the greatest statesmen of all time. But Octavian/Augustus was a chameleon, who abruptly changed colors, but did not change substance. His contemporaries were not really deceived by all of this and we should not be either. The convenient revival of republican institutions, the assumption of high sounding titles and the ostensible change in the source of his authority from the army to the constitution, did not change the facts of power. Power is no less effective, no less absolute, simply because it is disguised.

During his long 41-year reign, from 27 BCE to 14 CE, Augustus had the time to establish firmly his new system of government, and most of the institutions which he created endured for several centuries. He faced many problems and he developed many creative solutions for them. He reorganized the army into a permanent, professional military force, designed to stand guard at the borders of the empire, not to oppress the empire's population. He extended and straightened those boundaries to make them more rational and easier to defend. He established a 20 year retirement system for the soldiers, which was paid for by the state treasury, and this secured the loyalty of the soldiers to the state, or rather to the emperor, instead of to their generals.

The city of Rome, the capital of the extraordinary empire that Augustus ruled, had grown to over one million inhabitants by this period, and it had developed all the problems that go with a teaming and crowded metropolis. Vehicular traffic was so heavy in parts of Rome that pedestrians crossed the street at the risk of sudden death. Apartment buildings (*insula*) had been thrown up so quickly in order to accommodate the growing population that they often collapsed, killing scores of occupants. And street crime was at least as prevalent in late Republican Rome as it is in our modern cities—and up until this time, Rome did not even have a police force or a fire department.

Augustus attempted to solve, or at least to alleviate, these problems. He created a special force of 9,000 soldiers who were stationed permanently in the capital and were known as the Praetorian Guard. They served as the city's police force, as well as the emperor's personal body guard. Similar units were also assigned to other major cities of the empire. Augustus established a fire fighting department, built public baths, created building codes for apartment buildings, and developed other services required to make city life bearable and even enjoyable. Augustus also instituted the grain dole on a permanent basis to distribute free food to citizens too poor to buy it. And he built theaters, race tracks, and stadia to provide the public with entertainment, such as chariot racing, gladiatorial fights, and dramatic and comedic plays. This program was referred to by the Romans as "bread and circuses," the circus referring to the circuit of the chariot race track. The Romans believed this was necessary to keep the common people pacified and quiet. All this of course required an ever expanding bureaucracy to administer.

Although Augustus is not usually remembered for his conquests, more territory was added to the empire during his rule than under any other Roman ruler. His generals, including the future emperor Tiberius, advanced into central Europe annexing the area of modern Switzerland, Austria, and Bulgaria. A major defeat in the Black Forest of central Germany, however, resulted in the loss of three legions and convinced Augustus to make the Rhine and Danube Rivers the permanent frontier of the empire in Europe. In the East, Augustus negotiated a treaty with the Parthians and secured the return of the Roman standards lost by Crassus in 53 BCE without a major war. His arrangements in the East and Africa resulted in stability and peace in those regions for the next two centuries.

For these accomplishments Augustus must be counted among the greatest statesmen of all time. He found the Roman state divided against itself and on the verge of self-destruction, but he left it united under a firm but fair and basically unoppressive government, that produced a two century long era known as the pax Romana, the Peace of Rome, perhaps the most peaceful and prosperous period in the history of Western Civilization. In Augustus, the Mediterranean world celebrated an earthly redeemer, a savior, to whom it yielded a certain amount of liberty, but from whom it received the blessings of peace and prosperity. The rewards of this bargain were obvious to all: the millions of inhabitants of the Mediterranean basin enjoyed, for the first and the last time in their long history, peace and security behind consolidated frontiers. The establishment of one common economic order throughout the entire empire permitted the unprecedented growth of commerce, industry, and agriculture; and the freedom of movement and interaction between the many diverse cultures of the basin encouraged the exchange of intellectual and spiritual ideas as never before, and facilitated the spread of new movements, such as Christianity, throughout the entire area.

The Empire after Augustus

The history of the Roman Empire after Augustus is made up of elements of remarkable continuity as well as gradual transformation. Rome had many emperors, some amazingly competent, some mediocre, a few even insane. For two hundred years after the death of Augustus, his solution to the problem of ruling the Mediterranean worked remarkably well. Except for minor outbursts of violence, emperor succeeded emperor in peaceful continuity. But as time passed, the true nature of the imperial constitution, which Augustus managed to partially conceal behind the façade of republican forms, became clearer. And the nature of that constitution was simply this: the will of the emperor counted for much more than the will of the Senate, and the popular assemblies soon lost all of their elective and legislative functions and disappeared all together.

Julio–Claudian Dynasty

Constitutionally, the office of "emperor" did not exist, because Augustus's position was a package of specific powers granted to him personally by the Senate and the people for fixed periods. When he died, his powers terminated and it was up to the Senate and the people to appoint another princeps or revert to republican government by the annual magistracies. In theory, at least, the government of Rome was still a republic. But in practice, everyone realized that a return to the "free" Republic meant a return to the civil wars and chaos that had come so close to destroying the Roman state. Although Augustus faced a real paradox in attempting to create a dynasty, he behaved consistently within the ethos of the Roman aristocracy, in which the family is supreme. But the piecemeal and ephemeral nature of the emperor's powers proved to be the most destabilizing political element in the future history of the Roman empire. The problem was to reoccur again and again. Whenever the emperor died without an heir already in control of the imperial powers, civil war threatened and sometimes occurred.

Therefore, Augustus was constantly preoccupied throughout his rule with the question of his successor. One of the ironies of his life was that although he lived to the age of 76 (extraordinary in the ancient world), he was never in robust health and was always quite literally expected to expire at any moment. This, of course, kept the problem of succession in the forefront of affairs. However, the choice of successors open to Augustus was not unlimited. He could not simply chose the person whom he considered to be the best man for the job from among his followers. Given the structure of Roman society, his successor must come from among the highest social class—a patrician, or at the very least, a noble. More specifically, to avoid civil war among the soldiers, the successor must come from the Julian line. If this proved impossible, then the successor must be an adopted Julian with as much Julian ancestry as possible. Unfortunately, the longer Augustus lived, the more restricted his field of choice became. Indeed, he outlived almost all possible heirs.

In the absence of sons (he had only one child, his daughter Julia by his first marriage to Scribonia), he employed the time honored strategies of adoption and controlling the marriage of the women in his family. Judging from his action, it is clear that he intended to secure a blood relative as his successor. During the first years of his reign, his oldest male relative was Marcus Claudius Marcellus, the son of his sister Octavia by her first marriage, but he was only 11 years old in 31 BCE.

Figure 11.4: The Julio-Claudians after Augustus. Top, left to right: Tiberius, Gaius; Bottom, left to right, Claudius, Nero.

However, in 25 BCE he was made the heir apparent and was married to Julia: she was 14, he was 16. Marcellus began his political career at the age of 18, in 23 BCE, with election to the aedileship. Obviously, great things were planned for him, but he was never a healthy man and he died later that year, probably of tuberculosis.

Now Augustus was forced to turn to his loyal and faithful associate, Marcus Agrippa, who now married Julia: she was 18, he was 42. They had five children, three sons and two daughters. The first two sons, Gaius (born in 20 BCE) and Lucius (Born in 17 BCE) were adopted by Augustus and in 18 BCE arrangements were made for Agrippa to act as guardian if necessary. Everything seemed set for an orderly and peaceful transition in power, but it was not to be. Augustus outlived them all. Agrippa died in 12 BCE when Gaius was only 8 and Lucius was only 5 years old.

The young heirs must have a guardian, and the only logical place to turn was to the Claudian side of the family. Augustus's wife Livia had two sons by her first husband, Tiberius Claudius Nero. Her eldest son, also named Tiberius, was now aged 30 and his brother, Drusus, was age 26. In order for Tiberius to serve as guardian for the young Julians he was forced to divorce his wife Vipsania Agrippina, whom he loved dearly, and marry the widowed Julia. At the time of this marriage, she was 28, he was 31. Again, everything seemed prepared for an orderly succession. In 5 BCE, at age 15, Gaius Caesar was designated for the consulship for the year 1 CE, when he would be 21 and he was now admitted to the Senate. Lucius was to follow him in these honors three years later. Tiberius was to act as guardian if necessary.

In 1 BCE Gaius Caesar was sent on a mission to the East with proconsular *imperium* and the next year held the consulship as scheduled. However, tragedy struck again. In 2 CE Lucius Caesar was sent to Spain with *imperium*, but died at Massilia in route at age 19. In that same year Gaius was again dispatched to the East to represent Augustus in a conference with the Parthian king. While suppressing a revolt in Armenia he was wounded and died eighteen months later in Lycia at age 24. Again fate had defeated Augustus. His only real choice now was Germanicus, age 19, the son of Tiberius's brother Drusus and Antonia, the daughter of Octavia and Antony. Germanicus was married to Agrippina, the daughter of Julia and Agrippa, and thus their children, Augustus's great grandchildren, would preserve the Julian line on both sides of their family. But Germanicus was too young at this point to rule alone and the office of guardian to the heir had to be revived and filled again by Tiberius. Thus in 4 CE, barely four months after the death of Gaius Caesar, Augustus adopted Tiberius, and Tiberius adopted his nephew Germanicus, who thus became the grandson of Augustus.[5] This was the final arrangement that stuck and, during the last decade of Augustus's life, Tiberius, who now received the proconsular *imperium* and the *tribunicia potestas*, held powers nearly equal to those of Augustus and was, in reality, a co-emperor.

---

5. Much bitterness had developed between Augustus and Tiberius by this time. Julia had become tired of being passed from man to man like a bottle of wine at a banquet table. She began sleeping around and was finally involved in a scandal that resulted in her exile. Tiberius had been forced to divorce his beloved Vipsania for the unhappy union with Julia and now was forced to adopt Germanicus, which meant the rejection of his own son for that of his brother's. Tiberius's life after his divorce could not have been a happy one and he had attempted to retire into private life but was forced by Augustus to assume the responsibilities of the emperorship against his will. For his part, Augustus expressed his distaste at the arrangement when he announced it to the senate with the sarcastic words: "I do this for the commonwealth." It is no wonder that Tiberius was bitter and resentful and during the last decades of his life he experienced a deep depression.

Tiberius (14–37)

The reign of Tiberius is the first occasion when the powers designed by Augustus were passed on to someone else. By formally conferring the powers upon Tiberius, the Senate recognized the office of the emperor and the fact that the state was now a monarchy. Tiberius's reign was one of contradictions. Most of his last years were lived in a deep emotional depression. He left Rome in 27 CE and spent the rest of his life in isolation on the island of Capri, off the coast of Naples. There he allowed himself to come under the influence of unscrupulous men who pursued their own selfish ends and tarnished the reputation of Tiberius. Thus, he has not been treated kindly by history.

Despite minor troubles and mutinies among the troops stationed in Germany and Pannonia, Tiberius's first years were generally good. He remained faithful to the policies of Augustus and began the preparation of Germanicus to assume the emperorship. But unfortunately, Germanicus died in 19 CE while on a mission to the East. Then, as Tiberius sank deeper into depression he came to depend heavily on the commander of the Praetorian Guard,[6] Lucius Aelius Sejanus, to administer the day-to-day functions of the government. As Sejanus became more and more prominent, his statues were erected in public places and Tiberius openly praised him as "the partner of my labors." But Sejanus was an evil man who worked only for his own aggrandizement. He was gradually successful in eliminating almost all of the possible Julian heirs to the throne and then he secured a marriage to Livilla, the widow of Tiberius's son, Drusus. He seems to have attempted to play the role Agrippa had played during the reign of Augustus. Agrippa had been an outsider who became the emperor's designated successor through a combination of loyalty, necessity, and family alliance. But Sejanus was too clever for his own good, and Tiberius eventually discovered his motives. In 31 CE he was denounced before the senate and executed.

The Sejanus affair drove Tiberius even deeper into depression. Betrayed by his close friend and confident, who could he trust? He withdrew from public life even further. Only letters kept him touch with Rome, but the machinery of government established by Augustus continued to function smoothly. He died in 37 CE at the age of 78, leaving his young, inexperienced nephew, Gaius, the son of Germanicus, as his heir.

Even though Tiberius's reign produced turmoil and tyranny in Rome, out in the provinces it was a peaceful and well ordered time. He appointed competent governors who performed their jobs well, and there were no destructive wars. Indeed, the provinces had already settled into a pattern of peaceful prosperity—under the administration of the professional bureaucracy—that was generally not affected by the reign of good as well as bad emperors in far off Rome.

Gaius (Caligula) (37–41 CE)

We will never be able to know the real character of this young emperor, because the meager and universally hostile sources provide us with only a caricature of a megalomaniac given to cruelty and harebrained schemes. Gaius was born in 12 CE, the third of six children of Augustus's adopted grandson, Germanicus. He accompanied his father on military campaigns in Germany where the troops gave him the nickname "Caligula," meaning "little boots," because of the miniature soldier's

---

6. The praetorian Guard had been created by Augustus as his personal body guard and to keep order in the city of Rome. Augustus had billeted the troops discretely in small towns around Rome, but Tiberius, undoubtedly at the suggestion of Sejanus, concentrated all 9,000 troops within the city at the Praetorian Camp. For the rest of Roman history the guard was used by the emperors to intimidate the population of Rome.

uniform he wore. However, his childhood was spent in the atmosphere of suspicion and murder generated by the instability of the Julian family. When his father died in 19 CE, he was sent to live with his great-grandmother, Livia, and then after her death with his grandmother Antonia. In 31 CE he was summoned to Capri and was confined there under the watchful eye of Tiberius, his grand-uncle, until his accession to the throne in 37 CE. Thus, he had only a defective education and no experience at all for public office.

The beginning of his reign was astonishingly upbeat. He entered Rome amid scenes of wild rejoicing, and his first acts were generous: he paid all Tiberius's bequests and gave a cash bonus to the Praetorian Guard (thus setting a precedent). He recalled the exiles and honored his relatives. He was immensely popular, but within four years he was murdered by his own guards. What went wrong? All the ancient sources agree that the cause of his downfall was insanity. In October of 37 CE Gaius became seriously ill with a high fever, and afterward his personality changed radically. The ancients believed this illness to be the source of his insanity, but it may not have been the cause. Rather, his behavior was probably the result of an inexperienced young man thrust into a position of unlimited power, the true nature of which had been carefully disguised by Augustus. Gaius, however, had no tact or self-restraint whatsoever, and this led to behavior which struck his contemporaries as insane.

The government of Gaius much more resembled an oriental despotism than that of the earlier emperors. He was consul four times during his four-year reign. Another indication of his orientalism was his treatment of his sisters, especially Julia Drusilla, with whom he is reported to have committed incest.[7] During his illness of 37 CE, he named her his heir, but she died in 38 CE, at the age of 22. Caligula enforced public mourning throughout the Empire and, although there was no precedent in Roman history for the consecration of a woman, she was declared divine, under the name Panthea. During the later empire, however, many imperial women were given divine honors. For himself, Gaius accepted unprecedented honors, which came close to deification. He needlessly stirred up great unrest among the Jews in both Alexandria and Judea by attempting to have a statue of himself set up in the temple at Jerusalem.

Finally, on the 24th of January 41 CE, a conspiracy was successful, and he was murdered in the palace in Rome. His fourth wife, Milonta Caesonia, and his only child, a daughter of three years, were murdered with him. Thus ended the first—and perhaps premature—experiment in oriental absolutism: though it was unsuccessful, it demonstrated that the governmental system established by Augustus could support oriental despotism, even without any fundamental constitutional modification.

The difference between the reigns of Augustus and Gaius was only the difference between the personalities of the two men, not between their powers. The tact and moderation of Augustus made him see law as the voluntary limit on his own will, but Gaius made his will the law, and thus tore away all the legal fictions of the republican façade, revealing the *princeps* to be, in fact, the absolute master of the Roman state. When it comes to making a judgment on Gaius's personality, one must recognize that his conduct cannot be totally attributed to simple madness. Much of the responsibility must be attributed to the bad examples laid before him in childhood and in adolescence, which took the place of a good education and training for leadership that he never received. Also, the psychological insecurity and constant fear for his life during his enforced residence on the Island of Capri with the paranoid old emperor, Tiberius, must have permanently damaged and twisted his inherently weak mental and moral fiber.

---

7. His great-grandfather was Mark Antony. Some scholars think Gaius was attempting to imitate the Egyptian tradition of the brother-sister marriage in the Egyptian royal family.

Figure 11.5: The Claudian Aqueduct where it enters Rome at the Porta Maggiore.

Claudius (41–54)

The next emperor's full name is Tiberius Claudius Nero Germanicus, but he is known to history simply as Claudius. He was the elder brother of Germanicus, but he suffered from some kind of paralysis, which was considered a disqualification for public office by Augustus and Tiberius. Thus, he had hitherto been the most ignored member of the Julian family. His proclamation as emperor in 41 CE was largely an accident. After the murder of Caligula, he was discovered in the palace by a soldier, where he was hiding behind a curtain because he feared that he too would be murdered. He was dragged to the Praetorian camp and saluted by the Praetorian Guards as emperor while the senate was still discussing the possibility of restoring the republic. It may have been an accident, but it almost certainly prevented a long civil war.

Claudius, like Henry VIII, was incurably uxorious. Though he was unlucky in marriage, he could not bear to be without a wife: he was married four times and fathered at least five children. At the time of his accession, he was married to Valeria Messalina and had by her a daughter, Octavia, who later became Nero's first wife, and a son, Britannicus, who almost certainly was poisoned in 55 CE on Nero's orders. But Messalina was not a faithful wife, and Claudius alone seems to have been blind to her sexual extravagance. Also, it cannot be argued that she was very intelligent. In 48 CE, she was seized with an unhealthy desire for the consul of that year, a certain Gaius Silius, who likewise could not have been one of the more intelligent products of the Roman aristocracy. Messalina and Silius in combination, though they were never a real threat to the position of Claudius, did however foolishly destroy themselves. The climax of their affair came while Claudius was absent from Rome at Ostia, when the lovers openly went through the formalities of a marriage service. Needless to say this rather upset the imperial freedmen and they took counsel together to protect their own position as much as that of Claudius. Upon Claudius's return, the two lovers were forthwith put to death. Claudius then married his niece, Julia Agrippina, the daughter of Germanicus and the mother of Nero. This marriage was even more tragic than the previous one. In 50 CE, Agrippina persuaded Claudius to adopt her son Nero. Her argument was that Nero was four years older than Britannicus and could serve as his guardian. Four years later, on October 13, 54 CE, Claudius died suddenly. It was and still is believed that Agrippina handed him a dish of poisoned mushrooms, though there is no real proof for this. He was 64 years of age and, in fact, his health had been failing for some years. Sudden death due to strokes and heart attacks after the age of forty was not uncommon in the ancient world—as indeed it is not unknown today.

Claudius was the first emperor since Augustus to receive the distinction of deification. His greatest claim to honorable fame is that he followed in the footsteps of Augustus. He converted the absolute force of the Principate, which Gaius had used merely to gratify his own base desires, into the enlightened service of the empire. Claudius thus preserved the Augustan tradition of respect for republican forms, but he also had many faults, which give a certain unattractiveness to his personality. He was a glutton, a relentless joker, and he liked to gossip: he talked to everyone about everything in anyone's presence. As an administrator, he attempted to personally supervise even the minute details of his directives and thereby needlessly overburdened himself with work—about which he constantly complained: of course he had absolutely no administrative experience before he assumed the office of emperor. He was, perhaps, too trusting of those around him, especially his wives, but after all, this is merely a reflection of his own basic honesty and goodwill. In the end, these are all forgivable faults, and he atoned for them by his deeds, which indicate that he sincerely and keenly felt that the tremendous responsibility of ruling the world must be exercised for the benefit of the common good, not merely to satisfy his own personal desires and lusts.

Nero (54–68 CE)

Nero, a great-great-grandson of Augustus, was the last, and in many ways, the most colorful and interesting of the Julio-Claudian emperors. With the help of his mother, Agrippina,[8] and the support of the freedman Pallas, the young Nero succeeded to the Principate without opposition on the

---

8. This is Julia Agrippina (15–59 CE), the sister of Gaius and daughter of Germanicus and Agrippina, the daughter of Julia (Augustus's daughter) and Agrippa. She was thus the great-great-granddaughter of Augustus. It is quite easy to confuse the various "Agrippinas" of the Julio-Claudian family.

13th of October of 54, at the age of 17. In his inaugural speech he declared that he intended to rule *ex praescripto Augusti,* "as ordained by Augustus." He then demonstrated his modesty by declining additional honors; his piety by consecrating Claudius and expressing gratitude to his mother; his clemency by refusing to sign a death warrant. Because of his intense enthusiasm for art, flatterers hailed him as Apollo. Thus, the reign of Nero began with great promise and expectation.

But trouble was bound to arise between the artistic son and the overbearing mother, and it was not long in coming. During the early days of his reign, Agrippina exerted the most personal influence over Nero, while his former tutor, the philosopher Seneca, together with Sextus Burrus, the perfect of the Praetorian Guard, controlled the administration of the empire. However, the young emperor's friend, Marcus Salvius Otho, who was himself destined to be emperor, at least for a few weeks in 69, encouraged Nero to free himself from his mother's control. Agrippina retaliated by backing the claims of Britannicus, son of Claudius and Messalina, with the result that Britannicus was poisoned in 55 CE and Agrippina was sent into exile,[9] giving Nero's character free reign and the result is not a pretty picture.

Now Nero fell in love with the beautiful Poppaea Sabina, the wife of his friend Otho, who was dispatched to Lusitania (modern Portugal) as governor, where he remained until Nero's death. Poppaea now became Nero's mistress. It is alleged that she influenced Nero to murder his mother in 59 CE and to divorce, banish, and finally execute his first wife, Octavia in 62. There may be some truth in this. . . or it may be the product of embellishment by ancient writers. At any rate, he married Poppaea, who bore him a daughter in 63, which died four months later. She was pregnant again in 65, but she died when Nero, in a fit of temper, kicked her in the abdomen. The repentant emperor gave her a public funeral and divine honors.

In the year 64 CE, a fire destroyed about half of the city of Rome and Nero seized this opportunity to build himself a colossal palace in the burned out area of the city which he called the *Domus Aurea,* or "golden house." This palace was to cover the Palatine, Caelian and Esquiline Hills, about 125 acres in all. Rumors, probably unfounded, circulated that Nero himself had set the fire and had recited his own poems while the city burned. He tried to use the small Christian congregation in Rome as scapegoats in order to deflect the rumors away from himself, but by the end of the year 64, almost all the elements of the Roman population had reason to dislike him. Then, in 65, a conspiracy against Nero was discovered and its leaders were executed, but now Nero began to suspect everyone, and a series of judicial murders followed. In 66 he toured Greece where he graciously declared "the freedom of the Greeks." In 67, he competed in the Olympic Games where he personally won many victories—in fact, he won just about every event, he entered—a great athlete, as well as a great artist!

Back in Rome there was much unrest while Nero was absent, and a famine threatened because so many grain ships were diverted to Greece to carry supplies for his court. In the winter of 67/68, the freedman Helius, who had been left in charge at Rome, crossed over to Greece and convinced Nero to return home. He reached Rome in January of 68, but the situation continued to deteriorate. In March several generals, including Servius Sulpicius Galba, the governor of Spain, rose in revolt. Nero could probably still have saved himself by firm military action, but all he could think of was fantastic schemes of revenge, or else fantasize about reducing his enemies to tears by the power of his poetry. The Praetorian Guards were bribed by their commander to desert Nero

---

9. Agrippina was murdered in March of 59 CE at Baiae by a freedman, Anicetus, acting on Nero's instructions. Thus, Nero is known to history, among many other things, as a matricide. She wrote an autobiography which does not survive.

and proclaim Galba the emperor. Nero fled Rome and, on June 9th of 68, committed suicide: his last words were, "*qualis artifex pero,*" "what an artist dies in me!" He was a little over thirty years of age and he reigned for less than fourteen years: he was the last of the "sons of Aeneas," the last Julio-Claudian. It was, indeed, the end of a dynasty.

Nero's concept of the imperial authority as a principle of sovereign splendor, an omnipotent source of all good as well as all evil, was understood quite well in the East and, at least by the lower classes, in the West. His fame in history is preserved by the legends that grew up around his name. It was really only the Christians and the Jews, with their pretentious and overbearing moral conscience, who damned his memory. They, together with the official opinion of the ensuing Flavian Dynasty, passed down to the Middle Ages the demonic figure of Nero, around whom crystallized the most fantastic collection of legends attached to any of the Roman emperors, with the result that even today he is the best known of all the Roman emperors. He is also the most popular with Hollywood, where this demon Nero, has become a kind of morbid model by which all Roman emperors are portrayed—and this is a shame, because it falsely colors the public's perception of the ancient world.

The effects of the murder of Caligula were confined to the urban circle of Rome, but the opposition provoked by Nero was so widespread that for the first time it involved the armies stationed in the provinces. The Julio-Claudian dynasty had run its course and come to an end, but the Principate established by Augustus went on. The ensuing civil war was fought to create a new emperor, not to destroy the monarchy, and the survival of the imperial regime was never in question. The administration founded by Augustus and consolidated by Tiberius and Claudius continued to function and it demonstrated that it could now run on its own, or even with a madman or a lyre-playing artist at the helm.

The Flavian Dynasty (69–96)

The reign of Nero was followed by a civil war between the commanders of the provincial armies to determine who would be the next emperor. This civil war occurred primarily because there was no Julian left to ascend to the throne, but both in length and intensity it was mild when compared to the last decades of the Republic. Nonetheless, it was a period of anarchy.

The Long Year (69)

Nero committed suicide on June 9, 68; Vespasian was recognized as emperor by the Senate on December 22, 69. During the intervening eighteen months, three emperors, Galba, Otho, and Vitellius, mounted the throne of the Roman Empire and were, each in their turn, cut down, before Vespasian finally made his occupation of the office permanent. This short period between the death of Nero and the accession of Vespasian has fascinated historians from that time to the present. Perhaps more has been written about the year 69 than any other single year in the entire history of Western Civilization. It is usually known as "the year of the four emperors," or simply as "the long year."[10]

Servius Sulpicius Galba, the governor of Spain for eight years under Nero, entered Rome in October of 68, but was able to hold on to the emperorship for only a few months. When he adopted

---

10. Among the most useful of the modern studies is Wellesley, Kenneth, *The Long Year* (1976), Westview Press, Bolder, Colorado.

Figure 11.6: The Flavian Amphitheater, or Colosseum.

Lucius Calpurnius Piso as his heir, the disappointed Otho (ex-husband of Nero's second wife Poppaea) bribed the Praetorian Guard to proclaim him emperor, and they murdered Galba and Piso. Otho himself was on the throne only eight weeks, because Aulus Vitellius, commander of the powerful armies of the Rhine, had already been proclaimed emperor by his troops. Vitellius was victorious at the Battle of Cremona and Otho committed suicide. During his reign of seven months, Vitellius almost bankrupted the treasury with his sumptuous banquets and luxurious living. Out in the East, Titus Flavius Vespasian had been sent to Judea in 66 with a large army to suppress the Jewish revolt. Now his soldiers hailed him as emperor. He left his eldest son Titus in charge of the siege of Jerusalem[11] and set out for Rome. Vitellius's forces were defeated and on December 20, 69 he was killed. Vespasian founded the Flavian dynasty and restored peace to the Roman Empire.

Vespasian (69–79)

Vespasian was an efficient administrator. He provided a strong central government for Rome which further enhanced the powers of the emperor. The old republican institutions—the Senate and the Assembly—no longer retained any powers at all. But the consuls and other magistrates continued to exist, although they were now, in effect, appointed by the emperor.

---

11. Beset by violent factional strife and internal discord, Jerusalem remained defiant. Built on two hills and surrounded by formidable fortifications, the city proved to be a difficult obstacle to the pacification of Judea. The assault began in the spring of 70. Four weeks were required to breach the walls of the so-called New City, actually the suburb of Bezetha. A siege wall was constructed around the inner city and the Temple, but not until August was the outer Temple court reached and in the ensuing attack the Temple itself was burned to the ground and all the defenders were killed. In the final desecrating of the Temple a sacrifice was made to the Roman standards in the Temple court.

Vespasian encouraged rebuilding on the vacant areas created by the fire of 64, and he himself began work on several important buildings, including the famous Flavian Amphitheater (Colosseum) on the site of the lake of Nero's Golden House. His administration marks a turning point, a kind of coming of age, of the government of the Principate. From this point on the power of the emperorship will be used in a responsible and mature way to promote the general welfare of the state. Vespasian sought to promote merit over birth or wealth by offering subventions to senators not possessing the property qualifications of their rank. He also restored many cities throughout the empire and granted state salaries for the first time to teachers of Latin and Greek rhetoric. In contrast to his immediate predecessors, Vespasian died peacefully on June 23, 79. His last words are reported to have been, "Oh my! I think I am becoming a god." Indeed, he was deified immediately after his death and was interned in the Mausoleum of Augustus alongside the Julio-Claudians.

Titus (79–81)

From the very beginning of Vespasian's reign, Titus was designated the official heir apparent and he received virtually all the honors of the imperial office while his father was still alive—yet none of the sources indicate that he was ever considered a "co-ruler." Upon assuming the throne, Titus immediately had his father deified and the cult temple he built in the forum just below the Capitoline Hill is still partially standing today. The Colosseum was completed and dedicated by him with a 100-day festival which included mock sea battles on an artificial lake, wild beast hunts, and gladiatorial combats. He also began the construction of many other public projects and large sums were spent in the provinces as well, especially on road construction. This gained for him a reputation for generosity. But his reign was cut short by his sudden and unexpected death in 81, only 26 months into his reign. He was immediately deified by his brother and successor, Domitian.

Domitian (81–96)

Domitian, the second son of Vespasian, was about ten years younger than Titus. Although he received a good education, he was kept in the background during the reigns of his father and brother, because he was never intended for the throne. The two brothers were never close, but as Titus lay dying in September of 81, Domitian was proclaimed emperor in the Praetorian Camp.

He had problems with the aristocracy from the beginning, partly because he was considered to be an upstart outsider, and partly because of his insistence on micromanaging everything, particularly the economy, which made him appear autocratic and oppressive. For example, he rigorously collected the taxes (always unpopular) and established the office of "curator" to investigate financial mismanagement in the provinces. Yet, he spent lavishly on civic improvements, both in Rome and in the provinces. Another source of discontent among the aristocrats was Domitian's stern enforcement of public morals. In 85 he made himself *censor perpetuus*, censor for life, in order to enforce the *mos majorum* and encourage the traditional Roman religion. To this end he ordered all philosophers and foreign cults, with the exception the cult of Isis, of which he himself was a devotee, out of Rome. Some Christians and Jews may have been affected under this decree, but there is no indication that they were the object of his action. Later, however, stories of Christian persecutions, true or not, evolved and multiplied, but with no evidence to support them.

Mistrust between the emperor and the aristocracy continued to increase and at least 11 senators of consular rank were executed and many others were exiled. Several conspiracies, real or imagined, were suppressed by Domitian, but when suspicion finally spread to the personal staff of the emperor, they acted more or less in self-defense, and Domitian was assassinated on September

18, 96 in a palace plot. It was the end of the Flavian dynasty, the second imperial dynasty to rule the Roman world. The empire was governed efficiently during Domitian's reign, and he left the treasury with a surplus. Nevertheless, his reign was remembered by the Romans as a period of tyranny and illegal oppression.

The Age of the Five Good Emperors (96–180)

Following the Flavian dynasty a series of five excellent emperors ruled the Roman Empire for almost 85 years. They were called the "Five Good Emperors"[12] because, unlike their predecessors, they were able to win the support and cooperation of the Senate. Although Domitian did not designate an heir, no civil war ensued, and the stability established by the Flavians endured.[13]

Nerva (96–98)

A group of the conspirators who had murdered Domitian proclaimed a rather obscure man named Marcus Cocceius Nerva as the new emperor. Nerva seems at first glance an odd choice. He had never governed a province or commanded an army, he was 66 years old and well past his prime, but he was safe and innocuous, having cooperated with every regime all the way back to Nero. Furthermore, he had no children or other close relatives, and there was no possibility of him establishing a dynasty. In other words, he was no one's first choice but everyone's second choice. Some senators even seemed to believe Nerva could be used to re-establish the old republic and make the Senate once again the leading institution of the state. But of course that was merely a dream that had no basis in reality. The most important act of Nerva's brief sixteen-month reign was the adoption of Marcus Ulpius Traianus (Trajan) as his son and heir and co-emperor. About three months later, on January 28, 98, even before Trajan arrived in Rome, Nerva died and Trajan became the next emperor without opposition.

For almost a century thereafter, the throne of the Roman Empire passed peacefully and without opposition from one emperor to the next through the process of adoption. This is very strange in a monarchal form of government and some historians have seen this phenomenon as a conscious attempt by the Romans to solve the problem of succession. Each of these emperors, so the theory goes, abandoned dynastic considerations and searched the empire to find the best man to be his successor. According to this theory, then, the imperial monarchy became an appointive office by use of the institution of adoption. This all sounds reasonable, but the trouble is, it does

---

12. This designation does not mean that none of the previous emperors were good, but that these five, compared with Domitian before them and Commodus after them, conformed to the model established by those whom the ancient writers—who viewed the world through the eyes of the aristocratic class—considered to be the best of the previous emperors: Augustus, Vespasian, and Titus.

13. Edward Gibbon, in his great work, *The History of the Decline and Fall of the Roman Empire* (1776), calls this period the "happiest age of human history," and describes it in the opening paragraph of the three volume book thus: "In the second century of the Christian era, the Empire of Rome comprehended the fairest part of the earth, and the most civilized portion of mankind. The frontiers of that extensive monarchy were guarded by ancient renown and disciplined valor. The gentle but powerful influence of laws and manners had gradually cemented the union of the provinces. Their peaceful inhabitants enjoyed and abused the advantages of wealth and luxury. The image of a free constitution was preserved with decent reverence: the Roman senate appeared to possess the sovereign authority, and devolved on the emperors all the executive powers of government. During a happy period (A.D. 98–180) of more than fourscore years, the public administration was conducted by the virtue and abilities of Nerva, Trajan, Hadrian, and the two Antonines."

not fit the evidence, because it simply did not happen that way. In the first place, the whole adoptive principle, so-called, was a fluke of history, an accident. It was an accident because it was made possible, indeed it was made necessary, by the fact that none of these emperors happened to have a son or other close male relative. The first emperor (Marcus Aurelius), who did have a son of his own, made that son his successor, even though, as we shall see, he was far from being the best man for the job. Secondly, the adoptive principle, in itself, contradicts the concept of an appointive office. The fact that adoption was used as the method for transmitting the powers of the Principate was an affirmation, rather than a denial, of the dynastic principle. The Roman practice of adoptio, placed the adopted person, for all practical and legal purposes, in the same position as if he had been a biological child of the adopter. Therefore, we must not forget that, in the eyes of the Romans, the six emperors from Nerva to Commodus consisted of one unbroken dynasty, not a series of rulers who appointed their successors. The fact that these emperors were succeeded by adopted sons, instead of natural sons, in no way denies the dynastic principle. And thirdly, the idea that the "best man for the job" was selected for adoption is bit off the mark. In every case there were other considerations, and one of them was kinship to the emperor. It is true that Trajan was not related in any way to Nerva, but Hadrian was Trajan's first cousin once removed, and Marcus Aurelius was the nephew of Antoninus's wife, Faustina. It is true that these are not very close relatives and this may all seem very academic to modern ears, but if these emperors searched over all the empire to find the best man to adopt, they always seemed to find that man very close to the imperial palace. In other words, the adoptive principle, contrary to popular belief, affirms, rather than denies, the dynastic principle.

Trajan (98–117)

Trajan was a military man and he thus saw a military solution to most problems. The Dacians, who lived north of the Danube River, had been menacing the provinces of Pannonia and Moesia for about a decade. Domitian had attempted to buy their good behavior with large subsidies, but under their king Decebalus, the Dacians continued their hostile activities. So Trajan applied the military solution: in a series of two hard-fought wars between 101 and 106, Dacia was annexed and eventually so completely Romanized that even today the inhabitants of the area (modern Romania) speak a romance language.

Trajan was a capable and efficient administrator and remained on good terms with the Senate throughout his reign. He pursued an ambitious building program, both in Rome and around the empire. The remains of the Basilica Ulpia, where Trajan's Column still stands, and the great Trajan's Market, an ancient shopping mall, are among the most fascinating sites in modern Rome. Since Trajan had no close male relatives, his wife and female relatives played enormously important roles in the public life of his reign. His wife, Pompeia Plotina, and his sister, Matidia, were given the title of Augusta. Matidia's daughter, Sabina, married the future emperor Hadrian in the year 100. These women were honored throughout the empire and were involved in many significant decisions.

After seven years of peace, trouble developed in the East, and in 113 Trajan prepared for a decisive war with Parthia. He invaded Mesopotamia in 114, capturing Babylon and the capital of Ctesiphon and reaching the Persian Gulf in 116. The following year was devoted to putting down revolts among the newly conquered peoples. Trajan was now an old man of at least 64 and in 117 he began to make his way back home, but at Cilicia (in southeast Asia Minor) he suffered a stroke and died on August 9, after designating Hadrian his successor on his deathbed. He was recognized by the ancient Romans and by modern historians as one of the best emperors ever to rule Rome.

For the rest of Roman history each new emperor was hailed with the prayer, "may he be luckier than Augustus and better than Trajan."

Hadrian (117–138)

Hadrian's father died when he was only eight or nine years old, and his only male relative was Trajan, his father's uncle. Trajan and Plotina thus became surrogate parents to Hadrian. It was Hadrian who carried the news to Trajan of his adoption by Nerva in 97 and he was a close associate of the emperor until his death in 117. At that time he was serving as commander of the army of the East.

Hadrian's first act upon ascending the throne was to abandon Trajan's eastern conquests. But he did far more than this: Trajan had been a dynamic expansionist; Hadrian, by contrast, was a patient consolidator. In fact, Hadrian adopted a system of limits, which was, perhaps, one of the most important benchmarks in the history of the Roman Empire. With Hadrian's reign, the psychology of the Romans began to undergo a subtle, though very fundamental, change. The posture of the army was gradually shifted from the offensive to the defensive mode: philosophers, intellectuals, and writers—the thinkers of society—slowly stopped looking outward and began to turn their gaze inward upon themselves. Expansion gradually gave way to status quo, and sometime during the next few generations, the cares of this world became less important to the people of the Roman Empire than the concern for that "other world," whatever name you chose to give it. It was an extremely subtle change, and it began to appear during Hadrian's reign, though it is difficult, perhaps impossible, to discern to what extent Hadrian was the molder of this change or to what extent he was merely its product. At any rate, few historians will disagree that the empire, at least in the eyes of its own inhabitants, had now reached the limits of its human and natural resources, and the Romans must now settle down to defend its borders.

The major part of Hadrian's time and energy, during his entire reign, was devoted to reorganizing the defense of the empire. His foreign policy was aimed at providing secure frontiers and a peaceful interior. This necessitated the development of a new grand strategy of the empire. The Augustan defense strategy was based on a system of client states, situated beyond the actual borders of the empire, which served as buffers against the empire's enemies located still further out from the empire's center. Under this system, the Roman army's mission was first to maintain and support the regimes friendly to Rome within this client state system, and second, to assist these clients in any major wars against their common enemies, meaning, of course, the peoples who lived beyond the Roman influence. Under this system, the borders of the empire were often not clearly defined: Roman influence simply faded away as one traveled further and further away from the center of the empire, especially as one left the provinces. Sometimes, it was not completely clear whether a specific territory was Roman or not, particularly if that territory was located near the edge of Roman influence.

The more rigidly preclusive defensive system developed by Hadrian involved so-called "scientific" borders precisely demarcated wherever possible along natural barriers, such as mountains, rivers, or oceans, but otherwise a simple line drawn on the ground, so that all would know what was Roman and what was not. Where no natural boundaries existed, walls, moats, earthworks, forts, and other permanent defensive fortifications known as *limes*, were constructed. This was something new to Roman strategy; the army was now committed to face the enemy directly across precisely defined borders. More than half of Hadrian's twenty-one-year reign was spent traveling around the empire, organizing and inspecting these new defenses.

Hadrian was a man of extraordinary talents, certainly one of the most gifted rulers Rome ever produced. He was an accomplished public speaker, a student of philosophy, and he wrote both prose and poetry, but it was as an architect that he left his greatest mark. He rebuilt Agrippa's

Pantheon into the remarkable building that exists today. The main section of the building is in the shape of a drum capped by a coffered dome, pierced by an oculus, over 29 feet in diameter, which is the only source of illumination for the interior of the temple. The height and diameter of the room are identical and form a perfect circle in every direction. The concrete dome is the largest ever constructed until the 20th Century. Modern engineers have still not been able to determine exactly how such a feat was accomplished.

Hadrian's choice for a successor was a distinguished senator Tiberius Aurelius Fulvius Boionius Arrius Antoninus, mercifully known to history as simply Antoninus Pius. Hadrian was actually responsible for selecting the next two emperors because he had Antoninus adopt two young men, Lucius Verus and Marcus Aurelius, who became co-emperors upon Antoninus's death in 161. When Hadrian died on July 10, 138, his ashes were placed in his mausoleum which he had constructed across the Tiber, which still exists today as the Castel Sant'Angelo because it was used by the papacy as a fortress during the Middle Ages.

Antoninus Pius (138–161)

The twenty-three year reign of Antoninus Pius was a time of unprecedented peace and prosperity. His low-keyed style of administration was in marked contrast to those of his two immediate predecessors, Trajan and Hadrian. As a result of his gentle and efficient administration, he was remembered by his subjects as the most respected and loved of all the Roman emperors.

Antoninus's economic policy was conservative and he avoided waste while at the same time spending generously on public works, such as roads, harbors, and relief for fires, floods, and other

Figure 11.7: Marcus Aurelius.

natural disasters. In foreign affairs, Antoninus sought to maintain peace with the peoples bordering the empire, but there were nevertheless minor wars with the Britons, Moors, Dacians and revolts in Achaea and Egypt. His administration was more centralized in Rome than his predecessors'. In fact, he never even left Italy during his entire reign.

Antoninus and his wife, Faustina, had four children, two sons and two daughters, but only one daughter, Faustina the Younger, was still living when he was adopted by Hadrian. He married her to Marcus Aurelius, his heir apparent, in 145. When the empress, Faustina the Elder, died in 141 the Senate deified her and voted her a temple in the Roman Forum, which is still partially standing today. In her memory, Antoninus instituted a program to aid orphans, which used government money to make loans to farmers and set aside the money generated by the interest on these loans to care for orphaned girls. On the coinage these children were called *puallae Faustinianae*, "the girls of Faustina." When Antoninus died in March of 161 he was immediately deified by the Senate, and the Temple of Faustina was rededicated to both Antoninus and Faustina, as the surviving inscription over its porch indicates. A column of red granite was erected in Antoninus's honor in the Campus Martius. The marble base for this column is preserved in the Vatican Museum and includes the beautiful image of the apotheosis of Antoninus and Faustina.

Marcus Aurelius (161–180)

Marcus Aurelius and Lucius Verus became joint emperors, but Verus was always the junior partner and remained in the background until his early death in 169. Aurelius, on the other hand, is a unique figure in Roman history because he symbolized the philosopher-king ideal of Plato. He was a serious student of the stoic school of philosophy all of his life and he attempted to apply the principles of Stoicism not only to his own life but to his rule of the empire as well. He has left us a very interesting little book called simply *Meditations*,[14] which records his very personal reflections on life.

---

14. *Meditations* is a kind of personal journal, or dairy, not intended for publication. Marcus Aurelius simply jotted down from time to time anything that struck him as worth preserving. It has a "stream of consciousness" atmosphere about it. There is no plot, or organization or purpose to the book and the reader may look through it and read entries at random, as suits his mood. There are priceless little gems everywhere. For example: "To pursue the unattainable is insanity, yet the thoughtless can never refrain from doing so." Or: "Whatever you take in hand, pause at every step to ask yourself, 'Is it the thought of forfeiting this that makes me dread death.'" Here are some of his thoughts concerning fame: "Little then is each man's life and little the corner of the earth he lives in, and little even the longest survival of his fame with posterity, and that too passed through a succession of poor mortals, each one of them soon to die, with no knowledge of themselves even, let alone of a man who has died long ago.

"Shall mere fame distract you? Look at the speed of total oblivion of all and the void of endless time on either side of us and the hollowness of applause.... For the whole earth is but a point, and this what a tiny corner of our dwelling place, and how few and how paltry are those who will praise you.

".... but even supposing that those who are to remember you never die and their remembering is thus immortal—what is that to you? To the dead praise means nothing.... In a short time will come for you obliviousness of everything—and everything will be oblivious of you.

"Consider for example the times of Vespasian, and you will see all these things: people marrying, rearing children, falling ill, dying, making war, holding festivals, trading, farming, flattering, asserting themselves, suspecting, plotting, praying for other people's death, muttering about present conditions, making love, hoarding money, wanting the consulship, wanting the throne. Now that life of theirs exists no more anywhere. Pass on again to the times of Trajan. Again, all the same. That life is dead too. Words familiar once are now obsolete. So too are the names of those once renowned in song, now obsolete in a sense, Camillus, Caeso, Volesus, Dentatus, and a little later Scipio and Cato, then Augustus too, then Hadrian and Antoninus. For everything fades away and quickly becomes a myth; and soon complete oblivion covers them over. And this I say of those who shone in some remarkable way. For the rest, as soon as the breath left their bodies, they were unnoticed and unwept. How many a Chrysippus, how many a Socrates, how many an Epistetus has eternity already devoured?"

With the reign or Marcus Aurelius, the *pax Romana* was about to come to an end. Serious threats to the empire were developing in two widely separated areas: in the East, the newly resurgent Parthians seized Armenia and defeated two Roman armies; in the north, the German tribes, specifically the Marcomanni, the Quadi and the Sarmatians, were threatening to overrun the northern frontier. The tireless efforts of Marcus Aurelius were able to confine these wars to the periphery of the empire, but it was not clear how long such an effort could be sustained. Two simultaneous wars on widely separated frontiers was a nightmare for the Roman Empire. It is ironic that war dominated the reign of this peace loving emperor.

In 162, Marcus dispatched his imperial colleague, Lucius Verus, to the East with a large army to deal with the Parthians. But Verus was not the same kind of strong leader as Marcus himself: "indulgent" and "dilatory" are words that the ancients applied to him. However, Marcus provided him with able and talented generals, and the Roman armies recovered Armenia, invaded Mesopotamia, annihilated the Parthian army, and destroyed Ctesiphon, the Parthian capital. But the entire Roman Empire was to pay dearly for this success. Toward the end of the campaign a highly contagious plague appeared in the Roman army. In 166, Verus began his homeward journey and as the Roman army marched through Asia and Greece, the plague spread like wildfire through these provinces. Eventually, the plague was carried throughout Italy and Europe by the soldiers returning to their stations. The effects of this plague were no less devastating than the infamous black death of the Middle Ages. Between one third and one half of the population of the entire Roman Empire was swept away in a matter of a few years. Some areas of Europe were completely depopulated and had to be resettled later, more often than not by non-Roman peoples from outside the empire. The Roman Empire's population never fully recovered from this blow, and many scholars cite this disaster as one of the prime causes for the empire's eventual decline. The plague may well have touched off a vicious cycle of economic, social, and political decline that could not be reversed.

In 166, German tribes poured across the upper and lower Danube, looted the northern tear of Roman provinces, and even reached northern Italy itself. Two new legions were recruited as quickly as possible, and both Marcus and Verus led the army north to Aquileia. The barbarians sought peace and withdrew across the Danube: Italy, for the time being, was saved. After they returned to Rome, in early 169, Verus died suddenly of a stroke. Marcus now attempted to apply the same military solution to the German problem that Trajan had applied to the Dacians, permanent conquest of the area north of the Danube and the establishment of a more efficient frontier, further away from Italy, that could be defended with fewer soldiers. He probably would have continued west in a giant pincer movement, and finally have set the Elbe or even the Oder as the new Roman border. This would have given the Roman Empire a new frontier at least one third shorter and also several hundred miles further away from the center of the empire. At the same time it would have also lifted an enormous burden from the army, greatly improved the defense of the empire, and eventually Romanized several German tribes that had long been a thorn in the side of the Empire. It was a tremendous enterprise and Marcus very nearly succeeded. Indeed, he probably would have carried it off, except that he died in the process. This addition to the empire might very well have rejuvenated both its spirit and its economy to the extent of prolonging the *pax Romana* for many more decades or even centuries. But it was not to be. Instead, the reign of Marcus Aurelius ended in disaster. Immediately after his death, his son Commodus abandoned the entire campaign in order to retire to the pleasures of Rome. Thus, a lifetime of toil and planning was swept away by one childish whim. Marcus was deified by the Senate and sincerely mourned by the Romans, but the reign of the "philosopher king" ended in utter failure.

The Crisis of the Third Century (180–284)

From this point onward, the history of the Roman Empire is essentially a narrative of internal turmoil and external threat. A state as strong and firmly established as the Roman Empire possesses enormous restorative resources and can withstand even the most severe crisis, but when crisis feeds upon crisis, in a crescendo of disasters, even the most stable society is shattered. For more than two centuries,[15] scholars have attempted, without much success, to understand the causes of the events of 3rd Century. The general consensus has been that three principle elements contributed to the decline of the Roman Empire: a series of weak and corrupt emperors; a demoralized and paralyzed bureaucracy; and the militarization of the empire's government. But these proposals are vague and of little use. In reality they amount to more of a description of the process of decline than an analysis of its causes.

The Severan Dynasty (193–235)

In some superficial aspects, the end of the age of the Five Good Emperors resembles the end of the Julio-Claudian Dynasty. Like Nero, Commodus (180–192), the son of Marcus Aurelius, ascended the throne as a young (age 19), inexperienced man. Also like Nero, he was received with great expectation and the early part of his reign—under the influence of the wise advisors his father had provided—went extremely well. But soon the dark side of Commodus began to emerge. He indulged in the most extraordinary excesses. He believed himself to be the reincarnation of Hercules and began to dress in lion skins and carry a club, the symbols of that ancient Greek hero. Commodus may well have been insane during the last years of his reign. In any event, he became so oppressive and abusive of even those assistants and servants within the palace that on the last day of the year 192 the athlete Narcissus—the emperor's personal trainer, to use a modern term—strangled him to death in his bath.

After a year of civil war, intrigue, and assassination, Septimius Severus (193–211), a native of North Africa who was the commander of the army in the province of Pannonia north of Italy, became emperor and established the Severan Dynasty (193–235). But he had to spend the next 4 years defeating two other generals who had made a bid for the imperial throne at the same time. During his 18 year reign, Severus fought two important wars. In 198 he invaded Parthia and was completely victorious, but instead of attempting to annex the entire area, as Trajan had done, he only established a small new province, called Mesopotamia, just east of Syria. The other major war was in Britain, where he attempted unsuccessfully to push the Roman frontier north of the old boundary known as Hadrian's Wall, but he died there during the campaign in 211, at age 63.

Septimius Severus initiated the most far reaching reforms in the Roman government since the reign of Augustus. He radically lowered the importance and prestige of the Senate and elevated the importance of the military and the *equites* in the operation of the government. The praetorian prefect (commander of the imperial guard) became, in effect, the commander of all troops stationed in Italy, and Italy itself was reduced to the status of a province. (Or looked at another way, the status of the provinces became equal to that of Italy.) This was actually the culmination of the leveling or equalizing of the various geographical and cultural elements of the Roman Empire that had begun as early as the reign of Vespasian. The several legal reforms included the formal recognition of a social trend that had been developing for some time: the division of Roman citizens into

---

15. Since Edward Gibbon's classic work, *The Decline and Fall of the Roman Empire* (1776–88).

the privileged *honestiores* ("honorable" orders) and the *humiliores* ("humble" people).[16] Perhaps the most important change of all was army reform. The soldiers' pay was increased by half and they were permitted to marry while still in service. The size of the army was increased from 30 to 33 legions, and it was now possible for soldiers of the lower ranks to make their way up into high positions in the command structure through merit and service. During the 3rd Century the most promising and rewarding career would be in the military.

The Severan Women

A remarkable facet of the Severan Dynasty was the prominent role played by the women. In a very real sense, the last decades of the dynasty can be labeled the "rule of the Severan women." These women were members of the Julian family of Syria. Septimius Severus's second wife, Julia Domna, and her sister, Julia Maesa, were educated, shrewd, and politically astute. How did these two families, one which originated in North Africa, the other in Syria, become united? Early in his career, when Severus was governor of Syria, he developed a close friendship with Julius Bassianus, the de-

Figure 11.8: The Severan Women. Top, left to right: Julia Domna, Julia Maesa; Bottom, left to right, Julia Soaemias, Julia Mamaea.

---

16. The *honestiores* included senators, *equites*, municipal magistrates, and soldiers of all ranks. The *humiliores* included all others: people who did not have enough wealth to hold local offices, freedmen, and the various poor citizens of all types. For the same crime, a *humilior* might be exiled or beheaded, while a *honestior* would be sentenced to labor in the mines or crucified. Furthermore, *honestiores* could much more easily appeal to the emperor.

scendant of a long line of priest-kings of the ancient city of Emesa. The descendants of these kings had long since been Romanized and were now, in the late second century, one of the most prominent families in Syria. They were the hereditary high priests of Elagabal, the sun-god of Emesa. The current high priest, the friend of Severus, had two daughters. The youngest was named Julia Domna, and her horoscope foretold that she was destined to be the wife of a ruler. The ancient texts tell us that this was the reason that Severus chose her for his second wife when he became a widower in 186.

Once her husband became emperor, Julia Domna managed to gather into her hands power, influence, and accrual control over the administration of the government unprecedented for a women of that time. She immediately acquired the title Augusta, which was traditional for the empress, but eventually her title as it appears on official inscriptions expanded to read: *Julia Pia Felex Augusta, Mater Augusti et Castrorum et Senatus et Patriae,* "Julia, the Pius, the Fortunate (favored by the gods), the August, Mother of the Augusti, and the Army, and the Senate, and the Fatherland."

But there was a cloud gathering over the Severan Dynasty: the hatred between Julia Domna's sons, Caracalla and Geta. The entire imperial family was in Britain when Septimius Severus died in 211. On his deathbed he consigned the empire to both his sons as joint rulers, with the advice, "Avoid quarrels, pay your soldiers well and do not bother about anything else." But of course the two brothers did quarrel, and when they returned to Rome their rivalry became so vicious that there was even talk of dividing the Empire between them. This, of course, would have invariably resulted in a civil war. In an attempt to avoid bloodshed, Julia Domna invited her sons to her apartment in the palace for a private meeting to settle their differences in February of 212. Unfortunately, Caracalla had commissioned some of his soldiers to murder his brother, and although Geta ran to his mother for protection, they stabbed him to death even in her arms.

Yet, Caracalla, vile though he was, was no matricide and Julia Domna's ascendancy in the government of her son remained dominate. The guilt Caracalla suffered over the murder of his brother seems to have driven him into near insanity. He had delusions that he was the reincarnation of Alexander the Great and during the years 214 to 217 he attempted to retrace the steps of Alexander through the Near East. During this time, Julia Domna administered the affairs of the empire. In the spring of 217 the route of Caracalla's march took him into Persian territory and the events of the next months are not clear. Evidently, his soldiers had enjoyed marching around the East as conquering heroes, so long as they were within Roman territory, but were not so happy about engaging in a real war with Persia. In any event, in April of 217 Caracalla was murdered, by whom it is not clear, but the Praetorian Prefect, Marcus Opellius Macrinus, declared himself the new emperor. Julia Domna returned to Syria and died at Antioch a short time later, probably by her own hand. Her horoscope had promised her husband power, it had not promised her happiness.

Julia Domna had an older sister, Julia Maesa, whose husband was already dead. Julia Maesa had two daughters, Julia Soaemias and Julia Mamaea. They were both also widows and they both had an only son. The son of Soaemias, known to history as Elagabalus, was, at 15, the oldest male member of the Julian family and had already assumed the family's hereditary position as high priest of the sun-god Elagabal at Emesa. On this young boy hung the fate of the Severan Dynasty. A coup was engineered by Julia Maesa with the help of her two daughters. First a rumor was circulated among the soldiers in Syria that Elagabalus was really the son of Caracalla, and his mother was glad to confirm the story. That such a story would have an influence on the soldiers is an indication of the strength of dynastic feeling at the time. Next, the young boy was smuggled into the army camp and there the troops proclaimed him emperor. After losing two battles against the insurgents, Macrinus was murdered by his own men. The sources tell us that during one of these battles the tide of war was running against the Severans, and their cause was saved only when the three Julian women appeared on the battlefield and through their own bravery prevented the soldiers from deserting the field.

Now Julia Maesa took firm control of the government, and the Roman Empire was for the first time ruled by a woman. But soon the young Elagabalus developed an independent streak and his mother unfortunately was not willing to keep him under control. The sun-god of Emesa, Elagabal, was worshiped in the form of a black stone, and the young emperor brought this object with him to Rome and attempted to elevate his god to the supreme position in the religion of the empire. The sources are also filled with stories of the emperor's corruption and debauchery, stories similar to those told about Commodus and Nero.

At any rate, within four years the bizarre behavior of Elagabalus so upset the Romans that it became obvious to Julia Maesa that if the dynasty was going to survive Elagabalus would have to be replaced. So she cleverly prevailed upon Elagabalus to adopt his cousin, her other grandson, a boy of 13 named Gessius Alexianus Bassianus, who received the name Severus Alexander and the title of Caesar. Then, in 222, Julia Maesa and Julia Mamaea formed an alliance and bribed the Praetorian Guards to murder Elagabalus and his mother and proclaim Severus Alexander the new emperor.

Severus Alexander was the nominal emperor for the next 13 years, but the government was actually under the control of his grandmother and mother, although they remained in the background as much as possible and never attempted to assume power openly. After Julia Maesa died in 223, Mamaea continued to administer the government and Alexander was always under her guidance and control, for he never developed a taste for independent action as his cousin had done. Julia Mamaea received all the high sounding titles and honors that had been accorded to Julia Domna. The emperor even come to be called "Alexander, the son of Julia Mamaea" on official inscriptions and documents. And Alexander was rememberd as the very personification of the ideal ruler. The old religion was re-established, the Senate was restored to a position of respect if not power, and several far reaching legal reforms were realized to make Roman law more equitable and just.

However, there is one thing a female ruler cannot do: lead the army in combat. In 235 Alexander and Mamaea were forced to campaign against the marauding Germans in the North. Mamaea sought to avoid war by offering the Germans subsidies in exchange for a treaty of alliance. Unfortunately, the soldiers viewed this as a display of weakness and thought the money should be distributed to the Roman army, not to the barbarians. Thus, on March 18, 235, Alexander and his mother were murdered together in their tent by the soldiers, and the dynasty of the Severans came to an end.

The historian may search all the ancient literature and find not one statement condemning Severus Alexander. His record is spotless. Almost alone among the Roman emperors, he is never accused of murder, corruption, or debauchery. But the reality is that he reigned, he did not govern. Power was always in the hands of his grandmother and his mother and while in the accounts of the period, which were all written by male writers, Alexander received all the credit, his good reputation is certainly a testimony to the orderly, peaceful and intelligent government of the Severan women.

The Soldier Emperors (235–284)

The end of the Severan Dynasty opened the flood gates of crisis. For the next fifty years, the Roman Empire was caught up in a rip tide of simultaneous external attack and internal chaos. Emperors were made and unmade on the whim of the soldiers. From 235 to 284, no less than twenty men officially ascended the throne of the Roman Empire, but only one of them died a natural death. In addition, there were countless others (we do not even know the names of some of them) who are listed as "usurpers," because they never managed to receive the official sanction of the Senate. During the crisis of the third century the empire came perilously close to self-destructing. Whole regions broke away from the central control and were governed temporarily by their own emperors.

The causes of this situation were numerous and complex. The civil wars ravaged the economy. Constant warfare interfered with trade and agricultural production. The dependence of the constantly changing emperors on the favor of the army forced them to overtax and debase the coinage in order to raise funds to satisfy their soldiers. Landlords, farmers, and manufacturers lost all motivation to produce. Many farmers simply abandoned their land, and poverty and hunger became rampant. The plague, which had decimated the population during Marcus Aurelius's reign, returned with a vengeance and swept through the population. Beginning in Egypt where the population of Alexandria was reduced by half, it raged across the empire for fifteen years. At one point in Rome 5,000 people a day lost their lives to the plague.

With the Roman population thinned and the empire's armies fighting each other, the Germans in the West and the Persians in the East broke through the Roman frontiers and spilled into the Empire's territories. In 251, the Goths overrun the Balkans, defeated, and killed the emperor Decius. For several years they looted and ravaged the northern provinces unchecked. In 260, the emperor Valerian was captured by the Persians. He was abused and humiliated by the Persian king Shapur. Valerian was used as a human stepping-stool to assist Shapur in mounting his horse, and the emperor's body was later skinned

Figure 11.9: Panel from the Ara Pacis Augustae: Mother Earth (center) flanked by the sea wind riding a dragon (right) and the land wind riding a swan (left).

and displayed as a trophy. The western provinces even broke away and formed an independent empire for a time. The glories of the *pax Romana* were only a dim memory.

Intellectual and Cultural Life of Ancient Rome

During the early part of their history, the Romans gave only a low priority to intellectual pursuits. In fact, the Romans themselves were quite aware that other peoples, especially the Greeks, were superior to them in art and literature. As the Latin poet Virgil expressed it in his famous lines from the *Aeneid*:

> Others may softer mould the breathing brass,
> Or from the marble coax the living face;
> Others may more eloquently plead than you,
> Or trace the hzeavenly orbits, or name the stars.
> But yours, O Roman, be the empire of men!
> Be these your arts! Impose the law of peace,
> Sparing the meek, and trampling down the proud![17]

Latin Literature

However, even if the Romans did not match the Greeks in artistic and literary creativity, their works have a status and value of their own, and they are important especially because, for many centuries after the passing of the ancient world, Europe knew of antiquity only through Roman eyes. This is because after the passing of the ancient world, knowledge of the ancient Greek language was lost in Western Europe for a thousand years and, until the Renaissance, it was only through Latin literature that Europe knew its past.

Roman poetry, while by no means as original and as moving as its Greek model, should not be dismissed as simply a second-rate imitation. Lucretius's 7,400 line poem *de Reum Natura*, or "On the Nature of Things," was the first great achievement of pure Latin poetry. It was an account of Epicurean philosophy and had as its object the freeing of human beings from the fear of death by giving them an insight into the laws of nature. But beyond the philosophy, Lucretius's work is great poetry. It was dedicated to the goddess Venus, whom the Romans worshiped as Venus Genitrix, the "mother of the Roman state": The first lines of the introduction demonstrate the beauty and power of Lucretius's poetry, even in translation:

> O Venus, mother of the Roman people eternal,
> Delight of gods and men and giver of life,
> You cause the sail-filled sea to team beneath the gliding stars,
> You cause the sky to clear and tempests to be stilled.
> For you the Earth puts forth her gentle flowers,
> For you the ocean smiles and the fierce heavens soften into golden glow,
> And for you the renewing South wind brings forth the returning spring.
> O then, dear goddess, the songs of birds herald your coming,
> The stolid cattle bound the fertile plains
> And swim the swollen streams for the sake of love.
> Then through all the seas and plains and mountains
> Love warms the hearts of all the creatures

---

17. Virgil, *Aeneid*, 6.848–854, translation by John Dryden.

And each in its own way renews its race.
Therefore you alone, O Venus, control the sum of things.
Without you no living creatures come forth,
Without you nothing glorious or beautiful exists.[18]

Lucretius and the Epicureans in general have a reputation for being anti-religious atheists, but these lines do not express the views of atheism.

It was, however, during the Augustan period that Latin poetry achieved its pinnacle, and it is here that we find the most perfect harmony of form and content. The poems of the Augustan Age are concentrated and polished, not dashed off with a careless hand but realized with great intellectual labor. The most famous of all Latin poets is Virgil, and his fame rests first and foremost on his great epic poem, the *Aeneid*, which is the epic story of the origins of the Roman people and it interweaves myth and history in a masterly fashion. The example quoted above needs no further explanation.

Many other poets flourished during this period. Ovid, the greatest lyric poet of the age, produced two works of equal fame. Probably best known to modern readers is his humorous "The Art of Love," in which he offers the young man instructions in how to find, win, and hold the affections of a girl. Ovid never seems to have taken life very seriously and in almost every line of the poem his joyful and irreverent humor comes through. For example:

Every lover is a soldier, and Cupid has his encampments,
Its true. Atticus, every lover is a soldier.
The age for warfare is also the age for love—
An old lover is no more use than the old soldier.
The qualities a general looks for in a good soldier
Are those a girl looks for in her fellow.
Both can sit up all night, both can sleep on the ground,
The one guards his mistress's door, the other his general's. . .[19]

Ovid's other great work is the *Metamorphoses*, a poem in fifteen books, which is a collection of the most important myths of the ancient world. They are mainly concerned with transformation, or metamorphoses, of human forms into things such as animals, birds, trees, bodies of water, and so forth. Beginning with the first transformation of chaos into order, Ovid retells about 250 myths from remote antiquity up to the deification of Julius Caesar. The stories are thus unified by a mythological chronology. This poem often seems strangely modern, because Ovid makes no pretense of believing in the gods or in events about which he writes. His tone is playful and even flippant and his stories are fantastic and amusing. In reality, his stories often reveal human folly, weakness, and courage. For example, in book 4, he describes how Venus, who was married to Vulcan, the god of fire and metalworking, was caught by her husband having an affair with Mars:

The Sun sees all things first. The Sun, they say,
Was the first one who spied on Mars and Venus
When they were making love. The Sun, offended,
Went with the story to her husband, Vulcan,
Telling him all, the when, the how, the where,

---

18. *Lucretius, de Reum Natura*, 1.1–27, translation by the author.

19. Ovid, *Amores*, 1.9.1f, Translation by F. A. Wright.

And Vulcan dropped whatever he was doing,
And made a net, with such fine links of bronze
No eye could see the mesh: no woolen thread
Was ever so delicate, no spider ever
Spun filament so frail from any rafter.
He made it so the slightest touch would bend it,
The slightest movement make it give, and then
He spread it over the bed, and when the lovers
Came there again, the husband's cunning art
Caught them and held them fast, and Vulcan, lord
Of Lemnos, opened wide the ivory doors
And called the gods to come and see. They lay there,
The two, in bondage, in disgrace. And some one,
Not the least humorous of the gods in Heaven,
Prayed that some day he might be overtaken
By such disgrace himself. And there was laughter
For a long time in Heaven, as the story
Was told and told again.[20]

In the end, however, Ovid's robust love of life got him into trouble with Augustus: he was some-how—we don't know the details—implicated in the scandal with Augustus's daughter Julia and spent the last years of his life in exile far his beloved Rome. It was an especially cruel punishment for him.

Roman prose reached its peak during the late Republic with Cicero, the outstanding orator and one of the most prolific writers of ancient Rome. In fact, more writing by Cicero survives than by any other Latin writer. But Cicero was not a thinker of great originality, his real achieve-ments were the development of the Latin language and the enlargement of Rome's spiritual hori-zons. The fact that so much of his writing survives—speeches, personal letters, essays, and treatises on almost every subject—is not so much due to what he said as to how he said it. He is studied even today not so much for his philosophy as for his Latin.

Cicero also tried his hand at poetry, but with little success. He wrote a long epic poem about his own consulship, which, we must be thankful, does not survive. This assertion can be made with confidence because we do know the first line, which reads: "O Rome, how fortunate were you to have had me as your consul!" Had the entire poem survived, young students of Latin throughout the centuries would have been forced to suffer through over 700 lines of that drivel.

Roman Historians

Livy (Titus Livius), a Romanized Celt, wrote the first great history in Latin, called *Ab Urbe Con-dita*, or "From the Foundation of the City," in 142 books. In his preface, Livy says that he wishes to record the great achievements of the Romans, the sovereigns of the world, and to teach by exam-ple noble conduct and virtue. This attitude is, of course, rather in conflict with the point of view of modern historical thought, which seems most concerned with exposing the depravity of human nature and dealing exclusively with the most negative aspects of Western Civilization, but Livy has, nevertheless, exerted enormous influence on historiography.[21]

---

20. Ovid, *Metamorphoses*, 4.168–193, translation by Rolfe Humphries.

21. For an example of Livy's writing, see Cleve, Robert, *Early Western Civilization, Source Readings*, (2002), Kendall/Hunt Publishing Company, pp. 320–331.

Figure 11.10: Roman realism: portrait of an old senator.

Suetonius (Gaius Suetonius Tranquillus) wrote biographies of Julius Caesar and the first 11 emperors, called De Vita Caesarum, "The Lives of the Caesars." He served on the secretarial staff of both Trajan and Hadrian, which gave him access to the confidential documents of the palace. Unfortunately, Suetonius included all the gossip, innuendo, and rumor he could dig up on his subjects. Nevertheless, his biographies are among the most valuable sources we have for the personal lives of the Julio-Claudian and Flavian Dynasties.[22]

One of the most important and trusted historians of ancient Rome was Tacitus (Cornelius Tacitus), a member of the senatorial aristocracy. He began his career under Vespasian, served as praetor in 88 under Domitian and as consul during the reign of Nerva. He was appointed governor of Asia by Trajan for 112–113. Thus, he had wide experience in government. His historical works include: *De Vita Julii Agricolae*, a biography of his father-in-law Julius Agricola, governor of Britain for seven years; *De Origine et Siter Germanorum*, in which Tacitus describes the public and private lives of the Germans; *The Histories*, which covered the years 69–96, but unfortunately only the first four and a quarter books survive; *The Annals*, in eighteen books, which covers the reigns of Gaius, Claudius, and Nero, but only four and a half books remain.[23]

---

22. See Cleve, Robert, *Early Western Civilization, Source Readings*, (2002), Kendall/Hunt Publishing Company, pp. 380–388.

23. See Cleve, Robert, *Early Western Civilization, Source Readings*, (2002), Kendall/Hunt Publishing Company, pp. 407–432.

Figure 11.11: Flora, goddess of flowers, from Pompeii (Museo Archeologico Nazionale, Naples).

Three other important historians of Rome who wrote in Greek should be mentioned. Polybius gives us a unique view of the Roman Republic. He was one of the 1,000 hostages the Romans took from prominent Greek families in 167 BCE to ensure the good behavior of the Greeks. He lived with the famous Scipio family until 151 BCE and became familiar with Roman society and institutions. His history of the Romans was written in Greek for the Greek audience and thus provides us with the exceptional point of view of an outsider who is nevertheless extremely knowledgeable of his subject.[24] The history of Polybius is our most accurate and informative source for the history of the late Roman Republic.[25]

Dio Cassius, a prominent Greek senator held the consulship in 229 as the colleague of the emperor Severus Alexander, wrote a massive 80 book history of Rome from its origins down to his own time. Unfortunately, this work, titled *Roman History*, only partially survives. Dio attempted to provide a record of civil and military affairs in the traditional annalistic manner, that is, he arranged his material chronologically by consular year. He did not maintain the high standards of Polybius and Tacitus for accuracy, however, and errors and distortions are not uncommon in his history. He also makes free and casual links between events and the motives of historical characters, which are

---

24. Scholars never tire of pointing out the similar attitude between Polybius and Alex de Tocqueville, *Democracy in America* (1835–40), a book written by a Frenchman for the European audience.

25. See Cleve, Robert, *Early Western Civilization, Source Readings*, (2002), Kendall/Hunt Publishing Company, pp. 333–342.

Figure 11.12: Mosaic from Piazza Armerina, Sicily. "The Wild Boar Hunt."

his own opinions not derived from reliable sources. And unlike most earlier writers, who were adamantly anti-imperial, Dio fully accepts and supports monarchy over the old republican system.[26] In some ways this serves as a corrective for the bias of writers like Tacitus.

Finally, Plutarch (Mestrius Plutarchus), who lived in the late 1st and early 2nd centuries of the Common Era, wrote extensively on philosophy, ethics, biography, and other subjects, but his greatest achievement was the *Parallel Lives*, a series of biographies of Greek and Roman historical figures, of which twenty-three pairs survive. His intention was to illustrate either virtue or vice in the lives of his subjects. To achieve this, Plutarch provides first a biography of a Greek character and then a Roman character who seem in some way to be similar or to have experienced common situations. He then provides a comparison of them, explaining and illuminating the meaning of their lives. Nineteen of these comparisons survive.[27]

---

26. See Cleve, Robert, *Early Western Civilization, Source Readings*, (2002), Kendall/Hunt Publishing Company, pp. 390–406.

27. See Cleve, Robert, *Early Western Civilization, Source Readings*, (2002), Kendall/Hunt Publishing Company, pp. 154–237; 343–378.

Other Latin Writers

There were numerous others who wrote prose works on every conceivable subject: Vitruvius wrote *De Architectura*, a textbook on architecture, and Pliny the Elder wrote *Naturalis Historia* (Natural History), an exhaustive survey of the geography of the Mediterranean basin in 37 books. His nephew and adopted son, Pliny the Younger, has left us a large collection of personal and official letters.[28] These letters give us a unique insight into the everyday life of an aristocrat during the period of the *pax Romana*.

The most important Roman philosopher of the imperial period was the Stoic philosopher Seneca. He was not simply a dreamer who sequestered himself in his library, he was heavily involved in the politics of his day. He was the tutor and advisor of the young Nero and in this capacity amassed a large fortune. Unfortunately, in 65 he was, rightly or wrongly, implicated in a conspiracy against Nero and forced to commit suicide. He remained a true stoic to the end, however. He called together his closest friends and, while discussing the finer points of philosophic theory, opened the veins in his wrist and slowly departed from this world.[29] Seneca's philosophy was the product of a remarkably humanistic outlook, as in his insistence that the slave was also a human being, which goes beyond the thinking the of other ancient philosophers, even Plato and Aristotle.

Roman Technology

Unlike the Greeks, the Romans do not seem to have been interested in "pure science," that is, the investigation of the fundamental understanding of nature for its own sake, but they did seek a practical and technical knowledge of nature which could be applied to the solution of civic, governmental, or military problems—the Romans were always practical, not theoretical. While the Greeks are often thought of as dreamers, the Romans come across as the doers.

A long list of technical inventions and improvements produced by the Romans can easily be complied, but a few examples must suffice. The exploitation of concrete as a building material made possible the construction of great public buildings unlike any ever seen before or since until very modern times. The most enduring example is the famous Pantheon, discussed earlier as part of the building program of Hadrian.

The Romans also made use of some remarkable appliances: The abacus was a calculation board which in some applications was as fast and efficient as the modern electronic calculator. Various hoists, cranes, and tackle blocks were used in workshops and by construction crews to lift heavy loads. Military machines reached great complexity: the army employed an arrow gun which consisted of two tension arms joined by a string and capable of firing a four foot long arrow for 370 yards and piercing a hardwood shield to a depth of one foot. There was also a siege gun that could hurl stone balls a distance of 330 yards with great accuracy.

Roman engineers were also very good at constructing factories. Archaeologists have excavated a complex series of water mills at Barbegal, near Aries, France, which were capable of producing enough flour to feed 80,000 people a year. The waterwheels were over 6 feet in diameter and were

---

28. See Cleve, Robert, *Early Western Civilization, Source Readings,* (2002), Kendall/Hunt Publishing Company, pp. 433–463.

29. Seneca's death, which is modeled explicitly on that of Socrates, is described in vivid detail by Tacitus, *Annals* 15.62–4, who found it a bit theatrical and contrived.

geared to horizontal millstones which were powered by water channeled through an aqueduct. There were two channels, one on each side of the mills, which drove two millstones at each level. The Romans also used water wheels in reverse to pump water from a lower to a higher level. At the copper mines at Rio Tinto, Spain, a series of waterwheels lifted the water through successive reservoirs to the top. The wheels themselves were probably powered by treadmills driven by oxen.

In the field of medicine, the Romans did not make many original contributions. The building of the temple of Aesculapius, the Greek god of healing, on the Tiber Island in the 3rd Century BCE marked the beginning of the acceptance of Greek medical practices which continued for centuries. In the early period, doctors were usually Greek slaves and their social status was very low, but gradually specialists established themselves, and by the period of the empire those with the best reputations could command astronomical fees. The high position of doctors was finally secured when the emperor Antoninus Pius appointed state physicians for universal care to each of the fourteen regions of Rome, a form of socialized medical care. The range of medical instrumentation was highly developed and from Pompeii alone some 200 different types of medical instruments are known. In the field of public health, the provision of fresh water, public baths, and drainage on a scale unprecedented before this time gave protection against many health risks, such as malaria, that had hitherto been prevalent in the population.

Roman Religion

The Roman religion of the historical period was so heavily influenced, one might even say "contaminated," by Greek forms and values that it is difficult to uncover the Roman original. However, it is apparent that the early Roman peasantry believed themselves to be surrounded, protected, and threatened by numerous spiritual powers, which had to be placated with well defined rites, sacrifices, and ceremonies. The lord of the heavens and most powerful deity was Jupiter, who cast thunderbolts. At a very early date he was identified with the Greek Zeus. Juno was the protectress of women, and Minerva was the goddess of craftsmen. These three deities were a powerful triad, or trinity, worshiped together on the Capitoline Hill. Also important was Mars, who was originally an agricultural god of fertility, only later identified with the Greek Aries, god of war. Other important gods included Saturn, also an ancient god of agriculture, and Vesta, goddess of the hearth. Beyond these deities which were part of the state religion, the ordinary Romans worshiped a long list of spirits including the lares, spirits of each locality, and deities of the household, to name only the most important. In addition each aristocratic family in particular exhibited deep respect, if not outright worship, for the spirits of its dead ancestors.

The Romans always welcomed foreign deities into their pantheon. Their religious attitude included a deeply-rooted respect for the customs and deities of other peoples. They believed that it was of fundamental importance to maintain the *pax deorum*, literally the "peace of the gods," through sacrifices and prayers. The Roman concept of *pietas* meant more than just "piety:" It was the unqualified acceptance of one's obligations toward the gods, toward heaven, and toward one's ancestors. Octavian's revenge on the murderers of Caesar, his adoptive father, was in Roman eyes an act of *pietas*.

Yet, the Roman relationship with the gods, like the relationship of client and patron, was one of mutual obligations, and the duties on either side were governed by *fides*, or faith. If the human preformed his obligations, the god was duty-bound to perform his. This continuous and close contact with the gods was, for the Roman, not only a private matter, but also a public, political affair of state. To question the gods, to pray to them, to procure their favor, and also to thank them, were

Figure 11.13: The "Gemma Augustea," onyx cameo. Roman politics and religion: Tiberius (left) in triumph in the presence Augustus and the goddess Roma (seated); below, Roman soldiers hoist the spoils of victory in the presence of prisoners.

the supreme duties of the state, and these duties were satisfied by sacrifice, games, and the building of temples. To the historian Livy, for example, Roman domination of the world was due to the piety of Rome, and he said: "You will find that those who followed the gods had every success, while those who disregarded them were visited with misfortune."[30] It was a further characteristic of Roman religion that the individual's links with the gods was not direct but through an intermediary. It was the duty of the *paterfamilias* to communicate with heaven, on behalf of the family. It was the responsibility of the state priests, the *pontifices*, to communicate with the gods on behalf of the state. Thus, in ancient Rome, the spheres of politics and religion could not be separated, and even the idea of separation never seems to have occurred to anyone.

Beginning in the 3rd Century BCE, however, some fundamental changes took place in Roman religion. Foreign influences culminated in 205 BCE with the introduction of the cult of the great mother-goddess Cybele, from Phrygia in Asia Minor. This cult had certain ecstatic and orgiastic elements which provided the worshiper direct encounters with the gods, in contrast to the traditional

---

30. Livy, 5.51.5.

Roman religious forms, which required a priest as an intermediary between worshiper and heaven.[31] At almost the same time, the mystery cult of Dionysus, or Bacchus in Latin, appeared at Rome. This cult was even more "un-Roman": it involved the celebration of the Bacchanalia, an orgy of music and dancing in which the celebrants threw off all restraints. The resultant blurring of the barriers between the social ranks and the sexes was considered a grave threat to morality, tradition, and public order by the Roman Senate and led to the suppression of the cult, at least among Roman citizens.

To the Romans, secret meetings and cult vows were perceived as political conspiracies, and the continuing tolerance of the state toward such foreign cults was tempered by a desire to maintain an ordered society. The Christians would later get into trouble for this reason, as much as for their religious activities. By the time of the late Republic, the old Roman religion seemed to be losing its hold on the people, but then the disasters of the civil wars led to a renewal of religious feelings. There was a widespread conviction that all the sufferings and deprivations of the age were a punishment of the gods. It was at this point that Augustus began his work of systematic religious restoration which was a real religious revival. In Rome alone he restored eighty-two ruined temples and revived many half-forgotten festivals. At the same time, the cult worship of the emperor became an act of political loyalty, especially in the eastern provinces. However, it is a mistake to think that this so-called "emperor worship" happened as a result of state pressure applied from above. Augustus never issued a decree instituting the cult, but the government did tolerate it wherever it arose, especially in the east where the population had become accustomed to worshiping their rulers. Among Roman citizens, the cult took the form of the worship of the emperor's genius, which was something like the modern concept of the "guardian angel." The most important religious development during the early Empire was undoubtedly the spread of the mystery religions, which will be treated in more detail in the context of the discussion of the rise of Christianity in the next chapter.

Roman Art

Roman art has constantly been underestimated and at times even derided. It is often dismissed as derivative and imitative, useful only as a bridge to the lost Greek masterpieces. This is partly due to the Romans themselves. The lines of Virgil quoted above are a good example, but Cicero, Pliny the Elder, and other Latin writers were also disingenuous toward Roman artistic endeavors. However, Roman art became the paradigm for excellence during the succeeding Middle Ages and Renaissance, because for a long time after the passing of the ancient world, Europe perceived its past only through Roman eyes. But with the rediscovery of Greek art toward the end of the 18th Century, Roman art began to suffer again, and so-called "art experts" began to view Roman masterpieces only as second rate copies of Greek originals. This snobbishness was even applied to Hellenistic art. For well over a century the curators of the Louvre Museum have maintained, in the face of overwhelming evidence to the contrary, that the famous Venus de Milo, one of the greatest masterpieces of Hellenistic art, is really an example of classical Greek art. This silliness has gone so far that

---

31. This movement toward a more mystical relationship with the spiritual world has been interpreted by some historians as an early manifestation of a dissatisfaction with the traditional religion, but it is debatable whether this is evidence of a serious breakdown of the native Roman religion itself. These scholars often view ancient polytheism as basically being already dead by the time that Christianity arrived upon the scene. In actual fact, however, paganism remained an important force in the lives of the people for many centuries into the Christian era, as evidenced by the Medieval cult of the saints, the fascination with relics, witchcraft, etc.

very few art critics today will admit even the possibility of a Roman artistic masterpiece. The following brief and very cursory discussion, however, will attempt to present Roman art on its own terms, not from a preconceived position of contempt and derision.

Sculpture

Roman artists produced sculpture in a variety of materials, but the vast majority of surviving examples are in marble. Sculpture was created for a wide range of purposes: monuments; patriotic and religious displays; architectural decoration; and portraiture. If there is a single unifying aspect to Roman sculpture, it is its public attitude. Very little sculpture was produced for private display.

Roman contacts with the Greek world, beginning with the colonies in southern Italy and later through the conquest of Greece, cultivated an increasing admiration of the Greek classical style, but from the late Republic onward, a distinctive Roman style developed, which is most elegantly expressed in the reliefs that adorned major state monuments. Often these reliefs represent specific events and provide the historian with information not available from any other source. Trajan's Column, discussed in chapter 1, provides historians with details concerning the Dacian Wars that can be obtained from no other source.

The *Ara Pacis Augustae*, the altar of the Augustan Peace (Fig. 11.9), is one of the most beautiful and best preserved examples of this genre. The monument was voted by the Senate in 13 BCE to celebrate Augustus's return from Spain and Gaul.[32] The structure was constructed of white Italian marble. The altar itself stood within a square, walled enclosure, reminiscent of the early Roman open air shrines. The two entrances to the precinct were on the east and the west. The four panels flanking the entrances show purely mythological scenes. The two long panels on the north and south walls depict the actual processions of Roman officials, priests, and members of the imperial house, including Augustus himself, that took place on July 4, 13 BCE when the altar site was consecrated. Thus, we have a detailed three-dimensional record of an actual historical event. Although the reliefs are in the realistic Hellenistic style—with a minimum of Classical idealism—there is a logical organization and elegant simplicity that is purely Roman.

The striking realism of Roman portraiture, especially during the late republic, involves the accurate recording of facial characteristics including such unflattering features as wrinkles, warts, and moles (Fig. 11.10). These portraits were used in the competitive political environment of the Republic. However, the emperors, beginning with Augustus, favored the more idealized image of the classical Greek style, but still recognizably Roman. There are exceptions: the portraits of Vespasian are almost republican in their realism. The representations of the Julio-Claudians and the Flavians are mostly clean shaven, but beginning with Hadrian most imperial portraits are bearded. Many portraits of imperial women were produced, illustrating the important social and political roles played by these women. These images also record the constantly changing fashions in coiffure. In Egypt, during the late empire, mummy portraits painted on wood became popular. Roman portraits were rendered in a wide range of materials including silver, bronze, stone, terracotta, and glass. All in all, the Romans left a vivid record of themselves through their portraiture.

---

32. In Augustus's own words: "On my return from Spain and Gaul in the consulship of Tiberius Nero and Publius Quintilius [13 BCE] after successfully arranging the affairs in these provinces, the Senate resolved that an altar of the Augustan Peace should be consecrated next to the Campus Martius in honor of my return, and ordered that the magistrates and priests and Vestal Virgins should perform an annual sacrifice there." Res Gestae Divi Augusti, "The Achievements of the Divine Augustus," 12.2.

Figure 11.14: The Portland Vase.

Painting and Mosaics

In the late republican period, wealthy Romans collected Greek "old master" paintings, but by the time of the empire interest shifted to wall painting.[33] At Pompeii, which was buried during the volcanic eruption of Vesuvius in 69 CE, the walls of almost every residence were covered with wall paintings (Fig. 11.11), and the indications are that the painting styles changed constantly. The subject matter varied from the imitation of masonry or marble veneer, to elaborate illustrations of landscapes and cityscapes, to representations of mythological scenes, to fantastic images of unreal architecture and surreal juxtapositions of objects that are vaguely reminiscent of

---

33. This change was lamented by the elder Pliny, *Natural History*, 35.118: "Among artists great fame has been confined to painters of pictures only, a fact which shows the wisdom of early times to be the more worthy of respect, for they did not decorate walls, merely for owners of property, or houses, which would remain in one place and which could not be rescued from a fire. Protogenes was content with a cottage in his little garden; Apelles had no wall-frescoes in his house; it was not yet the fashion to color the whole of the walls. With all these artists their art was for the benefit of cities, and a painter was the common property of the world."

"modern" art. The evidence for the post-Pompeian period is much more sparse and difficult to analyze. In the 3rd Century, a style became popular in which the walls and ceilings were divided into panels by red and green lines on a white background. This style was adopted by the artists of the early Christian catacombs.

A related art form, mosaics, reached a high level of development by Roman artists (Fig. 11.12). Unlike Roman painting, most of which is lost, hundreds of mosaics survive in Italy, Sicily, North Africa, Britain, and other areas of the Mediterranean basin, and they provide us with information about Roman life not available from other sources. The largest mosaic surviving from ancient Rome was discovered in 1831 in Pompeii in the House of the Faun. It portrays the battle fought in 333 BCE between Alexander the Great and the Persian king Darius III at Issus. It is believed to be a reproduction of a 4th Century BCE Greek painting. The amazing achievement of light and shading is accomplished through the use of a very limited color range. The drama of the event is captured in every detail, especially in the expression of the faces of the two commanders.

Architecture

Roman architecture is the result of the synthesis of traditional Greek forms with the Roman arch and vault and the exploitation of a new building material, concrete. While the Greek Ionic and Corinthian orders remained important, distinctive Italian forms emerged by the 2nd Century BCE, the most successful being the Composite order, which combined the acanthus leaf Corinthian motif with the volutes of the Ionic order. New, purely Roman building types evolved, such as the amphitheater, the public bath, and the basilica. The development of the arcaded façade, utilized in the Theater of Marcellus and the Colosseum, had a strong influence on Renaissance and later architecture all the way down to the federal style employed in many of the early buildings of Washington D.C.

Glass

Glass was utilized for a wide variety of purposes by the Romans. It was used extensively for vessels and containers of course, but glass was also used for ceiling and wall decoration, inlaid panels for furniture and even for personal adornment in the form of hairpins, necklaces, ear and finger rings. The invention of glass blowing in the late 1st Century BCE transformed glass from a mere luxury product into an item of everyday use. The geographer Strabo tells us that a glass drinking cup can be purchased "for a copper coin" in the late 1st Century BCE.

One of the most beautiful examples of Roman glass art is the Portland vase (Fig. 11.14) in the British Museum, dating from the late 1st Century BCE. It is a blown amphora made of dark blue and opaque white layered glass. The outer layer of white was cut away to reveal the dark blue ground color and the figures were cameo-cut in relief to produce two detailed scenes which probably represent the wedding of Peleus and Thetis, the parents of Achilles. One cannot help but marvel at the great skill required to create such an object.

12

The End of the Ancient World

During the Crisis of the 3rd Century the Roman world declined but did not collapse. For two more centuries the Roman Empire continued to encompass the entire Mediterranean basin. Nevertheless, there had always been a cultural, economic, and even psychological division between the eastern and the western Mediterranean, and that division now became more prominent. The empire almost split into the seemingly natural eastern and the western entities during the late 1st Century BCE, but Augustus pulled it back from the brink. However, during the Crisis of the Third Century this problem again came to the forefront, and the empire seemed for a second time headed toward self-destruction, but in 284 the soldier emperor Diocletian began another reorganization which again suppressed this east/west dichotomy and allowed the empire to survive in tact until the late 5th Century. Thus began the transformation of the ancient world, and a major aspect of the transformation was the rise and spread of two new, monotheist religions: first Christianity and later Islam. The introduction of these new religions produced a degree of intolerance, violence, and bloodshed that had not been a part of the religious life of the Mediterranean world up to this time.

The Empire Reorganized

The real turning point between chaos and stability occurred in 285 when the political, military, and natural disasters of the 3rd Century began to be abated by the force of the Diocletian's reforms. Diocletian's solution was military despotism, and the result of his reforms was the transformation of the Principate of Augustus into an oriental monarchy known as the "Dominate," or "Tetrarchy." In fact, his reforms ensured the continuity of the Roman Empire in the East for another thousand years as a Christian state, usually called the "Byzantine Empire," but more properly known as the "Later Roman Empire."

Diocletian (284–305)

Diocletian was born in 236 or 237 in Dalmatia of very humble parents and received little education beyond elementary literacy. He grew up in a world engulfed in turmoil. Since Dalmatia was one of the prime recruiting areas for the army, it was quite natural for him to pursue a military career, but the army in which Diocletian served as young man was far different than the army of the high empire. The emperors of the 3rd Century were so insecure on their thrones that they granted inflationary pay raises to the soldiers. To pay for the increases, they were forced to debase the coinage until it was almost worthless. The only significant income of the soldiers now was the gold donatives distributed by newly proclaimed emperors. Thus, the soldiers were provided with a

Figure 12.1: Coin issued by Diocletian in 295 to commemorate the victory over the Sarmatians. Left, Diocletian's portrait on the obverse; Right, the reverse depicts the four members of the Tetrarchy sacrificing an archway of an army camp.

powerful motive to replace the emperors at frequent intervals. The resulting civil wars disabled the Empire's defenses and opened the borders to the invasion of the German tribes, Franks, Alamanni and Goths, from the north and the resurgent Persians from the East.[1]

Diocletian made his way up through the ranks by sheer merit and ability. In 282 the army of the Danube proclaimed the praetorian prefect Carus as emperor. Diocletian was appointed the commander of the praetorian cavalry and in 283 held the consulship. In 284, during a campaign against the Persians, Carus was killed by a lightening bolt and the empire was left in the control of his two young sons, Numerian and Carinus. Numerian soon died under mysterious circumstances and Diocletian was proclaimed emperor in his place. In 285 Diocletian defeated and killed Carinus in a battle near Belgrade and thereby gained control of the entire empire.

Diocletian's Reforms

Diocletian now faced extraordinary problems and took extraordinary steps to solve them. The army was mutinous and barbarized, and the empire was vulnerable to invasion. The economy was in shambles and the government was ineffective. Diocletian believed it was the responsibility of the emperor to solve these problems no matter how harsh or innovative the solutions might be.

The Army
Diocletian complety reorganized the command structure of the army. The existing fifty provinces were subdivided into approximately one hundred and grouped into twelve "dioceses" each under a "vicar." These dioceses were in turn grouped under four "prefectures," each governed by a "praetorian

---

1. In 226 Ardashir I, a Persian vassal king, rebelled against the Parthians, who had ruled the area since 257 BCE, and founded the new Persian dynasty known as the Sassanids. He then conquered several neighboring kingdoms, invaded India, subdued the rulers of the Punjab, and conquered Armenia. The Sassanids ruled Persia until 637 and were always a thorn in the side of the Roman Empire.

prefect." This significantly increased the imperial bureaucracy and enhanced the control of the government over the ordinary citizen. In order to prevent further insurrections of the generals in the field, the civilian and the military authority were separated. The army itself was divided into border troops, consisting of citizen militia, which served as a kind of early warning system for invasions across the frontiers, and a highly mobile field army commanded by the emperor himself, which could quickly respond to trouble anywhere within the empire. In the process, he transformed the office of the emperor into an oriental monarchy. Access to the emperor was restricted and he was no longer addressed as *Princeps* (First Citizen) or *Imperator* (General), but as *Dominus Noster* (Lord and Master). Those admitted into his presence were required to prostate themselves on the ground before him.

Now that the army, under Diocletian's control, could turn its attention to fighting off the empire's enemies instead of constantly fighting civil wars, the empire was quickly swept free of invaders. All of Rome's enemies were defeated in short order, and stability was re-established throughout the empire. In fact, the eastern frontier was actually expanded. Thus, it became obvious that the cause of Rome's troubles during the Crisis of the Third Century was not the ineffectiveness of its army by the failure in its leadership.

The Government

Diocletian also decided that the empire was too large to be ruled by only a single emperor and introduced the Tetrarchy, "the rule of four." In 285, he assigned the western half of the empire to his subordinate Maximianus as joint ruler and raised him to the rank of Augustus.[2] Both of the emperors adapted divine attributes. Diocletian was identified as Jupiter and Maximianus as Hercules. Each Augustus appointed a Caesar as an assistant: Constantius in the West was given rule of Gaul and Britain, under Maximianus; while Galerius was assigned the Balkan area under Diocletian. Thus, the Tetrarchy consisted of two Augusti, or senior emperors, and two Caesars, or junior emperors. This arrangement also addressed the constitutional problem of succession. Under Diocletian's plan, each Augustus would be succeeded by his Caesar, who would then name a new Caesar. It was a very rational solution, which operated smoothly and effectively—for a brief time, at least.

The Economy

At the time Diocletian became emperor the economy was practically prostrate. The coinage was virtually worthless. Agricultural production and trade was paralyzed. Inflation was rampant. Diocletian attempted to reissue gold and silver coins, but that program failed because there was simply not enough gold and silver available to restore confidence in the currency.[3] Inflation continued to mount.

In 301, Diocletian tried price control, a policy that has almost always proven a failure. His "Maximum Price Edict" was intended to stop inflation by setting a ceiling on the price of over a thousand items, including wheat, barley, rice, poultry, vegetables, fruits, fish, wines, clothing, bed linen, ink, and parchment. It also placed controls on wages. The text of this amazing edict

---

2. This practice in fact began the process which would culminate in the permanent division of the Roman Empire into western and eastern empires. Only the eastern empire would survive beyond the 5th Century, as the Christian Byzantine Empire.

3. One problem was that over the previous centuries vast treasuries of bullion had accumulated through donations in the temples all over the empire and had thus been taken out of circulation. In the ancient world, when money was "saved" it was taken out of circulation and thus became a drag on the economy. In the modern world, just the opposite is true. When money is saved, it is normally placed in an account with a bank or other financial institution and is then reinvested, thus generating economic activity.

has been pieced together from numerous fragments of inscriptions. The preamble sharply condemned speculators and profiteers who "rob the helpless public." Diocletian was particularly concerned about the purchasing power of the soldiers, who had only coinage to exchange in the market place, unlike civilians who could trade and barter their goods. The death penalty was prescribed for those who overcharged. However, this policy simply made the economy worse, because with prices fixed and the value of money falling, it was unprofitable to sell goods at the official price, and people either refused produce goods or sold them illegally on the black market, or relied on barter, which had always played an important role in the everyday economy. By the end of Diocletian's reign the edict was a dead issue and it was simply ignored thereafter.

Tax Reform

Increased revenues were necessary to meet the needs of the reorganized government. Diocletian simplified the tax structure by discarding many taxes and concentrating on two basic taxes that had been traditional throughout the Mediterranean for centuries: the land tax and the poll tax. Both agricultural labor and land were taxed according to standard units. A unit of labor was a *caput*, a unit of land was an *iugatio*. This seems simple and straight forward, but his system appears to have fallen much more directly on the small farmer than on the wealthy landlord. Nevertheless, the system did relieve the taxpayer from unexpected and unregulated taxes, and that was a benefit.

Religious Policy

Diocletian attempted to use religion as a unifying element. As the self-proclaimed representative of Jupiter, he sought to restore the ancient Roman faith and moral code. His motives for the persecution of the Christians are somewhat controversial, because his wife was a Christian. His goal was to ensure political conformity and uniformity among the population in order to enhance the security of the state. Constantine and later emperors would pursue the same policy of religious uniformity, but to the advantage of the new Christian religion, not to its detriment. This resulted in the persecutions of the pagan religion by the Christians, especially after Christianity became the official religion in 380, but the persecutions of the pagans are rarely discussed in history books.

Diocletian's persecutions of the Christians were touched off at a public sacrifice in 299. The will of the gods was to be solicited by the inspection of the entrails of the sacrificial animals, but the presiding priests reported that the presence of hostile influences had defeated the purpose of the sacrifice. Diocletian was furious and ordered everyone in the palace, including his Christian wife, to offer sacrifice to the traditional gods of the state, or be beaten. He then ordered all officers and men of the army to sacrifice or be dismissed from service. In 303, at his palace in Nicomedia, he issued an edict ordering the destruction of Christian churches and the burning of their sacred books. The edict was posted throughout the city but an enraged Christian tore down one of the posters and was arrested and burned at the stake. During the next days, two fires of unknown origin broke out in the palace and numerous Christian suspects were imprisoned and executed. Revolts occurred in Syria and Cappadocia and were ascribed to the Christians which led to more edicts, ordering the imprisonment of the Christian clergy and all Christians to sacrifice or face execution. However, these edicts were not enforced throughout the empire with equal severity. In Gaul and Britain, for example, only a few churches were pulled down, whereas in the East the persecutions were more severe and continued sporadically until 311.

Abdication

In 304, Diocletian visited Rome and celebrated the twentieth anniversary of his reign. Soon afterward, however, be became ill, probably from a stroke, and ceased to conduct the affairs of state. After he returned to his capital of Nicomedia, he formally resigned on May 1, 305 and retired to his palace at Split in Illyricum, where he spent the last eight years of his life. On the same day, Diocletian forced Maximianus, his colleague in the west, to resign at Milan. Their Caesars, Galerius in the East and Constantius Chlorus in the West, became the new Augusti. Galerius appointed his nephew Maximinus Daia as his Caesar, and Constantius begrudgingly accepted Flavius Valerius Severus, a friend of Galerius, as his Caesar, thereby passing over his own son, Constantine.

To Diocletian, it seemed that his new constitutional arrangement was operating smoothly, but in fact it was not. The strong personality of Diocletian was the only thing that held the system together and, without his presence, the whole complex structure began to collapse. Maximianus was resentful over his enforced retirement and waited for any opportunity to format trouble. His successor in the East, Galerius, died in 311 and Diocletian died the following year. A sad epilogue: Diocletian's widow, Prisca, and their only child, Valeria, now the widow of Galerius, were exiled by Maximinus and both were beheaded by his successor, Licinius.

Constantine (306–337)

Civil war broke out among Diocletian's successors and continued until Flavius Valerius Constantinus (the son of Constantius Chlorus), known to history as Constantine I, or "Constantine the Great" in Christian literature, seized the sole emperorship and reunified the empire in 324. Constantine is rightly recognized as the most important emperor of late antiquity. Indeed he laid the foundations of the Post-Classical Western Civilization.

Figure 12.2: Constantine. Fragment of the colossal statue from the Basilica of Constantine.

Long Road to Reunification

When his father, Constantius Chlorus Augustus, died in 306, his Caesar, Severus, was supposed to succeed him as Augustus under the Diocletian constitution, but the soldiers immediately proclaimed Constantine emperor, precipitating the civil conflict that eventually resulted in Constantine (Figs. 12.2 & 12.3) becoming the sole emperor in 324. From 324 to his death in 337, Constantine ruled the reunified empire, but in a real sense, the eastern and the western portions of the empire were never again fully unified, and by the 5th Century it was clear that only the eastern part of the empire was destined to survive.

Constantine made the city of Trier his residence and capital between 306 and 312. The Senate and praetorian guard in Rome backed Maxentius, the son of Maximianus. Although Constantine married Maxentius's sister, Theodora, and the two rulers co-existed peacefully for a time, they never trusted each other and open warfare broke out in 312. Constantine's victory over Maxentius at the famous Battle of the Milvian Bridge in that same year made him the sole ruler of the western half of the Roman Empire. He attributed his victory to his conversion to Christianity.

The Conversion of Constantine

Although it was one of the most important events of the 4th Century, the circumstances and motivations surrounding Constantine's adaptation of Christianity have been a point of controversy down to the present day. The basic question is, was his motive religious or political? The conversion was portrayed by early Christian writers as a sudden religious experience produced by divine supernatural intervention, but a closer examination of Constantine's career makes a different interpretation possible. Constantine, in fact, was exposed to Christian influence from an early age. His mother, Helena, was a Christian, but the extent of her influence on him during his formative years is uncertain. The problem is that information about her is scanty and distorted by the bias of the sources. The picture presented by Christian writers is of a virtuous Christian wife and mother, but the pagan sources say she was a concubine of low birth and questionable morals. The best evidence indicates that Constantine was born in 272 or 273 in the province of Moesia (now Serbia). If Helena was in fact his father's wife and not his concubine, she was nevertheless discarded for a more advantageous marriage to Theodora, the daughter of Maximianus, Diocletian's colleague in the West. At about this time, the young Constantine was sent to Diocletian's court at Nicomedia as a kind of hostage to ensure his father's good behavior as Caesar in the West. There he received an excellent education in politics and military science. Thus, the real influence of his Christian mother on his formative years is a point of contention. In any event, Constantine rejoined his father as soon as Diocletian and Maximianus abdicated.

An indication that his conversion may not have occurred suddenly in 312 is the fact that upon coming to power in 306, he immediately and unilaterally ended the persecution against the Christians in his territories, even providing restitution. However, the Christian writers emphasize a sudden conversion. Lactantius,[4] who was a member of Constantine's court, says that during the night before the Battle of the Milvian Bridge, Constantine was commanded in a dream to place the sign of Christ on the shields of his soldiers. Writing some twenty-five years later the church historian Eusebius[5] reports a different, more detailed account in his biography of Constantine. According to Eusebius, during Constantine's march toward Rome—neither the place nor time is

---

4. Lactantius, *De Mortibus Persecutorum*, 44.5–6.

5. Eusebius, *Vita Constantini*, 1.28–29.

Figure 12.3: Constantine from a coin issued in 319. Left, obverse, portrait; Right, reverse, two "Victorias" holding a votive shield above an alter. Pagan motifs continued to appear on Constantine's coins after he converted to Christianity.

recorded—the entire army was treated to a bizarre phenomenon in the sky: a cross of light and the words "by this sign you shall conquer." During the next night Christ appeared to Constantine and instructed him to place the sign on the battle standards of his army. Whatever the specifics of his experience, Constantine attributed his victory to "the God of the Christians" and committed himself to the Christian faith, although his understanding of the new religion at the time seems quite superficial. At any rate, after his victory at the Battle of the Milvian Bridge on October 18, 312, Constantine was supreme in the West, and in February of 313, Constantine and Licinius, now Augustus in the East, met at Milan to negotiate, among other things, an arrangement to share the rule of the empire. As a result, Licinius issued an edict of toleration, but did not convert to Christianity, and indeed even his toleration eventually gave way to renewed persecution.

The argument that Constantine's conversion was politically motivated is supported by his subsequent attempts to use the church as an instrument of his imperial policy. An abundance of evidence indicates that he did not become a sudden and exclusive believer in Christianity in 312. Yet, by the time of his baptism, which did not occur until the end of his life, he was clearly a believer. During his reign, the interaction between religious and political considerations were complex and open to differing interpretations. He was obviously too astute a politician to attempt the immediate suppression of the religion of 90 to 95 percent of his subjects, and of course he could not completely alienate the Senate, the imperial bureaucracy, and the army, all of which were still pagan to the core. As emperor, he continued to hold the office of *pontifex maximus* and proclaim the Unconquered Sun as his official patron deity. This god appears on his triumphal arch in Rome and on his coinage down to 323. He also struck coins in honor of Mars, Jupiter, and Hercules as late as 318. Thus, Constantine did not reign as a Christian emperor over a Christian empire.

Constantine's motives may have been more subtle than is generally recognized. At the time of his conversion, Constantine was facing a very serious political problem: how to unite under his sole rule an empire that had become deeply divided. Centuries before, Augustus had created a rationale for the monarchy. He had camouflaged the monarchy in republican form and positioned it behind a republican façade. The image was of a group of men ruling the earth like the group of gods ruled in heaven. The image projected by Augustus was of a republic, not a monarchy. The title by which he most wanted to be known was "*Princeps,*" an ancient republican term which meant senior citizen, or simply first among equals. It had the same connotation as "elder statesman" has in our society. Indeed the Roman government instituted by Augustus is often referred to as the "Principate." Well, this was all an image. Everyone *knew* that Augustus was a monarch. Everyone *knew* that the state was not a republic. Yet this was the image behind which the Roman emperors ruled for more than 300 years. The image was a state ruled by a group of men—consuls, praetors, etc.—just as heaven is ruled by a group of gods.

The problem for Constantine was that this republican façade had all but disappeared by now, leaving the monarchy exposed in the strong light of reality. When Constantine came to the throne, the emperor had no clothes, so to speak. It was perfectly obvious that the emperor now held all the power and the image of the republic was dead. Several of the emperors of the 3rd Century had groped toward a new image. The Roman Empire seemed to be moving slowly toward the oriental image of a state ruled by a god-king. That was the kernel of the reforms of Diocletian. He had taken the official name "Jovis"—which is a variation of Jupiter, the king of the gods in the Roman state religion—and he had surrounded himself with much of the oriental ceremony and ritual that supports a divine ruler. Indeed, the government after the reforms of Diocletian is often referred to as the "Dominate."

But during the Crisis of the 3rd Century another answer to this problem was also suggested: and that was to change the image not of the earth but of heaven to make it more accurately reflect the reality of this world. There was a tendency—a drift really—toward monotheism long before Christianity appeared upon the scene. There had long been a tendency to combine or synthesize the gods. For example, the Hellenistic god Sarapis, popular in the East, combined the attributes of many Greek gods like Zeus, Hades, and Aesculapius with Egyptian gods like Osiris. The emperor Elagabalus had attempted to make his local god from Syria supreme in the Empire. Elagabalus was mad, of course, but some of the emperors of the 3rd Century adapted the god called Sol Invictus as their patron. Sol Invictus, the "Unconquered Sun," was identified with Apollo and other gods. Some writers of the time even spoke of Sol Invictus in the singular as if he were the only god. This is a radically different approach. Under this image there would be only one god ruling in heaven, just as there is only one ruler here on earth—the emperor, who would not be divine in the oriental sense, but would be God's viceroy, that is God's designated representative.

Thus, the problem facing Constantine was to find a new framework, a new rationale for the monarchy, a new symbol for the unity of the empire, which was now on the verge of disintegration into its constituent parts. When it comes to the unity and control of a society, religion—or at least a common belief system—must always play a central role. Constantine, in his struggle for supreme power, repudiated the image of a divine king put forward by Diocletian. At first he turned to Sol Invictus, a deity who already had wide acceptance among the pagans.[6] Indeed this sun-god appears on Constantine's coins in the West to the end of his reign. But gradually another solution to the problem presented itself to Constantine in the new religion of Christianity, which was much more of a break with the past. He saw in this new religion the potential instrument by which he could unite the diverse elements of the empire under the rule of one all powerful emperor, ruling the earth in the name one all powerful God in heaven.

---

6. "Pagan" is a term derived from the Latin word *paganus,* "rustic, ignorant, untaught, country yokel, red neck, hillbilly." The early Christians used the word to refer to non-Christians in a derogatory and contemptuous manner. Today, as used by historians (and especially as used in this book), it does not have the derogatory overtones of its original usage, but is employed simply to designate the traditional polytheistic religions of the ancient world in the context of their relationship to Christianity.

And history has proven Constantine correct in his estimate of the political value of Christianity as a bulwark for divine right monarchy. Although his policy of using the new religion to support his throne failed in the long run to hold the empire together in the West, the eastern half of the Roman Empire continued to exist under a Christian emperor with the strong support of the Church, until 1453, a period of over 1,000 years. And Christianity itself remained the firm ally of totalitarian monarchy in Europe until very recent times.

Yet, Constantine's conversion proved to be an unmixed blessing for the early church. If he hoped to use Christianity to unify the empire, he was soon disappointed to discover that the new religion, although monotheistic in its theology, was not monolithic in its structure. Almost immediately upon declaring himself the champion of the Christians, Constantine was drawn into the petty rivalries and theological quarrels of the church's leaders. In Africa, for example, a controversy raged among the clergy over how to respond to the lapsi, those Christians who had succumbed to the pressure of the persecutions. The Donatists, who took their name from Donatus, a priest who had endured six years of prison and torture without submission, opposed the election of Caecilianus as bishop of Carthage, because he was too ready to grant forgiveness to those who had lapsed under persecution. Over the objections of the pope in Rome, the Donatists installed Donatus as bishop of Carthage. A crescendo of fanaticism split the African church, and the leaders of both sides appealed to Constantine. He convened two church councils in 313 and 314, which he chaired himself. The councils ruled against the Donatists, and Constantine ordered their suppression by military force and the confiscation of their churches. The results were not what Constantine had in mind, however, and by 321 he realized that persecution only intensified their fanaticism and he called off the army and left the Donatists "to the judgment of God." So the first attempt to impose peace and unity on the church was a dismal failure, but the internal struggle of the church's leaders for control over the church and the struggle of the Church against the secular government for control over society would frequently erupt into bloodshed and violence throughout the church's history.[7]

The ultimate goal of both Constantine and Licinius was sole power. The agreement reached in 313 was really the product of necessity, not of mutual goodwill. Conflicts erupted again in 316 and 317, which were patched up by new agreements, but tensions continued to grow. Finally war erupted again in 324 and Licinius was completely defeated. He was executed a few months later. Constantine was now the sole and undisputed mater of the Roman Empire.

Crisis in the Imperial Family

After the long struggle of absolute power was complete, the darker side of Constantine's personality came to the surface. He had two close members of the imperial family executed. In 326 he ordered the death of his oldest son, Crispus, who had been appointed Caesar in 317, had held the consulship three times, and had recently distinguished himself in the campaign against Licinius. A little later, Fausta, his wife and mother of his other three sons, was executed. These two deaths seem to be connected, but it is impossible to separate rumor from fact. One source[8] says that Crispus was "involved" with his step-mother, Fausta. Another source[9] reports that Constantine killed Fausta when his mother, Helena, rebuked him for the death of Crispus. Even if some involvement of

---

7. These conflicts continue even in the modern age. Witness the present bloodshed in Northern Ireland.

8. Zosimus, 2.29.1.2.

9. Aurelius Victor, *De Caesaribus* 42.11.12.

Helena cannot be excluded, the responsibility for the killings still rests with Constantine. Interestingly, shortly after these events, Helena went on a pilgrimage to the Holy Land. Though there is no clear cut evidence in the sources, some historians have suggested that this pilgrimage was an act of expiation, either for her own sins or those of her son.

Constantine's Government (324–337)

On November 8, 324, Constantine formally laid out the boundaries of his new capital city on the site of the ancient Greek city of Byzantium. His decision to move the capital of the empire from Rome to the East was as significant as his conversion to Christianity. Constantine named his new capital New Rome, but it quickly became known as Constantinople. The location he chose was a masterstroke, because it sat astride the cross roads of the two most important lines of communication in the Medieval world: the north-south route from northern Europe to the Near East and the beginning of the caravan routes to the orient and the water route connecting the Black and Mediterranean Seas. Furthermore, it was a nearly impregnable fortress. It was surrounded on three sides by water and on the fourth side, facing Europe, a great defensive wall was constructed. The new city quickly became the economic, political, and cultural center of the eastern Mediterranean.

Although the mystical values of the new religion were in many ways diametrically opposed to the humanistic ideals of the Classical Age, Constantine's adoption of Christianity did not lead to drastic reordering of society or a significant revision of the legal system. Even though he made the church an official agency of his government and entrusted some important administrative functions to the clergy, he retained most of the governmental reforms of Diocletian, especially the provincial administration and army organization. Some minor changes were affected, however. The praetorian prefects, for example, became the chief civilian ministers assisting the emperor. The economy was strengthened and inflation brought under control by a major reform of the currency. As a Christian, Constantine was able to confiscate the vast treasuries of the pagan temples and put the bullion back into circulation by instituting a new coin, the gold *solidus*, which remained standard of exchange for the Mediterranean area for centuries to come.

In the last years of his reign, Constantine was more aggressive in his suppression of paganism. We know of several temples which he ordered to be torn down, and most of the temple treasuries were confiscated into the imperial treasury. In the spring of 337, Constantine fell ill. He traveled to Nicomedia where he was baptized and at last officially received into the Christian faith. He died a few weeks later, on May 22. His body was placed in the Church of the Hole Apostles in Constantinople, as he had directed. His tomb was surrounded by stelae of the Twelve Apostles, symbolically making him the thirteenth Apostle. Before he died he had created no less than four Caesars, but did not designate a formal heir. In the next months there was a bloody purge of imperial family, which almost certainly had its roots in the religious strife between the Arian and Orthodox factions of the imperial court. It was not the first nor the last time that the conflicts between the factions of the "religion of peace" resulted in the spilling of blood.

The Rise of Christianity

The origin of Christianity, of course, predated Constantine by three centuries, but it spread widely throughout the ancient world only during the chaos of the 3rd Century and became an important element in the religious life of the Roman Empire only after Constantine became its champion and promoted it as the favored religion of his imperial government. Before the conversion of Constantine, no one could have predicted that Christianity would become the official state religion of the Roman Empire before the end of the 4th Century.

The Mystery Religions

The Christian subversion of classical civilization began during the golden age of the Roman Empire, during that era of history known as the *pax Romana*. This was the period which the great Enlightenment historian Edward Gibbon called, "that happiest age of human history," and, indeed, most of the pagan writers of the period, such as Pliny and Plutarch, did not seem to believe that a better state of existence than the Roman Empire during this golden age was either possible or even desirable. Only on the fringes of society did a few individuals began to speak vaguely of a better world, a world they perceived to exist, not here on earth, but in another sphere, in a spiritual realm, that could be entered only through the portals of death and only by conforming to the rituals, patterns, and behavioral constraints prescribed by a *soter*, or "savior," who had died and been resurrected and had thus conquered death. These individuals were the adherents to the so-called mystery cults, religions which were eastern in origin.

The mystery religions, or cults,[10] began to appear very early in the history of the Near East. We have already looked at one of these mystery religions in some detail, the cult of the Egyptian god Osiris and his wife, goddess Isis, which first appeared early in the history of Egyptian civilization and which gave hope of immortality beyond the grave to even the common Egyptian. As we saw, however, the religion of Osiris, in its ancient Egyptian context, was an affirmation of this world, rather than a subordination of it to the spiritual realm, as the later mystery religions became, because the Egyptians conceived of that other world to be exactly like this one, whereas the later mystery religions conceived of a much more spiritual and other worldly afterlife.

After the unification of the entire Mediterranean basin by the Romans into one political and economic unit, what has been described as a "host" of these mystery religions, cults which originated near or beyond the eastern periphery of the Roman Empire spread gradually across the ancient world. But as late as the 3rd Century, these cults still formed a kind of underground culture and were confined to small, isolated groups. Their alien ideas and often deviant lifestyles did not yet have any appreciable influence on the mainstream life of the Roman world. But they did have a certain appeal to some minority groups of the population.

Part of the attraction of these mystery religions was that they were "salvationist eschatologies." They were eschatologies because they claimed to explain the *eschatos*, or the "last things," that is, the ultimate purpose of human life. They were salvationist because they offered personal salvation in the form of life after death. All the mystery religions utilized basically the same formula for salvation: the association of the believer, through mystical rites, with a hero, or cult figure, who had conquered death.

This was a very ancient concept. Recall that at the very beginning of Egyptian civilization, some 3,500 years before the birth of Jesus, the pharaoh possessed immortality, in the form of life beyond the grave, due to his special relationship with the gods, specifically because of his association

---

10. The terms "religion" and "cult," as used in this discussion are almost synonyms. As used here, the term "cult" is a neutral term and means only "a system of religious belief or ritual, or the body of adherents to such a body of belief." Do not confuse this with the modern usage, especially in the news media, of the term "cult" to designate "a religion regarded as unorthodox, spurious and/or dangerous."

Figure 12.4: Cult figures of two popular mystery religions. Left, Mithras; Right, Isis.

with the sun-god Amun-Re. But this was an idea too attractive to be forever kept within the palace walls forever and eventually all of the Egyptian people, down to the lowliest peasant, came to believe that they too could gain personal salvation through association with the benevolent god Osiris, who had died and been resurrected by the efforts of his devoted wife, Isis. This ancient Egyptian religion, now in the 3rd Century of the common era, had been Hellenized and was known as the cult of Isis (Fig. 12.4). It had become the most popular of the mystery religions, especially among women, and it had spread all over the Mediterranean world.

Another popular religion of the 3rd Century was the cult of Mithras (Fig. 12.4), which was once thought to have originated in Persia as an offshoot of Zoroastrianism, the state religion of Persia, but is now believed to be based on astrology and the mythology of the constellations of the Zodiac. Mithraism was by far the most popular mystery religion within the Roman army and also had a strong following among bureaucrats and merchants. Mithraism, however, could never have become a universal religion because it excluded women. Other mystery cults centered around hero-savior figures such as Orpheus, Adonis, Dionysus, or Bacchus and Demeter, to name just a few. All of these heroes had conquered death.

The initiation rite into several of these cults involved the ritual slaughter of a bull on an altar which consisted of a perforated grating. The worshipers being initiated into the cult positioned themselves below this grating, and when the bull's throat was lanced, the warm blood of the slaughtered animal ran down over them and they bathed themselves in it. In this way their souls were cleansed of sin. This baptism of blood is known as a taurobolium, and it was practiced by the cults of Cybele (the "Great Mother Goddess"), Mithras, and others. Those that had undergone this cleansing were said to be "reborn for eternity."

Jesus

The hero or cult figure of all these mystery religions had died and been resurrected, and had conquered death. Jesus was such a hero. He too had died and risen from the dead; he too had conquered death. The cult of Jesus was in some ways similar, but in some ways different from the other mystery religions. Like the others, salvation for the Christians required a moral life, in addition to the usual rituals, mysteries, and sacraments. But unlike the other cults, Jesus—according to the Christians—was a historical person, a human being who had actually lived here on earth, while all the other cult heroes—according to the Christians—were only mythical figures. It must be recognized that the adherents to the other mystery religions fiercely disagreed with this statement, and indeed these kinds of statements were viewed by them as being extremely provocative. To the members of the other religions, their cult figure was just as real as Jesus was to the Christians. But the most important difference between Christianity and the other mystery religions was intolerance. The Christians believed, and they constantly proclaimed, that they possessed an absolute monopoly of truth, that they possessed a total and exclusive control of salvation. All other religions and beliefs were viewed by the Christians as enemies of the truth and manifestations of evil. Salvation, it seems, which had begun over 3,000 years before as the exclusive possession of the pharaoh, was now the exclusive possession of the Christians, or more accurately, the Church.

According to the tradition recorded in the Gospels, the first four books of the Christian New Testament, Jesus was born in Judea a few years before the beginning of the Common Era,[11] during a period of extreme religious and political turmoil in the area. During the centuries after the rebuilding of the Temple in Jerusalem (see chapter 4), Judaism had become an uncompromisingly monotheistic relationship between Yahweh and his chosen people. Of course the absence of the possibility of compromise always produces fanaticism and sectarianism, because there is no prospect that every individual in a community will think and behave exactly alike. Absolute conformity is impossible.

The two major Jewish factions active during the period of Jesus's career were the Sadducees, who represented the priesthood and the aristocracy, and the Pharisees, a group of teachers and preachers of religious law who, in a vague way, represented the tradition of the prophets. While the Sadducees believed that most of the religious law applied only to the priesthood, the Pharisees proclaimed that all 613 of Yahweh's commandments were binding on all Jews. They also expected the messiah, promised by Yahweh through the prophets, to appear at any moment and deliver the Jews from the domination of the Romans. In addition, there were several smaller splinter groups. Important among these were the Essenes, an almost monastic group that sought spiritual enlightenment through asceticism, repentance, and mystical confrontation with God.

It must be recognized that it is impossible to know anything definitive about the historical Jesus, since the only sources about him are the four Gospels, the earliest (Gospel of Mark) of which was written over thirty years after his death. We have no sources at all written by anyone who actually knew Jesus, or indeed anyone who knew anyone who knew Jesus. These Gospels themselves are full of historical inaccuracies, in part because they were not even intended to be factual historical records.

---

11. The Common or Christian Era was supposed to begin in the year of Jesus's birth. The original calculations are certainly incorrect, however, and most Biblical scholars now believe that Jesus was born in the year 4 BCE (or BC). As a substitute for "Anno Domini," or AD ("in the year of our Lord"), many academics, including this author, prefer to use "CE," which is understood to mean "Common Era."

The account contained in the gospels relates that when Jesus was about thirty years old, a reform preacher named John the Baptist proclaimed Jesus to be a teacher "mightier than I" and for the next three years Jesus preached, healed the sick, and cast out demons. He proclaimed that God had given him a mission to save humanity from sin. The teachings of Jesus contained several seminal principles: the brotherhood of humanity and the absolute submission to the will of God (exactly how the will of God is to be determined in any given situation is not explicitly stated); forgiveness and love of one's enemies; avoidance of hypocrisy; the immanent coming of the "Kingdom of God;" and the resurrection of the dead and the establishment of the Kingdom of Heaven.

The readiness of Jesus to relax the religious law for ethical reasons was anathema to the Sadducees, however. Jesus's entry into Jerusalem at Passover in the manor of the messiah and then his physically driving the money changers out of the Temple precincts was an unforgivable offense in the eyes the city's religious leaders. They arrested him and charged him with blasphemy before the highest court presided over by the Roman governor Pontius Pilate. Pilate, like any Roman governor, was primarily concerned with preserving peace and order in his province. He therefore sided with the local authorities and condemned the trouble maker to death by crucifixion, the normal Roman punishment for those guilty of sedition.

At first the death of Jesus seemed like the end of his mission to his followers. But after a few days rumors began to circulate that Jesus had risen from the dead and had appeared to some of his disciples and that he was truly a divine being. From this beginning the belief of Jesus's resurrection became the central theme of the Christian faith. The image of Jesus was transformed into the image of "Christ" (Greek for "Anointed One"), the divine son of God, sent to earth to suffer and die for the sins of humanity. Furthermore, the Christians came to believe that Christ would come again to judge the world at the end of time.

The triumph of Christianity within the Roman Empire represents one of the most remarkable cultural revolutions in all of human history. The victory of this new religion is all the more extraordinary because it advocated values which were diametrically opposed to those of classical humanist thought. The great pagan philosophers, for the most part, believed that the good life must be found here in the present world. *Carpe diem*, they taught, "seize the day," for there is no certainty about tomorrow, no hope at all of some imagined life beyond the grave. This life, right here, right now, is the most precious thing that any human being can ever possess. This was the classical humanist view. This was the view of life that was prevalent throughout the classical period. To the early Christians, on the other hand, this present world was a place of exile, a temporary existence through which humans pass on their way to another existence beyond the grave. Earthly life for the early Christian, then, was a pilgrimage in a foreign, a hostile, and often a hated land. To the Christian, the importance of this life paled in comparison with that eternal life beyond the grave. Obviously, both of these concepts of the meaning of human life cannot be correct. They are mutually exclusive, and one or the other must prevail. Therein lies the seeds for much future conflict and bloodshed.

The Persecutions of the Christians

The development of Christianity as an organized religion owes much to the missionary activities of Paul, who was originally Pharisee, but became a fanatical Christian after he underwent a dramatic conversion. Declaring himself the "Apostle to the Gentiles," he declared the Jewish religious law to be irrelevant to salvation. He established communities in the major urban centers along the

Figure 12.5: Christian painting from the catacombs, c. 350. Moses strikes the rock to produce water.

trade routes of the empire. However, the Christians' rigid and intolerant monotheism, which rejected the traditional gods, and their refusal to participate in the established public sacrifices and ceremonies of their pagan neighbors, was a grave insult and provocation to the mainstream elements of the empire's inhabitants. This bred hostility toward the Christians and led to persecution.

Why Were the Christians Persecuted?

The persecutions of the Christians by the pagans is one of the most misunderstood and misinterpreted events in the history of the Western Civilization. To consider the problem of the persecutions, four major aspects must be isolated and investigated. First, why did the pagans demand the persecution of the Christians? The first official intervention by the Roman Government[12] against the Christians, recorded in the secular sources, was the persecution of Nero, after the great fire which destroyed much of Rome in 64 CE. Both the historian Tacitus and the biographer Suetonius record this incident. The description of Tacitus is particularly important. He says that there were rumors that Nero himself had set the fire and that the emperor, in order to exonerate himself, blamed the

---

12. The Roman government was not the first to persecute the Christians. The New Testament Book of Acts, chapter 8, verse 1, informs us: "There was a great persecution against the church which was in Jerusalem, and they were scattered abroad throughout the regions of Judea and Samaria." Early Christianity made a bad first impression on just about everybody—it was so alien and divergent from the mainstream of ancient life that, when first encountered, it seemed like a madness.

Christians. It must be remembered that Tacitus, who lived through the tyranny of Domitian, is quite biased against the emperors and always wants the reader to believe the worst about them, whatever the truth may be, but he does not ever simply lie about a historical event. There is no doubt that Tacitus knows neither Nero nor the Christians really set the fire—it was an accident—but why did Nero try to blame the Christians? Because the accusation was creditable to most of the Romans and they therefore made a good scapegoat. Tacitus himself says that the Christians were "hated for their vices." The Christians, he said, deserved "exemplary punishment," not because they were necessarily guilty for this particular act of arson, but because "they hated the human race." In other words, the Christians were chosen as scapegoats by Nero because they were already believed by the public to be capable of even the most horrendous crimes, and to accuse the Christians of burning down Rome was a perfectly creditable accusation in the eyes of most Romans.

This was the year 64 and Jesus has been dead only for some 30 years. The Christian congregation in Rome could not have been very numerous and, in fact, the Christians were still viewed as a renegade sect of Judaism. Very few people outside the Jewish community knew anything substantial about them. In fact, Tacitus, a highly educated and informed scholar, who wrote his history more than a generation later, still did not know very much about them. He also realized that his audience was not familiar with them either and he felt it necessary to describe the Christians:

> Christus, the founder of this sect, had undergone the death penalty in the reign of Tiberius, by sentence of the procurator Pontius Pilatus, and the wicked superstition was checked for a time, only to break out once more in the capital itself, where all things horrible and shameful collect and find vogue.[13]

This at least partially explains pagan support for the persecutions. Of course it goes a great deal deeper than this one incident, but obviously the pagans perceived the Christians to be a criminal and anti-social element that was a direct threat to their values and to their way of life. When Tacitus described the Christians as hating the human race, he was referring to their mysticism and anti-humanistic attitude. From the very beginning, the humanists and the mystics recognized that their two modes of thought, their two lifestyles, their two fundamentally different ways of perceiving the very meaning of human existence, were simply not compatible—and subsequent history has demonstrated that Christianity possess neither the tolerance nor the inclination to allow other modes of thought to exist whenever it has acquired the power to eliminate them. One need not list here a catalog of inquisitions, crusades, and wars to support this point. So, viewed within the historical context, the Christian persecutions were an attempt by pagan society to defend itself, to preserve the way of life that had been prevalent in the Mediterranean area for several thousand years. From the pagan point of view, the Christians were the revolutionaries, the pagans were the defenders.

The Christians and the Law

Once the first group of Christians had actually been brought to trial and condemned on criminal charges, such as arson for example—regardless of weather or not the conviction was justified—the next logical step was to bring others to trial on charges of simply being Christian. In the

---

13. Tacitus, *Annals*, 15.44. Interestingly, this is the only mention of the name Pontius Pilatus (Pilate) in the secular sources and Tacitus almost certainly retrieved this story from Christian sources. Thus, this citation does not, in itself, provide firm historical evidence for the events related in the Gospels.

legal jargon of the time, the crime was "*nomen Christionum*," literally "the name of Christian." This is rightly viewed by modern standards as a gross miscarriage of justice. But it is difficult for the modern observer to view these events objectively, that is, through the eyes of the vast majority of the inhabitants of the ancient world. The Christians were the "winners" of this conflict, and the modern observer tends to see everything through Christian eyes—that is, whatever the Christians did was automatically righteous and whatever the pagans did was automatically evil. This is the version of these events that the early Church fathers sincerely believed, and this is the perception of the persecutions embraced by the modern media, the version enthusiastically advocated by Hollywood, the image that permeates almost all Post-Classical Western literature, and it is the version embraced by almost all history "documentaries" broadcast on educational TV. Because of bias, it is difficult for us to view this issue with anything approaching objectivity.

However, the action taken against the Christians did not seem unjust to the pagans themselves—no more unjust than the modern charge of conspiracy, for example, under which individuals can be imprisoned even when no crime has been committed. The law of *nomen Christionum* was also similar in some ways to modern anti-racketeering laws—it was aimed at protecting society. And remember the historical context: the pagans were the original inhabitants of the ancient world, the Christians were the revolutionaries. In the historical context, the Christians, not the pagans, were the disrupting and destabilizing force. It was the Christians who were trying to destroy the old values and the old way of life.

So, from an early date, Christians were punished simply on the charge of *nomen Christionum*. But how prevalent and widespread were the persecutions? The religious sources give the impression that Christians were persecuted with great efficiency, from the very beginning of their existence, continuously right up to the time that Constantine made Christianity the favored religion of the empire in 312. But the problem with this view is that it simply does not reflect historical reality. We know of no official persecutions at all by the Roman government from the secular sources until the those of Nero in the year 64. But even this persecution was strictly a local affair in the city of Rome and did not affect the provinces at all. There was no general, empire-wide persecution until the one conducted by the emperor Decius, which lasted little more than a year beginning in 250. Between 64 and 250 then, there were only isolated, local persecutions, and most of these individual outbreaks were quite brief. The second general persecution lasted for less than 3 years from 257 to 259 under the emperor Valerian. Finally the third and last systematic persecution was during the reign of Diocletian, for approximately 2 years in the West (303–304), but continued sporadically in the East until 311. During these three centuries, then, there were long periods when the Christians enjoyed peace over most of the empire.

A specific example clearly illustrates the infrequency of the actual persecution of the Christians during the 1st and 2nd centuries. In the year 112, during the reign of Trajan, a man named Gaius Pliny—known to history as Pliny the Younger—was governor of the province of Bithynia, a province far out in northeastern Asia Minor. He was a lawyer and an imperial bureaucrat who had served for many years as legal advisor to the emperor and had also held several high government administrative posts. As a lawyer he had persecuted numerous cases in Roman courts. In short, he knew his way around the Roman government and was an expert lawyer. Shortly after he reached his post of governor of the province of Bithynia, there was an outbreak of charges brought against Christians in his court, and Pliny consulted the emperor concerning the exact procedure to follow. His letter and the emperor's reply are very informative:

Pliny to the Emperor Trajan[14]

It is my custom to refer all my difficulties to you, Sir, for no one is better able to resolve my doubts and to inform my ignorance.

I have never been present at an examination of Christians. Consequently, I do not know the nature or the extent of the punishments usually meted out to them, nor the grounds for starting an investigation and how far it should be pressed. Nor am I at all sure whether any distinction should be made between them on the grounds of age, or if young people and adults should be treated alike; whether a pardon ought to be granted to anyone retracting his beliefs, or if he has once professed Christianity, he shall gain nothing by renouncing it; and whether it is the mere name of Christian which is punishable, even if innocent of crime, or rather the crimes associated with the name.

For the moment this is the line I have taken with all persons brought before me on the charge of being Christians. I have asked them in person if they are Christians, and if they admit it, I repeat the question a second and third time, with a warning of the punishment awaiting them. If they persist, I order them to be led away for execution; for, whatever the nature of their admission, I am convinced that their stubbornness and unshakeable obstinacy ought not to go unpunished. There have been others similarly fanatical who are Roman citizens. I have entered them on the list of persons to be sent to Rome for trial.

Now that I have begun to deal with this problem, as so often happens, the charges are becoming more widespread and increasing in variety. An anonymous pamphlet has been circulated which contains the names of a number of accused persons. Among these I considered that I should dismiss any who denied that they were or ever had been Christians when they had repeated after me a formula of invocation to the gods and had made offerings of wine and incense before your statue (which I had ordered to be brought into court for this purpose along with the images of the gods), and furthermore had reviled the name of Christ: none of which things, I understand, any genuine Christian can be induced to do.

Others, whose names were given to me by an informer, first admitted the charge and then denied it; they said that they had ceased to be Christians two or more years previously, and some of them even twenty years ago. They all did reverence to your statue and the images of the gods in the same way as the others, and reviled the name of Christ. They also declared that the sum total of their guilt or error amounted to no more than this: they had met regularly before dawn on a fixed day to chant verses alternately among themselves in honor of Christ as if to a god, and also to bind themselves by oath, not for any criminal purpose, but to abstain from theft, robbery and adultery, to commit no breach of trust and not to deny a deposit when called upon to restore it. After this ceremony it had been their custom to disperse and reassemble later to take food of an ordinary, harmless kind; but they had in fact given up this practice since my edict, issued on your instructions, which banned all political societies. This made me decide it was all the more necessary to extract the truth by torture from two slave-women, whom they call deaconesses. I found nothing but a degenerate sort of cult carried to extravagant lengths.

I have therefore postponed any further examination and hastened to consult you. The question seems to me to be worthy of your consideration, especially in view of the number of persons endangered; for a great many individuals of every age and class, both men and women, are being brought to trial, and this is likely to continue. It is not only the towns, but villages and rural districts too which are infected through contact with this wretched cult. I think though that it is still possible for it to be checked and directed to better ends, for there is no

14. Pliny the Younger, *Letters*, 10.96.

doubt that people have begun to throng the temples which had been almost entirely deserted for a long time; the sacred rites which had been allowed to lapse are being performed again, and flesh of sacrificial victims is on sale everywhere, though up till recently scarcely anyone could be found to buy it. It is easy to infer from this that a great many people could be re-formed if they were given an opportunity to repent,

Trajan to Pliny[15]

You have followed the right course of procedure, my dear Pliny, in your examination of the cases of persons charged with being Christians, for it is impossible to lay down a general rule to a fixed formula. These people must not be hunted out; if they are brought before you and the charge against them is proved, they must be punished, but in the case of anyone who de-nies that he is a Christian, and makes it clear that he is not by offering prayers to the gods, he is to be pardoned as a result of his repentance however suspect his past conduct may be. But pamphlets circulated anonymously must play no part in any accusation. They create the worst sort of precedent and are quite out of keeping with the spirit of our age.

The remark at the beginning of Pliny's letter that "I have never been present at an examina-tion of Christians" is quite astonishing. This is clear evidence that the persecution of Christians was so rare that even this experienced lawyer and civil servant knew nothing about them. The fact is that before the late 3rd Century, the Christians were not numerous enough in most areas of the empire for government officials to even take note of them. Another interesting aspect of this event is that the Christians were suspected of political conspiracy because of their secret nocturnal meet-ings. It is noteworthy that the emperor instructs Pliny that, to be valid, charges must be brought by individuals against other individuals and that the trial must be held in open court in order for the accused to have the opportunity to clear himself. Also, there are to be no mass roundups or sweeps of the countryside by the army (as in Hollywood "documentaries"), nor is the investigation to be pressed beyond specific complaints, and most important, anonymous denunciations are to be ignored completely. On the other hand, no crime need be committed to incur punishment, for the "name of Christian" alone is a sufficient crime to incur punishment. It is important to remember that before the time of the general persecutions, which began in 250, the only procedure for prosecuting Christians was accusatory, not inquisitional. Those brought before the court by responsible citizens were to be tried, but there was to be no general round ups of suspects.

Why Were the Christians Singled Out?

Since during the first three centuries of the Common Era the Christians were only one of a "host" of mystery religions, why were the they singled out for persecution? The most frequent charge against the Christians was their refusal to sacrifice "to the gods"—and not specifically to the gods of Rome, but simply "to the gods." Why was this considered such a horrible crime? Because it struck at the very heart of the pagan value system. Keeping the gods propitiated, or satisfied, that is, maintaining the *pax deorum* ("peace of the gods"), was necessary to ensure the health and pros-perity of the state, as well as the individual members of society. Therefore, everyone had an interest in preventing the gods from being insulted. On a more personal level, the refusal of the Christians to participate in the public rituals necessary to maintain the goodwill of the gods, separated the

15. Pliny the Younger, *Letters*, 10.97.

Figure 12.6: Christian painting from the catacombs, c. 350. "Sinners in Hell."

Christians into a category of "them" in contrast to "us" and thereby alienated them from the rest of society. This in itself made them an easy target. But this was not true of the other mystery religions. While they performed their own rituals of worship necessary for their personal salvation, they did not reject or insult the other gods, nor did they arrogantly set themselves apart from the rest of society as the Christians did. The other mystery religions, for the most part, remained within the mainstream of pagan life.

But what about the Jews, who also refused to sacrifice to the gods? Why were they not persecuted in the same manner as the Christians? The answer is quite simple. The Jews were not perceived by the Romans as revolutionary, while the Christians were. The Jews' refusal to worship the gods was formed in a quite different context than the Christians' refusal. Remember that the Romans had great respect for something known as the *mos majorum:* the "custom of our ancestors" (see chapter 10). When the Romans admonished the Jews to worship the gods, the Jews could reply that to do so was against their *mos majorum,* they had never worshiped the gods and could not do so now. It would be in conflict with the custom of their ancestors. The Romans were basically tolerant and could understand this—they may not like it, but they could understand it. A people obeying their own customs was not a threat, it was not revolutionary, and the Jews did not seem intent on destroying pagan civilization, they did not seek to convert others to their religion, they were simply conforming to their *mos majorum.* And the Romans believed that to interfere with another people's *mos majorum* was in itself a breach of *pax deorum,* that harmony between heaven and earth that was so important. A compromise was thus easy to reach. The Jews could simply offer prayers for the health and prosperity of the emperor and the state to their own god in accordance with their own customs and everything would be fine. Thus, the Jews were not persecuted for observing their own religion, though they did frequently get into trouble on political grounds.

But when the Christians were admonished to worship the gods, their response was quite different. The Christians arrogantly and provocatively replied that those gods were evil daemons and the Romans must denounce their gods and their wicked *mos majorum* and beg forgiveness from the new and revolutionary god of the Christians or else this upstart god would send them all to burn in hell for eternity. The old pagan gods and the old pagan values of the *mos majorum* must be abolished, and the new god and the new values of a convicted criminal named Jesus, who had been executed for his crimes against humanity and against the gods, must now be worshiped in their place. Imagine how provocative this was to the Roman pagans. It is quite extraordinary, under these circumstances, that the Roman response to Christianity was not more violent than it was.

Voluntary Martyrdom

Finally, the fourth aspect that must be considered is the part martyrdom played in the persecutions. Suffice it to be said that there is ample evidence that the Christians frequently presented themselves as willing, even enthusiastic, candidates for execution. It is impossible to enter into the mind of people who lived almost 2,000 years ago and know what they were thinking, but their behavior is well reported. Evidence from both secular and religious literature relates that at the trials of Christians it was sometimes impossible to restrain members of the audience from also voluntarily confessing their guilt. This attitude undoubtedly increased the severity of the persecutions because it made it more difficult for the authorities to terminate the trials once they had begun. This is evident from the letter of Pliny the Younger quoted above: "Now that I have begun to deal with this problem, as so often happens, the charges are becoming more widespread and increasing in variety."

Numerous examples of how this voluntary martyrdom erupted could be catalogued, but two will suffice. During the reign of Marcus Aurelius (161–180), in the province of Pergamum in Asia Minor, two Christians named Carpus and Papylus, were put to the torture by the proconsul, but steadfastly refused to offer sacrifice to the gods. They were therefore sentenced to be burned alive. In antiquity executions were held in public and the community was encouraged to watch. The purpose was to set an example. In effect the government was saying: "Look, this is what happens when you commit this crime." After the fire was lit and the flames began to flare up around the two being executed, suddenly a woman from the crowd named Agathonice ran forward shouting "praise be to God!" and jumped into the flames and expired with the two men. This may seem like suicide to modern sensibilities, but Agathonice is today counted as one of the martyred saints in heaven.

About the same time, across the empire in Carthage, in the council chamber of the proconsul Saturnius, a trial of a group of Christians proceeded with the usual melancholy drama: confession of Christianity, refusal to sacrifice, even refusal of the customary time to reconsider, and finally the sentence of execution—whereupon several members of the audience jumped up shouting "praise be to God!" and ran down the isle to the judge's podium to be executed along with those already convicted.

For whatever reasons, many of the early Christians behaved as if they wanted to die and get this life over at the earliest possible moment. In the modern media and literature, this attitude is portrayed as eliciting great sympathy from the contemporary pagans, but this is not correct. Remember that the pagans were humanists and believed that this life is the most precious thing any human could possesses. To witness people needlessly throwing their lives away, produced contempt rather than sympathy in the pagan mind. This behavior could only increase the severity and duration of the persecutions, because it made it more difficult for the authorities to terminate the trials of Christians, once they had begun. From the point of view of the civil authorities, they were not conducting religious persecutions, they were attempting to maintain public order and tranquility by punishing the provocative behavior of those who deliberately insulted the gods by refusing to offer sacrifice. Insulting the gods was a threat to the community as a whole as well as to each individual member of the community. Whoever offered sacrifice returned home unmolested, and there is no evidence whatsoever that the officials concerned themselves with a Christian's beliefs or prior activities. The Christian desire for martyrdom must have been tremendously frustrating for those Roman authorities who were charged with the responsibility for maintaining order out in the provinces.

The Triumph of Christianity

Since the 18th Century movement called "The Enlightenment," an almost immeasurable quantity of scholarly effort and energy has been expended investigating the question: "Why and how did Christianity triumph over seemingly insurmountable opposition to become the only religion permitted to exist within the Roman Empire and, later, its successor states?" After all the analyses and debates have been completed, after all the books and articles and pamphlets have been written, it all comes down to four major proposals to explain the triumph of Christianity over paganism:[16] (1) the appeal of the promise of salvation and the fear of punishment; (2) the rational Christian theology; (3) the strong organization of the Church; (4) the support and the coercion of the government. All the arguments of theologians and historians, all the verbiage that has flowed from the pens of pundits and from the pulpits by fanatics, are only variations and embellishments of these four fundamental proposals. But do all four of these proposals have equal value? It is important to examine each of them in some detail.

The Appeal of Christianity

Many scholars, especially theologians, give great credit for Christianity's success to something they call simply "appeal." Christianity, they say, had more appeal to the masses than did the other mystery religions. In fact, those who advance this argument almost always assume that some form of salvationist religion was destined to replace ancient polytheism, and their argument seeks only to explain why it was Christianity and not one of the other mystery religions. They maintain that no one really ever believed in all those pagan gods and goddesses anyway. Everyone in the ancient world was actually waiting and yearning for the "right" religion to be revealed to them, and when Christianity came along it was accepted with overwhelming enthusiasm and joy. However, it is quite easy to gather an abundance of evidence that paganism did not simply die a natural death, but in fact was bludgeoned

---

16. Edward Gibbon, in the famous chapter 15 of *The Decline and Fall of the Roman Empire* (1776–1688), was the first writer to analyze the problem of Christianity in a historical context—in contrast to a religious event—and he proposed five major reasons for its success; the zeal of the early Christians in spreading the faith; the promise of immortality; the claims of miraculous powers; the ethical standards of early Christianity; and organization of the church on the model of imperial Rome. Some of the other historians who have dealt with the problem (in English) are Merivale, *Conversion of the Roman Empire* (1865); A. C. McGiffert, "The Influence of Christianity upon the Roman Empire," *Harvard Theological Review* (1909); J. Klusner, *From James to Paul* (1943); Ramsay MacMullen, *Christianizing the Roman Empire,* Yale University Press, London (1984).

Figure 12.7: Mother and child motif in 3rd Century art. Left, Isis and Horus; Right, Mary and Jesus.

to death.[17] The pagan belief system was a viable and vigorous tradition in the lives of millions of human beings for many thousands of years longer than Christianity has existed. It did not simply fade away of its own accord. However, we need not go into all of that here. For the sake of discussion, we can concede this point and look at this argument of appeal on its own terms.

Put into its simplest, and therefore its crudest form, this arguments proposes that Christianity was more appealing, and thus acquired a larger number of converts than the other salvationist religions because it was the "right" religion, whereas the others religions were the "wrong" ones. Of course these scholars put their arguments into much more sophisticated clothing for the history books. They argue, for example, that Christianity was superior to the other mystery cults because its founder was a historical person, because it had higher moral standards, because it incorporated from the Jews their rich collection of religious law and literature, because it promised the meek that they will inherit the earth—although they must leave it in hands of the powerful and the arrogant for the foreseeable future, but eventually they will inherit.

All the other mystery cults, say these scholars, had fatal disadvantages when compared with Christianity. Some of them, like Mithras, appealed only to men—indeed only men were allowed in the Mithras religion. Others, like Isis, appealed mostly to women, and still others, like Cybele,

17. Geffcken, Johannes, *The Last Days of Greco-Roman Paganism* (1978), North Holland Publishing Co., Amsterdam, p. vii: "No Scholar of ancient history. . . will now believe the dogma of earlier days, that there is a direct connection between the coming into existence and the spread of Christianity on the one hand and the decline of paganism on the other. The exact opposite is the case." See also Vermaseren, Maarten J., "Paganism's Death Struggle, Religions in Competition with Christianity," from *The Crucible of Christianity*, edited by Arnold Toynbee (1969), World Publishing Co., New York City.

demanded unrealistic sacrifices or changes in lifestyle. The priests of the goddess Cybele, for instance, worked themselves up into a frenzy and castrated themselves as part of their initiation into the priesthood—indeed an abrupt and nonreversible change in lifestyle.

But upon closer examination, this whole argument of appeal is revealed as the product of a shallow and ethnocentric thinking. As a matter of fact, up until the year 313, when Constantine made Christianity the favored religion of the Roman empire, there is no evidence whatsoever that Christianity was any more popular within the general population than the other mystery cults. Of course, Christianity seems emotionally more appealing to us today than any of those other strange mystery religions, about which we actually know very little, except what the early Christian writers, who were their enemies, tell us. That is not a very unbiased source of information. Because of our cultural background and education, Christianity seems more appealing, more "correct," more "natural," than all those other strange religions that ceased to exist many centuries ago.

The truth is that many important aspects of the competing mystery cults were absorbed into the Christian religion. For example, the priests of Cybele castrated themselves as part of their initiation into the priesthood, which may at first seem to us very strange and even amusing, but what about the oath of celibacy taken by Roman Catholic priests as an important part of their initiation into the priesthood? Is this not a symbolic form of self-castration? And where did this practice originate? Was it part of Christianity's Jewish heritage? No indeed, Jewish religious leaders are expected to be family men, not celibate.

In fact, when one analyzes Christian customs and practices, one discovers almost nothing original in them. Almost every individual facet of Christian belief or practice can be found in one or another of the mystery religions, or in pagan practices far older than Christianity. An obvious example is the Christmas holiday. No one really has the slightest clue concerning what day of the year Jesus was born. The celebration of his birthday on December 25th is purely and simply the result of a successful takeover of the very popular pagan festival called the feast of the Saturnalia. It celebrated the winter solstice, the shortest day of the year, the day when the sun reaches its farthest movement south and begins to travel back northward, meaning that the days will now become longer and eventually winter will pass and spring will come again. The Saturnalia was celebrated with the exchange of gifts, feasting with family and friends on special foods, etc. Why would the Christians be interested in this pagan holiday? Because when pagans converted to Christianity they refused to give up many of their former practices. When the Christian priest looked out on his congregation in late December and saw many empty seats, he asked "where are the members of my congregation?" Someone told him, "Well, they are down the street at the temple celebrating the Saturnalia." What was the answer to this problem? Well, of course, a counter feast. Thus, Christmas was born.

The second most important Christian holiday, Easter, celebrates Christ's resurrection, but it does not even occur on a fixed date. It is actually derived from the pagan festival of spring. The date for Easter is decided by an astrological formula: the first Sunday after the first full moon after the Jewish Passover. So, the date of Easter is determined, among other things, by the phase of the moon. Thus, it turns out that these Christian holidays were developed to prevent worshipers from deserting the church to celebrate pagan festivals. These were deeply imbedded in the pagan way of life, and the people would not easily give them up after becoming Christians, so the festivals were absorbed into Christianity along with the new converts. The argument that Christianity had more appeal than the other mystery cults, or even paganism in general is not valid. In fact, a rational argument could be made that Christianity did not have as much appeal as the pagan cults and thus was forced to absorb many customs and practices from them in order to overcome its lack of appeal.

Christianity's Rational Theology

The second proposed explanation for the success of Christianity is its rational theology. Christianity is often said to be the triumph of truth and rationality over the superstition of polytheism. However, like all religions, the basic and most important aspects of Christian theology are not rational at all and must be accepted on faith. No new religion was ever discovered through scientific research. The development of this so-called rational theology by the early church fathers took place over a period of centuries—in fact this process is still in progress today. That is what theologians do.

As early Christianity came into contact with the Greek communities in the East, the Greeks naturally began to subject Christian beliefs to the rational principles of their philosophy, which they had developed over many centuries and which had deep roots in Greek culture. In defense, the Christian leaders, most of whom were Hellenized and had a Greek education, began to employ the same rational modes of thought to explain and clarify Christian doctrine. Therefore, the Christian theology which developed through this process was a compromise between Christian mystical irrationality and Greek philosophic rationalism, rather than a triumph of Christian reason over pagan superstition, as is so often argued. The interaction of Christianity and Greek culture was very much a two-way street.[18] Each changed the other in fundamental ways through what anthropologists call cultural interpenetration. This interaction always occurs when divergent cultures come into contact. In any event, rationalism as a reason for the triumph of Christianity among the masses is not a strong argument. No doubt it had some effect on the small, elite educated class, but not among the broad, uneducated masses. The rational argument rarely carry the day in matters of religion. Actually, Christian theology is only rational in the way it manipulates the basic tenants of the faith. Those tenants are not in themselves any more rational than the beliefs of the pagan religions. Thus, the development of rational theology does not explain the triumph of Christianity.

The Organization of the Church

However, the third reason proposed by scholars for Christianity's triumph over paganism, its superior organization, does have merit. If the rational framework for theology was a Greek contribution, organizational and administrative techniques were the contribution of the Romans. During the first 3rd or 4th centuries of its existence, the church organized itself on the model of the empire itself, based on a hierarchy of deacons, priests, and bishops. In fact, the church became a state itself, a state within the state, with its own administrative structure, tax system, welfare program, judicial process, etc. This was all made possible by the umbrella of the *pax Romana*, which allowed free movement throughout the Mediterranean area. The spread of one single religion across such a heterogeneous population would be unimaginable except in the context of the Roman Empire.

There is no need here to go into all the details of the church hierarchy and bureaucracy which were developed by the early church, but it is obvious that this organization gave the church the strength, resilience, and endurance which enabled it to survive some very serious defeats and setbacks that might otherwise have destroyed it and also permitted it to take quick and tenacious advantage of its victories. But organization alone cannot account for Christianity's complete triumph. Something more was necessary.

---

18. A detailed discussion of this process is contained in Jaeger, Werner, *Early Christianity and Greek Paideia* (1961). Oxford University Press, London.

The Support of the Government

So now we come to the fourth proposal on our list, government support and coercion. The single most important reason that Christianity triumphed over great odds was that it gained the support of the government of the Roman Empire. No religion anywhere has achieved universal success, that is, become the sole religion of a people or complex civilization, without the active support of the government and the ruling class. Left to their own inclination, the general population of any complex civilization will never willingly and of its own volition unite within one single religion anymore than everyone in a nation will spontaneously join the same political party. Such an event requires coercion, it requires the application of force from the government. This fact is often ignored by historians.

The single most important event that assured the triumph of Christianity was the conversion of the emperor Constantine. At the time Constantine made Christianity the favored religion of the Empire, in 313, it is estimated that somewhere between 5% and 7% of the Empire's population was Christian, and this was after almost three centuries of missionary effort by the Christians. This is not evidence of Christianity's overwhelming popularity and appeal with the masses. Christianity had, by early 4th Century, achieved about as much expansion as it ever would have achieved without active government support. If you read the writings of the early church historians, writers such as Eusebius, it is evident that they knew this. Eusebius states clearly that the reason the church triumphed was the conversion of Constantine.[19]

But on the other hand, 5% of the population is not an insignificant figure when it comes to gaining control of the government. The Bolsheviks, for example, seized control of the Russian government in 1917 when less than 3% of the population was Communist. If you accept the premise that individuals can influence history, then it follows that even a small group of very determined and dedicated and well organized individuals can have an even greater influence upon history. And if that small group gains control of the power structure of society, as the Christians did in 313, or as the Communists did in 1917, the influence of that small group can be decisive. Throughout its subsequent history, Christianity managed to spread only by first converting the rulers or the upper classes of societies, and then conversion of the people was a simple matter. In no case have Christian missionary efforts been successful until the ruling class has accepted Christianity and given active government support and coercion to the conversion of the masses. Therefore, the Christian revolution within the Roman Empire was engineered from above, not from below, as is often imagined.

The Transformation of Europe

During the 4th and 5th centuries of our era, as the western half of the Roman Empire slowly disintegrated and disappeared from history and the eastern half of the Roman Empire was gradually transformed into the Christian state that modern scholars call the Byzantine Empire, a subtle but very fundamental change occurred in the spirit and outlook of Western Civilization. This change was at least as important and far-reaching as the change that occurred in Roman society around the 3rd and 2nd centuries BCE, when they came into contact with the Greeks. Indeed, this transformation in Western Society was so pervasive that it is still to this day reflected in almost every aspect of life in Western Civilization both and private.

---

19. Eusebius, *Ecclesiastical History*.

Figure 12.8: The Image of Humanity. Left, Late Classical; Right, Early Christian.

The Rise of Mysticism

This change can easily be demonstrated by an analysis of the literature and art of the period. Indeed, plastic artists are often the most penetrating observers and accurate recorders of the spirit of their own times. Note, for example, Figure 12.8, which is a depiction of human beings from the late classical period on the left and a rendition of the same subject from the early Christian era on the right.

The image of the human form rendered by the classical artist is one of strength, confidence, beauty—even godliness, because the figure on the left is the goddess Roma, The other seated figure is Augustus. Humanism is the essence of this artist's vision, and this is the expression of the spirit of the artist's age. For the most part, classical thinkers believed that the meaning of life must by found here in this world in the human context, and they believed that human beings had the strength to meet that challenge. Oh, it is true that most classical philosophers believed that the human being possessed a soul, an almost indefinable quality that separates humans from the "lower" animals. A few of them, Plato comes first to mind, even speculated that the human soul might have an existence independent from the body, that it might even live on after the death of the body. But for the most part, classical philosophers believed that the true meaning of human life must be found here on this earth in this human context, because "man is the measure of all things." The very essence of classical humanism is embraced in this one simple phrase, the famous quote from the philosopher Protagoras. In the final analysis, then, at least in the view of the humanists, each of us is responsible for our own life, and it is what we do now, right here in the present, that counts, not what happens in some world of the spirit about which we can never know anything for certain.

In contrast, the artist of the early Christian age holds a starkly different image of the human form, which reflects a fundamental change in the zeitgeist of the age. If the essence of humanism can be described in one phrase, the essence of early Christianity can be described in three words: "guilt, guilt, guilt!" This image of Adam and Eve, on a Christian fresco from the catacombs of Rome, painted in the late 2nd or early 3rd Century, would hardly be recognized as human by the classical artist. This is not the image of godliness. It is true that in the view of the early Christian, man was *created* in the image of god, but they believed that image very quickly degenerated into a vile, evil, and hopelessly depraved being. These very first two human beings committed the first sin against god, the eating of the forbidden fruit depicted here, and all their descendants are forever tainted and degraded by that act. Now, in the view of the Christians, all human beings come into this world already convicted of that original sin, already condemned to an eternal punishment of unbelievable horror. Now each human being stands utterly alone before the tribunal of an awful, omnipotent, and omniscient God. Now there is no inner human strength upon which to draw, because now no fraction, no particle of his fate remains under his own control. Now the depraved human being has only one choice: he must beg and pled for his salvation from a god so powerful and so sovereign that the feeble human mind can never hope to understand him. This represents the triumph of mysticism and the decline of humanism in Western Society at the end of the ancient world. This was the essential transformation, the fundamental change that occurred in Western Civilization during the 4th and 5th Centuries of the common Era. This new zeitgeist affected every aspect, every nuance of the history of the Post-Classical period, the period that once was known as the Dark Ages, but must now be referred to by the politically correct term Middle Ages or Medieval Period.

The Successor Societies

With the demise of the Roman Empire in the West, three new successor societies inherited the territories and the traditions of Greco-Roman civilization. They were: Western Christianity, or Roman Catholicism, in western Europe; Eastern Christianity, or Greek Orthodoxy, in Asia Minor, the Balkan peninsula and Russia; and Islam in North Africa and the Middle East. Each of these societies was different from Roman civilization in two fundamental aspects: one was economic, the other was cultural.

Economically, their agricultural systems rested on peasant farmers, who were not exactly free in the modern sense of that word, but they were not outright slaves either. Slavery continued, of course, in all three societies, but it become much less important economically. Agricultural production now depended on a new type of involuntary servitude, know as serfdom in western Europe. Under serfdom the farmers were tied to the land, and come to be conceived of as much a part of the land as the trees and meadows. Perhaps serfdom was not so inhuman and brutal a form of servitude as outright slavery—for one thing individuals could not be bought and sold, which prevented families from being split up on the auction block, but weather or not the serfs of the Middle Ages enjoyed a better life than the slaves of the ancient world is really a matter of opinion.

Culturally, each of these new civilizations were overshadowed by its own vision of an afterlife and the hope of personal salvation, provided by one of the branches of Christianity or Islam. Under these religious systems, even the most miserable serf could believe that if he did God's will here on earth, which for most members of society meant, in effect, performing as one's master demanded, then he could ultimately attain eternal life. For this reason, these belief systems have been referred to as the "higher religions."

The Barbarian Migrations

Many other changes accompanied the fall of the Roman Empire in the West. Some of these changes may have been causes of the fall of the Empire, some of them may have been results of the fall, and others may have simply occurred simultaneously.

For one thing, there was a vast migration of peoples throughout the entire area of these three civilizations. Celts, Germans, and Slavs moved in from the North and the East. Arabs moved in all directions from the Arabian Peninsula. Many other peoples shifted and enlarged the area of their former settlements. The violence and destruction which accompanied these migrations, especially in western Europe and North Africa, destroyed the Roman governmental structure and plunged Europe into what can only be described as the status of pre-civilization.

The structure of the social and political institutions of Europe were also changed in fundamental ways. Both barbarian and Roman elements were combined and evolved into a socio-political system known as "feudalism." The barbarian kingdoms that slowly emerged from the shambles of the provinces of the Western Roman Empire formed a kind of skeleton of the modern state system of Europe. The peoples who invaded the provinces of the western Roman Empire during the 5th and later centuries were called "barbarians" by the Romans. They were called barbarians because, in the eyes of the Romans, they were completely uncivilized. Although it is politically incorrect nowadays to speak of a people being "uncivilized," let the facts speak for themselves: they did not lead a settled life; they did not live in cities; they did not have a written language; they possessed only primitive, tribal political and social institutions. Thus, according to all the normal definitions of the term civilization, these peoples were definitely not civilized. And when they overrun the western provinces of the Roman Empire and destroyed the cities upon which Roman civilization was based, western Europe descended into the abyss of barbarism and darkness from which it could not recover for a millennium. Indeed, when some observers look at the state of the Mediterranean area today, they conclude that this area has not even in the 21st Century recovered the security, the common civility and the prosperity that it possessed during that period known as the *pax Romana*.

But it is a mistake to think of the "barbarians" as a single people: in fact the term refers to a whole multitude of different peoples. These peoples had wandered for centuries beyond the northern frontiers of the Roman Empire, but had hitherto exerted only a minor influence on the cultural life of the ancient world. Celtic tribes inhabited the island fringes of northern Europe: These included the Gaels of Ireland and the Picts of Scotland, culturally and linguistically related to the Gauls and the Britons, who had long ago been included in the Roman cultural system. But more numerous and formidable than the Celts were the Germanic peoples, who controlled a great territorial arch stretching from Scandinavia across northern Europe to the Black Sea. These German tribes had been in contact with the Mediterranean civilizations for centuries and they were the most advanced of the barbarian peoples. Beyond this band of Germans lived a group of the most primitive and perhaps the most numerous of all the barbarian peoples, the Slavic tribes. The Germanic tribes had pressed against the Roman frontiers for centuries, because their poor economy and primitive agricultural technology, coupled with their ever expanding population, forced them to constantly search for new lands to plunder. And, as we have seen before, the peoples living outside the highly developed and civilized areas conceive the wealth and splendor of civilization as simply a kind of natural resource to be harvested whenever they are powerful enough to do so.

Although the Romans were almost always successful in resisting the armed invasions of the barbarians, they nevertheless admitted large numbers of them into imperial territory. After all, this was only in accordance with the long observed Roman policy of inclusion. The Romans had always sought to include more and more peoples within their cultural and political system, this was the policy and the process that had created the Roman Empire in the first place. Thus, it is incorrect to conceive of this influx of barbarians into Roman territory as exclusively, or even primarily, due to armed incursions, because it was accomplished for the most part by a steady and relentless infiltration and often peaceful migration.

At first the barbarians came as slaves or prisoners of war, then as free peasants to settle on lands deserted after the plagues of the 3rd Century, then they came as mercenary soldiers in the imperial army and finally as officers of the army. However, this barbarian penetration acquired a new urgency and a new violence in the 4th Century, when a new factor was added to the equation. Hordes of a nomadic people from central Asia, the Huns, began to conquer and ravish the Germans themselves and, in order to find protection from this onslaught, the Germans turned against the Roman frontiers with renewed determination. Unfortunately, this occurred at a time when the Roman Empire was weakened by internal troubles and was no longer able to provide the strong and efficient defense of its borders that it had done for so many centuries. For reasons that are not fully understood by modern scholars, but certainly are related to a population explosion if far off central Asia, the Huns swept out of their Asian homeland and terrorized Western Europe. By 375 they had subjugated the Ostrogoths (the "east Goths"), who inhabited the area that is now the Ukraine and pushed the Visigoths (the "west Goths") against the Danube frontier.

Then the greatest leader the Huns ever produced, a man named Attila, known as the "scourge of God" to the Christians, appeared on the historical scene. Attila reorganized the Huns into an army which was literally a nation of horse back, a nation that could ride for days without dismounting. Attila led this army into Western Europe where he ravished and plundered the Roman provinces Gaul and Italy and brought the Empire to the brink of dismemberment. However, in 453, Attila died suddenly (incidentally, while in bed with a Roman princess), and with his death the Huns vanished from history even more quickly than they had appeared. But like that other great invasion of Italy by Hannibal almost 675 years earlier, the Huns set into motion a massive process of migration that did not end even when the force that had initiated it was removed. Indeed, before the cycle of migration, set into motion by the Huns, had run its course, the Roman Empire in the West lay in ashes, and the period that Gibbon called "that happiest age of human history" had vanished with it.

By 410 the Visigoths had sacked Rome itself; soon afterward the Franks conquered Gaul and the Vandals conquered Spain and North Africa, where they established a kingdom in 429 and then plundered Rome for fourteen days in 455. Finally, on September 4, 476, Odoacer, one of the barbarian officers in the imperial army which now consisted mostly of barbarian mercenaries, simply deposed the last Roman emperor[20] in the West and established the barbarian kingdom of Italy. This year, 476, is commonly given as the date of the fall of the Roman Empire, although in reality it was a minor event. Most of the people living in Italy in 476 probably did not experience much of a change in their daily life. Rome was not built in a day, and it did not fall in a day either.

---

20. The emperor's name was Romulus Augustulus. Ironically, the first and last emperors of Rome were both named Romulus, though they ruled over 1,200 years apart.

The Emergence of Western Europe

From the ashes of Rome's western provinces gradually arose several barbarian kingdoms, which, as stated earlier, formed a kind of skeleton or outline of the political map of modern Europe. However, the details of the histories of these kingdoms are too complex, tedious, and irrelevant to relate here in detail. The barbarian kings did not view their positions as rulers in the same way as the Roman emperors had. Whereas the emperors viewed the empire as a commonwealth to be ruled for the mutual benefit of all its inhabitants, the barbarian kings perceived of kingdoms as their personal estates to be administered for their own selfish advantage. Their aversion to urban life caused the Roman administrative and economic infrastructure to disintegrate and disappear. The center of social, economic, and cultural life shifted to the countryside, a critical change which facilitated the demise of classical civilization.

The Germans, however, did not exterminate the Roman populations of the territories in which they settled. They did not even establish an exclusively German aristocracy. Rather, they gradually intermarried with the Romans and slowly the old and new inhabitants became indistinguishable. But on the cultural level, everything sank down to the lowest common denominator. The cities, upon which Roman culture and civilization was based, disappeared. A thousand years of classical knowledge and tradition were lost forever. Literacy and just simple, common civility all but vanished from western Europe: during the early Middle Ages, not one person in a thousand, *not one tenth of one percent* of the population, could read and write.

Germanic Society

One of the striking contrasts between the Romans and the Germans was their attitude toward children. Classical culture was based on literacy and learning, which required heavy investments in the education of the young. Despite the aura of affluence, classical society was poor, and parents opted to make that investment only in a limited number of offspring. Families were small and the population was stable. The illiterate Germans, on the other hand, practiced another option: they reared many children, but invested little in their upbringing. Children of the rich and the poor were reared with equal indifference. Indeed, in the early Middle Ages there is no real concept of childhood, the art of the time depicts children simply as miniature adults. This contrast in the cultures of the two peoples assured that the Germans would eventually overwhelm the Romans by reason of shear numbers.

The German social and political structure was still primarily tribal in form and spirit. Before the invasions, the Germans did not have true kings, but chieftains, and the German chief occupied an ambiguous position in relation to the tribe and its members. The chief was primarily a military leader and high priest. His power rested not on prerogative or law, but on the naked violence he could threaten or apply. This tribal organization of German society left to the family the responsibility for avenging the injuries done to its members. Eventually, custom replaced the crude "eye for an eye" vendetta with a scale of compensations that could be demanded for a person's life, arm, eye, etc., but the responsibility for avenging a crime against its members remained the responsibility of the family, not the tribal chief. Because the family was sometimes too weak to protect its members, several families often formed association, called *comitatus*. Young freemen would join the following of an established chief and fight for him in exchange for a share of the booty and for protection. This personal tie between chief and follower, based on mutual obligations, resembles the later medieval relationship between lord and vassal. This is hardly an accident.

Customary Law

Without a written language, how did the Germans create and enforce contracts? Obviously, not very efficiently. To create and record contractual obligations, the Germans—and the Medieval world after them—relied heavily on symbolic gestures performed in public. The transfer of real property, for example, was accomplished when the former owner publicly and ceremoniously transferred a clod of dirt from his own hand to the hand of the new owner; witnesses could later testify as to what had happened. But depending on testimony is a very uncertain method of solving contractual disputes. Therefore, the Germans determined the guilt or innocence of individuals by investigating their character or appealing to magic. In a practice called compurgation, twelve "good men," who knew nothing about the facts in dispute, would swear to the honest reputation of the accused. Or, more often, the accused would undergo an ordeal, such as running barefoot over hot irons or immersing his hand in a vessel of boiling water; if no harm came to the person, he was declared innocent. Another method was to have the two contenders in a legal issue to simply duel to the death before the court. The assumption was that God would not allow the innocent party to be vanquished. Obviously, all of this is a far cry from the principles of equity and fairness of Roman law.

To set and maintain government policies, the Germans relied on the old and respected men of the community to recall and state the ancient customs. This explains one of the most distinctive features of tribal government: the use of councils and assemblies. The German chief, like the Medieval king afterward, never made important decisions alone, but always acted in an assembly or council of freemen, who could help him recall the customs and aid him in making judgments. The councils also served to bestow legality on the chief's decisions. All of these practices influenced the later development of medieval institutions. The medieval king, like the German chief, was always expected to make his major decisions with the advice of the great men of the realm. The use of juries in trials is based on the assumption that the entire community, represented by a jury of sworn men, and not a judge alone, should determine when a law was broken.

German Religion

German religion displayed much the same attitude of pessimism and fatalism that we saw in early Mesopotamia. The Germans conceived of nature as a cruel and hostile force, and religion was a method of at least partially placating and appeasing those forces. The German pantheon consisted of two sets of gods. Minor deities and spirits—these were both good and evil—inhabited the forests, streams, fields, and seas. It was these deities that directly affected human affairs, and it was these that the ordinary person felt compelled to deal with. Through incantations, spells, or charms the Germans attempted to influence the actions of these spirits. For example, they believed that spirits inhabited certain evergreen trees in the forest and it was necessary to make offerings of shiny trinkets, bits of food, and other objects, which were tied with strings to the trees, in order to prevent the spirits from doing harm to humans. Even after the Germans were converted to Christianity, they would not give up this practice, and indeed we still practice this magical ritual today—especially at Christmas time. This is, in fact, the origin of the Christmas tree. These magical practices were foreign to Roman paganism, but they strongly influenced the popular religion of the Middle Ages and indeed for a long time afterward.

The higher gods, on the other hand, lived in the sky and took only a remote interest in the affairs of humans. The chief, or king, of the gods was Woden (or Oden), god of magic and victory. The days of the week in all the Germanic languages, including English, are named after these gods: Wednesday is named for Woden; his wife Friia gives her name to Friday; Tuesday is named after Tyr, the god of war;

Thursday after Thor, god of thunder. According to Germanic religion, warriors who died on the battlefield were transported immediately to Valhalla, the great banquet hall of the gods in the sky. This means that war was a holy activity and that death on the battlefield offered the only possibility of salvation.

But in keeping with their pessimistic outlook, the Germans believed that in the not too distant future, the entire company of the gods and heroes were doomed to a massive destruction by fire during a cosmic event called the "twilight of the gods." At that time the whole universe, including both heaven and earth, would be consumed by fire, and the ravaged cinder would sink into the sea and cease to exist.

In summation then, the successful invasions of these barbarian peoples of the western provinces of the Roman Empire led to the triumph of a vulgar, non-literate culture over the literate, urban civilization of the classical world. Although the barbarians had a great respect for Roman civilization, and in fact for many centuries after its destruction, barbarian kings, like Charlemagne, attempted to resurrect it, their aversion to urban life, coupled the sheer destruction with which their invasions were accomplished, brought all culture in western Europe down to the lowest common denominator. The inevitable result was that, for all practical purposes, life in western Europe reverted to a level of pre-civilization: during the early Middle Ages, no urban area in western Europe (outside of Italy) had a population of 10,000. The governmental structure, which had been so painstakingly built up by the Romans over the centuries, vanished with the cities, and throughout the countryside the weak were forced to seek the protection of the strong; "might makes right" replaced the rule of law, and the people descended into the darkness of superstition and apathy. But far more important than all of this was the fact that literacy, culture, and just plain common civility all but disappeared from western Europe. The Middle Ages was a time of illiteracy, superstition, and ignorance. Even that greatest hero of the Middle Ages, Charlemagne, who attempted to re-establish classical culture, who produced something scholars like to call "the Carolingian Renaissance," was so utterly illiterate that he could not even sign his own name. If this period does not deserve to be called the "Dark Ages," it is difficult to dignify it with the name "civilization."

Byzantium

The Byzantine Empire is the name given by historians to the eastern half of the Roman Empire that survived as a Christian state for a thousand years after the fall of the Roman Empire in the West. However, the very name "Byzantium" is a historical misnomer. The inhabitants of the eastern Empire did not recognize a break in the continuity between their civilization and that of the ancient Roman Empire. They did not call themselves Byzantines, they called themselves Romans until the very end of their history, even after the city of Rome had slipped forever from their power, even after they had adopted Greek as their official language.

The Influence of Byzantium on the History of Western Europe

Byzantium had a lasting and important influence on the history of Western Europe. Byzantine scholars preserved the ancient Greek Byzantine classics, by coping them from papyrus to parchment. The knowledge of ancient Greece and of Greek literature was lost completely in Western Europe and was not recovered until the Renaissance. Had the texts not been preserved by the Byzantines, they would have been lost completely, and our knowledge of ancient Greece would be severely limited. The eastern empire held the line against the inroads of the barbarians from the North and the East. Otherwise, Europe would have been even worse off than it was during the Middle Ages. But even more importantly, Byzantium was the bastion of the defense of Europe against Islamic aggression. Without the survival of the Byzantine Empire in the East, European civilization would have been caught between an Islamic invasion from two fronts and probably would have succumbed completely to Muslim expansion. Had that occurred, we would not even have a Western Civilization to study. So Byzantium not only preserved the legacy of Western civilization, it is almost certainly responsible for its survival during those dark centuries of the Early Middle Age.

The West also owes a debt to Byzantium for the preservation of another priceless legacy: Roman law. Although Roman "civil law" was lost completely in the West during the Middle Ages, it was later reintroduced from the East and eventually went on to become the basis of the law codes of all Western European nations, except Britain. Today, Roman civil law is the basis of the legal systems of large areas of the world, including all of South and Central America and even such unexpected nations as the Philippines and Japan.

The theology of the Christian religion in the West is still based on the first seven church councils, which were held before the Roman West split off from the Orthodox East. In spite of all the theological controversies and developments of the Middle Ages, the doctrines which emerged from those councils is still today the basis of almost all the major Christian churches and sects, even the Protestant denominations. The basic tenants of the trinity and the duel nature of Christ were crystallized under the influence of Greek thought during the early councils.

Finally, in the decades just prior to the fall of the Byzantine Empire, which occurred in 1453, many of the scholars in Constantinople, fully understanding that their civilization was doomed, sought refuge in the West. Most of them moved to Italy, taking their precious manuscripts and the knowledge of the ancient world with them. Europe by that time was just emerging from the dark centuries of the Middle Ages, and the influx of these scholars and the knowledge of the classical world was an important factor which helped to touch off the period of Italian history known as the Renaissance—a word that literally means "re-birth."

Constantinople and the East

The term "Byzantine Empire" is a term invented by modern historians to distinguish the later Roman (Christian) Empire from the earlier phase of Roman history. It is, in fact, one of those lies that historians impose on history. The inhabitants of the eastern empire did not recognize a break in the continuity between their civilization and that of the ancient Roman Empire. They did not call themselves Byzantines, they thought of themselves Romans until the very end of their history. Long after the city of Rome slipped forever from their power, even after they had adopted Greek as their official language, they still knew themselves as Romans.

The first Christian emperor of the Roman Empire, Constantine (303–337), transferred the capital of the Empire from Rome in 324 to a new city he built on the Bosporus, at the site of the ancient Greek town of Byzantium. The study of "Byzantine" history traditionally begins with this event, although the western part of the empire did not fall for another 150 years (476). Constantine's motives were both religious and military. Rome was still a pagan stronghold and he wanted to build a new Christian capital, uncontaminated by a pagan presence. But undoubtedly, more important than this were his military intentions. The provinces of the East were the wealthiest, the most populous, and the most urbanized provinces in the empire, and they had a much longer history of civilization than the provinces of the West. And the eastern provinces had made a much more rapid and complete recovery from the ravages of the plagues and political crises of the 3rd

Century. Indeed, many of the western provinces never recovered their former population levels after the plagues. In short, the Roman Empire could not survive at all without these eastern provinces, but they were now menaced on every side by many enemies: the newly rejuvenated Persians beyond the Euphrates River; the German tribes beyond the Danube River; and the German pirates in the Black sea. Therefore, it was more important for the survival of the empire as a whole to defend the East than to defend the West, and for these reasons the imperial capital was moved to the East (see "Constantine's Government" above).

But certainly of prime importance to the empire's survival, Constantinople, unlike Rome, had the best natural defenses of any city in the Mediterranean basin. A fortress capital is essential for a civilization that is on the defensive. So long as Constantinople remained unconquered, the empire remained unconquered. Constantinople was, in fact, invincible until the invention of the cannon made possible to breach its walls. But by that time, a thousand years had passed and Europe had recovered from its long decline and the torch of Western Civilization was passed to Europe. That, in a sense, was the destiny of the Byzantine Empire.

The Development of Christianity

The early Church faced four major obstacles: the rival mystery religions (which provided the same mystical solace but remained within the mainstream of ancient society); the pagans (who adhered to the traditional polytheistic and humanistic tradition); the Jews (from whom the Christians originated); and the heretics (dissenters from Church orthodoxy). The early Church leaders who confronted these opponents are known as the "Church Fathers," or sometimes as the "Christian Apologists."[21]

By the 2nd Century of the Common Era the Jews and the Christians had parted company and most Christians were Gentiles. However, the Christians adopted much of the Jewish tradition: the organization of the believers into congregational units; the Sabbath (which the Christians transferred to Sunday); and the adoption of the Jewish literary tradition which formed the Christian Old Testament (which became the companion of the Christian scriptural texts, the New Testament). Ironically, this debt to Judaism did not preclude anti-Semitism on the part of the Christian community.[22]

Early Christianity could have followed several different theological directions, and there were many controversies. The final theology adopted by the Church is known as orthodox ("true"), while the other possible courses are known as heresies ("contrary to truth"). Some important early heresies were: the Gnostics (who believed they had received a special *gnosis*, or "knowledge"); the Montanists (who followed the 2nd Century prophet Montanus); the Arians (followers of Arius, who believed Jesus was human, not divine); and the Monophysites (who believed that Christ had only one divine nature). All these and other "incorrect" views were debated and rejected by the Church Fathers. Although these terms and concepts seem strange and obscure to us today, any one of them could have become Christian orthodoxy.

The final solution was the doctrine of the Trinity, the product of such complex and intricate philosophical reasoning that it can be truly understood by only a few, but nevertheless it remains the fundamental core belief of the Christian religion. The Trinity postulates that God is both one

---

21. The most important of the Christian Apologists: Clement of Rome, Bishop of Rome c. 88–101; Justin of Neapolis (Justin Martyr), c. 100–165; Tertullian of Carthage, c. 155/160–after 200; Origin of Caesarea, c. 185–c. 254; John Chrysostom of Antioch, c. 347–407; Jerome of Palestine, c. 347–419/420; Augustine of Hippo (North Africa), 354–430.

22. Justin's *Dialogue with Trypho* established the tradition of Christian anti-Semitism. Around 400, Saint John Chrysostom delivered eight *Sermons Against the Jews and Gentiles* at Antioch, which accused the Jews of the murder of Jesus and provided support for many of the anti-Semitic arguments of later centuries.

and three at the same time, or "three in one." The one God includes the three "persons" of Father, Son, and Holy Spirit. All can act separately and each is whole and complete, but yet at the same time they form a single One. The hallmark of a devout and true Christian is the acceptance and belief in this doctrine, even when the believer cannot fully understand it.

During the period when this Christian theology was developing, the Roman Empire slowly separated, both culturally and politically, into the Greek East and the Latin West. The Church split along with the empire. Constantine's Edict of Milan in 313 made Christianity legal and tolerated. During his subsequent reign he gradually made Christianity the favored religion of the state, transferring government support from paganism to the new faith. Government resources that had formally been devoted to building temples and financing the public festivals now flowed into the Church coffers. Soon the government began to discriminate against non-Christians in the army and the bureaucracy. Temples were looted and destroyed. Often the rage against the pagans became as violent and ugly as the Christian persecutions had been. For example, the famous female philosopher Hypatia of Alexandria (370–415) was viciously murdered by a Christian mob, who dragged her through the streets into a church where they stripped and mutilated her body and then burned it. The Christians of the city praised the patriarch Cyril for this deed and "hailed him as 'the new Theophilus,'" for he had destroyed the "last remains of idolatry in the city."[23]

Only one emperor after Constantine was a pagan. Julian "the Apostate" (361–363) attempted to restore the traditional religion. He was raised a Christian in the imperial court, but became resentful of the Christianizing imperial family who had slaughtered all the heirs to the throne accept him. Unfortunately for the future of paganism, he did not live long enough to affect much reform. During a campaign against Persia in 363 he was killed. The succeeding emperors continued to forcibly Christianize the empire. In 391 Theodosius I ordered the destruction of the temples in Alexandria and the Christian mobs also burned the great library, established over 500 years before by the Ptolemies. In the next year Theodosius outlawed all pagan sacrifices, which was the death blow to Paganism and effectively made it illegal. Christianity was now the official state religion.

As the empire became more Christian, the power of the Church increased. In the East the Church was kept under the firm control of the emperors, but in the West the church leaders began to invade the secular sphere. By 390 the bishop of Milan had excommunicated an emperor. By the 5th Century the bishop of Rome, now called the "Pope," was acting like an emperor: Pope Innocent I (401–417) negotiated with the Goth Alaric, and Pope Leo I (440–461) persuaded Attila the Hun to halt his invasion of Italy and spare the city of Rome from devastation. As the Roman Empire in the West faded into obscurity, the Church rushed into the Power vacuum left behind. Christianity was triumphant, but chaos, ignorance, and disorder descended upon western Europe.

---

23. John, Bishop of Nikiu, *Chronicle*, 84.87–103. The event is graphically detailed by Mangasarian, Mangasar Mugurditch, "The Martyrdom of Hypatia, or The Death of the Classical World," *The Rationalist*, May 1915: "The next morning, when Hypatia appeared in her chariot in front of her residence, suddenly five hundred men, all dressed in black and cowled, five hundred half-starved monks from the sands of the Egyptian desert—five hundred monks, soldiers of the cross—like a black hurricane, swooped down the street, boarded her chariot, and, pulling her off her seat, dragged her by the hair of her head into a—how shall I say the word?—into a church! Some historians intimate that the monks asked her to kiss the cross, to become a Christian and join the nunnery, if she wished her life spared. At any rate, these monks, under the leadership of St. Cyril's right-hand man, Peter the Reader, shamefully stripped her naked, and there, close to the alter and the cross, scraped her quivering flesh from her bones with oystershells. The marble floor of the church was sprinkled with her warm blood. The altar, the cross, too, were bespattered, owing to the violence with which her limbs were torn, while the hands of the monks presented a sight too revolting to describe. The mutilated body, upon which the murderers feasted their fanatic hate, was then flung into the flames."

Figure 12.9: Coin of Julian the Apostate. Left, portrait; Right, bull with stars, a pagan symbol.

Justinian and Theodora

After Constantine, the next great emperor of the Byzantine Empire was Justinian (527–565). He and his wife, Theodora, are two of the most colorful individuals of all history. Justinian himself seems to have been the weaker of the pair, but his will was stiffened by his ambitious wife, Theodora. Justinian was the son of a peasant. Theodora was the daughter of a circus bear trainer, and she became a famous actress and prostitute before she was 20 years old. She is said, at least by her enemies, to have traveled through the major cities of the empire, earning her way as a prostitute. In her early twenties, however, she returned to Constantinople, where she mended her morals but lost none of her charm, it seems, and married Justinian. Well, of course all these stories were circulated by her enemies, of course, and they may or may not be true. The point is that both Justinian and Theodora were outsiders to the social establishment of the capital and thus had no inclination to respect its conventions. In this regard, both of them resemble several other active rulers of history—Catherine the Great, the German empress of Russia, Napoleon, the Corsican emperor of France; or more recently, Eva Perón, the lower class first lady of 20th Century Argentina. The list could be expanded.

Theodora's influence on her husband was decisive. In 532, five years after Justinian became emperor, the popular athletic factions of the Hippodrome[24] rose in rebellion. The rioting mobs burned down most of the city. Justinian was terrified and prepared to flee, but Theodora urged him

---

24. When Constantine established the city of Constantinople, one of his major undertakings was the construction of the Hippodrome in the tradition of the Circus Maximus in Rome. It is estimated that the Hippodrome of Constantine was about 492 feet long and 426 feet wide. Its stands were capable of holding 100,000 spectators. The racetrack was U-shaped, and the Emperor's box, with four bronze statues of horses on its roof, was located at the eastern end of the track. These horses, which were cast in the 5th Century BCE and brought from Greece, were looted during the Fourth Crusade in 1204 and can today be seen atop St. Marks's Cathedral in Venice. The track was lined with other bronze statues of famous horses and chariot drivers, none of which survive. Throughout the Byzantine period, the Hippodrome was the center of the city's social life. Huge amounts were bet on chariot races, and the whole city was divided between fans of the Blue and Green chariot racing teams. Frequently rivalry between Blues and Greens became mingled with political or religious factions, and riots which sometimes amounted to civil wars broke out in the city between them. The most severe of these was the Nike riots of 532, in which 30,000 people were said to have been killed.

Figure 12.10: Mosaics from Revenna of Justinian (above) and Theodora in religious procession. Notice that the emperor and empress have halos.

to choose death rather then exile: "Once you put on these purple robes, it is better to die in them than to live out an ignominious life in exile." Justinian's resolve was strengthened, he remained in the city, the rebellion was eventually crushed, and he went on to rule until 565, another 33 years.

Justinian set three major goals for himself: the restoration of the Western provinces; the reform of Roman law; and a grandiose building program to rebuild and glorify Constantinople. The attempt to accomplish these goals is the story of Justinian's reign. In pursuit of the first goal, armies were sent against the Vandals in Africa, the Ostrogoths in Italy, and the Visigoths in Spain. These campaigns met with both success and failure. At the approach of the Byzantine army, the Vandal kingdom in North Africa collapsed like a house of cards, and by 554 Byzantine rule was establish in both Africa and Italy. The southern tip of Spain was also conquered. But in the end, Justinian could not reconcile the theological differences that had developed between East and West and could not gain the support of the Church in the West. After Justinian's death, the western provinces again slipped from control of Constantinople. This was the last serious attempt to restore the old Roman Empire, and for this reason Justinian is sometimes referred to as "the last Roman."

However, Justinian's efforts to reform the legal code met with more lasting success. A committee of lawyers, under the direction of the emperor, brought all the laws of the Roman Empire into a systematic code called the *Corpus Juris Civilis*, literally the "Body of Civil Law."[25] It is difficult to exaggerate the importance of the *Corpus Juris Civilis*. This book became for all subsequent ages the richest source of information concerning the greatest glory of the Roman Empire: its legal institutions and thought. The modern legal systems of all Western nations, except the British commonwealth nations and the United States, are based on Roman law as represented by the *Corpus*, and even legal systems of such unlikely nations as the Philippines and Japan are based on civil law. English Common law, the basis of our legal system, is strongly influenced by the *Corpus*.

After the devastation of the rebellion of 532, Justinian wanted to rebuild Constantinople as a capital worthy of a great empire. His most spectacular project was the great church of Hagia Sophia, or "Holy Wisdom." The building still stands today in Istanbul. It was transformed into a mosque by the Turks when they captured the city in 1453. This building was so impressive during the Middle Ages that it was thought to be a miracle. Indeed, the building was intended to impress visitors with the majesty of the Byzantine Empire. Of course today it is much less impressive because the Muslims stripped it of the beautiful mosaics that once adorned the dooms and the walls of the church. Visitors during the Middle Ages often remarked that the huge dome seemed to float on a bed of light. It must have been very impressive.

After Justinian

In the years following Justinian's death the empire went over to the defensive. There was a devastating war with the Persians. After years of bitter fighting they were overwhelmingly defeated in 627, but this turned out to be a mixed blessing because Persia was so weakened that it became an easy victim of the Muslims a few years later, and the Muslims were a far more serious threat to Byzantium than the Persians would ever have been. Had Persia been strong enough to withstand Muslim aggression it could have become a buffer state between Islam and Christendom.

The Muslims overrun most of Asia Minor and laid siege to Constantinople itself in 669. Survival of Byzantium was tenuous and uncertain for several decades. It was not until 718 that the siege was broken by the use of a secret weapon called Greek fire. Evidently, this weapon was a

---

25. The term "civil" here refers to "citizen," indicating that this is domestic law in contrast with international law.

highly flammable liquid substance which was ignited as it was sprayed under pressure on enemy ships and set them on fire. After the siege of Constantinople was broken, Asia Minor was slowly reconquered from the Arabs.

The Byzantine Empire had another revival under the warrior emperors of the 9th through the 11th centuries. Under an energetic line of emperors known as the Macedonian Dynasty, the Byzantines pushed the Muslims back into Syria and extended control into southern Italy, the Balkans, and the Caucasus. The Orthodox Christian religion spread northward into Russia.

Theological Differences between East and West

The Eastern Orthodox Church developed under the close control of the emperor. Just the opposite occurred in the West, where the vacuum of public authority following the collapse of the Roman Empire in the West gave the pope a position of leadership in secular affairs. Put into its simplest terms (always a dangerous thing to do): in the East the emperor controlled the Church as well as the secular government, whereas in the West the pope controlled the Church and often the secular government as well—and control over secular affairs was always the goal of the Roman Church. These contrasting philosophies of government deeply affected the character of the two major branches of Christianity.

The theological differences between the two churches seem insignificant to us today, but they were important enough to the people of the Middle Ages to cause a split between the churches that shows no signs of healing even today. The creed of the Christian religion was worked out and adopted in its final form at the Church Council of Nicaea in 325, before the eastern and western churches split apart. It is known as the Nicene Creed and still today defines the basic doctrine of just about every Christian sect. Later however, the Catholic Church added two phrases to the creed, which the Orthodox Church, even today, refuses to accept, because they have not been approved by a council of the whole Church.

The most important addition was the one Latin word *filioque*, "and the son." Therefore the disagreement is known as the "*filioque* dispute." The dispute involves the relationship among the members of the trinity, that is, the complex way in which Christianity defines monotheism (see above). The Nicene Creed defines each of the three persons of the Trinity. The *filioque* controversy swirls around the definition of the Holy Spirit. The original Nicene Creed simply affirmed the existence of the Trinity but did not define it precisely. There was still a lot of debate about this complex and irrational concept. After all, how can there be both *one* and *three* gods at the same time? So another church council was held in Constantinople in 381 to settle the debate. The result was the Nicene-Constantinopolitan Creed, which defined everything very neatly. In this creed the Holy Spirit is defined as "the Lord, the Giver of Life, who proceeds from the Father. . ." You might think that this would settle the debate once and for all, but some centuries later the Catholic church, after it had split away from the eastern Church, added a single word to that definition and the Catholic creed reads: the Holy Spirit "who proceeds from the Father and the Son (*filioque*)." The Orthodox Church has never accepted this addition.

Other theological differences developed as well. The Orthodox Church did not accept the Catholic belief in purgatory, a kind of half-way house between heaven and hell, where the soul stops to suffer for the sins committed on earth before entering paradise. The Orthodox Church permitted divorce for adultery and the ordination of married men into the priesthood, although bishops had to be celibate. But even more important than these theological differences were the difference in the organization of the two churches and their respective relationship to the secular authority. During the early Middle Ages the Catholic Church began to separate itself from secular authority and to develop its own centralized government under the papacy. By the 12ᵗʰ Century the pope had become the absolute ruler of the Catholic Church, which he governed with the same kind of elaborate bureaucracy that a secular ruler governs a state. The pope even attempted, with considerable though temporary success, to establish his absolute authority over the apparatus of the secular governments of the emerging kingdoms of Western Europe. The Eastern Orthodox Church, on the other hand, remained under the authority of the emperor and, in fact, became an arm of his government. In the East, the Church depended on the secular government to defend and protect its interest, and the state made full use of the Church's great wealth and spiritual power for its own ends. This union and cooperation between church and state gave the Byzantine Empire a critical advantage in its struggle against the barbarians to the North and the Muslims to the South.

In the West quite the opposite situation prevailed. Society was torn apart by savage disputes and almost permanent struggle between church and state for control of the governing power, and this measurably weakened the response of Western Civilization to the continued inroads of the barbarians invasions. Thus, whereas Christianity seemed to strengthen the East in its struggle for survival, is seemed in some ways to weaken the West in its struggle. The East survived as a viable and creative civilization for a thousand years, whereas the West descended into the stagnation and brutality of a thousand year dark age. Many factors were responsible for the different fates of the East and the West, such as geography, the stronger urban base of the east, etc., but the divergent role which Christianity played in the two areas of the Roman Empire was also an important and critical factor.

Islam

Around the year 610, in the little Arabian town of Mecca, a merchant's son named Muhammad (?570–632) began to preach repentance and reform. Gradually he developed his teachings into a new system of religious belief that is called Islam. This religion had an explosive impact upon world history. Within a century after Muhammad's death in 632, his followers had conquered territories larger than the old Roman Empire. Today, Islam is the religion of about 1/8 of the world's population.

Muhammad's Life

The harsh environment of the Arabian peninsula profoundly influenced the culture and the history of the Arabs, who produced and spread by the sword this new religion. The area is mostly steppes, wasteland, and desert—indeed one of the hottest and driest deserts in the world is located in the southern part of the peninsula, called the "Empty Quarter." But over the centuries the Arabs adopted to this harsh environment and they were arrogantly proud of their family structure, of their race, language, and way of life. Ancient civilizations from the Assyrians to the Persians to the Romans had attempted, but failed, to dominate the Arabs in their fierce desert home.

Before the appearance of Muhammad, the traditional pagan religion of the Arabs gave no promise of an afterlife and offered no mission of world conquest. Both Christianity and Judaism had won some scattered converts in the Arabian peninsula, but neither had been able to gain the adherence of the upper classes. That is always the key to success for a religion. The achievement of Muhammad consisted of fusing pagan, Jewish, and Christian ideas into a single Arabian religion.

The prophet was born about 570 at Mecca. His father died before his death, his mother died when he was six, and he was raised by his uncle. He was probably illiterate, because his knowledge of the Christian and Jewish scriptures is quite inaccurate—he obviously knew them only through hearsay. At the age of 25, Muhammad married a rich widow and was thus freed of economic concerns. He then began to devote his time to religious meditations in the deserts outside Mecca.

The desert played an important and critical role in the religions of the Near East. In Jewish literature we hear of prophets "crying out in the wilderness;" in Christian literature there is the image of Christ undergoing the temptations in the desert; and Christian monasticism was born in Egypt, when certain holy men went out into the desert to live there as hermits in order to do battle with the forces of evil. The desert is very conducive to religious experience and is an ideal place to experience religious enlightenment. So, in the year 610, the angel Gabriel spoke to Muhammad and he continued to receive revelations in this manner for the rest of his life. After this momentous event, Muhammad began to preach publicly about moral reform, but at first only his wife and a small group of relatives accepted his teachings.

The problem was that Mecca was already the center of a pagan cult. The cult at Mecca involved the worship of a sacred stone called the Kaába, the "cube." Pilgrimages by the surrounding people to Mecca to worship the Kaába provided a livelihood for much of the population. The leaders of Mecca therefore viewed Muhammad's exhortations to moral reform as a threat to their economic and social position. Rejected in his native city, he accepted an invitation in 622 from the rival trading town of Medina, 270 miles to the north.

This event is called the Hegira, or "flight," and 622 is the year 1 on the Muslim calendar. It was a turning point in Muhammad's career for two reasons: first, he became the political as well as the religious head of an important town, which gave him a base for the military expansion of his new

©Mehmet Biber
Figure 12.11: The Kaába at Mecca.

religion; and secondly, his responsibilities as a secular ruler affected the character of his religious revelations, which now became less concerned with morality and more concerned with the application of political power.

Muhammad was quite successful at Medina. He told his new flock that god ordered them to conquer and convert their neighbors by force, and through war and conquest the new religion grew rapidly. He took control of Mecca in 630, but in order to avoid conflict with the ruling class there he prudently received a revelation that his followers should continue to worship the black stone. Indeed, a pilgrimage to Mecca to worship at the site of the kaába is still a very important aspect of the Islamic religion. By the time of his death in 632, Muhammad had set his Arab followers upon the course of war and conquest that, in a very real sense, has not stopped to this very day.

Islamic Theology

Well, what are the tenants of this religion that believes its destiny is to conquer the world? Muhammad, unlike Jesus, was not considered to be divine, but simply a prophet, who passed on to his followers the word of God, or "Allah," as it was revealed to him by the angel Gabriel. Yet, that is still a pretty potent position. Muhammad is not divine, but he is not an ordinary human being either, and he is not treated as such by the Muslims. A human being who has a hotwire directly into the mind of God is someone very special. His prophecies were collected, around 657, into a book called the Koran, whose true author is therefore Allah. The teachings of the Koran are uncompromisingly monotheistic, and involve constant repetitions of set formulae praising Allah for his power, knowledge, mercy, justice, and concern for his people.

The chief obligations of the believer is submission to the will of Allah. In fact, Islam, the proper name for the religion, means simply "submission." The will of Allah is revealed in the Koran. But unlike Christianity, Islam did not recognize a separate clergy and church for the interpretation of the scripture. In Islamic theology, Allah is the direct ruler of the faithful on earth. He legislated for them in the Koran and administered the earthly government through his prophet Muhammad and his successors. Thus, under the Islamic system, there can be no separation of state and religion, there can be no secular government, there is only one sacred and indivisible community of Allah. To this day, religion and politics are inseparable in Muslim countries. Indeed, Muslims consider Islam to be one community, and their first loyalty is always to Islam. Even in the 21st Century, there are only a few Islamic nations, like Turkey, Egypt, and Pakistan, which have made even half-hearted attempts to develop secular governments. But these attempts are only cosmetic, there is no real freedom of religion in any Islamic country. And it is no wonder that this unity of politics and religion is so hard to break, it is a powerful instrument in the hands of any ruler.

Beyond its rigid insistence on stark monotheism, Islam is an extremely simple re-interpretation and combination of Jewish, Christian, and pagan ideas. All three of these traditions influenced Islam's religious and legal code, which regulates diet and behavior. Muhammad is simply the last of a long line of prophets that began with Abraham and includes such names as Jesus. From Christianity comes the concepts of the last judgment, personal salvation, heaven and hell, charity to the poor, and the concept of a universal religion. Universality, of course, means intolerance, which the Muslims have refined and pursued with at least as much fanaticism as the Christians. Christianity perhaps also suggested the figures of Satan and the evil daemons, with which the Muslims are just as fascinated as the Christians. From the Arabic pagan tradition comes the Islamic worship of the Kaába at Mecca and the requirement of a pilgrimage to that holy city.

But Islam also reflects the strong racial and cultural attitude of the Arabs. Allah, it seems, speaks only Arabic. The Koran is written in Arabic, and Allah can properly be addressed only in Arabic. Islam is the final revelation of God and it brings to completion the message of God, which was only partially revealed to the prophets of the Jews and the Christians. The Arabs were a semi-nomadic people to whom Allah gave the mission of converting the world. Muhammad replaced Christ as the supreme prophet, and the Arabs replaced the Jews as God's chosen people, which gave them the right to God's holy places, including Jerusalem, where they built a great mosque, called the Dome of the Rock, directly over the site of the old Jewish temple—a site that just happens to be sacred to two other religions. The present conflict in the Middle East, and indeed, around the world, between Arab and Jew, between Muslim and Christian, between believer and infidel, is a deeply-rooted cultural and religious rivalry that shows no signs of abating anytime in the near future. This conflict is grounded in long ingrained cultural values and arrogances, which in fact have little to do with Israel or Palestine. If the Palestine problem did not even exist, the conflict between Islam and the rest of the world would still be no less virulent and bloody.

CHAPTER

13

The Early Middle Age (800–1000)

By the mid 5th Century, the Mediterranean world was deeply divided between the East and the West. By 467, the Roman political structure in the West had collapsed, although the Mediterranean economy remained reasonably integrated until the late 6th Century. Gold coinage still circulated, but primarily to finance a declining luxury trade in items such as silk, spices, and jewelry. By 650, however, even the economic unity of the Mediterranean world was broken. The cities of Italy, Gaul, and Spain, now ruled by bishops, continued to decline and would soon disappear altogether as the population declined—the inhabitants of Western Europe moved out into the countryside during the 7th Century. At the same time the Roman taxing system collapsed, and the coinage systems of Western Europe also broke down and the economy reverted to a primitive barter system. Slowly, Western Europe descended into the chaos, confusion, and superstition that once was called the "Dark Age."

Feudalism

At least a cursory acquaintance with feudalism is essential for an understanding of the medieval world. Feudalism was a political and social system based on customary contracts for the disposal of land in exchange for honorable service. Although it was not, in itself, an economic system, it was based on the "manorial" economy that must be included in any discussion of feudalism. Politically, feudalism meant the fragmentation, or the division of the powers and the functions of the state among the lords of the land, that is, the great landowners. Socially, it meant a personal, mutually dependant relationship between the lords, or landowners, and the vassals, or tenants of the land, involving the granting of landed estates by the lords to their vassals in exchange for military or other service. The manorial system of agriculture was based on large estates, called manors, which were worked by gangs of serfs, who were tied to the land and were, in reality, little better off than slaves.

Feudalism became prevalent throughout Europe during the Carolingian Period—the 8th and the 9th centuries—however, the origins of feudalism extend far back into the histories of both the Roman and Germanic societies and the process by which feudalism replaced the urban society of late antiquity is a complex one. All the social and political elements necessary for feudalism to function were already present in both the Germanic and the Roman societies. Yet these elements lay dormant in ancient society for centuries and were emphasized and developed to produce the new system of feudalism only at the end of the antiquity as a result of the convergence of certain historical trends.

Figure 13.1: Pepin's Reliquary, so called for reasons now forgotten. Christ between John and Mary. The chest was made c. 1000 of gold and precious stones, presumably to contain the foreskin of Christ.

However, it is important to realize that the rise of feudalism occurred simultaneously with and was part of the transformation of Western Europe from ancient civilization to barbarism that was discussed in the last chapter. Feudalism did not congeal out of thin air, it arose to meet a need—it came into existence to provide a semblance of social order and political structure in the period that bordered on utter chaos. And like all historical periods, its beginning was not a sharp clear-cut event that one can date to a specific year, but rather it required several centuries to develop into its mature form. As feudalism gradually rose to dominate the political and social fabric of society, urbanism gradually decayed into a predominately rural lifestyle, classical humanism transformed into Christian mysticism, and literacy all but disappeared. All these aspects of the historical experience of Western Civilization are interrelated and cannot be separated, although we must discuss all of them separately.

On the surface of events, at least, four tendencies help to explain the rise of feudalism: First, the concentration of land ownership into the hands of a small, elite aristocracy. Almost continuous warfare and the resulting chaos in the countryside, after the disappearance of Roman government, reduced the small farmers to ruin and forced the weak to seek protection of the strong. This produced a gradual transformation of the free peasant farmer into the serf, who was tied to the land of his lord and protector. During the centuries of constant, almost annual raids by the barbarians into Western Europe, it became impossible for the small farmer to exist without the protection of the great landowner who had the resources to resist the invaders. Year after year the farmer's crops were destroyed and his farm pillaged. Eventually he simply surrendered his holdings to the landlord and remained on the land as a tenant/surf in exchange for the landlord's protection against the barbarian raids.

Second, the breakdown of *both* the Roman provincial administration and the Germanic tribal organization led to the development of personal dependence upon private individuals for protection. Why did this occur? First of all, the barbarian incursions into the Empire's territory were so violent that they destroyed the cities and with them the Roman administrative infrastructure that was based on the cities. This led in turn to the collapse and disappearance of government. At the same time the German tribes settled on the land. As we have seen before, whenever tribal, nomadic nations adapt a settled way of life, their tribal political structure becomes irrelevant and collapses. Thus, the simultaneous disappearance of the Roman government and the breakdown of the Germanic tribal structure led to chaos in the countryside. The weak had no choice but to seek the protection of the strong, and the local landowner assumed the functions of the government.

The third important tendency was the replacement of the Roman system of taxation and bureaucratic administration with a barter system involving exchange of military or other honorable service for land grants. With the disappearance of government, the landlord became responsible for the functions of the state and the protection of his property and people. The Romans had provided these governmental services by employing tax collectors, who went out into the countryside and collected taxes. The revenue thus obtained, was then used to hire soldiers, administrators, and bureaucrats to provide protection, justice, and all the other services that governments normally provide. How could the landowner in this new situation provide these same services? He could not levy taxes. For one thing, there was no money in circulation. The minting of coins, the actual creation of money, is one of the functions the now defunct Roman government preformed, but all that is gone now. The landlord of the Early Middle Age could not pay for the services of those he must have to assist him in order to maintain a semblance of law and order. All he has is his land. However he can grant the use of a portion of his land to an able-bodied man in exchange for his service. That man could use the land grant for his economic support, which then freed him to serve the landlord. This is a form of barter, a method of compensating a person for his service without the exchange of money. It was very primitive by ancient Roman standards. It represents the retrogression from urban civilization to feudalism that marked the end of the ancient world.

Finally, the attachment of the executive, judicial, and legislative powers of the government directly to the land resulted in the division of these powers among those who held the land. Whoever possessed the land also exercised the powers and responsibilities that once belonged to the government. Thus, feudalism developed as a way to avoid chaos and anarchy.

Patronage, Comitatus, Beneficium

These four tendencies facilitated the establishment of feudalism in Western Europe during the Early Middle Ages, but like all social and political phenomena, feudalism did not simply develop suddenly out of thin air. In a sense, history never seems to invent anything completely new, but always elaborates, re-interprets, and builds on what has gone before. The historical roots, or context, of feudalism is to be found in an interaction between Germanic and Roman social institutions and customs, which can be traced back beyond the origins of written history.

One of the most important of these institutions was patronage. As far back into Roman history as we can see with any accuracy—say to the 5th Century BCE—patronage was already so ingrained in Roman society that the sources take it for granted, and the writers feel no need to offer an explanation. In the ancient world freedom and servitude had a rather different meaning than it does in our modern society. We conceive of freedom in quite absolute terms. Either a person is free or he is not. For example, after serving his term in prison, the ex-felon walks through the prison gates and suddenly becomes free. Although the choices and options open to him may be severely restricted when compared to those available to, say, a wealthy businessman or a successful lawyer, in our mind's eye, he is just as free as other members of society. This is perhaps a cruel hoax we play on ourselves in order to reconcile our ideology of equality with the reality of inequality.

To the Roman mind, however, there was no absolute freedom, or absolute servitude, but rather an almost infinite gradation of degrees of both freedom and servitude. The Romans knew instinctively that the imperial slave, who was highly educated and was a trusted agent of the emperor, who might be dispatched out to the provinces to manage an imperial estate and who might amass an impressive fortune and even own other slaves, was not in the same condition of servitude as the slave who toiled endlessly in the horribly inhuman conditions of the Spanish lead mine and might have a life expectancy of eight months. Both of these individuals were chattel property, both could be bought and sold at will—the imperial slave was worth quite a bit more money than the mine slave, of course. In short, both were slaves but their degree and condition of servitude was quite different. Similarly, there were degrees of freedom. For instance, there were differences between freedmen and freeborn citizens, between upper and lower class citizens, between male and female, and so forth across the social spectrum. The institution of patronage was the Roman social institution for dealing with these different degrees of freedom and servitude.

Patronage was not enforced by written law, but rather by inescapable custom, a force much stronger than law. Patronage was, in fact, so strongly ingrained into Roman society that law never became necessary for its implementation. Put into the simplest possible terms, patronage was a personal relationship based on mutual obligation. It always involved the protection of a weaker party (called the *cliens*, or client) by a stronger party (called the *patronus*, or patron), in exchange for loyalty and service. The freedman automatically became the client of his former master. The freeborn citizen inherited his patron from his father. The enemy soldier, by the act of surrender to a Roman general, became that general's client. In this way, every individual in Roman society had his niche, his place in the scheme of things. This gave everyone a sense of belonging, a sense of security.

Now in the late western Roman empire, as the political institutions of the state began to break up and fade away, it became the practice of even well-to-do Romans to commend themselves to a member of the landed aristocracy and, in exchange for loyalty and service, to obtain a degree of protection against the severe imperial taxation and oppression. This practice became universal as the barbarian invasions increased the need of the weak for protection.

German society also had an institution, known as *comitatus*, which filled much the same need. The *comitatus* was a group of young nobles or freemen who were bound to the chieftain by strong obligations to serve him in exchange for food, shelter, military training, and leadership. It is not at all difficult to see how Roman patronage and German comitatus meshed together very easily when the two cultures came into contact. In fact, the two practices probably descend from a common Indo-European origin.

A second Roman root of Medieval feudalism was the practice of *beneficium*. Under Roman law land was held in full property, very much like it is in the U.S. today. But during the late antiquity a practice grew up, without the sanction of law, under which land was granted for a stipulated period, say for life, in exchange for service or other consideration. This practice was called *beneficium*. After the barbarian invasions and the decline of the money economy, this practice was taken over by the great landowners, who granted parcels of land, or *beneficia*, to their nobles or officials for life or the duration of the office, in lieu of a money salary. The landholders, in turn, dealt with their own retainers in a similar way, by subdividing this land still further.

Classical Feudalism

During the Early Middle Ages the *beneficium* became known as a fief and the client became know as the vassal. But this embryonic feudal structure of the great nobles and their armed retainers did not really undermine the state so long as strong kings, such as Charlemagne, ruled. But later, when warfare between the Carolingians themselves and against the invading Norsemen, Magyars, and Arabs, caused the Frankish state to decay into chaos and disorganization, the local populace sought protection by placing itself under the protection and control of the local counts and dukes, who tended to assume more and more independence from the king. Gradually, the Frankish kingdom split into its component parts of France, Germany, and Italy, and each of these areas disintegrated into a multitude of feudal duchies, counties, and bishoprics, each with its own vassals and sub-vassals. Thus, classical feudalism emerged.

The king was at the apex of the feudal hierarchy and he, in theory at least, owned all the land. Directly beneath the king were the crown vassals, or the "tenants-in-chief," who bore titles such as duke, count, margrave, archbishop, bishop, and abbot. Yes, the church became part of the feudal hierarchy. Thus, the dukes of Normandy, Burgundy, Aquitaine, Brittany and the counts of Flanders, Anjou, Maine, Champaign, Blois, and Toulouse were the immediate vassals of the king of France. They in turn had their vassals, who were thus sub-vassals to the king. At the bottom of this broad, pyramid-shaped feudal hierarchy were the knights, the backbone of the feudal army. The military strength of a lord depended on the number of knights he held in direct vassalage. As a rule, vassals owned allegiance only to their immediate lord, and royal authority became restricted only to the territory over which the king himself had direct control.

Feudal Obligations

The relationship between lord and vassal was a contractual one and involved obligations and duties of each to the other. The obligation of the vassal to provide military service to his lord was limited in both space and time. Forty days service a year became the excepted rule, after which the lord was obliged to compensate the cost. The vassal was also obliged to supply certain kinds of financial support to his lord. There were originally three types of *auxilia*, or aids: (1) funds for the ransom of his lord if he were captured; (2) for the knighting of his eldest son; (3) and for the dowry of his eldest daughter. But in practice aids were levied on all possible occasions. The vassal also had to provide the lord with entertainment or hospitality at least three times a year. Finally, the vassal owed his lord *consilium*, which involved not only advice, but also actual assistance in the administrative and judicial work of the government. Failure of the vassal to fulfill any of his obligations resulted in the forfeiture of his fief.

The lord's obligation to his vassal included the protection of his life, property, and honor and a guarantee of justice in his court. Failure to fulfill these responsibilities justified the vassal in renouncing his allegiance or bringing a charge against the lord in the king's court.

Originally the fief was granted for a stipulated period, or for life, but by the end of the 10th Century the hereditary fief was the general rule, although there were exceptions, especially for church fiefs. The son who inherited a fief owed relief, usually a sum of money, to the lord and he must do homage and fealty—a ritual of public avowal of allegiance and loyalty. A minor heir was under the lord's wardship until he reached majority; a female heir was under the lord's wardship until he found her a husband.

Manorialism

Below all of this aristocratic hierarchy, which after all, comprised probably less than 5% of the population, was the lowly serf, whose endless toil supported the whole feudal system. The basic economic unit of Medieval Europe was the manor, which was in theory the fief of an individual knight, while the lords of higher rank held many manors under their direct control, frequently hundreds or even thousands. The smallest manorial estates were between 300 and 400 acres in size. Each was comprised of one or more villages, the land cultivated by the serfs, the common forest and pasture lands, the land belonging to the parish church and finally the lord's domain, which of course included the best farm land on the manor. All the cultivated land was divided into three main blocks of fields: one for spring planting, one for fall planting, and one to lay fallow.[1] These three blocks of land were rotated each year so that a given block of soil was unused each third year. This was the famous three-field system of agriculture. It was, of course very inefficient to cultivate only two thirds of the land at a given time, but it was the best that the technology of the Middle Ages could accomplish. The holdings of each serf consisted of land, generally about one acre each, located in each of the three fields. But the cultivation of all the land on the manor was done collectively by the manor's entire gang of serfs.

Except for the noble, his family, the parish priest, and perhaps a few administrative officials, the entire population of the manor fell into the class of serf. A few slaves remained, but their number continuously diminished, because they did not fit well into the feudal economy. What slaves remained were mainly used as household servants in the manor house.

The individual obligations of the serfs involved both direct taxes and forced labor, and they are too numerous to catalog here. Suffice it to say that the serf's life was not an easy lot. During the growing season he toiled from sunrise to sunset, but his rewards were few indeed. His home was a hovel plastered with mud. A hole in the thatched roof let out the smoke. His floor was the bare earth, which was often cold and damp. The serf's bed was a box filled with straw, his easy chair was a 3-legged stool. His diet consisted of black bread, supplemented in summer by a few vegetables from his garden, plus porridge, that is grain boiled until it is digestible, and from time to time a little salt meat, which was often half putrid. When the crops failed, starvation was by no means unknown. The serf was always illiterate and often the victim of superstitions and dishonest stewards. The serf was, in short, a despised creature. It was said that all serfs were shifty, dull-witted, mean, squint-eyed, and ugly; it was said they were "born of ass's dung," and "the devil did not want them in hell because they smelled too bad." Remember that the serfs made up at least 85% of the entire population of the Early Middle Age. This is not a pretty picture.

The Frankish Kingdom

The Franks were a west Germanic tribe who entered the late Roman Empire as *foederati*[2] and established a lasting presence in an area the area that is France and Germany today. The word *frank* meant "free" in their language. There were initially two main subdivisions within the Franks, the

---

1. The field that "lay fallow" actually was planted in "green manure." That is, the fallow field was sewed in some form of leguminous plant, such as pea, vetch, clover, alfalfa, etc., and plowed under while still green in order to enrich the soil. In this way the Medieval farmer could maintain the fertility of the soil. This technique is sometimes used in "organic" farming today.

2. *Foederati* (Singular: *foederatus*) were barbarian tribes, which the Romans subsidized in exchange for providing soldiers in the Roman armies. *Foederatus* was derived from the Latin word *foedus*, which indicated a binding treaty of mutual assistance between Rome and another people for perpetuity. At first, the Roman subsidy took the form of money or food, but as tax revenues declined in the 4th and 5th centuries, the *foederati* were billeted on local landowners, which came to be identical to being allowed to settle on Roman territory. The loyalty of the tribes and their leaders was not always dependable and at times they rose in rebellion. By the 5th Century Roman military strength was almost completely based on *foederati* units. The English word "federation" is derived from the Latin *foederati*.

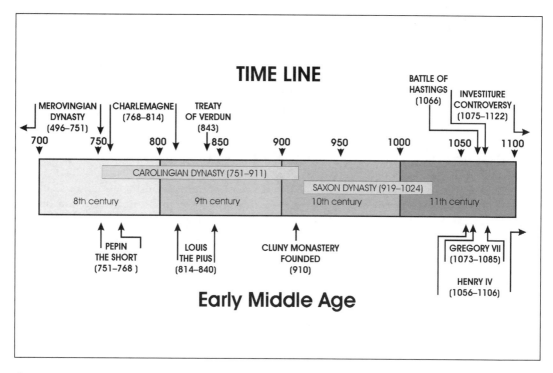

TIME LINE

Early Middle Age

Figure 13.2

Salian ("salty") and the Ripuarian ("river") Franks. By the 9th Century, if not earlier, this division was in fact virtually non-existent, but continued for some time to have implications for the legal system under which a person could be tried.

Early Frankish history is obscure. There are few sources, and they are not dependable.[3] Modern scholars of the period have suggested that the Frankish people emerged from the unifications of various earlier, smaller Germanic groups inhabiting the Rhine valley and lands immediately to the east. Around 250 a group of Franks took advantage of the weakened Roman Empire and penetrated south as far as Spain. They plundered the region for about a decade before being expelled from Roman territory. About forty years later, the Franks brought the Scheldt region (modern Belgium) under their control. The Roman finally managed to pacify them, but they were not expelled and by 358 a considerable part of Belgium was given to the Franks. From this time on they become *foederati* of the Roman Empire. A region roughly corresponding to present day Flanders and the Netherlands became a Germanic region down to the present day, although Duch is spoken there now. The Franks thus became the first Germanic people to permanently settle on Roman territory. From this base they gradually conquered most of Roman Gaul. At first they helped defend the border as Roman allies. For example, when a major invasion of mostly East Germanic tribes crossed the Rhine 406, the Franks fought against these invaders.

---

3. Our main source is Gregory of Tours, who quotes from lost sources like Sulpicius Alexander, Frigeridus and from oral sources of the Franks around him, all of which must be taken with a healthy dash of scepticism.

The Merovingians

Gradually the Franks became rulers over an increasing number of Gallo-Roman subjects. In 452, the Roman general Aetius called upon his Germanic allies on Roman soil to help fight off an invasion by the Huns. The Salian Franks answered the call, the Ripuarians fought on both sides as some of them lived outside the Empire. At this time Merovech[4] was king of the Franks.

Clovis, the grandson of Merovich, consolidated the various Frankish kingdoms in Gaul and the Rhineland by 486 and ended Roman control around Paris. Then Clovis became locked in a bitter conflict with two other Germanic tribes, the Burgundians and the Visigoths, for control of the rest of Gaul. The events of this period illustrate once again how closely religion and politics were intertwined in the lives of the people of the Early Middle Age. Clovis was still a German pagan, while the other Germanic peoples were Arianian Christians. However, most of the Roman population of Gaul were Roman Catholic Christians. In 496 Clovis converted to Roman Catholicism, which won him the powerful support of the papacy and the Roman church in his struggles against the heretic Arians. With great suffering and bloodshed, the Burgundians were conquered by 500, the Visigoths by 507, and all of Gaul, excpet Provence, was subjugated to Clovis's control. These bloody conquests were supported by the Catholic clergy as a holy war to stamp out what they considered to be the dangerous heresy of Arianism. Clovis founded the Church of the Holy Apostles at Paris and made Paris the capital of his Kingdom. The Merovingians thus built the most stable of the successor-kingdoms in the west.

The Merovingians adhered to the Germanic practice of dividing their lands among their sons, and the frequent division, reunification, and redivision of territories often resulted in murder and warfare within the leading families. So, on Clovis's death in 511, his realm was divided between his four sons, and over the next two centuries the kingship was shared between his decendants. The Frankish area expanded further under Clovis's sons, eventually covering most of what is today France, but including areas east of the Rhine River as well. After a temporary reunification of the separate kingdoms under Clotaire I, the Frankish lands were once again divided in 561 into Neustria, Austrasia, and Burgundy. The chief officer of each kingdom was the Mayor of the Palace. During the 8th Century the Merovingian dynasty degenerated into a line of kings known as the "lazy kings." While these kings spent their time in the pursuit of pleasure, the Mayors tended to wield the real power in the kingdom, laying the foundation for the new dynasty, the Carolingians.

The Carolingians

This office of Mayor of the Palace became hereditary in the Carolinian family, and eventually the Carolingians seized the kingship itself. They managed to do this through an alliance with the papacy, and this illustrates how the Catholic Church, unlike the Orthodox Church in the East, managed to insinuate itself into the secular affairs of the kingdoms of Western Europe. From the middle of the 7th Century on, the Merovingian king became a figurehead distinguished by his beard, long hair, crown and throne, but exercising little royal power. When King Theuderic IV died in 737, he was not replaced. Charles Martel ruled instead as Mayor of the Palace. Charles Martel died in 741 and was succeeded by his sons Pepin the Short and Carloman. The brothers installed another king,

---

4. Merovech was a chief of the Salian Franks in the 5th Century. He is considered a semi-legendary individual, as not much information survived about him. Gregory of Tours records that he was the son of Chlodio and father of Childeric I. His descendants called themselves Merovingians, or the House of Merovech. Some scholars believe that Merovech may have been the namesake of a certain god honored by the Franks prior to their conversion to Christianity, a being described as part human, part bull and part sea-creature.

Childeric III in 743, largely to assuage the concern of other Frankish leaders about their growing power. Carloman withdrew from politics in 747 and retired to the monastery of Monte Casino. In 751, Childeric III also wisely "decided" to retire to a monastery and Pepin the Short had himself proclaimed king in November 751, thus officially ending the Merovingian Dynasty.

Pepin the Short (751–768)

Having displaced the Merovingians, it was in the interests of the Carolingian Kings to depict their predecessors as useless anachronisms. Hence, the earlier Merovingians were depicted as evil and brutal tyrants while later Merovingians were propagandized as lazy and simple incompetents. In order to legitimize his act of usurpation, Pepin requested the pope to give his blessing. Pepin's reasoning was that since he had all the responsibility for ruling the kingdom and did all the work, the actual title of king should be his as well. The pope (Stephen II) not only recognized Pepin as "King of the Franks," but gave him the additional title "Protector of the Roman Church." Pepin then marched into Italy with his army and seized the central area of Italy from the Lombard Kingdom, which he turned over to the pope's personal rule. This act was legitimized and recorded in a document known as the "Donation of Pepin," and it consisted of most of central Italy. This was the beginning of what came to be known as the Papal States, of which only the tiny state of the Vatican remains today.[5] This was surely an equal exchange, a win–win situation, so to speak: the pope gave Pepin someone else's crown and Pepin gave the pope someone else's land.

Upon his death in 768, the kingdom was once again divided between Pippin's sons, Charles and Carloman. However, Carloman withdrew to a monastery and died shortly thereafter, leaving sole rule to his brother, who is known to history as Charlemagne, "Charles the Great."

Charlemagne (768–814)

Beginning in 772, Charlemagne launched a series of campaigns against the pagan Saxons to the north. He continued and expanded the practice of Christian rulers conquering and converting their non-Christian neighbors by armed force. Catholic missionaries from Gaul, Ireland, and Anglo-Saxon England had been entering Saxon lands since the mid-8th Century, often with armed backing, but the Saxons had consistently resisted the missionary efforts. But the application of massive military force by Charlemagne turned the tide. After many years of valiant resistence, the important Saxon leader Widukind was baptized in 785 as part of a peace agreement, but other Saxon leaders continued to fight. Charlemagne achieved an important victory in 787 at Verdun, and ordered the wholesale killing of thousands of pagan Saxon prisoners. After several more uprisings, the Saxons were only defeated for good in 804. These campaigns expanded the Frankish kingdom to the Elbe River, something the Roman Empire had attempted and failed to accomplish.

During the same time, Charlemagne conquered the Lombards and brought northern Italy into his empire. He confirmed the Donation of Pepin and promised the papacy of continued Frankish protection. Later campaigns incorporated Bavaria into the Frankish kingdom, and by 796 Charlemagne had conquereed modern Austria and parts of Croatia. By 800 he was the undisputed

---

5. At about this time a fraudulent document known as the Donation of Constantine was "discovered" in the Vatican, which claimed to have been written by Constantine back in the 4th Century. It purports to be a grant of land by Constantine to Pope Sylvester (314–335). This document was believed to be a legitimate for more than ten centuries. The rule of the pope over the Papal States was confirmed by Pepin's son, Charlemagne, on the basis of this phony document.

Courtesy of the Granger Collection.

Figure 13.3: The coronation of Charlemagne. Pope Leo III crowns Charlemagne ``Emperor of the Roman Empire'' on Christmas day, 800.

ruler of an empire that included what is now France, Swizerland, Belgium, The Netherlands, Germany, northern Italy and parts of Austria and Spain.[6]

Charlemagne seems to have been more adapt at conquering pagans than in conducting relations with the papacy. In the late 790s, Pope Leo III (795–816) was in serious trouble. The office of the papacy had become a prize to be won in the feuds and battles between the noble Roman families. In 799 a rebellion against the pope broke out and Leo was attacked, beaten, and imprisoned for a time by his family's rivals. When he escaped, he fled Rome and appealed to Charlemagne. The opposing faction brought criminal charges against the pope to Charlemagne, which placed him in the position to arbitrate between the two sides. On 23 December 800 he convoked a council of prelates and nobles. Leo took an oath affirming his innocence and the council absolved him of wrongdoing. Although the Roman Church had always maintained that no secular authority had power over the church, with a royal army nearby, no one could dispute the findings of the council.

This would appear to be a victory for secularism, "but wait, there is more." Two days later, the king attended Christmas mass at St. Peters. The pope himself said the Mass before the assembled Frankish nobles and local Romans. As Charlemagne arose from prayer before the altar, the pope set a crown on his head. The people in the church cried out the traditional acclamation that greeted a

---

6. The great threat from this quarter was Islam. Most of the Iberian peninsula had fallen to Muslim aggression. The few Christians who remained were in the North and they appealed to Charlemagne for help. In 778, Charles led a great army over the Pyrenees. He managed to win back a few cities, and he established a Frankish presence beyond the Pyrenees known as the Spanish March, but he was unable to win a decisive victory, was unable to negotiate anything substantial, and finally had to return to Gaul with not much accomplished. Nevertheless, this did mark the farthest advance into Europe by the Muslims from the direction of Africa.

new Roman emperor. By this act, Charlemagne was made emperor of the Romans. He was the first in the West to claim this title since Odoacer the Goth usurped the throne from Romulus Augustulus in 476. It was a momentous event and it has caused controversy from that day to this. Charlemagne is said to have been surprised by this caronation, declaring that he would not have come into the church had he known of the pope's plan. However, some historians believe that the pope would not have dared to act without Charlemagne's knowledge.[7] It appears that Leo made the most of the situation as it was handed to him. To be protected from his enemies, he needed the support of the Roman emperor, and Charlemagne was the obvious candidate for that position. But by crowning the emperor himself, Leo further insinuated the papacy into the business of making kings. From that Christmas day on there would be a tension between pope and emperor, and a controversy over who had the authority to crown the emperor.

Yet, the significance of the coronation of Charlemagne goes beyond the conflict between Church and state. It may appear to be a fruitless and pompous effort to resurrect the old Roman Empire in the West, but in fact it marks the arrival of a new competitor to the Byzantines. This entity would come to be called the Holy Roman Empire,[8] and its existence meant that the West as well as the East would inherit the classical tradition. It also marks the union of the Roman and the German societies. Until now, these two societies had been separate, though intertwined, but increasingly now on the dividing line would be between East and West. The lands west of the Elbe and the Adriatic would be regarded by others as a single society: Western Christendom, with its religious capital at Rome and its secular center north of the Alps. This new society was still in its rough infancy under Charlemagne and there were dark times ahead, but it would prove strong enough to survive as the basis of the future European Civilization. It was a society clearly distinct from both Byzantium and Islam. In this sense, the coronation of Charlemagne marks the beginning of "European history."

Charlemagne did, in fact, take his title seriously and attempted to play the role of a Roman emperor. He endeavored to promote classical learning and Christian wisdom by gathering scholars to his court. This effort is lovingly savored by some historians of the period as the "Carolingian Renaissance." This term refers to the often-rejected but just as frequently resuscitated idea that a flowering of literature, the arts, architecture, jurisprudence, liturgical, and scriptural studies occurred during and shortly after the reign of Charlemagne, that this flowering was consciously nurtured by the court, and that its flowering was connected to the resurrection of the title of Emperor for Charlemagne in the year 800. In reality, this so-called renaissance was only a brief revival of classical learning, laboriously fanned into flame, but alas, there was no longer suitable fuel to sustain such a glow, and the feeble light soon disappeared again. The "Carolingian Renaissance," was thus little more than a ripple in the steady decline of civilization in Western Europe—but it did designate a direction.

---

7. Although Charlemagne would naturally have wanted the pope's support and recognition of his political position as legitimate, and he may have even envisioned the resuscitation of the old Roman Empire in the West, it is also logical to assume that he would resist actually being crowned by the pope. It set the precedent that the Church had the prerogative to install secular rulers, and by implication to depose them. The struggle between church and state for the control of society has deep roots in the history Western Civilization. However, all is speculation, because we simply do not know the precise circumstances of Charlemagne's coronation as emperor.

8. This name is meant to imply that the Roman Empire in the West is now under the domination of the Church, but historians never tire of pointing out that the Holy Roman Empire was neither holy, nor Roman, nor even an empire: it was only a loosely knit conglomeration of feudal entities that never throughout its long history functioned as a unified state.

Charlemagne's Successors

Charlemagne had several sons but only one survived him: Louis the Pius (814–840), so nicknamed because of his patronage of the Church. Sole inheritance in this instance was a matter of chance, rather than intent, as the Carolingians still adhered to the Germanic custom of the equal inheritance of all surviving sons. Louis was a good but an unremarkable king and there were no great crises or important wars during his 26 year reign. His principal accomplishment was to preserve and further his father's accomplishments.

Louis had three sons. His settlement of their estates demonstrates how far the Franks still had to go in political understanding, for he divided the Frankish empire among the three of them, splitting the empire his predecessors had brought together with so much toil. However, the division of the empire made perfect sense to the Franks. The titles, privileges, and lands of Louis belonged to him, not to some abstraction known as the State. They were his in the same sense as his hounds and horses, and so the division had nothing to do with ethnicity, language, or nationality—it was based strictly on value and revenue. Charles the Bald received the western portion of the empire and ruled the Franks. Louis the German got Germany. Lothair got Italy and a strip of territories between Germany and France. All three were unhappy with the arrangements and went to war after Louis's death, but in 840, at Verdun, the three agreed on the final arrangements, which weren't much different from the original bequests.

This agreement is known as the Treaty of Verdun, and it is one of the most important treaties in the entire history of Europe. A glance at the modern map of Europe reveals that an outline of this division still remains: the Kingdom of Charles the Bald developed into France, the Kingdom of Louis the German developed into Germany, and the "Middle Kingdom" of Lothair, the least stable of the three kingdoms, eventually disintegrated into Italy, Switzerland, Belgium, Luxemburg, and the Netherlands. But over the centuries there were many efforts to resurrect the old Middle Kingdom and, in a sense, France and Germany have fought over its territory right down to the Second World War.

The Frankish practice of dividing the realm among all the sons led to further splits, not only of land but of rights and powers. No new Charlemagne emerged from these families to unite the lands anew, and many of the kings were incompetent and lazy, as indicated by their names: Louis the Fat, Charles the Simple, etc. Yet this was a time that required competency and leadership. The century between 850 to 950 was filled with the worst of the Viking invasions from the north, the Moslem pirate raids from the south, and Magyar incursions from the east. Against these pressures the Carolingians could not stand. Charlemagne's great empire fragmented into a kaleidoscope of contending feudal units. The monasteries were plundered, the towns burned. Even the very title of emperor was lost again for a time, and when it reappeared it was taken by a German king.

The Role of the Church in the Early Middle Age

The importance of the role played by the Roman Church in the history of Western Europe, beginning especially in the Carolingian Period, can hardly be understated. The "role played by the Church," does not refer to the influence of the Christian religion on the life and spirit of the age. That was of critical importance, of course, and it has already been discussed in some detail in the last chapter. But the subject to be discussed now is quite different and perhaps even more important: the role played by the organized Roman Church in shaping the political, social, and even the economic structure of Medieval Europe. This will be much more of a description of a struggle for power than a discussion of religious principles. It was during the early centuries of the Middle Ages that the struggle between the Church and the secular authority for the ultimate control over the power structure of the state first became evident. It should not really surprise us, however, that the leaders of the Church would seek to gain control over the state, because the urge, indeed the drive, to control both private and public behavior, actions, and even mental attitudes of all members of society is an inherent and essential aspect, of the nature of Christianity, and when that drive to control was harnessed by the strong organization of the Church, the conflict between church and state was inevitable and, in fact, had already been taking place less openly from the time that Constantine had recognized Christianity as the favored religion of the Roman Empire back in 313. This struggle between church and state is one of the central themes of the history of the entire Middle Ages. And like many other aspects of this period, it is not a pretty picture.

Church and State

During the Early Middle Age, the only individuals in Europe who could read and write at all were a few elite members of the clergy—most priests of the period were illiterate. Less than one person in a thousand, less then one tenth of one percent of the population could read and write. This in itself gave the church an immense amount of power. For one thing, it was from among this very small group of clergymen that all the thinkers and intellectuals of the period were to be found. And it was this group that exerted the most profound and critical influence on the development of the civilization of Western Europe, that civilization destined to rise from the ashes of the Roman Empire. This monopoly gave the church a tremendous advantage in its struggle with the secular authority for supremacy in the state, because it was from among the leaders of the Church that the king must chose his most efficient and effective assistants to help him run his government. Thus, in the Kingdom of the Franks, the bishops of the church also functioned as the administrators of the secular affairs of the kingdom. In this situation the question arises: to whom did these bishops owe their first loyalty—to God? To Caesar? Or perhaps to the Pope?[9]

However, in any confrontation between church and state, a strong monarch, with the power of a loyal army behind him, could overcome this disadvantage. Charlemagne was such a monarch. Although he was a genuinely devout man and determined to rule as a Christian prince, he was also determined to maintain secular control of the church. But under his successors, the bishops began to claim the dominate role in the government and, in the end, they succeeded in setting themselves up in a position of superiority to the king himself.

How did this happen? In the old Frankish kingdom of the Merovingians, that is, before the Mayor of the Palace, Pepin the Short, usurped the Frankish throne, and founded the Carolingian dynasty, the Frankish church was under the tight control of the king. Clovis (481–511), the founder of the barbarian Merovingian dynasty, had been a Germanic pagan until 496, when he converted to Catholic Christianity. As recounted above he established his capital at Paris and founded the Church of the Holy apostles there which became the headquarters of the Frankish Church.

---

9. This is a fundamental question in western society that, in truth, has never been fully solved. The recent controversy concerning the insertion of the words "under God" into the Pledge of Allegiance and the inclusion of the motto "In God We Trust" on the currency comes to mind.

But from the beginning, Clovis and his successors claimed the right to appoint the bishops of the Frankish Church. Like the emperors of the East, they viewed the church as the religious arm of their government. At first the bishops attempted to resist the king's intervention in their election, claiming that it was contrary to the ancient tradition of the church. But gradually they came to accept it and for all intents and purposes the bishops of the Frankish Church were chosen by the king. These appointees were often court favorites. When an office fell vacant the king nominated one of the clerics from the royal chapel or sometimes even a layman. These members of the king's court would take orders from the king rather than from the pope and many of them continued to lead the same secular lifestyle as before their appointment to the bishopric.

After the line of kings descending from Clovis degenerated into the "lazy kings," and the Mayor of the Palace took effective control of the kingdom, this practice continued. Obviously, reform was necessary and it began under Pepin the Short. A papal delegate—a representative of the pope—was accepted into the court and gave advice upon which the king took action. This gave the pope some influence in the choice of the bishops, but the kings refused to give up their strict control over the Episcopal elections, and it was their wishes that still dominated the choice of bishops. However, some important reforms were accomplished. All the Frankish bishops were placed under four regional archbishops. The result of this change was a more efficient and better organized church, it came even more under the direction and domination of the king, because these archbishops were appointed by him.

Charlemagne continued the work of reform, but his object was to organize the Frankish church not merely as a framework for the religious life of his empire, but as an integral organ of his government. To Charlemagne, as indeed to everyone in the Middle Ages, there was little difference between religious and secular power. As the king of the Frankish state, Charlemagne saw it as his duty as a Christian prince to watch over the spiritual life of his subjects. He saw himself as both a political and a religious leader, and it was his duty to guard the safety of his subject's souls as well as their bodies. Therefore, the church was to be his agent in the performance of this sacred mission. He was, after all, the viceroy of God here on earth, and he ruled his kingdom by divine appointment.

Charlemagne's reforms consisted of another complete reorganization of the Frankish Church, which took the form of a return to the old Roman provincial divisions. Within each ecclesiastic province, the perish priests were grouped under several regional bishops, who were in turn directly under the provincial archbishop, who resided at the provincial cathedral, his administrative headquarters. At the top of this hierarchy of priests, bishops, and archbishops was Charlemagne himself and he wielded almost absolute power over the entire church. The archbishop, who now had authority over the bishops in their provinces, had to give an annual account of themselves to Charlemagne. Many of these bishops and archbishops were appointed from the nobility, others were from the clergy of the royal chapel, and still others were famous scholars or writers. Although himself totally illiterate, Charlemagne had great respect for scholars. Very few of these appointees, however, had received any training or experience to prepare them for the priesthood, or for a career in church administration. Moreover, Charlemagne entrusted his bishops with both civil and religious duties, which made them an integral part of his governmental structure. But their secular and administrative duties left them little time to evangelize the inhabitants of their dioceses, even though some of these areas had only recently been conquered and had large populations of non-Christians. Therefore, the spiritual activity of the Church was left almost completely in the hands of the monks.

Monasteries

In Charlemagne's day monasticism developed some of the features that were to persist for many centuries. Christian monasticism began in Egypt during the 3rd Century when a saintly man named Anthony entered the desert to live a solitary life of rigorous asceticism and to do battle with the spiritual forces of evil. However, this form of hermitic or solitary monasticism had serious difficulties. It was hard for a hermit to find food and water in the desert, but even more importantly a hermit, living alone in the desert, is unable to participate in the common prayer and public worship required of Christians. In addition, the harsh life of the desert produces severe psychological distortions in the weak hearted. Nevertheless, hermetic monasticism became very popular and many, many men moved out into the desert to imitate Anthony.

Indeed, the imitators of the most famous hermits became so numerous that they began to form de facto communities. Pachomius, another of these hermitic monks, had acquired so many followers that he grouped them into a community and drew up the first monastic rule, which enjoined his followers to practice chastity, poverty, and obedience to the abbot, a Semitic word that simply means "father." This type of communal monasticism quickly spread into other lands, and by the 5th Century it had achieved a powerful presence throughout Christendom, but it was practiced in a confusing variety of forms.

The monk who brought uniformity and order into the monastic movement was St. Benedict (480?–543?) of Italy. In 525 Benedict founded a new monastery at Monte Cassino in central Italy and near the end of his life drew up his famous "rule" for monastic life. The Benedictine rule was, in fact, a constitution, and monasteries were thus the one social group of Medieval Europe who possessed a written charter. In this sense, the rule is similar to the municipal charters granted by the Roman government to the cities of the Empire, and this is yet another example of the survival of Roman organization genius in the Church.

The Benedictine rule endowed the abbot with full authority over the community, which amounted to sovereignty. He was elected by the monks, a touch of democracy, but he held his position for life and could not be replaced. While his decision was final and could not be appealed, the abbot was duty bound to consult regularly with the elder brothers and even with all the members on important matters. The Benedictine rule included regulations to cover every aspect of monastic life, both spiritual and practical. For example, a monk could take his final vows only after a one-year trial period to test his suitability to monastic life. Other regulations governed the daily schedule, setting aside certain hours for manual labor, in which all monks must participate. "Idleness is the enemy of the soul," according to St. Benedict.

During Charlemagne's reign numerous monasteries were founded in his kingdom and each devoted itself to evangelizing the countryside. Many of these institutions also became centers of culture—in fact they were often like islands of civilization in a sea of barbarism and the monks exerted an extraordinary influence on every aspect of Medieval life. Not only did they preserve copies of some of the Latin literary masterpieces, but they saved, developed, and spread ancient technology that would otherwise have been lost. The most obvious example of this is agriculture. The agricultural technology, which the barbarians brought with them when they overran the European provinces of the Roman Empire was far inferior to that practiced by the Romans. While it would seem to be an easy and logical process for the barbarians to acquire the superior agricultural technology from the Romans among whom they settled, we often do not realize just what a delicate thing technology really is, how closely it is tied to the culture that creates it, and how easily it can be lost.[10] During the chaos and disruption of the 5th and 6th centuries farming, like every aspect of life, was barbarized and much of the practical "know-how" was forgotten. Throughout the Early Middle Age, the monks were the most successful agriculturalists. As monasteries developed and managed ever larger estates, they restored and preserved the ancient farming methods and developed new strains of both plants and animals better suited for the harsh environment of northern Europe. The monasteries thus set an example of good farming practices from which the surrounding laymen could benefit. In fact, Medieval governments often grew to depend upon monastic farms to supply the food and other commodities for their administrators and armies.

Also, monks were almost the only people during the Middle Ages who were literate, and the monasteries usually maintained both libraries and schools for training young monks. The monks also organized scriptoria, or writing offices, in which the manuscripts that were needed for the church or for education were copied. Most of the ancient Latin literary works, of both pagan and Christian origin, which survive today were preserved in copies made in monasteries.[11]

Because the monks maintained the only schools and libraries in all of Europe, they were virtually the only intellectuals in society. Secular rulers therefore recruited their counselors and administrative officials from the monasteries and nearly all the administrative records we have from this period were written by monastic scribes. In fact, our modern word "clerk," which means an office worker who keeps records, comes from the Latin word *clericus*, which means clergyman.

But beyond all this, there are two other reasons why the monasteries played such an important role in Medieval society. One reason is that their strongly communal organization enabled the monks to cope more effectively with the problems of a turbulent age than any other segment of the population. During the Early Middle Age, the monastery was the only institution left that resembled an urban community. True, a monastery was not a actual city—for one thing it was not composed of families—but it did perform some critical functions for Medieval society that cities normally perform for a civilization, such as education and cultural transmission from one generation to the next. And its communal organization meant that the monastery was self-sustaining. Essential tasks within the monastic community were divided among the members: some monks worked the earth; some arranged for the defense of the community; while some were left free to read and study. This division of labor was unknown in the countryside where the surfs performed all tasks. Yet, specialization is vital to progress.

Another contribution of the monasteries to Medieval society was their powerful stimulus for both economic and cultural change. Early Medieval society was desperately poor and, like all poor societies, its only real hope of improvement was to save and invest part of the current production, meager though it was, in the future. Monasteries were the great savers and investors of the Middle

---

10. Consider, for example, just how few people actually know how to make computer chips. And think of the consequences to society if that know-how was suddenly lost. How long would it take our society to recover?

11. The Medieval monasteries have received a great deal of well-deserved praise for preserving the heritage of the ancient world. But at the same time it must be understood that less than 1% of the literary works of antiquity survive today. And those few that do survive are not a random selection from the total mass of ancient literature, but were in fact carefully chosen for survival by the Medieval Christian monks. No one can seriously believe that these manuscripts were chosen in anything resembling an objective manor. Since Christianity and paganism were enemies, the pagan literary sources that we have today were chosen by enemies of paganism—and yet, these manuscripts are all we have to reconstruct the history of the ancient world and the part that Christian bias played in their survival must be taken into account. It must also be remembered that the original literary works themselves have not survived and we must therefore rely on copies made by Christian monks who were, to say the least, hostile to their contents.

Figure 13.4: Illustration from Gospel Book of Abbot Wedricus, c. 1147. St. John the Evangelist.

Ages, and this helps explain their economic success. Their ascetic lifestyle rejected both the classical aversion to manual labor and the barbarian love of violence. Thus, by rejecting both the classical and the barbarian value systems, the monks prepared the way for the acceptance of new values and new cultural traits later during the High Middle Ages.

Church-State Relations after Charlemagne

After the death of Charlemagne there was a sharp reaction to his policy of tight government control of the Frankish Church. The bishops eagerly planned religious reforms which would throw off all government control over their activities and leave the Church free to pursue its spiritual mission. But unfortunately, like their contemporaries, the bishops were incapable of separating in their minds the religious and the secular functions of church and state and, therefore, they began to claim a preeminent role for the church in secular affairs. The concept of the separation of church and state, which seems so familiar to us—though it is still far from perfectly realized—was not yet a part of the political thought of Western Europe. In the minds of the people of the Middle Ages there was a natural unity of the religious and the secular authority. The idea that the ruler of the state and the ruler of the Church could each pursue their own interests independently and peacefully never occurred to them. Either the prince or the bishop had to be in absolute control of society. These are the same politico-religious views that had existed under Charlemagne, except that they were turned upside down and now the clergy saw its role as superior to that of the secular sovereign. The bishops now elaborated a basically theological theory of their superior position which was finally put into practice and was even sometimes accepted by the secular rulers themselves.

The advisors of Charlemagne, for the most part, still adhered to the principles of Roman law, which favored imperial absolutism. In the old Roman Empire the emperor was also the *pontifex maximus*, the chief priest of the state religion. Now Christianity was the state religion, but it was organized into a church, on organization separate and independent from the organization of the secular government. The pope had appropriated that title of *pontifex maximus* for himself. In 800, Pope Leo had crowned Charlemagne emperor of the Roman Empire, but he had retained the office of chief priest for himself. This was, in essence, the crux of the state-church struggle throughout the Middle Ages, the attempt to reunite these two offices as they had been during the Roman Empire.

The monastic schools, which produced the so-called Carolingian Renaissance, created a small elite group of educated clergymen. This new group of intellectuals was trained in cannon, or church, law. Cannon law proclaimed the superiority of the spiritual power over temporal power. It stated quite clearly that the bishop was superior to the king, because on the day of judgment the bishop would have to account to God for the king's actions, just as he would for the other members of his congregation. But the clergy of the 9th Century went even further. They constructed a theory of the Christian state, founded on the ideas expressed by St Augustine[12] in his 5th Century discourse, *The City of God*. Augustine had reasoned that peace and justice produce perfect order, which to him meant obedience to God's design. This order must be realized both in the family and in the state. The state must be founded on that perfect justice which gives both man and God their due. Thus, the state must be founded on Christian principles. From this it follows, as the Church fathers had repeatedly affirmed, that the bishops were the leaders of the Church and that all state institutions must be imprinted with Christian principles. The next logical step was for a pope to proclaim: "power is granted from on High. . . so that the earthly kingdom shall be at the service of the Kingdom of Heaven."

So in the 9th Century Western Civilization came full circle. In the ancient pre-Greek world of the New East and Egypt, human beings were simply the slaves of heaven, with no rights, purpose, or vision of their own, except as agents and servants of the divine will. From there the West advanced to the humanistic concept of the Classical period that "man is the measure of all things." In the 9th Century, Western Civilization moved back to the view that the only purpose of humanity is to serve God. Humanism and mysticism seem to be two mutually exclusive concepts that seem always to be in a state of struggle. And although the pendulum will swing back toward humanism and reason during the early modern period, it appears that today, at the beginning of the 21st Century, the West is poised to move back in the direction

---

12. St. Augustine, bishop of Hippo, in North Africa, from 395 to 430, was the leading theologian of the West. Much of his voluminous writing was a defense of orthodoxy against contemporary heretical groups. He was convinced that all truth was spiritual, derived from God and that acceptance of truth (identical with "faith" to him) was dependant on God's divine grace (the undeserved love of God). Augustine is rightfully considered to be the founder of Christian mysticism. For him (as with Socrates), truth was to be found by each person within himself, in his soul, and this spark of divine truth would bring him into communion with his maker and provide him with peace and happiness. But this was only possible through the aid of God's grace (Socrates' "inner voice?"). In his best known book, *The City of God*, Augustine presents the symbolic struggle between two cities, the city of those who do God's will and the city of the forces of this earth. Thus, reality is viewed as the eternal struggle between the spiritual and the worldly, a feature of Christianity to this day.

of mysticism once again. Enslavement to the will of God is the vision of humanity being put forward today by the fundamentalist Christian sects, as well as the Islam, as a model for the future world order.

But the bishops and clergy of the 9th Century carried Augustine's ideas, expressed in *The City of God,* much further than Augustine himself did. In 829, the successor to Charlemagne, Louis the Pious, convened a synod, (conference of bishops) at Paris and put to them the question: "What is nature of his duties as a Christian king?" Those bishops were only too happy to answer that question! They replied with a detailed explanation of what came to be known as "Political Augustinianism." This doctrine holds that because the purpose of life is peace in this world and salvation in the next, it was the duty of the king to ensure that his subjects adhered to the "correct" principles of Christianity. The king's power was given to him by God for this purpose, it was not his property, but rather his ministry. And anyway, the temporal power of the king was merely the secular arm of the spiritual power. And the spiritual power belonged to the bishops, who wielded the "power of the keys"—that, is the keys to the Kingdom of Heaven. The bishop was therefore superior to the king and it was the bishop's duty-given to him by God-to instruct the king as to where his duty lay, to prevent him from sinning or leading the people into sin, to admonish him and instruct him. The pope was the head of the Church, to which the king belonged like every other Christian, and the pope was responsible only to God.

The opposing view, which had always been practiced in the Eastern Empire, is called Caesaropapism. This view holds that the king or emperor is God's viceroy here on earth, and it is he who must answer to God on judgment day. Thus, the Church is simply his agent, necessary to carry out his God-given mission. Although this extreme view was never openly or seriously advocated in the West, the underlying concept nevertheless furnished the impetus, in modified form, for the efforts of the secular rulers of Europe to gain control over the churches in their states during the early modern period. It was one of the driving forces of the Protestant Revolt.

The battle lines are drawn, then, between secularism and mysticism. Either the Church must be the arm of the secular government and the prince has the supreme power over both state and church, or the secular government is merely an arm of the Church and the pope is the supreme ruler of all Christendom and the princes of Europe are only the pope's agents in carrying out his divine mission. Obviously, these two positions are totally incompatible and are bound to lead to a bloody showdown.

This struggle between the two different views of the relationship of state and church is one of the most important aspects of the Middle Ages. It was a long, bitter, and bloody struggle. Before it was over, an emperor of the Holy Roman Empire was deposed from his throne by the pope and forced to stand barefooted in the snow outside the pope's window begging for forgiveness. But both sides scored victories and suffered defeats. At another point in the struggle a pope was placed in chains and led into captivity by an emperor. How was the question finally resolved? It never was really settled. The participants in the struggle, after many centuries, eventually became so exhausted that the struggle simply became less important and less central to Western Civilization.[13]

---

13. Unfortunately, today this struggle seems to be reviving. We see indications all around us. Future historians may well view the "9-11" attack on the World Trade Center in 2002 as an early battle of the renewed struggle between humanism and mysticism. Are we poised for another bloody round of religious wars? Will our children and grandchildren live in a world drenched with the blood and suffering of this renewed struggle? The signs do indeed appear ominous.

The Holy Roman Empire

The struggle between church and state ragged continuously throughout the Middle Ages all over Europe, in France, England, Spain, etc., but the history of the Holy Roman Empire presents the best example. The empire was called "holy" and "Roman" because it was an association between the Roman Catholic Church and what was supposed to be a revival of the old Roman Empire in the West. But this Holy Roman Empire was always more of an ideal than a reality. It represented a yearning for the dimly remembered unity, peace, and security of the *pax Romana*. This ideal of a universal state which includes all civilized humanity under one just, stable, and peaceful government, is the heritage of Rome. It is an ideal toward which Western Civilization has never stopped striving. In our own day the United Nations and the European Union are very important examples of efforts to achieve that universal state.

After the division of Charlemagne's empire by the Treaty of Verdun in 843, the Carolingian dynasty went through a long period of decline and finally ended with the death of Louis IV, the Child in 911. He was the last direct descendant of Charlemagne in Germany. However, the ideal of the empire remained, and the German nobles elected Conrad, Duke of Franconia, who was not a Carolingian, as the new emperor (911–919). Unfortunately, his seven year reign was a complete disaster, but on his deathbed he recommended Henry, Duke of Saxony, as his successor and he became Henry I, the Fowler (919–936). Henry designated his son, Otto, to be his successor. He is known as Otto I, the Great (936–973, emperor after 962), and his reign is generally considered to be the true beginning of the Holy Roman Empire. He consolidated the German state, and made significant advances for cause of secularism. During his reign, Otto defeated revolts by his half-brother, his younger brother, and his son, and expanded the boundaries of his empire through constant war.

The success of Otto I was possible, in part, because the papacy suffered under a series of weak popes during this period. The papal office had become the captive of the local Crescenti family, who maintained control of Rome and the Papal states for most of the 10th Century. Otto became involved in Vatican affairs when Pope John XII requested his protection against the Crescenti. Otto had, in fact, been waiting for some excuse to invade Italy, which he considered an integral part of his empire. He easily broke the power of the Crescenti and the grateful pope crowned him Holy Roman Emperor in 962. However, in the best German tradition, Otto proceeded to make the pope subject to the power of the emperor. In fact, by requesting protection of the German king, the pope had simply exchanged one master for another, more powerful, master. Once he was emperor, Otto confirmed the Papal States as the sovereign territory of the papacy, but extracted a promise from the Romans not to elect a pope without imperial consent. This proclamation is known as the *Privilegium Ottonianum* and it opened an era of German domination over the papacy. Otto then called a synod at Rome which deposed John XII on trumped up charges and installed the emperor's choice as successor—a layman who took the name Leo VIII (963–964). This event marked the beginning of a period of about a century in which the German emperors or by their vassals, the counts of Tusculum, dominated papacy.

During the early 11th Century, however, the German emperors again became preoccupied with internal problems and made only rare visits to Italy. The empire was not really a state but rather a confederation of the old Germanic tribes of Bavarians, Alamanns, Franks, and Saxons. The Empire as a political union only survived because of the strong personal leadership of Henry and

Otto. Although formally elected by the leaders of the Germanic tribes, they were in practice able to designate their successors. This changed, however, after Henry II died in 1024 without children. After some debate, the tribes elected Conrad II, the first of the Salian Dynasty.

While the emperors were thus preoccupied, the papacy fell under the domination of their nominal vassals, the Counts of Tuscany, and the papal throne degenerated into infamy and debauchery. Finally, in 1045, the papal office was actually sold for cash by pope Benedict IX to his godfather, who became Gregory VI. We are told that Gregory purchased the papal throne "in order to reform it," but he reigned less than a year and by 1046 the throne was claimed by no less than three rival popes simultaneously. This incident reminds one, on course, of the sale of the throne of the Roman Empire in 192, more than 800 years earlier. The amazing thing is that in neither case did such run-away degeneracy marked the end of the throne.

Ironically, this period of papal degeneracy and corruption saw the foundation, in 910, of the Abby of Cluny by William the Pius, Duke of Aquitaine. Cluny, unlike other monasteries, was completely free of feudal controls and was directly under the pope. Branches of Cluny, called daughter monasteries, spread rapidly through France and Germany. The monks of Cluny advocated three major reforms: (1) celibacy of the clergy; (2) abolition of lay investiture; (3) and the end of simony (the sale of church offices). Cluny also spearheaded the efforts to restore the central authority of the Church and elevation of the position of the pope to the supreme lawgiver and judge of all Christendom.

But the methods employed to pursue these admirable goals seem strange to the modern mind. In support of the these efforts, various decrees, and documents, most of them forged, began to appear. For example, the so-called Truce of God (1040) was an attempt to limit feudal warfare to certain days and seasons of the year, much in the same way we limit hunting season today. This may seem a bit silly at first glance, but actually it was a practical approach. If the Church's right to outlaw fighting on certain days could be established, that authority could than be expanded until the peace of God became universal. However, the use of deceit and forgery in pursuit of these admirable goals might lead some to question the sincerity of reformers. And it might be noted that the Church never came out against warfare per se, it only condemned those acts of violence which could not be used to further its own needs. The Church always condoned and encouraged the slaughter of thousands of heretics in its attempts to establish its own unquestioned authority. And as we shall see, the Church would soon be preaching crusades against the Muslims. So it is difficult not to believe that the Church's main interest was always the pursuit of its on power.

Henry III, the Black (1039–1056, emperor after 1046), ruled the Holy Roman Empire for 17 years while imperial authority was at its height. He was heavily influenced by his wife, Agnes of Poitou, and he was a sincere reformer, although he retained a firm hand on the Church. In 1046, he deposed all three popes that claimed the papal throne after its purchase by Gregory VI and installed his own nominee, Clement II (1046–1047), who was the first of a series of reforming popes—but this act was at the same time a reaffirmation of the emperor's right to nominate the pope. Clement's first act was to crown Henry emperor. Pope Clement II lost no time beginning the work of reform. He called a synod in Rome in January of 1047, which degreed that the buying and selling of church offices was punishable by excommunication. Unfortunately, he died later in 1047, before his reforms had gone further. Henry III named four more reforming popes during his reign and they worked toward renewing the strength of the papacy. The renewed papacy was, however, to be a nemesis for Henry's successors.

The Investiture Controversy (1075–1122)

The Investiture Controversy was the most important political crisis of the 11th Century. It was a struggle between the emperor of the Holy Roman Empire and the pope over which of them had the supreme power over the other—it was, in short, the struggle between state and church par excellence. The term also refers to related controversies in other European countries, most notably in England, regarding the dual allegiance of bishops to their sovereign and to the pope. It began with a dispute about lay investiture of bishops and abbots. Such prelates held land and often exercised secular as well as ecclesiastical functions and for this reason lay secular rulers had an understandable interest in their appointment and frequently invested[14] them with their various offices. The controversy had its roots in the Cluniac reform movement, which demanded that the Church free itself from secular influence. This upset the established relationship between emperor and pope. Initially the emperor had taken on the role of protector of the Church and assumed the title of emperor in return, but the pope now began to claim a superior role for himself in several aspects: not only did he demand the right to appoint all clergy (who frequently had important secular responsibilities) in the Empire, but he claimed the right to select and unseat the emperor himself.

The details of the long struggle are too complex to be related here, but it culminated during the reign of Pope Gregory VII (1073–1085). Gregory was at least as ambitious as any of the secular rulers of Europe. His program embodied the three Cluniac reforms enumerated above: elimination of simony; observance of clerical celibacy; and abolition of lay investiture. In order to enforce supreme papal authority on the entire church administration, Gregory appointed a group of legates to supervise local church affairs throughout Europe. The term legate is significant: it is a Latin term that goes all the way back to the Roman Empire when the Roman emperors appointed legates, or personal representatives, to rule the imperial provinces in their name. This system of papal legates is still in use by the Roman Catholic Church today.

The pope's antagonist in this effort was Henry IV (1056–1106), who had succeeded his father, Henry III, at the age of six, which necessitated a regency from 1056 to 1060. During the emperor's minority the papacy, the German nobles, and the high ecclesiastical leaders all took advantage of the weakened throne to increase their power at the expense of the imperial authority. In 1062, Archbishop Anno of Cologne even abducted Henry and assumed the regency himself, which had been held by Henry's mother, Agnes.[15] Anno proceeded to enrich himself from the royal lands and revenues. He allowed Archbishop Adalbert of Hamburg-Bremen to share in the plunder, and Adalbert soon became sole regent. Henry attained his majority in 1065, but Adalbert retained the regency until jealous nobles persuaded Henry to dismiss him in 1066. It is not difficult to understand why Henry IV did not trust the Church leaders.

Henry's first task was to restore his authority within the Empire. The duchies had become accustomed to their independence and Henry had to put down several revolts, the most serious one in Saxony. By 1075 he was able to turn his attention to Italy. He disregarded Gregory VII's opposition to lay investiture and invested a new bishop in Milan. Gregory supported the previous bishop, which had been installed by a revolutionary movement within the city and threatened to depose

---

14. Investiture: The act or ceremony by which a feudal lord granted a fief to a vassal. In the ceremony attending the consecration of a bishop, he was invested with ring and crozier (staff), the symbols of his office.

15. Henry's mother, Agnes of Poitou, was regent from the death of Henry III in 1056 to 1062. She spent her last years in a cloister in Italy where she encouraged monastic reform.

Henry. In response, Henry convened a council at Worms in January of 1076, which declared Gregory deposed. Not to be outdone, Gregory summoned a synod a month later in February and declared Henry excommunicated[16] and deposed and absolved his subjects of their oaths of fealty.

Seeing an opening for increasing their independence from the imperial throne, a powerful coalition of German nobles, including the rebellious Saxons, agreed in October to withdraw their recognition of Henry's authority unless he obtained absolution by February. His position would be decided in a diet to be held at Augsburg in February of 1077 under the chairmanship of the pope. What strange bedfellows politics make! But Henry was a little too clever for both Gregory and the nobles. He crossed the Alps in the dead of winter and met Gregory at Canossa, in northern Italy, in January of 1077. Standing barefoot in the snow outside the pope's window, the emperor presented himself as a humble and submissive penitent, begging for forgiveness. Now it is a cardinal principle of the Christian religion that no one, not even the pope, can refuse pardon and forgiveness to a truly and sincerely repentant sinner. Clearly Gregory would have refused if he could have done so, but under Christian doctrine he had no right to do so. After stalling for three days, Gregory finally absolved Henry of his sins.

The fortunes of the two men were quickly reversed. The rebellious German nobles were still determined to depose Henry, which indicates that their motives were political, not religious, all along. They elected the Rudolf, Duke of Swabia, as anti-king and plunged the empire into a civil war. Gregory remained neutral until March of 1080, when he excommunicated Henry again and recognized Rudolf as king. But this time it didn't work; Gregory's use of the Church power for political purposes was exposed. Henry was now supported by a powerful coalition and a large number German and Italian bishops joined him in declaring Gregory deposed and in electing an anti-pope, Clement III.[17]

Rudolf died in 1080, but by this time the revolt was broken and in 1081 Henry carried the war to Italy. He occupied Rome in 1084 and installed Clement III as pope and was crowned emperor by him. Gregory fled south into the kingdom of the Normans and acquired allies there. After Henry withdrew from Rome the Normans under Robert Guiscard brought Gregory back to Rome and plundered Rome for several days. When the Normans withdrew from Rome, Gregory did not dare remain in the city, due to the hatred he had gained from the Romans because of the Norman atrocities.

Gregory VII died in exile at Salerno in 1085. Most of his trusted assistants and advisors had renounced him and those still faithful to him in Germany had shrunk to small numbers. His life's work was based on the belief that the Church was founded by God and entrusted with the task of embracing all humankind in a single society in which divine will is law; that the Church is supreme over all human structures, including the secular state; and that the pope, as the head of the Church, is God's regent on earth and disobedience to the pope is disobedience to God. However,

---

16. Excommunication: exclusion from membership in the church and from the communion of the faithful. In Medieval society this, in effect, placed the excommunicate outside the protection of the law and meant that all oaths of allegiance previously sworn to him were no longer either valid or enforceable.

17. This is complicated. Already the archbishop of Ravenna, Wilbert was elected pope and took the name Clement III after the synod of Brixen deposed pope Gregory VIII. The reason for calling the synod in the first place was Gregory's treatment of Henry. Wilbert gained strong support after he crowned Henry IV emperor in Rome in 1084. Outside of the Holy Roman Empire, however, most people continued to recognize the papacy of Gregory and, after he died in 1085, his successor Urban II. Today Clement III (1080–1100) is regarded as not having been validly elected pope and is thus counted as an anti-pope. He is not listed at all in the Church's official list of popes. The Clement III listed there was pope between 1187 and 1191.

the enforcement of this doctrine would require the Church to annihilate not merely the Holy Roman Empire but all the nations of Europe. Since this was not possible in practice, Gregory adopted a different course; he acknowledged the existence of the state as a dispensation of divine providence, but the subordination of the state to the Church was to him a fact that admitted of no discussion and which he never doubted. He wished to see all important matters referred to Rome; appeals were to be addressed to the pope himself; the centralization of ecclesiastical government in Rome naturally involved the curtailment of the powers of the bishops. Since the bishops refused to submit their traditional independence, Gregory's papacy was not only a struggle against the secular authorities of Europe but also against the higher ranks of the clergy.

Henry survived Gregory by more than 20 years, but they were far from happy years for him. His stubborn support of Clement III against Gregory's successors made even his own family turn against him, because they felt he was endangering the monarchy. He had to face revolts by his vassals, led first by his eldest son, Conrad, then by his second son and successor, Henry, and finally even by his second wife. By 1100, he had lost Italy and had few supporters left even in Germany—only the growing urban communities of the north remained loyal. He was forced to flee his capital in 1106, excommunicated again and died soon afterward. Henry IV thus did not even receive a Christian burial. Such were the heights and depths of fortune for Henry IV, emperor of the Holy Roman Empire. These events cause one to wonder why human beings in every age of history expend such energy and effort seeking fame and power when it so rarely produces happiness or contentment.

The partial settlement—more like a truce—of the investiture issue was accomplished under the next emperor, Henry V (1106–1125). In 1122 a compromise was reached, known as the Concordat of Worms, under which the emperor invested the bishops with their temporal authority, that is land and secular power symbolized by the scepter, while the pope invested them with their spiritual authority, symbolized by the ring and staff. In this way each party had a veto on the other's appointments. This was a clear gain for the papacy. The power of the pope, vis-à-vis the emperor, was on the rise.

The Holy Roman Empire after the Salian Dynasty

Henry V was the last emperor of the Salian family as he left no direct heir when he died in 1125. In the bitterly fought election that followed the church forces managed to deny the throne to Henry's nearest relative, Fredrick, Duke of Swabia, and instead elected Lothair II, Duke of Saxony (1125–1137). Lothair was thus under the heavy influence of the clergy and, even worse, he died without heir. During the ensuing decades the struggle between Welf and the Hohenstaufen families for the imperial throne plunged Germany into chaos, especially when emperors like Conrad III and Fredrick Barbarossa were absent on the crusades.

During the 12th Century the popes continued to pursue the goals of Gregory VII: the centralization of the church authority in Rome; independence and, if possible, dominance over the secular authorities; and consolidation of the papacy's secular base in central Italy. One of the methods that the church used to infringe on secular governments was to expand the jurisdiction of ecclesiastical courts. Before the advent of Christianity, the judiciary function had always been completely in the hands of the government. But from the beginning the church fathers had insisted that the church must have the exclusive privilege to try and punish the members of the clergy. And beginning with the emperor Constantine, the secular governments had made this concession to the church. But during the Middle Ages the church attempted to expand its jurisdiction over persons and disputes that definitely were not of a religious nature.

The reformers of the 12th Century insisted that certain persons in addition to the clergy, such as widows, orphans, crusaders, and wards of the church, should be judged only in ecclesiastical courts. The church had long sought exclusive jurisdiction over such religious matters as sacrilege, heresy, and marriage. Church leaders had believed from the beginning that it was their god-given duty to force all members of society to conform to the exact standards of thought, belief, and behavior that they, guided by God, considered to be correct. But during the 12th Century, the ecclesiastical courts sought to gain jurisdiction over wills, contracts, and other civil affairs, no matter who the parties might be. This brought the ecclesiastical courts into direct rivalry and conflict with the secular courts of the king. The Church developed a complex system of courts in which judicial decisions could be appealed to Rome and taken completely out of the national systems. This was but one of the ways the church sought to dominate the secular government of Medieval Europe.

Centralization of church authority gained in other ways as well. The popes exerted a progressively stronger control over the canonization of saints, which had hitherto been a local matter. The church gained a stronger and stronger voice over the appointment of bishops. The Concordat of Worms, in 1122, was but one step in this direction. By the end of the 12th Century, papal approval was generally accepted as essential for the valid election of a bishop. The papacy also imposed tithes—which were in reality a tax—on the clergy and the churches all over Christendom. The outlines of a centralized financial administration began to take shape, although it was still quite rudimentary.

The successful establishment of celibacy for the clergy set them apart from the laity to a degree previously unknown, and was in contrast to the Eastern Church. These restrictions have continued to influence the life of Catholic priests down to the present day. The church reforms also influenced Medieval society. The reform clergy gave powerful support to the efforts of secular rulers to suppress private warfare and establish internal peace—at least whenever and wherever internal peace was in the interests of the Church. However, the Church never hesitated to support and advocate violence and warfare when pursued in the Church's own interests.

It is ironic, however, that these church reforms contained the seeds of the revival of humanism, because the Church also set about to build an educational system for its clergy. The bishop's school and then the university were the result of these efforts. As the revival of intellectual activity proceeded, the dispute between church and state stimulated speculations about the nature of Christian society and an investigation into the ancient sources which defined its character. This, in turn, slowly led to the belief that humanity need not accept the world the way it is, but could correct its evils and imperfections. In other words, there was a new emergence of confidence in human ability to improve this world. This is a humanistic attitude that once awakened has not yet been abandoned.

Everyday Life in the Early Middle Age

The daily life of Europe during the early Middle Age was a blend of Roman, Germanic, and Christian practices and values. Christian values and ideals had not yet taken deep root.

The Family

Marriages were arranged by the father to promote the interest of the extended family. Wives were expected to be faithful to their husbands—it was important to know who was the child's father—but aristocratic men often kept concubines, sometimes slave girls, but more often free women from their estates. Even Charlemagne, that "most Christian king," had a large number of concubines. Life was far more communal than in classical times. The lord and his family lived together with crowds of vassals and servants. Everyone ate together in the common hall at the manor house. The nobles amused themselves with music, dance, and games. In times of peace the noble's main pastime was hunting, which was intended to keep him ready for his real purpose in life: warfare.

The Church increasingly insinuated itself into family life, however. Under German custom, marriage was a civil arrangement, but priests tried to bring it under the umbrella of the church by adding their blessing and making it a sacrament. The church even required that a girl over fifteen must give her consent to her guardian's choice of a husband, which doesn't sound like much progress to modern sensibilities, but the Germans considered it quite an imposition. The church also attempted to make marriage monogamous and permanent. A Frankish council in 789 decreed that marriage was an "indissoluble sacrament" and condemned concubinage and easy divorce. However, this prohibition was only slowly accepted by the Germans, both the nobles and the common people. Indeed, concubinage survived late into the Middle Ages. Charlemagne had a number of wives and many concubines, but his devout son, Louis the Pius, began to emphasize monogamy and urged married men to give up their concubines. The church, however, was never able to persuade the nobles to make the sacrifice.

The Christian ideal, of course, was the celibate life.[18] The early church fathers believed a sexless life was far superior to marriage. Paul made this very clear in his famous letter to the Corinthians:

> It is good for a man not to touch a woman. Nevertheless, to avoid fornication, let every man have his own wife, and let every woman have her own husband. Let the husband render unto the wife due benevolence: and likewise also the wife unto the husband. . . . For I would that all men were even as myself. But every man hath his proper gift of God, one after this manner, and another after that. I say therefore to the unmarried and widows, it is good for them if they abide even as I. But if they cannot contain, let them marry: for it is better to marry than to burn.[19]

Children

There was a stark contrast between the Roman and the German attitude toward children. The Romans limited their families through various forms of contraception and infanticide, primarily the exposure of unwanted children, but they invested a great deal of resources in the education and

---

18. This attitude toward sex does not appear to be part of Christianity's "rich Judaic heritage," but rather an influence of one or more of the other mystery religions. The cult of Cybele and Attis, for example, was centered around the legend of the Phrygian shepherd Attis, a young man of unusual comeliness, who was beloved of the Mother of the Gods, Cybele. It is doubtful that their love was ever consummated, which is probably why Attis fell in love with a nymph. Cybele was so outraged by his infidelity that she caused him to become insane. In this condition he castrated himself and died. After death he was reborn and reunited with the Mother Goddess. Attis and Cybele were worshiped as a pair. "If Christians believed that Jesus died on a cross as the only way to pacify his father's anger at humankind, it was no more absurd for the devotees of Attis and Cybele to worship a jealous goddess and her mutilated son." Godwin, Joscelyn, *Mystery Religions of the Ancient World* (1981), Harper and Row, San Francisco.

19. I Corinthians, 7.1–8 (excerpts), King James translation.

upbringing of a limited number of children. Classical art abounds with the figures of little innocent children playing and frolicking through scenes of the serious adult world. In contrast, there
are no real children at all in Early Medieval art, only miniature adults. The Germans possessed no
concept of childhood in the classical sense. Ironically, once the Germanic tribes abandoned their
nomadic life and adopted the sedentary lifestyle of the Middle Ages, they also adopted the practice
of infanticide, particularly female infanticide, to limit the size of their families. Even though the
church condemned infanticide, it was not able to stop the practice, especially among the poor and
the victims of seduction who did not want to keep illegitimate offspring. One method employed
by the priests was to encourage people to abandon unwanted children in churches.[20] These children were usually taken to monasteries and convents and raised as monks and nuns. With smaller
families, the Germans began to invest more in their children's education, though during the Early
Middle Age this was limited to vocational training to prepare them to fit their adult roles. A prominent example of this is the intense training and discipline given to young aristocrats to prepare
them for the knighthood.

Food and Diet

The staple food for both aristocrat and serf during the Early Middle Age was bread. Ovens were
kept busy turning out the loaves. Sometimes a porridge of barley and/or oats supplemented the
peasant diet. Of course the upper classes enjoyed more variety in their diet. Pork was the major
meat. Domestic pigs were allowed to run freely through the forests to find their own food and
were rounded up in the fall for slaughter. The meat was smoked and cured with salt for consump-
tion during the winter months. Wild game from the hunt was roasted for the aristocrat's table (serfs
were normally forbidden to hunt on the lord's domain). Beef and Mutton were occasionally consumed, but cows, oxen, and sheep were more valuable for other purposes than food. During the
Carolingian period, dairy products became more prevalent. Milk, because it spoiled quickly, was
usually made into cheese and butter. Chickens were raised for both meat and eggs. Vegetables were
an important element of the diet, including beans, peas, lentils, garlic, onions, carrots and turnips.
Honey was used as a sweetener, while spices and herbs were especially important because the lack
of refrigeration meant that half spoiled meats could be made palatable. Gluttony and drunkenness
were not uncommon in Carolingian society, and the art of the period often depicts people with
potbellies. Wine and ale were the favorite beverages. Monasteries allotted monks a daily ration of
one and a half quarts of wine, for instance. Yet, malnutrition was widespread among the common
people throughout the Middle Ages.

---

20. Some things, it seems, never change. In an attempt to prevent the deaths of unwanted babies, in 2001 California
passed the "Abandoned Baby Law" permitting mothers to legally and anonymously abandon new born babies in
hospitals, with no questions asked and suffer no retribution.

14

The High Middle Age (1000–1300)

The term High Middle Age denotes the cultural and economic improvement in the life of Western Europe which occurred in the 11th, 12th and 13th centuries. But, no spectacular event marks the beginning of this period. Indeed historians do not even agree on the exact date of the beginning of this period. Many scholars date the beginning of the High Middle Ages from 1050, but a majority agree to round it off even further to the year 1000. One difficulty is that the transition from the Early to the High Middle age was gradual and uneven across Europe. Nevertheless, with the waning of the Viking, Magyar (Hungarian), and Arab invasions around the 1000, Europe experienced a new creative energy.

Differences between the Early and the High Middle Ages

By comparing Europe before and after the year 1000, this year emerges as a watershed date between two contrasting periods of history. Before that time Western Civilization changed only

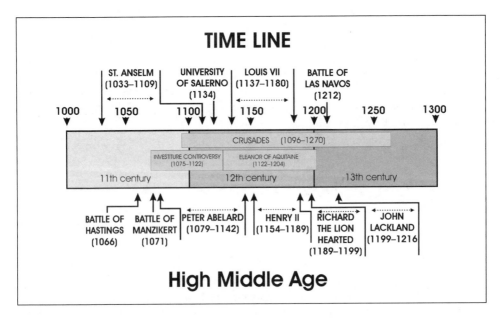

Figure 14.1

slowly, almost imperceptivity. Europe's population was small and its economy was overwhelmingly agricultural. Trade was almost non-existent and there no towns of any consequence anywhere outside of Italy. Governments were weak and unstable, art and literature were in a state of decay—few works were produced anywhere in Europe before 1000 can be called masterpieces.

But during the first decades of the 11th Century, change began to occur rapidly and on every level. Population, which had been declining since the late Roman Empire, began to increase. People cleared and settled new land, thereby extending Europe's settled and cultivated areas in every direction. Commerce began to revive, and the expansion of commercial wealth—as contrasted with landed wealth—sparked the beginning of the revival of urban life, for the first time since the death of the Roman Empire in the West. In the political sphere, rulers reorganized their governments in an effort to adapt the institutions of feudalism to the new environment. Philosophers became active for the first time since the demise of classical culture, and they began a penetrating examination of the Christian theology, and even the Church itself underwent a major internal reform. Finally, artists once again became productive, though still primarily in the service of the Church. From the beginning of this period called "The High Middle Age," European society showed signs of growth, both in its human population and in its geographic areas of settlement. Moreover, for the first time during the Middle Ages a small but growing number of people were now engaged in trade and commerce.

Population Islands

During the Early Middle Age, Europe's population was small and was distributed unevenly across the countryside. The people tended to concentrate into rural communities often separated from one another by vast stretches of wilderness. These are called "population islands" by demographers.[1] The evidence indicates that within these population islands there was some population pressure but no absolute growth of population during the Early Middle Age. Demographers have not been able to isolate all the factors responsible, but a number of complex causes can be discovered. The average size of the family in the 9th Century was small—fewer than five persons per family. Men significantly outnumber women. Female infanticide was practiced extensively and also many women died in childbirth and as result of the hard labors they had to perform. "Natural childbirth" has today become quite fashionable and many modern women seem to believe that there is something a little mystical about it. During the Middle Ages all women practiced natural childbirth and it didn't work very well. Perhaps as many as one of three women died during childbirth. In addition, just as indeed in many agricultural societies today, the most strenuous, the dirtiest, and the most dangerous work was reserved for the women. For various reasons, known and unknown, in stark contrast with the modern world, women did not survive well in the early Middle Ages.

Why did the people not spread out from these impacted settlements and clear new farms in the surrounding wilderness? Many factors were responsible: the restraints of feudalism; serfs were bound to the land on which they were born; and the strong bonds of kinship kept members of a family from splitting up. The institution of feudalism, in fact, could not accommodate an expanding population. Another important factor was the continuing barbarian invasions which made it necessary to find safety in the close settlements surrounding Medieval fortresses and castles. These invasions also promoted the traditional fear of the wilderness. Every family could relate stories of

---

1. Demography: the study of human populations especially with reference to size and density, distribution, and vital statistics

family members who had wandered out into the wilderness and never returned. Medieval mythology describes the terrible fire-breathing dragons which inhabited the wilderness and which have become a popular subject for modern movies and computer games.

However, during the early decades of the 11th Century the pattern of settlement began to change. Peasants began to move out of the old population islands and to open up new frontiers in the wilderness areas. What caused this change? Well, by the late 10th Century the invasions of the Vikings, Magyars, and Arabs were waning and the new security made the wilderness less intimidating. Landlords and princes began to encourage the settlement of the wilderness areas they controlled. They offered land—more accurately, the use of land—to new settlers under favorable terms and provided protection during the work of settlement. The motive for this "enlightened" policy on the part of the aristocracy was to increase their rents. The Church, which was now Europe's largest landlord and controlled more land even than the aristocracy, also sought to increase its revenues.

New Horizons

These changes imply that a new self-confidence was emerging among both the secular and the ecclesiastical leaders of Europe. Instead of merely reacting to the day-to-day events, as they did during the Early Middle Age, they now began to analyze their situation, evaluate their needs, and to act rationally in order to obtain them. This is the first evidence that the humanistic rationalism of classical antiquity was beginning to find its way back into the European mind. It was indeed a very small spark, and it would incubate for five more centuries before it exploded into the creative and humanistic activity of the Renaissance. But it is a beginning.

The opening of these new lands encouraged population growth. Children became an economic asset to families engaged in the hard work of clearing land. Women survived better than before—perhaps because of a decline in female infanticide, but certainly the work demanded of them did not become less. More land in cultivation meant more food. More food meant more people. During the 11th Century, for the first time since the fall of the western Roman Empire, Europe's population experienced substantial and sustained growth. All over Europe, in France, England, and Germany, the peasants leveled forests and drained marshes, in a movement similar in some ways to the frontier period of the United States.

In the low countries on the North Atlantic coast, in the delta of the Rhine and Meuse rivers, new land was claimed from the sea by building dikes and polders. Approximately half of modern Netherlands consists of land that is below sea level. Reclaiming this land from the sea began during the High Middle Age. Much of the area was inundated twice a day by the tides and even the higher areas were flooded on an irregular basis by the flooding of the rivers. The area was inhabited by the Frisians,[2] who lived by raising livestock and trade, since the cultivation of wheat for bread was impossible in the wetlands. Soon, the Frisians erected artificial hills, known as terps or warffs on which they built their farms and stables. Around 1000, they began to connect the terps by earthen walls, enclosing stretches of land which remained dry even when the area around was

---

2. The Frisians became part of the Roman Empire in 38 BCE, during the reign of the emperor Tiberius. During the Medieval migrations the Anglos and the Saxons settled among them and changed their culture significantly. In 734 the Frisians were defeated by the Franks at the Battle of the Boom River, but they continued to maintain their culture. They were coerced to convert to Christianity by Charlemagne, although earlier missionary activity by St. Wilfrid (678), St. Willibrord (690) and St. Bonifatius (754) had been unsuccessful.

inundated. These were the first dykes. As more dykes were built, windmills were constructed which used wind energy to pump the water out of the low-lying areas. Canals were dug to facilitate the outflow of water and to serve as waterways. This process required centuries of labor. Today the Dutch proudly say: "God created the earth. The Netherlanders created the Netherlands." The task of building dykes and digging canals required well-organized labor. In Medieval Frisia, every farmer had to contribute to the work: "He who does not want to work on the dyke has to leave." All low-lying areas had to be protected by dykes in all directions against the rivers and swamps. The dykes also served as lines of defense. Feudal armies did not feel comfortable marching through the marshes, because the canals were obstacles to horses even in times of peace, but during a battle the riders could easily be isolated. Not surprisingly, the low-lying parts of the Netherlands never became feudalized to any degree, and the majority of the population maintained their status as freemen.

German peasants and knights pushed eastward beyond the former borders of the Frankish Empire into territories which were thinly inhabited by Slavs, Prussians, and Lithuanians. For example, some Germans crossed the Elbe River and established the Principality of Brandenburg. Others advanced along the shores of the Baltic Sea. Still others pushed through the middle Danube valley and founded the principality of Austria. By the mid 13th Century this "drive to the East," as it is known, had more than tripled the area of German settlement over what it has been during the Carolingian period.

Settlers also began to move into the Iberian Peninsula, which had been overrun by the Muslims in the 8th Century. In the mid 11th Century, Christian kings, whose kingdoms were then confined to the extreme north Spain, began an offensive against the Muslims to liberate the peninsula. These kings actively recruited Christian settlers for the territories they re-conquered and gave them land under favorable terms. It was a long struggle, but Christian domination of the peninsula was confirmed in 1212 at the Battle of Las Navos de Tolosa, where the allied Christian army defeated and expelled the Muslim army back into North Africa. Thereafter, only the Principality of Granada in the south remained under Muslim rule. The Spanish frontier then remained almost unchanged for the next 280 years.

In Italy also the pioneers pushed the Christian frontier southward. Important to this effort were the Normans, a fascinating people who came out of Scandinavia in the 8th Century as perhaps the most savage, uncivilized group of all the barbarians and converted to Christianity in the early 10th Century. A group of them settled on the coast of France opposite Britain, in an area still known today as Normandy. The leader of this group, William the Conqueror, led them across the channel and conquered England in 1066. But the story of the Normans hardly ends there. During the 11th Century another group of Normans moved into the Mediterranean and began fighting against the Muslims who had earlier overrun Sicily and parts of southern Italy. By 1124, after a hundred years of fighting, they had driven both the Muslims and the Byzantines out of southern Italy and Sicily and established the Norman Kingdom of Naples and Sicily, sometimes known as The Kingdom of the Two Sicilies.

European influence moved into the Mediterranean as well. The early leaders of this expansion were the commercial cities of Pisa and Genoa in northwest Italy. In 1016, fleets from these two cities freed Sardinia from Islamic rule, and in 1115 a Christian army, carried by a fleet from Pisa, drove the Muslims from the Balearic Islands.

In some areas of Europe the growth in settlement began to shift the balance between the free and serf classes. This transformation was accelerated by the fact that in order to attract settlers onto previously uncultivated lands the landlords had to offer generous terms, often guaranteed by a written charter. Many landlords established free villages on their property. The peasant who settled in a free village paid only a small, fixed rent for the lands he cleared and was not, like the serf, required to labor for the landlord. Furthermore, he could leave the village whenever he wanted to and sell his interest in the land and his house at their market value. Most important, under feudal custom, a runaway serf who resided in a free village for one year and one day, without being claimed by his owner, was henceforth legally free.

For several reasons the conditions of the serfs also improved during the High Middle Age. Emancipation was considered a religiously pious act, and this was a period of religious enthusiasm. The increase in the population meant that landlords need not keep the entire labor force tied to the soil. But another factor contributed to the decline of serfdom: since the newly settled lands with their free villages strongly encouraged the serfs to desert their lords for a better life, only more humane treatment, not brute force, could hold the serfs on the lord's land. Also, the revival of trade enabled some serfs to sell their own produce on the open market and thus earn money with which to buy their freedom. Finally, serfdom was sometimes a hindrance to the landlord as well as the serf. Lords who wished to raise rents or to change the method of cultivation on their estates were blocked by the feudal customs which made the obligations of both serf and lord fixed and immutable. Feudalism had developed to meet the needs of a static society, not one in a state of change. In order for a landlord to free himself to reorganize his lands, he had to free the serfs. But this presented a problem: often the serfs viewed emancipation as eviction from the land that they had a right to occupy under the feudal contract. At times during the High Middle Ages there were even riots of serfs protesting their eviction. However, by the 13th Century serfdom had disappeared in large areas of France, Spain, Italy and western Germany, although some vestiges of it remained as late as the 18th Century.

The character of aristocratic life also changed during the High Middle Age. Most landlords now rented their lands to peasants (whose feudal obligations were thereby transformed into a payment of rent in lieu of forced labor) to cultivate, which means they become rent collectors instead of direct managers of the land. This new role freed the aristocrats to live away from home for extended periods. They could travel as pilgrims or crusaders to distant lands and spend a great deal of time mingling with their peers at the court of the king or one of the great nobles. This new freedom of the aristocracy promoted the growth of a courtly society which in turn produced a richer culture.

Life continued to be very hard for the peasant, of course. But there is evidence that life expectancy in the 13th Century increased to around 40 years. And although female infanticide declined, in the peasant village men still outnumbered women.

The Beginning of Trade

Europe from the 9th to the 12th centuries was still overwhelmingly rural and agricultural. By far the majority of the inhabitants of the period lived in the countryside. Towns of any size were still rare: before 1200 no town in Western Europe reached a population of 30,000. In the modern world, an urban center of 30,000 is thought of as a small village, but in the Middle Ages it was perceived as a mega-city.

The first revival of both trade and towns occurred in Italy—where, unlike the rest of Europe, the towns never completely disappeared. The leaders of Medieval commerce were the northern towns of Venice, Pisa, and Genoa. During the 10th and 11th centuries, the Venice was Europe's most powerful commercial and navel power. The Venetians obtained charters from the Byzantine emperors which gave them complete freedom of action in the Byzantine Empire, and by the end of Byzantine civilization the empire's economy was completely under the domination of the Venetians. During the 12th Century, Pisa and Genoa negotiated formal trade agreements with Islamic rulers which allowed them to establish trading posts in the Middle East and North Africa.

What types of items were involved in this trade? The East shipped to Europe a whole series of materials known under the generic name "spices"—the famous spice trade. These so-called spices included not only pepper, spices, and medicine, but also perfumes, dyes, ivory, precious stones, and rare metals. Manufactured items such as fine linens, brocades, and silk were also imported from the East. In exchange, Europe sent to the East mostly raw materials and agricultural materials, such as wood, iron, grain, wine, and other commodities. Wood, a by-product of clearing the wilderness, was almost like trash in Europe, but at the same time very valuable in the Near East. But by the late 12th Century, however, Europe began to export a few manufactured items as well, such as fine woolen cloth.

Medieval Towns

The first towns of Italy, then, were commercial centers. Elsewhere, however, towns developed around the administrative centers of the bishops, dukes, counts or other feudal lords. These administrative centers were originally nothing more than fortresses or walled enclosures into which the surrounding rural population could gather during periods of attack. In fact, the original meaning of the English word "borough" and the German word "burg" is fortress. In time, permanent colonies of merchants and craftsmen grew up around many of these fortresses to form the first Medieval towns.

As the merchants of the emerging cities became wealthier, they naturally sought to gain control of their own fate. The most serious problem they faced was the remoteness of the ruling nobles, who remained on their rural estates and led a lifestyle far removed from that of urban society. The feudal lords outside of Italy harbored nothing but contempt for the commercial activities of the urban merchants. Although these lords exercised oppressive powers of taxation and demands for military service, they offered the townspeople only awkward justice and careless protection of their commercial rights and property. Therefore, the wealthy commercial families of the towns banded together and obtained autonomy, and sometimes complete freedom, from the lords through various methods, including usurpation, purchase, and outright revolt. Some sites gained sovereignty which gave them the status of "free cities," although most achieved only autonomy, which gave community leaders the right to judge and tax themselves and manage their own affairs independently of the lord's interference.

As the urban population increased it also began to develop its own aristocracy, but the urban societies of Italy and the rest of Europe progressed in contrasting directions. The urban aristocracy of Italy included many nobles and great landlords who lived at least part of the year in the city and participated in its commercial activities. Many of the great commercial families of Italy had their origin in the landed aristocracy. In the north, however, the nobles kept to their rural estates and viewed with disdain the growing commercial wealth of the cities. Handling money seemed disgraceful and demeaning to them. Thus, the commercial aristocracy of the north had its origins in the lower classes—quite the opposite of Italy. This divergence in the composition of the urban societies of the two areas will play an important role in the flowering of the Renaissance during the 15th and 16th centuries.

Merchants and shopkeepers formed themselves into associations, known as guilds, to protect their economic interests. In the beginning these guilds were unspecialized. Most of the towns of

Figure 14.2: Illustration from the *Trés Riches Heures du Duc de Berry* (the Book of Hours of the Duke of Berry), painted between 1412 and 1416. Winter scene (February) shows peasant women warming their legs before a fireplace while outside peasants are occupied cutting wood, taking produce to market, etc.

the 12th Century still had only one guild, which included all craftsmen. Soon, however, these guilds began to multiply and to specialize in specific crafts, such as leatherwork, weaving, black-smithing, etc.

Perhaps the most distinctive feature of urban society, even at this early stage, was the lack of rigidity separating the classes. Vertical social mobility was easier in the city than in any other part of Medieval society, with the possible exception of the Church. The urban aristocracy constantly admitted new members. As individuals reached a certain level of wealth and power through commercial activity, they automatically became members of the urban upper class. Beginning in the 12th Century, then, these Medieval towns exerted a growing influence on the culture of the Middle Ages.

The Early Centralized Kingdom: France and England

The first stage on the long road from the decentralized feudal organization of Medieval Europe to the modern nation-state system was the emergence of centralized kingdoms out of the hodge-podge of feudal principalities, jurisdictions, and authorities into which Europe had disintegrated by the 9th Century. Although the same process of consolidation occurred, at uneven rates and with local variations, throughout Europe, the best examples of this process are France and England. To better understand the complex process, a review of the important events leading up to the High Middle Age is necessary.

France from 843 to 1204

After the death of Charlemagne's son, Louis the Pious, his empire was divided into three kingdoms by his three sons. This was accomplished by the Treaty of Verdun in 843 (see chapter 13). Charles the Bald became the king of an area that roughly encompassed modern France. But neither Charles nor his descendants were strong rulers and the kingdom soon dissolved into its constituent feudal units, each region developing its own unique cultural diversity.

The largest and most important of these regions were ruled by great nobles, who bore the title of Duke or Count. They were, in theory, the direct vassals of the king, but in practice they were independent rulers and maintained only a fictional loyalty to the king. These noble magnates developed their own systems of justice and even frequently engaged in warfare with one another. The king was powerless to intervene. In other words, the great nobles exhibited all the trappings of sovereign rulers.

The Capetian Dynasty

By the year 987, all the direct descendants of Charles the Bald had died out, leaving the throne of France vacant. Although the great nobles had no intention of yielding obedience to the king, the ideal of the Frankish kingdom still remained strong, so the nobles gathered and elected a new king. However, it was of prime importance to them to prevent the throne from falling into the possession of any one of their own members, because it would give that individual the advantage in the struggle for power and threaten the independence of all the nobles. In fact they wanted to keep the throne as weak as possible so that the king could not interfere with them. Thus, the man they chose as king was a certain Hugh Capet, who bore the title "Duke of the Franks," but was one of the weakest of the nobles. The name, Capet, which literally means "cape," was derived from the cloak that Hugh wore when he was abbot of St. Martin de Tours earlier in his life. The descendants of Hugh Capet held the French throne until 1792—though not always through the direct line.

Hugh Capet was elected king of France primarily because of his small possessions, which consisted only of the Ile-de-France ("Island of France"), i.e. the little town of Paris and the surrounding region, made him no threat to the independence of the great nobles. The Roman church immediately put pressure on him to submit to the imperial authority of the Holy Roman Emperor, which would have kept France, in theory at least, as part of the Holy Roman Empire. But Hugh Capet refused and his election symbolized the final demarcation, or separation, between France and Germany.

For the next century or so, the successors of Hugh Capet made no dramatic efforts to enlarge the royal power. Indeed, during this early period the Capetian dynasty's most important achievement was simply to transform the kingship from an elective to a hereditary office. This was accomplished by the good fortune of managing to produce heirs at the right moment and arranging for the new heir to be crowned before the old king died. They got away with it because the crown was not a rich enough prize to arouse the ambitions of the powerful nobles. By the time that the crown became truly important, the hereditary principle had already been firmly established.

During the next centuries, however, the Capetians completed three main tasks that brought all of France, either directly or indirectly under the king's control: (1) they mastered and pacified their own domain, the Il de France; (2) they brought additional territories under direct royal authority;

(3) and they made their overlordship of the tenants-in-chief real, rather than merely theoretical. They used no hard and fast formula to accomplish this. They had no master plan to consolidate their kingdom. Indeed their final success was due to a combination of ingenuity and just plain good luck. Unlike the German emperors, they almost always maintained rather good relations with the papacy and they did not pursue grandiose schemes or set unrealistic goals, which would attract the attention of the great nobles. They extended their power gradually through marriage, through the confiscation of fiefs when vassals died without heirs or when vassals violated their feudal obligations. Their strategy was to build a kingdom composed of a substantial core of royal domain, surrounded by loyal and obedient vassals. This took a great deal of time and patience, in fact, more than three centuries were required to transform France from a collection of feudal principalities into a centralized kingdom.

The first Capetian king to work seriously toward the consolidation of the Ile-de-France was Philip I (1060–1108), who was able to make some modest additions to the royal domain. His son, Louis VI, "the Fat" (1108–1137), pursued an even more vigorous policy. He successfully brought under his control the petty nobles of the Ile-de-France. They had been harassing travelers who sought to cross the royal lands by charging outlandish customs tolls. Louis the Fat promoted the colonization of forests and wastelands by establishing free villages. The economic growth thus achieved added to his resources. He staffed his growing administration with new men from the middle ranges of society, not members of the older, entrenched, and unreliable nobility. By the end of his reign, Louis the Fat had established effective control of the lands of the Ile-de-France, and this gave future kings a firm power base from which to operate.

But his son, Louis VII (1137–1180), could do little with this new power. In the words of a contemporary, he was "a very Christian king, but somewhat simple-minded." And Louis VII had to deal with a new and serious problem, the expansion of the so-called Angevin Empire of Henry Plantagenet, the Count of Anjou, who also became the Duke of Normandy and Aquitaine in France, as well as the king (Henry II) of England. This strange combination of titles means that Henry II, who was the sovereign of England was also, as Duke of Normandy and Aquitaine and Count of Anjou, the vassal of the King of France. Henry actually controlled more of France than Louis. This was a sure formula for trouble, since there was no possibility that one king will behave as a loyal vassal to another king.

Eleanor of Aquitaine (1122–1204)

Now one of the most formidable and interesting women of the entire Middle Ages—Eleanor of Aquitaine—moves onto the historical stage.[3] She was born in 1122, the eldest daughter and heiress of William X, Duke of Aquitaine. Because William had no sons, she was his heir and when he died in 1137, Eleanor became the Duchess of Aquitaine at the age of 15. In July of that same year she married Prince Louis, the heir apparent to the French throne. The marriage, of course, had been arranged by her father before his death. One month later, in August of 1137, her husband succeeded to the French throne as Louis VII and Eleanor became Queen of France. This would seem to be more than any young lady of 15 could wish for—but we shall see that Eleanor was no ordinary young lady.

From the political point of view, the marriage had great possibilities, but from the psychological point of view, the match had problems from the beginning. The union offered the possibility that

---

3. A 1968 movie, *The Lion in Winter*, directed by Anthony Harvey and starring Peter O'Toole as Henry II and Katharine Hepburn as Eleanor of Aquitaine, depicts a single episode (Christmas, 1183) in the life of Eleanor.

the large and wealthy duchy of Aquitaine could be added to the royal domain some day, but for the moment the two territories were merely juxtaposed and everything depended on how the king got on with his wife—and therein was the rub, for Louis and Eleanor were simply not compatible. While Louis VII was a man of sensitivity and piety, he was not particularly intellectual and Eleanor was simply more than he could cope with. She was one of the most educated people of her time, extremely well read, fluent in several languages, including Latin, yet she was sensual, coquettish, and full of amorous energy. And to make matters worse, Louis fell passionately in love with her, which gave her overwhelming influence over his policies.

Early in his reign, Louis VII got into trouble with the Church over the appointment of the bishops in the French church. This was uncharacteristic of the French monarchy, which normally maintained good relations with the Church. When Louis insisted on appointing a layman as Bishop of Bourges, Pope Innocent II excommunicated him. All the evidence indicates that Louis's religious policy at this time was decisively influenced by Eleanor. Although Louis was later able to get the excommunication lifted, in 1147, when the Second Crusade was proclaimed, Louis agreed to participate along with Conrad III, emperor of the Holy Roman Empire, in order to be completely reconciled with the Church. Eleanor, of course, insisted on going along to the Holy Land with him. In any event, it is doubtful if Louis would have left her alone in Paris, because of her amorous nature, to put it delicately.

Needless to say, Eleanor loved every minute of the two-year-long trip. She visited the colorful and exotic cities of Constantinople and Antioch, rich and wonderful beyond anything to be found in Europe. The sophisticated urban life of the East was so much more in tune with her personality than the primitive and damp castles of Europe. In 1148, while the royal couple were at Antioch, a scandal broke out concerning Eleanor's relations with her young uncle, Raymond of Poitiers, Prince of Antioch. Louis hastily packed his wife off to Jerusalem, but had to leave her alone there while he led his army in the siege of Damascus. While he was gone there is an unconfirmed rumor that Eleanor bestowed her favors on a handsome Moorish slave. Not all of the stories told about her are necessarily true, yet they are not only indicative of her personality but typical of the controversy which always surrounds a strong woman. Aristocratic men of the period also "slept around," of course, but their activities did not create the same kind of scandals as the such activities did for a woman.

Although the Second Crusade did not achieve all of its goals, Louis returned to France in 1148. About two years after their return, Eleanor gave birth to a second daughter, but this was a disappointment because it was a male heir that the king wanted. This led to increased friction between the royal couple. The lack of a male heir was far from being the only problem, however. Eleanor was as exasperated by Louis's piety as he was frustrated by Eleanor's amorous affairs. Louis managed to get a divorce in 1152 on grounds that the couple were too closely related. They were distant cousins.[4]

The Angevin Empire

This divorce was to bring Louis great misfortune and unimaginable humiliation, because as soon as she was free, Eleanor married Henry Plantagenet, the Count of Anjou, and the duchy of Aquitaine passed under his rule, as her husband. Henry was the son of Matilda, the daughter and heiress to

---

4. Of course, this was simply a pretext. Outright divorce was against Church law and had to be disguised as "annulment," a judicial pronouncement declaring a marriage invalid for some reason that rendered it legally non-existent. This means that any children born during the invalid union were technically illegitimate.

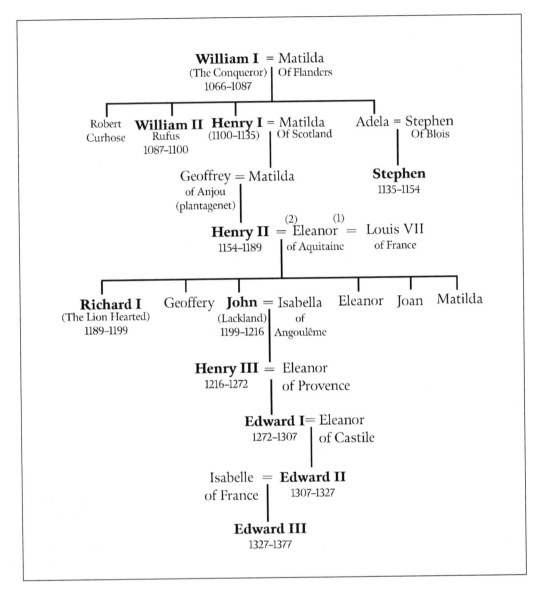

Figure 14.3: The Norman and Plantagenet kings (simplified).

King Henry I of England, the son of William the Conqueror (see Fig. 14.3). Thus, as a consequence of this marriage, Eleanor's second husband ruled not only England, but the entire western half of France as well, and although Henry was Louis's nominal vassal in France, he was immensely more powerful than Louis himself. What sweet revenge for Eleanor! And to rub salt into the wound, so to speak, Eleanor proceeded to bare Henry no less than five sons and three daughters. Three sons and all of the daughters survived into adulthood. Furthermore, this marriage initiated a 400 year long struggle between France and England that caused untold bloodshed and wasted the uncountable treasure of both kingdoms.

Although Eleanor's marriage to Henry was a great success politically, on a personal level it was not much more satisfactory than her marriage to Louis. Henry was about 20 years younger than Eleanor and, like all aristocrats, he liked to dally around with the young ladies of the court. Although Eleanor was known to amorous affairs from time to time, she not the type of woman to put up with such relationships involving her husband. Thus, when her three sons, Richard and Geoffrey and John, revolted in 1173, she did everything in her power to aid them. She was detained while trying to cross the English Channel to join them in France and was placed under house arrest for 16 years. Nevertheless she continued to hold the title of Queen of England and even appeared with the king at court on state occasions.

After Henry's death and the accession of her son, Richard the Lion Hearted, Eleanor enjoyed great prestige again and considerable influence over affairs of state. In fact, she ruled England in Richard's name for several years while he was away on the Third Crusade. In 1191, she joined him in Sicily to conduct his bride, Berengia of Navarre, so that they could be married there. She frustrated a plot by her other son, John Lackland, against Richard and later even reconciled the two brothers. But Richard is proof that one does not have to be intelligent to be king, and he stupidly attempted to return from the Second Crusade through Germany and was captured by Leopold V of Austria and held for ransom. Eleanor collected the money in a special tax on the English and paid for his release, which was not attained until 1194.[5]

When Richard died in 1199 from a wound received in a skirmish in France, Eleanor helped secure the succession for her other son John by putting down an uprising in Anjou which attempted place her grandson Author on the throne. Eleanor indeed wielded tremendous influence on the history of her age. Her own court at Poitiers was famous for its cultivation of chivalry and the patronage of troubadours.[6] The idea of romantic love first blossomed in France and England during her lifetime, leading many historians to believe that it was Eleanor who introduced this dangerous disease, which has been the curse of romantics to this very day. She is to thought to have brought it back from the East after her visit there during the Second Crusade. Eleanor's last years were spent at the Abby of Fontevrault, in France, where she died in 1204, at the age of 82. Her body was buried there beside the tombs of her husband, King Henry II, and her son, King Richard the Lion Hearted.

Anglo–Saxon England

England has already been discussed as part of the story of Eleanor of Aquitaine, but it is now appropriate to review England's history before this period. Early in the 5th Century, when the Roman legions were withdrawn from Britain, in a vain attempt to save the provinces of Western Europe, the island was almost immediately inundated by Jutes, Picts, Angels, and Saxons. Seven Anglo-Saxon kingdoms slowly emerged from this chaos and during the 6th and 7th centuries most of England was reconverted to Christianity.

---

5. While in captivity Richard wrote the following verse:

No one will tell me the cause of my sorrow
Why they have made me a prisoner here.
Wherefore with dolour I now make my moan;
Friends had I many but help have I none.
Shameful it is that they leave me to ransom,
To languish here two winters long.

6. A class of lyric poets and poet-musicians, often of knightly rank, who flourished from the 11th to the end of the 13th Century, chiefly in the south of France and the north of Italy and whose major theme was courtly love.

Danelaw

Then came yet other waves of barbarian invasions, first the Danes, later their cousins the Vikings. These new invasions were resisted by the Anglo-Saxon kings, led by the monarchs of Wessex, located in the southern end of the island. Finally, one of these Anglo-Saxons, Alfred the Great, defeated the Danes in 878 and forced the Peace of Wedmore on the invaders, under which the Danish king Guthrun became a Christian and divided England between himself and Alfred. The area under control of the Danes was called the "Danelaw." Alfred was given the name "Great" because of his efforts to spread Christianity, not so much for his military exploits. However, his son, Edward,[7] began the re-conquest of the Danelaw and this was completed by Alfred's grandson, Ethalstan. These were the first true kings of England.

But a new wave of invasions broke across England around 991. The collection of Danegeld, a kind of land tax, began to be collected by the English king Ethelred II and paid to the Vikings as tribute. The Danegeld tax was a symbol of humiliation and Ethelred lost all credibility with his subjects. Finally, in 1013, Sven, king of Denmark, was recognized by the English as their king and Ethelred fled across the channel to Normandy, the home of his wife, who was the daughter of the Duke of Normandy. Sven's son, Canute, became a kind of "emperor," on the model of Charlemagne, over a northern empire that included Denmark, Norway, and England. But his reign was short, his sons were incompetent, and his dynasty ended in 1042.

Thereupon, the most important of the tenants-in-chief of England, Godwin, Earl of Wessex, had Edward III, the Confessor, elected king of England. Edward was the son of Ethelred, who had fled to Normandy, and he had been raised in the Norman court. He was also married to the daughter of Godwin and very much under Godwin's influence. After Godwin's death his son Harold became the Earl of Wessex and continued to weld influence over the king. Unfortunately, during one of his trips along the coast of England, Harold was driven ashore in Normandy by a storm and fell into the hands of William, Duke of Normandy and cousin of Edward the Confessor, the King of England. William forced, or tricked, Harold into taking an oath promising to aid him to attain the crown of England, which he said Edward had promised him. Of course after his release Harold repudiated the oath because it was obtained under duress, but nevertheless it seems to have had a debilitating psychological effect on him.

Upon Edward's death, Harold was chosen king by the English noblemen,[8] but William led the Normans across the channel and defeated Harold at the Battle of Hastings on Oct 14, 1066. Thus, England became Norman. In the best feudal tradition, William divided England among his vassals, retaining about 1/6 of the total land under his direst control. He created about 170 tenants-in-chief and numerous sub-vassals. But unlike the feudal systems of Germany and France, William required a direct oath of primary vassalage to the crown from all vassals, high and low. In addition, a royal survey was conducted in order to record information regarding the size, resources, past and present ownership of every parcel of land in the kingdom. The results were recorded in the famous Domesday Book,[9] a unique record for taxation and administration. Nothing else like it exists on

---

7. This is King Edward the Elder, King of Wessex (899–924), not Edward I, the Plantagenet king of England (1272–1307)

8. It should be noted that neither of these men had a strong claim to the English throne by heredity: Harold II was elected king by the Anglo-Saxon nobles, while William claimed that Edward the Confessor, the legitimate king of England, had voluntarily granted him the crown.

9. The Domesday Book was commissioned in December of 1085 by William the Conqueror. The first draft was completed in August 1086 and contained 13,418 settlements in the English shires (counties) south of the rivers Ribble and Tees, the border with Scotland at that time. The Domesday Book can be viewed on the Internet at www.domesdaybook.co.uk/.

the continent. The Normans, however, did not destroy Anglo-Saxon culture, but settled down in England as a ruling elite. Norman Culture and language, itself a blend of French and Scandinavian, had a significant influence on Anglo-Saxon culture and language. The result of all this mixing is modern English.

William the Conqueror's Successors

The second Norman king, William II (William "Rufus"), the second son of William the Conqueror, reigned from 1087 to 1100. William II was a passionate, greedy ruffian. He was designated king by his father on his deathbed, while the eldest son, Robert, received Normandy, and Henry, the youngest, received cash. This was a compromise between the new custom of primogeniture and the old Germanic custom of dividing the estate equally between all the sons. William ruled England with a strong hand and aroused hatred of all sections of society, particularly the church, for which he had utter contempt. He extracted huge sums of money from the church through the sale of church appointments and by leaving high offices vacant so that their revenues would flow to him. Although he appointed St. Anselm to the archbishopric of Canterbury in 1093, he soon quarreled with him over the question of investiture and finally sent him into exile in 1097. William II was killed by an arrow while on a hunting party in 1100, and there is strong evidence that his death was no accident.[10] The English throne was immediately seized by his younger brother, Henry.

Henry I (1100–1135)

Henry was the youngest son of William the Conqueror. He used the conflicts of his elder brothers, Robert Duke of Normandy and William Rufus, to his own advantage by changing sides when it was in his interests. This displeased his brothers, and even though they were rivals, neither wanted Henry to become King of England or Duke of Normandy. To ensure this, they signed a treaty at Caen stating that if either of them died without producing an heir, they would be succeeded by the other.

However, the death of William Rufus came just at the right time for Henry to claim the English throne for himself. Duke Robert was returning from the first Crusade and was not in a position to oppose Henry's claim to the throne. When the news of William's "accidental" death in the New Forest reached him, Henry hurried to Winchester to demand the keys to the royal crown and other royal treasures. The treasurer William De Bretevil at first refused to admit him, reminding Henry of the treaty signed in Cean by his elder brothers Robert and William Rufus, but under threat of death, the treasurer handed over the keys. On 5th of August, 1100, only three days after his brother's death, Henry was crowned at Westminster Abbey.

Henry's first problem was the threat of invasion by his brother Robert from Normandy, and the last thing he needed was distractions in the north of England, and so on 11 November, 1100, Henry married Matilda of Scotland, the daughter of Malcolm III, king of the Scots. When Robert returned from the Crusades he began his plans to invade England and landed an army at Portsmouth in July, 1101, but was unable was make any headway and a treaty was signed allowing Henry to remain as king of England as long as he paid Robert an annual fee for the privilege.

---

10. In a sense, this event can be interpreted as a message that the English people will repeatedly send to their monarch until the monarchy finally understands. The message is simply this: unlike the French, the English people will never tolerate tyranny and the abuse of their human rights for very long. Indeed, no English speaking people on earth have ever accepted dictatorship or tyranny for any appreciable length of time.

In 1105 Henry invaded Normandy. His aim was to remove his brother whose incompetent rule was bringing Normandy under threat of invasion from its neighbors. It wasn't until September 1106 at the battle of Tinchebrai that Henry finally defeated Robert, who was captured and spent the remainder of his life in prison. For the rest of his reign, Henry not only had to guard his English lands from invasion but also Normandy as well.

Henry's plans for a united realm of England and Normandy by marrying his son William Audelin to the daughter of Count Fulk of Anjou, came to grief in 1120. While attempting what should have been an easy crossing of the channel, William's ship ran aground and the prince was drowned. Henry was a widower[11] and although he remarried after the death of William, he had no more children. Henry only had one other legitimate child, Matilda. Matilda had been married at the age of eight to Henry V, the German Emperor, but he died in 1126, and Matilda returned to her father's side. Concerned that he had no male heir, Henry asked the Barons to agree that Matilda should become queen after his death. He then married Matilda to Geoffrey of Anjou.

Dynastic Crisis

When Henry died in 1135 the control of his kingdom was in dispute and it lead to civil war. The problem was that Henry I had a sister, Adela. She had married Stephen, the count of Blois and she had a son, Stephen. His father, the Count, was killed on Crusade, and Stephen was looked after by his uncle, the King of England. The king bestowed a great deal of land on Stephen and he soon became extremely wealthy and powerful. In 1125 Stephen married Matilda, who was next in line to inherit the lands around Boulogne. This gave Stephen control of a major port on the Channel and control over trade between the two countries.

When King Henry I died, the claimant to the throne was his daughter, Matilda. Although it had been agreed that Matilda would rule with her husband, the Count of Anjou, the Barons neither wanted a female ruler nor a ruler from Anjou. The decision was taken that Stephen's elder brother Theobald should become ruler, but Stephen crossed to England and was crowned at Westminster on 22nd December, 1135. Matilda, now married to the Count of Anjou, was away from England at the time of her father's death, but she was not prepared to accept Stephen as king. Not all of the Barons were happy with their new king and a few were willing to support Matilda's claim. Robert, Earl of Gloucester, an illegitimate son of Henry I and step-brother to Matilda, was in a good position to claim the throne himself. Being illegitimate had not stopped William the Conqueror. But Robert was happy to assist Matilda in her cause and in May of 1138, Robert declared his allegiance to Matilda.

In February of 1141, Stephen laid siege to Lincoln Castle, owned by the Earl of Chester. A relief force lead by Robert captured Stephen and moved him to Bristol where he was held. In April Matilda was elected Queen and moved to London for her coronation, but the London citizens disapproved and of her drove out before she could be crowned. Stephen's wife sent an army to assist her husband who was still a captive and during a siege Robert, Earl of Gloucester was captured. The captives, Stephen and Robert, were exchanged and Stephen resumed his position as King.

---

11. His first wife, Matilda of Scotland, died in 1118. She was remembered as one of the strong women of the Middle Ages, in the tradition of the later Eleanor of Aquitaine. Her marriage to Henry in 1100 provided him with a politically desirable link to Matilda's ancestor Alfred the Great. Her life makes clear that she possessed outstanding talents. She was educated in the convents of Romsey and Wilton. She was an active partner in the administration of Henry's cross-channel realm, served as a member of his *curia regis* and on occasion acted with vice-regal authority in England while Henry was in Normandy.

Figure 14.4: Illustration from the *Trés Riches Heures du Duc de Berry* (the Book of Hours of the Duke of Berry), painted between 1412 and 1416. Harvest scene (June) shows peasants mowing a meadow with the Hotel de Nesle, the duke's Parisian residence, in the background.

Matilda and Robert, escaped capture and moved to the West where Robert's forces were in control. Stephen was unable to force Matilda out and the country was effectively split down the middle. In 1147 Robert Earl of Gloucester died, however, depriving Matilda one of her most powerful allies. This was a major blow to Matilda and in the following year she returned to Normandy never to see England again.

But her cause was not lost. Matilda had a son also named Henry, who as the grandson of Henry I had an excellent claim to the throne. In 1147 and 1149, he attempted to invade England to drive Stephen out, but both attempts failed and Henry returned to Normandy where he concentrated on building up his future power. In 1151 Henry inherited both the County of Anjou and the Duchy of Normandy giving him huge resources and power. In 1153 Henry again invaded England in an attempt to get Stephen's agreement that he should become king after Stephen's death. Stephen wanted his own son Eustace to become king, but in that same year Eustace died and Stephen reluctantly agreed to Henry's wishes. Thus, the dynastic crisis was resolved and Stephen lived out the rest of his life as King of England, and after his death in October of 1154, Henry was crowned king, as Henry II.

Henry II (1154–1189)

Thus, in 1154, Henry Plantagenet became Henry II , the master of a hybrid empire that included England, Normandy, Anjou, Maine, and Lorraine by inheritance; Poitou, Aquitaine, and Gascony by marriage to Eleanor of Aquitaine and Brittany; Wales, Ireland, and Scotland by a loose feudal bond. The story of how this occurred has been related above in the context of the life of Eleanor of Aquitaine. This so-called Angevin Empire dwarfed the modest territory controlled by the king of France. But Henry II and his successors experienced difficulties in maintaining order throughout these heterogeneous territories. The French territories were a source of power and prestige to the English monarchy, but also a grave burden. Not until the end of the Hundred Years War in 1453, when England lost its last foothold in France, was the English monarchy finally free to devote its full efforts to the governing of England. This latter period of English history will be treated in the next chapter.

The Crusades (1096–1270)

The Crusades are grossly misunderstood in today's politically correct world. Muslim propaganda has almost completely succeeded in picturing the Crusades as an atrocious and unprovoked aggression on the part of the Christian West against a peaceful and innocent Islamic East. As usual, the truth is not so simple or one sided.

First, exactly what were the Crusades? They were a series of eight official, and several unofficial, military expeditions from Western Europe against the Muslims in the Near East, which occurred between 1096 and 1270. The stated purpose was to recover the Holy Land from the Muslims, but in fact there were probably as many motives for going on a crusade as there were individual crusaders. In order to understand how something so utterly improbable and fantastic could occur, we need to look in some detail at the state of affairs in both Western Europe and in the Byzantine Empire to the east on the eve of the Crusades.

Europe before the Crusades

Western Europe in the late 11th Century consisted of a number of loosely knit feudal states, which were just beginning the process of developing into centralized kingdoms—the first step on the road to modern nationhood. Europe had suffered through some dark times, but on the whole, things were beginning to look a little brighter.

In northern Europe the so-called Holy Roman Empire was anything but an empire in the traditional sense of the word. In theory, at least, the emperor was the sovereign ruler of a vast area which included most of north-central Europe and northern Italy, but in practice, most emperors had little or no authority outside of their feudal domain, which at this time was the Duchy of Swabia. In fact, the Holy Roman Empire in the 11th Century had almost completely dissolved into its constituent feudal components. It reality the Empire was made up of a hodgepodge of principalities, duchies, counties, free cities, and bishoprics, numbering well over 1,000 states, which were independent and sovereign in everything but name.

As for France, during this period, as we have seen, it was still a divided kingdom. Although the French king, who ruled from Paris, had theoretical sovereignty over most of what is modern France, he was in fact much less powerful than many of his own chief vassals, and the English king actually ruled the western half of France as a kind of fictional vassal to the French king. England, now under Norman rule, was much more unified than France, but was in some ways still a weaker power than many of the mainland duchies.

During the 11th Century, Spain was in the process of being re-conquered from the Muslims who had overrun the Iberian peninsula back in the 8th Century. The area that had so far been re-taken was divided between four kingdoms: Leon-Castile, Navarre, Aragon, and Catalonia.

Italy was nothing like the nation state we are familiar with today. In the late 11th Century Italy was divided into numerous principalities: some of them were independent; others were, at least in theory, part of the Holy Roman Empire; several states in the central part of the peninsula were ruled directly by the pope; and still others were part of the Norman Kingdom of the Two Sicilies, itself only a very loosely unified feudal state.

So, the political map of Europe on the eve of the Crusades was both similar to and different from the map of modern Europe. Actually, the political structure of 11th Century Europe was a kind of skeleton of the modern European state system, which was only beginning to take shape. But on the whole, things in Europe were beginning to look up again after the long period of decline during the Early Middle Age: the population was growing; for the first time in many centuries there was a surplus of food and energy beyond what was necessary for mere survival; the people were beginning to look outward again, to take an interest in what might be happening beyond the narrow confines of their own village, beyond the horizons of their own particular valley. The people of Europe, in fact, during the 11th Century were beginning to awake from that long sleep, which used to be called the "Dark Age."

The Byzantine Empire on the Eve of the Crusades

But out in the East, the ancient Byzantine Empire was in deep trouble. Yet, in the late 11th Century, what was left of Byzantium was still by far the most civilized and culturally advanced portion of Christendom. Back in the 9th Century, what had once been the eastern half of the Roman Empire had consolidated itself into a more or less homogeneous Greek state. It permanently lost Egypt and Syria to Arab aggression and much of the northern Balkans was overrun by various Slavic tribes. What remained of Byzantium by the 9th Century was the rich hinterland of Anatolia—or Asia Minor—plus the Greek homeland. This empire was ruled by a line of emperors who traced their origins back to Augustus, back to the ancient Republic of Rome, back even to Romulus. Indeed, they traced their cultural heritage back to the classical Greece of Homer. And the capital of this empire was the jewel of the Medieval world, the great fortress city of Constantinople.

The contrast between the Eastern Empire and Western Europe was immense. It is difficult for us today to really conceive of how truly vast these differences were between the two Christian worlds. Picture, on the one hand, the sophisticated, worldly urbanite, shopping in the bustling markets of Constantinople, or attending the chariot races in the huge hippodrome, and on the other hand, the culturally deprived surf, working in the turnip fields or huddled in the wretched farming villages of Western Europe. There was an enormous difference separating them; indeed, a distance not only of space, but a distance of time and of spirit and of cultural legacy. The inhabitant of the Byzantine Empire could trace his heritage directly back to Rome and Athens, back even to the Troy of Homer. But the peasant living in the wretched village of Western Europe could hardly remember his grandfather's name. It is not surprising, then, that the Medieval European and the Byzantine never really understood or trusted one another. Nor is it really surprising that, in the long run, the fall of the Byzantine Empire, that richest and most civilized part of the Christian world, was due perhaps as much to the barbaric greed and treachery of the Western Christians as to the savagery of the invading Turks. In 1204, as we shall see, the Christian knights of the 4th Crusade captured and sacked Constantinople with such brutal ferocity that it never recovered from the damage, and was thus a far easier target for the Islamic Turks than it would have otherwise been.

The Byzantine Empire had almost succumbed to the Arabs back in the 8th Century, but after staving off that disaster, had pulled itself together and then suddenly in the 9th Century exploded into what was probably the most brilliant and glorious period of its history. Under the first 7 emperors of the great Macedonian dynasty,[12] the period from 867–1025, the imperial Byzantine armies pushed the empire's frontier eastward to the banks of the Euphrates, throwing the Muslims temporarily on the defensive, and eastward through the Balkans, annexing Bulgaria and Dalmatia, and even establishing a small province in Italy as a refuge for the Orthodox Christians driven out of Sicily by the Arabs.

But alas, the Macedonian dynasty eventually declined, then died out, and the Byzantine Empire declined along with it. During the heady days of prosperity, the over development of the imperial bureaucracy stifled initiative and disabled the empire's defenses. Whole armies were disbanded in order to obtain money to pay the civilian bureaucrats. Then, when external danger again threatened, in the form of the invading Turks from the East, mercenaries had to be hired for the empire's defense, which were even more expensive than the old citizen army and much less dependable.

Finally, in 1071, at the Battle of Manzikert, north of Lake Van, the Seljuk Turks annulated the Byzantine army and captured the emperor (Romanus IV Diogenes). Even though this battle, in itself, was not the end of Byzantium, most historians consider it to be one of the pivotal events in the history of the Byzantine Civilization, that ranks in importance with the Battle of Salamis, for example. This defeat so crippled Byzantium that it could never again offer effective or sustained resistance to the advance of the Islamic Turks. And indeed, once Byzantium was gone, Christian Greece and the Balkans would soon fall under Turkish domination as well. In fact the advance of the Turks was not checked until they reached the outskirts of Vienna in central Europe. But the Byzantine Empire had recovered before and probably could have recovered again after the defeat at Manzikert, with a little assistance from the West. But the Western Christians did not understand, did not appreciate the invaluable contribution of Byzantium to the security of western Europe. The empire had, in fact, protected Europe from the Muslim advance for many centuries.

Thus, on the eve of the crusades, Constantinople was hard pressed. The present emperor, Alexius I (1081–1118), was in desperate need of soldiers for the defense of the empire against the Muslim Turks. Many of the mercenaries he had in his army were Turks themselves and were not really very dependable for warfare against their own kinsmen. Alexius, perhaps a bit naively, believed that Christians from the West would be more dependable and he attempted to recruit mercenaries from Western Europe. He wrote to Robert, Count of Flanders, in 1089 and the Count promised

---

12. There is much controversy concerning the origin of Basil I, the founder of the Macedonian dynasty. While Greek sources speak of the Armenian or Macedonian extraction of Basil I, and Armenian sources assert that he was pure Armenian, while Arabic sources call him a Slav. On the one hand, the generally accepted name "Macedonian" is applied to this dynasty, but on the other hand, some scholars still consider Basil an Armenian, and still others, especially Russian historians prior to the late nineteenth century, speak of him as a Slav. However, the majority of modern scholars consider Basil an Armenian who had settled in Macedonia, and speak of his dynasty as the Armenian dynasty. In recent years scholars have succeeded in determining that Basil was born in the Macedonian city of Charioupolis, but his life previous to his succession was very unusual. As an unknown youth he came to Constantinople to seek his fortune, and there attracted the attention of the imperial court because of his tall stature, his enormous strength, and his ability to break in even the wildest horses. The emperor Michael III took him into his confidence, became completely subject to Basil and soon proclaimed him co-ruler. Basil repaid the emperors favors in a most brutal way. When he noticed that Michael was becoming suspicious of him, he ordered his men to slay his benefactor, and then proclaimed himself sole emperor (867–86).

to send 500 Flemish knights. And with this same object in mind, he corresponded with Pope Urban II (1088–1099). Indeed Alexius did desperately need soldiers from the West, but he expected to hire them individually and to integrate them into his own army. He had no idea, even in his worst nightmares, that great hordes of what appeared to the Byzantines to be little more than semi-barbarians would stream out of Western Europe and materialize before the walls of Constantinople. With the Turks already breathing down his neck, another foreign army on imperial territory was the last thing in this world that Alexis needed.

Dieu Io Volt! ("God wills it!")

The first calls for help from Constantinople after the Battle of Manzikert, reached a Europe already caught up in a fever pitch of religious fanaticism. The re-conquest of Spain by the Christians had just gained its initial successes and the Spanish Christians now held between one fifth and one quarter of the Iberian peninsula. The Spanish Christians imitated, probably unconsciously, the Muslim *jihad*, or holy war, with its doctrine that the highest morality is to die fighting on behalf of God. The simple fact is, the Christian ruling class in Western Europe had never learned to do anything very well except to fight. This was the legacy of the long series of foreign invasions that had washed across Europe during the Early Middle Age.

The papacy had watched the progress of the *reconquista*, as the Spanish holy war was called, with intense interest and had come to believe that the Church's interests could be served by a general imitation of this war on other fronts. The doctrinal question of a holy war and the shedding of blood on behalf of the Christian religion was not a problem for the popes of this period—and anyway, most Europeans viewed the continuing struggle against the Muslims as a defensive effort against a long string of aggressions from the East. True, early Christianity had exhibited strong pacifist tendencies, but that was before Church leaders had gained the power to use force. Once the Church had that power, its use was quickly justified.

When the first appeals for help from Constantinople reached Western Europe in the years immediately after the Battle of Manzikert (1071), Pope Gregory VII was locked in his bitter struggle with Henry IV, emperor of the Holy Roman Empire (see above). If Gregory had not been preoccupied with Henry he undoubtedly would have turned Alexius's plight to the papacy's advantage, but the continuation of the investiture controversy precluded Gregory from organizing an expedition. The launching of the First Crusade was the work of another pope—no less ambitious than Gregory VII. This was Pope Urban II, who occupied the papal throne between 1088 and 1099. In addition to the obvious motive of regaining the Holy Land for Christianity, Pope Urban had at least four other important goals in mind: first to unite the Catholic Church after the bitter and divisive disputes between Gregory VII and Henry IV; second, to increase papal authority in general; third, to work toward ending the separation of the Western and the Eastern churches; and finally, his last goal was a bit more subtle. The increasing population in Western Europe and the adoption of primogeniture had produced a large number of landless knights. These were usually the younger sons of aristocrats who were left out when the oldest son inherited the father's title and estate. This situation had created a large number of knights who were, in effect, unemployed. Since these knights had limited opportunity for conquest at home, Urban quite rightly saw in these restless, out of work knights a reservoir of manpower for foreign ventures. He believed that if he could tap their military skills and energies for a foreign venture it would lead to a more peaceful Europe by draining off manpower available for domestic wars.

The pope planned his proclamation of a crusade with great care. He summoned a council of bishops and abbots at Clermont in central France in 1095 and he urged the attending clergymen to bring with them the prominent secular lords of their provinces. At the council, Urban made a highly emotional appeal to "the race of the Franks" to join in a crusade to the Holy Lands. His speech was one of the most skillful and effective examples of rhetoric in all of European history.[13]

He touched on every motive, both religious and worldly, that a French knight might have for taking up the cross. Urban painted a grim picture of the sufferings of Christian pilgrims in the Holy Lands at the hands of the Turks. He mentioned the imminent danger to Byzantium of the Muslim aggression. He reminded the French knights of their reputation for courage and piety and called upon them to rescue the Holy Sepulchre from the infidels. He offered his listeners the prospect of carving out kingdoms for themselves in Palestine, a land, he said, is "flowing with milk and honey." He promised papal protection for the property and family of any crusader during his absence from home. And finally, because the pope is the keeper of the keys of the kingdom of heaven, he promised all crusaders an indulgence from their sins.[14] This meant that when the crusader died, he could go directly to heaven and not have to stop off in purgatory like other Christians to suffer for the sins they committed on earth.

The People's Crusade (1096)

The response to Urban's speech was overwhelming, as evidenced by the cries of "*Dieu Io Volt!*" ("God wills it!") from the audience. This became the war cry of the First Crusade. After the speech, Bishop Adhémar of Le Puy handed out crosses made of cloth that were sewn onto the clothes of those who vowed to take part in the crusade. However, immediately following the council of Clermont, even before the military units could be formed, an incredible thing happened. A popular preacher, named Peter the Hermit, began preaching a crusade in central and northern France, creating unprecedented enthusiasm wherever he went. He journeyed about the countryside on the back of a decrepit old mule, clad only in a hermit's robe, and bearing a crucifix in his hand. And everywhere he went he was greeted with the cry, "God wills it! God wills it!" The result of this little bit of insanity was the so-called "People's Crusade." It was not at all what Pope Urban had in mind. Peter the Hermit led a motley and undisciplined multitude of 40,000 men, many of them

---

13. There are no records of exactly what Pope Urban said, but we have an account of the chronicler Fulcher of Chartres, who was present and heard him. Here is an excerpt from his *History of the Expedition to Jerusalem*:

> . . . For your brethren who live in the east are in urgent need of your help, and you must hasten to give them the aid which has often been promised them. For, as most of you have heard, the Turks and Arabs have attacked them and conquered the territory of the Romans as far west as the shore of the Mediterranean and the Hellespont. They have occupied more and more lands of those Christians and have overcome them in seven battles. . . On this account I, or rather the Lord, beseech you as Christ's heralds to publish this everywhere and to persuade all people of whatever rank, foot-soldiers and knights, poor and rich, to carry aid promptly to those Christians and to destroy that vile race from the lands of our friends.

Thatcher, Oliver J. and McNeal, Edgar Holmes, *A Source Book of Medieval History* (1905), Charles Scribner's Sons, New York, p. 513.

14. This inducement of indulgence had a certain similarity to the Muslim doctrine that a warrior who died fighting for the faith proceeds directly into paradise. The practice was to be abused in later centuries. By the 12th Century, the Church was awarding indulgencies for vicarious crusading-that is, for supporting crusaders through monetary assistance. In other words, the person did not actually have to go on a crusade himself, but could simply sponsor someone else. By the 14th Century the papacy was selling indulgences outright, without even a crusading pretext. This abuse will be one of the factors leading to Martin Luther's reformation in the 16th Century.

runaway serfs armed with nothing more than pitch forks, through Eastern Europe toward Constantinople. There were no plans, everything was trusted to God. They lived off the countryside and they indulged in the wildest excess of plunder and pillage. They repeatedly had to be restrained by armed force. Their progress through Eastern Europe left a wide path of destruction and suffering. Probably about half of them died of hunger and exposure before the ragged hoard reached Constantinople. The emperor of the Byzantine Empire looked down from the walls of Constantinople at this hoard of beggars and immediately gave directions to his navy to transport them across the Bosporus into Asia Minor, where the Turkish army and Turkish bandits slaughtered them without mercy and they disappeared from history. Thus ended the "People's Crusade." It all unfolded, undoubtedly, just as God willed it.

The First Crusade (1096–1099)

The first official crusade consisted of no less than four armies from Germany, France, and the Norman Kingdom of Sicily, which rendezvoused at Constantinople in 1096. The total force was about 30,000 men, including about 5,000 cavalry. This first crusade was a loose alliance between feudal nobles, mostly French, rather than a compact army. There were too many leaders involved to name them all here, but the two most important were both named Godfrey—Godfrey of Bouillon and Godfrey of Lorraine.

Of course, this was not at all what the Alexius, the Byzantine emperor, had in mind when he asked for help from the West. To the Byzantines, this crusading army was nothing more than another semi-barbarian hoard that had to be dealt with. For centuries, the Byzantine emperors had dealt with barbarian peoples who invaded their territory and they had learned that they could not employ the rules of civilized diplomacy with them, but had to make use of the barbarians' own customs. And that is what happened now. Even though Byzantium was not a feudal society and did not observe feudal customs, Alexius demanded that all the crusaders take a feudal oath of allegiance to him and pledge to restore to him all captured towns and territories which had formerly belonged to the Byzantine Empire. In return, the emperor promised financial assistance. The crusaders agreed. It should be noted that any territory the crusaders were likely to enter in the Near East had at one time belonged to Byzantines, because they considered themselves Romans.

In the spring of 1097 the crusaders were ferried across the Bosporus by the Byzantine navy and gained a series of stunning victories over the Turks. Their first target was Nicaea, which had fallen to the Turks ten years earlier and was now the capital of the Turkish state of Rhüm. After a two month siege, aided by Byzantine troops and the Byzantine navy, the city fell to the crusaders and was returned to Byzantine sovereignty, but the emperor would not allow the crusaders to pillage the city, a move that caused bitterness between the Byzantines and the crusaders. The crusaders soon headed across Anatolia toward Antioch. The army was not equipped to deal with the lack of water and the freezing cold it encountered crossing the mountains, which prompted a diversionary movement that resulted in the capture of Edessa, a Christian Armenian kingdom that stretched from the coastal plain of Cilicia all the way to the Euphrates River. The possession of Edessa, deep within Muslim territory, provided the crusaders with a secure base for further campaigns.

The siege of Antioch began in October of 1097. The city was strongly defended and was famous for never having fallen except through treachery. It was so large that the crusaders could not fully surround it and settled down to blockade the main gates. The siege dragged on through the winter of 1098 and the crusaders ran short of food and supplies. Many died of starvation and disease, many more fled home. The crusaders sent out forging expeditions, one of which ran into Muslim relief force and in the ensuing battle did sufficient damage to the Turks to cause them to abandon their relief attempt. The defense of Antioch was under the command of the Armenian Firouz, who had converted to Islam. He now negotiated with the crusaders and allowed them to enter Antioch, just before another even stronger Muslim army arrived. Now the crusaders themselves were besieged behind the walls of Antioch and there seemed no hope of survival.

However, now a "miracle" occurred. A Provençal peasant named Peter Bartholomew, claimed that Christ and St. Andrew had appeared to him in a vision and told him the lance that had pierced the side of Christ was buried beneath the alter of the Church of St. Peter. The peasant was allowed to supervise the digging and duly found the lance. The crusader leaders knew Peter to be a fraud, but the foot soldiers believed that a miracle had occurred and this caused their morale to surge. The commanders took advantage of this to launch a desperate attempt to break the siege. The morale of the Muslim troops was at this point as low as the crusaders morale was high, and they broke under the fierce attack and the crusaders were triumphant. Antioch was not returned to Byzantine control.

With the major regional power destroyed, the journey south to Jerusalem was uneventful. Jerusalem, however, was strongly fortified. The Muslim governor, Iftihar ad-Daula, had expelled the Christians living there and desolated the surrounding countryside to make it impossible for the crusaders to live off the land. His garrison of Arab and Nubian troops far outnumbered the crusaders and there was an Egyptian army on its way. The Crusaders set up their positions along the northern and western walls and began to construct siege equipment. Before these preparations were complete, however, one of the many mystics that permeated the army persuaded the leaders to attempt an assault. God, he said, would not fail them. The attack wasa disaster.

The crusader army now settled down to the business of conducting a traditional siege. The entire army, encamped before the walls of Jerusalem, were now caught up in spiritual fever with miracles, portents, and signs occurring daily. In one of these, the dead Bishop Adhémar appeared before a priest, Peter Desiderius, and told him that the crusaders must humble themselves before they would be allowed to enter Jerusalem. The leaders were convinced and organized a fantastic procession. Lead by priests chanting and holding their sacred relics before them, the entire army marched in slow, solemn procession barefoot around Jerusalem. Six days later the final assault began. The night before the attack Godfrey of Bouillon and Robert of Normandy stealthily moved their forces to an undefended part of the wall. It was from their positions that, after more than a day of continuous fighting, the crusaders forced their way into the holy city on July 15, 1099.

There followed several days of wild pillage and terrible carnage. The crusaders raged through the streets of Jerusalem, killing everyone they came upon. Thousands of Muslims, Jews, and even Christians of both sexes and of all ages were put to the sword by the crusading soldiers of the cross—almost as a kind of sacrifice to God. Not everyone was killed. Some were made captive and used as laborers to cart the bodies out of the city. But eventually, the sack of Jerusalem ran its course—either because the soldiers became tired or because they ran out of victims—and order was restored to the city. With that, most of the crusaders visited the tomb of Christ, packed their loot, and returned home.[15]

---

15. Two views of the capture of Jerusalem:

Excerpt from Ibn Al-Athir, quoted in *Arab Historians of the Crusades-Selected and Translated from the Arabic Sources*, translated from the Arabic by Francesco Gabrieli and from the Italian by E. J. Costello (1969) University of California Press, Berkeley

The Crusader States

But a few of the more adventurous crusaders remained and established four principalities: Jerusalem, Tripoli, Antioch, and Edessa. These states did not become ecclesiastical states as Pope Urban II had intended, but feudal states on the European model. Indeed, the second ruler of Jerusalem had himself crowned King Balwin I. In all four of these states a feudal hierarchy of fief holders made up the governing class. But unlike the feudal states in Europe, this hierarchy was a small minority governing a large heterogeneous native population. During the course of the 12th Century, the crusaders who settled in the Holy Land developed a distinct culture. In certain superficial respects, such as dress and food, this cultural became orientalized. A few crusaders even learned to speak Arabic. In military tactics and castle construction, much was borrowed from the Byzantines and the Muslims. War with the surrounding Muslims was the general rule, but it was frequently interrupted by periods of truce, and the crusaders learned to ally themselves with friendly Muslim rulers and take advantage of the divisions and rivalries between the surrounding Muslim states. When not fighting, Muslims and crusaders were often quite friendly neighbors.

Yet, in the fundamental aspects of life, such as religion and language, the crusaders remained European. Documents and correspondence, for example, were always written in Latin and, al-

---

After their vain attempt to take Acre by siege, the Franks moved on to Jerusalem and besieged it for more than six weeks. They built two towers, one of which, near Sion, the Muslims burnt down, killing everyone inside it. It had scarcely ceased to burn before a messenger arrived to ask for help and to bring the news that the other side of the city had fallen. In fact Jerusalem was taken from the north on the morning of Friday 22 sha'ban 492 [15 July 1099]. The population was put to the sword by the Franks, who pillaged the area for a week. A band of Muslims barricaded themselves into the Tower of David and fought on for several days. They were granted their lives in return for surrendering. The Franks honored their word, and the group left by night for Ascalon. In the Masjid al-Aqsa [mosque near the summit of the city] the Franks slaughtered more than 70,000 people, among them a large number of Imams and Muslim scholars, devout and ascetic men who had left their homelands to live lives of pious seclusion in the Holy Place. The Franks stripped the Dome of the Rock [the mosque built on the rock located in the ruins of the ancient Jewish temple from which Mohammed was believed to have ascended to heaven] of more than forty silver candelabra, each of them weighing 3,600 drams, and a great silver lamp weighing forty-four Syrian pounds, as well as a hundred and fifty smaller silver candelabra and more than twenty gold ones, and a great deal more booty. Refugees from Syria reached Baghdad in Ramadan, among them the qadi Abu l-Muzaffar al-Harawi. They told the Caliph's ministers a story that wrung their hearts and brought tears to their eyes. On Friday they went to the Cathedral Mosque and begged for help, weeping so that their hearers wept with them as they described the sufferings of the Muslims in that Holy City: the men killed, the women and children taken prisoner, the homes pillaged. Because of the terrible hardships they had suffered, they were allowed to break the fast.

Excerpt from Raymond D'Aguilers: *Historia Francorum Qui Ceprint Jerusalem*, translated by John H. Hill, Laurita L. Hill.

Now that our men had possession of the walls and towers, wonderful sights were to be seen. Some of our men (and this was merciful) cut off the heads of their enemies; others shot them with arrows, so that they fell from the towers; others tortured them longer by casting them into the flames. Piles of heads, hands and feet were to be seen in the streets of the city. It was necessary to pick one's way over the bodies of men and horses. But these were small matters compared with what happened in the Temple of Solomon, a place where religious services are normally chanted. What happened there? If I tell the truth, you would not believe it. Suffice to say that, in the Temple and Porch of Solomon, men rode in blood up to their knees and bridle reins. Indeed, it was a just and splendid judgment of God that this place should be filled with the blood of the unbelievers, since it had suffered so long from their blasphemies. The city was filled with corpses and blood.

though the crusader states were not formally attached to any European power, they were in every other respect European colonies. It is easy to think of the crusades as a kind of dress rehearsal for the age of modern colonialism.

The Second Crusade (1147–1149)

The Second Crusade was occasioned by the fall of Edessa to the Muslim king Zengi in 1147 and was preached by St. Bernard of Clairvaux at the urging of Pope Eugenius III. A formidable expedition, led by King Louis VII and Queen Eleanor of France and Emperor Conrad III of Germany, marched overland to Constantinople. Conrad's army arrived at Constantinople first, but relations with the Byzantine emperor Manuel I were not good and the Germans were convinced to cross Asia Minor and march toward Edessa without waiting for the French. Conrad split his army into two divisions; one was destroyed by the Turks in October of 1147, the other was massacred early in 1148.

Relations between the emperor and the French were somewhat better, but Manuel refused to help them with his own troops and had them swear to return to the empire any territory they captured. The French joined the remnants of Conrad's army at Nicaea but suffered a heavy defeat in 1148, just as the Germans had. The remains of both armies managed to get to Syria by sea and attack Damascus. The siege of Damascus began in July of 1148 but ended in failure in less than a week. Conrad and Louis returned home, although as noted earlier, Eleanor thoroughly enjoyed the entire trip, so perhaps the project was not a total loss.

The Second Crusade was, in fact, a double failure, because Europe became temporarily dismayed and the whole crusading idea was temporarily discredited, whereas the Muslims, who had braced themselves to meet what seemed like a major threat, were encouraged by the outcome. In fact, the Muslims now went over to the offensive. In 1187 the city of Jerusalem fell and within two years most of the kingdom was also lost.

The Third Crusade (1189–1192)

Europe was disturbed by these events and something of the former crusading spirit was revived, which occasioned the Third Crusade. But once again, there was no unified command and this caused the project to be much less successful than it could have been. This crusade, amazingly, was made up of three separate armies under three separate commanders: King Philip Augustus of France; Emperor Fredrick Barbarossa of Germany; and King Richard the Lion Hearted of England.

The Third Crusade began in 1189 as an attempt to reconquer the Holy Land from Saladin. Egypt after 1169 was ruled by the powerful Seljuk Turks, whose great champion Saladin made it his life's mission to drive the Christian power from Palestine. Control of both Egypt and Syria allowed Saladin to surround the Crusader kingdom; on July 4, 1189 Saladin won the Battle of Hattin, and on October 2 Jerusalem surrendered. Thereafter, Christian power was restricted to Antioch, Triople, Tyre, and Margat.

Pope Gregory VIII wished to enlist the help of the kings of England and France to take back what had been lost; in response, Henry II of England and Philip II of France ended their war with each other, and both imposed a "Saladin Tithe" on their subjects to pay for a new Crusade. However, Henry died in 1189 and the leadership of the English contingent fell to his son, Richard the Lion Hearted.

Frederick I Barbarossa, emperor of the Holy Roman Empire, also responded to the Pope's call, and was the first to depart in 1189. Frederick faced opposition from the Byzantine Emperor Isaac II, who had made a secret treaty with Saladin. Frederick passed through Byzantine land as quickly as possible, and captured the Seljuk capital of Iconium on May 18, 1189. Unfortunately for his crusade, the emperor drowned in the Saleph River on June 10, 1190.[16] Although the German army was larger than Saladin's, without his leadership his troops immediately began to break up, and those who remained were quickly defeated in battle when they reached Syria.

Richard and Philip travelled by sea. They rondevoued and spent the winter in Sicily, where they engaged in constant quarraling and in the spring of 1191, each king embarked seperately for the Holy Land. On the way, Richard stopped at Cyprus, where he took offense at his treatment by the independent Byzantine ruler of the island. By the end of May, he had conquered the whole island, which he later sold to Guy of Lusignan, the nominal King of Jerusalem. Meanwhile, Philip had arrived at Tyre and allied himself with Conrad of Montferrat, who also claimed the kingship of Jerusalem. The two besieged Acre in April, 1191, with help from the remnants of Frederick's army, and Richard arrived to take charge of the siege in June. Saladin's army attempted unsuccessfully to break the siege, and the city was taken on July 12. The three Christian commanders now fought for power among themselves; Leopold of Austria, the German commander, wanted to be recognized equally with Richard and Philip, but Richard removed Leopold's banner from the city. Philip, also frustrated with Richard, left the Holy Land in August.

On August 22, Richard executed the 3,000 Muslim prisoners he still had in his custody at Acre, because he felt Saladin was not honoring the terms of Acre's surrender. Richard then decided to take the port of Jaffa, which he would need to launch an attack on Jerusalem. While on the march, Saladin attacked him at Arsuf, but Richard won a resounding victory. By January of 1192, Richard was ready to march on Jerusalem, but Saladin had reinforced his army and fortified the city. Richard came within sight of Jerusalem twice, but each time retreated in the face of Saladin's larger army. Saladin then attempted to retake Jaffa in July, but was defeated by Richard's now much smaller force. In September of 1192, Richard and Saladin finalized a treaty by which Jerusalem would remain under Muslim control, but which also allowed unarmed Christian pilgrims to visit the city. Richard left for England at the end of September, ending the Third Crusade.[17] The failure of the Third Crusade to recapture Jerusalem would also lead to the call for the Fourth Crusade six years later.

---

16. Barbarossa fell off his horse while crossing the river, dressed in his full metal armor, and sank to the bottom of the river, never to be seen again.

17. The Germans who remained in the Holy Land after the Third Crusade formed the basis of the Teutonic Knights, a crusading order of knights under Roman Catholic religious vows which was formed at the end of the 12th Century in Palestine to give medical aid to pilgrims to the holy places. They received Papal orders for crusades to take and hold Jerusalem for Christianity. They were based at Acre.
Christian military orders also had appeared following the First Crusade. The foundation of the Templars in 1120 provided the first in a series of tightly organised military forces which protected the Christian colonies in the Middle East, as well as fighting non-Christians in Spain and Eastern Europe. The principle feature of the military order is the combination of military and religious ways of life. Some of them like the Knights of St. John and the Knights of St. Thomas also cared for the sick and poor. However, they were not purely male institutions as nuns could attach themselves to a convent of the orders. One significant feature of the military orders is that clerical brothers could be, and indeed often were, subordinate to non-ordained brethren.
The role and function of the military orders has sometimes been obscured by the concentration on their military exploits in Syria, Palestine, Prussia, and Livonia. In fact they had extensive holdings and staff throughout Western Europe. The majority were laymen. They provided a conduit for cultural and technical innovation, for example the introduction of fulling (a step of clothmaking involving the process of beating, rolling, and pressing hair into a compact mass of even consistancy) into England by the Knights of St. John, or the banking facilities of the Templars. Joseph von Hammer in 1818 compared the Christian military orders, in particular the Templars, with certain Islamic models such as the Shiite sect of Assassins. In 1820 Jose Antonio Conde suggested they were modelled on the ribay, a fortified religious institution which brought together a religious way of life with fighting the enemies of Islam. However popular such views may have become, others have criticized this view suggesting there were no

Dates of the Crusades

Peasant (Peoples's) Crusade	1096
First Crusade	1096–1099
Second Crusade	1147–1149
Third Crusade	1189–1192
Fourth Crusade	1202–1204
Children's Crusade	1212
Fifth Crusade	1218–1221
Sixth Crusade	1228–1229
Seventh Crusade	1248–1254
Eighth Crusade	1270

Figure 14.5

The Fourth Crusade (1202–1204)

The Fourth Crusade was preached by Pope Innocent III (1198–1216), with the objective of attacking Egypt, whose rulers now controlled all the territory around the crusader states in Palestine. However, this expedition never reached Egypt, but instead turned against the Byzantine Empire. After the failure of the Third Crusade, there was little interest in Europe for another one and indeed the Fourth Crusade was the last of the major crusades to be directed by the Papacy, because the Popes were losing much of their power to the Holy Roman Empire and other European monarchies. The later crusades were all directed by secular rulers, and Papacy even lost control the Fourth.

In 1198, Pope Innocent III called for a new Crusade, which was largely ignored among European leaders. The Germans were struggling against Papal power, and England and France were still engaged in warfare against each other. However, due to the preaching of Fulk of Neuilly,[18] a crusading army was finally organized at a tournament held at Ecry by Count Thibaud of Champagne in 1199. Thibaud was elected leader, but he died in 1200 and was replaced by an Italian count, Boniface of Montferrat. Boniface and the other leaders sent envoys to Venice, Genoa, and other city-states to negotiate a contract for transportation to Egypt, the object of their crusade. Genoa was uninterested but Venice agreed to transport 30,000 crusaders, a very ambitious number.

---

such ribats around Palestine until after the military orders had been founded. Thus, the Muslim military organizations may be imitations of the Christian orders. In any event, the innovation of fighting monks was something new to Christianity.

18. A famous French preacher whose sermons and alleged miracles gave him a popular following in Northern France. Pope Innocent III appointed him to preach the Fourth Crusade. Tremendous crowds come to hear him, but he lost his credibility when the suspicion spread that he had misused some funds he had collected. Unscrupulous evangelists, it seems, have been a part of Christian culture from the beginning of its history.

By 1201 the crusader army was collected at Venice, though with far fewer troops than expected. The Venetians, under the aged and possibly blind doge[19] Enrico Dandolo, would not let the crusaders leave without being paid the full amount agreed to originally, but the crusaders could only pay half, and only by reducing themselves to extreme poverty. The Venetians barricaded them on the island of Lido until they could decide what to do with them.

At this point Dandolo and the Venetians succeeded in turning the crusading movement to their own purposes. Dandolo, who made a very public show of joining the crusade during a ceremony in the church of San Marco di Venezia, had the fleet instead attack the Hungarian port of Zaraa, a former Venetian possession on the coast of Dalmatia. The King of Hungary was a Catholic and had himself "taken the cross," meaning he too had agreed to join the crusade. Many of the crusaders were opposed to this, and some, including a force led by the elder Simon de Montfort, refused to participate altogether and returned home. The citizens of Zara made reference to the fact that they were fellow Catholics by hanging banners marked with crosses from their windows and the walls of the city, but nevertheless the city fell after a brief siege. Both the Venetians and the crusaders were immediately excommunicated for this by Innocent III.

Boniface, meanwhile, had left the fleet before it sailed from Venice, and had visited his cousin Philip of Swabia. The reasons for his visit are a matter of debate; he may have realized the Venetians' plans and left to avoid excommunication, or he may have wanted to meet with Alexius Angelus, Philip's brother-in-law and the son of the recently deposed Byzantine emperor Isaac II. Alexius had fled to Philip when his father was overthrown in 1195, but it is unknown whether or not Boniface knew he was at Philip's court. In any case, Alexius offered to pay off the Crusaders' debt to Venice, if they would restore his family to the Byzantine throne, an offer Boniface found difficult to refuse. Boniface may also have had in mind the former land holdings of his brother Conrad of Montferrat, who had married a daughter of emperor Manuel I but had been driven out of the empire around 1190. Alexius returned with Boniface to rejoin the fleet at Corfu after it sailed from Zara, and the Venetians, when they learned of Alexius's idea, were particularly pleased with it. They also had been personally offended by the Byzantines in recent years, as thousands of Europeans (including many Venetians) had been killed in riots against their merchant communities in Constantinople in 1182.

The Crusaders were still reluctant to attack fellow Christians, but the clergy accompaning the expedition convinced them that the Orthodox Byzantines were almost as bad as the Muslims: they had allied with Saladin against the Third Crusade, and had done nothing to aid the Second Crusade and they should be punished for their lack of support. Unfortunately, Alexius Angelus had overstated his importance and it was quickly discovered when the crusaders arrived at the walls of Constantinople that the citizens preferred a usurper to an emperor supported by the hated "Latins." The crusaders and Venetians decided to place Alexius on the throne by force, and an amphibious assault was launched on the city in 1203. Unexpectedly, emperor Alexius III panicked and fled, and the citizens of Constantinople reluctantly welcomed Alexius Angelus back into the city. He was crowned emperor as Alexius IV, and his father Isaac II was restored as co-emperor.

The crusaders were opposed to Isaac, as they had never met him and did not believe he was part of their deal with Alexius, but the Byzantines did not want Alexius, who was just as unknown

---

19. Doge: the chief magistrate in the republics of Venice and Genoa.

to them, to rule by himself. Isaac soon realized that Alexius's promises were impossible to keep, and Alexius was forced to abrogate his promise to pay the Venetians as the imperial treasury was empty. Alexius also had to deal with the growing hatred by the citizens of Constantinople for the "Latins" in their midst. Factions opposed to the Latins frequently attacked any crusader they could find, and Alexius had to tell his allies to leave and set up camp on the other side of the Golden Horn. Nevertheless, there was still fighting in the city, and during an attack by the crusaders on a mosque (which they were shocked to find in the Christian city), a large part of Constantinople was burned down. Opposition to Alexius IV grew, and one of his courtiers, Alexius Ducas Murtzuphlos, soon overthrew him and had him strangled to death. Alexius Ducas took the throne himself as Alexius V; Isaac died soon afterwards, probably naturally.

The Crusaders and Venetians, incensed at the murder of their supposed patron, attacked the city once more in 1204. Alexius V, who had a much larger army, although it was much more poorly trained, marched his troops outside Constantinople and seemed to prepare for an all-out assault on the crusader force. As the crusaders panicked and armed everyone they could find, including cooks who wore their pots as helmets, Alexius V turned around and marched his army back into the city. It is possible that his foot soldiers were afraid of the western knights, who had defeated them earlier in the year in skirmishes outside the city, but the actual reason for Alexius's refusal to fight is unknown. Although Innocent III had again warned them not to attack, the papal letter was suppressed by the clergy on the scene, and the crusaders prepared for their own attack, while the Venetians attacked from the sea; Alexius's army stayed in the city to fight, but Alexius himself fled during the night.

The crusaders were eventually able to knock holes in the walls, large enough for a few knights at a time to crawl through; the Venetians were also successful at scaling the walls from the sea. The crusaders, while attempting to defend themselves with a wall of fire, ended up burning down even more of the city than they had during their first attack. Eventually, the crusaders were victorious and inflicted a horrible and savage sacking on Constantinople for three days, during which many ancient works of art were stolen or destroyed.

According to a pre-arranged treaty, the empire was apportioned between Venice and the Crusade's leaders, and the Latin Empire at Constantinople was established. Boniface was not elected as the new emperor, although the citizens seemed to consider him as such; the Venetians thought he had too many connections with the former empire because of his brother's land holdings, and instead placed Baldwin of Flanders on the throne. Boniface went on to found the Kingdom of Thessalonica, a vassal state of the new Latin Empire. Meanwhile, Byzantine refugees founded their own successor states, the most notable of these being the Empire of Nicaea under Theodore Lascaris and the Despotate of Epirus. It was not until 1261 that the Byzantines finally recovered their city and put an end to this infamous fiasco.

The Children's Crusade (1212)

In the year 1212 an incident occurred that simply could not be believed, except that it is well documented as a historical event. In that year, two young boys about 12 or 13 years old, Stephen, a peasant boy in France, and Nicholas, a peasant boy in Germany, began to preach a Children's Crusade.

Not a great deal is known about the Children's Crusade other than it was a major disaster. The person who seemed to be in charge was a boy called Stephen of Cloyes. He was a shepherd and in 1212 he was 12 years of age. With a peasant's background, he would not have been able to read or write and at his age he would have done very basic work around a farm. In May 1212, he turned up at the court of King Philip of France and told him that he had a letter from Christ ordering him to organize a crusade. Not surprisingly, King Philip was not impressed by the 12 year old and told him to go away and come back when he was older. But Stephen went around preaching to other children about his letter from Jesus and his desire to go to the Holy Land to capture Jerusalem. He told his followers that crossing the Mediterranean or any other waterways was easy as the waters would part and they would walk across because they were protected by God. By June, Stephen is said to have gathered 30,000 followers around him, all children.

As they marched south through France, they clearly had no idea of what to expect. Adults cheered them along the route. It was believed that their innocence would make their success a certainty. The Church was not so sure. The Children's Crusade was never officially endorsed by the pope but neither did he stop it. It is possible that the Church believed that the actions of the children might shame kings and emperors into getting a real crusade going to capture Jerusalem.

Of course the Children's Crusade was doomed to failure. Many of the children had never walked such distances before and the journey from Vendome to Marseilles caused many children to drop out and even die of exhaustion. The sea did not part as Stephen had promised and they had to cross the Mediterranean Sea by boat. Amazingly, the children boarded seven boats in Marseilles and that was the last anything was heard of them. However, many years later a priest returned from traveling around northern Africa and claimed to have met some of the surviving children, now adults. He said that two of the seven ships had sunk killing all on board and that pirates had captured the other five ships and sold the children into slavery. White skinned children were considered to be a valuable prize in Algerian and Egyptian slave markets.

The German Children's Crusade also took place in 1212. This was led by a boy named Nicholas, and he had about 20,000 followers. His dream was exactly the same as Stephen's—take Jerusalem for Christianity. This crusade also included religious men and unmarried women so it was not fully a Children's Crusade. Their journey south from Germany to Italy included a very dangerous crossing of the Alps and many died of the cold. Those that survived pushed on to Rome. Here, they met the pope. He praised their bravery but told them that they were too young to take on such a venture. With this, some of them returned to Germany but few of them survived the journey back. Many stopped off at the Italian port of Pisa and boarded ships for the Holy Land. No one knows for sure what happened to them, but they were probably sold into slavery.

Fifty thousand children sacrificed like animals on an altar! Why did their parents allow this to happen? Why did the Church not stop it? Where was the voice of reason? It is something that can only be explained as the product of religious fanaticism and uncontrolled crowd hysteria. But that is really no explanation at all.

The Later Crusades

Pope Innocent III spent most of his papacy preaching a Crusade. When he began, he was trying to mobilize an expedition to recover Jerusalem in the wake of the failure of the Third Crusade. Henry VI's crusade had died with him. The Fourth Crusade had gone woefully wrong. After that, Innocent was preoccupied with the Albigensians[20] and preached a Crusade against them.

---

20. A Catharistic sect of southern France flourishing primarily in the 12th and 13th centuries. It is difficult to form any precise idea of the Albigensian doctrines, as all the existing knowledge of them is derived from their opponents, and the few texts from the Albigenses contain very little information concerning their beliefs and moral practices. What is certain is that they formed an anti-sacerdotal party in opposition to the Roman Church, and raised a continued protest against the corruption of the clergy. The Albigensian theologians, called *Cathari* or *perfecti* were few in number; the mass of believers were not initiated into the doctrine at all-they were freed from all moral prohibition and all religious obligation, on condition that they promised by an act called *convenenza* to become "hereticized" by receiving the *consolamentum*, the baptism of the Spirit, before their death.

He also preached a Crusade in Spain. He called for yet another one at the Fourth Lateran Council in 1215, but by then he was at the end of his years and he died in 1216 without seeing the results.

Three days after Innocent's death, a new pope was elected as Honorius III. He immediately took up where Innocent had left off, writing letters to the monarchs of Europe. Few answered the call, and those who did sent only very small armies. Response was better among the French and German barons, and the Frisians agreed to provide a fleet. The Crusaders were to assemble in Italy in 1217 and set out from there, but the Frisians were late arriving, and the army had to wait out the winter.

A portion of the army sailed in April, 1218 and arrived in Acre with most of the leaders. There they decided that the best course of action would be to attack Egypt. King John of Jerusalem knew perfectly well that there was no point in attacking Jerusalem as long as Egypt was strong, whereas with Egypt under Latin control, then the Muslims could not hold Jerusalem for very long. The great wealth of Egypt must also have been an attraction.

The Fifth Crusade did manage to capture the fortress of Damietta in the Nile Delta in 1219, but due to poor leadership it was soon badly defeated and had to withdraw. A striking and bizarre episode of the Fifth Crusade was the appearance in Egypt of St. Francis of Assisi. This saint of peace, who supposedly could talk to the birds, appeared on the bloody battlefield, preached to the soldiers and then visited the Sultan of Egypt, who received him with courteous respect but, of course, did not allow him to preach.

The Sixth Crusade was the work of the emperor Fredrick II. He took the crusader vow in 1215 when he was still a youth, but as he grew older he must have thought better of it because he repeatedly gained delays by pleading illness. Finally, in 1227 he embarked, only to fall ill again and have to return. For this he was excommunicated by the pope. But then he set out on his crusade without obtaining a reconciliation with the Church. Thus, the Sixth Crusade was led by a man under excommunication. Little better than an infidel himself in the eyes of the Church! He reached the Holy Land and managed to negotiate a treaty which turned over Nazareth, Bethlehem, and Jerusalem to the Christians. Fredrick entered Jerusalem in 1229 and had himself crowned king. This act, of course, automatically brought the holy city of Jerusalem under the pope's interdict! Fifteen years later Jerusalem was sacked by the Turks and a few months after that it was again under the control of Egypt.

Before the final demise of the crusader states in 1291, there were two more official crusades, both conducted by King Louis IX of France, but neither of them accomplished much. In fact Louis himself died during the Eighth Crusade (1270). But the crusading idea died hard. Even after the fall of the last crusader state in 1291, various projects were elaborated and some expeditions actually set out. The papacy never ceased urging. Long after Europe had forgotten about the Muslim danger, the crusading idea remained. It was even in the minds of the Portuguese and the Spanish explorers when they struck off toward the new World. And of course, the first English settlers to reach North America are still today called pilgrims. And it all began with that stirring speech of Pope Urban II at Clermont in 1095. Surely, no speech in the annals of Western Civilization has had a greater effect on history.

The Birth of the University

The reorganization of the cultural and intellectual life of Western Europe during the 11th and 12th centuries was so far reaching that it still affects many aspects of our life today. The most important of these changes were the products of the new urban lifestyle which was now beginning to emerge in the medieval towns, and this is yet another demonstration that cities are central, indeed indispensable, to the process of civilization itself. During this period of change a new institution assumed the leading role in the intellectual life of Western Society, a role it has maintained to this day. This institution was the university and it ranks as one of the most important contributions of the Middle Ages to the society in which we live today.

The Bishop's School

Up to about 1050, that is to the beginning of the High Middle Age, monastic schools dominated the educational and intellectual life of Western Europe. But the monastic devotion to prayer, asceticism, and mystical meditation was not really favorable to original thought, and the isolation of the monasteries restricted the experience of the scholar and made it difficult to exchange ideas, a process which is essential to intellectual progress. During the first decades of the 11th Century, however, the growth of Medieval towns brought about a decline in the importance of the old monastic schools, which had played such an critical role in the preservation of culture during the dark days of the Early Middle Age. Now, the bishop's school, sometimes called the cathedral school, assumed the intellectual leadership of Europe. The cathedral center was originally not a town at all, but simply the residence and administrative headquarters of a bishop, in much the same way that a castle was the residence of a great secular lord. The urban revolution of the 11th and 12th centuries resulted from the permanent settlement of merchants and craftsmen around these castles and cathedral centers to form the first Medieval towns.

Traditionally, bishops had been obliged to provide for the education of their own clergy, but the disappearance of urban life and the sheer chaos of the Early Middle Age, produced by the barbarian invasions, had prevented these schools from assuming a prominent role in the cultural life of western Europe. From the late 11th Century, however, four major factors served to stimulate and revitalize the cathedral school: (1) the growth of Medieval town, which provided facilities for classes; (2) the Gregorian church reforms, which emphasized the value of an educated clergy; (3) the shock of the investiture controversy, which led to an inquiry into the ancient relationship between church and state; (4) and finally, the craving for knowledge resulting from the more intimate contact with non-Christian cultures and ideas produced by the crusades.

Structure of the Early University

The cathedral schools were at first so fluid and flexible that they seemed to have no structure at all. It was not really an organized school in the modern sense of the term. The special officer of the cathedral, known as the *scolasticus*, was in charge of the school. He simply invited learned men, called "masters," who possessed specialized knowledge, to lecture to the students who had gathered at the cathedral center to pursue their love of learning. From that point, both students and masters made their own arrangements with each other.

The students very early formed themselves into guilds. This student organization is the direct ancestor of the student union which operates in all modern institutions of higher learning today. In the first universities the student guilds hired and paid the masters. In other words it was the students, not the faculty, that ran the early cathedral school, and students insisted on getting their money's worth. For example, many guilds had a rule that if the professor did not speak fast enough he would be not be considered cost effective and would be dismissed. The famous law school at Bologna in Italy even had a rule that the professors must obtain permission from the students before going out of town!

Figure 14.6: Lecture in a Medieval university. Notice the similarities to a modern classroom: most students pay close attention, but a few carry on private conversations while one takes a nap.

The interesting life of the young students at these early universities is painted for us by the letters, songs, and verses they left behind. Most of this literature is concerned with wine, women, and song, not the pleasures of seeking knowledge. Many of the letters are obviously model letters, analogous to modern form letter, composed for a fee by the masters of rhetoric for students not yet sufficiently elegant to write their own letters. For example, a student wrote home from Oxford:

> This is to inform you that I am studying at Oxford with the greatest diligence, but the matter of money stands in the way of my progress, as it is now two months since I spent the last of what you sent me. The city is expensive and makes many demands; I have to rent lodgings, buy necessities and provide for many other things I cannot here specify. Wherefore I respectfully beg you that by the promptings of divine pity you may assist me, so that I can complete what I have so well begun. For you must know that without Ceres and Bacchus, Apollo grows cold.

No doubt this letter was quite impressive to the student's parents—especially the last sentence, since they probably had no inkling of its meaning. If the student can send home a letter that the parent cannot understand, then he is obviously getting an education!

Another aspect of student life in the Medieval universities that seems familiar to us today was the disputes between the students and permanent residents of the towns where the schools were located. Often resentment developed between the students and the townspeople because the student's clerical status gave them immunity from local police and courts. The permanent residents could only appeal to the bishops for redress of their complaints, which often, then as today, seemed to be of little concern to the school authorities. This resentment sometimes broke out into riots and violent protests, another feature of university life that is all too familiar today. Eventually, however, the Church sought to impose a minimum order on the academic chaos of the early schools and to protect innocent young students from incompetent teachers (actually the Church was more concerned with unorthodox than incompetent teachers), the 12th Century schools gradually began to insist that that masters possess a certification of their expertise, called *licentia docendi,* a "license to teach," which was awarded by the cathedral scholasticus. This certificate of competency is the ancestor of the modern university degree.

By the late 12th Century these universities were distinguished from lesser schools by three major factors: (1) they drew students from great distances, not just the surrounding districts; (2) their teachers were specialists in one specific subject, not teachers of all subjects as in the elementary schools; (3) and they offered degrees in both general and more advanced specialized curricula. Basically, the Medieval university offered a program of instruction in the "seven liberal arts." These subjects were astronomy, geometry, arithmetic, music, grammar, rhetoric, and dialectic. The university also offered advanced programs in one or more of the called the "higher disciplines": theology, law, and medicine. This basic division between undergraduate and graduate studies still exists in the university today.

In the Medieval university, completion of the liberal arts curriculum allowed the student to apply for the license to teach, but most students continued their education by specializing in one of the graduate fields of study, medicine, theology, or law, which consisted of two independent subfields: civil law and canon (church) law. Then, as today, the most popular branch of study was law, because it promised a lucrative career in the royal government or with the Church.

Thus, the Medieval university was both similar and different from the modern institution of higher learning. When one hears the word "university," the first image that comes to mind is of a permanent campus with stately buildings, an established infrastructure and a stable, well organized administration and faculty. Actually, the Medieval university was none of those things. It was a guild, or privileged corporation of teachers and students, which operated under the patronage of a bishop. Its classes were held in rented rooms and it was thus a highly mobile institution. On more than one occasion, when the members of a university were dissatisfied with local conditions, they won concessions from the townspeople simply by threatening to move elsewhere. On occasion these threats were actually carried out. Cambridge University, which is the second oldest university in England, was founded by a group of students from Oxford, which is the oldest one, when they became so incensed with poor conditions at Oxford that they moved to Cambridge and obtained the sponsorship of another bishop.

By the 14th Century universities were flourishing at Bologna (founded 1088), Paris (1150), Oxford (1167), Naples (1224), Cambridge (1281), and Montpellier (1289). Within a century, others followed at Prague (1348), Krakow (1364), Vienna (1365), Heidelberg (1385), and Cologne (1388). Some of these universities, such as those at Paris and Cambridge, were now dominated by the guilds of their liberal arts faculties, while others, like Bologna, were still governed by their student guilds. The student guild at Bologna managed to reduce the local price of food and lodgings by threatening to move to another town. Bologna was a graduate school specializing in the study of law, and its students, who had already completed their undergraduate liberal arts programs, were determined to secure the training necessary to pursue successful careers in law.

Graduate Studies

From the 13th Century onward, the graduate schools of Europe began to turn out the leading intellectuals, secular and ecclesiastical bureaucrats, and pioneering scientists and physicians. A brief survey of these programs is in order.

Medicine

The chief medical school of Medieval Europe was the University of Salerno in southern Italy. When the Roman Empire in the West disappeared, the public health care system fell by default to the church. By the 6th Century, a network of ecclesiastic hospitals were established in southern Italy. A Church-controlled medical school to provide doctors for these hospitals appeared around 900 at Salerno, south of Naples. However, Pope Leo IX, as part of his reforms against the secular priesthood, forbade clerics to follow "worldly occupations," and this precluded prelates and deacons from practicing medicine. The school begin to look to the state for support. In 1134 the Norman King Ruggero II turned the institution over to laymen and it thus became the oldest state-supported medical school in Europe. In 1224, Emperor Frederic II, who made southern Italy and Sicily part of the Holy Roman Empire, at least temporarily, designated Salerno as the only institution in his realm authorized to license teachers and practitioners of medicine. Thus, medicine was the first science to come completely under secular control.

There are good reasons why the University of Salerno became the most important medical school of the Middle Ages. Its geographical location in southern Italy was an area of vigorous cultural intermingling where scholars were able to draw from the medical heritage of both Islam and Byzantium, and it thus benefited from Greek, Arabic, Hebrew, and Latin influences. The greatest medical scientist of the ancient world was Galen, who worked in the 2nd Century of the Common Era, and his writings were used as the basic textbook at Salerno, but important works by Arab physicians were also utilized.

In general, Medieval medicine was a bizarre mixture of cautious observation, common sense, and gross superstition. On the one hand, we encounter the rather good advice that a person should eat and drink in moderation—advice which physicians still dispense today and which now as then was usually ignored. But on the other hand, we are informed that onions will cure baldness, that the urine of a dog will cure warts, and that all a woman needs do to prevent conceiving is to tie a red ribbon around her head during sexual intercourse.

Yet, in spite of such nonsense, some progress was made in medical science and, interestingly, women physicians played a significant part in these medical advances. During the Middle Ages obstetrics was almost exclusively in the hands of midwives, who were trained for it as for a trade. All the achievements of ancients in this field were forgotten, and it was only after anatomical studies had been resumed and surgery had made some progress that things began to improve. The most important advances in obstetrics at Salerno were made by the female physician Trotula (d. 1097?). She wrote works on obstetrics and gynecology which remained authoritative for several centuries. "At times Trotula's advice seems uncannily modern, emphasizing the importance of cleanliness, a balanced diet and exercise, and warning against the effects of anxiety and stress"[21] Little is known about her life except that she had a husband and two sons who were

---

21. Alic, Margaret, *Hypatia's Heritage: A History of Women in Science from Antiquity Through the Nineteenth Century* (1986), Beacon Press, Boston, p.51.

also physicians and faculty members at Salerno. Other significant contributions were made in the fields of medical herbs and human anatomy. Both animal and human dissections were performed at Salerno and the work done there laid the foundations of modern European medical science.

Law

Medieval legal scholarship addressed two distinct bodies of material: civil law and canon law. The legal structure of medieval society was based on Germanic oral law and custom, because Roman law almost completely disappeared after the fall of the western empire. Customary law remained strong throughout the Middle Ages because it governed the relationships among the feudal aristocracy and determined the obligations of the serfs. But from the late 11th Century onward a revival of the study of Roman law occurred at Bologna and then spread to other universities. Europe was then exposed to a legal system, which was coherent, logical, and, most importantly, written, not based on custom. Because the Roman system was obviously superior, it slowly began to replace Germanic law throughout western Europe.

Roman Civil Law

The origin of Roman law in Europe was the *Corpus Juris Civilis*, the compilation of Roman law by the Byzantine emperor Justinian back in the 6th Century. This book was unknown in the West, however, until it appeared at Bologna in the last quarter of the 11th Century. Since the tradition of Roman law had never entirely disappeared from Italy, it provided the most logical environment for its revival. The university at Bologna remained the most important center of Roman legal studies throughout the Middle Ages. From there it spread across western Europe.

Bologna, however, remained the "Harvard Law School of the Middle Ages." It was in the University of Bologna that the most able scholars worked. The problem was that the Roman law code of the *Corpus Juris* could not be applied directly to Medieval European society, because it had been developed in a far different environment and time. Its provisions must be carefully interpreted to accommodate it to new circumstances. This was accomplished by writing commentaries, clarifications, and elucidations to supplement the original codes. About the middle of the 13th Century all these commentaries were brought together into a comprehensive book by the Bolognese scholar Accurisius known the *Glossa Ordinaria*. Thereafter, the *Glossa Ordinaria* became the authoritative supplement to the *Corpus Juris* in the courts of Roman law.

By the 13th Century, Roman law was beginning to make significant inroads in most of Western Europe, as lawyers trained in civil law were appointed to high positions in the courts of France, Germany, and Spain. These lawyers were critically useful to kings attempting to transform their states into centralized kingdoms, because Roman law was an excellent vehicle for elevating the king's position and enhancing his power. It is true that Roman law had originally developed during the Roman Republic and possessed an element of constitutionalism, but during the long centuries of the Empire, when Roman law underwent its most important development, it acquired a very autocratic basis. The theory is that sometime at the beginning of the imperial period the Roman people voluntarily voted to vest their sovereignty in the emperor and thus Roman law recognized the ruling prince to be above the law. Indeed, under the Roman legal system, law emanates from the prince.

It was only natural, then, for European kings to attempt to adopt Roman law and as it gained an increasingly firm hold on the states of continental Europe, it tended to make their governments more systematic and at the same time more absolute. In France, for example, civil lawyers played a

Figure 14.7: Illustration from the *Trés Riches Heures du Duc de Berry* (the Book of Hours of the Duke of Berry), painted between 1412 and 1416. Grapes being harvested by peasants (September) and carried into the beautifully detailed Chateau de Saumur.

significant role in the process that transformed the feudal Capetian monarchy into a royal autocracy. And, as we shall see, the development of the parliamentary constitution in England owed much to the fact that a limited monarchy was already strongly established before Europe felt the full impact of the Roman law revival.

Canon Law

The study of canon law developed alongside Roman law and drew a great deal from it. Methods of scholarship and court procedure were quite similar in both systems. But there was one major difference: whereas Roman law was based on a single source, the *Corpus Juris Civilis*, canon law derived its authority from many different sources, including the Bible, the writings of the church fathers, the decrees of Church councils, and papal decrees.

Like civil law, canon law became a serious scholarly discipline in 11th Century Bologna and later spread to other major universities. The study of canon law received a strong stimulus from the investiture controversy and the subsequent Church-state struggles. Quite naturally, the papacy turned to canon lawyers to support its claims of superiority with legal documentation. However, medieval canon law scholars were far more than mere papal propagandists. They grappled with the extremely tough problems of systemizing their sources, explaining what was unclear, reconciling what seemed contradictory. In other words, their task was to impose a logical order on the immense variety of decrees, opinions, and precedents on which canon law was based: they must accomplish for canon law what Justinian's lawyers accomplished for Roman law back in the 6th Century. Their task was daunting indeed.

The definitive collection of canon law was completed at Bologna around 1140 by the great canon lawyer Gratian.[22] Its formal title is the *Concordia Discordantium Canonum* ("The Concord of Discordant Canons"), but it is usually known simply as the "Decretum." It is an orderly body of almost 4,000 canons derived from particular passages of the Bible, the Church fathers, and from papal and councilor decrees. The Decretum was very successful and was considered the official law book of the Catholic Church until 1917.

Theology

Medieval scholars called theology "the queen of the sciences." Theology had also dominated the thought of the Early Middle Age, but the monastic scholars were mostly interested in biblical interpretation. They tried to extract four traditional levels of meaning from the Holy Scriptures: literal; moral; allegorical; and mystical. But they did not attempt to construct a rigidly logical system of theology.

During the High Middle Age, however, the scholars associated with the universities explored the relationship between rationalism and theism, between reason and revelation. In the context of the religious environment of the time, this was a very dangerous activity, to say the least. A system of theological reasoning called "scholasticism" was developed by applying the ancient principles of dialectic to Christian theology. Dialectic, sometimes called the "Socratic method," involves analyzing the logical relationships among propositions in a dialogue or discourse. While the monastic theologian

---

22. Almost nothing is known about Gratian. It is often claimed that he was a Camaldulese monk and taught at a monastery in Bologna, but this has been proven to be a myth. Here is an excerpt from the Decretum:

On Marriage (dictum post C. 32. 2. 2)

The response is as follows: The first institution of marriage was effected in Paradise in such a way that there would have been "an unstained bed and honorable marriage" [Heb., xiii. 4] resulting in conception without ardor and birth without pain. The second, to eliminate unlawful movement, was effected outside Paradise in such a way that the infirmity that is prone to foul ruin might be rescued by the uprightness of marriage. This is why the apostle, writing to the Corinthians says, "On account of fornication let each man have his own wife and each woman her own husband" [I Cor., vii. 2]. It is for this reason that the married owe a mutual debt to each other and cannot deny each other. So the apostle says, "Do not defraud one another except perhaps by consent for a time in order to give yourselves [more readily] to prayer. But return to it again lest Satan tempt you. [However I say this] on account of your incontinence" [I Cor., vii. 5]. Therefore, given that they are admonished to return to the natural use because of incontinence, it is clear that they are not commanded to join together solely for the procreation of children. Yet marriage is not to be judged evil on that account, for what is done outside of the intention of generation is not an evil of marriage, but is forgivable on account of the good of marriage which is threefold: Fidelity, Offspring, and Sacrament.

Translation by Paul Hyams, Cornell University.

attempted to discover what was true, the scholastic theologian sought to learn how the various propositions of faith joined together to form a complete, consistent, and logical theological system. It goes without saying that pointing out inconsistencies to a true believer is in itself a grave and unforgivable provocation.

The first thinker to explore the theological application of dialectic was St. Anselm of Canterbury (1033–1109). Anselm defined his own intellectual interests as *fides quaerens intellectum* ("faith seeking understanding"), by which he meant faith seeking to find logical consistency among its various beliefs. For example, he tried to show that there is a necessary and logical connection between the traditional Judeo-Christian dogma that God is a perfect being and the other dogma that he really exists. In his important work, *Proslogium*, he asserts that the idea of the perfect being—"than which nothing greater can be thought"—cannot be separated from its existence. For if the idea of the perfect Being, thus present in consciousness, lacked existence, a still more perfect Being could be thought, of which existence would be a necessary metaphysical predicate, and thus the most perfect Being would be the absolutely Real. In its most simple form, this first version of the ontological argument is as follows:

1. The term "God" is defined as the greatest conceivable being.
2. Real existence (existence in reality) is greater than mere existence in the understanding.
3. Therefore, God must exist in reality, not just in the understanding.

Anselm's main intuition is that the greatest possible being has every attribute which could make it great or good. Existence in reality is one such attribute. Anselm's actual argument is often reconstructed as a *reductio ad absurdum* (reduction to absurdity). *Reductio* arguments have two parts: a target argument, and a concluding argument which reduces the target argument to absurdity. His argument begins with some general assumptions which include the idea that (a) God exists in the understanding, (b) Existence in reality is greater than existence in the understanding alone. The first assumption simply means that we understand and can consistently think about the concept of God (whereas we could not think about the concept of a square circle, for instance). The second means that a real X is greater than an imaginary or merely conceived X.[23]

Although this argument for God's existence does not sound like a very great achievement today, its importance lies in the fact that it marks the beginning of the revival of logical inquiry in metaphysics after an absence of many centuries and it is thus of great historical interest. The scholastic concern with dialectical relationships resembles classical Greek thought, but with an important exception: the Greeks sought to find order among observed propositions; the scholastics sought to find order among propositions presented by faith, that is, by divine revelation. Later they would take further propositions from the ancient pagan philosophers and eventually from their own observations. Scholastic thought, then, assumed that the human intellect was powerful enough to probe the logical and metaphysical patterns within which even God must operate.

---

23. Gaunilo, a contemporary monk of Anselm, wrote an attack on Anselm's argument titled "on behalf of the fool." He offers several criticisms, the most well known is a parody on Anselm's argument in which he proves the existence of the greatest possible island. If we replaced "an island than which none greater can be conceived" for "something than which nothing greater can be conceived" then we would prove the existence of that island. Gaunilo's point was that we could prove the existence of almost anything using Anselm's style of argument. The ontological argument is therefore unsound.

Peter Abelard (1079–1142) is often called the father of Scholasticism. He brought a new rigor and popularity to dialectical theology. Abelard came to the University of Paris in the early years of its intellectual growth, and his brilliant teaching helped give that university its reputation as Europe's leading center of philosophical and theological studies. Using what became the classical method of scholastic argumentation, he posed formal questions with the citations of authorities on both sides of the issue. Abelard assembled 150 theological questions in this way. For each question he arranged statements from the Bible, church councils, and the church fathers. In every case there were conflicts and inconsistencies. He made no effort to reconcile these discrepancies, but left the authorities standing in embarrassing juxtaposition. His method was an ingenious retort to those who maintained that it was enough to simply hold fast to the ancient writings. The title of Abelard's book was *Sic et Non*, "Yes and No," and it implied that one must either enlist the dialectic method to reconcile these conflicts or concede that the Christian faith is a tissue of contradictions. Needless to say, the Church authorities did not appreciate his efforts. His writings on the trinity were condemned in 1121. Eventually pressure from the Church caused him to recant his positions and he made peace with the Church before his death.[24]

By the end of the 12th Century, Scholasticism, as developed in Paris, was the predominate system of studying theology because it seemed to offer a certain avenue to truth. Another important factor in Europe's intellectual life was that after the middle of the 12th Century translators working in Spain and Sicily introduced European scholars to the hitherto unknown works of Aristotle, which had been translated into Arabic in the East. Even though these texts were incomplete and faulty, due to the fact that the Arabic translations were filtered through the Islamic cultural tradition, they were still influential because Aristotle's philosophy was built on reason alone and his assumptions drove Western scholars to examine their own works of faith through dialectic. The difficulties of reconciling Aristotelian reason and logic with Christian revelation and divine grace remained the central philosophical problem in the 13th Century.

---

24. Abelard is perhaps more famous today for his love affair with Heloise (1100/01–1163/4) and its disastrous consequences, which resulted in her giving birth to a son (called Astrolabe), to Abelard's castration by Heloise's angry relatives, and to both their retreats to monastic life. Heloise was one of the most literate women of her time, and an able administrator: as a result, her monastic career was notably successful. Abelard, an intellectual jouster throughout his life was notably less happy as a monk. He incurred the displeasure and enmity of abbots, bishops, his own monks, a number of Church councils and St. Bernard of Clairvaux. The last months of his life were spent under the protection of Peter the Venerable of Cluny, where he died. The tomb of Abelard and Heloise can be visited today in the Pére Lachaise cemetery in Paris.

CHAPTER

15

The Late Middle Age (1300–1500)

In contrast to the High Middle Age, which was a time of promise and optimism (it is sometimes called the "times of feasts"), the Late Middle Age was a period of adversity and setbacks ("times of famine"). From about 1300 until the late 15th Century, Europe suffered through a series of calamities and disasters of appalling severity. Much of it was brought on by natural environmental changes, what the people of the Middle Ages called "acts of God." Poor agricultural technology and misguided farming practices led to soil exhaustion, accentuated by a climatic change which produced several centuries of colder temperatures and increased rainfall.[1] The result was recurrent famines. Then came further suffering in the form of a pestilence known as the "Black Death," which spread quickly across Europe and drastically reduced the population. Tragically, many of Europe's problems during this period were not caused by acts of God, but were the result of the incessant warfare which raged across the continent, producing unnecessary hardship and desolation. The destruction of warfare coupled with the mortality of famine and plague reduced large stretches of Europe to an almost wilderness condition, where packs of wolves roamed the countryside and even sometimes invaded the outskirts of the cities. Yet, there was another, more encouraging aspect to the Late Middle Age. In spite of these hardships the people did not abandon themselves to apathy and despair, but attempted to overcome their adversities. Civilization did not collapse. Indeed, the people of Europe extended and preserved the most enlightening achievements of the High Middle Age. Thus, in a very real sense, the most important theme of the Late Middle Age is the perseverance and eventual triumph of the human spirit.

Depression and Plague

The economic depression of the Late Middle Age descended gradually and unevenly across Europe. During the late 13th and early 14th centuries a number of related trends resulted in a deep economic slump: shrinking population; contracting markets; an end of the availability of new land for

---

1. Change of climate is at the same time one of the most important and one of the least understood factors in history. Sudden—and not so sudden—changes in temperature, rainfall, sunshine, etc. have been a factor in human history from its beginning, but has for the most part been ignored by historians, mainly because the process is so little understood. Climatic change was an important factor in the calamities experienced by Europe during the Late Middle Age, just as it was in the demise of several civilizations of the ancient world, but none of these events have been investigated to any significant extent by historians. The modern attempts to deal with "global warming" (which would have been called an "act of God" by the people of another age) by treating it as simply an unnatural man-made phenomenon which can be controlled by human behavior, exhibits little more knowledge of the normal process of the earth's climatic changes than that of the Middle Ages.

development; and an increasing mood of pessimism and retrenchment. The expansion and prosperity of the High Middle Age outpaced the natural resources and technological competence of European civilization, and by the 14th Century the continent clearly suffered from the effects of overpopulation. All the fertile lands had been occupied and now the newly cleared lands were only marginally productive. Population growth could be accommodated only by lowering the standard of living of the peasants through the subdividing of their land into smaller and smaller plots.[2] A series of cold, rainy years resulted in poor harvests, and mass starvation spread across northern Europe and England. The size of families decreased drastically during the first decades of the 14th Century, and thus the population of most areas was already in decline before the onset of the Black Death.

The Great Famine of 1315

In 1798, the English political economist Thomas Malthus (1766–1834) wrote that, since production increased arithmetically (2, 4, 6, 8, 10) and population increased geometrically (2, 4, 8, 16, 32), the population of a region or the world will eventually increase until there are not sufficient resources to support it.[3] From 1000 to 1300, the total production of Europe had increased steadily. Although there were local food shortages in which many people died of starvation, the standard of living in Western Europe as a whole rose even while the population had steadily increased. By the beginning of the 14th Century, however, the population was growing to such an extent that the land could provide enough resources to support it only under the best of conditions. There was no longer any margin for crop failures or even harvest shortfalls. At the same time, however, the western European climate was undergoing a change, with cooler and wetter summers and earlier autumn storms. Conditions were no longer optimum for the kind of agriculture practiced at this time.

A wet Spring in the year 1315 made it impossible to plow all of the fields that were ready for cultivation, and heavy rains rotted some of the seed grain before it could germinate. The harvest was far smaller than usual, and the food reserves of many families were quickly depleted. People gathered what food they could from the forests: edible roots, plants, grasses, nuts, and bark. Although many people were badly weakened by malnutrition, the evidence suggests that relatively few died. The Spring and Summer of 1316 were cold and wet again, however. Peasant families now had less energy with which to till the land needed for a harvest to make up for the previous shortfall and possessed a much smaller food supply in reserve to sustain them until the next harvest.

---

2. It is interesting to recall the similar phenomenon which occurred toward the end of the Greek Dark Age in the 8th Century BCE. See chapter 5.3.

3. Malthus, Thomas, *An Essay on the Principle of Population* (1798):

> I think I may fairly make two postulata.
> First, That food is necessary to the existence of man.
> Secondly, That the passion between the sexes is necessary and will remain nearly in its present state.
> Assuming then my postulata as granted, I say, that the power of population is indefinitely greater than the power in the earth to produce subsistence for man.
> Population, when unchecked, increases in a geometrical ratio. Subsistence increases only in an arithmetical ratio. A slight acquaintance with numbers will shew the immensity of the first power in comparison of the second.
> . . . . I see no way by which man can escape from the weight of this law which pervades all animated nature. No fancied equality, no agrarian regulations in their utmost extent, could remove the pressure of it even for a single century. And it appears, therefore, to be decisive against the possible existence of a society, all the members of which should live in ease, happiness, and comparative leisure; and feel no anxiety about providing the means of subsistence for themselves and families.

By the spring of 1317, all classes of society were suffering, although, as might be expected, the lower classes suffered the most. Draft animals were slaughtered, seed grain was eaten, infants and the younger children were abandoned. Many of the elderly voluntarily starved themselves to death so that the younger members of the family might live to work the fields again. There were even reports of cannibalism, although it is impossible to know if these were more a product of rumor-mongering than fact.[4]

Although the weather pattern returned to normal by the summer of 1317, a quick recovery was impossible. Records of the time indicate that a bushel of seed was required to produce four bushels of wheat. At the height of the hunger in the late Spring of 1317, starving people had eaten much of the grain normally set aside as seed, as well as many of their draft animals. Even so, any of the surviving people and animals were simply too weak to work effectively. However, there were consequently fewer mouths to feed because about ten to fifteen percent of the population had died, many from pneumonia, bronchitis, tuberculosis, and other sicknesses that starvation had made fatal. It was not until about 1325 that the food supply returned to a relatively normal state, and population began to increase again. Europeans were badly shaken, however. The death rate had been high, and even nobles and clergy had perished from hunger. The world now seemed a less stable and "gentle" place than it had before the Great Famine.

The Black Death of 1347–1351

During the next few years, the European economy slowly improved, and agricultural and manufacturing production eventually reached pre-famine levels. This return to normalcy was suddenly ended in the year 1347 by a disaster even worse than the Great Famine.

Since the failure of Justinian's attempt to restore the Western Empire in 540–565, Europe had been relatively isolated, and intercommunication among its villages slight. Although many diseases were endemic (that is, they were always present), contagious diseases did not spread rapidly or easily. So the last pandemic (an epidemic that strikes literally everywhere within a short time) to strike Europe had been the one brought to the West by Justinian's armies in 547. By the 14th Century, however, the revival of commerce and trade and the growth of population had altered that situation. There was much more movement of people from place to place within Europe, and European merchants traveled far afield into many more regions from which they could bring home both profitable wares and contagious diseases. Moreover, the diet, housing, and clothing of the average men and women of Western Europe were relatively poor, and a shortage of wood for fuel after most of the forests had been cleared during the High Middle Age, made hot water a luxury and personal hygiene substandard.

The Black Death appears to have been a combination *bubonic plague*, which was carried by black rats—or rather the fleas the rats carry—and *pneumonic plague,* which results when a person with a respiratory infection contracts bubonic plague, and this form is spread by direct contact. The Black Death did not originate in Europe. Outbreaks of the pestilence are recorded in China as early as 46 CE. In 468, over 140,000 people died in the Chinese cities of Honan, Hopei, and Shantung. The disease traveled slowly across the Near East and reached the Crimea in 1346, when it seems to have mutated into a more vigorous form, spreading quickly through Turkey and the islands of the Aegean to the continent of Europe.

---

4. One of *Grimm's Fairy Tales* relates the story of Hansel and Gretel, abandoned in the woods by their parents during a time of hunger. They were taken in by an old woman living in a cottage made of gingerbread and candy. They saw that the old woman was bringing in wood and heating the oven, and they discovered that she was planning on roasting and eating them. Gretel asked the woman to look inside the oven to see if it was hot enough, and then pushed her in and slammed the door.

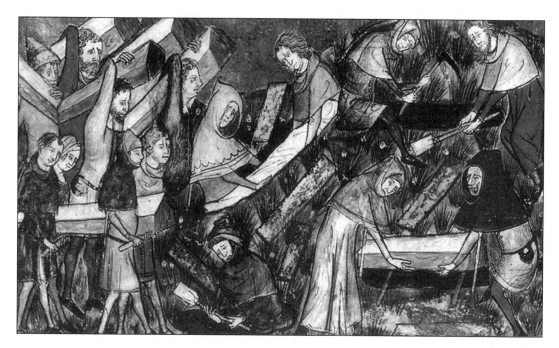

Figure 15.1: Mass burial of Black Death victims.

From the Mediterranean ports the Black Death advanced across Europe with terrifying rapidity, which may be explained, in part, by the lively trade in rat-infested grain and by the fact that the population was already weakened by malnutrition. It reached Sicily in 1346, Italy early in 1347, and by the end of 1347 it struck Marseilles, France. The next year it attacked Spain and spread throughout Germany. It arrived in London in 1348 and spread somewhat more slowly through Britain, reaching Scotland in 1359.

People tried to protect themselves by carrying little bags filled with crushed herbs and flowers over their noses, but to little effect. Those individuals infected with bubonic experienced great swellings of their lymph glands and took to their beds. Those with the respiratory form of the disease died quickly, but not before developing evident symptoms: a sudden fever that turned the face a dark rose color, a sudden attack of sneezing, followed by coughing, coughing up blood, and death. The mortality rate cannot be determined with any accuracy, but the most severely effected parts of Europe suffered a population decline of between two thirds and three quarters, although some cities were less seriously infected and a few areas escaped the plague entirely. The population of Europe appears to have continued its decline for the next century and a half.

The Black Death finally played out in Scandinavia about 1351, but another wave of the disease came in 1361–1362, which was known as the "children's plague" because it struck especially hard on the young people born since the first outbreak of the pestilence. It returned in 1369, 1374–1375, 1379, 1390, 1407 and several times after that until—for some unknown reason—the Black Death weakened and was replaced by waves of typhoid fever, typhus, or cholera. Europe continued to experience regular waves of such mortality until the mid-19th Century. Although bubonic plague is still endemic in many areas, including New Mexico in the American Southwest, it does not spread as did the Black Death of 1347–1351. The effects of that plague and its successors on the men and women of Medieval Europe were profound: new attitudes toward death, the value of life, and of one's self-worth. It kindled a growth of class conflict, a loss of respect for the Church, and the emergence of a new personal spirituality that profoundly altered European attitudes toward religion. Still another effect was a new cultural vigor, which favored the national languages, rather than Latin, as the vehicle of intellectual and literary expression. An example of this movement was Giovanni Boccaccio's *The Decameron*, a collection of tales written in 1350 and set in a country house where a group of noble young men and women of Florence have fled to escape the plague raging in the city. These were natural disasters, but they were made all the worse by the inability of the directing elements of society, the princes and clergy, to offer any effective leadership during these crises.

Effects in the Countryside

The population "die back" produced by the Black Death solved the problem of agrarian overpopulation in Europe and at the same time presented new problems: now there was abundant arable lands but an extreme shortage of cultivators. The services of peasants were in high demand and their economic condition swiftly improved. The labor shortage resulted in an upward spiral of wages for agrarian workers and meant that peasants could obtain land at much reduced rents. Some peasants were even able to acquire estates of their own and hire laborers to farm them. Landlords attempted to hold down the wages artificially through collective action and by legislation. In England, for example, the Statute of Laborers in 1351 aimed at freezing the wages of workers, but these efforts achieved little success. Landlords still had to compete for labor and were often forced to pay "black market" wages to obtain workers. Supply and demand, as always, worked its way relentlessly through the market. Many landlords were forced to free their serfs in order to induce them not to abandon the fields for better opportunities. Most serfs ascended to the status of tenant farmer during this period, and by 1500 the demise of the old manorial system was evident, though some vestiges of serfdom hung on for another two centuries, particularly in eastern Germany and Poland.

Effects on the Towns

The cities of Western Europe recovered from the trauma of the famines and the Black Death more quickly than the countryside, where deserted villages and stretches of unworked, overgrown fields remained a common site for many decades. However, even as late as 1500 the urban populations remained much smaller than they had been in 1300. Nevertheless, cities became relatively more important to the civilization of Europe than they had been during the High Middle Age, due in part to the large and continuing migration of people from the countryside into the towns and cities.

Ironically, many of the newcomers joined the growing numbers of urban unemployed, even though there was still an acute shortage of agricultural workers in the countryside.[5] The gap between

---

5. A somewhat similar situation seems to be developing in the modern U.S. economy: growing unemployment and homelessness in the cities, while a labor shortage in the countryside facilitates a surge of illegal migration from outside our borders. The situation is further exacerbated by the "export" of middle class jobs to foreign countries. The only solution to this problem appears to be a radical and drastic lowering of the American standard of living in order for U.S. labor to compete on the global job market. Employers are understandably reluctant to hire highly trained engineers and technicians locally at $40,000 to $60,000 annual cost when they can have the same jobs performed in India or China for well under $4,000. Will the solution to this problem be the lowering of annual U.S. wage levels for skilled labor to under $4,000? Only time will tell. One is reminded of a similar economic situation in Italy soon after the Mediterranean basin became "globalized" by Roman imperialism in the 1st Century BCE and large numbers of the same Roman citizens who accomplished the unification of the ancient world were transformed into homeless and unemployed urban mobs. The marketplace appears to be the relentless master of the economy in all ages of history.

the rich and the poor classes increased as the urban elites attempted to maintain their positions. The merchant guilds and the aristocracy jealously guarded their shares of the declining wealth, creating deep social unrest, which resulted in riots and rebellions, for example the workers' rebellion in Florence in 1378, the French Jacquerie uprising of 1358, and similar conflicts in Germany, Spain, the Netherlands, and England. The English Peasant Revolt of 1381 was particularly bitter and bloody, resulting in the severed head of the Archbishop of Canterbury being carried around the streets of London on a stick. Although many towns and cities were torn apart by these riots, in general the rich merchants and the aristocracy managed to retain their privileged status. The kings, as we shall see, were able to play these groups off against each other to their own advantage, resulting in the emergence of the centralized kingdoms of Europe, the first stage in the development of the modern nation-state.

The Rise of Capitalism

A major reorganization of the European economy occurred during the Late Middle Age, which involved the collapse of the guild system and its replacement with the "proto-capitalist" system of production.

The Guild System

Medieval manufacturing centered around the family shop, which consisted of a master craftsman, his wife, one or two employees, and perhaps a couple of children who were learning the trade. The master bought the necessary raw materials, fabricated his product, and sold it retail. The shop was at the same time a residence, dormitory, workshop, warehouse, and retail store. The local masters of each town or city formed themselves into guilds, which served many economic and social functions.

The economic functions of the guild were far reaching. It set and policed the standards of quality for the products or services its members provided. It rigidly controlled the prices to be paid for materials and labor, as well as the minimum price of the product. In order to control the price, the guild set production quotas for its members to ensure that production would be sufficient to meet the demand but not large enough to glut the market. The guild also acted as a kind of credit union for its members by insuring loans, and pooling capital to share the risks of doing business. For example, if a merchant sent out a shipload of goods, there was always the risk that his merchandise could be lost in a shipwreck and cost him the entire value of his goods. However, if eight members of the guild united and divided their shipments between eight ships, then the loss of one ship would mean only the loss of one eighth of each merchants shipment.[6]

The guild also established and enforced minimum educational standards for apprentices. Masters were expected not only to teach their apprentices the skills of their profession, but also how to read and write and enough arithmetic to keep books. There were two steps in the education of a master: apprenticeship and journeymen. The arrangement for apprenticeship involved a formal contract. When a boy was about seven years of age, his parent entered into a formal contract with a master and paid a substantial fee for his education. The usual agreement was for a seven year apprenticeship. The

---

6. Modern companies evolved from this practice, which is why they sell *shares* of *stock* to the public.

master promised to educate and train the boy and, at the end of seven years, provide him with a new suit of cloths, a tool kit for his trade, and enough money to begin the period of traveling and gaining experience as a journeyman.[7] The guilds provided a board to examine candidates for journeyman and master. The candidate for master was required to provide an example of the guild's product and if it was judged good enough the board granted him the title of "Master." The example was known as his "master-piece." This system of examination ensured the competence of all the masters of the guild. Recall that the universities were originally guilds and it is still today necessary for the candidate for a Master's degree to present a thesis for the approval of an examination board.

The guild was also a fraternal organization. Its members contributed to a fund that paid for funeral expenses and the upkeep of widows and orphans of deceased members. Each guild honored its own patron saint, just as in antiquity each trade had its own patron deity, even sometimes constructing its own church, as did the stevedores of 13th Century Barcelona when they constructed the church of Santa Maria del Mar. The guild also provided a representative on the town council. The city of London, for example, is still governed by a Lord Mayor and his council, who sit in the Guildhall.

Free cities had to defend themselves and the artisan militias were an important part of their defense. Over time, however, urban guilds gave up fighting in the field in favor of hiring mercenary armies to defend them. The guilds provided other important civic services including provision for the neighborhood fire watch and fire-fighting equipment and manpower. They also contributed to the town treasury, participated in local festivals, and maintained charitable institutions, such as public schools, hospitals, orphanages, etc.

The Collapse of the Guild System

The guild system was cooperative and non-competitive and therefore adapted to an expanding economy. However, after 1250 the economic expansion in Europe slowed and the guilds had to face a new competitive environment. The guilds reacted in a variety of ways. They restricted the admission to master's status to avoid competition, they reduced labor costs by cutting the wages of journeymen and extending the years required for apprenticeship and lowered working conditions. Because of their restricted income, the guild members reduced their civil services and contributions to charities. Worst of all, the quality of their products became lower due to the use of cheaper materials and shady workmanship. However, even these measures were insufficient in the long run. The guild was designed to promote the common good in a stable economy and to protect a number of small businesses, which precluded the development of larger business to achieve the efficiency of size.

When the markets began to shrink after 1350, the craftsmen had to lower their costs in order to compete. Two systems of "proto-capitalist" production developed. Under the putting out method the merchants would rent the necessary equipment to peasant families, sell them raw materials, and purchase the finished product. This process was common for the production of candles, clocks, pewter ware, stockings, hats, and especially weaving. It continued to be common until the end of the 19th Century. Under the factory system, merchants would concentrate equipment in a warehouse "factory," acquire raw materials from their own farms or through agents, hire workers for wages only, ignore any production quotas, and compete rather than cooperate. This method was employed primarily for products that required several steps to manufacture or used heavy materials. It eventually developed into the factory system of the Industrial Age and is still prevalent in the modern era.

---

7. Many guilds stipulated that its members must provide their apprentices with new clothes once a year, usually at Easter. Even today clothing stores still hold major sales just prior to the Easter holidays.

The artisan guilds fought the development of these proto-capitalist systems, but were unable to compete economically and eventually disappeared, although there were class wars in many towns. Some guilds persisted for a longer time, however, especially those in retail and the small-scale service and repair trades. It was only with the advent of shopping centers and supermarkets after World War II that butchers and bakers lost their professional status, while some groups such as plumbers have managed to keep that status even today by transforming their guilds into unions. The professional guilds developed into the American Medical Association, the American Bar Association, while the silver-smiths and gold-smiths became the economy's bankers.

The proto-capitalists of the Late Middle Age did not support civic services, so urban life deteriorated. The workers' standard of living dropped, and this reduced their ability to buy the goods they produced. The European consumer markets became quite restricted and this led to a general depression of the 15th Century. Production was now uncontrolled and cycles of inflation and depression became common. The wealth and economic power concentrated into ever fewer hands. The demise of the manorial system in the countryside and the development of capitalism in the cities altered the structure of society. The non-aristocratic section of the population split into proprietors and proletariat, the lower levels of which merged with the pauper class. Something of the same thing began to take place among the aristocracy, where the gap between the great magnates and the squires continued to increase. The Medieval social structure based on classes determined by birth was already beginning to be replaced by the modern social structure based on economic classes.

The Church in the Late Middle Age

During the 13th Century, the idea of the Universal church in Western Europe was at its apex. By 1200, the Roman Catholic Church had grown into an organization possessing both spiritual and secular power. Although by now the church enjoyed many advantages, it also had to deal with many serious problems, in fact, the same kinds of administrative, political, and foreign affairs problems which all European governments of the time had to grapple with. However, the church was fortunate that during most of the 12th Century the popes were individuals of ability and foresight, men who could effectively administer a far-flung, diverse, and often worldly institution, in effect, a kind of empire.

In 1198, Innocent III (1198–1216) was elected pope at the young age of 37. He became one of the most famous popes of all time and, like Gregory VII, he was really more of a statesman and ruler than a churchman. Innocent III spent his tenure in the papacy patiently and tirelessly building up the worldwide authority of the Church. He not only claimed the supreme voice in all matters touching on faith and morals, but also the ultimate authority over civil and political disputes not even covered in cannon law. He acted as arbitrator in the struggle between the Hohenstaufen and the Welf families for the throne of the Holy Roman Empire; he forced King John of England to acknowledge papal rights and appointed Stephen Langton, against John's wishes, to be the bishop of Canterbury. Furthermore, John was forced to acknowledge the pope's overlordship and England became a papal fief for almost a century, with English kings paying feudal dues to the popes. Innocent also intervened in the political affairs of the Iberian Peninsula and succeeded in making the popes the feudal overlords of the Kingdom of Castile as well as of Sicily. Innocent greatly strengthened the administration of the Church's realm. In fact, he achieved what most of the kings of Europe had so far failed to do: he applied the monarchal principle within the Church; that is, he established the Vatican as the central governing authority and the final source of political power over the entire church institution.

In judicial matters, Innocent III obtained recognition by the secular governments of the supreme and final appellate jurisdiction for the papacy. This meant the results of almost any trial in Europe could be appealed right out of the national court systems to Rome, which of course gave the church tremendous authority over the internal affairs of the European kingdoms. He also insisted on the careful collection of Church dues and tithes, which in effect amounted to an income tax on all of Europe, and this vastly increased the revenues and the financial power of the popes.

Innocent III applied equal force and energy to spiritual matters: in 1215, he convened the Fourth Lateran Council and imposed on it his own views concerning ecclesiastical discipline and dogma. This council issued some seventy canons which defined the doctrine of transubstantiation,[8] required bishops to maintain cathedral schools and took steps to suppress heresy. The Fourth Lateran Council is considered by church historians to be one of the most important of all church councils. Innocent III also took vigorous action to stamp out heresy: a case in point was the Albigenses, which was discussed in the last chapter.

The practice of inquiring into the faith of those who were suspected of heresy had been applied occasionally in earlier periods by local ecclesiastical courts, but it first came into broad and harsh use during Innocent III's papacy. In 1233, the Court of the Inquisition became a permanent institution of the Church under Gregory IX (1227–1241). The Inquisition was charged with inquiring into the views of individuals who were suspected of being nonconformists. Suspects were usually tried by torture, and those individuals found guilty were turned over to the secular authorities for punishment, which ranged from confiscation of property to imprisonment, exile, and burning at the stake. As discussed already, the Fourth Crusade and the Children's Crusade both occurred during Pope Innocent III's reign. It was the infamous Fourth Crusade that captured Constantinople and contributed to the fall of the Byzantine Empire.

For more than half a century, the successors of Innocent III managed to maintain the dominant position of the Roman Church. They maintained the church's monarchal structure in tact; they enforced Rome's judicial supremacy; they preserved the church's financial hold on Europe; and they kept Europe's rulers, for the most part, subservient to the papacy. However, they failed, just as Innocent had, to regain the Holy Land through crusades and they failed to turn the capture of Constantinople into a real victory for Catholicism. Although a puppet "Latin Empire" was established, the Greek Orthodox patriarch moved to the city of Nicaea and refused to submit to the authority of the Pope. Finally in 1261, the Latin Empire itself collapsed, the Byzantines reoccupied Constantinople and the Patriarch resumed his work in the capital; nothing of substance, except the weakening of the Byzantine Empire, was accomplished by this disgraceful act of blatant aggression against the eastern Church.

The Holy Roman Empire

During the last two decades of the 12th Century, the Holy Roman Empire reached a new apex of power under Hohenstaufen emperors like Frederick Barbarossa (1152–1190) and his son Henry VI (1190–1197). Barbarossa settled the struggle over the secular authority in Germany in favor of the

---

8. Transubstantiation: the miraculous change by which, according to Roman Catholic and Eastern Orthodox dogma, the elements of the eucharist during their consecration literally become the body and blood of Christ, while keeping only the appearances of bread and wine.

imperial crown—at least temporarily. He continued the policy of extending German settlement eastward into former Slavic lands. In Italy he was less successful, however. There he was opposed by the popes and the growing commercial towns of northern Italy: Venice, Pisa, and Genoa. He was more successful in southern Italy, where he managed to marry his son Henry to the heiress to the Kingdom of the Two Sicilies. This was the Norman kingdom that included southern Italy as far north as Papal States. It had become a model feudal state and the dominant Mediterranean power after the Normans drove both the Muslims and the Byzantines from Sicily and southern Italy. By this marriage, the German emperors gained possession of southern Italy as well as large portions of the Mediterranean and they seemed to have the papacy caught within the jaws of a powerful vice.

Barbarossa's policies were carried on by his son Henry VI, but unfortunately, he died prematurely in 1197, when his son and heir, Frederic, was less than three years old. The prestige and power of the emperorship were largely destroyed by the German nobles during the minority of Frederic. Frederick II (1215–1250) ranks with Eleanor of Aquitaine as one of the most remarkable and colorful individuals of the Middle Ages. He grew up in Sicily, where Christians, Muslims, Byzantines, and Jews lived side by side; where peoples, cultures, and languages mixed together; where science as well as art flourished as nowhere else in Europe at that time. In short, Sicily in the early 13th Century was on the leading edge of change and progress.

Frederick learned from all these varied cultures and grew up to be an individual of extreme intellectual independence who did not really fit into the age in which he was born. He became a freethinker and a skeptic; he is said to have rejected all religions as frauds; he became a poet and a scientist; he was probably the world's foremost authority on falconry; yet he was also a brilliant ruler. He tried to organize society on a rational basis; he wrote a book on birds and conducted anatomical studies of animals and human bodies with the detached curiosity of a scientist. A contemporary called him *stupor mundi*, "the wonder of the world."

But alas, he was a man out of tune with the spirit of his age. So few individuals are ever able to rise above the limitations of their culture and when they do they are rarely understood by their contemporaries. It is not surprising that even before Frederick died, his work had mostly crumbled away. The power of the Holy Roman Empire was actually broken by Innocent III, who feared the combined might of Germany and Sicily. After the death of Henry VI, in 1197, Innocent secured the election of Otto IV (1208–1215), a member of the rival Welf family, to the imperial throne. This maneuver, however, was not entirely satisfactory from the pope's point of view, because Otto was just as insistent on German rights in Italy as any Hohenstaufen had been. The pope, therefore, eventually turned to Frederick II, who had become the King of Sicily. In 1214, Otto IV suffered a severe defeat at the hands of France's King Philip Augustus, the ally of Frederick. Innocent could not prevent Frederick from gaining the imperial throne and he became the Holy Roman Emperor in 1215.

Germany, however, was not the center of Frederick's world and he spent only a few years there. His neglect allowed the central administration to dissolve into the hands of the princes and great lords. In the meantime, Frederick focused his attention on Italy and Sicily. He tried to revive full imperial authority in northern Italy, but only with mixed results. However, in southern Italy and Sicily he built a modern bureaucratic, centralized government supported by an efficient and well balanced tax system. It is strange to use the word "modern" to describe a 13th Century kingdom, but it is the only term which applies to the situation. He even minted Europe's first gold coin since antiquity.

As already related, Frederick led the Sixth Crusade. He was handicapped most of his life by chronic strife with the popes, who excommunicated him no less than five times. The Church consistently put pressure on him to lead a crusade. Eventually, even though still under an edict of excommunication, in 1228 he led an expedition to the Holy Land and through negotiations with his friend, the Sultan of Egypt, he obtained possession of Jerusalem and the Holy Places under the terms of the Treaty of Jaffa. Many church scholars refuse to designate this expedition as a crusade, since Frederick was an excommunicate and because he won Jerusalem without any significant fighting. Nevertheless, Frederick was formerly crowned King of Jerusalem in 1229 and the West was able to retain the Holy City until 1244. After his return, his struggle with the popes continued: the principle issue was the control of northern Italy and Sicily; in truth, the objection of the Church to Frederick was far more political than religious.

The Interregnum and the Hapsburgs

With the death of Frederick II in 1250, the Holy Roman Empire ceased to function as a major power in European affairs. The framework, or the skeleton, of the Empire continued to link Germany and Italy, but the real authority and power of government fell into the hands of the local princes in Germany and the growing city-states in Italy.

The period between 1254 and 1273 is known as the Great Interregnum, because several rivals contended for the title of emperor and Germany descended into near chaos. Finally, in 1273, the princes of Germany elected Rudolf of Hapsburg (1273–1291) as the first member of that family to hold the emperorship. But instead of building the imperial power by uniting Germany and bringing the nobles under control, Rudolf pursued a selfish policy of increasing his own ancestral possessions. For the most part, his successors also sought to use the office of emperor for their own narrow dynastic advantage. So now even the institution of the emperor contributed to the break up of the Empire.

One of the most significant events of the 14th Century was the issuance of the Golden Bull by Charles IV in 1356,[9] which defined the constitution of the Holy Roman Empire as it would remain in effect until 1806. The right of naming the emperor was given to seven "electors:" the Archbishops of Mainz, Trier, and Cologne; the Count Palatine of the Rhine; the Duke of Saxony; the Margrave of Brandenburg; and the King of Bohemia. Although three of the seven electors were bishops, it assigned no role at all to the pope in naming or crowning the emperor. Thus, it was a victory of the secular forces for the independence of the imperial authority from the papacy, but it did little to really unite the Empire politically or economically.

---

9. Charles IV was King of Bohemia (1346–78), German king (1347–78), and Holy Roman emperor (1355–78). The son of John of Luxemburg, Charles was educated at the French court and fought the English at Crécy, where his father's heroic death made him King of Bohemia. Pope Clement VI, to whom he had promised far-reaching concessions, helped secure his election (1346) by the imperial electors as anti-king to Holy Roman Emperor Louis IV. Louis's death in 1347, the popular desire for peace, which was fostered by the ravages of the Black Death, and the absence of a strong leader to unite the opposition enabled Charles to make good his claim to the crown by 1349. In 1355 he journeyed to Rome, where, on Easter Sunday, he was crowned emperor by the papal legate (the pope was then residing at Avignon). His coronation with papal approval ended years of conflict between popes and emperors, during which time the imperial rulers had tried to regain control of Italy and the papacy. Although the emperors continued to be crowned at Rome, they were henceforth excluded from Italian affairs. At the same time, Charles's Golden Bull of 1356 ended papal interference in the Holy Roman Empire by eliminating the need for papal approval and confirmation of emperors. Although he had virtually renounced imperial pretensions in Italy through his treaty with Clement VI, Charles nevertheless supported the plans of Urban V to return the papacy from Avignon to Rome. The historian Lord Bryce wrote that the Golden Bull "codified anarchy and called it a constitution." Indeed, Germany remained disunited until Bismarck's efforts in 1871.

Switzerland

Another significant event of the 14th Century was the development of the Swiss Confederation of cantons, or districts, which won virtual autonomy from the Empire. In the late 13th Century, Emperor Frederick II had granted autonomy to two cantons and given them a responsibility for guarding the Saint Gotthard Pass through the Alps, which was the shortest route from Germany to Italy. The territory of modern Switzerland was technically part of the old Duchy of Swabia, and in the late 13th Century the Habsburg princes attempted to consolidate their possessions in the duchy by subjugating the Swiss cantons. To resist the Hapsburgs, three cantons joined together in the Perpetual Compact of 1291. This formed the nucleus of what eventually became the 22 cantons of present day Switzerland. But the Swiss had to fight to preserve their autonomy, and over the centuries they acquired a reputation for being among the best fighters in Europe.

Italy

In Italy the "free city" became the dominant political unit during the Late Middle Age. Although the Holy Roman Empire claimed sovereignty over much of the Italian peninsula north of Rome, almost all of the principle cities and many of the smaller ones gained the status of free, self-governing city-states. However, the smaller cities always found it difficult to maintain their independence. Small towns were centered around family run industrial and commercial businesses and it was impossible for them to compete with the huge corporations of the large cities like Venice, Genoa, and Florence, to name the three most important. Also, the rising cost of warfare made it hard for the small city-states to defend their independence. These pressures produced two political tendencies in Italy: first, very strong governments, which at times became true despotisms, replaced what had heretofore been relatively weak feudal governments; second, regional states, or principalities, dominated both politically and economically by one large city, began to absorb the numerous free and competitive small city-states.

Perhaps the best example of these trends and the most effective despot of the period was the ruler of Milan, Gian Galeazzo Visconti (1378–1402), who made Milan, for a short time at least, the strongest state in northern Italy. By shrewd negotiations and skillful warfare, Visconti secured the submission of Verona, Vicenza, and Padua, which gave him an outlet to the Adriatic Sea. He then seized the university city of Bologna, purchased Pisa, and through a variety of ways made himself the master of Siena, Perugia, Spoleto, and Assisi. During all of this aggression, Visconti managed to prevent his two chief enemies, Venice and Florence from joining in an alliance against him. At this point, Visconti seemed on the verge of uniting all of Italy for the first time since the fall of the Roman Empire. His real success stemmed from his ability to wring enormous tax revenues from his subjects and his uncanny political skill. In 1380, he secured an appointment from the emperor as imperial vicar in Italy, a mainly ceremonial title, but it nevertheless gave legitimacy to his conquests. In 1395, he became the Duke of Milan, which made him the only duke in Italy. Just one more obstacle, Florence, seemed to remain in the way of his assumption of the title of King of Italy—but Visconti died unexpectedly in 1402 at the age of 51. He left only two minor sons, who were incapable of defending their inheritance, and the state that he had built soon collapsed.

But even those states that escaped the despotism of a ruler like Visconti moved toward stronger governments and the formation of regional states. The government of Venice, which was republican in form, fell under the domination of a small oligarchy of the wealthiest families. A group known as the Council of Ten ruled the Venetian state and ruthlessly suppressed all opposition to the government. During most of the Middle Ages Venice stood aloft from the affairs of Italy and concentrated its energies on maritime commerce and overseas territories. But during the 14th Century the growth of the strong states on the mainland threatened to engulf Venice also, and beginning in the early 15th Century it adopted a policy of territorial expansion in Italy in order to protect itself—the old story of "defensive imperialism." By 1405, Padua, Verona, and Vicenza, which had recently been Visconti possessions, were Venetian dependencies.

Florence was the other important republic in northern Italy. There a single family, rather than an oligarchy, gained control of the city's political process. Although Florence, like Venice, retained its republican form of government, in the year 1434, a successful banker named Cosimo de'Medici established a kind of boss rule over the city. In a style of politics that reminds one of the modern political machines of Chicago and New York, or even of the tyrants of the ancient Greek city-states, Cosimo de'Medici cultivated the support of the middle class by appointments to office and other forms of political patronage. Another way he gained their support was through tax policies that favored the lower and middle classes. By policies such as this and by consistent concern for the welfare and the glory of the city, the de'Medici family was able to control Florence for several generations.

But unlike the Visconti, the goal of the de'Medici was not military conquest or the political domination of Italy. They were bankers, and their main concern was commerce. Thus, they sought to promote a stable atmosphere which would promote business and commerce and, coincidently, their own profit—though their policies were not selfishly exploitative. The foreign policy of the de'Medici was based on friendly and peaceful relationships with the other cities and states of Italy and not to be perceived as a threat to the existence of other states.

Cosimo's grandson, Lorenzo the Magnificent, ruled Florence between 1478 and 1492, and was even more famous than his grandfather. Lorenzo's lifetime is usually regarded as the golden age of Renaissance Florence. With splendid festivals, elegant social life, beautiful new buildings, and lavish support of scholars and artists, Lorenzo set the Renaissance style for all of Italy, and indeed eventually for Europe as well.

In southern Italy, the political situation was the most complicated of all. During the 13th Century, the papacy, as was its custom, intervened constantly in the seething cauldron of southern Italian politics. The pope invited Charles of Anjou, the younger brother of King Louis IX of France, to establish a dynasty over southern Italy and Sicily after the end of Hohenstaufen rule there. The pope's motive was not so much to produce stability in that kingdom as to enhance the influence of the Church over its government. The papal policy of encouraging violent aggression whenever it seemed to be in the Church's interest has a long history: in fact, it is a consistent policy that goes all the way back to the deal struck between Pepin the Short and Pope Stephen II in 754, which gave the church's blessing to the usurpation of the Frankish throne by Pepin in exchange for the establishment of the Papal States through an act of naked aggression known as the "Donation of Pepin."

Nevertheless, this papal policy of encouraging aggression frequently had mixed results, that is, it often caused a great deal of suffering and bloodshed without measurably increasing the Church's power. By 1268, Charles of Anjou was able to establish his dominion over the Kingdom of Sicily, and Naples and was duly crowned king by the pope. But as so often happens, the people of such a territory do not always agree with the choice of their rulers made by outsiders. In 1282, the people of Sicily revolted against their new masters and appealed to the Spanish king of Argon for help. And so it was that papal meddling resulted in a bloody and bitter hundred and fifty year struggle between Spain and France for the domination of Sicily and Naples. Finally in 1435, Alfonso V, the Magnanimous, reunited Sicily and southern Italy under the rule of the Spanish kings of Aragon.

Avignon and the Great Schism

In central Italy, the Papal States for a time degenerated into near chaos. The papacy continued, however, to envision Europe as a united Christendom in submission and obedience to Rome. But in reality, the Christian community of Europe was now torn by powerful forces which worked to undermine and weaken papal authority and influence. These forces eventually culminated in the Reformation of the 16th Century, but the troubles had their roots deep within the history of the 14th and 15th centuries. The kings in the emerging nation-states of Western Europe—the prime examples being France, England, and Spain—became increasingly resentful of the papacy's often arrogant claims to sovereignty over the churches in their countries. It was the goal of these kings to unify their territories into strong centralized kingdoms, and this necessitated the unity of every facet of national life, including religion. They thus viewed with suspicion the church organization which demanded the loyalty of their subjects to a foreign power. Since the church owned so much property within these emerging kingdoms—as much as one half of the total land in some of them—it was essential that the kings gain the ability to tax that property. But both the kings and the church had so far avoided an open conflict over this problem by developing the fiction whereby the king would "ask" and usually receive a "gift" from the local managers of the church property equal to what the taxes on the property would have been. But in 1296 Pope Boniface VIII forbade all clergy to make such gifts without papal permission. The English simply ignored the order, but King Philip IV, the Fair, of France, retaliated by forbidding the church to export coin from his kingdom to Rome. Then, in 1301, when Philip arrested a papal legate for treason, this struck directly at the sovereignty of the pope and the immunity of his representatives. Pope Boniface threatened to excommunicate Philip, but the king sent one of his principal advisors to Rome and, with the help of a Roman faction opposed to Boniface, the emissary broke into the papal palace and arrested the pope. Although the pope was rescued shortly afterward, he was a broken man and he died a few months later.[10]

Philip's victory over the papacy was complete in 1305, when French influence within the College of Cardinals managed to have a Frenchman, Clement V (1305–1314), elected pope. Clement claimed that the political disorders in the Papal States made Rome unsafe for him, and he moved the papal court to Avignon. Avignon was technically in the Holy Roman Empire, but by language and culture it was a French city, and the French king exerted heavy influence there. The popes who followed Clement all expressed the desire and intention to return to Rome, but they remained in Avignon because they claimed that the unsettled conditions in Italy would not permit the papal government to function effectively. And so for 72 years the popes lived in Avignon under the shadow of the French monarchy. This period, from 1309 to 1377, is known in Church history as the "Babylonian Captivity."

The end of this period resulted in yet another controversy that almost split the Catholic church into two parts. In 1378, Pope Gregory XI reluctantly returned to Rome but died there a short time later. The people of Rome feared that the next pope would once again leave Rome and deprive them of the revenues and prestige resulting from the presence of the papal court. A mob of Romans threatened the meeting of Cardinals with personal violence if they did not elect an Italian pope. They elected Urban VI (1378–1389), a man from Naples who was of both Italian and French ancestry. However, seven months later, a majority of the Cardinals declared

---

10. Contrast Pope Boniface in chains in 1301 with Henry IV standing in the snow outside Pope Gregory's window begging for forgiveness in 1077. The Church was not always victorious.

that the election had taken place under duress and was therefore invalid: they therefore elected Clement VII (1378–1394), who promptly returned to Avignon. This was the beginning of the Great Schism, or division, of the Catholic Church, a period of 40 years in which there were two, and later even three popes, all with their own college of Cardinals, all claiming to be the one true pope.

All of Western Europe became divided into two hostile camps. Each pope excommunicated the other and those who supported him, so that all Catholic Christians were, at least technically, excommunicated from the Church. The Church eventually attempted to solve this perplexing problem by means of a general council which would take over the Church and reform it. The two groups of Cardinals managed to convene a council at Pisa in 1409. This council asserted its own primacy over the Church by deposing the two popes and electing another. But this only made matters worse, because now there were three popes, all claiming to be the rightful pope. If this were carried to its logical conclusion, there would soon be as many popes as there were bishops! Fortunately, a few years later another council did manage to solve the controversy. The Council of Constance (1414–1418) was the largest international gathering of the Middle Ages. It forced all three popes to resign and then elected a Roman Cardinal, who took the name Martin V (1417–1431). Thus, the Great Schism was finally ended and the Catholic Church was again united under one pope who resided in Rome. The Council of Constance also decreed that a general council was supreme within the church and directed that new councils be summoned periodically, but this effort did not democratize the Church. A series of strong popes and the basic inability of large councils to develop concise programs prevented councils from exerting any great influence over the church, and the papacy remained the supreme and unquestioned power center of the Roman Catholic Church. Thus, on the eve of the Renaissance, Italy was no longer a land of numerous small free cities, rather, it was now divided into five territorial states: the Duchy of Milan; the Republic of Venice; the Republics of Florence; the Papal States; and the kingdom of Sicily and Naples.

The Rise of the Centralized Kingdoms

A glance at the political map of Late Medieval Europe reveals that a skeleton or outline of the modern nation-state system was already beginning to take shape. What began to develop during the Late Middle Age was the centralized kingdom, which was the first step of the long journey to modern national statehood. The best way to understand how the centralized kingdom came into being is to look at the two archetypal examples: France and England.

Both France and England began from common feudal roots but developed in different directions during the Late Middle Age and early Modern Period. It is true that eventually both France and England did achieve representative democracy, but whereas England, because its monarchy was limited from the beginning, achieved democracy through relatively peaceful evolution, France, because its monarchy became absolutist, had to undergo the bloody suffering and horrible terror of a major revolution. But that is getting ahead of the story.

It should be emphasized that the political development of these two states was not necessarily typical of the other Western European states. In fact, in many ways they were atypical and extreme, when compared to the other European states. One can almost say the other European states fall somewhere between these two poles of development. But there is both good reason and strong precedent for choosing the most extreme examples available for study. When we discussed the ancient Greek civilization, in chapter 6, we gave the most careful and critical attention to the political institutions of Sparta and Athens, not because their governmental institutions were typical of the other Greek city-states, but precisely because they were unique, because they represented the two extreme poles of Greek political ideals and potential. By studying Sparta and Athens, we discovered the entire range and diversity of Greek political institutions. In much the same way, we can gain at least a rudimentary acquaintance with the range and diversity of European political development when we look at the development of the political institutions of these two diverse states of Europe: France and England.

As a starting point, we can observe that all the states of Western Europe began their political development toward nationhood with roughly the same types of feudal institutions—although as with all sweeping general statements such as this, one should be careful not to carry such simplistic assertions too far. At any rate, both France and England began their journey toward nationhood from feudal bases, that is, with kings, who had to struggle for power with their great nobles, and with incipient national assemblies—in England called the Parliament, in France called the Estates-General. In France, however, unlike in England, the assembly never developed into a dominant institution, but was pushed aside by the growth of absolutist, divine-right monarchy. It is not because France and England were so different at the beginning, they were not, but rather because as they developed, each society emphasized different institutions, each society channeled its energy in different directions, towards different goals.

In fact, the earliest development of the monarchy followed a quite similar course in both countries. In both France and England there were certain clergymen and political philosophers quite ready to support the principles of divine right absolutism. Both countries developed a prosperous middle class, which the king could play off against the nobility, to his own advantage. And both monarchies had to deal with the opposition of stubborn religious minorities—the Calvinist Huguenots in France, the obstinate Puritans in England.

Yet, there was at least one major difference: geography. England enjoyed the advantage of geographic semi-isolation, which normally isolated it from foreign invasion. In fact, English soil has not known the burden of a foreign army since the Norman Conquest of 1066. Invasion of the British Isles across the narrow English Channel is by no means an impossibility, the Romans, the barbarians, and the Normans all did it, but the sea certainly presents a formidable defense and the English felt secure enough from foreign invasion that their kings could not justify the maintenance of large standing armies. The English kings did, of course, maintain a formidable navy, but ships cannot be used, like armies, to overawe the populace and stifle incipient revolutions, especially in island areas.

France, on the other hand, like most of the continental nations, faced almost constant threat of invasion. Its northeastern and eastern frontiers are not natural geographic boundaries and they are easily penetrated by foreign armies. For this reason, it was easy for the French kings to argue the necessity of maintaining massive armies of professional soldiers. But such troops, necessary as they are for the national defense, could also be used to oppress and regiment the French people themselves, to nip domestic disturbances in the bud, to convince the people that resistance to the central authority would be fruitless in any event. However, one must not place undue emphasis on this difference in geographic situation as a cause for the development of such different types of government in the two countries. Many other factors were also at work.

The Feudal Constitution

The first step on the long road toward the development of the modern nation-state system of Europe was the emergence of centralized kingdoms from the hodge-podge of feudal units and authorities. By the High Middle Age, Europe had disintegrated into thousands of small feudal states. However, this tendency toward decentralization was reversed as the kings of the Late Middle Age began to reassert their authority and power.

The governmental systems of medieval Europe were based on what can be called feudal constitutions, which involved a multitude of partnerships in the exercise of political power. Although the king enjoyed the supreme dignity, he was far from being an absolute ruler. In exchange for supposed loyalty and service, the king had conceded a large share of the responsibility and authority for government to a wide range of privileged persons and institutions. These included the great secular and ecclesiastical princes (the dukes, counts, archbishops, etc.), free cities, and even favored guilds, such as the universities.

The emergence of these feudal relationships, however, produced a more ordered life in Western Europe during the 11th and 12th centuries, but it was based on a very delicate equilibrium. To maintain internal, as well as international peace, all the various members to the feudal partnership must remain rigidly faithful to their obligation. Actually, it went much deeper than that. Peace depended on all members to the feudal partnership holding identical concepts and understandings as to exactly what these various obligations and relationships were, because not only an outright breach of faith, but even a disagreement over exactly what the obligations were, could lead to war—and although Europe during the High Middle Age did lead a more stable life than during the Early Middle Age, war was, nevertheless, very frequent.

Many forces could upset the equilibrium of these feudal governments. One of the most obvious causes of instability to any feudal arrangement is the failure of dynasties to perpetuate themselves. Any family, sooner or later, simply through the law of averages, will experience a generation in which there is no direct male heir. And when that happens, there are bound to be disagreements over which of the other family lines is the rightful heir. Countless European wars have been fought over these problems. They were called "wars of succession." The Norman conquest of England and the War of the Roses, both fought over the succession to the throne of England, are but two examples.

France

The growth of royal power in France was the product of gradual evolution, which began with the origin of the Capetian dynasty (987). The first kings of this dynasty exercised real power only in the small area immediately surrounding the town of Paris, an area called the Ile-de-France. The efforts of these early kings, such as Philip I and Louis VI to extend their power through marriage alliances and the use of the feudal courts, the humiliation of Louis VII because of his inability to cope with the formidable Eleanor of Aquitaine, was discussed in chapter 14.

The problem facing the French kings of the 13th and 14th centuries was how to exert royal power over their vassals, who behaved as if they were independent rulers. The kings attempted to accomplish this in three major ways: (1) by substituting a national taxation for the old feudal obligations and using this revenue to hire professional soldiers and bureaucrats; (2) by assuming for themselves the sole power to administer justice throughout the kingdom; and (3) by restricting the authority of the pope to regulate ecclesiastical affairs within the kingdom. In other words, the monarchy attempted to usurp the power of the other two parties to the feudal partnership, that is, the great nobles and the Church.

Of course, to make any changes in the old feudal arrangements legitimate they must be formally agreed to by all concerned parties, because feudal relationships and obligations are contractual and a contract cannot be altered by only one party to the agreement—changes must be approved by all parties. Here is where the feudal assembly came into the picture. It was originally simply a meeting of all the concerned parties to the feudal arrangement to negotiate changes in these feudal contract.

Philip IV, The Fair (1285–1314)

Philip IV, called "Philip the Fair," reorganized the kingdom's financial system. He established the state revenues on a more regular basis by changing nearly all of the old feudal obligations into direct taxes. This revenue was then used to establish a professional army to replace the old feudal levies. This change is one of the elements that characterize the gradual transition of the medieval feudal state into the centralized kingdom, the first step on the road to the modern European nation state, and it is by no means unique to France. The same process, as we shall see, took place in England at an even earlier date (Henry II, 1154–1189). Actually, this transition met with almost no opposition on the part of the royal vassals, because it was much more convenient to pay an annual tax than to fulfill the feudal obligation of military service.[11]

In addition to changing feudal obligations into direct taxes, Philip the Fair devised new taxes, especially on the property and goods of the merchants. Actually, this too was not as difficult as one might expect, because these middle class merchants had no real place in the old feudal system, they had originated after the feudal contract was already in place. Since they were under no feudal obligations which could be transformed into direct taxes, it was necessary to impose new taxes on them in order to bring their contributions to the state revenue into line with that of the other propertied classes. The merchants could hardly complain about it, because it was only fair. But fair or not, it set an important precedent that the king had the right to impose new taxes on his subjects.

The growing popularity during this period of Roman law also supported the king in this, because Roman law contained the principle of the absolute sovereignty of the ruler. This is one of the fundamental contrasts between France and England: the English will consistently appeal to English common law against the prerogatives of the king, whereas the French kings will consistently appeal to Roman law against the rights of the French people. Under Roman civil law the ruling prince is above the law and, in fact, the law emanates from the ruler. On the other hand, English common law was based on the old Germanic customary law, which recognized the king as possessing only that limited power and authority which was specifically granted to him by feudal arrangements with those people he governed. These two conflicting and contrasting concepts of the law and the role of the prince in the state are at the very root of the difference between absolutism and constitutionalism.

---

11. There is a temptation in any society to transform the obligations of citizenship into the payment of taxes. It makes life more convenient for all concerned. A step in this direction occurred in our society over 40 years ago, when the military draft was abandoned and our military establishment, which was made up of citizens from every walk of life who served temporarily, was transformed into a professional military. Now we just pay our taxes and we don't need to worry about our obligation to our country, and the government hires others to perform our service. Very convenient. Also very dangerous. History illustrates that the loyalty of the professional army is quite different than the loyalty of the citizen militia. Our society has yet to come face-to-face with this fact, but will inevitably be forced to face it sooner or later.

Figure 15.2: Battle of Crécy, Hundred Years War. The English, on the right, use long bows against the French crossbow. The English long bowman could fire up to ten arrows while the French cross bowman loaded his weapon by cranking the handle.

The Estates-General

The third element of Philip's fiscal reforms was an attempt to tax the possessions of the Church and, while he got away with the first two reforms easily enough, this one resulted in an angry quarrel with the pope. In order to marshal the support of his subjects for his cause, Philip, in the year 1302, convoked what has become known as the first meeting of the Estates-General, the medieval feudal assembly of France.

The Estates-General was an assembly made up of the three broad groups of the French population: the clergy, the nobles, and the representative of the townspeople. They were known respectively as the 1st, 2nd, and 3rd estates, or classes. The idea of an assembly was not exactly new. Feudal levies on the nobles and the clergy had always been negotiated in local meetings of these two estates. Likewise, taxes of the townspeople had been achieved through negotiations between the towns and royal agents. Therefore, provincial estates meetings had been called frequently during the 13th Century. The convocation of the Estates-General simply meant the substitution of national for local negotiations and certainly did not imply the principle of consent or control of the people over the taxation authority of the king. Representative councils or assemblies composed of members of the various classes, such as the Diet in Germany and the Cortes in Spain, were quite common throughout medieval Europe, but few of them developed into major organs of the government, like the Parliament in England.

Philip the Fair increased royal revenue in France ten fold during his 30 year reign. This meant over taxation of all classes, harmful effects on French economic life, and the estrangement of public opinion. Anti-tax leagues were organized and local assemblies drew up lists of grievances, but nothing was ever really accomplished by this opposition. The Estates-General was summoned on two other occasions by Philip, but because the bourgeoisie, that is the growing middle class of the towns, and the nobility distrusted each other, no effective measures were taken and no permanent constitutional restraints over the king's growing power occurred. The king had the upper hand so long as the various classes that made up the French population were not united. The Estates-General was not, of course, intended to be an independent legislative assembly, but merely a council of advisors to the king, in the old feudal tradition. It was only under the later influence of 18th Century liberalism that the French people came to look on it as a true national assembly. On the other hand, since the Estates-General did include representatives of elements outside the nobility, its establishment may be considered another stage in the transformation of the French government from a feudal to a national institution. It is significant that the middle classes in England, in contrast to France, united with the nobles against the royal power, while in France the bourgeoisie and the aristocracy were never able to form an alliance and in the end both separately succumbed to the growing power of the monarchy and finally that power became absolute.

The Estates-General was convoked by Philip IV's successors more or less regularly up until 1614, but the climax of its power occurred during the Hundred Years War (1338–1453). In 1356, the English achieved a devastating defeat of the French at Poitiers. The French king, John II, together with one of his sons, Philip of Burgundy, two brothers, and a multitude of French aristocrats, were taken prisoner by the English. Charles, the 18-year-old son of King John and the heir apparent, became regent during his father's captivity. It became his responsibility to negotiate the release of the king. Just prior to this period, during 1348–1350, the Black Death had reduced the population of France by about a third and this coupled with the English defeat brought about the collapse of the French financial system, reduced the royal authority to a mere shadow of it former self, and caused civil chaos to reign throughout France. Then, in 1357 the Estates-General had to be summoned to raise money for the ransom of King John. With the French monarchy at its weakest level in generations, this was the golden opportunity for a move toward representative government in France and indeed an attempt was made in that direction.

The Great Ordinance

The Estates-General of 1357 passed a law known as the Great Ordinance, which provided for the supervision of both the levy of taxes and expenditure of state revenue by a standing committee of the Estates-General. This was a very promising, revolutionary piece of legislation, and on the face of it, there seems no reason why it could not have been France's Magna Carta. There seems no reason why such a committee could not have evolved into a cabinet system of government in the tradition of the English Parliament. However, the Estates-General, unlike the Parliament, was badly divided against itself, and its members had no real coherence or skill in self-government. In contrast, the members of the English Parliament, as we shall see, had long experience in both local and national government. As mentioned previously, the 2nd and 3rd estates, that is, the nobility and the middle class, never trusted each other and were never able to work together against the expansion of royal power. As for the 1ˢᵗ estate, the clergy, it was itself a house badly divided. The lower clergy came almost completely from the 3ʳᵈ estate, while the bishops and abbots came from the noble class.

Triumph of Absolutism in France

After the passage of the Great Ordinance, a radical faction of the Estates-General backed a rival claimant to the throne, forcing Charles to flee from Paris, but he was able to create a powerful coalition against Estates-General. In 1358 he returned to the capital and re-established himself with a firm hand, the Great Ordinance was completely discredited and discarded, and no reduction of the powers of the French monarchy resulted. Representative government in France was simply not destined to be at this time. The strategy of the English Parliament was much the same: first gain control over royal taxation and fiscal policy and then assume the authority to determine who shall be king, although the English achieved these objectives much more slowly and deliberately. The English attempt was successful and is remembered as the "Glorious Revolution," while the French attempt was a miserable failure and is hardly remembered at all. At any rate, by his decisive action in putting down this incipient constitutionalism, Charles made it clear that the future of France lay with the absolutist monarchy, not with constitutional government. When Charles later became king he was known as Charles the Wise.

After the exhausting struggle of the Hundred Years War, absolutism continued to grow in France during the 22 year reign of Louis XI (1461–1483), who revitalized the monarchy and the country. He forced higher taxes on his subjects but sweetened the bitter dose, at least for the middle class, by granting them favors and giving them responsible posts in his administration. He thus continued the successful royal policy of playing one class off against the other to the king's advantage. He enlarged the army, but used it only for the most extreme emergencies as he preferred secret diplomacy to open war—a policy which earned him the nickname "the Universal Spider." He successfully countered the threat of the Dukes of Burgundy to assert their independence, and defeated their attempts to resurrect the old Middle Kingdom between France and Germany. Louis XI managed to extend the royal domain over all of present day France, except Flanders and the Duchy of Brittany. Even Brittany was brought under royal control during the reign of his son, Charles VIII (1483–1498).

Francis I (1515–1547) had to face the attempts of Hapsburg ruler Charles V to destroy the balance of power in Europe. France was caught between the vice of the Spanish and German holdings of Charles V, who was both emperor of the Holy Roman Empire and King of Spain. The vice almost closed, but in the end France emerged intact. While the trend toward absolutism continued, France was still but imperfectly tied together under Francis I. Provinces like Brittany, which had only recently come directly under the French crown, retained their own local Estates-General, their own local courts and many other privileges. The nobility still held on to feudal memories and attitudes, although it had lost most of its governmental functions to royal appointees. And the national bureaucracy was still a rudimentary patchwork by modern standards. Francis I was the last strong king of the House of Valois. After the death of Francis I, his wife, Catherine de Medici (1519–1589), ruled France in fact if not in name through the reigns of her sons, Francis II and Charles IX.

The trend toward absolutism continued, however, and finally culminated in the reign of the "Sun King," Louis XIV (1643–1715), who uttered those famous words, "I am the state." Louis XIV and his age go beyond the period covered by this textbook, but it is important to note just

Figure 15.3: The Palace of Versailles, built by Louis XIV. It was the largest royal residence in Europe and not only housed members of the king's government, but also served as home for thousands of French nobles.

how far the absolutist monarchy of France developed. Louis XIV entertained the most exalted notions of himself and his position as king. Not only did he believe that he was commissioned by God to rule over France, but he regarded the welfare of the French state to be intimately bound up with his own personality. He choose the sun as the official emblem of his reign to indicate his belief that France derived its glory and sustenance from him just as the planets derive their light and life from the sun.

Louis XIV built a great palace outside Paris at Versailles, with two great wings, one culminating in the bedroom of the king, the other culminating in the bedroom of the Queen. He gathered all the great nobles of the kingdom there at his court and kept them occupied with useless entertainment and senseless extravagance, while he ruled the kingdom utilizing his middle class appointees. With all power in the hands of the king, the nobility became little more than a decoration of the state. Each morning, the greatest lords of the realm, the dukes, counts, and margraves, lined up outside the king's bedroom door and literally fought with each other for the privilege of helping the king put on his stockings! Of course, all of this could be dismissed as some kind of pitiful but ludicrous mental disorder, except for the fact that 20 million French people apparently took it all very seriously.

England

In order to understand how England developed politically in such a different direction than France, it is necessary to review the origins of the English. After the Romans were forced to withdraw their troops from Britain, in the year 405, in a vain attempt to defend the heart of their empire against the barbarian onslaught, the island was quickly overrun by several successive waves of Germanic barbarian peoples, known as Jutes, Picts, Angles, and Saxons, all of them even more primitive than the Goths, Vandals, and Franks who invaded Gaul and Spain. Britain quickly descended into the abyss, into the darkness of pre-civilization and we know very little about the events of this period, which used to be called the "Dark Ages." Eventually, however, a line of Anglo-Saxon kings gradually gained control over the central and southern part of Britain, roughly the area we today call England. Two latter waves of barbarians from Scandinavia—the Danes and the Vikings—were not able to overrun all of England, although they did establish a base temporarily in the northern part of Britain.

The Norman Conquest

Then in 1066, as we have learned, the Normans, also a Scandinavian people, originally known as the Norsemen who had settled on the coast of France during the early 10th Century, were led across the English Channel by William the Conqueror and defeated the Anglo-Saxon "Good King Harold," as he was called at the battle of Hastings. The Normans, however, neither destroyed the Anglo-Saxon culture nor radically changed the political and social institutions of England, but rather settled down to enjoy their conquests as a ruling elite. Norman culture and language—itself now a hybrid of Scandinavian and French—thus had a significant influence on the Anglo-Saxon culture and language. In fact, the blending of all these cultures—Angle, Saxon, Scandinavian, French, and more—is what we call today English.

William left all the institutions of local government in England intact. It is easy to understand why, because the English government was a much more centralized system than any of the feudal kingdoms on the continent. Anglo-Saxon England was already organized into local units known as shires, which correspond to modern counties. Each shire was supervised by a representative of the crown known as the sheriff, who had primary responsibility for looking after the king's interest. The sheriff administered the local royal estates, collected the local taxes, summoned and commanded the shire's contingent of the national militia when called into duty by the king, and presided over the shire court. All of this administrative infrastructure was adapted intact by William. The real impact of the Norman conquest was felt by the upper levels of Anglo-Saxon society. The great nobles, as well as most of the lesser nobles, lost their estates, which William redistributed among his own followers from the continent.

However, William did make one significant change in the political structure of England. He redefined the relations between the king and his vassals and sub-vassals. Whereas on the continent the lesser nobles, the sub-vassals, received their fiefs and owed their loyalty to their lords, William insisted that all English land be considered as a fief held directly from the king, and therefore the primary loyalty of even the lowest ranking knights was directly to the king, not to the king's vassals. Obviously, this made Norman England a much more centralized state than the contemporary feudal kingdoms on the continent. So at this early stage, England appears to be ahead of France in developing divine-right absolutism.

The Domesday Book

In another action which also had far-reaching consequences and further strengthened the royal prerogatives, William, in 1086, had a comprehensive survey made of all the lands of England, and the results were recorded in the so-called "Domesday Book" (see discussion in chapter 14). This survey is unique among the European feudal kingdoms and it served two main purposes: it gave the king a clear record of all his own holdings as well as those of his vassals; and it allowed him to calculate exactly how much feudal service the land could support. In short, the Domesday Book was an official tax assessment.

The Feudal Councils

In order to maintain close contact with his vassals, William instituted the Curia Regis, (Great Council). Essentially this body was an assembly of the great lords of the realm, the barons, bishops, abbots, etc. For the nobles, the Great Council fulfilled the feudal obligations of giving the king advice, one of the services a vassal owes to his lord. However, since the Great Council could not be kept permanently in session—its members had their own estates and affairs to manage—a small council, a kind of standing committee of the Great Council, consisting only of those persons who were in permanent attendance at the court, came into existence. The purpose of the Small Council was to carry on the functions of the Great Council whenever it was not in session. The Great Council is the direct ancestor of Parliament, while the Small Council evolved into the administrative bureaus and the cabinet of the royal government.

The Norman and Plantagenet Kings

The later Norman kings, William II, Henry I, and the dynastic crisis which resulted in the reign of Henry II and his queen Eleanor of Aquitaine, have been discussed in chapter 14 (see Fig. 14.3). However, a look at the political reforms of these kings is necessary here. William the Conqueror was succeeded in 1087 by his eldest son William Rufus, or William II, who became one of England's worst kings. He terrorized his subjects and antagonized the church. In the year 1100, after 13 years of misrule, he was assassinated and his brother Henry I became king and ruled for 35 years. Henry I further centralized the government of England and increased the royal power. The most important of his reforms was the extension of the royal courts, thereby setting into motion the process of the gradual replacement of the individual feudal courts by the king's law, which came to be known as "common law," that is, the law which is common to the entire kingdom.

Unfortunately, the end of Henry's reign resulted in a dynastic crisis, because he had no sons. He made his only daughter, Matilda, his heir and married her to Geoffrey Plantagenet of Anjou, a French nobleman. This is the origin of the Plantagenet dynasty of England. However, Stephen of Blois, the son of William the Conqueror's daughter, Adela, also laid claim to the throne. Stephen was the Count of Blois, the nephew of Henry I and the grandson of William the Conqueror. Henry I required his nobles to take an oath that they would recognize his daughter Matilda as regent for her son Henry when he died, but they repudiated their oaths, because of their dislike of the Angevins and because they believed Stephen would be an easy-going monarch. They were right, Stephen became king in 1135 and his 19 year reign was weak and marked by constant attempts of Matilda to place her son, Henry, on the throne. Eventually, in 1153, Stephen agreed that Henry should succeed him when he died—which he did in the next year.

Henry II, as we have already learned, married Eleanor of Aquitaine, who was the divorced Queen of France and heiress of Aquitaine. Thus, in 1154, Henry Plantagenet became Henry II, ruler of a hybrid empire which included England, Normandy, Anjou, Main, and Loraine by inheritance and Aquitaine, Poitou, and Gascony by marriage to Eleanor. This meant that about half of France was under the control of the King of England. We have already learned about Henry II's reign and his humiliation of Louis VII, the king of France and Eleanor's first husband. He did indeed exert considerable influence on the history of France, but in England he left an even greater and more permanent mark, because he carried to completion many of the reforms begun by his grandfather, Henry I.

He completed the task of making royal justice the common law of the entire kingdom. He did this through the use of itinerant, or traveling, royal justices, who were endowed with all the authority of the king himself in matters of justice. Each judge was assigned a group of shires, and traveled on a regular circuit through these shires to investigate and punish crimes against the king's law. Upon arrival in a shire, the royal judge would impound "12 good men" of the community and inquire of them under oath what crimes had been committed since his last visit and who they suspected of committing these crimes. This sworn inquest is the ancestor of the modern grand jury, which hands down indictments against those suspected of breaking the law. In the 12th Century of Henry II, those individuals indicted by the 12 "good men" were still tried by the ancient ordeals of fire and water—this is a hold over from Germanic tribal law and illustrates the different origins of English common law and Roman civil law. However, a Church council finally condemned these trials by ordeal in 1225 and thereafter, the so-called petty jury, or small jury, also made up of 12 men from the community, decided the guilt or innocence of the accused—just as it still does in all common law countries today.

These itinerant judges did not forcibly interfere in civil disputes, that is, disputes between private individuals, but they did offer the services of the royal courts in settling them. The great superiority of royal justice in civil matters was that it relied not on ordeals or duels, but on sworn inquests before juries. While Henry made no effort to suppress feudal courts in civil maters, the superior justice offered by the royal courts meant that royal justice gradually became the only law available. The king's law, in fact, became the common law of England.

The central administration and royal bureaucracy also grew under Henry II's reign. The great officers of the royal government, the chancellor or secretary, and the exchequer or treasurer developed in Henry's reign. Henry II also, like Philip the Fair of France, began the practice of allowing his vassals to pay a money substitute in lieu of their personal military service due under feudal law. This payment was gradually transformed into a regular tax and was, in fact, the origin of the national tax in England.

Henry II also tried to bring the English clergy under royal authority, which caused a bitter conflict with the Archbishop of Canterbury, Thomas Becket. In 1170, the archbishop was murdered in his church during a service by some of the king's overzealous knights. This incident made a lasting impression of the English people. The tomb of Thomas Becket became the object of pilgrimage in Chaucer's *Canterbury Tales*, and was the subject of T.S. Eliot's famous play *Murder in the Cathedral*, to mention but two examples. There is, however, no evidence that Henry himself was directly involved in the murder. It seems to have been the result of actions of a group of overzealous knights. Henry eventually was forced to repent, and although he was unable to dominate the Church, the English monarchy was the strongest in Europe at the time of his death in 1189.

The next king was Richard I, the Lion Hearted (1189–1199). He was the eldest of Eleanor's spoil-brat boys and he promptly began to waste England's resources on crusades, reckless campaigns in France, and personal luxuries. In fact, during his entire 10 year reign, he spent only a few months in England. But his absence was probably more positive than negative, because it allowed the institutions which had been created by his predecessors to develop undisturbed by his meddling. Eleanor ruled England while Richard was gone and seems to have done a much better job than he would have done.

Richard was followed on the throne by his younger brother, John Lackland (1199–1216), another of Eleanor's spoiled sons. He was nicknamed "Lackland" because his father, Henry II, considered him so incompetent that he left him no territories at all. Yet, ironically, John lived to become king and inherit it all. He was said by a contemporary to be "cruel, weak of will and without counterbalancing virtues." John's arrogance and brutality caused increased opposition from the nobles as well as the Church. After a series of defeats in France, he was much in need of money and he tried to arbitrarily increase taxes on his vassals. Now as we have seen, there is no basis for this in feudal law for the king to arbitrarily impose new taxes on his subjects. Since feudal law is based on contract, the only legal way to change the terms of the contract is for all parties to agree. Philip the Fair (1285–1314) may have been able to arbitrarily force his will on the French nobles, but the English will demonstrate time and time again that they will not submit to such actions by their king. Consequently, the nobles of England rose up in revolt and, in the year 1215, forced King John to sign the Magna Carta, or Great Charter, at Runnymede. By this charter the nobles enforced the terms of their feudal contract with the king.

The Magna Carta

It is tremendously important to understand the principle at work here, because it sheds light on our modern system of government. The basic concept of our own modern democratic system, the principle that those being taxed must consent to that taxation, that they cannot be taxed without their consent, goes all the way back to the feudal contract system of the Middle Ages, and, although basically the same feudal systems were in operation all over Europe, the Magna Carta was produced only in England. Well, what was so important about this document? Its purpose was to protect the nobles—the nobles, not the people yet—from the arbitrary power of the king. The document guaranteed this protection in three major ways: (1) The nobles were not to be tried except by a court of their own peers; (2) They were not to be imprisoned except by "due process of law; and (3) They were not to be subjected to new taxes without their consent, which was to be given in the Great Council, the king's traditional advisory council.

It is important to understand that the Magna Carta was in no way democratic, nor was it intended to be. Above all, the nobles did not aim at the destruction of the monarchy, but rather they wanted to enforce their rights under the feudal contract with the king. Without a monarch, there would be no contract, no rights to protect. However, rights that could be demanded by the nobles could and were later demanded in other segments of the population and through the centuries of experience, the ideas contained in the Magna Carta—not the Magna Carta itself—were transformed into a generalized formula of constitutional procedure which became the modern English constitution. And those principles embedded in the Magna Carta are familiar to us today as the basic guarantees of our own political freedom: trial by jury; due process of law; no taxation without consent. And it all began in an open meadow outside London called Runnymede on June 15,

1215, when King John was forced to sign the Magna Carta. But this act did not bring immediate peace to England. The pope declared the charter void, because it was signed under duress and civil war continued until John's timely death a year later in 1216.

The next king, Henry III (1216–1272), was only 9 years old when he came to the throne. This gave the nobles a chance to share in the regency. The Church also played an important role. Henry III, in fact, remained a weak ruler throughout his 56 year reign. Under the influence of the Church and his wife, Eleanor of Provence, he permitted an influx of French and Italian appointments to the exclusion of the native English. But, as the English nobles will demonstrate again and again, unlike their peers on the continent, they will never allow the king to arbitrarily disregard their rights.

The Provisions of Oxford

A reaction set in and in 1258 the nobles forced Henry III to sign the Provisions of Oxford, which committed the king to regular consultations with the nobles. Notice that a subtle but important change has taken place in the feudal relationship. The feudal duty of the vassal to provide the king with advice has been transformed into the duty of the king to consult with his vassals. The relationship between the king and his vassals is being turned upside down. It was during Henry III's reign that the Great Council of nobles became known as the Parliament.

Very soon after signing the Provisions of Oxford, representatives of the knights and townspeople were also summoned for consultation. The reasoning was that if the king must consult with his nobles, he should also receive advice from other groups of his subjects. All the great lords of the realm could be called into session, but the rest of the population could hardly be gathered together in one spot, so they were asked to send representatives. At first these representatives met together with the lords, but they were overawed by the presence of the nobles and did not feel free to discuss issues and make candid recommendations, so they asked permission to meet separately. Thus, parliament became divided into the upper and lower houses, that is the House of Lords and the House of Commons, as it still is today.

The next king was Edward I (1272–1307) and during his long reign he surrounded himself with able ministers and frequently consulted Parliament. In 1295 he summoned the so-called "Model Parliament" with the famous phrase: *quod omes tangit, ab omnibus approbetur,* "let that which touches all, be approved by all." After this date, Parliament always functioned as a permanent institution of the English government. This was 60 years before the French unsuccessfully attempted to pass the Great Ordinance (1357).

Edward II (1307–1327), the next king, was bored by the duties of kingship and during his reign England degenerated into near chaos. He made very bad appointments and was dominated by his ministers, who were unpopular, and this led to another reaction of the nobles. In 1311 Parliament appointed a group of more than twenty bishops and barons, calling themselves the Lord Ordainers, to reform the government and restrict the appointments to the king's household. The aim was to curtail Edward II's tendency to give power and influence to his favorites. The key royal favorite, Piers Gaveston, Earl of Cornwall, was banished, and the Lord Ordainers forced Edward to sign a series of reform ordinances which required Parliamentary consent for royal appointments, for a declaration of war and for the departure of the king from the realm.

Nevertheless, Edward continued to demonstrate his incompetence. He lost a war with Scotland. He could not even control the internal affairs of his kingdom. Edward came under the domination of a new court favorite, Hugh le Despenser. Things got so bad that his wife, Isabella of France, with the cooperation of the English nobles, brought in foreign troops and forced Edward to abdicate at the Parliament of Westminster in 1307. Edward II was murdered in prison 8 months later. The English continuously demonstrate that they will not submit for long to tyranny or incompetence. It took a long time, but in the end, the English monarchy got the message.

His son, Edward III (1327–1377), was only 15 years of age when he came to the throne and, of course, there was a regency, which was headed by a certain Mortimer, who just happened to be the queen's lover. It was during Edward III's reign that the Hundred Years' War (1338–1453) broke out with France. This long war, the early success of England and the final victory of France, is significant to parliamentary history because the necessities of war finances played into the hands of Parliament and allowed it to exert increasing influence over the government. Whenever the king was in need of money he had to consult Parliament. And Parliament's attitude was always something like this: "Alright, we will be happy to talk to you about more money for your war, but first there are a few other things we need to settle." This was not exactly blackmail, but the kings must have thought of it in those terms at times. The Parliament successfully asserted its right to consent to all non-feudal taxes (1340), to approve all ministers appointed by the king (1341), and to force all money to be spent for the purpose for which it was granted (1344). Finally, in 1376 the so-called Good Parliament, for the first time, actually impeached royal officials, in this case two notorious war profiteers.

The next king, Richard II (1377–1399), made an attempt at absolutism. Richard was only 10 years of age when he became king. He remained on very good terms with Parliament during the first 20 years of his reign and the power and influence of Parliament continued to increase. But in 1397, Parliament demanded a financial accounting of his government and Richard became furious. He had the person responsible for proposing the bill and three other lords condemned for treason. He then forced Parliament to delegate all its powers to a committee friendly to the king and he proceeded to behave as if he was an absolute monarch, in the French style. He imposed heavy taxation, unlawful executions, and a general reign of terror. Of course, there was another uprising of the nobles, this time led by the king's nephew, Henry of Bolingbroke. In 1399, Henry had Richard II thrown into the Tower of London, where he later either died or was murdered.

Parliament now elected Henry himself king. He is known to history as Henry IV (1399–1413). His real power was based on a vote of Parliament and backed by public opinion, which was far different from attempting to rule by divine right, like the French kings, or indeed, like Richard II had done. During the reigns of the next two kings, Henry V (1413–1422) and Henry VI (1422–1461), Parliament almost completely dominated the royal government. The Hundred Years' War with France was not popular in England, and parliamentary resistance to grants for its continuance led to a series of victories for France.

War of the Roses

After the end of the Hundred Years' War in 1453, which terminated English rule in France, a dynastic war broke out in England between the House of Lancaster, whose coat of arms was a red rose, and the House of York, whose coat of arms was a white rose. Naturally this war is known as the War of the Roses (1455–1485). Actually, this was not so much a civil war between the English people as a kind of private war between these two contenders for the throne, and the nation as a whole took little part. There is no need to recite all the details of the gradual growth of Parliamentary power during this period. Suffice it to say that the culmination of the War of the Roses was the crowning of Henry VII (1485–1509) as the first king of the House of Tudor in 1485.

House of Tudor

With the Tudors (1485–1603) there was a reaction against parliamentary dominance of the royal government. The disgust of the English people, produced by the turmoil of the long, dreary conflict of the York and Lancaster families, was so great that they welcomed, as people always do, a strong central government as an alternative to anarchy. The middle class, especially, desired the protection of a stable government. One of the lessons of history is that when forced to choose, people will invariably choose tyranny over anarchy.

It is perhaps this factor more than anything else, this strong desire of the various groups of the population for peace and stability, that accounts for the remarkable success of the Tudors in regulating the religion of their subjects and bending them to the royal will. But it should be pointed out that the most successful Tudors, Henry VIII (1509–1547) and Elizabeth I (1558–1603), gained their absolutist-like power by shrewdly maintaining a semblance of popular government. Whenever they desired to exact measures of doubtful popularity, they regularly went through the formality of obtaining parliamentary approval. When they wanted more money, they manipulated procedure in such a way as to make the appropriations appear to be voluntary grants by the people's representatives.

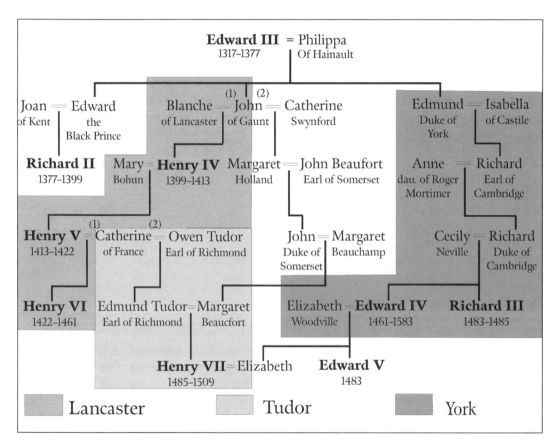

Figure 15.4: The houses of Lancaster and York.

On the other hand, it is true that under the Tudors the Parliament became little more than a rubber stamp for the monarch. Parliaments were convoked irregularly; the length of sessions were limited to brief periods; elections were tampered with in order to stack the House of Commons with royal favorites; members were cajoled, flattered, and bullied in order to obtain their support. Nevertheless, throughout the Tudor period, the people of England nurtured the deep-seated belief that the governed had an inherent right to a voice in their government, and the Tudors never dared to openly question that right. In this sense the English monarchy never approached the level of absolutism of the continental monarchies, especially of France.

And by the time the Tudor period ended with the death of Elizabeth I in 1603, the stage was set for the events that would eventually lead up to the glorious revolution of 1689 and the complete victory of Parliament as the dominant organ of the English government and the transformation of that government into a constitutional monarchy. But all of that is beyond the purview of this textbook.

CHAPTER

16

The Renaissance

What Was the Renaissance?

There are few periods of history in which human achievement shines so brightly as that age we call the Renaissance. But, as is the case with most periodizations of history, there is no general agreement among scholars concerning exactly what this complicated age was, or even precisely when it occurred. As a historical period, its beginnings are blurred, its end is almost indefinable. A few historians date the beginning of the Renaissance as early as the 13th Century; others date it to the 14th Century; but most date it from mid 15th Century; some historians hold that it was set into motion by the fall of Constantinople in 1453; or by the invention of the printing press in 1451. Of course, either of these last dates place the beginning of the Renaissance squarely in the center of the 15th Century.

And if there is little agreement as to when the Renaissance occurred, almost no one agrees about what the age actually was. To one historian it represents the birth of the modern age; to another it was the rebirth of interest in the classics; to still another it was the emancipation of the West from centuries of darkness, or a transitional period from medieval to modern times; or simply a time of unusual creative activity.[1]

---

1. Many Western Civilization textbooks take the Social Studies approach that the Renaissance, and indeed, Western Civilization, is nothing special or unusual and attempt to diminish its importance. Typical of this attitude is Coffin, Judith G., et al, *Western Civilizations* (2002), page 453:

> The prevalent modern notion that a "Renaissance period" followed Western Europe's Middle Ages was first expressed by numerous Italian writers who lived between 1350 and 1550. According to them, one thousand years of unrelieved darkness had intervened between the Roman era and their own times. During these "Dark Ages" the muses of art and literature had fled Europe before the onslaught of barbarism and ignorance. Almost miraculously, however, in the fourteenth century the muses suddenly returned, and Italians happily collaborated with them to bring forth a glorious "renaissance of the arts."
> Ever since this periodization was advanced, historians have taken for granted the existence of some sort of "renaissance" intervening between medieval and modern times. Indeed, from the late eighteenth to the early twentieth centuries many scholars went so far as to argue that the Renaissance was not just an epoch in the history of learning and culture but that a unique "Renaissance spirit" transformed all aspects of European life—political, economic, and religious, as well as intellectual and artistic. Today, however, most experts no longer accept this characterization because they find it impossible to locate any

To the author, however, the Renaissance represents a time when Western Civilization recovered at long last from its long, precipitous, thousand-year plunge, a time when the human spirit awoke at last from its long sleep and began to concern itself once again with *this* world and *this* life; and finally, it was a time when the quality of human existence once again made life worth living, at least for a fortunate few. Indeed, within at least a few small areas of Western Europe, human life approached that level of culture and achievement attained over a thousand years earlier by the Greco-Roman civilization. In short, the Renaissance represents a victory, isolated though it was, of civility over barbarism.

The Social Studies establishment and most of the historians who specialize in the study of Medieval history, of course, vehemently disagree with this view, but let the facts speak for themselves. It is quite easy to demonstrate how different life during the Renaissance was from that of the preceding age. Before 1400, no one in Europe even thought of building a permanent theater and staging a secular play in it; by 1600 theaters were springing up in every city and accomplished playwrights were writing dramas for them. Before 1400, no artist would have dared to paint a picture of the naked human body; by 1500 Botticelli had not only painted one of the most beautiful nudes ever rendered in paints, but had made it to represent the pagan goddess Venus. In 1350, not one person in all of Western Europe could read and understand the ancient Greek language; by 1500 there were hundreds who could and the Greek classics, lost to the West for a millennium, were being eagerly studied again. During the Middle Ages, Aristotle (who was known only through incomplete and corrupt translations from Greek into Arabic and then into Latin) was the ultimate authority in all fields of non-religious thought. To clinch any argument one had only to cite a passage from Aristotle, the ultimate authority—authority settled all arguments during the Middle Ages. However, in 1536, the French humanist Peter Ramus (1515–1572) took as his doctoral thesis, "Everything Said by Aristotle Is Wrong."[2] Not much respect for authority there. Whatever one's

---

truly distinctive "Renaissance" politics, economics, or religion. Instead, most scholars reserve the term "Renaissance" to describe certain trends in thought, literature, and the arts that emerged in Italy from roughly 1350 to 1550 and then spread to northern Europe during the first half of the sixteenth century.

As noted in the Preface to this book, the author rejects this condescending and pedestrian point of view.

2. Peter Ramus was born in 1515 in northern France. Despite his family's poverty he was able to put himself through the University and graduate with a Master of Arts degree at age 21. His works attacked Aristotle, the teaching system at that time and also supplied new definitions and interpretations of rhetoric. His master's thesis was entitled "Whatever Aristotle Has Said Is a Fabrication." After several years of being banned for his works, he was appointed professor of eloquence and philosophy in the College of France. A Catholic at birth, Ramus was swept up in the Protestant reform of 1562. During the following religious wars Ramus fled to Germany and Switzerland. He eventually returned to France and was murdered on the third day of the Massacre of St. Bartholomew.

His two most important volumes were *The Structure of Dialect* and *Remarks on Aristotle*. Ramus felt that Aristotle was wrong concerning the theory that dialect and rhetoric are intertwined and could not to be separated. Aristotle believed that to master rhetoric was to master dialect. Ramus believed the opposite. In Ramus's view, dialect was not based upon truth, but rather based upon probability, leaving room for the rhetor to persuade. Scientific logic is based on truth, not dialect. Ramus was a foundationalist, that is, a person who believes that there is complete, ultimate knowledge, or truth, for everything and every situation. Ramus, however, only believed this in the scientific sense.

Prior to Ramus, rhetoric was defined in a five part system—invention, style, memory, arrangement, and delivery. These are known as the five cannons of rhetoric. Ramus, however, reduced his definition of rhetoric to simply ornamentation. Basically this means that rhetoric is not what you say but how you say it. Instead of five cannons, Ramus had only delivery and style. He then defined dialect as the discovery of argument and the

view of history, these were great changes, and unlike many other eras of change, the people living through this one realized that something unusual was happening, and they themselves believed they were living in a world born anew.

Yet, to the average person the word Renaissance indicates more than anything else a time of unparalleled artistic achievement. The names Michelangelo, Raphael, Botticelli, Titian, and the rest are familiar to anyone who has ever visited a major art museum. Painting, sculpture, music, architecture, literature, jewelry, furniture—all the major and minor arts registered artistic triumphs on a scale not approached since antiquity.

And much that occurred in the renaissance is still with us today. For instance, when the Russian ambassador to the United States presents his credentials in Washington, he is carrying out a tradition of diplomacy that took shape in Renaissance Italy. When the accountant in a large international cooperation balances the company's assets and liabilities, he may use a modern computer, but he follows a system of accounting developed in 15th Century Italy. When a scientist in a modern medical center examines a sample of diseased lung tissue under a microscope, he is perpetrating a tradition of scientific observation outlined by Leonardo de Vinci. The debate presently taking place at Harvard and Berkeley and Stanford over what subjects should be required of college students is, in fact, a distant repercussion of an experiment in education begun in Italy in 1453. The modern landscape architect, who plots the placement of trees and shrubs in a formal garden, is merely the modern exponent of an art that developed—or was rediscovered—in Italy five hundred years ago. Depending on one's point of view, it may be either reassuring or dismaying to discover that the women of the Italian Renaissance bleached their hair, wore heels so high that they had to be helped along the street by servants, and spent unconscionable sums of money on jewelry and constantly changing fashions.

By the mid-15th Century, then, the basis of the Italian Renaissance was in place. Economically, there was an expanding trade and industry; cities and individuals were newly rich; politically, there was a new freedom and energy loose in the land. The mood was one of change, of improvement; old restraints and Medieval dogmas were crumbling; there was a zeal to recover the knowledge contained in the classics of ancient Rome and Greece, for building upon that knowledge a new civilization better than any civilization known before. And beyond all this, there was a new rivalry: between cities; between princes; between artists; all competing with each other to be the best, to do whatever they did better than anyone else. Italy possessed the greatest concentration of gifted individuals seen in the West for a thousand years, and the conjunction of these people and these times produced the Renaissance, an outpouring of creative energy that was unlike anything seen in Western Europe in a thousand years.

---

arrangement of these arguments. Ramus also defined logic in his own terms. The general principle being, the simplification of everything, going from general to particular. Take something and split it into two categories, then split each of the two categories and so on. The multiple divisions would eventually create something both conceivable and extramural. This form of logic leads back into his foundationalist belief that eventually there is an ultimate truth.

Despite all this, Ramus's most important work lies in his heavily influential theories on education. Prior to Ramus, education was basically the same as from the day of the Greek Sophists. At the university level, students would go into one classroom and then different teachers would come in and teach on their respective subject. Ramus believed that it would be better for the student to only associate one room with one subject. The system he developed is what we use today. It is because of Ramus that we have different department buildings now, in our Universities. It was these thoughts and those concurring opposition to Aristotle that caused him to be banned from France.

The Renaissance in Italy

The Renaissance was not exclusively Italian, but certainly it began there, and it developed there, and nowhere else did the brilliance of achievement shine so bright. It is not an exaggeration to say: in the 15th Century the Italians opened wide a door on a bright new world, and Western Civilization has been exploring that world ever since. To understand the character of the Renaissance, a period which played such an important part in shaping the modern world, requires a familiarization of Italian society of the time.

Urban Society

One basic characteristic clearly distinguished Italy from other areas of Europe during the 14th and 15th centuries and that was the number and size of the cities, especially in the north—and this can be demonstrated by accurate census figures for the first time since the fall of the Roman Empire. In the year 1377, for example, less than 10% of the people of Europe lived in urban centers with a population larger than 3,000. This percentage was fairly typical for most of Europe, except Italy, where about 26% of the population lived in urban areas. The cities of Italy were also the largest in Europe. Venice, for instance had a population of over 120,000 inhabitants in a census of 1338—a mega-city by Medieval standards.

This urbanization affected all levels and all facets of Italian culture. The more than one quarter of the population, which was nonagricultural, depended for its support on commerce and industry. All levels of Italian society participated in commerce, including landlords, nobles, and knights, the same classes that remained on their rural estates in northern Europe and would have nothing to do with commercial activity.

Moreover, success in urban occupations required a much higher level of training and education than was needed for an agricultural lifestyle. Therefore, many of the Italian cities provided public schools in order to assure themselves of an educated citizenry. Frequently even girls were given an elementary education, since literacy was an essential skill for the wives of shopkeepers and merchants. In fact, the upper and middle class population of the cities of Italy in the 15th Century approached a level of literacy not known in Europe since the days of the Roman Empire.

Finally, many of the cities of Italy were self-governing and offered their citizens the opportunity—indeed placed upon them the responsibility—to participate in governmental process of their cities. In fact, such participation was essential to the protection of the interests of many of the great urban families. Political life required the mastery of the arts of communicating with one's fellow citizens at meetings and debates. Thus, the study of the ancient art of rhetoric became popular. To sum all this up, Italian urban society in the 14th and 15th centuries was remarkably well educated and committed to active participation in the affairs of business and of government.

Women in the Renaissance

Although the cities of Italy were populous, the households that made up these cities tended to be small and unstable. We have some firm census figures on which to base this assertion. At Florence in 1427, the average household contained only 3.8 persons; at Verona in 1425, 3.7 persons; and at Bologna in 1395, 3.5 persons. In all of these cities, then, the urban households during the early 15th Century consisted, on average, of less than 4 persons.

A major factor contributing to this small household size was the marital customs of the period. Urban males tended to be much older than their brides when they married. Most men postponed marriage until they were in their thirties, and an increasing percentage of Renaissance males did not marry at all. This was due in part to economic factors, such as the lengthy apprenticeships required of males for the urban trades; extended absences from home on commercial ventures; and the need to accumulate capital before starting a family. And there were undoubtedly social factors at work that we are now unable to isolate. On the other hand, women were much younger, on the average less than 18 years of age, at the time of their marriage. The most common age for marriage of urban girls in the Florentine census of 1427 was 15.

This kind of marriage pattern produced several important social and cultural results: Because of the short life expectancy of the time (below 40 years), the pool of prospective grooms, that is of men approximately 30 years or older, was much smaller than the pool of prospective brides, that is, girls in their middle teens. The fathers of families with several girls faced serious competition in the search of scarce husbands, and the brides therefore usually entered into marriage under unfavorable terms. In particular, girls—or at least their families—had to pay substantial dowries to acquire husbands. Families with many daughters to marry faced financial ruin. This was one reason why girls were married off as young as possible, in order for their fathers and families to settle their uncertain futures as soon as possible. Those girls who could not be married before the age of 20 were considered unmarriageable and they had no honorable alternative but to enter convents. Thus, the convents of Renaissance Italy became warehouses for these women which society rejected, many of them still in the prime of their lives. Needless to say, these embittered and socially discarded women did not make the most ideal nuns. In the words of a contemporary, St. Bernardine of Siena, these unwilling nuns were "the scum and the vomit of the world." On the other hand, it may be assumed that the opinion of these nuns toward their convents was not much higher.

Because of the wide age difference, the urban marriage was likely to be short and usually ended with the death of the husband. The young widow seldom remarried. The husbands, in fact, discouraged their wives from remarrying after their deaths because it was believed that remarried widows would neglect the children of their first union. Therefore, Renaissance husbands usually wrote wills that gave widows special concessions that would be lost in the event of remarriage. Such concessions included the use of the family estate, the right to serve as guardians for their children, and often a sizable pension or annuity. In addition, the dowry paid by her father at the time of her marriage became the sole property of the widow.

Thus, for the first time in her life, the widowed woman was freed from male tutelage and at the same time acquired economic independence. In Florence, in the 1427 census cited above, more than half of the female population age forty or over were widows. The city literally teemed with widows, some of them wealthy enough to influence the urban culture. Indeed, wealthy widows commissioned some of the greatest artistic masterpieces of Florence. So to the question: were Renaissance women better off than their Medieval processors, there is no simple answer. If one looks at the urban widows, then the answer is certainly yes, but if the question refers to the thousands of young nuns in the convents, then the answer is no.

Renaissance Humanism

At the heart of the Renaissance was the intellectual movement known as humanism, sometimes in this context it is referred to as "civic humanism." In its most basic sense Renaissance humanism meant classical scholarship, the ability to read, understand, and appreciate the writings of the ancient world.

Although knowledge of Roman writers, like Virgil, Ovid, and Cicero, was not totally absent from the medieval world, there was a significant quantitative increase in Latin texts available to Renaissance scholars. The Latin works of Livy, Tacitus, Lucretius, and many more were rediscovered. Even more important, however, the literature of classical Greece and Byzantium became known to Italian scholars in their original language for the first time in a millennium. Even the texts of the Bible in their original Greek and Hebrew languages could now be studied by Renaissance scholars for the first time.[3] Furthermore, whereas the Medieval thinkers had perceived that pre-Christian texts would simply complement and confirm their own Christian assumptions, the intellectuals of the Renaissance began to use the knowledge from these classical texts in new ways. The people of the Renaissance became acutely aware of the unbridgeable gulf of time separating them from the ancient world. At the very same time that they came to understand the glory and magnificence of the ancient world they realized that that world was gone forever and could never be recovered. This "shock of recognition" is a fundamental aspect of Renaissance humanism. The similarities between the ancient city-states and those of Renaissance Italy made the ancient sources models of thought and action for their own time. All of this drove Renaissance culture toward a new secularism.

Renaissance humanists developed a program of education designed to replace the Medieval emphasis of logic and metaphysics with the study of the "humanities," which they believed would produce virtuous citizens capable of functioning in the new secular society.[4] These Renaissance concepts concerning the purpose and function of education in society were heavily influenced by the ancient Greek practice of *paideia*. Although the dictionary gives the meaning of *paideia* as "education," this term cannot be accurately translated into English by a single word. Basically, *paideia* means to instill *arête* into the young person through education and training. Unfortunately, *arête* is perhaps even more difficult to translate than *paideia*. Although it is usually translated simply as "virtue," it means much more than that. It includes the attributes of valor, manly beauty, dignity, and even excellence of workmanship and skill—but always in the moral sense of goodness, reputation, and merit. In short, *arête* includes all those things the Greeks considered to be the highest and best elements of their culture, and *paideia* was the method of passing those elements from one generation to the next.

The Greeks employed an analogy to demonstrate the function of *paideia*. The young person was compared to an unworked lump of clay. The potential of a lump of clay can be realized only through the skill of the potter's hands. The potter fashions the clay into a vessel that corresponds, as nearly as his skill can duplicate, to the image of the vessel, which he holds in his mind. In the same way, *paideia* forms the young person into the adult citizen and causes him to conform as nearly as possible to the idea of excellence, or *arête*, which the society holds in its collective mind. The attainment of *arête*, of virtue, of excellence, was the purpose of *paideia*, and therefore of education.

---

3. An ancient Latin version of the Bible, known as the Latin Vulgate, is the only version that the Roman Church admits to be authentic. The Vulgate translation was made by Jerome at the close of the 4th Century at the instigation of Pope Damasus I. It takes its name from the phrase *vulgata editio*, "the edition for the people" (cf. Vulgar Latin), and was written in an everyday Latin used in conscious distinction to the elegant Ciceronian Latin, of which Jerome was also a master. Jerome translated the Old Testament mostly from the Hebrew and Chaldaic, and revised the New Testament from an older Latin version. At first, Jerome did not want to include the Deuterocanonical books. However, Augustine of Hippo argued for their inclusion, and Pope Damasus insisted on it, so these books were included, thus keeping its Old Testament canon the same as the Septuagint, which was at that time the translation most widely used by Greek-speaking Christians. Renaissance scholars, however, now had access to the original Greek versions of the books of the New Testament, for the first time since antiquity.

4. This attitude is still referred to today as humanism, or even "secular humanism."

Through *arête* the individual attained freedom, that is freedom to operate successfully and productively within the society. The ancients did not understand our modern concept of freedom "from" society, but only understood freedom "within" society. The ancient Greek concept of educating or molding an individual into free person, of freeing, or liberating, the individual into society is the concept the Renaissance educated attempted to create, and it is the antecedent of our modern "liberal" education.

Unfortunately, the modern university has come to be thought of as a vocational school, rather than a liberal arts institution and that was not at all what the Renaissance educators had in mind. If one wished to train for a job or acquire craft skills, one became an apprentice or attended a vocational school. The humanists contended that the proper role of education is to liberate the individual through the process of perfecting him, something far more important than mere job training.

The curriculum believed most suited for the molding of a young person into a free and responsible adult was called the *studio humanitatis*, or "the study of humanity." It was designed to develop in the student those qualities of intellect and behavior, which truly distinguish human beings from the lower animals. The ideal product of the humanist education is what used to be called the "Renaissance man," a person trained in the classics, who possessed both the wisdom needed to know the right path to follow in any situation and the eloquence required to persuade his fellow citizens to follow him in that path.

Thus, Renaissance humanism exhibited three distinctive characteristics: First, it rejected the emphasis which the Medieval schools placed on professional training, whether in theology, law, or medicine, and advocated a liberal education based on a knowledge of moral philosophy and a command of eloquence. Second, humanism stressed the supreme importance of the Latin and Greek languages and a knowledge of the classical authors as the models of eloquence and the storehouses of wisdom. Third, humanism affirmed the possibility of human improvement through education and study. While true perfection, of course, can never be realized, progress toward that ideal is attainable. This attitude is in stark contrast with that of the Medieval world.

Political History of Italy during the Renaissance

The various city-states of Italy assumed diverse forms of government that ranged from monarchy to republic. The Kingdom of Naples, consisting of the entire southern half of the Italian peninsula, was a standard feudal monarchy. Milan and Savoy, however, were autonomous duchies; the area around Rome and the northeastern Italian peninsula were a series of semi-autonomous states under the direct control of the pope—the Papal States. The popes of the later Middle Ages and the Italian Renaissance could scarcely be considered churchmen; drawn from the nobility, they were ruthless politicians whose central goal was the expansion of their political power. Finally, Venice and Florence were republics, nominally ruled by senates but in reality ruled by a small group of nobility and wealthy capitalists.

Florence

The humanist movement began in Florence in the early 14th Century. The area around Florence, called Tuscany, had been the center of Italian culture throughout the High Middle Age. The most significant writers of the High Middle Age and the Renaissance were Tuscans, including Dante, Boccaccio, and Machiavelli. So important is this area for Italian culture that after the unification of Italy in the 19th Century, the Tuscan dialect became the official language of Italy.

While most of the city-states made significant contributions to Italian culture, the most important cultural and intellectual activity throughout the Renaissance occurred in Florence. Its rulers sought to glorify their wealth and power by subsidizing literature, philosophy, science, architecture, and the arts. Historians of the Renaissance have traditionally believed that the phenomenal growth of wealth in these small city-states was directly responsible for the flowering of literature, scholarship, and the arts during the Italian Renaissance, as the aristocracy and the wealthy sought to enhance and legitimate their power by patronizing the arts and scholarship.

Although Florence was nominally a republic, the chaos that followed the Ciompi Rebellion (1378)[5] continued for almost five decades until Cosimo de'Medici (1389–1464), the wealthiest of the Florentines, secretly gained control of the city. He exercised his power behind the scenes and spent large sums of money wildly on poets, scholars, painters, and sculptors. It was Cosimo who founded the Platonic Academy and provided the resources that revived Neo-Platonism in the western tradition.

His son, Lorenzo de Medici (1449–1492), ruled Florence openly as a totalitarian ruler. He, as did his father, sought to legitimate that rule by dumping vast amounts of resources into the arts, literature, and scholarship. However, his son, Piero de'Medici, did not have the strength or the shrewdness of his father, and the Medici were overturned by the establishment of a Florentine Republic under the puritanical monk, Savonarola.[6]

The Treaty of Lodi and the French Invasions

Renaissance Italy was constantly plagued with internal conflict, but simple power and military ability was not enough. The states were small and numerous and out of this tension grew a sophisticated and devious kind of diplomacy. The only way to successfully maintain territorial integrity was to make alliances with allies that one could not fully trust. The most important of those alliances was the one struck between Florence and the states of Milan and Naples, both bitter enemies of each other, known as the Treaty of Lodi (1454–1455). The purpose of the alliance was to check the growing power of Venice, and a frequent fourth party in this alliance was the pope himself who also came into conflict with Venice over the northernmost Papal States.

---

5. The Ciompi Rebellion in Florence in 1378 was an attempt by day-laborers and shop owners, mostly in the textile trades, and others of the *popolo minuto* (common people) to achieve a political voice. The goal of the uprising was to address inequalities rather than a complete upheaval of the constitution, and the new regime was successful for three years. Three new guilds were created and the committee of priors was adjusted. Although the *popolo grasso* (wealthy aristocrats) eventually regained power in 1381, Florentine politics would continue to be influenced by the idea of popular uprisings.

6. Girolamo Savonarola (1452–1498) was a Dominican priest and, briefly, ruler of Florence. He was known for religious fanaticism, anti-Renaissance preaching, and his book burning and destruction of art. Oddly, Lorenzo de'Medici was both a target of Savonarola's preaching and his patron. After the overthrow of the Medici in 1494, Savonarola was the sole leader of Florence, setting up a democratic republic. His chief enemies were the Duke of Milan and Pope Alexander VI, who issued numerous restraints against him, all of which were ignored. In 1497 he and his followers carried out the famous Bonfire of the Vanities. They sent boys from door to door collecting items associated with moral "laxity": mirrors, cosmetics, "lewd" pictures, "pagan" books, gaming tables, fine dresses, and the works of "immoral" poets, and burnt them all in a large pile in the Piazza della Signoria of Florence. Notoriously, fine Florentine Renaissance artwork was lost in Savanarola's bonfires, including paintings by Sandro Botticelli. On May 13, 1497, he was excommunicated by Pope Alexander VI and in 1498 he was simultaneously hanged and burned. He was charged with uttering prophecies, sedition, and religious error. The Medici regained control over Florence.

This delicate balance, however, collapsed when pope Alexander VI (1492–1503), Florence, and Naples betrayed Milan at the time Naples invaded that country. This is perhaps one of the single most important bad moves in the history of the Renaissance. The ruler of Milan, Ludovico il Moro, fearful that Florence of the Papal States would militarily support Naples, asked the French king for help.

Charles VIII of France (1483–1498) was more than willing to help Milan. The French had dynastic claims over Italian territory; throughout the 15th Century, however, they were content to do nothing about them. Charles VIII, however, marched through Florence, the Papal States, and Naples as a conqueror in 1495. The speed and efficiency of Charles's march through Italy, as well as the seemingly unstoppable power of an alliance between France and Milan, struck terror in the hearts of all the other city-states. At the instigation of Ferdinand of Aragon, King of Sicily and Spain, the League of Venice was formed in 1495 consisting of Spain, Sicily, Venice, the Papal States, and the Holy Roman Empire. Even Milan's ruler, Ludovico il Moro, was terrified by the swiftness of Charles's conquests and joined the League of Venice the year after it was created. Charles did not really stand a chance against such a coalition and he was soon driven out of Italy. The forces behind this conflict, however, endured well into the 16th Century and helped inflame such radical cultural changes as the Reformation in Germany.

The French, however, pressed their claims again under the leadership of Louis XII (1498–1515). They were assisted by Alexander VI, the pope from the Borgia family that had originally supported the Neapolitan invasion of Milan. Like Ludovico il Moro, Alexander VI saw an alliance with France as a way to solve the papacy's perpetual rivalry with Venice. The Papal States extended far to the north on the eastern coast of the Italian peninsula where they came very close to the territory controlled by Venice. These regions had always been a problem to the popes, and Venice actively encouraged their disloyalty. Even though Venice was an ostensible ally, Alexander VI nevertheless quit the League of Venice and allied himself with Louis XII. This alliance was enough to again shatter the delicate balance of power among the states of Italy. In 1499, Louis XII conquered Milan and in 1500 Louis XII and Ferdinand of Aragon conquered Naples and divided it in half between them. The power of France allowed Alexander VI to conquer all the cities of Romagna, the area of northern Italy along the Adriatic coast, and quell any rebellion that might happen in the future.

The Papal States

History has not been kind to the popes of the Italian Renaissance, especially the three "worldly" popes, Alexander VI (1492–1503), Julius II (1503–1513), and Leo X (1513–1521). The papacy from the mid-14th Century to the mid-16th Century consisted, with a couple interruptions, of a long series of greedy, political, devious, and sometimes sex-crazed popes interested in temporal power far more than religious principles. However, as usual, there is another side to the coin, so to speak. These men occupied the papal throne during both an exciting and frightening time. Without going into details about their individual lives, the popes of the Renaissance pursued a remarkably consistent set of objectives and sincerely believed that those objectives outweighed every other consideration. From the mid-14th Century to the Reformation years, the popes and the Papal States government pursued four central objectives: (1) to reassert the supreme authority of the pope over Christians; (2) to bring about a uniformity of Christian belief by stamping out heresy; (3) to recover political power of the Papal States so that the papacy could remain politically neutral and unaffected by European and Italian power politics; and (4) to protect Christianity from Islam, primarily by driving the Ottoman Turks out of Europe and freeing Constantinople from Turkish domination.

The Muslim Threat

The fear of Islamic aggression was very real. To Europeans of the time it appeared that the Ottoman Turks would eventually conquer all of Europe, and these fears came perilously close to becoming reality. Church officials, including the pope, realized that this would mean nothing less than the complete destruction of Christianity and Western Civilization. The Ottomans were one of a number of Turkish tribes that migrated from the central Asian steppe. They were initially a nomadic people who followed a primitive shamanistic religion. Contact with various settled peoples led to the introduction of Islam, and under Islamic influence, the Turks acquired their greatest fighting tradition, that of the gazi warrior. Well-trained and highly skilled, gazi warriors fought to conquer the infidel, acquiring land and riches in the process. While the gazi warriors fought for Islam, the greatest military asset of the Ottoman Empire was the standing army of formally Christian soldiers, the Janissaries. Originally created in 1330 by Orhan (d.1359), the Janissaries were Christian captives from conquered territories. Educated in the Islamic faith and trained as soldiers, the Janissaries were forced to provide annual tribute in the form of military service. The conquest of Thrace gave the Ottomans a foothold in Europe from which future campaigns into the Balkans and Greece were launched, and Adrianople became the Ottoman capital in 1366.

Over the next century, the Ottomans conquered an empire that included Anatolia and increasingly larger sections of Byzantine territories in Eastern Europe and Asia Minor. Ottoman expansion into Europe was well underway in the late 14th Century. Gallipoli was conquered in 1354 and at the Battle of Nicopolis in 1394, the Ottomans crushed a vast crusading army, taking many European

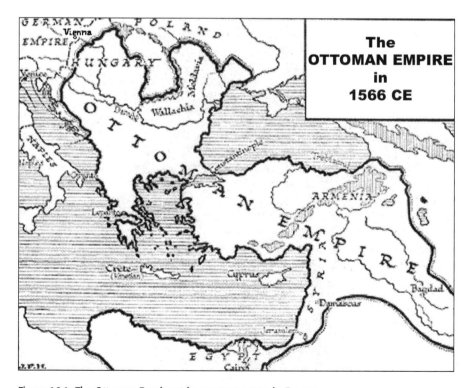

Figure 16.1: The Ottoman Empire at its greatest extent in Europe.

leaders hostage. The disaster was so great that the first survivors to return to France were imprisoned as liars. But Nicopolis was only the beginning. The appearance of the Tatars under Tamarlane early in the 15th Century temporarily delayed Turkish advances, but the Ottomans soon resumed attacks on Eastern Europe. A Hungarian-Polish army was decimated at Varna in 1444 by Murad II (c.1403–1451) and Ottoman conquests were virtually unchecked during the reign of his son, Mehmed II the Conqueror (1432–1481)

Constantinople itself was captured in 1453, sending a shockwave across Europe. With the fall of Byzantium, a wave of Byzantine refugees fled to the Latin West, carrying with them the classical and Hellenistic knowledge that provided additional impetus to the burgeoning humanism of the Renaissance, but the Muslim advance continued. Athens fell in 1456, and Belgrade narrowly escaped capture when a peasant army led by the Hungarian Janos Hunyadi held off a siege in the same year. Nevertheless, Serbia, Bosnia, Wallachia, and the Khanate of Crimea were all under Ottoman control by 1478. The Turks commanded the Black Sea and the northern Aegean, and many prime trade routes had been closed to European shipping. The Islamic threat loomed even larger when an Ottoman beachhead was established at Otranto in Italy in 1480. Although the Turkish presence in Italy was short-lived, it appeared as if Rome itself must soon fall into Islamic hands. In 1529, the Ottomans moved up the Danube and besieged Vienna. The siege was ultimately unsuccessful, and the Turks, for the first time, began to retreat. Although the Ottomans continued to instill fear well into the 16th Century, internal struggles began to undermine the once overwhelming military supremacy of the Ottoman Empire. The outcome of battles was no longer a foregone conclusion and Europeans began to score victories against the Turks.[7]

The Late Renaissance

At any rate, each of the Renaissance popes pursued these goals differently, and all of the sordid history of the papacy in the Renaissance arose from these rather intelligent and laudable goals. The most important of these objectives, as far as the popes were concerned, was the maintenance of papal neutrality by shoring up the pope's control of the Papal States.

By 1500, the only major Italian players left were Venice and the Papal States. In 1503, the Papal States came under the rule of Giuliano delle Rovere, or Julius II (1503–1513). Julius had two overwhelming goals: the eviction of the Venetians from Romagna and the eviction of the French from Italy. Both the Venetian presence in the Papal States and the French presence in Italy threatened to make the papacy a pawn of either the Venetians or the French. Julius accomplished his first goal in 1509 and permanently secured papal power in Romagna. However, two years later, Julius allied himself with Venice and Ferdinand of Aragon in the second Holy League. With their combined strength, they drove the French out of Italy by 1512.

Julius II, like Alexander VI before him, conducted himself more like a despotic politician than like the leader of the Christian religion. It was Julius II who inspired open criticism by the humanists of the Northern Renaissance, including Erasmus, who questioned the spiritual authority of a person and an office that had become overwhelmingly secular. Most scholars consider the growth of the

---

7. In several of his pronouncements leading up to the destruction of the World Trade Center in 2001, Osama bin Laden cited the Turkish defeat, i.e., the failure of the Ottomans to conquer all of Europe in the 16th Century, as one of the unforgivable insults to Islam which justifies the use of terrorism against the West.

Papal States in the High Renaissance to be one of the direct causes of the European Reformation. Yet, this was the same pope who commissioned Michelangelo to paint the Sistine chapel, one of the greatest achievements of Western art.

France, as you might imagine, was not finished with Italy. Under Francis I (1515–1547), France invaded Italy yet again but was eventually defeated by the forces under Pope Leo X in 1516. The Papal States and France cut a deal which gave the King of France control over his clergy and the pope control over church councils. It was the last significant moment in Italian Renaissance history; the Reformation, one of the most significant events in European history, was on the eve of its eruption, awaiting a cold morning at the end of October 1517, to permanently change the face of European culture. During this time, Italy would be successively invaded by France, Germany, and Spain, in a titanic struggle over the floundering city-states. No politician like Alexander VI or Julius II could stand in the way, and in 1527, the Holy Roman Emperor, Charles V, sacked Rome—as so many invaders had done before him—and brought the power of the Papal States to its close.

Renaissance Scholarship

Francesco Petrarch (1304–1374)

Any survey of Renaissance thinkers and writers begins with Francesco Petrarch, the first great exponent of humanism. Born of an exiled Florentine family in 1304, Petrarch was urged by his bourgeois father to study law. Petrarch came upon the works of Cicero in the course of his reading and was led to a passion for all the classics. When his father died, he gave up law and turned to a life of scholarship. But his love of the pagan classics in no way diminished his Christianity, for he believed he could harmonize classical genius with divine revelation—the result is sometimes referred to as "Christian humanism."

It was Petrarch who first undertook the collection of ancient manuscripts. He persuaded others to join him in a search through monastic and cathedral libraries that took him all over Italy and into France and Germany as well. His private library, the first of its kind, became a model for scholars and educated gentlemen. His enthusiasm was contagious. Following his example many sons of the wealthy families took up the search and began to build their own libraries. Affluent patrons became interested and by the 15th Century had founded such famous libraries as the Laurentian in Florence, St. Mark's in Venice, and the Vatican in Rome.

Petrarch lived only a generation after Dante, but in these two figures we can see the shift from medieval to modern times. His irrepressible pursuit of fame culminated in a spectacular ceremony in Rome in 1341, and he was crowned with a laurel wreath as the foremost poet and scholar of his time, thus becoming the first "poet laureate" of modern times. By his inexhaustible industry in scholarship he brought the mind of Western Civilization into sympathetic contact with classical antiquity. In the ensuing centuries humanism came to mean the cultivation of the human personality so that the individual, with liberated intelligence and talent, could lead a life of dignity, self-reliance, and creativeness. Francesco Petrarch died in 1374. His "Letter to Posterity" epitomizes the humanist attitude:

> Greetings. It is possible that some word of me may have come to you, though even this is doubtful, since an insignificant and obscure name will scarcely penetrate far in either time or space. If, however, you should have heard of me, you may desire to know what manner of man I was, or what was the outcome of my labors, especially those of which some description or, at any rate, the bare titles may have reached you.

To begin with myself, then, the utterances of men concerning me will differ widely, since in passing judgment almost everyone is influenced not so much by truth as by preference, and good and evil report alike know no bounds. I was, in truth, a poor mortal like yourself, neither very exalted in my origin, nor, on the other hand, of the most humble birth, but belonging, as Augustus Caesar says of himself, to an ancient family. As to my disposition, I was not naturally perverse or wanting in modesty, however the contagion of evil associations may have corrupted me. My youth was gone before I realized it; I was carried away by the strength of manhood; but a riper age brought me to my senses and taught me by experience the truth I had long before read in books, that youth and pleasure are vanity—nay, that the Author of all ages and times permits us miserable mortals, puffed up with emptiness, thus to wander about, until finally, coming to a tardy consciousness of our sins, we shall learn to know ourselves. In my prime I was blessed with a quick and active body, although not exceptionally strong; and while I do not lay claim to remarkable personal beauty, I was comely enough in my best days. I was possessed of a clear complexion, between light and dark, lively eyes, and for long years a keen vision, which however deserted me, contrary to my hopes, after I reached my sixtieth birthday, and forced me, to my great annoyance, to resort to glasses. Although I had previously enjoyed perfect health, old age brought with it the usual array of discomforts.

My parents were honorable folk, Florentine in their origin, of medium fortune, or, I may as well admit it, in a condition verging upon poverty. They had been expelled from their native city, and consequently I was born in exile. I have always possessed an extreme contempt for wealth; not that riches are not desirable in themselves, but because I hate the anxiety and care which are invariably associated with them. I certainly do not long to be able to give gorgeous banquets. So-called convivial which are but vulgar bouts, sinning against sobriety and good manners, have always been repugnant to me. I have ever felt that it was irksome and profitless to invite others to such affairs, and not less so to be bidden to them myself. On the other hand, the pleasure of dining with one's friends is so great that nothing has ever given me more delight than their unexpected arrival, nor have I ever willingly sat down to table without a companion. Nothing displeases me more than display, for not only is it bad in itself, and opposed to humility, but it is troublesome and distracting.

I have taken pride in others, never in myself, and however insignificant I may have been, I have always been still less important in my own judgment. My anger has very often injured myself, but never others. I have always been most desirous of honorable friendships, and have faithfully cherished them. I make this boast without fear, since I am confident that I speak truly. While I am very prone to take offence, I am equally quick to forget injuries, and have a memory tenacious of benefits. In my familiar associations with kings and princes, and in my friendship with noble personages, my good fortune has been such as to excite envy. But it is the cruel fate of those who are growing old that they can commonly only weep for friends who have passed away. The greatest kings of this age have loved and courted me. They may know why; I certainly do not. With some of them I was on such terms that they seemed in a certain sense my guests rather than I theirs; their lofty position in no way embarrassing me, but, on the contrary, bringing with it many advantages. I fled, however, from many of those to whom I was greatly attached; and such was my innate longing for liberty, that I studiously avoided those whose very name seemed incompatible with the freedom that I loved.

I possessed a well-balanced rather than a keen intellect, one prone to all kinds of good wholesome study, but especially inclined to moral philosophy and the art of poetry. The latter indeed, I neglected as time went on, and took delight in sacred literature. Finding in that a hidden sweetness which I had once esteemed but lightly, I came to regard the works of the poets as only amenities. Among the many subjects which interested me, I dwelt especially upon antiquity, for our own age has always I repelled me, so that, had it not been for the love of those dear to me, I should have preferred to have been born in any other period than our own. In order to forget my own times, I have continually striven to place myself in spirit in other ages, and consequently I delighted in history; ,not that the conflicting statements did not :offend me, but when in doubt I accepted what appeared to me most probable, or yielded to the authority of the writer.

My style, as many claimed, was clear and forcible; but to me it seemed weak and obscure. In ordinary conversation with friends, or with those about me, I never gave any thought to my language, and I have always wondered that Augustus Caesar should have taken such pains in this respect. When, however, the subject itself, or the place or listener, seemed to demand it, I gave some attention to style, with what success I cannot pretend to say; let them judge in whose presence I spoke. If only I have lived well, it matters little to me how I talked. Mere elegance of language can produce at best but an empty renown.

Later Florentines

Subsequent Florentine thinkers, such as Leonardo Bruni (c. 1370–1444) and Leon Battista Alberti (1404–1472), agreed with Petrarch on the need for eloquence and the study of classical literature, but also believed human beings should be active and useful to society. This period marked the emergence of individuality, when ambition, fame, and even the striving for wealth, were thought of as noble and desirable characteristics. Humanists now argued that human progress involved gaining mastery over the earth and its resources. For example, in his *On the Family* (1443), Alberti argued that the nuclear family was instituted by nature for the well being of humanity. Unfortunately, he relegated women to a purely domestic role, asserting that "man is by nature more energetic and industrious" and woman was created "to increase and continue generations, to nourish and preserve those already born." However, such attitudes were fiercely resisted by a few notable women humanists, such as Onorata Rodiana,[8] Queens Isabella of Spain and Elizabeth I of England, Charlotte Guillard,[9] and Marguerite de la Roque.[10]

Lorenzo Valla (1407–1457)

As the humanist movement gained in prestige, it spread from Florence to the other principle cities of Italy. One of the best known humanist scholars was Lorenzo Valla. He studied Latin under

---

8. Onorata Rodiana was a talented fresco painter, who was commissioned by a Marquis to do some extensive work in his palace. Accosted by one of his staff, she stabbed her assailant and then fled. The Marquis eventually called off his hounds, but Onorata had, in the meantime, joined a band of "condottieri"(mercenaries for hire). Onorata soon became leader of her own mercenary band and over the next 30 years she excelled not only at painting frescoes, but at banditry and died with a sword in her hand fighting invading Venetians in 1472.

9. Charlotte Guillard inherited Soliel d'Or, a prestigious publishing house, when her husband died prematurely. Soon re-married to a bookseller, she worked tirelessly to expand her business and to make her publishing house the most prestigious in Paris. She hired women as editors and published long lists of humanist histories, references, and textbooks. Her company is still in business today.

10. Marguerite de la Roque wanted a bit of adventure and when her cousin, Roberval, and his friend, Jacques Cartier, decided to explore Canada, she went along. Life onboard ship was a bit boring so she had an affair and soon found herself pregnant. Roberval accused her of betraying their family honor and tossed her off the ship and onto a small isolated island in the St. Lawrence River. In short order she buried her child, her maid and her lover. She, however, survived three winters alone living like a starving hermit before a passing ship finally rescued her. Once back in France she opted for a more sedate life of teaching.

Leonardo Bruni and Greek under Giovanni Aurispa, two of the most imminent humanist scholars of their day. He taught rhetoric for a time at the University of Pavia, but when he wrote an open letter criticizing the jurist Bartolo and ridiculing the shortcomings of contemporary jurisprudence, he was forced to leave Pavia. In 1433 he began a long service in the court of the king of Naples and finally returned to Rome in 1448 as a secretary in the papal chancery. Most modern scholars agree that in terms of sheer intellectual power and originality, Valla was the ablest of all the Renaissance humanists. He had a keen intellect and a driving ambition to excel at scholarship. In every field that he touched, he tended to take unconventional, even extreme, positions.

Humanists from Petrarch onward became aware that many classical texts contained omissions, interpolations, and textual errors as a result of simple scribal mistakes that had accumulated through centuries of recopying. Thus, humanists sought not only to find lost works but also to detect and remedy textual errors, either through comparison of multiple manuscripts or through conjecture based on their sense of the author's style or the general context. Yet even at its best, the early humanistic work of criticizing and emending ancient texts was haphazard. Lorenzo Valla developed the tools of historical and linguistic criticism and analysis to interpret ancient records and documents. In the words of Charles Nauert:[11]

> Valla hit upon the second of the two truly new ideas of Renaissance thought (the first being Patriarch's discovery of historical discontinuity). This idea, which no ancient or medieval thinker had clearly seen, was that human language, like everything else outside of the material world, is a cultural artifact, so that language undergoes historical development and changes with the passage of time....
>
> The most famous exercise of his critical method was a tract he wrote on behalf of his employer King Alfonso of Naples when the king was at war with the pope. His *Declamation on the Forged Donation of Constantine* (c. 1440) attacked the authenticity of a document that formed an important part of the medieval popes' claim to possess political (rather than only religious) authority over all of Western Europe. The Donation purports to be a grant of political authority by the first Christian emperor, Constantine, to Pope Sylvester I. It is a blatant forgery made in the eighth century (four centuries after Constantine). But it had been included in the collections of canon law and had been cited by papal apologists during their conflicts with the medieval German emperors. A few critics had cautiously wondered about its authenticity. But Valla did not merely wonder. He subjected the document to intensive critical examination, applying general principles of both historical and linguistic criticism, two ways of thinking little practiced in the Middle Ages. First Valla advanced purely theoretical objections. Such a grant would never have been made by a competent emperor like Constantine, and even if it had been offered, a saintly pope like Sylvester would have refused it, for he had no worldly ambition. This rhetorical thrust at the political ambitions of the current pope could have been made by any medieval defender of royal power. Valla's second line of argument was more innovative, involving a basic principle of historical criticism. This was the demand for independent corroboration. If Constantine really did transfer control over the Western provinces, where are the other evidences of Sylvester's rule? Where are the laws, charters, and other documents issued in his name, and the

11. Nauert, Charles G., *Humanism and the Culture of Renaissance Europe* (1995), Cambridge University Press, Cambridge, pp. 36-40.

lists of officials he appointed? Where are the coins struck bearing his image? Which contemporary or later chroniclers recorded the events of Sylvester's reign? Turning to the text itself, he subjected it to close verbal analysis. For example, 'Constantine' speaks of his new capital of 'Constantinople', but that name was never used in his time. Again, the alleged emperor speaks of the *optimates* as if they were Roman nobles, but any student of Roman history should know that they were an aristocratic political faction during the civil wars of the late republic, centuries earlier. Most telling of all, however, is Valla's devastating application of philological science: the language used in the document is not the Latin used in genuine documents of the fourth-century imperial chancery but shows characteristics of a much later phase in the degeneration of classical Latin. For example, why did the author use the medieval word *banna* for *flag*, when any Roman would have written the correct word, *vexillum*? Leaving aside the question why Constantine, a layman, would presume to grant a bishop authority to ordain priests, why in the document does he use the medieval term *clericare* for *ordain*? Valla also pointed out grossly unclassical grammatical forms. In short, the document must be a forgery. Both historically and linguistically, it contains gross anachronisms. The Middle Ages had absolutely no sensitivity to anachronism, as art historians and literary historians have repeatedly noted, because it was quite innocent of the concept of historical discontinuity and periodization that Petrarch had invented.

Valla's critical attack was devastating, though in fact the papacy did not quit citing the Donation in defense of its political claims for several centuries. In 1519, the German humanist Ulrich von Hutten published Valla's treatise as Evangelical propaganda against the popes. But Valla did not conceive his tract as an attack on the papacy at all, only as an attack on the *political* claims that the current pope was making against the king of Naples.

These same tools of historical criticism, developed by Valla in the 15th Century, are still used by scholars today to probe the ancient world.

By the beginning of the 16th Century the cause of humanism had been won. With few exceptions, the monastic libraries had yielded their treasures of ancient manuscripts to the educated public. Even by the late 15th Century the leaders of Italian intellectual were no longer the humanists but rather the philosophers, who were now able to use the classical heritage to enrich develop their own philosophical systems.

Renaissance Art

Perhaps the most towering achievement of the Italian Renaissance was in the realm of the visual arts. During the Renaissance, as in the ancient classical world, art was a public thing, expected to be available to the people to enjoy as they strolled through the cities, attended church, or when they visited public buildings. While upper-class boys pursued humanistic literary studies to prepare them for public life, they were discouraged from pursuing a career in the plastic arts. Michelangelo's father dismissed his son's interest in art as "shameful." On the other hand, peasant boys had little opportunity for an art career, unless they were "discovered," like Giotto, by an influential patron. In fact, the majority of Renaissance artists came from artisan families and began, like Botticelli, as apprentices. Late in the Renaissance artists began to gain a measure of new respect, as wealthy patrons stopped viewing them as mere manual laborers.

The idea of rebirth lies at the heart of all Renaissance achievements: artists, scholars, scientists, philosophers, architects, and rulers believed that the way to greatness and enlightenment was through the study of the Golden Age of the ancient Greeks and Romans. They rejected the more recent, medieval past, which constituted the "Gothic" era, meaning "barbaric." Instead of this,

Figure 16.2: Giotto, "Jesus Entering Jerusalem."

inspired by humanism, they looked to the literary and philosophical traditions, and the artistic and engineering achievements, of Greco-Roman antiquity. There is not time to pursue a detailed discussion of Renaissance art in a book of this nature, but a cursory description of the most famous Renaissance artists is in order.

Giotto (c. 1267–1337)

The Florentine painter and architect Giotto di Bondone is recognized as the first genius of art in the Italian Renaissance. Yet, in fact, Giotto still had one foot in the Middle Ages, so to speak, that is, he was a transitional figure between the humanistic art of the Italian Renaissance and the Gottic style of the Late Middle Age. Giotto lived and worked during a time when the spirit of the Italian people was first being freed from the shackles of Medieval restraint. In the tradition of his Medieval predecessors, he dealt almost completely with traditional religious subjects, but in the spirit of Renaissance humanism he gave these subjects an earthly, full-blooded life and force. He was born about 1266 in the village of Vespignano, near Florence. His father was a small landed farmer. Giorgio Vasari, one of Giotto's biographers, tells how Cimabue, a well-known Florentine painter, discovered Giotto's talents. Cimabue supposedly saw the 12-year-old boy sketching one of his father's sheep on a flat rock and was so impressed with his talent that he persuaded the father to allow Giotto become his apprentice.

Figure 16.3: Giotto, "The Mourning of Christ."

The earliest works of Giotto's are a series of frescoes[12] on the life of St. Francis in the church at Assisi. The human and animal figures are realistic and the scenes expressive of the gentle spirit of this patron saint of animals. In about 1305 and 1306 Giotto painted a notable series of 38 frescoes

---

12. The first fresco-type paintings date back at least 30,000 years ago to the paintings created in the Chauvet cave in France. Some 15,000 years ago frescoes were created in other caves in Lascaux, France and Altamira, Spain. These early examples of fresco painting are testimony of the long and varied history of this art form. By 1500 BC the techniques of fresco painting evolved to painting on wet plaster, allowing more flexibility in the use and location of frescoes for decorative purposes. The earliest known examples of such frescoes around 1500 BC are to be found on the island of Crete in Greece. Frescoes were also painted in ancient Greece, but few of these works have survived. In southern Italy, at Paestum, which was a Greek colony, a tomb containing frescoes dating back to 470 BC has been discovered. Roman frescoes, found in Pompeii and Herculaneum and dating from the first century CE, include remarkably realistic scenes of homes and gardens. The most celebrated frescoes in Western Europe were painted by the great Italian masters, beginning with Giotto. This term "fresco" indicates the only pictorial technique where no agglutinants (egg, oil, glue, acrylic resin, etc.) are used to fasten the pigments to the painted surface. The pigments are mixed with water, deposited on skated lime mortar, freshly applied on a wall. On contact with the air, the lime undergoes a transformation called carbonatation, which creates a fine sheet of limestone and traps the pigments, fixing them in a durable way to the underlayer.

Figure 16.4: "The Birth of Venus."

in the Arena Chapel in Padua.[13] The frescoes illustrate the lives of Jesus Christ and of the Virgin Mary. The compositions are simple, the backgrounds are subordinated, and the faces are studies in emotional expression. Two of these frescoes, "Christ Entering Jerusalem" (Fig. 16.2) and "The Mourning of Christ," (Fig. 16.3) are among the most famous paintings in Western art.

Giotto executed commissions from princes and high churchmen in Rome, Naples, and Florence. In the Bargello in Florence he painted a series of his Biblical scenes and among the bystanders in the paintings is a portrait of his friend the poet Dante. The Church of Santa Croce, also in Florence, is also adorned by Giotto murals depicting the life of St. Francis. In 1334 the city of Florence honored Giotto with the title of Magnus Magister (Great Master) and appointed him city architect and superintendent of public works. In this capacity he designed the famous campanile (bell tower). He died in 1337, before the work was finished.

In common with other artists of his day, Giotto lacked the technical knowledge of anatomy and perspective that later painters mastered. Yet what he possessed was infinitely greater than the technical skill of the artists who followed him. He had a grasp of human emotion and of what is significant in human life. In concentrating on these essentials he created compelling pictures of people under stress, of people caught up in crises and soul-searching decisions. Modern artists often seek inspiration from Giotto. In him they find a direct approach to human experience that remains valid for every age.

---

13. Called the "Arena Chapel" because it occupies the site of an ancient Roman arena.

Figure 16.5: Botticelli, "Primavera."

Sandro Botticelli (1445–1510)

Botticelli's "Birth of Venus" (c. 1485, Fig. 16.4) and "Primavera" (1477–78, Fig. 16.5) are often said to epitomize for modern viewers the artistic spirit of the Renaissance. Ironacally, Sandro Botticelli remained little known for centuries after his death. Then his work was rediscovered late in the 19th Century by a group of artists in England known as the Pre-Raphaelites. He was one of the most individualistic painters of the Italian Renaissance. His ecclesiastical commissions included work for all the major churches of Florence and for the Sistine Chapel in Rome. His original name was Alessandro Di Mariano Filipepi. The name we know him by was derived from his elder brother Giovanni, a pawnbroker, who was called Il Botticello ("The Little Barrel"). Botticelli was apprenticed to a goldsmith. Later he was a pupil of the painter Fra Filippo Lippi. He spent his entire life in Florence except for a visit to Rome in 1481–82. There he painted wall frescoes in the Sistine Chapel at the Vatican. In Florence, Botticelli was a protege of several members of the powerful Medici family, for whom he painted many family portraits.

The most original of his paintings, however, are those illustrating Greek and Roman legends. Botticelli's sharply contoured, slender form and rippling sinuous line, for which he is famous, was influenced by the precise draftsmanship he acquired during his training as a goldsmith, but his sophisticated understanding of perspective and anatomy never overshadows the sheer poetry of his vision. Nothing is more gracious, in lyrical beauty, than Botticelli's mythological paintings "Primavera" ("The Allagory of Spring") and "The Birth of Venus," where the pagan story of the goddess' origin is depicted with reverent seriousness and Venus is the Virgin Mary in another form. But it is also

Figure 16.6: Leonardo da Vinci, "Mona Lisa."

significant that art critics have never agreed on the actual subject of "Primavera," but though scholars may argue, we need no theories to make "Primavera" appealing to us. In this allegory of life, beauty, and knowledge united by love, Botticelli catches the freshness of an early spring morning, with the pale light shining through the tall, straight trees, already laden with their golden fruit: oranges, or perhaps the mythical Golden Apples of the Hesperides.

Leonardo da Vinci (1452–1519)

Leonardo da Vinci, painter, draftsman, sculptor, architect, and engineer whose genius, perhaps more than that of any other figure, epitomized the Renaissance humanist ideal. He is thought of today as the true "Renaissance man." His "Last Supper" (1495–97, Fig. 16.7) and "Mona Lisa" (1503–06, Fig. 16.6) are among the most widely popular and influential paintings of the Renaissance. His notebooks reveal a spirit of scientific inquiry and a mechanical inventiveness that were centuries ahead of his time. He is such in interesting and important figure that his life deserves a somewhat more detailed discussion.

Leonardo da Vinci was the illegitimate son of a 25-year-old notary, Ser Piero, and a peasant girl, Caterina. Leonardo was born in 1452, in Vinci, Italy, just outside Florence. His father took custody of the little fellow shortly after his birth, while his mother married someone else and moved to a neighboring town. They kept on having kids, although not with each other, and they eventually supplied him with a total of 17 half sisters and brothers.

Figure 16.7: Leonardo da Vinci, "The Last Supper."

Growing up in his father's home in Vinci, Leonardo had access to scholarly texts owned by family and friends. He was also exposed to Vinci's longstanding painting tradition, and when he was about 15 his father apprenticed him to the renowned workshop of Andrea del Verrochio in Florence. Even as an apprentice, Leonardo demonstrated his colossal talent. Indeed, his genius seems to have seeped into a number of pieces produced by the Verrochio's workshop from the period 1470–1475. For example, one of Leonardo's first big breaks was to paint an angel in Verrochio's "Baptism of Christ," and Leonardo was so much better than his master that Verrochio allegedly resolved never to paint again.

Beginning in 1482 he worked for Ludovico Sforza, the Duke of Milan, for 17 years, leaving only after Duke fall from power in 1499. It was during these years that Leonardo reached new heights of scientific and artistic achievement. The Duke not only kept Leonardo busy painting, sculpting, and designing elaborate court festivals, but also designing weapons, buildings, and machinery. From 1485 to 1490, Leonardo produced a series of studies on many subjects, including nature, flying machines, geometry, mechanics, municipal construction, canals, and architecture. His studies from this period contain designs for advanced weapons, including a tank and other war vehicles, various combat devices, and submarines. Also during this period, Leonardo produced his first anatomical studies. His Milan workshop was a veritable hive of activity, buzzing with apprentices and students.

Alas, Leonardo's interests were so broad, and he was so often compelled by new subjects, that he usually failed to finish what he started. This lack of "stick-to-it-ness" resulted in his completing only about six works in these 17 years, but they included the masterpieces "The Last Supper" and "The Virgin on the Rocks." Yet he left dozens of paintings and projects unfinished or unrealized. He spent most of his time studying science, either by going out into nature and observing things or by locking himself away in his workshop cutting up bodies or pondering universal truths.

Between 1490 and 1495 he developed his habit of recording his studies in meticulously illustrated notebooks. His work covered four main themes: painting, architecture, the elements of mechanics, and human anatomy. These studies and sketches were collected into various codices and manuscripts, which are now hungrily collected by museums and individuals.[14]

After the invasion by the French and Ludovico Sforza's fall from power in 1499, Leonardo was left to search for a new patron. Over the next 16 years, he worked and traveled throughout Italy for a number of employers, including the dastardly Cesare Borgia.[15] He traveled for a year with Borgia's army as a military engineer and even met Niccolo Machiavelli, author of "The Prince." About 1503, Leonardo reportedly began work on the "Mona Lisa." On July 9, 1504, he received notice of the death of his father, Ser Piero. Through the contrivances of his meddling half brothers and sisters, Leonardo was deprived of any inheritance. The death of a beloved uncle also resulted in a scuffle over inheritance, but this time Leonardo beat out his scheming siblings and wound up with use of the uncle's land and money. From 1513 to 1516, he worked in Rome, maintaining a workshop and undertaking a variety of projects for the Pope. He continued his studies of human anatomy and physiology, but the Pope forbade him from dissecting cadavers, which truly cramped his style.

Following the death of his patron Giuliano de Medici in March of 1516, he was offered the title of Premier Painter and Engineer and Architect of the King by Francis I in France. His last and perhaps most generous patron, Francis I provided Leonardo with a cushy job, including a stipend and manor house near the royal chateau at Amboise. Although suffering from a paralysis of the right hand, Leonardo was still able to draw and teach. He produced studies for the Virgin Mary from "The Virgin and Child with St. Anne," studies of cats, horses, dragons, St. George, anatomical

---

14. Bill Gates recently purchased the Codex Leicester for $30 million.

15. Cesare Borgia (1475–1507), Duke of Valencia, Dark Prince of Romagna, the illegitimate son of Pope Alexander VI (Rodrigo Borgia) and brother to Lucrezia Borgia. Cesare was initially groomed by his father for a Church career and was elevated by his father to the rank of Cardinal by the age of 22. Alexander VI staked the hopes for the Borgia family on Cesare's brother Juan, who was made captain general of the military forces of the papacy. When Juan was assassinated, Alexander was forced to substitute Cesare, despite the fact that this conflicted with Cesare's vows. Cesare's career was founded entirely upon his father's ability to distribute patronage. Appointed commander of the papal armies, Cesare was sent by his father to subdue the cities of Romagna in central Italy. Though in theory subject directly to the pope, the rulers of these cities had been practically independent or dependent on other states for generations. Alexander VI hoped that by subduing them his son would create a new central Italian state that would rival Naples, Florence, Milan and Venice. It was during this time that Cesare Borgia briefly employed Leonardo da Vinci as military architect and engineer at one point. Though an immensely capable general and statesman, Cesare could do nothing without continued papal patronage and the death of his father ended his own career. Gravely ill at the time that his father died in 1503, his political enemies, led by pope Julius II, were able to seize and imprison him. Exiled to Spain, in 1504, he escaped from a Spanish prison two years later and joined his brother-in-law, King Jean d'Albret of Navarre. Serving Navarre as a soldier, he died at the siege of Viana in 1507, at the age of thirty-one. Cesare Borgia was greatly admired by Niccolo Machiavelli, who knew him personally. Machiavelli used many of his exploits and tactics as examples in *The Prince*. A few scholars, however, have argued that Machiavelli's praise for Borgia was a parody, to cover up the actual anti-hero of the work, Ferdinand II of Aragon.

studies, studies on the nature of water, drawings of the Deluge, and of various machines. Leonardo died on May 2, 1519 in Cloux, France. Legend has it that King Francis was at his side when he died, cradling Leonardo's head in his arms.

The "Portrait of Mona Lisa," also known as "La Gioconda," the wife of Francesco del Giocondo, is in the Louvre Museum, Paris. This figure of a woman, dressed in the Florentine fashion of her day and seated in a visionary, mountainous landscape, is a remarkable instance of Leonardo's unique sfumato technique of soft, heavily shaded modeling. The Mona Lisa's enigmatic expression, which seems both alluring and aloof, has given the portrait universal fame. Reams have been written about this small masterpiece by Leonardo, and the gentle woman who is its subject has been adapted in turn as an aesthetic, philosophical, and advertising symbol, entering eventually into the irreverent parodies of the Dada and Surrealist artists. The history of the panel has been much discussed, although it remains in part uncertain. According to Vasari, the subject is a young Florentine woman, Monna (or Mona) Lisa, who in 1495 married Francesco del Giocondo, and thus came to be known as "La Gioconda." The work should probably be dated during Leonardo's second Florentine period, that is between 1503 and 1505. Leonardo himself loved the portrait, so much so that he always carried it with him until eventually in France it was sold to Francis I.

From the beginning "The Mona Lisa" was greatly admired and much copied, and it came to be considered the prototype of the Renaissance portrait.[16] In his essay "On the Perfect Beauty of a Woman," the 16th Century writer Firenzuola says that the slight opening of the lips at the corners of the mouth was considered in that period to be a sign of elegance. Thus Mona Lisa has that slight smile which enters into the gentle, delicate atmosphere pervading the whole painting. To achieve this effect, Leonardo uses the sfumato technique,[17] a gradual dissolving of the forms themselves, continuous interaction between light and shade and an uncertain sense of the time of day.

Raphael (1483–1520)

Raphael (Raffaello Sanzio) is best known for his Madonnas and for his large figure compositions in the Vatican in Rome. His work is admired for its clarity of form and ease of composition and for its humanistic idealism. After the complexities of the personalities of Leonardo and Michelangelo, it is a relief to find in Raphael a genius whose daily life was basically like the mainstream members of his society. He was born in the small town of Urbino, an artistic center, and received his earliest training from his father. Later, he trained under Pietro Perugino (active 1478–1523) who, like Verrocchio and Ghirlandaio, was an artist of considerable gifts. But while Leonardo and Michelangelo quickly outgrew their teachers and show no later trace of influence, Raphael was an absorber of wide ranging influences.

There are still echoes of the gentle Perugino in an early Raphael like the diminutive "St George and the Dragon," (Fig. 16.8) painted when he was in his early twenties. The little praying

---

16. It became even more famous in 1911, when it was stolen from the Salon Carré in the Louvre. It was recovered 27 months later when the perpetrator, Vincenzo Perugia, attempted to sell it to the Uffizi Gallery in Florence for $100,000.

17. Sfumato: a term coined by Leonardo to refer to a painting technique which overlays translucent layers of colors to create perceptions of depth, volume and form. In Italian sfumato means "blended" with connotations of "smoky."

Figure 16.8: Raphael, "St. George and the Dragon."

princess is very Peruginesque, but there is a fire in the knight and his intelligent horse, and a nasty vigor in the convincing dragon that would always be beyond Perugino's skill. Even the horse's tail is electric, and the saint's mantle flies wide as he speeds to the kill.

Raphael returned to the subject of the Madonna and Child several times throughout his short 37 year life. The "Alba Madonna" (Fig. 16.9), for example, has a Michelangelesque heroism about it, yet a tenderness that is uniquely Raphael. The figure group iserfully composed in tondo form,[18] which expresses fulfilment in the watchful face of Mary. The world stretches away on either side, centered on the figures, and the movement sweeps graciously onwards until it reaches the furthest fold of Mary's cloaked elbow. Then it floods back, with her body inclined towards the left, and the meaning is perfectly contained: love is never stationary, it is given and returned. The entire meaning of the composition would be altered if Mary's head was inclined toward instead of away from the infant child.

---

18. Tondo form means unity. Raphael posed the figures of the Madonna in a complex 3-D polygon, rather than in the tightly-constructed pyramid of the earlier paintings, giving his figure group both freedom and expressive power.

Figure 16.9: Raphael, "The Alba Madonna."

The "School of Athens" (Fig. 16.10) is the most famous example of the large figure frescoes for which he is so famous. It was painted for Pope Julius II when Raphael was 27 years old. So enthusiastic was the pope when he saw the painting that Raphael received the commission to paint the entire papal suite. The *Stanza della Segnatura* was to be Julius's library, *Bibiotheca Iulia*, which would house a small collection of books intended for his personal use. The ancient Roman practice of furnishing libraries with portraits of great poets and philosophers was revived in 15th Century Italy. Raphael revolutionized this practice in the *Stanza* by harmoniously arranging large groups of people as one unit in his fresco compositions. In the "School of Athens," philosophers from different epochs are arranged as colleagues in a timeless academy. Those that have been positively identified using accurate historical evidence are: Plato, Aristotle, Socrates, Pythagoras, Euclid, Alcibiades, Diogenes, Ptolemy, Zoroaster, and Raphael. Plato is in the center pointing his finger to the heavens while holding the *Timaeus*, his treatise on the origin of the world. Next to him, his younger pupil Aristotle holds a copy of his Ethics while describing the earth and the wide realm of moral teaching with his extended hand in an elegant horizontal gesture. The architectural setting, however, is not classical Athens, but ancient Rome, with which Raphael was familiar from the abundant ruins visible all over Italy.

Figure 16.10: Raphael, "The School at Athens."

Michelangelo (1475–1564)

Michelangelo (Michelangelo di Lodovico Buonarroti Simoni) was a sculptor, painter, architect, and poet, who exerted an unparalleled influence on the development of Western art. He was universally acknowledged as a supreme artist in his own lifetime, but contemporaries all too often present us with only his outward manner, his muscularity and gigantic grandeur, but miss the inspiration. Michelangelo resisted the paintbrush. He thought of himself as a sculptor, which for him was "the making of men," analogous to divine creation. As a well-born Florentine, a member of the minor aristocracy, he was temperamentally resistant to coercion at any time. Only the power of the pope, tyrannical by position and by nature, could force him to paint the Sistine Chapel ceiling, the world's greatest single fresco. His contemporaries spoke about his *terribilità*, which means, of course, not so much being terrible as being awesome. There has never been a more literally awesome artist than Michelangelo: awesome in the scope of his imagination, awesome in his awareness of the significance—the spiritual significance—of beauty. Beauty was to him divine, one of the ways God communicated Himself to humanity.

David

The unique genius of Michelangelo's art is wonderfully realized in his monumental "David" (Fig. 16.11), commissioned in 1501 by the Guild of Wool Merchants of Florence. Michelangelo broke away from the traditional way of representing David as the winner of his encounter with the giant, with Goliath's head at his feet and the powerful sword in his hand, but portrays David as the

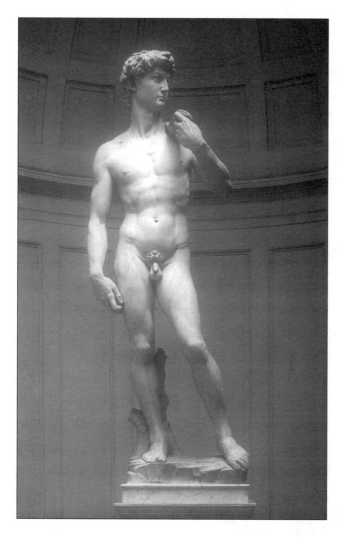

Figure 16.11: Michelangelo "David."

youth in the moment immediately preceding the battle. Perhaps he is depicted just at the moment when he has heard that his people are hesitating, and he sees Goliath jeering and mocking them. Michelangelo envisions David as in the most beautiful representation of the Greek hero, a combination of manly strength, human intelligence, and elegant dignity. The right-hand side of the statue is smooth and composed while the left side, from the outstretched foot all the way up to the disheveled hair is openly active and dynamic. The muscles and the tendons are developed only to the point where they can still be interpreted as the perfect instrument for a strong will, and not to the point of becoming individual self-governing forms. Once the thirteen and a half foot statue was completed, a committee of the highest ranking citizens and artists decided that it must be placed in the main square of the town, in front of the Palazzo Vecchio,[19] the Town Hall, although it had

19. It has since been replaced by a modern copy and the original removed to Galleria dell Accademia.

Figure 16.12: The Sistine Chapel.

originally been designed for display in the cathedral. It was the first time since antiquity that a large statue of a nude was exhibited in a public place.[20] This occurred thanks to the confluence of two forces, which by a fortunate chance complemented each other: the force of an artist able to create, for a political community, the symbol of its highest political ideals, and a community that understood the power of such a symbol. "Strength" and "Wrath" were the two most important characteristic of the ancient patron of the city, Hercules. Both these qualities, passionate strength and wrath, were embodied in the statue of David.

---

20. Amazingly, this occurred less than a decade after Savonarola's infamous Bonfire of the Vanities, in which he and his followers destroyed art works depicting the naked human body as indecent and immoral. How quickly the political climate of a society can change.

Figure 16.13: Michelangelo "The Creation of Adam."

Sistine Chapel

Although he considered himself a sculptor, it is the Sistine Chapel frescoes (Fig. 16.12) that display the full range of Michelangelo's genius. He was commissioned by Pope Julius II in 1508 to repaint the ceiling,[21] which originally contained golden stars on a blue sky. The work was completed between 1508 and 1512. He returned some 23 years later and painted the "Last Judgment" on the wall behind the alter, between 1535 and 1541, this commissioned by Pope Paul III Farnese (1534–1549).

To be able to reach the ceiling, Michelangelo needed a support. The first idea was by the Vatican architect Bramante, who wanted to build for him a special scaffold suspended in the air with ropes. But Michelangelo suspected that this would have left holes in the ceiling once the work was ended, so he built a scaffold of his own, a flat wooden platform on brackets built out from holes in the wall, high up near the top of the windows.

The first layer of plaster applied to the ceiling began to grow mold because it was too wet. Michelangelo had to remove it and start again, but he tried a new mixture, called intonaco, created by one of his assistants, Jacopo l'Indaco. This one not only resisted mold, but also entered the Italian building tradition and is still in use.

Michelangelo was employed to paint the twelve Apostles, but when the work was finished there were more than 3,000 figures, organized into a huge complex of panels, nude youths, medallions, prophets, and sibyls, distributed to accommodate the uneven architectural framework, but still compelling in its artistic unity. The central ceiling area is subdivided by five pairs of supporting girders, and Michelangelo organized this around nine panels enclosing scenes from Genesis. The sequence begins with the "Creation of the World," over the chapel entrance and ends with the "Drunkenness of Noah" over the alter at the far end of the chapel. From the

---

21. Michelangelo had earlier been commissioned to decorate the tomb of Pope Julius II, which perhaps would have been his greatest achievement had he carried it out as planned.

Figure 16.14: Michelangelo, "The Fall of Man."

last panel of the ceiling the eye then moves naturally to the "Last Judgment" on the wall behind the alter, which, although painted almost a quarter of a century later, must have been part of the plan from the beginning. Thus, Michelangelo depicted the entire sweep of human history from the creation to the end of time.

A detailed survey of the Sistine Chapel would fill an entire book; thus, a cursory discussion of a few major scenes will have to suffice to encourage the student to pursue the subject further on his own. "The Creation of Adam" (Fig. 16.13) is one of the most compelling and familiar images in Western art, unrivaled by any other artist. The subject is nothing less than the passing of the divine spark of life—the soul—from God into the body of Adam. The first human being, created in God's image, is shown at the first instant consciousness. He opens his eyes for the first time and his body tenses as he strains toward not only his creator but toward Eve, who is enclosed by God's left arm, still waiting to be created. The eyes of Adam and Eve, the first two human being meet at the instant of creation. The entire scene is powerfully electrified by a brilliant flash of energy, by a primordial shock of recognition.

"The Fall of Man and the Expulsion from the Garden of Eden" (Fig. 16.14) is the sixth of the nine panels in the chorological order of the narrative. The rhythm of the whole composition flows from left to right.[22] Eve grasps the apple boldly, but Adam's eager reach expresses greed as much as curiosity. In spite of rocks and the barren tree stump, Eden—the term signifies bliss—is voluptuous and full of delight; the bodies are plump and smooth, the foliage above their heads is luxuriant. It is striking that the angel with the raised sword pointing the way out appears a twin of the tempter and, like her, issues from the Tree of Life. Good and Evil have divided and become a dual power.

To understand the artistic power that has gripped the viewers of this composition for over almost five centuries, it must be remembered that it expresses ideas that conform to the Catholic thinking

22. It has been noted that the composition's three sections, the fallen pair to the left, the pair expelled from Paradise to the right, and the anthropomorphized tree of knowledge with the female tempter in the center join arms at the top to form the letter M. Was this intended to be Michelangelo's signature?

of Michelangelo's time. The theory of evolution would not be put forward for several hundred years. The story in Genesis was considered history.[23]

At first glance, this painting may not look very dramatic. Adam and Eve are tempted and make the mistake that costs them Eden. However, we need to think of what exactly was lost by this act. In Catholic theology, the time before the fall was also a time of peace and happiness, without sickness or even death. God created man in his own image. Humans were created good, and established in friendship with the Creator and in harmony with each other and the world around them. As long as human beings remained in divine favor they would not have to suffer or die. However, humans clearly suffer now, they are prone to illness, and they age and die. But the God of goodness and did not create humankind to exist in this state, so how did it happen? It is the result of the "original sin." God had commanded Adam: "Of every tree in the garden thou mayest freely eat: but of the tree of the knowledge of good and evil, thou shall not eat of it: for in the day that thou eatest thereof thou shall surely die." But, of course, Adam and Eve did eat of the forbidden fruit and God cast them out of Eden because of it.

Michelangelo dramatically demonstrates what this transition means to humanity: his art speaks to us on a personal level; it explains how the sorry state of affairs of our own world came to be. On the left side of the image, Eden is a richer green, symbolized by the leaves of the tree. On the right side, the land is flat, barren, more like a savanna. Eve is reclining on the Eden side, to indicate the rest and the lack of any need that was present in paradise. On the other side, both Adam and Eve are walking, to signify their lack of rest or ease. The dividing line between Eden and sorrow is the tree and especially the snake. It is the serpent who suggests the evil but who could not cause it. Humans had to agree. Humans are responsible for their own predicament—this is the terrible message of guilt Christianity imposes on its believers. The snake may also represent wisdom in the ancient world, so valued by the Renaissance humanists, a wisdom gone wrong, because it is a wisdom not of God.

The contrast between the left and right sides of the composition is a powerful expression of the change that took place with the expulsion. Compare the change in Eve. Before the fall, pictured on the left, she looks physically healthy, very strong, beautiful, alert, assertive, curious, and intelligent. In contrast after she is expelled from Eden, she looks aged, unwell, and frightened. Her arms cover her breasts out of deep emotion, and perhaps shame. Adam has not fared well either. He looks older, and stressed compared to how he looked at creation. Adam would not have aged until the fall, it is a consequence of original sin. Also the angel doesn't simply threaten with the sword—the sword is not on the back but on his neck: Adam can never go back, he cannot even look back. Compare the face of Adam in the creation scene with that of expulsion scene. Michelangelo is saying that Adam's tragedy is our tragedy. He represents all of us who have rejected what is good, wise, and loving. Our lives are poisoned as a result. We are all guilty.

When Michelangelo returned to the Sistine Chapel over twenty years later to paint "The Last Judgment" (Fig. 16.15), Western Civilization was in spiritual, political, and social crisis: the Protestant Revolt (or the Reformation, depending on your point of view) was sweeping across the continent and the bright optimism of Renaissance humanism was being replaced by the gloomy pessimism of religious warfare and social turmoil. And of course, Michelangelo was twenty years older and maturity effects every artist's outlook. The radiant vitality of the ceiling fresco was replaced by the somber foreboding of "The Last Judgment." Now, humankind, blessed and doomed alike, huddle together is desperate groups, pleading for mercy from a vengeful God. Christ, accompanied

---

23. For a review of the Genesis story of creation see Cleve, Robert, *Early Western Civilization, Source Readings* (2002), Kendall/Hunt Publishing Company, Dubuque, pp. 45-49.

Figure 16.15: Michelangelo,
"The Last Judgment."

by Mary, appears in the center of the composition. He is a wrathful judge, not a forgiving savior. St. Bartholomew is seated on a cloud, just below and slightly to the right of Christ, holding his own skin to represent his martyrdom, at which he was flayed alive. The face of that skin, however, is not the saint's but Michelangelo himself. This grim image symbolizes the terrible burden of guilt that must be borne by the Christian. The fact that this deeply religious man, who conceived and executed the Sistine Chapel ceiling masterpiece was so driven by his feelings of guilt and unworthiness to paint his self-portrait in this context says so much more than any words can express.[24]

---

24. "The Last Judgment" was the object of a heavy dispute between Cardinal Carafa and Michelangelo: the artist was accused of immorality and intolerable obscenity, having depicted naked figures, with genitals in evidence, inside the most important church of Christianity, so a censorship campaign (known as the "Fig-Leaf Campaign") was organized by Carafa and Monsignor Sernini (Mantua's ambassador) to remove the frescoes. The Pope resisted. After Michelangelo's death, a law was issued to cover genitals ("Pictura in Cappella Ap.cacoopriantur"). So Daniele da Volterra, an apprentice of Michelangelo, thereafter nicknamed "Braghettone," covered the genitals with perizomas (briefs), leaving unaltered the complex of bodies. When the work was restored in 1993, the restorers chose not to remove the perizomas of Daniele; however, a faithful, uncensored copy of the original, by Marcello Venusti, is now in Naples, at the Capodimonte Museum. Numerous masterpieces from antiquity in the Vatican Museum have likewise been disfigured by fig leaves. It is ironic that when one visits the museum, these disfiguring fig leaves draw attention to the "offensive" parts of the human anatomy they are intended to hide.

The Underside of the Italian Renaissance

While we like to think of the Italian Renaissance as representing the best of Western culture, several less stellar practices were introduced during this period. The rapidly expanding mercantile culture produced class divisions far more destructive than those of earlier periods and the legal status of women declined seriously in the process. The Italian Renaissance was also the period that Europeans rediscovered slavery. The market in human slave labor in southern Europe began as early as the 12th Century. Initially the Spaniards were the key traffickers in human life, but as the Italian city-states grew, their demand for slaves also grew and they became one of the largest consumers of human slaves. The slavery that they practiced was not yet racial slavery: most slaves sold in Italy were provided by Muslim slave traders from Spain, North Africa, Crete, the Balkans, and the Ottoman Empire. There was a trickle of black slaves into Spain, Portugal, and Italy, but they were only a very small minority.

Almost all the slaves in Renaissance Italy were domestic servants and most wealthy families in the cities had at least one. When a slave was acquired, the owner acquired full rights, including the right to sell and "enjoy," that slave. For the most part, the slaves were incorporated into the household and their children were always born free. In many cases when a slave owner produced a child with a slave, the slave owner would raise it as a legitimate child. A more insidious side of slavery was developing, however, in this period. In the Venetian sugar cane plantations in Cyprus and Crete, a new kind of "plantation slave" emerged. Since sugar is a labor intensive industry, this new type of slave was acquired for purely economical reasons: the cheapest labor possible.

The Renaissance in the North

"Europe beyond the Alps," a phrase which means all of Europe outside Italy, did not undergo the same type of cultural transformation that occurred in the Italian peninsula. For one thing, the rest of Europe did not have the many large cities and the high percentage of urban dwellers in the 15th Century that supported the humanistic movement in Italy. Moreover, unlike Italy, the physical monuments and languages did not constantly remind the inhabitants of their classical heritage. In Italy, even today, it is almost impossible anywhere to walk more than a few yards without being reminded of antiquity—the remains of the ancient world are everywhere. On the other hand, many parts of northern Europe, particularly northern Germany, had never been a part of the Roman Empire, had never been brought into the Greco-Roman cultural system. And even areas like France, England, and Spain, which at one time were highly Romanized, had now for many centuries been under the influence of Germanic culture, whereas Italy had, throughout the Middle Ages, maintained at least a tenuous relationship with the eastern empire and its strongly classical heritage.

The culture of the north was dominated by the landed aristocrats of the rural courts, rather than by the urban society of the cities; by the chivalrous knight, rather than the busy merchant. Humanism and the true classical Renaissance, which required a literate, educated laity, did not reach the north until the last decades of the 15th Century. In fact, it has been rightfully argued that the changes which occurred in northern Europe during the 14th and 15th centuries, unlike what was happening in Italy, was not a Renaissance at all, but rather the decline, the decay even, of medieval European civilization. In this view, those very same classical influences, those same ancient

Figure 16.16: Hans Baldung Gruin, "Girl and Death" and "Woman and Death." Examples of the "cult of death."

ideals and concepts which produced that wonderfully liberating and positive cultural advancement in Italy that we call the Renaissance, produced in northern Europe the decadence, decay, and despair which usually mark the passing away of a civilization.

The "Defective Sense of Reality"

In 1919, the Dutch historian Johan Huizinga wrote a book titled *The Waning of the Middle Ages*,[25] in which he carefully examined the culture of the court of the dukes of Burgundy, who were among the wealthiest and most powerful princes of the north. Huizinga studied the courtly life and manners of the Burgundians and analyzed their views on love, war, and religion. He found in that society an extreme tension and a frequent violence, but he found little of the balance and serenity that had marked Medieval society in the earlier centuries. Now, its members exhibited what Huizinga called a "defective sense of reality," that is, an acute inconsistency of values and actions and a great emotional instability.

The defective sense of reality that was most apparent in the extravagant and bizarre cultivation of chivalry. Chivalry was the rules of conduct, the code of honor, of the Medieval knight. But in terms of military value and utility, the heavily armored knight was becoming, indeed had already

---

25. Huizinga, Johan, *The Waning of the Middle Ages* (1919), is one of the most important books on the history of the Middle Ages ever written. Today, almost a century later, it is still in print and is often required reading for university history courses.

become, far less important than the foot soldier, armed with the longbow, the pike and, increasingly, the firearm. But in spite of this obvious obsolescence, the aristocratic classes of the north continued to *pretend* that the knightly virtues of a bygone age still governed all questions of state and society. This was the prime example of what Huizinga labeled the defective sense of reality. The aristocrats of northern Europe refused to take into account such lowly and unworthy considerations as the role played by such things as money, the type of arms, and the number of soldiers possessed by a country in determining the outcome of wars. For example, before the Battle of Agincourt between the French and the English in 1445, a French knight told his king that he should not use his infantry contingents made up of Parisian townsfolk, because it would give his army an unfair advantage; rather the battle should be decided strictly on the basis of the chivalrous valor of the knights. A defective sense of reality.

This was the age of the perfect knight and of grand feats of arms. King John of Bohemia insisted that he be in the front ranks of battle so that he should better strike at the enemy: but he needed his soldiers to guide him to the front, for John was blind.[26] A defective sense of reality.

Such feats of renowned knights won the admiration of poets and chroniclers, but they affected the outcome of battle hardly at all. Yet the age was marked by the formation of even new orders of chivalry, such as the Knights of the Garter and the Burgundian Knights of the Golden Fleece. The assumption was that these orders could reform the world by their intensive cultivation of knightly virtues. A defective sense of reality. A special order was founded for the defense of the honor of women and knights tool lunatic oaths to honor their ladies, such as keeping one eye closed for extended periods, often several years. Obviously rational people did not fight wars or make love in this artificial way. But the people of northern Europe seem to have believed that they could somehow will this world into the phantom shape that existed only in their dreams. They confused the real world with world of their dreams. It was a defective sense of reality.

Huizinga noted that both knights and commoners showed a morbid fascination with death, which he called the "cult of decay" (Fig. 16.16). Reminders of the ultimate victory of death and the explicit treatment of decaying flesh are frequently encountered in both the literature and the plastic arts of northern Europe during this time. One popular subject was the danse macabre, or the "dance of death," which depicted people from all levels of society, the priest and the thief, the aristocrat and the peasant, all dancing that final dance. They were usually shown as rotting skeletons, with the flesh dripping from their bones. Another popular theme all over Europe was the pieta, the virgin Mary weeping over the body of her dead son.

---

26. Brereton, Geoffrey, translator, *Jean Froissart, Chronicles* (1968), Penguin Books, New York, pp. 89–90 "The noble and gallant King of Bohemia, also known as John of Luxembourg because he was the son of the emperor Henry of Luxembourg, was told by his people that the battle had begun. Although he was in full armor and equipped for combat, he could see nothing because he was blind. He asked his knights what the situation was and they described the rout of the Genoese and the confusion which followed King Phillip's order to kill them. "Ha," replied the King of Bohemia, "That is a signal for us." . . . Then the King said a very brave thing to his knights: "My Lords, you are my men, my friends and my companions-in-arms. Today I have a special request to make of you. Take me far enough forward for me to strike a blow with my sword." Because they cherished his honor and their own prowess, his knights consented. . . . In order to acquit themselves well and not lose the king in the press, they tied all their horses together by the bridles, set their king in front so that he might fulfill his wish and rode towards the enemy. The good king. . . came so close to the enemy that he was able to use his sword several times and fought most bravely, as did the knights with him. They advanced so far forward that they all remained on the field, not one escaping alive. They were found the next day lying around their leader, with their horses still fastened together."

Figure 16.17: Albrecht Dürer, "The Four Horsemen of the Apocalypse." The four horsemen who will bring vengeance on the damned on Judgment Day: Conquest, holding a bow; War, holding a sword; Justice, holding the scales; and Death or Plague, riding a pale horse and trampling a bishop.

This morbid interest in death and decay reveals an unbalanced concern for the material aspects of life, in fact, it indicates an excessive attachment to the material things of this world, a kind of inverse materialism. Yet this was the "Age of Faith," supposedly an intensely religious age, a time when the ageless world of the spirit was far more important than this transitory material world. This represents an acute inconsistency of values. Indeed, the cult of decay represents a growing religious dissatisfaction. Clearly, Christianity was failing to provide consolation to the people of northern Europe during the 14th and 15th centuries and a religion that fails to console is a religion in crisis.

Yet another sign of the unsettled religious spirit of the age was the fascination with the devil, demonology, and witchcraft. The most enlightened scholars of Germany argued at great length concerning whether witches could ride through the air on sticks and about their relations with the devil. One of the most famous witch trials of the period was held at Arras, France in 1460. Scores of people were convicted of participating in a witches' sabbat, of giving homage to the devil, even having sexual intercourse with him (a breath-taking experience, if the accounts of the time can be believed!). Large numbers were burned at the stake before the trials ran their course.[27]

Finally, there was the "cult of the saints," another manifestation of the survival of paganism. The passion of the people to have physical contact with the objects of religious devotion—a pagan characteristic—resulted in an obsession with relics of the saints. More often than not these relics were fabricated rather than authentic, but they became a major commodity of trade, and some princes accumulated collections of relics numbering in the thousands. As described by Will Durant:[28]

> The official prayers of the Church were often addressed to God the Father; a few appealed to the Holy Ghost; but the prayers of the people were addressed mostly to Jesus, Mary, and the saints. The Almighty was feared; He still carried, in popular conception, much of the severity that had come down from Yahveh; how could a simple sinner dare to take his prayer to so awful and distant a throne? Jesus was closer, but He too was God, and one hardly ventured to speak to Him face to face after so thoroughly ignoring His Beatitudes. It seemed wiser to lay one's prayer before a saint certified by canonization to be in heaven, and to beg his or her intercession with Christ. All the poetic and popular polytheism of antiquity rose from the never dead past, and filled Christian worship with a heartening communion of spirits, a brotherly nearness of earth to heaven, redeeming the faith of its darker elements. Every nation, city, abbey, church, craft, soul, and crisis of life had its patron saint, as in pagan Rome it had had a god. England had St. George, France had St. Denis. St. Bartholomew was the protector of the tanners because he had been flayed alive; St. John was invoked by candlemakers because he had been plunged into a caldron of burning oil; St. Christopher was the patron of porters because he had carried Christ on his shoulders; Mary Magdalen received die petitions of perfumers because she had poured aromatic oils upon the Saviour's feet. For every emergency or ill men had a friend in the skies. St. Sebastian and St. Roch were mighty in rime of pestilence. St. Apollinia, whose jaw had been broken by the executioner, healed the toothache; St. Blaise cured sore throat. St. Corneille protected oxen, St. Gall chickens, St. Anthony pigs. St. Médard was for France the saint most frequently solicited for rain; if he failed to pour, his impatient worshipers, now and then, threw his statue into the water, perhaps as suggestive magic.
>
> The Church arranged an ecclesiastical calendar in which every day celebrated a saint; but the year did not find room for the 25,000 saints that had been canonized by the tenth

---

27. The affair began at Langres in 1459, when a hermit was arrested. Under torture, he admitted attending a sabbat, and named a prostitute and an elderly poet of Arras as his companions. The hermit was burned at the stake. The inquisitor arrested and tortured his accused accomplices, resulting in a widening pool of accusations, arrests, tortures, and confessions, which spread quickly through Arras. The inquisitor was spurred on by two fanatical Dominican monks, who believed that one third of the population of Europe were witches and if they had their way almost all the population of Europe would have been murdered. Anyone against the burning of witches was in their opinion also a witch. The victims were placed on a rack and the soles of their feet were put into the flames. They confessed to whatever the inquisitors wanted. They also named innocent people in accordance with the inquisitors leading questions and torture. The inquisitors lied to the victims by promising them their freedom in exchange for a confession, but they were then sent to the stake where they were denounced in public and burned alive. Eventually the witch hunt took a toll on the business of the Arras, an important trade center. By the end of 1460 the Duke of Burgundy intervened and the arrests stopped. In 1461 the Parlament (court) of Paris demanded the release of those imprisoned.

28. Durant, Will, *The Age of Faith* (1950), Simon and Schuster, New York, pp. 742–744.

century. The calendar of saints was so familiar to the people that the almanac divided the agricultural year by their names. In France the feast of St. George was the day for sowing. In England St. Valentine's Day marked the winter's end; on that happy day birds (they said) coupled fervently in the woods, and youths put flowers on the window sills of the girls they loved. Many saints received canonization through the insistent worship of their memory by the people or the locality, sometimes against ecclesiastical resistance. Images of the saints were set up in churches and public squares, on buildings and roads, and received a spontaneous worship that scandalized some philosophers and Iconoclasts. Bishop Claudius of Turin complained that many folk "worship images of saints; . . . they have not abandoned idols, but only changed their names." In this matter, at least, the will and need of the people created the form of the cult.

With so many saints there had to be many relics—their bones, hair, clothing, and anything that they had used. Every altar was expected to cover one or more such sacred memorials. The basilica of St. Peter boasted the bodies of Peter and Paul, which made Rome the chief goal of European pilgrimage. A church in St. Omer claimed to have bits of the True Cross, of the lance that had pierced Christ, of His cradle and His tomb, of the manna that had rained from heaven, of Aaron's rod, of the altar on which St. Peter had said Mass, of the hair, cowl, hair shirt, and tonsure shavings of Thomas a Becket, and of the original stone tablets upon which the Ten Commandments had been traced by the very finger of God. The cathedral of Amiens enshrined the head of St. John the Baptist in a silver cup. The abbey of St. Denis housed the crown of thorns and the body of Dionysius the Areopagite. Each of three scattered churches in France professed to have a complete corpse of Mary Magdalen; and five churches in France vowed that they held the one authentic relic of Christ's circumcision. Exeter Cathedral showed parts of the candle that the angel of the Lord used to light the tomb of Jesus, and fragments of the bush from which God spoke to Moses. Westminster Abbey had some of Christ's blood, and a piece of marble bearing the imprint of His foot. A monastery at Durham displayed one of St. Lawrence's joints, the coals that had burned him, the charger on which the head of the Baptist had been presented to Herod, the Virgin's shirt, and a rock marked with drops of her milk. The churches of Constantinople, before 1204, were especially rich in relics; they had the lance that had pierced Christ and was still red with His blood, the rod that had scourged Him, many pieces of the True Cross enshrined in gold, the "sop of bread" given to Judas at the Last Supper, some hairs of the Lord's beard, the left arm of John the Baptist. . . . In the sack of Constantinople many of these relics were stolen, some were bought, and they were peddled in the West from church to church to find the highest bidder. All relics were credited with supernatural powers, and a hundred thousand tales were told of their miracles. Men and women eagerly sought even the slightest relic, or relic of a relic, to wear as a magic talisman—a thread from a saint's robe, some dust from a reliquary, a drop of oil from a sanctuary lamp in the shrine. Monasteries vied and disputed with one another in gathering relics and exhibiting them to generous worshipers, for the possession of famous relics made the fortune of an abbey or a church, The "translation" of the bones of Thomas a Becket to a new chapel in the cathedral of Canterbury (1220) drew from the attending worshipers a collection valued at $300,000 today. So profitable a business enlisted many practitioners; thousands of spurious relics were sold to churches and individuals; and monasteries were tempted to "discover" new relics when in need of funds. The culmination of abuse was the dismemberment of dead saints so that several places might enjoy their patronage and power.

The cult of the saints was perhaps even more than a defective sense of reality, it was a flight from reality.

Nominalism

Even the intellectuals of northern Europe seemed to undergo a crisis of confidence. The Scholasticism of the High Middle Age, which arose with the birth of the Medieval universities, was based on the assumption that it was within the power of human reason to construct a universal philosophy, that is, a philosophy that would do justice to all truth, a philosophy that would reconcile all apparent conflicts between the truths which are derived from different sources, such as the Bible, church law, observation of the natural world, etc. This was a very optimistic view. But this style of thinking changed during the 13th and 14th centuries. Many scholastic theologians came to be more interested in analysis, or breaking things apart, rather than synthesis, or putting things together, as they had earlier. As they continued their investigation of the philosophical and theological foundations of Christianity, many scholastics lost their original unbounded confidence in human reason.

The most original philosophical thinkers of the early Renaissance in the north were the nominalists. They are called nominalists because they denied the existence of the universal natures, those ideal forms postulated by Plato. The ancient Greek philosopher had developed the theory that all visible, tangible things of this world are unreal and transitory; they are only imperfect copies of the perfect and universal "forms" or "ideas" that exist somewhere else—Plato never was very clear about where, perhaps in the realm of the spirit.[29] Why did Plato believe that the perfect ideas exist? Because the mind perceives them. For example, we know a chair when we see it—although no two chairs are exactly alike—because the mind perceives "chairness," or what Plato called the idea of "chair." Therefore, when we see a chair here in this world we recognize it as a copy of the idea of chair. Plato believed these perfect ideas really do exist somewhere. The nominalists denied that these idea exist.

The most important of the Medieval nominalists was the English Franciscan William of Ockham (1285?–1349?). The fundamental principle of his logical method came to be called "Ockham's razor" and it stated that between alternative explanations for a given phenomenon the simplest explanation is always to be preferred. This is also the "principle of economy, and Ockham used it to attack the problem of Plato's ideal forms. The simplest way to explain the existence of an individual object is to affirm that it exists. The mind can detect similarities between objects and group them into classes and categories—such as the class of chairs. These categories can further be manipulated in logically valid ways, but this offers no certain evidence that ideal forms exists, either in this world and any other.

Therefore, the area the human mind can function, according to Ockham, is severely limited. To the nominalist, the universe is an aggregate or mass of independent individual objects, not a collection of imperfect copies of ideal forms. The proper approach to dealing with the universe is through direct experience and observation, not through speculations about ideal or abstract forms, the very existence of which cannot be proven. But any theology based on observation and reason would obviously be very limited. Ockham believed that it was still possible to prove the existence of God, for example, but not whether there are many gods or one. Any important information about God, then, must be received through revelation, not detected through observation.

---

29. See Plato, "The Allegory of the Cave," in Cleve, Robert, *Early Western Civilization, Source Readings* (2002), Kendall/Hunt Publishing Company, Dubuque, pp. 251–256.

Figure 16.18: Pieter Bruegel the Elder, "The Triumph of Death."

The nominalists lacked the high assessment of human powers made by the scholastics and did not share their confident belief in the ordered and autonomous structure of the natural world. Living in a disturbed and pessimistic world they reflect a crisis of confidence in natural reason and in themselves, which is in stark contrast to the contemporary humanists in Italy. Yet, William of Ockham (1285–1349) in England and Francesco Petrarch (1304–1374) in Italy were contemporaries—but what a difference in outlook!

Mysticism

In the north, religion remained the central concern for the men and women of the 13th and 14th centuries, but now new forms of piety and religious practice begin to appear. Mysticism, which is the inner and personal sense of direct communion with God, had previously been almost totally confined to the monasteries, but now it began to appear outside the monastery walls, sometimes in heretical forms, that is, forms unacceptable to the Church. The Franciscan and Dominican orders organized special branches for laymen and tried to deepen the spiritual life of their members. This was in essence an effort to open the monastic experience to the lay world and to expose everyone to what had hitherto been restricted to the spiritual elite.

The most active center of lay mysticism was the Rhine valley. The Dominican preacher Meister Eckhart sought to bring his congregation into mystical confrontation with God. According to him, the believer should cultivate within his soul something he called the "divine spark." To accomplish this he must banish all thoughts from his mind and achieve a state of pure passivity, he must make the mind a blank slate. Then God will come and dwell within him. Eckhart stressed the futility of dogma and traditional acts of piety, such as charity and penitence. God is too great to be contained in dogmatic categories, too sovereign to be moved by traditional piety.[30] This, of course, comes dangerously close to heresy in the eyes of the Church, because if a believer can go directly to God for salvation there is no need for a church or priest as a go-between. The most basic doctrine of the Church is the requirement of the priest and the sacraments as the conduit of God's saving grace. Therefore, the Church can never condone a practice that makes itself irrelevant and unnecessary.

The simplicity of this new lay mysticism was a reaction against the pomp and splendor that had come to come to surround the popes and prelates and religious ceremonies. Likewise, the rules concerning fasts, abstinences, devotional exercises, the cult of the saints, the selling of indulgences and pardons, all seemed irrelevant to the true religious needs of these mystics. Without the proper state of the soul these traditional acts of piety were meaningless. On the other hand, if the soul was in the proper state for receiving God's grace, these traditional act of piety were unnecessary, even a hindrance and a distraction.

The Rhenish mystics, as they were called, managed to stay within the Catholic Church, but some other efforts at mysticism ended in outright heretical attacks on the religious establishment. These heresies were produced by the difficulties of the Church in adapting its organization and teachings to the demands of a changing world. The problem facing all religion is the fact that, like it or not, societies change, while the principles and practices prescribed by religion are timeless and immutable. Therefore, if a religion cannot find someway to accommodate to the changes that occur in society, it sooner or later becomes irrelevant and dies. In effect, almost all established religions suffer from this "social lag."

The most important heretic of this period was the English Dominican, John Wycliffe, who was influenced by the subservience of the Avignon papacy to France. In 1365 he denounced the payment of Peter's pence, which was an annual tax given by the English people to the papacy. Wycliffe argued that the scriptures alone declared the will of God and that neither the pope, the cardinals, nor scholastic theologians could tell the Christian what he must believe. He also attacked the dogma of transubstantiation, which asserts that the priest at mass performs a miracle which literally changes the substance of the bread and wine into the flesh and blood of Christ. In addition, Wycliffe attacked the powers, position and privileges of the priesthood and the authority of the pope to exercise jurisdiction over the church and even to hold property. He believed the chief responsibility for ecclesiastical reform rested with the prince, and that the pope could exercise only as much authority over the national church as the prince allowed. Although Wycliffe's ideas show many similarities to later Protestantism, his heresy does not seem to have had a direct influence on Church history. Late in his life Rome required him to appear and defend himself but he was too infirm to obey. He died in 1384 and was buried at Littlerworth, but 44 years after he died the Pope ordered his bones exhumed and burned. A heretic, it seems, is not safe even after entering the grave. Intense persecution stamped out his followers and teachings.

Yet another heresy arose in Bohemia when a Czech priest named John Huss (1369–1415) mounted an equally dangerous attack on the established church. Actually, Huss's ideas are not very clear, but he held that the Church included only those individuals who were predestined to go to

---

30. Regarding the requirement to eat only fish on Fridays, Eckhart commented: "You can't bribe God with a stinking fish!"

heaven and also questioned transubstantiation. For this Huss was burned at the stake in 1415. After his death Huss's followers, known as Hussites, refused to submit to the emperor or the Church. However, they soon split into several different rival sects and a civil war ragged between them in Bohemia from 1421 to 1436, with no clear cut outcome—except that they thereby destroyed themselves and saved the Church the trouble.

And so we end this short survey of the history of the West with Europe poised for a great adventure into the "New World" beyond the ocean and for the terrible suffering and destruction of the religious upheavals of the Protestant Revolt in Europe itself.

Epilogue

When we began the story of Western Civilization, far back in the Paleolithic Age, we found that humanity consisted of a few miserable bands of "hunters and gathers," wandering through an untamed landscape, painfully eking our a hand-to-mouth existence, always at the mercy of the elements, always a plaything of chance. We traced the so-called "progress" of humanity from that humble estate, through a series of sometimes agonizing but always complex adventures, which we called "civilizations."

The first of these civilizations developed in Mesopotamia, the "land between the rivers." Because of the endless warfare and natural disasters these peoples had to endure, they developed a pessimistic outlook on life and conceived of themselves as little more than the mere playthings, slaves even, of the gods. From the beginning to the end of their history, the geographical setting of the Near East made it a theater for war, aggression, bloodshed, and suffering. All of this was interpreted by the people as the wrath of the gods. When asked why the gods behaved in such a manner toward them, they were not able to give a clear answer. It is not given to human beings to understand the ways of the gods.

But in spite of this, humanity persevered and the societies which developed in Mesopotamia, one after the other, each built upon the legacy of its predecessor. The Sumerians built the world's first urban civilization by bringing the southern Mesopotamian plain under cultivation through the use of irrigation and constructed an impressive network of cities with names like Legash, Eridu, Kish, and Ur. The Semitic leader, Sargan, conquered the entire area and established the world's first empire, the Akkadian Empire, but after only three generations it was destroyed by invading barbarians from the foothills of the Taurus Mountains. The wrath of the gods again. After a period of confusion, a new people known as the Babylonians, led by their king Hammurabi, remembered for his great code of laws, established a new empire, but it too, after a period of prosperity, was destroyed by another people, the Indo-European Hittites, based in Anatolia.

Then we looked at the ancient and mystical civilization of Egypt, which was centered on the river valley of the Nile. The Greek historian Herodotus called Egypt "the gift of the Nile," and certainly the rhythm of the annual flooding of the Nile River made the Egyptian civilization prosperous, secure, and optimistic. From the beginning of their history the Egyptians seemed to be possessed by a vision of eternal life which colored and shaped the entire structure of their society. At first the king, or Pharaoh, due to his special relationship to the gods (he was the son of the sun god), monopolized this vision of an afterlife and the people, perhaps deriving a deeply religious experience from their labor, toiled to build the great pyramids, true wonders of the ancient world, which made it possible, they believed, for the pharaoh to assume his rightful place among the other gods after his departure from this world. But soon this vicarious experience was not enough and the Egyptians began yearn for an afterlife for themselves. Eventually, through the spread of the cult of the savior god Osiris and his faithful wife Isis, even the lowliest Egyptian peasant came to believe that he too could attain immortality in the next world. The key to this wonderful accomplishment was the association of the believer with the benevolent god Osiris, who had conquered death through resurrection (in the world of the spirit) and could share that conquest with his followers. That simple formula has been employed by successive religions down to this day. Fortified by this optimistic outlook, the Egyptians constructed the longest and most stable society in human history, spanning an unbroken period of over 3,000 years.

Eventually, however, Mesopotamia, the Levant, and Egypt were all brought under the domination of the brutal and militaristic Assyrians, who for a time ruled and ruthlessly exploited the entire Near East from their imperial capital of Nineveh, on the banks of the upper Tigris river. But the Assyrians were too much of a tyranny to hold sway permanently and in 612 BCE a coalition of the conquered peoples rose up and destroyed their master. The Assyrians disappeared from history. During this time, the Israelites carved out a small, short-lived kingdom in the Levant and began a long intellectual journey toward monotheism, which became the basis of three major modern religions: Judaism, Christianity, and Islam. After another period of confusion, the Indo-European Persians established a vast and somewhat more benevolent empire over the Near East from Egypt in the West to the Bosporus in the North to the Indus Valley in India to the East. Within this framework the Near East enjoyed peace for a time.

Our story then focused on Greece, which is often awarded the title of the birthplace of Western Civilization, and certainly it is impossible to overstate the importance of the influence of the ancient Greeks on our modern society: weather it be science or art, literature or philosophy, education or democracy, every important facet of our culture can be traced directly or indirectly back to ancient Greece. Yet the history of Greece was compressed into such a small space and time that their achievements make them appear larger than life to us. It seems impossible that so few people achieved so much is such a short time, because what they produced became the basis, the very foundation, of the Western Civilization in which we live in today.

Next our story turned westward to Italy where we met the Romans: statesmen, conquerors, empire builders, and lawmakers. Beginning at a little village on the banks of the Tiber River, the Romans brought the entire Mediterranean basin into one political and economic system, which produced an era of progress, prosperity, and peace—known as the pax Romana—a feat never achieved before or since. But though the roman Empire seemed permanent, the change is the only permanent element of human history and the Roman Empire also eventually declined and passed away, leaving three successor civilizations in its wake: Western Christendom, Byzantium, and the Islam. Western Europe was plunged into a dark abyss of barbarism from which it did not emerge for more than a thousand years.

Well, each of the civilizations we have studied, after a time, crumbled and disappeared. . . they are no more, but each of them left strong legacies, which to this day effect our own mode of thinking and our style of living in all kinds of important as well as trivial ways. The fact that we sit on chairs instead of floor mats is a legacy of ancient Egypt. The fact that we measure out our days, not to mention our class schedules, in 60 minutes hours instead of 100 minute hours is a legacy of the mathematicians of ancient Sumer. The fact that we wear trousers and dresses instead of robes and veils is a legacy of the outcome of the Medieval struggle between Christian and Muslim for the control of Europe. Western science, for example, can be traced back to the ancient Greek philosophers of the 6th Century BCE and the age of science and all that it entails, occurred only in Western Civilization, nowhere else.

At any rate, this is not the end of the story, but the present volume stops here, with Western Civilization poised, on the one hand, for centuries of bloody religious warfare within Europe itself, and on the other hand, for a stimulating adventure into a vast new world (new to the West, at least) beyond the seas, that will spread Western civilization into every continent.

And so it is time to inquire, "What does it all mean?" Well, long before the first tendencies toward what we today call civilization appeared on this spaceship earth, the human brain had already evolved to a state of intellectual capacity, sophistication, and potential equal to what it is today. There is no evidence that the long 6,000 year experience of civilization has made us more intelligent, has improved our morals (whatever that word means), or even made us feel much more secure, and certainly there is no evidence that we have learned any important lessons from what has happened to us over these thousands of years, because it is obvious that we insist on making the same mistakes over and over. . . and over again.

What has the human race accomplished then? If some mythical traveler from another world should happen to stop temporarily on our planet and aghast and mystified at the maddening pace and the infinite variety of human activity, should ask that ultimate question, "What are you doing here? What is the object of all of this? What does it all mean?" What answer could we provide him? It is yet to be proven that the historian could give him an answer he could understand. History indeed, at least so far as the author understands it, does not prove that the human animal is driven by anything more than a kind of blind instinct toward continuous and eternal activity. The Greek historian Thucydides said of the Athenians: "They were born into this world to take no rest themselves and to give none to others."[1] Perhaps the same statement should be made regarding humanity's relationship with the universe.

At any rate, the best response that a historian could make to this mystified space traveler would be to fall back on the classic statement of the mountain climber who, when asked why he climbs the mountain replied simply, "because it is there." The historian can give no more reasonable explanation to the burning question of why the human race, during the past 6,000 years, has moved from those small Neolithic villages of Jarmo and Jericho, moved through the amazingly diverse and exciting stages of ancient civilizations, moved through the desperate and exasperating darkness and despair of the Medieval experience, moved through the brilliant and exciting adventure of the Renaissance, and finally continued through the agonizing, frustrating, but immensely rewarding stages of the modern era, all the way down to the 21st Century, no more reasonable explanation for all of this than simply, "we did it because we could." It was simply an unending effort to realize the potential of the humanity. It is what we are, it is what we do. And has that potential yet been realized? The answer is certainly no. There is no reason to believe that all of this human activity and effort will diminish any time soon, especially now that humanity has turned its gaze face toward the stars.

But all of this is more of an observation than an explanation, because in fact history cannot reveal to us the purpose of life. That is not the historian's mission. History is not a window into the future. History is exactly what it purports to be: a study of the past. But if history cannot reveal the meaning of life and cannot tell us what the future will bring, it is still critically important to us, because history can tell us what roads we have traveled in the past, and we desperately need to know and understand where we have been in the past in order to understand where we are in the present. Only then can we make intelligent decisions concerning which roads to take into the future. But nothing we can learn about our past will reveal with any certainty what the future holds. This can be affirmed with confidence, because every prediction that has ever been made has proven wildly wrong.[2] However, history can, if properly used, provide us with a handle, a tool, to help us grasp the reality of the present, and for that reason, history is certainly worth our attention.

---

1. Thucydides, 1.70.

2. At the New York World Fair in 1939, the visitors were asked to fill out a survey and make predictions concerning the future achievements of science and technology to the end of the 20th Century. Well over 50% of the respondents predicted a cure for cancer by the year 2000, but of the thousands of responses, not a single person predicted that a human being would walk on the moon.

Index

Page numbers in *italics* refer to figures.